TO THE PROFESSOR

This product is available in two versions with software, to give you the software configuration most appropriate for your department and your students.

#21000–3 *Business Applications for the IBM-PC with VP-Planner, dBase III/III+, and WordPerfect* with SOFTWARE SITE LICENSE AGREEMENT.

Under this option, we send you 5 1/4 inch disks containing the VP-Planner, dBase III/III+ and WordPerfect software. You can either load on to a hard disk, make a backup copy, or use it to create individual floppy disks for students. Labels are provided for identifying these individual student disks. Also included in the package is a keyboard template for WordPerfect.

The Student Version software that accompanies this text is versatile and provides most of the same features as the full-scale products. However, it does have the following limitations:

VP-Planner	Each worksheet is limited to 60 columns by 90 rows and the multidimensional database feature is inoperable.
dBase III/III+	Each file is limited to 31 records. There is no printed user's guide, tutorial on disk, utility disk, or applications generator supplied. Otherwise it offers fully functional software.
WordPerfect	Documents are limited to 50,000 characters. Printed copy will contain ''WPC'' at random points. Advanced printing features are not allowed. The thesaurus and speller are limited and there is no tutorial on disk or printed user's guide.

If you choose to adopt the site license version of the text, please call Chris Cole for details at 1-800-848-1567. In Ohio, call 614-258-8441.

#21035–6 *Business Applications for the IBM-PC with VP-Planner, dBase III/III+, and WordPerfect* with Software Disks.

With this version, actual student software is included with each copy of the text. The package also includes a WordPerfect keyboard template.

For further details regarding this product, call Chris Cole, or contact your local Merrill representative.

Business Applications Software for the IBM PC

Alternate Edition with VP-Planner, dBase III/III Plus, and WordPerfect

Lon Ingalsbe
Portland State University

Merrill Publishing Company
A Bell & Howell Information Company
Columbus Toronto London Melbourne

To my wife Marita, and our children Marguerite, Claire, and Brent.

Cover art: © Merrill, Illustration by Illustrated Alaskan Moose

Published by
Merrill Publishing Company
A Bell & Howell Information Company
Columbus, Ohio 43216

This book was set in Frutiger and Century Schoolbook.

Administrative editor: Vern Anthony
Production editor: Pamela Hedrick-Bennett
Text designer: Cynthia Brunk
Cover designer: Cathy Watterson

Library of Congress Catalog Card Number: 87–73205
International Standard Book Number: 0–675–21000–3
Printed in the United States of America
2 3 4 5 6 7 8 9—91 90 89 88

Important: Please read this page before using the dBASE III Plus program, a copy of which is being made available to you for use in conjunction with this Textbook pursuant to the terms of this Agreement for educational, training and/or demonstration purposes. By using the dBASE III Plus program, you show your agreement to the terms of this license.

EXCLUSIONS OF WARRANTIES AND LIMITATIONS OF LIABILITY

THE COPY OF THE dBASE III PLUS PROGRAM MADE AVAILABLE FOR USE WITH THIS TEXTBOOK IS A LIMITED FUNCTIONALITY VERSION OF dBASE III PLUS, AND IS INTENDED SOLELY FOR EDUCATIONAL, TRAINING AND DEMONSTRATION PURPOSES. ACCORDINGLY, THIS COPY OF dBASE III PLUS IS PROVIDED "AS IS," WITHOUT WARRANTY OF ANY KIND FROM ASHTON-TATE OR MERRILL. ASHTON-TATE AND MERRILL HEREBY DISCLAIM ALL WARRANTIES OF ANY KIND WITH RESPECT TO THIS LIMITED FUNCTIONALITY COPY OF dBASE III PLUS, INCLUDING WITHOUT LIMITATION THE IMPLIED WARRANTIES OF MERCHANTABILITY AND FITNESS FOR A PARTICULAR PURPOSE. NEITHER ASHTON-TATE NOR MERRILL SHALL BE LIABLE UNDER ANY CIRCUMSTANCES FOR CONSEQUENTIAL, INCIDENTAL, SPECIAL OR EXEMPLARY DAMAGES ARISING OUT OF THE USE OF THIS LIMITED FUNCTIONALITY COPY OF dBASE III PLUS, EVEN IF ASHTON-TATE OR MERRILL HAS BEEN APPRISED OF THE LIKELIHOOD OF SUCH DAMAGES OCCURRING. IN NO EVENT WILL ASHTON-TATE'S OR MERRILL'S LIABILITY (WHETHER BASED ON AN ACTION OR CLAIM IN CONTRACT, TORT OR OTHERWISE) ARISING OUT OF THE USE OF THIS LIMITED FUNCTIONALITY COPY OF dBASE III PLUS EXCEED THE AMOUNT PAID FOR THIS TEXTBOOK.

LIMITED USE SOFTWARE LICENSE AGREEMENT

DEFINITIONS

The term "Software" as used in this agreement means the Limited Use version of dBASE III Plus which is made available for use in conjunction with this Textbook solely for educational, training and/or demonstration purposes. The term "Software Copies" means the actual copies of all or any portion of the Software, including back-ups, updates, merged or partial copies permitted hereunder.

PERMITTED USES

You may:

—Load into RAM and use the Software on a single terminal or a single workstation of a computer (or its replacement).
—Install the Software onto a permanent storage device (a hard disk drive).
—Make and maintain up to three back up copies provided they are used only for back-up purposes, and you keep possession of the back-ups. In addition, all the information appearing on the original disk labels (including copyright notice) must be copied onto the back-up labels.

This license gives you certain limited rights to use the Software and Software Copies for educational, training and/or demonstration purposes. You do not become the owner of and Ashton-Tate retains title to, all the Software and Software Copies. In addition, you agree to use reasonable efforts to protect the Software from unauthorized use, reproduction, distribution or publication.

All rights not specifically granted in this license are reserved by Ashton-Tate.

USES NOT PERMITTED

You may not:

—Make copies of the Software, except as permitted above.
—Rent, lease, sublicense, time-share, lend or transfer the Software, Software Copies or your rights under this license except that transfers may be made with Ashton-Tate's prior written authorization.
—Alter, decompile, disassemble, or reverse-engineer the Software.
—Remove or obscure the Ashton-Tate copyright and trademark notices.
—Use the Software or Software Copies outside the United States or Canada.

DURATION

This agreement is effective from the day you first use the Software. Your license continues for fifty years or until you return to Ashton-Tate the original disks and any back-up copies, whichever comes first.

If you breach this agreement, Ashton-Tate can terminate this license upon notifying you in writing. You will be required to return all Software Copies. Ashton-Tate can also enforce our other legal rights.

GENERAL

This agreement represents the entire understanding and agreement regarding the Software and Software Copies and supersedes any prior purchase order, communication, advertising or representation.

This license may only be modified in a written amendment signed by an authorized Ashton-Tate officer. If any provision of this agreement shall be unlawful, void, or for any reason unenforceable, it shall be deemed severable from, and shall in no way affect the validity or enforceability of the remaining provisions of this agreement. This agreement will be governed by California law.

Preface

The advent of the microcomputer is bringing revolutionary changes to the information environment of today's businesses. As these changes continue to affect every aspect of the business organization, many individuals, untrained in the discipline of programming theory, will be expected to use microcomputers to perform their everyday tasks.

This textbook is designed for any course in information systems, business, accounting, or related fields where learning to use applications software as a problem-solving tool is necessary. The text has been carefully conceived to provide students with hands-on experience with microcomputers so that they can become functional with the applications software as quickly as possible. Every portion of the text has been extensively class-tested with students of varying degrees of sophistication with microcomputers. The result is a text that will work equally well with students who have extensive programming background as with those who have little or no exposure to the computer and to computer fundamentals.

Scope and Sequence

This text has been organized in five self-contained modules that take students command-by-command through the use of the software, the capabilities of the program, and its advantages/disadvantages for given applications. The modular format allows the instructor to choose which packages to teach and in what order.

Each module has been organized in an easy-to-follow format that has been developed for maximum flexibility:

- Each module begins with an introduction that effectively introduces the student to the key fundamentals and terminology of the application.
- *Tutorial exercises* take the student step-by-step through the basics of the software, introducing them to essential commands, concepts, and structures. The objective of this section is to bring students to an initial level of competency with the software.
- The *Operation and Command Summary* is an alphabetic index of commands, functions, and control keys with brief explanations and/or examples. This summary is both an effective reference guide and review

source. The summaries have been tabbed throughout the book so that the students can locate them easily.

- *Additional topics* are covered to explore important advanced topics that are more appropriately taught by example than tutorial. These sections are based on examples that will allow students to enter the data provided to further their understanding.
- The *Hints and Hazards* section presents tips for improving efficiency and avoiding frustrating pitfalls in the use of the software.
- *Study questions* test the students' understanding with carefully thought-out questions that focus on conceptual issues involved in using the software.

Text Organization

The text begins with an introduction to the fundamentals involved in using microcomputers and applications software. This section covers the use of microcomputers in business, microcomputer operations, and the basics of DOS. A discussion of the most important DOS commands and DOS utility programs is included, as well as an explanation of concepts that are common to various applications software (including file creation and maintenance, numeric and string data expressions, and relational and logical operators). General exceptions to these rules are explained where they occur. The student will need to refer to this section of the manual periodically to review important concepts as they apply to specific microcomputer applications.

Software Coverage

The software applications chosen for this text include the key software packages that students will use once they are on the job.

VP-Planner® is a powerful spreadsheet software that may be used to teach students all of the popular spreadsheet skills and operations. Knowing these skills and operations is rapidly becoming a job requirement for many organizations and a growing number of college courses are requiring students to use spreadsheets in their course work.

WordPerfect® is still the most popular word processing software ever. Learning to use a word processing application is immediately useful to students who will use it to write papers, résumés, and written assignments.

dBase III® is perhaps the most important software application for students to learn since the majority of the data processing problems faced by today's organizations concern effectively managing, manipulating, storing, and retrieving database-type data.

BASICA has been included for those who are in transition from BASIC programming to applications software or require their students to have prior knowledge of BASIC and plan to review the subject. This section is also a valuable resource for students who want to learn some programming skills to enhance their use of applications software.

The final module of the manual introduces a subject neglected in other texts of this type. *Data Transfer between Applications* provides instruction on how to move data from one software application to another. For students willing to experiment with the subject, this module provides the opportunity to gain a conceptual understanding of the basics of data structure as well as the ability to use applications software to the greatest extent of its processing power.

Design Features

Because it is important for students to check their work against what is happening on the computer screen while they are learning, we have included accurate representations of the screens throughout every instructional step of each module. These screen representations provide immediate feedback regarding student's correct interaction with the software, as well as signaling errors or hazards that many have occurred while the student was inputting data. These should be checked at every stage while the student is working through software.

The use of color in this text has been designed for maximum instructional benefit. Every time the text signals hands-on work at the keyboard, the type appears in blue rather than black. The explanations, then, are distinct from the tutorial sections, and students are easily prompted as to when they are next expected to enter data with the keyboard. Further, the use of color separates the computer's response from the user's input, making it easy for the students to see the results of their input.

Acknowledgments

In 1982, the Earle A. Chiles Foundation provided a grant to the School of Business, Portland State University, for the purchase of a microcomputing laboratory to be used by students and faculty. Without this far-sighted action, and the Foundation's continued support, this manual would not have had the opportunity to be written.

After five years of use here at PSU, the manual has evolved through four rewrites to its present form. Its continued success at reaching its learning objectives is due largely to the constructive feedback of over 4,000 PSU students and their instructors.

A special acknowledgment is appropriate for Brent Simonson, PSU 1985 graduate. Without Brent's research, writing, technical expertise, and desire for excellence, much of the material in this manual would have suffered.

I thank all of the faculty and staff of our School of Business for the support and encouragement they have given me over the years. Without it, the additional task of writing this manual would have been overwhelming.

When it became time to have the manual published, a new group of individuals became involved in helping produce the finished product. These individuals reviewed the manuscript and then provided many valuable additional comments and suggestions. I would like to thank the following people for the thought and effort they contributed to this project: David Cooper, University of Connecticut; Darlene Lanier, Louisiana State University; Dan McNamara, College of St. Thomas; James Kasum, University of Wisconsin; Leonard Chochrek, University of Texas at El Paso; Robert McGeein, Bowling Green State; Larry Hegstad, Pacific Lutheran University; Michael Dunlap, University of Williamette; Paula Hall, University of South Carolina; Tom Haresign, Southampton College; Sue McDonough, Josten's Educational Systems, Inc and Southern Ohio College.

Finally, the staff of Merrill Publishing Company deserve special recognition for their efforts to produce this text. Their attention to detail, concern for pedagogical issues, and commitment of resources have resulted in producing the best possible finished product. In particular, I'd like to thank Pam Hedrick-Bennett, production editor, and Vern Anthony, administrative editor, for their efforts.

Contents

Learning VP-Planner

FUNDAMENTALS OF USING MICROCOMPUTERS

Microcomputer Systems | Types of Applications Software

MICROCOMPUTER OPERATIONS

Getting Started—Example Session, Part I | Using the Computer at the DOS Operating Level—Example Session, Part II | Creating a Spreadsheet—Example Session, Part III | Saving a Spreadsheet—Example Session, Part IV | Summary

THE BASICS OF DOS

The DOS Diskette | DOS | Summary

COMPUTERS WITH HARD DISK DRIVES

Introduction to Hard Disks

DOS OPERATION AND COMMAND SUMMARY

DOS Quick Reference Command Summary | DOS Control Keys

IMPORTANT DOS UTILITY PROGRAMS

FORMAT.COM | CHKDSK.COM | DISKCOPY.COM | DISKCOMP.COM | COMP.COM

Fundamentals of Using Microcomputers

Microcomputer Systems

The three major components to any computer system are hardware, software, and their user(s). Microcomputer systems differ from other computer systems because they usually are designed for a single user. In this manual you will be considered the user. Your role is to gain a functional understanding of how you can use the hardware and software of the systems covered here to solve business-related problems.

Microcomputer Hardware

The tangible portion of a microcomputing system is a piece of office equipment with individual parts referred to as microcomputer hardware. The hardware consists of five basic devices, as shown in the following drawing.

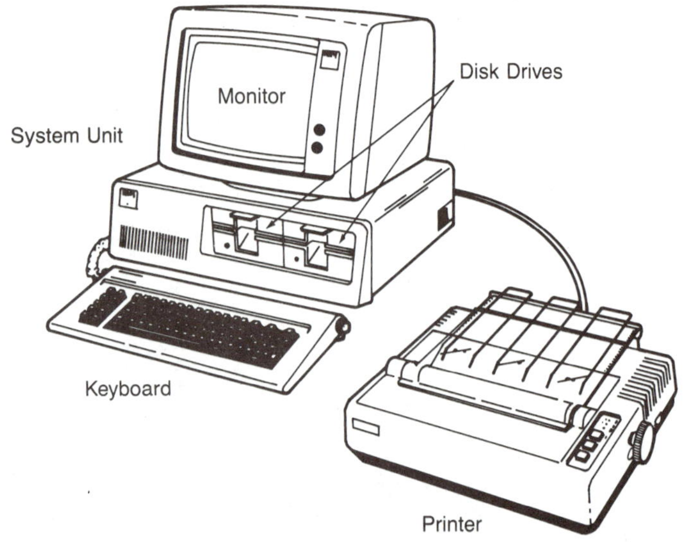

The devices that comprise the microcomputer hardware perform the following functions:

- *Monitor*—Displays data transmitted between the user and the computer.
- *System unit*—Processes data.
- *Keyboard*—Provides the user a means to input data to the computer.
- *Disk drive(s)*—Stores data on magnetic media.
- *Printer*—Produces hard-copy output for the user.

Microcomputer Software

A microcomputer's hardware requires software in order to make it a usable tool. With software, the microcomputer gains flexibility and can become the type of tool the user desires. The microcomputer system's ability to change its nature differentiates it from all other office equipment.

To understand the role of software, it is useful to divide it into five general, although not clear-cut, categories: operating systems; programming languages; canned programs; utility software; and applications software.

Operating Systems

A microcomputer's operating system software usually is purchased with the microcomputer, and is required if the microcomputer is to use any other of the software discussed here. It is the operating system software that, in effect, allows the computer to become any one of various business tools.

Examples of operating system software include MS DOS, CP/M, and UNIX. IBM's Disk Operating System (PC DOS) is the operating system software discussed and used throughout this manual.

Programming Languages

Programming languages cause the computer to become an all-purpose tool, able to solve an endless variety of problems, or behave in any number of ways. In this respect, programming languages are referred to as having "high power."

The trade-off for high power is that programming languages are low level, which means the user needs to write extensive sets of instructions, under rigorous constraints of logic and language syntax, to make the computer perform even the simplest tasks.

Because of their low level, programming languages typically are difficult to learn, cumbersome to work with, and time-consuming for the average person to use. Learning a programming language does, however, serve as an excellent introduction to other types of software by providing a basic understanding of programming theory and how microcomputers work.

Examples of programming languages include BASIC, Pascal, and COBOL. The programming language BASICA is covered in this manual.

Canned Programs

Canned programs cause the microcomputer to act in a specific manner or to solve specific types of problems. When the microcomputer is used with canned programs, the user generally is presented a set of instructions by the microcomputer and is expected to type the needed data from the keyboard. The microcomputer then responds with a solution or report. Canned programs for microcomputers include software for corporate accounting, income tax planning, production scheduling, project management, and inventory control.

Canned programs are considered to be high-level/low-power. They are relatively easy to use, but restrict the user to solving only the particular problem or performing the particular task for which that canned program is designed. Since businesses and their methods of operation typically are unique, a company often finds itself either compromising the manner in which it prefers to do its business or having to purchase (at great expense) a custom-made canned program.

Utility Software

Utility software programs also are quite specific and relatively easy to use. The tasks they perform, however, are best described as tasks of directing or converting data. For instance, three examples of utility software are communications, graphics, and proofreaders. Communications software is used to send and receive data between computers, while graphics software converts numbers into graphs, and proofreaders scan text to find spelling errors and allow them to be corrected.

As business managers and professionals become more sophisticated in their use of microcomputers, this general category of software becomes increasingly important.

Applications Software

Applications software is by far the most significant category of software for current business use of microcomputers, and it is the category of software on which this manual concentrates.

Applications software lie between programming languages and canned programs in their power and ease of use. They make the microcomputer a flexible tool, capable of performing a variety of important tasks, but do require a higher level of user sophistication.

Since applications software is the major subject of this manual, the following section describes this category in greater detail.

Types of Applications Software

The three fundamental types of applications software have familiar office counterparts. They cause the computer to perform standard business functions.

Spreadsheets

Spreadsheet applications software enable the microcomputer to create an electronic version of the accountant's standard spreadsheet. VP-Planner® is the spreadsheet application covered in this manual.

With a spreadsheet application, the user is presented an electronic representation of a spreadsheet on the monitor screen, and is provided a means to enter data into the spreadsheet.

To compare a standard spreadsheet with an electronic one, consider the following situation. At the request of your boss, you are to prepare a simple forecast for net earnings given the following information. Sales will begin in January at $100,000 and are expected to grow at a rate of 10% per month for six months. Cost of goods sold (COGS) will be 65% of sales. Using a piece of paper, a pencil, and a desktop calculator, you construct the following forecast.

	SALES	COGS	NET
January	100,000.00	65,000.00	35,000.00
February	110,000.00	71,500.00	38,500.00
March	121,000.00	78,650.00	42,350.00
April	133,100.00	86,515.00	46,585.00
May	146,410.00	95,166.50	51,243.50
June	161,051.00	104,683.15	56,367.85
		Total	270,046.35

The boss calls and tells you that an error has been made. Sales are expected to start at $95,000. This, of course, affects each month's sales, which in turn affects each month's cost of goods sold, and each month's net. The result is that you must make and record eighteen new calculations.

If the spreadsheet originally had been made with the microcomputer, you would not need to do any manual recalculation because the formulas used for the calculations may be entered into the spreadsheet when it is created.

For example, when you enter January's cost of goods sold, instead of using a calculator to multiply that month's sales by .65 and then writing the answer on paper with a pencil, you would use the computer's keyboard to type something similar to .65*SALES into the appropriate place in the microcomputer spreadsheet.

	SALES	COGS	NET
January	100000.00	.65 * SALES	

The microcomputer spreadsheet does not display the formula you enter. It instead displays the answer to the formula.

	SALES	COGS	NET
January	100000.00	65000.00	

Later, if that month's SALES are changed, a new answer obtained from the formula (.65*SALES) automatically will be calculated and displayed under January's COGS.

	SALES	COGS	NET
January	95000.00	61750.00	

Since all but one (January's sales) dollar entries can be expressed with a formula, it takes the computer less than two seconds to recompute and display the answers for the entire spreadsheet for any changes made to its beginning (January's) sales. With a microcomputer's spreadsheet it also is possible through a little trial-and-error to answer the question, "What does the sales figure need to be in January to net a six-month total of $xxx,xxx.xx?"

Its built-in calculator function is the fundamental strength of spreadsheet applications software, but is certainly not its only advantage.

Spreadsheet applications packages currently are used primarily in budgeting and accounting. Their use is increasing in other areas of business, including cost benefit analysis, production scheduling, strategic market planning, forecasting human resources requirements, and more. Any problem that can be solved with a number/formula-based model is a likely candidate for spreadsheet applications software.

Word Processors

Word processors are the type of applications software that turn the microcomputer into a tool resembling an office typewriter. WordPerfect is the word processing application covered in this manual. Unlike spreadsheets, or database management systems, word processors have little or no ability to deal with numbers or formulas. They are designed to deal with text.

When the microcomputer is used with a word processing application, the user is presented a blank "page" on the monitor screen and can type sentences and paragraphs on it by using the computer's keyboard. Whatever the user types appears on the monitor screen much as it would appear on a piece of paper in a typewriter.

The main difference between typing and word processing is that with word processing the act of typing the text is separate from printing it. After the user has finished typing the text, the microcomputer is instructed to print the text on paper. The advantage is that nothing is committed until it is printed. The user can move freely through the word-processed "pages" shown on the monitor screen, stopping wherever it is appropriate to insert, delete, copy, or move a word, group of words, or even entire pages of text.

With word processing, the user can format the text in professional, attractive, and efficient ways. Paragraphs already typed may be automatically adjusted to fit within new margins. Entirely separate texts or parts of texts may be merged to form new composites for form letters, contracts, or résumés. Topic headings may be automatically centered on the page, key words can be typed boldface or underlined, and line spacing can be changed at any time.

Professionals have been the major users of word processing applications software for microcomputers. Lawyers, professors, and journalists have had a real need for this type of application. Perhaps the fastest growing segment of microcomputer word processing users are students preparing to enter the business community. They are learning about word processing as they create written assignments on the microcomputer.

Database Management Systems

Database management systems (DBMS) are the applications software programs that turn the microcomputer into a tool resembling an office filing cabinet. dBase III and dBase III Plus are the database management system applications covered in this manual. When the microcomputer is used with DBMS applications software, the user begins by creating a database. A database, simply defined, is a collection of related data kept in the form of records. A well-known database would be your city's telephone directory. In this database you will find the name, address, and telephone number (three pieces of related data) for each individual listed in the directory. The three pieces of data comprise the record for each individual, and the collection of records comprises the database—the telephone directory.

The fundamental difference between a database created and maintained with a DBMS application and one created and maintained without a computer is the order in which the database's records must be organized to be useful. For instance, the telephone directory gives three pieces of related information (data) for each record.

NAME	ADDRESS	PHONE
Anderson John	1234 S.W. Maple Street	244-3876

The data items for each record are related since not only do the address and the phone number belong to that person, but the person and the phone number also belong to that address, and the person and address belong to that phone number. In order for you to access any of the data for a particular record in a conventional telephone directory, you must know the first piece of data (the person's name). The records in the telephone book are organized to answer the question, "What is the address and/or telephone number for John Anderson?" It is difficult to answer the question, "What is the address that belongs to the phone number 244-3876?" or "What is the name of the person living at 1234 S.W. Maple Street?"

With the microcomputer, how the records are organized is less important because, compared to you, the microcomputer is extremely fast at searching through data. It does not need to have the database records arranged in any particular order to find a specific record in a reasonable amount of time. If the entire telephone directory were entered as data into a database created and maintained with DBMS applications software, a command like

```
DISPLAY NAME FOR ADDRESS = "1234 S.W. Maple Street"
```

would cause the computer to print out John Anderson's name on the monitor screen in a short time.

There are two related advantages to keeping a database on the microcomputer with DBMS. The first is the ability of the microcomputer to reorganize the records in the database. A DBMS is able to organize (sort) the records in the database by any of the data items in a record. The second advantage is the ability of the DBMS to quickly perform counting and totaling operations for the records in the database.

The telephone directory is a very simple example of a database that has little to do with filing cabinets. Other databases in business include employee records, customer/client records, shipping and receiving invoices, and production reports. Such databases usually are kept in filing cabinets in an organized manner. They may be organized by date, alphabetically, or even alphabetically by date by department. Often two or more files of the same database, each organized differently, are necessary for the business to access the information it needs. In such cases, the microcomputer, using database management system applications software becomes a valuable business tool.

The DBMS applications software programs available today approach programming languages in their power. They are, however, more difficult to learn and use than the other types of applications software. As a result, the uses of DBMS in business, despite their potential, are limited. As the overall level of user sophistication increases, the DBMS applications will likely become a more important use of the microcomputer in business.

Integrated Software

Some software is marketed under the title of "fully integrated software." The idea behind integrated software is that several basic functions will be performed by one software. Two such fully integrated software are Symphony and Framework.

Although integrated software has been on the market for several years, it has not enjoyed the same level of market acceptance that applications software has enjoyed. The reasons lie in the complexity, the cost of adding hardware to a microcomputer system to use them, and the fact that most users do not need the full extent of features it offers.

There is a trend, however, for the newer versions of popular applications software to provide features that are integrative in nature. For instance, WordPerfect Version 4.2 is "integrated" to the extent that it is able to perform very limited math calculations in a spreadsheet-like manner and perform some sort and search operations like a database management system. WordPerfect also provides an internal spelling checker, thesaurus, and some graphics capabilities like the counterpart utility software provide. This is all in addition to WordPerfect's strongest feature of being a word processing software.

A major advantage of integrated software is its ability to move data from one type of processing to another. The last section in this manual, "Data Transfer Between Applications," points out that a user who has an understanding of a few fundamental concepts can transfer data between separate applications software without the need for integrated software.

MICROCOMPUTER OPERATIONS

How the three major components of a microcomputer system interrelate while the system is in use will now be examined. A step-by-step example of a simplified typical session, using the microcomputer to create a spreadsheet, will be used to show the relationships. The example will present cross-application consistencies of microcomputer operations. A general description of what occurs in the example is followed by an explanation of the terms used and concepts involved.

Getting Started—Example Session, Part I

You begin by sitting down at the microcomputer and inserting a diskette into the disk drive on the left side of the computer. You turn on the computer and its monitor. After a few moments a red light on that disk drive comes on and you hear a "whirring" sound. Shortly, an A> (A prompt) appears on the monitor screen. You have just booted DOS.

The Roles of Software and Hardware

The Role of Software

The best definition of *software* is that they are sets of instructions (called programs) for the computer's hardware to follow. The user gives the programs to the computer as they are needed. Once the computer receives a set of instructions, it follows *(executes)* them until it is given a different program to execute.

The Role of Hardware

Computer Memory

Inside the computer system unit is hardware constituting memory. *Memory* is space available to hold software and the results or data created as the user operates the computer while it executes programs. The two types of memory inside the computer are:

1. A portion of memory called *Read Only Memory* or *ROM*.
2. *Random Access Memory* or *RAM*.

ROM is a part of memory that has special programs permanently etched into it. The programs in ROM memory relate, in large part, directly to the computer rather than to anything you might want the computer to do. You can consider ROM a sort of subconscious memory for the computer.

The computer's RAM memory is used to temporarily hold software, which is usually kept in a permanent form on the magnetic surface of a disk enclosed in a plastic jacket. The disk and its jacket together are called a *diskette*.

Before the computer is turned on, RAM memory can be thought of as empty space available to hold data. The model here and its subsequent development illustrate the concept.

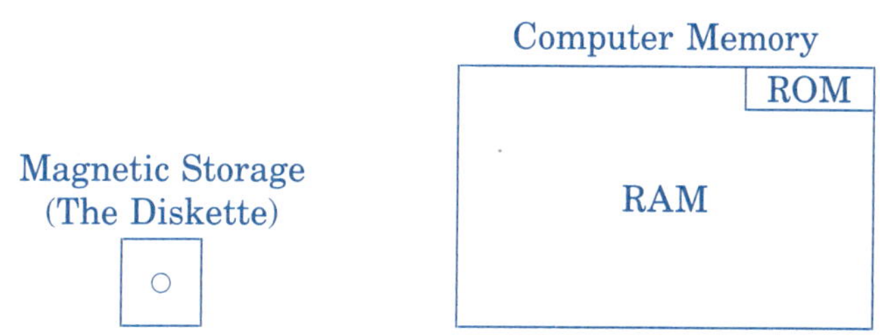

When you first turn on the computer there is a short wait while ROM helps the computer get started. The programs in ROM instruct the computer to check its parts to see if any are missing or not working, to check to see if any attachments are connected, and to perform other "housekeeping" chores necessary for the computer to function properly while it is being used. ROM then instructs the computer to check the disk drive to see if a diskette is there.

Computer Disk Drive(s)

A disk drive is a device attached to the computer system unit. It is similar to a phonograph turntable in operation. It spins the diskette placed in it so that a reading head can scan across the diskette to read the data on it.

If software is stored on the diskette, it is stored as a distinct set of data under a specific name. The data comprising the software are kept on the diskette as a *file* and the name of the data is referred to as the file's *filename*.

The Software DOS

The *disk operating system (DOS)* is the operating system software for the microcomputer. When the computer checks its disk drive, it has been instructed by ROM to look for a file with the filename COMMAND.COM. This file is one part of an interlinked group of files collectively called DOS.

DOS software instructs the computer how to operate its disk drives so that it can find other files that may be on a diskette. It also instructs the computer how to respond if the user types certain messages (called *DOS commands*). The DOS software must be in RAM before any other applications software may be used with the microcomputer.

In this example DOS was on the diskette that you placed in the disk drive. You know the computer has found and automatically read DOS into RAM when the A> appears on the monitor screen. The act of reading DOS into RAM is a copying process and is referred to as *booting, reading,* or *loading* the system. The data are not physically moved off the diskette, but rather the computer creates a copy of the data and places it into RAM memory.

The DOS Operating Level

Reading DOS from the diskette into RAM memory uses up part of the space available there to hold data.

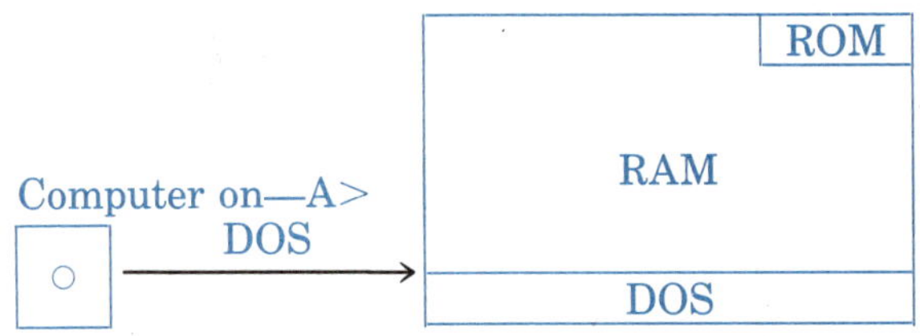

At this point the computer is at the *DOS operating level* or the *system level.* The computer is now able to perform several small but important tasks, and is able to read other software into RAM memory.

Using the Computer at the DOS Operating Level—Example Session, Part II

After you see the A> on the monitor screen you use the keyboard to type **DIR.** You then tap the Enter key. The computer responds by putting on the monitor screen:

```
A>DIR
COMMAND   COM     17792    10-20-83
VP        COM     59446     2-13-87

        2 File(s)
A>
```

You then type VP.COM and tap the Enter key again. Once more you see the disk drive light come on and hear a whirring sound. In a moment the screen displays a spreadsheet that looks something similar to:

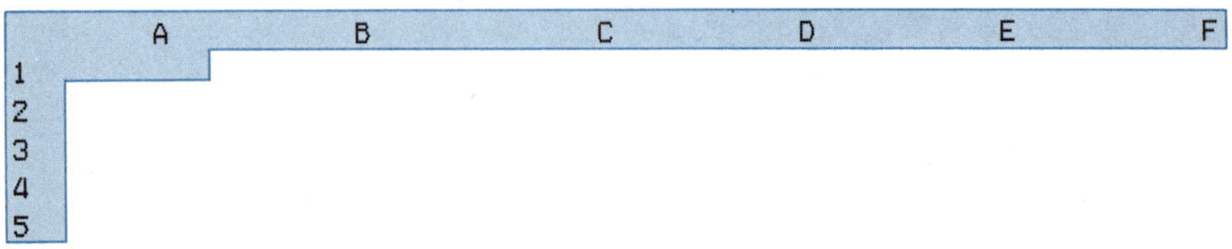

DOS's A> Prompt

DOS's A> indicates that it is your turn to use the computer's keyboard to send messages (commands) to the computer. The computer uses the monitor screen to display the command you are giving it, and to display the results of having executed a command after you have sent it to the computer by tapping the Enter key.

With different software, many of the keys of the keyboard take on different uses. A description of the important keys and how they are used is given in each section for each software covered in this manual.

Entering a DOS Command

In this example you used the keyboard to type **DIR** and then sent the command to the computer by tapping the Enter key. **DIR** is the DOS command that causes the computer to list a directory of the files found on a diskette. The listed directory includes the filename, size of the file measured in bytes, and the date stamp of each file found on that diskette.

COMMAND.COM was the first filename listed and is the filename for the DOS program already mentioned. The directory tells you that its size is nearly 18,000 bytes, which is roughly equivalent to 18,000 characters of data, and that it originally was dated in October 1983.

The second filename listed, VP.COM, is the one for the application software VP-Planner, which will be the spreadsheet application used in this example.

Loading Software into RAM

When you typed VP.COM and tapped the Enter key, the computer did not recognize your message as a DOS command. Therefore, it set out to do the second thing the microcomputer can do at the DOS level of operation—it started spinning the diskette in the disk drive to look for a file with the name VP.COM. When the computer found the file, it read that software into RAM memory.

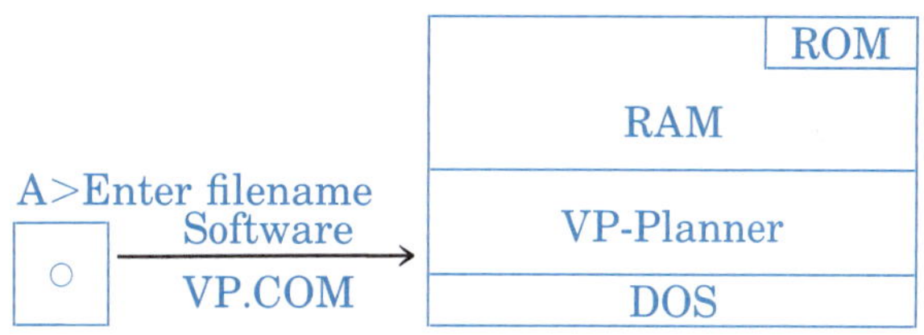

The Software Operating Level

Once the software named VP.COM was read into RAM, the screen became transformed and began to resemble a spreadsheet. The computer now is said to be at the *software operating level,* the level at which you may use the commands of the software currently held in RAM. As you use these commands, you usually end up creating something—a spreadsheet, a letter, a database, or a program of your own such as a BASICA program. To proceed with this example, you will create a small forecasting spreadsheet.

Creating a Spreadsheet—Example Session, Part III

The screen now appears as a mostly blank area with a large rectangle in the top left corner (called the *pointer*). The pointer can be moved around on the screen by tapping certain keys on the keyboard.

The pointer's current location is indicated at the bottom of the screen by column letter and row number. Each location is referred to as a cell of the spreadsheet, and the contents of the cell on which the pointer is currently located are displayed next to the display of the current cell location.

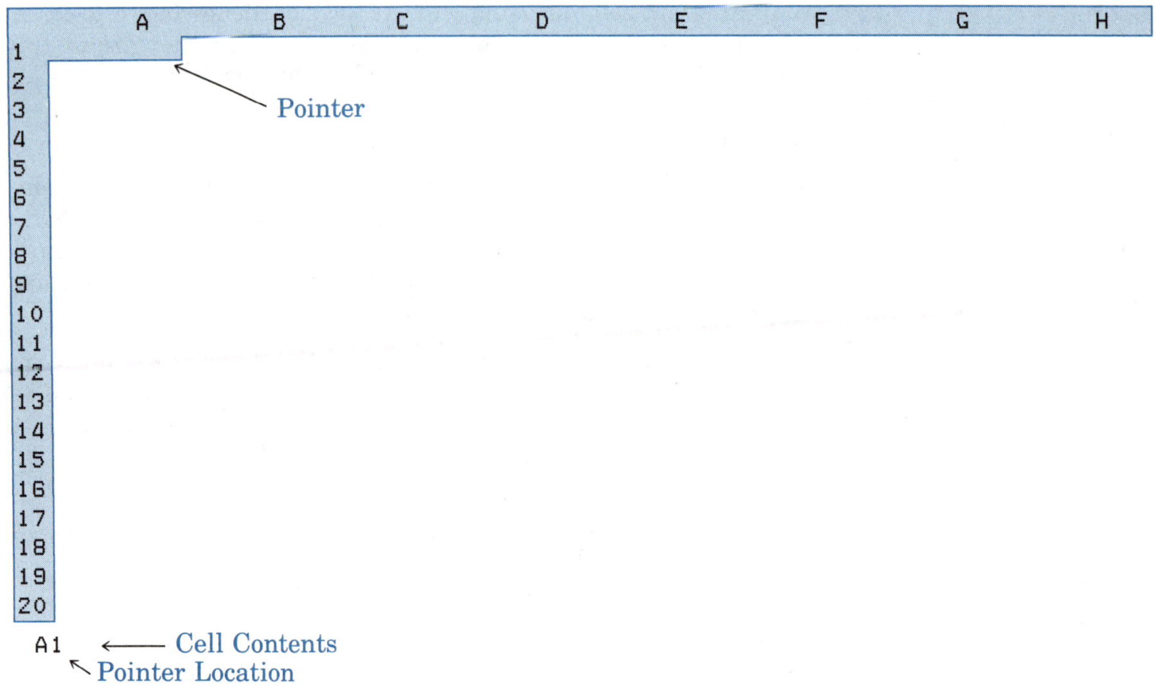

You move the pointer to the B column, second row and type SALES.

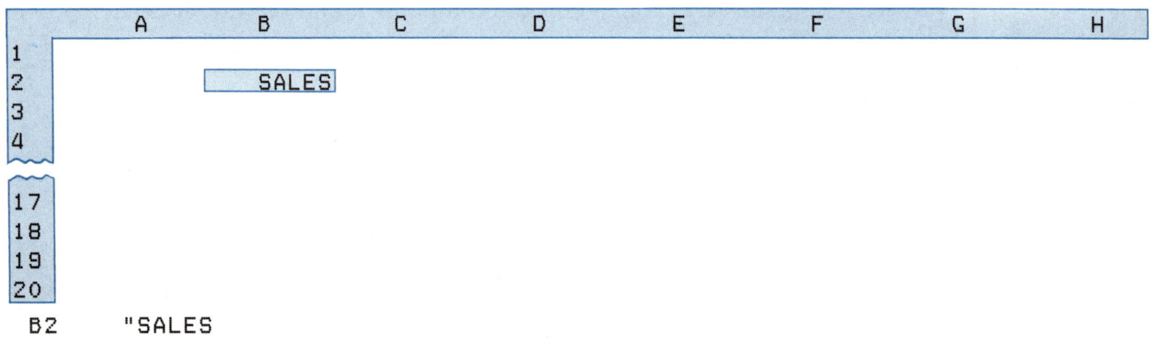

You continue across the row typing in the column labels, and then down the A column typing the row labels for the spreadsheet you are creating.

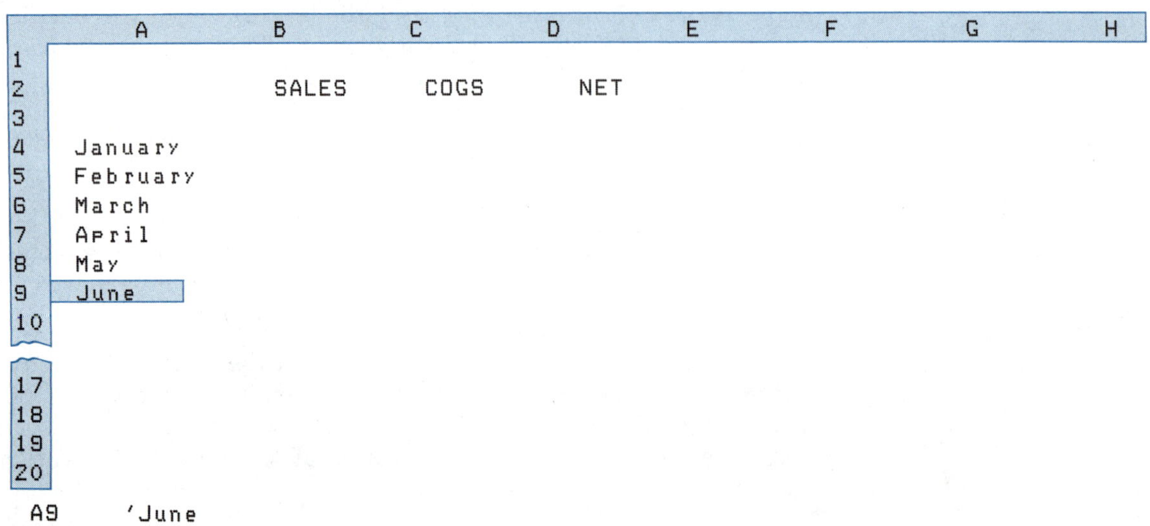

Next, you move to the cell B4 and enter the number 100000.

	A	B	C	D	E	F	G	H
1								
2		SALES	COGS	NET				
3								
4	January	100000						
5	February							
6	March							
7	April							
8	May							
9	June							
10								
17								
18								
19								
20								

B4 100000

Since sales will increase by 10% each month, your next step is to move to cell B5 and enter a formula to compute February's SALES. That formula takes the form 1.1*B4. This formula tells the computer to display in cell B5 the results of multiplying 1.1 times the value displayed in cell B4.

	A	B	C	D	E	F	G	H
1								
2		SALES	COGS	NET				
3								
4	January	100000						
5	February	110000						
6	March							
7	April							
8	May							
9	June							
10								
17								
18								
19								
20								

B5 1.1*B4

The calculated results, not the actual formula, are displayed in the spreadsheet. The formula may, however, be seen at the bottom of the screen as the contents of the current cell.

With the appropriate formula entered into cell B5, your next task is to copy that formula into the rest of the cells in the column. You tap the slash (/) key, and the bottom of the screen changes. It now displays:

	A	B	C	D	E	F	G	H
1								
2		SALES	COGS	NET				
3								
4	January	100000						
5	February	110000						
6	March							
7	April							
8	May							
9	June							
10								
17								
18								
19								
20								

B5

2Worksheet 3Range 4Copy 5Move 6File 7Print 8Graph 9Data 0Quit

This is a menu of VP-Planner commands. You select the /Copy command and use it to copy the formula into the cells B6 through B9.

Your next task is to enter the formulas to reflect the fact that cost of goods sold is 65% of sales and the net is the difference between sales and COGS; then you copy those formulas into the appropriate cells. When you are finished, each cell has the following contents.

	A	B	C	D	E	F	G	H
1								
2		SALES	COGS	NET				
3								
4	January	100000	.65*B4	+B4-C4				
5	February	1.1*B4	.65*B5	+B5-C5				
6	March	1.1*B5	.65*B6	+B6-C6				
7	April	1.1*B6	.65*B7	+B7-C7				
8	May	1.1*B7	.65*B8	+B8-C8				
9	June	1.1*B8	.65*B9	+B9-C9				

The spreadsheet is displayed on the monitor screen as:

	A	B	C	D	E	F	G	H
1								
2		SALES	COGS	NET				
3								
4	January	100000	65000	35000				
5	February	110000	71500	38500				
6	March	121000	78650	42350				
7	April	133100	86515	46585				
8	May	146410	95166.5	51243.5				
9	June	161051	104683.2	56367.85				

Creating a File

This example of creating a spreadsheet using VP-Planner demonstrated several important fundamentals. To start, you created the spreadsheet by entering data into the spreadsheet's cells. As you entered the data you created a file in RAM memory. The file used up a portion of the space available in RAM and could be represented in the model as:

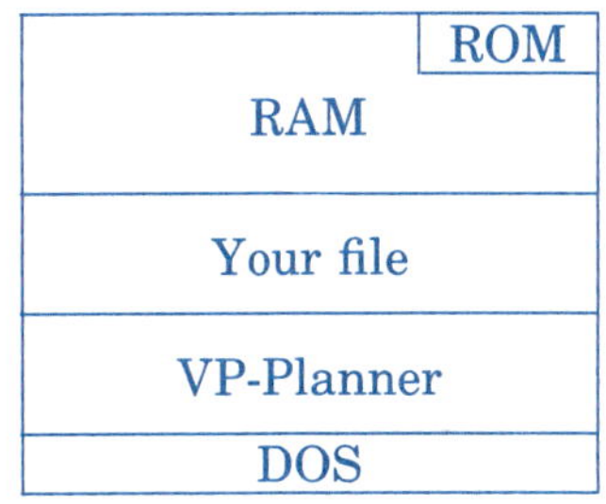

Variables

Using this model to take a close look at your file in RAM, you can see it is composed of several distinct areas of RAM memory called memory locations. Each memory location holds a spreadsheet data item and has a unique memory location name. With the spreadsheet applications, a memory location's name can be considered the same name as the spreadsheet cell holding the data.

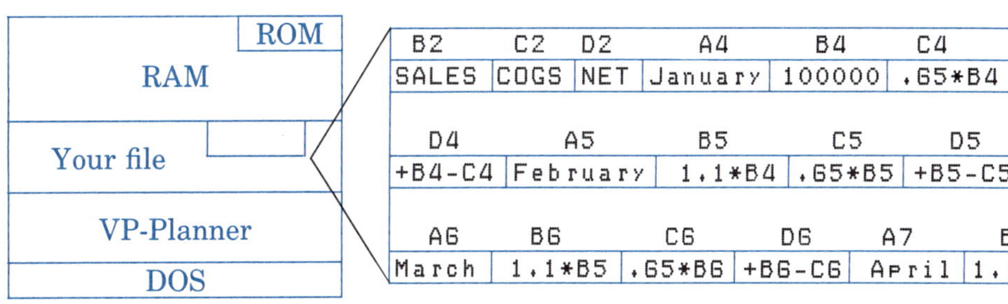

Programmers call these memory locations *variables.* It is fundamental when you use a computer that when you enter data or cause the computer to create data (e.g., use the /Copy command to enter data into cells), that those data items are held by the computer in variables. Each variable has a unique name known as its *address.* The act of entering data into a variable is called *assignment.*

After data items have been assigned to variables you can refer to them by using the addresses of the variables in which they are held. It is important for nonprogrammers to understand this concept since there are general rules about how assignment may or may not be done and about how the computer treats data held in variables.

Data Entry vs. Command Modes

When you are using the microcomputer system, for example, when you are creating a spreadsheet, a text, or a database, you will find that you are doing one of two things. You either are directly entering data (assigning data to variables) or you are entering software commands.

In this example, as you moved the pointer around the spreadsheet and typed labels and formulas, you were directly assigning data. As soon as you tapped the slash (/) key, however, you began using VP-Planner's commands. Until you were finished using these commands you were not able to enter data into variables by using the pointer and keyboard. There were two modes: a *data entry mode* and a *command mode*. The same two modes are apparent in every software covered in this manual. Beginning users can avoid many common problems if they understand this fundamental concept and remain aware of it while they use the computer.

Numeric vs. String Data

A numeric data item is a number, while a string data item is a group of characters. An expression is composed of numeric or string data items. Whether you are entering data into a variable or using it in a software command, your data take one of two forms—a numeric expression or a string expression.

When two or more data items are used in an expression they are connected with operators. Examples of operators are the mathematical operators for addition (+) and subtraction (−).

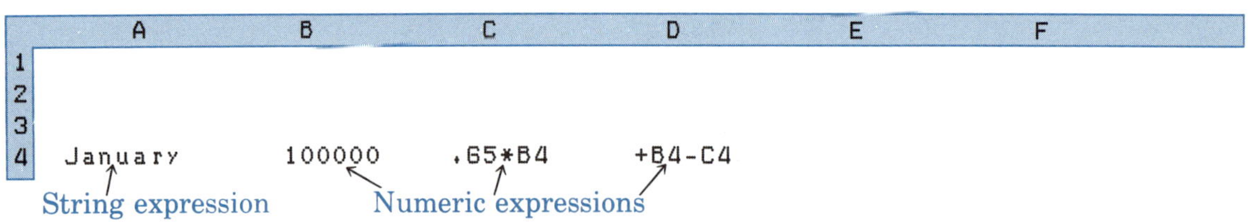

In this portion of the example spreadsheet, the variable A4 held a *string expression,* and the variables B4, C4, and D4 held *numeric expressions.* The simplest string expression is a single group of characters such as the group of letters that spell *January.* All of the string expressions used in the spreadsheet were of this type. The simplest numeric expression is a single number. The cell B4 holding the number 100000 was the only cell in the spreadsheet holding the simple type of numeric expression. Both simple expressions were made up of a single data item.

More complicated expressions are made up of data items and operators whose value can be determined by the computer. For example, the data held in cell C4 (.65*B4) is a numeric expression composed of two numeric data items (a number and the address of a variable holding a number) connected with the proper operator for multiplication. The computer can determine the value for this expression as it performs the operation of multiplication.

When the applications software being used deals with both numbers and strings, these two types of data cannot be mixed within a single expression of this type. When an expression is to be assigned to a variable, the computer needs to know in advance if that variable will be holding a string or a numeric expression.

The only applications software in which separation of types of data is relatively unimportant is word processing. Word processing typically deals only with string data.

Numeric Expressions

The items in a numeric expression may include numbers and/or the names of variables holding numeric expressions. The operators in the expression may include the following *mathematical operators.*

Operation	Operator
Exponentiation	^
Multiplication	*
Division	/
Addition	+
Subtraction	−

The formulas in the example spreadsheet are numeric expressions that use such operators. When the computer evaluates the expressions, it arrives at the answer to the formulas by performing the mathematical operations involved. The computer normally uses a specific order of precedence in performing mathematical operations. The order is:

- First — Any operations in parentheses.
- Second — Exponentiation (^).
- Third — Multiplication (*) and/or division (/).
- Fourth — Addition (+) and/or subtraction (−).

For example, to answer the question, "How much money do I need to deposit in the bank today in order to have *D* number of dollars in the bank *N* number of years from today if the bank pays me a yearly interest rate of *I* percent?" you may use the following formula:

D = ending dollars
I = interest rate
N = number of periods

$$D \times \frac{(1 + I)^N}{I}$$

To enter the formula so that the computer is able to evaluate it correctly, you would type:

```
D*((1+I)^N/I)
```

When the computer evaluates the numeric expression it will use the numeric values held in the variables named *D, I,* and *N* to arrive at the answer. Of course it is your responsibility to make sure the variables used in the formula have the correct values in them, and that you are using the correct variable names in your expression.

String Expressions

The most common form of string expression is the simple one of a single group of characters. Several issues, however, can be confusing to the beginning user regarding exactly what these simple string data items are.

A group of characters means a group of any characters, including spaces; all special characters such as ?, #, $, ^, *, (, −, =, +, !; and numbers. So, even though a data item such as "1235 S.W. Fulton Park Blvd." contains separate words and numbers, it is still only a single simple string data item.

The basic difference between numeric expressions and string expressions is that the computer does not perform mathematical operations on string data. This is important since some data items look like numbers but need to be treated like strings.

A good example is a telephone number, such as 244-7163. If you wanted this data item entered into your spreadsheet, DBMS, or BASIC program, you would need to be sure that the variable used to hold it was specified in advance to hold string data. Otherwise, the computer automatically would subtract 7,163 from 244 and subsequently use the results of that mathematical operation. In the case of a spreadsheet it would display -6919 in the cell into which the telephone number was entered.

Occasionally string expressions of the form "Hello" + "there" are used. Although the operator used in the expression is a plus sign, the operation is not the mathematical operation of addition. The operation is the string operation called *concatenation*. The result of the computer's evaluation of this string expression would be "Hellothere".

Functions

Both numeric and string expressions may contain *functions*. Functions can be described as built-in shortcuts to accomplish what would otherwise require a long numeric or string expression. Sometimes functions accomplish what might otherwise be impossible. Functions usually take the form:

XYZ(expression)

The function's name (in this case, XYZ) is followed by parentheses containing an expression which is referred to as the function's argument. When the computer evaluates a function it is said to return a value from its argument.

For example, all of the software covered in this manual except WordPerfect have some form of the Integer function which returns the integer value of its argument. In the spreadsheet applications, if you entered the numeric expression @**INT**(10/3) into a spreadsheet cell, the computer's evaluation of the expression would return the integer 3, and the computer would display that value in the cell.

Logical Expressions

A string or numeric expression can take a form in which the computer's evaluation of it results in whether or not that expression is true. When an expression takes this form the computer evaluates it as being equal to zero (0) if the expression is false, or equal to 1 [more accurately, not equal to zero (0)] if the expression is true.

For instance, if you were to move the pointer to a spreadsheet cell and enter the numeric expression $1 > 2$ the computer would display a zero in that cell since 1 is not greater than 2.

Logical expressions are important because they enable the computer to make a decision. Every software covered in this manual provides the user with options to enter data or use commands that are conditional. But the ways in which these options are presented to the user vary so much in their syntax (the exact manner in which the data item or command is typed) that only a general discussion of how conditions work is included here.

Conditions

The operators used in logical expressions are called *relational operators* since they are used to describe a relationship—such as greater than, less than, or equal to—between two data items. The two data items must be the same type, either numeric or string. The most common forms of these operators are shown in the following table.

Relationship	Operator
Greater than	>
Less than	<
Equal to	=
Equal to or greater than	>=
Equal to or less than	<=
Not equal to	< >

The general form of a condition is:

> If a relationship is true,
> the computer will perform a certain action.
> Otherwise,
> the computer will perform another certain action.

For instance, with a spreadsheet application it is possible to enter an expression that effectively says:

> If the value displayed in cell D9 is less than 45000
> display in this cell the value of zero.
> Otherwise,
> display in this cell the difference between
> the value displayed in D9 and 45000.

A spreadsheet function is used and the exact syntax for the expression is:

```
@IF(D9<45000,0,D9-45000)
```

Relationship to test — True action — False action

In the following example spreadsheet, this logical expression might be used to display "PROFITS" given the new information that fixed costs are $45,000 per month.

	A	B	C	D	E	F	G	H
1								
2		SALES	COGS	NET	PROFITS			
3								
4	January	100000	65000	35000	0			
5	February	110000	71500	38500	0			
6	March	121000	78650	42350	0			
7	April	133100	86515	46585	1585			
8	May	146410	95166.5	51243.5	6243.5			
9	June	161051	104683.2	56367.85	11367.85			

It is sometimes surprising to beginning users that logical expressions can test relationships between string data. For example, the expression:

"Anderson John" < "Anderson Larry"

is perfectly acceptable to the computer and would be evaluated as true. The ability to test relationships between strings is the basis for the computer's ability to sort data items such as names and addresses and to search for particular string data.

Logical Operators

Logical operators usually are used to connect two or more relationships into a single expression. The computer then evaluates the total expression as either true or false. If the total expression is evaluated as true, one action is performed. If the total expression is evaluated as false, another action is performed. The most commonly used logical operators follow.

Logical connection	Operator
The relationship(s) must be false in order for the total expression to be true	NOT
All relationships must be true in order for the total expression to be true	AND
Any relationship may be true in order for the total expression to be true	OR

The logical operator NOT is primarily used in special cases in which simply reversing the relational operators is not possible or desirable. The logical operator NOT could be used, for example, in the expression:

IF NOT D9 >= 45000

It accomplishes the same thing as:

IF D9 < 45000

The other two logical operators, AND and OR, often are used in expressions. The general forms of these logical operators are:

IF relationship AND relationship is true,
perform a certain action.

or

IF relationship OR relationship is true,
perform a certain action.

In the first case, IF relationship AND relationship, both relationships must be tested and evaluated as true in order for the total expression to be evaluated as true. For example, the total expression

IF 400 < 500	AND	"Able" < "Baker"
true		true

will be evaluated by the computer as true. Notice that the use of logical operators permits both types of data (numeric and string) to be used as long as data type is consistent within a given relationship.

In the second case, IF relationship OR relationship, either or both relationships may be evaluated as true for the total expression to be evaluated as true. For example, the total expression

IF 500 > 600	OR	"Able" < "Baker"
false		true

will be evaluated by the computer as true.

Many beginning users have trouble deciding which of these two logical operators to use when they are trying to accomplish a task. One method that can be very useful in helping answer this question uses the following rules: AND means to multiply; OR means to add; and true means not equal to zero.

IF 400 < 500	AND	"Able" < "Baker"	
true = 1		true = 1	
1	*	1	= 1 – the total expression's value is = 1 (true)
	AND means multiply		

IF 500 > 600	OR	"Able" < "Baker"	
false = 0		true = 1	
0	+	1	= 1 – the total expression's value is = 1 (true)
	OR means add		

With the operator AND, only if both relationships are evaluated as true (equal to 1) will the total expression be evaluated as true (equal to 1). If either relationship is false (equal to 0), the results of multiplication will make the total expression false (equal to 0).

With the logical operator OR, if either relationship is evaluated as true (equal to 1) the total expression will be evaluated as true (equal to 1). Only if both relationships are false (equal to 0) will the results of addition make the total expression false (equal to 0).

Using this approach, you can use an example case in which you want the true action to be performed, and easily evaluate it yourself to see if it passes the test.

Precedence of Logical Operators

Logical operators have an order of precedence just like mathematical operators. In complex expressions where several logical operators are being used, the expression usually is evaluated according to the order:

- First — NOT
- Second — AND
- Third — OR

so that the expression:

relationship AND relationship OR relationship AND relationship

is evaluated in the order:

(relationship AND relationship) OR (relationship AND relationship)

The order may be altered through the use of parentheses in the same way that mathematical operations' order may be altered. When parentheses are used, the expression takes on an entirely different meaning.

relationship AND (relationship OR relationship) AND relationship

Saving a Spreadsheet—Example Session, Part IV

You are satisfied with the forecasting spreadsheet you have created and are ready to quit using the microcomputer. First you insert a formatted diskette into the disk drive on the right side of the computer. Then you tap the slash (/) key and the Main menu of commands appears.

	A	B	C	D	E	F
1						
2		SALES	COGS	NET		
3						
4	January	100000.00	65000.00	35000.00		
5	February	110000.00	71500.00	38500.00		
6	March	121000.00	78650.00	42350.00		
7	April	133100.00	86515.00	46585.00		
8	May	146410.00	95166.50	51243.50		
9	June	161051.00	104683.15	56367.85		
10						
17						
18						
19						
20						

A1

2Worksheet 3Range 4Copy 5Move 6File 7Print 8Graph 9Data 0Quit

You select the /Files Save command and the computer displays the prompt at the bottom of the screen:

```
          A              B            C             D             E            F
 1
 2                     SALES        COGS           NET
 3
 4  January         100000.00     65000.00      35000.00
 5  February        110000.00     71500.00      38500.00
 6  March           121000.00     78650.00      42350.00
 7  April           133100.00     86515.00      46585.00
 8  May             146410.00     95166.50      51243.50
 9  June            161051.00    104683.15      56367.85
10
11

17
18
19
20
A1    Enter File Name:
```

You decide to name this spreadsheet data file FORECAST. You type the name and tap the Enter key. You again see the right disk drive light come on and hear the whirring sound.

Next you enter the /**W**orksheet **E**rase command and the spreadsheet you created disappears from the screen. You then enter the /**Q**uit command and the blank spreadsheet disappears from the screen. You are left with only DOS's A> on the monitor screen.

Next you type **DIR** B: and tap the Enter key. The computer responds by putting on the monitor screen:

```
A>DIR B:
FORECAST  WKS     1097     3-07-88

        1 File(s)
A>
```

Saving Your Work

The computer's RAM memory is known as *volatile* memory. *Volatile* is defined as "easily turned to vapor." Any software or data being held in RAM memory is "vaporized" the instant the computer is turned off.

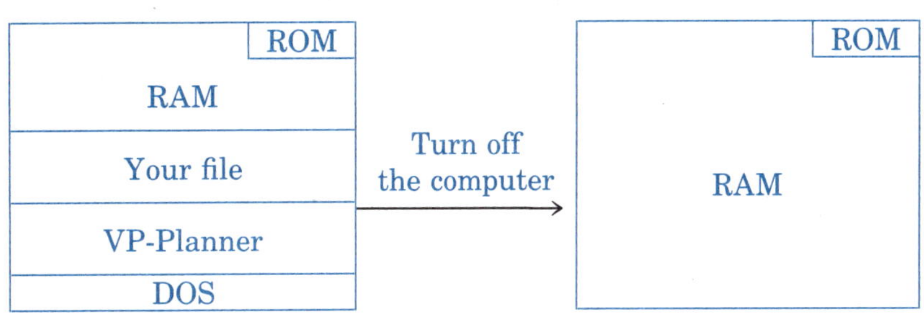

With DOS and VP-Planner this is not a problem because both softwares already exist in a permanent form on a diskette. If they are erased from RAM memory, you need only have the computer read them back into RAM memory. Your file, however, was created in RAM memory and must be saved in a permanent form to be used again later.

Naming a File

Every software covered in this manual has commands used to save a copy of your files created in RAM memory onto a diskette. In each case you must name the file in order for a copy of it to be saved. Every software covered here also has commands to read your files back into RAM memory. The computer uses the name you give your file to determine which file to retrieve from the diskette.

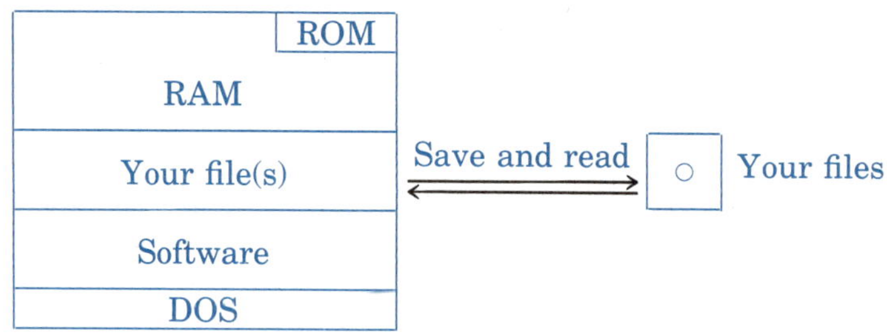

Filename Extensions

In the example, when you used the /**F**ile **S**ave command the computer prompted you to name your spreadsheet data file. After you named the file FORECAST, the computer made a copy of the spreadsheet data and recorded the copy on the diskette under the filename "FORECAST.WKS."

The .WKS following the filename is called a *filename extension* and was added by the computer according to the instructions of VP-Planner. It was added so that later, when you wanted the data read back into RAM memory, the computer would know it was looking for a .WKS file—a spreadsheet data file originally created using VP-Planner. All of the softwares covered in this manual instruct the computer to add extensions to the filenames.

Saving and Resaving Data

The beginning user may be confused about what the computer does when it saves data to a diskette and such confusion can lead to extra and unnecessary work. The computer rarely physically moves data. Instead, it makes a copy of the data, and then places that copy in the new location. In the example, after you entered the commands to save your spreadsheet data, and the computer executed the commands, you had two identical sets of data—one in RAM memory and a copy stored on the diskette.

The data set copied onto the diskette was a copy of the data that were in RAM memory at that time. If after saving it you made any changes to the spreadsheet data in RAM memory, those changes would not be made to the copy on the diskette. You need to save the data again in order for those changes to be made to the copy on the diskette.

Saving the data again with the same filename that you used previously (FORECAST) updates the copy on the diskette for any changes you may have made to the copy in RAM memory. When you update, the old copy on the diskette is replaced by a new one.

It is a good habit to resave your data (update the copy on the diskette) every fifteen minutes or so.

How the Computer Saves Your Data

When the computer saves your data on the diskette, it takes the copy it has made and divides it into blocks of data. It then looks for room on the diskette for those blocks and saves them one block at a time. As it stores the blocks of data it records where they can be found and where they came from (the name of the file) in a special area of the diskette called the file allocation table (FAT). When you later want that file read back into RAM memory, the computer uses the FAT to locate the blocks. It then copies them into RAM memory in the order in which they were stored.

Formatted Diskettes

The term *formatted* was used to describe the diskette you inserted into the disk drive in the example. When you first purchase a diskette it is unformatted. Before the computer can save blocks of data onto a diskette, the diskette must be formatted.

Formatting a diskette establishes where data may or may not be saved, configures the file allocation table for the diskette, and marks defective areas (if any) so that data will not be saved there. A special utility program with the filename FORMAT.COM is on the DOS diskette purchased with the computer. This program is used to format a new diskette to the specifications of the IBM PC and to the version of DOS being used. You need only format a diskette once, but, until it is formatted, the computer will not be able to save data on it.

Erasing Data and Software from RAM Memory

In the example, after you saved your spreadsheet you used two commands of VP-Planner, /**W**orksheet **E**rase and /**Q**uit. These commands have their command counterparts in every software covered in this manual.

The first command (/**W**orksheet **E**rase) was used to erase your data from RAM memory, but it left the VP-Planner spreadsheet software there.

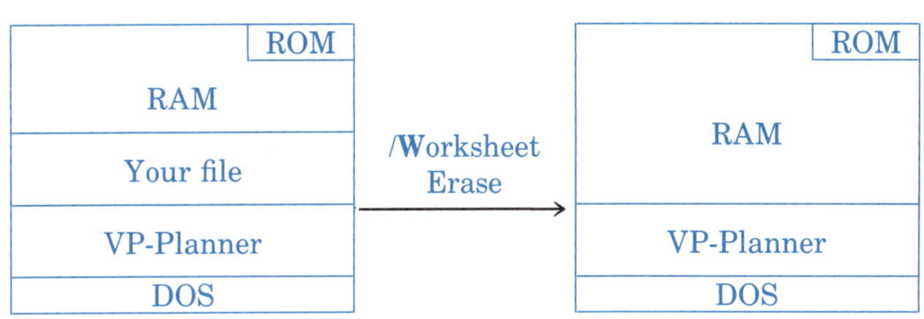

It allows you to create a new spreadsheet in RAM memory using VP-Planner.

The second command that you used (/**Q**uit) erases any spreadsheet data that may be in RAM memory, and also erases the applications software, VP-Planner, from RAM memory.

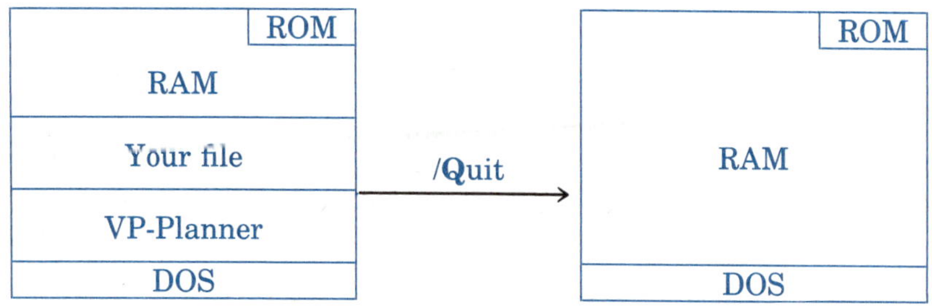

/**Q**uit returns you to the DOS level of operation. Then you may use the commands of DOS or type the filename of another software for the computer to read into RAM memory.

Returning to DOS

In the final step of the example you typed the DOS command **DIR** B:. This variation of DOS's **DIR** command tells the computer to list a directory of the files found on the diskette in the disk drive on the right side of the computer.

When the computer listed the directory you saw that the file you created using VP-Planner was saved under the name you gave it, with the extension added by the computer, and that it used up approximately 1,000 bytes of the space available to hold data on that diskette.

Summary

To illustrate spreadsheet application software an example of a simple spreadsheet was used to show how the computer may be used to automatically recalculate for changes made. The same example then was expanded into an example session to further explain some of the cross-application concepts and fundamentals of using the microcomputer.

If you were to create the spreadsheet, show it to your boss, and then move the pointer to January's sales and instruct your boss how to change the dollar figure there, you have, in effect, created a canned program for your boss's use. It is easy to use (high level) but has a limited use (low power). To create it you used the applications software, VP-Planner, which is not as easy to use, but is considerably more powerful. You can create many different spreadsheets with your knowledge of this applications software.

The creators of VP-Planner used a programming language to create it. The same programming language could be used to create other applications software for other purposes, such as word processing or database management. The programming languages used are very low level, very high powered. The computer is a very flexible general purpose tool that can be used at a variety of levels to perform a variety of tasks.

The DOS Diskette

The DOS diskette and the IBM manual for DOS usually are purchased with the computer. While the packaging and manual suggest that a single thing called DOS is on the diskette, there are, in fact, three separate things on the DOS diskette.

The DOS diskette has on it the software with the filename COMMAND.COM. This file with two or more (depending on the version of DOS) hidden files—files protected from your access to them—comprise the disk operating system for the IBM Personal Computer (PC DOS). The DOS diskette also has on it several DOS utility programs. The manual refers to the utility programs as DOS external commands, but they actually are separate small software programs. Finally, the DOS diskette includes the software named BASICA.COM, which is a programming language software.

DOS

The software DOS automatically is read into RAM memory when the computer is turned on. You know that DOS has successfully been read into RAM memory when an A> appears on the monitor screen. Once DOS is read into RAM memory, the computer is able to read other software into RAM memory. In addition, the computer is able to execute some important DOS commands.

DOS Commands

The DOS commands are used for file maintenance. With DOS you can erase, copy, rename, or view any particular file on a diskette. You also can check how many files are on a diskette and how much space is left on the diskette for saving files. In short, DOS provides you the means to keep your diskette clean, neat, and organized. The following table provides short descriptions for the important DOS commands.

Command	Description
DIR	Lists a directory of all files on a diskette. Directory includes filename.ext, size in bytes, and date/time stamp.
TYPE	Displays the contents of a file on the monitor screen.
ERASE	Erases a file from the diskette.
COPY	Produces a copy of a file.
RENAME	Renames a file.
A: or **B:**	Changes the current drive (the default disk drive status).

File Specifications

To use the commands of DOS you must identify files by entering their file specifications. A file's specification is composed of three parts: the device name of the disk drive where the file may be found; the filename you gave the file when it was created; and the filename extension added by the software when the file was created.

```
B:myfile.WKS
```

Disk drive → B: Filename → myfile Extension → WKS

Disk Drive Device Names

The hardware of a personal computer may include more than one disk drive. Although disk drive device names may be altered, it is standard that the disk drive located on the left front of the system unit has the name A:, the disk drive located on the right front of the system unit has the name B:, and any other drive has the name C:.

Filenames

The user assigns a filename to a file when it is created. The safest rules to follow when naming a file are to use one to eight characters, start with a letter, and use no special characters. A filename may be composed of letters and numbers as long as the first character is a letter. No spaces or special characters may be included in the name.

Filename Extensions

Filename extensions are added to the filename at the time the file is created by the software that is being used at the time. Each type of file will be given a different filename extension by the software to identify it by type.

Example DOS Command

To demonstrate how the three parts of a file specification may be used in a DOS command, the following example uses the **ERASE** command of DOS, which causes the computer to erase a file from a diskette.

```
A>ERASE B:myfile.WKS
```

Here the file to erase is in the B: drive. It was named "myfile" by the user and the software (in this case, VP-Planner) added a .WKS filename extension to identify it as a spreadsheet data file.

Default Drive Status

When you first load DOS, the default disk drive status is A:. Default disk drive status means that when a file specification used in a DOS command does not indicate the name of the disk drive, the computer automatically will look to the A: drive for the file.

You can change the default disk drive status by entering the desired device name. For instance, typing A>**B:**↵ (↵ means tap the Enter key) will change the default disk drive status to the B: drive. Any further command excluding a disk drive name will cause the computer to look to the B: drive for the file of concern.

When the default disk drive status is changed, DOS's prompt changes to reflect the change. In the last example, (A>**B:**↵), the new prompt shown on the monitor screen will be B>.

Wild Card Characters

Wild card characters may be used in place of parts or all of the filename and/or filename extension in a DOS command. Two such characters are the question mark (?) and the asterisk (*). The question mark has the effect of saying "accept any character in this position" and the asterisk has the effect of saying "accept all remaining characters here."

Expanding on the previous example of the **ERASE** command, typing

```
A>ERASE B:*.WKS
```

would cause the computer to erase all .WKS files from the diskette in the B: drive. Typing

```
A>ERASE B:myfile.*
```

would erase all files with the filename "myfile" regardless of their filename extensions. Typing

```
A>ERASE B:*.*
```

would erase all files from the diskette in the B: drive.

If there are three .WKS files on the diskette named myfile1, myfile2, and myfile3, typing

```
A>ERASE B:myfile?.WKS
```

would erase all of those files.

Wild card characters may be used together within a file specification in any manner and order that the computer is able to evaluate.

COMPUTERS WITH HARD-DISK DRIVES

Introduction to Hard Disks

Many microcomputers come equipped with a disk drive that has a disk permanently mounted and sealed within it. The disk drive is referred to as a "fixed" or "hard" disk drive. It usually operates under the DOS device name C:.

The disk found inside a hard-disk drive functions in much the same manner as a floppy diskette. It is made of magnetic storage media, it must be formatted before data may be saved on it, and it is spun within the disk drive while a reading head scans across it during read/write (loading and saving) operations.

The major difference between a hard disk and a floppy diskette is storage capacity.

Disk Storage Capacity

A standard floppy diskette is able to store about 360,000 characters (360 kilobytes) of data on its surface. While different types of hard disks are able to store different amounts of data, the smaller hard disks generally have about 10 million characters (10 megabytes) of storage capacity. Some models of hard disks are able to store over 100 million characters (100 megabytes) of data on their surface.

The vast storage capacity of a hard disk provides a valuable convenience to the user, but using a hard disk is not without its problems. To make efficient use of the storage capacity of a hard disk, the user must practice good file management technique . . . the art of organizing related files of data.

An Overview of Subdirectories

To assist the user in the management of files on a hard disk, DOS (Version 2.0+) provides commands that may be used to group files together so that they can be dealt with separately from other files on the hard disk. The files are grouped together onto disk subdirectories.

It is useful to think of subdirectories as a partitioning of the hard disk into separate disks upon which files may be stored. Each subdirectory (disk) is given a unique name by the user at the time it is created. Later, when the user wants to deal with the files on a particular subdirectory, he or she enters a DOS command to change over to that subdirectory (disk).

To further explain the use of subdirectories and their value to managing the files on a disk, the following uses a typical example of what might be done when one first acquires a microcomputer with a hard disk.

An Example of Hard Disk File Management

Computer Hardware Configuration

A computer with a hard-disk drive installed also will have at least one other floppy diskette drive installed. The floppy diskette drive operates under the DOS device name A:.

It is important to note that when the computer is first turned on or is rebooted with ^Alt-Del, it is the A: drive that the computer will first look to for the software DOS.

If the diskette in the A: drive has DOS on it, it will automatically be read into RAM memory and, after any initial prompts have been answered, an A> (A prompt) will appear on the screen.

Formatting a Hard Disk

In the example here, it is assumed that the hard disk has yet to be formatted and the diskette in the A: drive is the DOS diskette purchased with the computer. *Formatting any disk or diskette erases all files that may have pre-*

viously existed on the disk or diskette. (See FORMAT.COM for more information.) With the DOS diskette in the A: drive, you type:

```
A>FORMAT C:/S
```

This will load the DOS utility program FORMAT.COM into memory. The C: used in the command specifies that it is the hard disk you want formatted and the **/S** instructs the FORMAT program to copy DOS from the diskette in the A: drive onto the disk in the C: drive after the format operation is complete. When finished, the screen will appear similar to:

```
A>FORMAT C:/S
WARNING, ALL DATA ON NON-REMOVABLE DISK
DRIVE C: WILL BE LOST!
Proceed with Format (Y/N)?y

Formatting . . . Format complete
System transferred

10584064 bytes total disk space
   65535 bytes used by system
10518528 bytes available on disk
```

Changing the Current Drive

After the hard disk is formatted, you may cause it to become the current drive by typing:

```
A>C:↵
```

At this point the A> changes to C> to indicate that the C: drive is now the current drive, the default drive to which DOS will look when executing any DOS command or reading a software file into RAM memory.

If you now enter the DOS command DIR, the screen will display

```
 C>DIR

 Volume in drive C has no label
 Directory of C:\

COMMAND  COM    23210    7-25-86  4:49p
        1 File(s) 10518528 bytes free
```

The Root Directory

So far in the example, the hard disk has only one directory with one visible file (COMMAND.COM) on it. The directory is called the "Root Directory" and can be thought of as one disk residing on the hard disk.

Booting the Computer from the Hard Disk

Remember that when the computer is first turned on, or is rebooted with ^Alt-Del, the computer will first look to the A: drive for DOS. If there is no diskette in the A: drive (or the A: drive door is left open), the computer will next look to the root directory of the C: drive for DOS.

In the example, DOS has been successfully copied onto the root directory of the C: drive. Now, to load DOS from the C: drive simply requires that the A: drive is left empty or the A: drive door is left open when the computer is started.

Files on the Root Directory

You will want to keep the number of files you have in the root directory of the hard disk to a minimum. DOS and perhaps a few necessary DOS related files are all that should be kept there. Examples of DOS related files you may want to keep in the root directory include the following.

CONFIG.SYS The DOS file CONFIG.SYS is used to override the default input/output attributes of DOS. It is simply a text file that you may create with a word processing software, or in the same manner that the AUTOEXEC.BAT file is created in the Introduction's Hints and Hazards section.

The CONFIG.SYS file is particularly important if you intend to use dBase III or dBase III Plus, and it should be on the root directory. The recommended contents of the CONFIG.SYS file are:

```
FILES = 20
BUFFERS = 24
```

VDISK.SYS The VDISK.SYS program is a DOS utility software found on the DOS diskette. It is used to create what is called a "phantom" or RAM disk drive. It is particularly useful when the microcomputer has only one floppy diskette drive in addition to its C: drive. VDISK.SYS configures a portion of the computer's RAM memory into what is essentially a temporary disk drive. It will assign a DOS device name to the drive (usually D:). You then may use the RAM drive (D:) for temporary storage of data while using the computer.

It is important to note that the RAM drive is not a real disk drive, and any data on it will vaporize the instant the computer is turned off. Therefore, you must copy any data you want to keep onto a real disk or diskette before turning off the computer.

Also, the RAM drive reduces the amount of RAM memory available for processing data. If the software you are using requires a large amount of RAM memory, you may not be able to use it and the RAM drive at the same time.

To use VDISK.SYS to create a RAM drive at the time the computer is booted, copy the VDISK.SYS program onto the root directory. You then must add the following line to your existing root directory CONFIG.SYS file, or create a root directory CONFIG.SYS file with the line in it.

```
DEVICE = VDISK nnn
```

The "nnn" represents the size of the RAM drive you want created. For instance, DEVICE = VDISK 256 will create a 256 Kilobyte RAM disk drive.

In the example, assume that the preceding files have been created or copied onto the root directory. Now, if the **DIR** command is entered while the C: drive is the current drive, the screen will display:

```
 C>DIR

 Volume in drive C has no label
 Directory of C:\

COMMAND   COM    23210     7-25-86   4:49p
CONFIG    SYS       46     7-25-87   4:35p
VDISK     SYS     3307     3-07-85   1:43p
        3 File(s) 10510336 bytes free
```

Making a Subdirectory, the MD\ Command

To continue with the example, you now copy a word processing software onto the hard disk. However, before doing so, a subdirectory will be created using the DOS command **MD** (Make Directory). The directory will be named "WORDS." At the C> the following is typed and entered:

```
C>MD\WORDS
```

When done, the **DIR** command is entered again and the screen displays:

```
C>DIR

 Volume in drive C has no label
 Directory of C:\

COMMAND   COM    23210     7-25-86   4:49p
CONFIG    SYS       46     7-25-87   4:35p
VDISK     SYS     3307     3-07-85   1:43p
WORDS        <DIR>         7-25-87   4:50p
        4 File(s) 10506240 bytes free
```

The last item in the directory indicates that a subdirectory has been created. Again, it is useful to think of subdirectories as separate disks residing on the hard disk. At this point in the example there are two such disks—one named "WORDS" and the other the root directory.

Subdirectory Names

The names you choose to name your subdirectories must follow the same rules as those used in naming files—that is, one to eight characters, start with a letter, and include no special characters such as spaces or commas.

In addition, it is recommended that you keep your subdirectory names descriptive, but as short as possible in length.

Changing to a Subdirectory, the CD\ Command

In much the same manner as one changes the current disk drive by entering A:, C:, etc., you are able to change current subdirectories by using the

CD (Change Directory) command of DOS. Changing subdirectories is roughly equivalent to changing disks in the C: drive. Here, to change to the subdirectory WORDS, you would type:

```
C>CD\WORDS
```

Now if you enter the command **DIR,** the screen will display:

```
C>DIR

  Volume in drive C has no label
  Directory of C:\WORDS

.            <DIR>        1-01-80  12:18a
..           <DIR>        1-01-80  12:18a
        2 File(s)  10506240 bytes free
```

The information on the screen indicates that, as yet, there are no files on the subdirectory WORDS. The two <**DIR**>s listed indicate that you are currently working with a subdirectory and make reference to the root directory.

Changing the DOS Prompt

When using subdirectories, it is essential that you are aware of which subdirectory is current at any point in time. A very useful feature of DOS is the ability to use the **PROMPT** command to change its C> (C prompt) to display the information. To do so you enter:

```
C>PROMPT = $P$G
```

In the example, the command changes the C> to be C:\WORDS>. This is such a useful feature that, if your particular computer does not automatically display the subdirectory information, it is recommended that you put this command line (PROMPT = PG) in an AUTOEXEC.BAT file on the root directory. (See AUTOEXEC.BAT files, Introduction's Hints and Hazards section.)

Copying Files from the A: Drive to a C: Drive Subdirectory

At this point in the example, you are ready to copy your word processing software onto the WORDS subdirectory of the C: drive. To do so, you may put the word processing diskette into the A: drive. You then may change the current drive to A: by entering A:↵ and then copying all the files in the A: drive to the C: drive by entering the command:

```
A>COPY *.* C:
```

It is important to note that even though the C: drive was no longer the current drive, the subdirectory WORDS on the C: drive remained the current subdirectory. That is, if you consider a subdirectory as being like a separate disk, the WORDS disk was left in the C: drive when the A: drive was made current. Therefore, the A>COPY *.* C: command caused all files on the diskette in A: drive to be copied onto the WORDS subdirectory (disk) in the C: drive.

If you now change the current drive to be the C: drive, WORDS will still be the current subdirectory and the **DIR** command will display something similar to:

```
C:\WORDS>DIR

 Volume in drive C has no label
 Directory of C:\WORDS

.              <DIR>       1-01-80   12:18a
..             <DIR>       1-01-80   12:18a
WP        EXE    264113   12-04-86    3:09p
WPHELP    FIL      1508   12-04-86    3:09p
LEX       WP       8535   12-16-86    3:01a
README    WP       1304   12-03-86   10:08a
TH        WP       2051   12-03-86    9:44a
        7 File(s)   10215424 bytes free
```

The files now listed on WORDS represent the various files associated with the word processing software used in the example.

Changing Back to the Root Directory

To make the root directory the current directory, you may enter the command **CD**—that is, the Change Directory command with no subdirectory specified. In the example, if you entered the command **CD** and then **DIR**, the screen would display:

```
C:\>DIR

 Volume in drive C has no label
 Directory of C:\

COMMAND   COM    23210      7-25-86  4:49p
CONFIG    SYS       46      7-25-87  4:35p
VDISK     SYS     3307      3-07-85  1:43p
WORDS        <DIR>          7-25-87  4:50p
        4 File(s)   10215424 bytes free
```

At this point, the relationship of the root directory and WORDS might be graphically represented as:

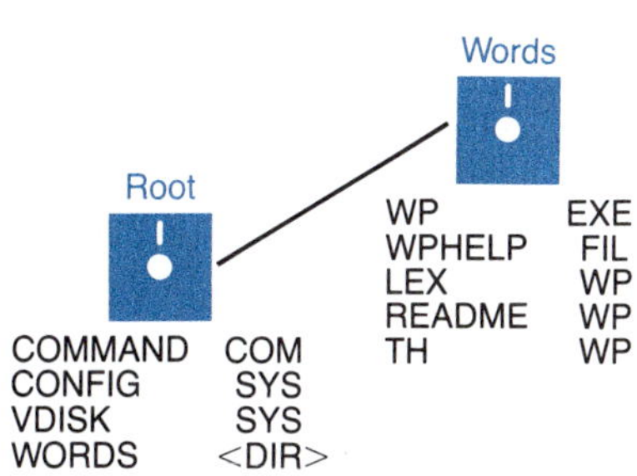

Making Several Subdirectories

To expand on the example, the preceding steps could be taken to make separate subdirectories for several different software. For instance, if you also plan to use a spreadsheet software, database management software, and several of the DOS utility programs, you may use the steps discussed in the example to create a partitioned hard disk that would be graphically represented as:

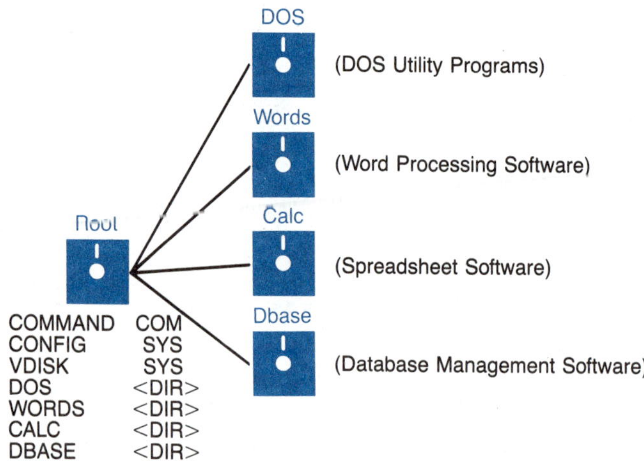

Here, four subdirectories, each containing the associated files of a software or collection of utility programs, exist on the hard disk. To load a particular software or utility program into RAM memory, you first change to the appropriate subdirectory with the **CD** command and then enter the filename of the software or program you wish to load. For instance, if you wanted to do word processing in the example, you could first type:

```
C:\>CD\WORDS←
```

You then would enter the filename of the word processing software found on the WORDS subdirectory:

```
C:\WORDS>WP←
```

Hard Disks in a Microcomputing Laboratory

Software found on hard disks in a computing laboratory will most likely be organized into subdirectories, one software in each subdirectory. To use such software you will need to familiarize yourself with the disk's subdirectory names and/or any other procedures necessary to access the software. In addition, you will probably be required to store your data (the text, spreadsheet, and/or database files created while using the software) onto floppy diskettes, which you will keep with you. To do so, you will need to put your floppy diskette in the computer's A: or B: drive, and use an appropriate software command to ensure that your file(s) are saved on it.

The following is a quick summary of commands that may be used for the software covered here.

VP-Planner After loading the spreadsheet software, type **/FD**← to call the File Directory command and then enter **A:**← or **B:**← to specify the A: or B: drive, respectively.

WordPerfect After loading the word processing software, type the F5 Function key to List Files. Next, type the = (equal) key to Change default directory. Then, type **A:**← or **B:**← to specify the A: or B: drive, respectively.

dBase III After loading dBase, at the Dot (.) prompt type **SET DEFAULT TO A:↵** or **SET DEFAULT TO B:↵** to specify the A: or B: drive, respectively.

BASICA Before loading the programming language, use the **CD** command to make the subdirectory with BASICA on it the current subdirectory in the C: drive. Next change the current drive to A: or B: by typing **A:↵** or **B:↵** and then type **C:BASICA↵** to load the programming language software.

Hierarchical Directories

In cases where you plan to store your files on the hard disk of a computer, you may want to create additional subdirectories for their storage. In fact, it is recommended that you create separate subdirectories for your files if you choose to keep them on the hard disk. To demonstrate how separate subdirectories for your files may be made and organized, the example will be continued. While the example focuses on the use of word processing software, the following discussion is transferable to the use of the other applications software you may intend to use.

Here it is assumed that while using your word processing software you intend to create various membership forms for an organization to which you belong, business correspondence (resumes, cover letters, references, etc.), and written assignments for two courses you are currently taking. Since all of the files will be word processing files, you will create subdirectories that are directly linked to the subdirectory on which your word processing software resides. To do so you use the **MD** (Make Directory) command and type:

```
C:\>MD\WORDS\FORMS
C:\>MD\WORDS\WORK
C:\>MD\WORDS\CLASS
C:\>MD\WORDS\CLASS\MGMT
C:\>MD\WORDS\CLASS\ACCT
```

When done, the hard disk will be partitioned in a manner that would be graphically represented as:

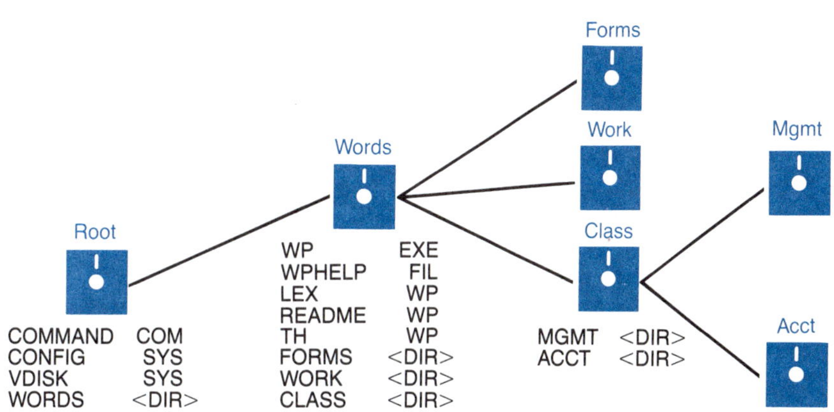

The graphic representation illustrates the concept of hierarchical subdirectories. Here, the subdirectories MGMT and ACCT "belong to" CLASS. FORMS, WORK, and CLASS belong to the subdirectory WORDS, and the subdirectory WORDS belongs to the root directory. This is known as a "parent/child" relationship.

The ability to relate subdirectories in this manner serves as a means to further organize subdirectories, and, therefore, further organize the files found on a hard disk.

DOS Paths

Notice that when making a "child" directory such as MGMT, all "parent" directories are listed in the **MD** command, and they are listed in the order in which they occur from the root directory forward. The list is known as a "path." A path describes the subdirectories through which one must pass to reach a particular destination subdirectory.

Using Paths in DOS Commands

In the previous discussion, "The Basics of DOS" (pages 27–29), it was stated that DOS commands require file specifications composed of three parts:

```
B:myfile.WKS
```

Disk drive Filename Extension

When subdirectories are in use, a fourth part to the file specification (path) is added to the file specification:

```
B:\path\myfile.WKS
```

Disk drive Path Filename Extension

Whether or not you need to include the path in the file specification depends upon which subdirectory is current at the time you enter the DOS command. The rule to use is as follows: the default path for the command will be that path which leads to the current subdirectory.

To demonstrate, assume that a file named ASSIGNA has been created and resided on the \WORDS\CLASS\MGMT subdirectory, and it is your objective to erase the file while the root directory is the current directory. The proper DOS command to use would be:

```
C:\>ERASE\WORDS\CLASS\MGMT\ASSIGNA↵
```

However, an alternate approach would be to use the **CD** (Change Directory) command to make the \WORDS\CLASS\MGMT subdirectory the current subdirectory by typing:

```
C:\>CD\WORDS\CLASS\MGMT↵
```

Then, type the command:

```
C:\WORDS\CLASS\MGMT>ERASE ASSIGNA↵
```

Summary

The following DOS Operation and Command Summary is designed for you to use when you work on other materials in this manual. You can refer to it whenever you need to do so.

DOS OPERATION AND COMMAND SUMMARY

DOS Quick Reference Command Summary

You will find helpful the following reference to commonly used variations of the DOS commands. The action desired is listed to the left, the exact command syntax to the right. The conventions for user supplied data are fn = filename, ext = filename extension.

Action desired	Command Syntax Current drive is A:	Current drive is B:
DIR		
Directory of A:	A>**DIR**	B>**DIR** A:
Directory of B:	A>**DIR** B:	B>**DIR**
TYPE		
Display a file on A:	A>**TYPE** fn.ext	B>**TYPE** A:fn.ext
Display a file on B:	A>**TYPE** B:fn.ext	B>**TYPE** fn.ext
ERASE		
Erase a file on A:	A>**ERASE** fn.ext	B>**ERASE** A:fn.ext
Erase a file on B:	A>**ERASE** B:fn.ext	B>**ERASE** fn.ext
Erase all files with same .ext on A:	A>**ERASE** *.ext	B>**ERASE** A:*.ext
Erase all files with same .ext on B:	A>**ERASE** B:*.ext	B>**ERASE** *.ext
COPY		
Copy a file A: to B:	A>**COPY** fn.ext B:	B>**COPY** A:fn.ext
Copy a file B: to A:	A>**COPY** B:fn.ext	B>**COPY** fn.ext A:
Copy all files with same .ext from A: to B:	A>**COPY** *.ext B:	B>**COPY** A:*.ext
Copy all files, same ext., from B: to A:	A>**COPY** B:*.ext	B>**COPY** *.ext A:
Copy all files from A: to B:	A>**COPY** *.* B:	B>**COPY** A:*.*
Copy all files from B: to A:	A>**COPY** B:*.*	B>**COPY** *.* A:
Copy a file from A: to A: with a different name	A>**COPY** fn.ext fn2.ext	B>**COPY** A:fn.ext A:fn2.ext
Copy a file from B: to B: with a different name	A>**COPY** B:fn1.ext B:fn2.ext	B>**COPY** fn1.ext fn2.ext
Copy a file from A: to B: with a different name	A>**COPY** fn1.ext B:fn2.ext	B>**COPY** A:fn1.ext fn2.ext
Copy a file from B: to A: with a different name	A>**COPY** B:fn1.ext fn2.ext	B>**COPY** fn1.ext A:fn2.ext
RENAME		
Rename a file on A:	A>**RENAME** fn1.ext fn2.ext	B>**RENAME** A:fn1.ext A:fn2.ext
Rename a file on B:	A>**RENAME** B:fn1.ext B:fn2.ext	B>**RENAME** fn1.ext fn2.ext
A: or **B:**		
Change current drive	A>B:	B>A:

DOS CONTROL KEYS

1 Function keys
2 Escape key
3 Control (Ctrl) key
4 Shift key
5 Alt key
6 Shift key
7 Print Screen (PrtSc) key
8 Number Lock (Num Lock) key
9 Scroll Lock (Break) key

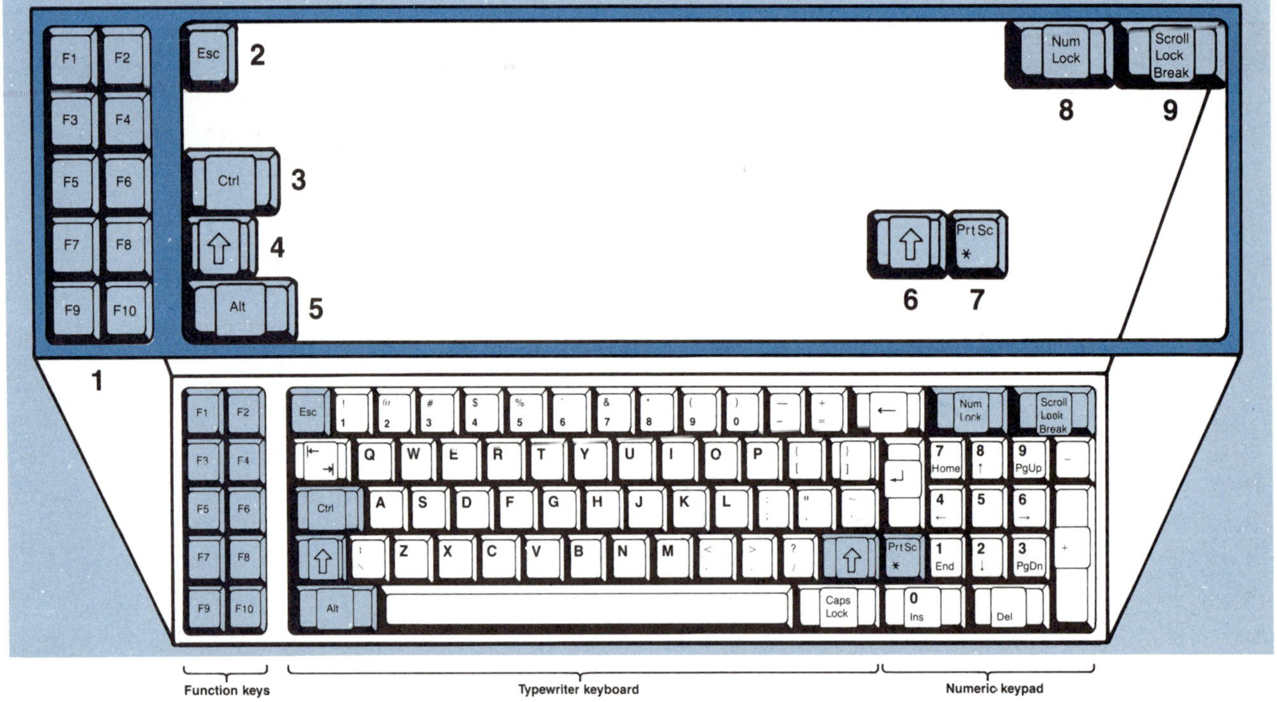

NOTE: The ^ character is a convention meaning "press and hold the Ctrl key and then tap the next key shown."

KEY COMBINATIONS

^Alt-Del Three-key combination. Press and hold the Ctrl and Alt keys, and then tap the Del key. Erases all data from RAM and reloads DOS.

^Break Interrupts any DOS command operation. Returns to the A>.

^Num Lock Pauses any DOS operation. Tapping any key will resume that operation.

^PrtSc Toggles ON/OFF an echo of screen output to the printer.

Shift-PrtSc Prints screen on the printer.

OTHER CONTROL KEYS

Enter Key Enters the current line into memory for the computer to act upon.

Escape Key Aborts current line without entering it as a DOS command or filename.

Num Lock Key Toggles ON/OFF ten-key numeric keypad to cursor control keys.

Function Keys 1, 3, 6

F1 Types out last command, one character at a time.

F3 Types out all of last command.

F6 Types out End of File character **^Z.**

IMPORTANT DOS UTILITY PROGRAMS

If you display a directory of the DOS diskette you will see that it includes several DOS utility programs:

Filename	Extension	Number of bytes used (disk space)
FORMAT	COM	6912
CHKDSK	COM	6400
DISKCOPY	COM	2576
DISKCOMP	COM	2188
COMP	COM	2534
.	.	.

DOS utility programs may be loaded into RAM from the DOS diskette to perform various operations. After a DOS utility program has completed its execution it erases itself from RAM memory. Therefore, if the operation is to be done more than once, the utility program must be reloaded into RAM memory. The following sections briefly describe these programs and the syntax associated with them.

NOTE: Several versions of DOS are available and the exact operation of the DOS utilities will vary from version to version. However, the essence of the operations will be consistent.

FORMAT.COM

It is important to note that a newly purchased (blank) diskette is unformatted. The user must format a diskette and the formatting operation performed by FORMAT.COM must be done to every new blank diskette. Once a diskette has been formatted to the specific type of computer and operating system being used, it need not be formatted again. If it is formatted again, any files that may have been on it will be erased.

Here is what you might see on the monitor screen as you successfully format a new diskette:

```
A>FORMAT
Insert new diskette for drive A:
and strike any key when ready

Formatting...Format complete

   362496 bytes total disk space
   362496 bytes available on disk

Format another (Y/N)?N
A>
```

Alternate forms:	`A>FORMAT B:`	Formats the diskette inserted into the B: drive.
	`A>FORMAT/S`	Formats and copies DOS over to the new diskette.

CHKDSK.COM

Another very useful DOS utility program is the CHKDSK (Check Disk) program. Executing CHKDSK will provide information about the space in use on the diskette being checked. It also performs housekeeping to better organize the blocks of data making up the files on the diskette.

Executing the CHKDSK program causes the computer to report the total disk space and the disk space remaining (available) on the diskette. It also reports the computer's total RAM memory and the RAM memory that is available (total RAM memory less the RAM memory being used by DOS). Here is an example of what you might see if you load and execute the DOS utility program CHKDSK while the DOS diskette is in the A: drive:

```
A>CHKDSK

179712 bytes total disk space          ←— S.S./D.D 5 1/4" diskette
 22528 bytes in 3 hidden files         ←— The rest of DOS
128512 bytes in 23 user files          ←— Other files on the diskette
 28672 bytes  available on diskette    ←— Space left on the diskette
262144 bytes total memory              ←— Total RAM memory
237568 bytes free                      ←— RAM memory left
```

This example tells you that 26 disk files are using about 84% of the total disk space on this particular diskette. The remaining 16% is still available for additional files. It is a good habit to CHKDSK your diskettes periodically to avoid running out of disk space in the middle of a save operation.

Alternate forms:	`A>CHKDSK B:`	Checks the disk in the B: drive.
	`A>CHKDSK B:/F`	Checks the disk in the B: drive and converts any lost data into files (versions DOS 2.0 +).

DISKCOPY.COM

This program is used to copy all of the diskette files form one diskette to another. The diskette from which you are copying is referred to as the *source diskette;* the diskette to which you are copying is called the *target diskette.* When the computer finishes a DISKCOPY, both diskettes are identical. If the target diskette had any files on it they were erased and replaced by the files from the source diskette. It is a good habit to use this DOS program to maintain a backup diskette for diskettes with important files on them. Here is an example of DISKCOPY:

```
A>DISKCOPY A: B:
Insert source diskette in drive A:

Insert target diskette in drive B:

Strike any key when ready

Copying 9 sectors per track, 1 side(s)

Copy complete

Copy another (Y/N)?N
A>
```

Alternate forms:

DISKCOPY	User switches source and target diskettes in and out of A: drive.
DISKCOPY B: A:	Source diskette in B:, target diskette in A:.

DISKCOMP.COM

This DOS program is used to compare two diskettes to assure that they are identical. Here is an example of what a successful DISKCOMP will look like:

```
A>DISKCOMP A: B:
Insert first diskette in drive A:

Insert second diskette in drive B:

Strike any key when ready

Comparing 9 sectors per track, 1 side(s)

Diskettes compare ok

Compare more diskettes (Y/N)?N
A>
```

Alternate forms:

DISKCOMP	User switches first and second diskettes in and out of the A: drive.

COMP.COM

This program, which is similar to DISKCOMP, is used to compare two files to assure that they are identical. The general form for executing the program is:

```
COMP X:filename.ext X:filename.ext
```

Microcomputing Laboratory

Hint To make sure your time on the microcomputer is productive, come prepared. Read through the tutorials and code your assignments before you come to the laboratory to key them in.

Hazard Do not bring food or drinks of any kind into the laboratory. Do not smoke in the laboratory.

Hazard Do not attempt to copy any software or data onto your diskette without the explicit approval of your instructor and the full knowledge of the microcomputing staff.

Diskettes

Hint Use a soft felt-tip pen to put your name, class, and other identification on the label of the diskette.

Hazard Keep your diskette dry, unbent, and away from magnetic fields. Magnets are found in your car's dashboard speaker, the computer's monitor, and in the sensing devices used to detect theft from bookstores and libraries. Do not touch the exposed surface of the diskette.

If you suspect that your diskette has been damaged do not put it into the computer's disk drive. Ask the person in charge for assistance.

Microcomputer Hardware

Hint If you are not the last person to be using the microcomputer for the day, turn off the monitor screen but not the computer when you are through. Before you leave make sure that all data (except DOS) have been erased from RAM memory.

Hazard Never attempt to insert or remove a diskette from the computer's disk drive while that disk drive's light is on.

Hazard Do not pound on the keyboard. It is an electronic device, not a mechanical one. If the same key needs to be repeated, press and hold it down. The keys are automatically repeating.

Microcomputer Software

Hint Some software are designed in sections that are loaded into RAM memory as needed. When this is the case, the diskette with the software on it must remain in the disk drive. WordPerfect and dBase III are designed this way. Depending on how you use it, VP-Planner also may need to remain in the disk drive.

On the other hand, DOS and BASICA are read entirely into RAM memory when they are loaded. Once they are read into RAM memory a diskette with these softwares on it may be removed from the disk drive.

Hint The software commands you are able to use are the commands of the highest level of software in RAM memory.

Hazard When you first boot DOS, if you see something like

```
The IBM Personal Computer Basic
Version C1.00 Copyright IBM Corp 1981
62940 Bytes free
OK
```

instead of the A>, you have not successfully booted DOS. It is most likely that the diskette is not firmly seated in the disk drive, or the disk drive door is not closed.

Numeric Expressions

Hint A common error in numeric expressions is the occurrence of unmatched parentheses. The computer's response to this error is usually somewhat cryptic. Check your expression for the same number of left and right parentheses.

Logical Expressions

Hint Upper-case and lower-case alphabetical characters are evaluated differently by the computer; for example, "A" is not equal to "a." When you use a logical expression to check a string relationship, the case as well as the letters must match for the expression to evaluate as true.

Saving Your Data

Hint Save or resave your data every fifteen minutes or so. You may want to purchase another diskette to use as a backup diskette for important files.

Hazard Always follow these rules when naming your data files: use one to eight characters; start with a letter; and use no special characters (spaces, commas, colons, etc.).

Using DOS

Hint A file specification used in a DOS command must have the filename extension specified. However, unless two or more files have the same filename, a software to be loaded into RAM does not need to have its filename extension specified.

Hint Most softwares covered in this manual have their own commands to perform the same file maintenance operations DOS performs. Since the command syntax of a given operation varies from application to application, it is generally easier for multi-application users to learn and use the commands of DOS.

Hint A series of DOS commands and software filenames may be put into a file with a .BAT (batch file) filename extension, and then executed by the computer in the order of their appearance when that .BAT file's filename is typed and entered from the DOS level of operation.

.BAT files may be created by using a word processing software (or any other software) or, by using a method described in the following example in which a variation of the **COPY** command is used to create a file directly from the keyboard.

This variation of the **COPY** command has the form:

```
COPY CON:filename.ext
```

CON: is the device name for the keyboard (console).

```
A>COPY CON:go.BAT
CHKDSK B:
PAUSE
DIR B:
PAUSE
VP
^Z
```

^Z ← This character (End Of File) is produced by tapping the F6 Function key.

In this example, a batch file is created that first will perform a CHKDSK operation on the diskette in the B: drive.

The next DOS command, **PAUSE,** typically is used only in batch files and causes the computer to stop executing the commands in the file until the user taps a key on the keyboard. This command is the next command executed by the computer.

When the user taps a key the computer continues by listing a directory of the files found on the diskette in the B: drive, and then it pauses again.

The last entry in this batch file is the filename for VP-Planner. When this is executed by the computer the spreadsheet application will be loaded into RAM memory and the user is left at the software operating level.

To cause the computer to execute these commands the user types and enters the filename of the batch file at the DOS level of operation. The following is an example of the output that this .BAT file might produce.

```
A>go

A>CHKDSK B:

     362496 bytes total disk space
      33792 bytes in 12 user files
     328704 bytes available on disk

     163840 bytes total memory
     139056 bytes free


A>PAUSE
Strike a key when ready . . .
```

THE FUNDAMENTALS KEY TERM GLOSSARY

Address The unique name of a variable.

Applications Software A software designed to perform a general type of task, e.g. word processing.

Assignment The act of entering data into a variable.

Booting The copying process that reads DOS into RAM. Also known as *reading* or *loading*.

Canned Programs Programs prepared by manufacturers in a ready-to-use form that cause the microcomputer to act in a specific manner or to solve specific types of problems. The user is generally presented with a set of instructions by the microcomputer and is expected to type in data from the keyboard.

Concatination A string operation in which two or more string items are joined.

Commands The message the user sends to the computer to make the computer perform specific operations.

Command Mode The mode in which the user enters software commands.

Database A collection of related data kept in the form of records.

Data Entry Mode The mode in which the user assigns data to variables.

Database Management Systems An application software that manages the storage, access, maintenance, and manipulation of records in a database.

Disk Drive A motorized unit that stores data on electronic media (diskettes) and allows that data to be retrieved.

Disk Operating System (DOS) The software that manages and controls the overall operation of the computer and its peripherals.

Diskette The magnetic storage medium that holds software and the user's data in permanent form.

DOS Operating Level The operating level of the computer after DOS has been loaded. The computer at this level is able to perform several small but important tasks and is able to read other software into RAM memory. Also called *system* level.

Execute The act of the computer carrying out the user's instructions.

File A set of data stored on a diskette.

Filename The name given to a file.

Filename Extension A sequence of characters, preceded by a period, added to the filename and used by the computer to locate a particular file.

Formatting The process that establishes where data can or cannot be saved on a diskette, configures the file allocation table, and marks defective areas (if any) so that data will not be saved there.

Functions Precoded routines that perform a series of operations or calculations. Functions are often shortcuts to accomplish what would otherwise require a long numeric or string expression.

Hardware The physical equipment of the computer, including mechanical, magnetic, and electronic devices.

Keyboard The typewriter-like device that provides the user a means to input data to the computer.

Integrated Software An applications software that performs several different functions. For example, VP-Planner combines the features of spreadsheets with limited word processing and database management.

Loading See *Booting.*

Logical Expression A string or numeric expression that the computer evaluates as either being true or false.

Logical Operators Operators that are used to connect two or more relationships into a single expression.

Memory The space available in a computer to hold software and the results or data created as the user operates the computer.

Monitor The hardware of the computer that displays data transmitted between the user and the computer.

Numeric Expression An expression made up of characters that the computer recognizes as a number or a series of numbers, on which mathematical operations may be performed.

Operating System See *Disk Operating System (DOS).*

Printer An output device that provides hard-copy for the user.

Programming Languages Software with a set of rules, statements, symbols, and syntax used to cause the computer to solve a variety of problems or to behave in a number of ways.

Random Access Memory (RAM) The working memory of the computer that temporarily holds software, and user's data.

Read Only Memory (ROM) The part of the computer's memory that contains permanent special programs that relate directly to the computer's functioning.

Reading See *Booting.*

Relational Operator An operator that describes a relationship (such as greater than, less than, or equal to) between two data items.

Software A set of instructions, procedures, and routines for a computer's hardware to follow.

Software Operating Level The level in which you may use the commands of the software that is currently held in RAM.

Spreadsheet Applications Software An application program that causes the microcomputer to create an electronic version of the accountant's spreadsheet.

String Expression A group of characters that the computer recognizes as a character-type data item.

System Level See *DOS Operating Level.*

System Unit The hardware of the computer that processes data.

Utility Software programs that primarily perform the tasks of directing or converting data.

Variables Locations in the RAM memory that hold specific data items.

Volatile A term (meaning easily turned to vapor) that in computer jargon refers to a memory in which data or software is lost when the computer is turned off.

Word Processing Applications An applications software used to store, edit and manipulate text.

MODULE OUTLINE

INTRODUCTION

Spreadsheet Basics

TUTORIAL EXERCISES: PART I

The VP-Planner Entry Menu | EXERCISE 1: Selecting a Command from a Menu | EXERCISE 2: Viewing the Spreadsheet | EXERCISE 3: Entering Labels into a Spreadsheet | EXERCISE 4: Introduction to Using VP-Planner Commands | EXERCISE 5: Ranges of Cells | EXERCISE 6: Relative vs. Absolute Cell References | EXERCISE 7: Using the Pointer to Enter a Formula | EXERCISE 8: Rejustifying a Range of Labels | EXERCISE 9: Adding Data to the Spreadsheet | EXERCISE 10: Introduction to @ Functions | EXERCISE 11: Finishing the Spreadsheet | EXERCISE 12: Saving a Spreadsheet | EXERCISE 13: Quitting VP-Planner

TUTORIAL EXERCISES: PART II

EXERCISE 1: Loading a Spreadsheet | EXERCISE 2: Formatting a Spreadsheet | EXERCISE 3: Global Change of Column Widths | EXERCISE 4: Altering the Spreadsheet | EXERCISE 5: More on Viewing the Spreadsheet | EXERCISE 6: Modeling with a Spreadsheet | EXERCISE 7: Other Yearly Summaries | EXERCISE 8: Printing a Spreadsheet | EXERCISE 9: Resaving Your Spreadsheet | EXERCISE 10: Exiting VP-Planner | EXERCISE 11: Back to DOS

VP-PLANNER OPERATION AND COMMAND SUMMARY

VP-Planner Quick Reference Command Summary | VP-Planner Control Keys | /**W**orksheet Commands | /**R**ange /**C**opy /**M**ove Commands | /**F**ile Commands | /**P**rint Commands | /**G**raph Commands | /**D**ata Commands | VP-Planner Spreadsheet Functions | VP-Planner Keyboard Macro Commands

SPREADSHEET DESIGN

Separate Kinds of Data in Separate Spreadsheet Areas | Spreadsheet Documentation | Mapping Out the Spreadsheet | Spreadsheet Templates | Mixed Cell References

VP-PLANNER FUNCTIONS

Mathematical and Statistical Functions | Engineering and Scientific Functions | Financial Functions | Date Functions | Logical Functions

VP-PLANNER GRAPHICS

VP-Planner Graphics Overview | Creating the Five Basic Graph Types | Adding Options to a Graph

/**D**ATA **S**ORT, /**D**ATA **Q**UERY, AND DATABASE FUNCTIONS

Database Structure and Terminology | The /**D**ata **S**ort Commands | The /**D**ata **Q**uery Commands | Database Functions

VP-PLANNER KEYBOARD MACROS

What is a Keyboard Macro? | Creating a Simple Macro | Cautions about Macros | Representing Special Keystrokes in a Macro | Interactive Macros | Building a Macro Library | How VP-Planner Executes a Macro | A Menu of Macros—The /**XM**range~ Command | Advanced Macro Commands

Learning VP-Planner

INTRODUCTION

VP-Planner® is a software application capable of performing several different functions. As an *integrated software,* VP-Planner combines the features of spreadsheets, database management systems, graphics software, and a built-in programming language whose programs are called *macros.* VP-Planner also has some word processing capabilities.

VP-Planner's most popular feature is its spreadsheet. As you will recall from the introduction, a spreadsheet is a kind of worksheet with columns and rows which many of you have performed calculations on manually with paper, pencil, and calculator. The following section begins by introducing you to basic spreadsheet concepts, followed by a two-part tutorial exercise section. Part I focuses on the essential concepts and operations involved in creating and using an electronic spreadsheet. Part II exposes you to techniques, commands, and operations that will enhance your spreadsheet skills.

The tutorial exercises are followed by an operation and command summary that briefly describes the full range of commands and control keys available with VP-Planner. Each major set of descriptions of commands is prefaced with an abbreviated reference guide.

Following the operation and command summary, discussions on the topics of spreadsheet design, mixed cell references, and VP-Planner's functions conclude the section's material on VP-Planner's spreadsheet feature.

The remaining discussions deal with VP-Planner's other features—graphics, databases, and macros. Each discussion includes several specific examples of how to perform the various operations.

Spreadsheet Basics

Spreadsheet Layout

In the VP-Planner spreadsheet, letters are used to designate columns and numbers are used to designate rows. You specify a particular position (or *cell*) in the spreadsheet by column letter and row number. For example, the cell G3 is located in column G, row 3.

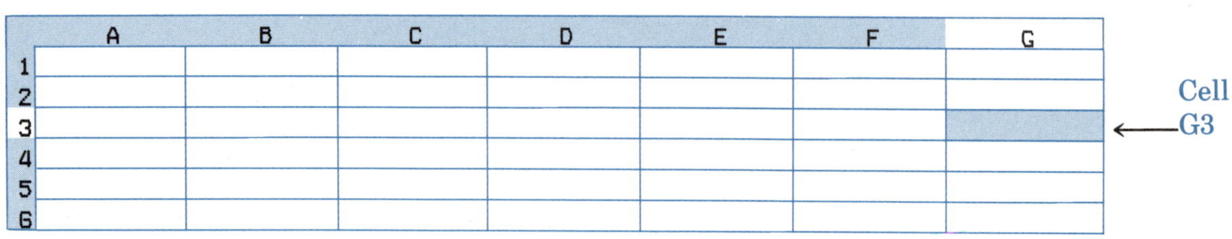

Entering Data into a Spreadsheet

You have the option of entering a simple string expression (called a *label*) or a numeric expression (called a *value*) into each cell. VP-Planner determines which of these two data types is being entered into a cell at the first keystroke of a data entry operation. If the first keystroke is any of the following, VP-Planner assumes you are entering a value into the cell.

0 1 2 3 4 5 6 7 8 9 + – . (@ # $

If the first keystroke is any other keyboard character, VP-Planner assumes you are entering a label into the cell.

In the following example, the spreadsheet shows some labels and values. Notice that labels automatically justify to the left side of the cell, and values justify to the right side. The values in this case are constants, the number 1200. Values also may take the more complex form of spreadsheet formulas.

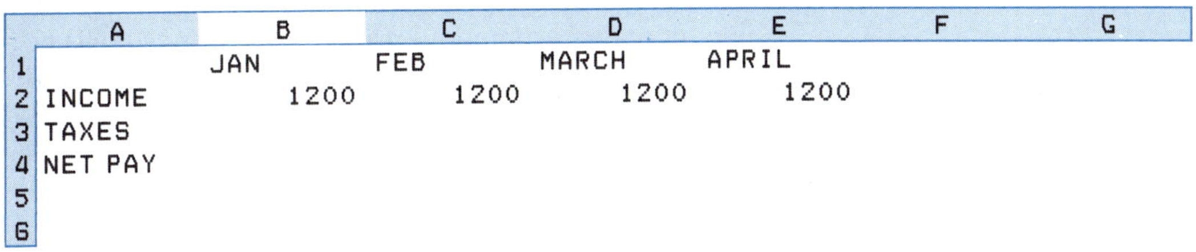

Formulas

To determine taxes and net pay you may enter formulas into each of the cells within rows three and four. For instance, if you assume a 25% tax rate, you may enter the formula .25*B2 as the value in January's tax amount (cell B3) and the formula +B2 – B3 in cell B4 for January's net pay.

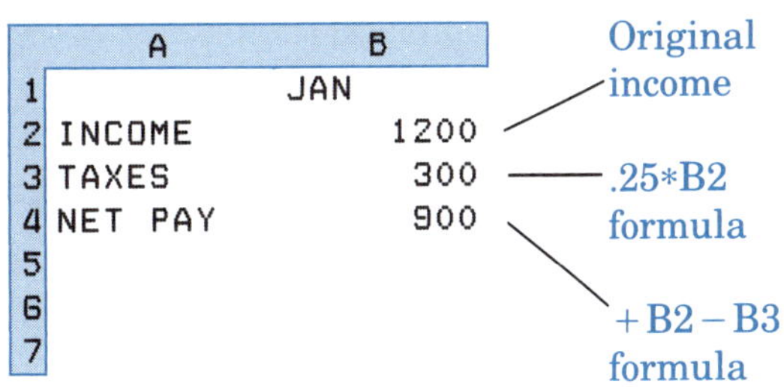

Although formulas become the contents of cells B3 and B4, VP-Planner will display 300 and 900 (the evaluation of the expressions) there. If you later change January's income (B2), the values displayed for January's taxes (B3) and net pay (B4) will change automatically.

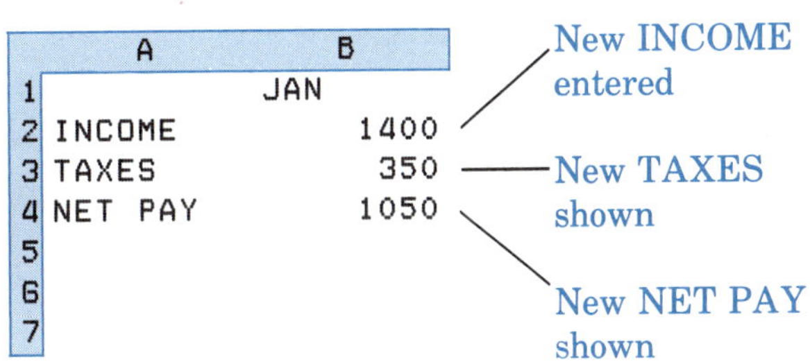

Window Lines

VP-Planner reserves four lines (collectively called the *control panel*) at the bottom of the screen. The lines indicate menu options, messages, the location of the cell pointer (current active cell), and the actual content of the current active cell (formulas as opposed to display values).

Command Structure

When you use VP-Planner, you are either directly entering data (labels or values) into the spreadsheet's cells or you are executing a VP-Planner command.

To manipulate the data in a spreadsheet, VP-Planner provides *menus* from which you select commands. These menus often are connected in a layered fashion: one menu command providing *(calling)* another submenu of commands. Sometimes a final command operation will require that you pass through several preliminary menus to reach the desired one.

Calling the Main Menu

When you tap the Slash key (/), you enter VP-Planner's command mode by calling the Main menu. The menu is displayed in the third line of the control panel at the bottom of the screen. To select a command, you may either type the first letter of the command, press the function key assigned to the command, or move the command pointer (shown here on "Worksheet") to the desired command and press the Enter key. (When a command is referred to in this tutorial, the first letter of the command, the portion you would need to type to execute the command, appears in bold type.)

The message line displays a listing of the submenu or a brief explanation of the command the pointer currently indicates. In this example, with the command pointer on "Worksheet," its submenu of commands would appear on the screen as follows.

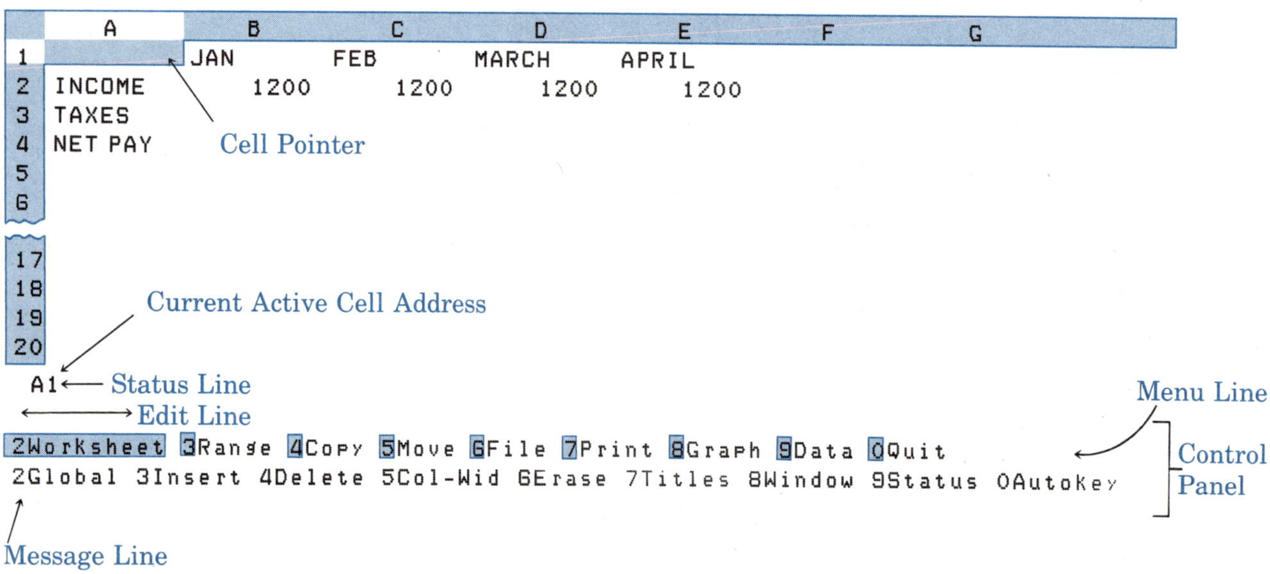

Working through Command Submenus

If you select "**W**orksheet" from the Main menu, the submenu for the command moves to the menu line and becomes the menu from which to select. An explanation for the submenu command that the pointer currently indicates is displayed on the message line.

```
      A          B          C          D          E          F          G          H
1             JAN        FEB        MARCH      APRIL
2  INCOME        1200       1200       1200       1200
3  TAXES
4  NET PAY
5
6

17
18
19
20
  A1

2Global 3Insert 4Delete 5Col-Wid 6Erase 7Titles 8Window 9Status 0AutoKey
2Format 3Label-Prefix 4Col-Width 5Recalculation 6Protection 7Default
```

If the command pointer is moved one command to the right, the explanation changes:

```
      A          B          C          D          E          F          G          H
1             JAN        FEB        MARCH      APRIL
2  INCOME        1200       1200       1200       1200
3  TAXES
4  NET PAY
5
6

17
18
19
20
  A1

2Global 3Insert 4Delete 5Col-Wid 6Erase 7Titles 8Window 9Status 0AutoKey
2Row 3Column
```

If you now select the **I**nsert command, a third menu that allows you the option of inserting a column or a row into the spreadsheet appears on the menu line and becomes the menu from which to select.

This process of working through submenus often requires a series of steps progressing toward the end command operation. The series of steps may be viewed in a tree structure format as:

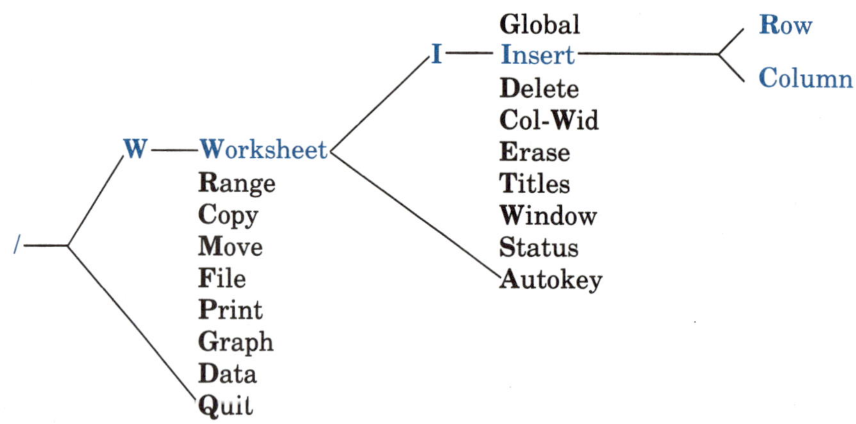

Backing Up or Aborting a Command Operation

When executing a final command operation involves several steps, it is useful to know that tapping the Esc key will cause VP-Planner to back up one menu or command operation. Pressing the key marked Ctrl, and then tapping the key marked Scroll Lock (Break) will abort a command operation and return you to the ready mode.

Learning VP-Planner

VP-Planner can require the completion of a number of steps in specific order to perform a particular command operation. As you use this application software, you will become familiar with the steps involved. Careful study of the tree diagrams and command summaries will help you master the command sequences.

Getting HELP

VP-Planner also has an on-line help facility that tries to anticipate your questions and provides a screen of information about the command(s) you are trying to use. You can gain access to a *help screen* at any time by tapping the F1 Function key. Each help screen provides information and a selection of other help screens from which to choose. You can select other help screens by pressing the F5 Function key followed by the number corresponding to the screen you wish to view and then pressing Enter. Tapping the Esc key exits you from the help screen mode and returns you to where you left off. If you use the help screen facility, leave the VP-Planner system diskette in the disk drive.

The following tutorial explains how to use the pointer and pointer control keys.

TUTORIAL EXERCISES: PART I

REQUIRED MATERIALS

1. An IBM DOS diskette
2. A VP-Planner program (system) diskette
3. Your files diskette
4. This manual
5. Other ______________________________

Tutorial Conventions

During this tutorial you will enter specific labels and values and use various VP-Planner menu commands to create an electronic spreadsheet. The following are the conventions that this tutorial's instructions will use.

↵ When you see this symbol, press the Enter key located on the right side of the keyboard and marked with a bent arrow (↵).

[ ] Do not type brackets when the tutorial includes them in its instructions. Type only what is inside the brackets.

HOW TO GET OUT OF TROUBLE

If you want to:	*Then:*
■ Erase characters before you have entered them into a cell . . .	■ Tap the Backspace key (←) located just above the Enter key.
■ Erase the existing contents of a single spreadsheet cell . . .	■ Move the pointer to the cell and type [/**RE**↵].
■ Back up a command operation or command menu . . .	■ Tap the Esc key once (the Esc key is located on the top row, far left side).
■ Stop any command operation and return to the data entry mode . . .	■ Press and hold the Ctrl key (middle left) and then tap the Scroll Lock key (top far right).
■ Stop the tutorial and continue it later . . .	■ Type [/**FS**filename↵]. Watch the disk drive light to make sure the spreadsheet has been saved. Then type [/**QY**] to quit VP-Planner.
■ Continue the tutorial after you have stopped it . . .	■ Load VP-Planner into RAM memory and then type [/**FR**filename↵].

Getting Started

1. Insert the DOS diskette into the A: disk drive (the disk drive on the left) and close the disk drive door.
2. If the computer already is on, press and hold the Ctrl and Alt keys and then tap the Del key. If it is not on, then turn on the computer and the monitor.

In a few moments DOS will be loaded automatically.

3. Answer DOS's date and time prompts.
4. When you see the A>, remove the DOS diskette from the A: disk drive.
5. Insert your files diskette into the B: disk drive (the disk drive on the right). Be sure to close the disk drive door.
6. Insert the VP-Planner program (system) diskette into the A: drive and close the door.
7. Type [VP↵].

Your screen should look like this:

```
                VP - PLANNER

                Copyright 1985, 1986
Kent Brothers, David Mitchell, James Stephenson
Stephenson Software Inc. -- All rights reserved

 Published by Paperback Software International

          Licensed for the exclusive use of
           Registered Single-User Licensee

 1   Worksheet Only
 2   Multidimensional Database with Worksheet
 3   Create/Edit Multidimensional Database
 4   Path for Multidimensional Files
 5   Directory Listing
 6   Quit

 Enter selection:
```

The VP-Planner Entry Menu

VP-Planner is comprised of a spreadsheet program, a multidimensional database program, and three utility programs. The Entry menu allows the user to select which program to enter. The remainder of this text will deal only with the WORKSHEET program because the multidimensional database deals with more advanced concepts.

EXERCISE 1: Selecting a Command from a Menu

Using the Command Pointer

The reverse video display around the command "WORKSHEET" is VP-Planner's *command pointer*. On the far right side of the keyboard is a numeric keypad including four keys with arrows on them. VP-Planner has programmed the arrow keys to move its pointers, as shown in the illustration on page V-9.

Three methods allow you to select a command from a menu. You can move the pointer to the desired command and then tap the Enter key, you can type the first letter or character of the desired command, or you can press the function key corresponding to the number appearing at the left of the desired command.

Loading the VP-Planner Spreadsheet

"WORKSHEET" is the command used to enter the spreadsheet portion of VP-Planner.

1. Use the ↑ and ↓ arrow keys to move the pointer through the Entry menu.
2. Now, move the pointer to WORKSHEET and press ↵.

VP-Planner's spreadsheet is 9,999 rows deep and 256 columns wide (90 rows deep and 60 columns wide if you are using the educational version).

EXERCISE 2: Viewing the Spreadsheet

After entering the spreadsheet by issuing the WORKSHEET command, you will be looking at a small portion of the total spreadsheet. For now, you may only make entries to or alter the content of the cells that appear on the display. You may think of the video display as a window through which the "active area" of the spreadsheet is accessed.

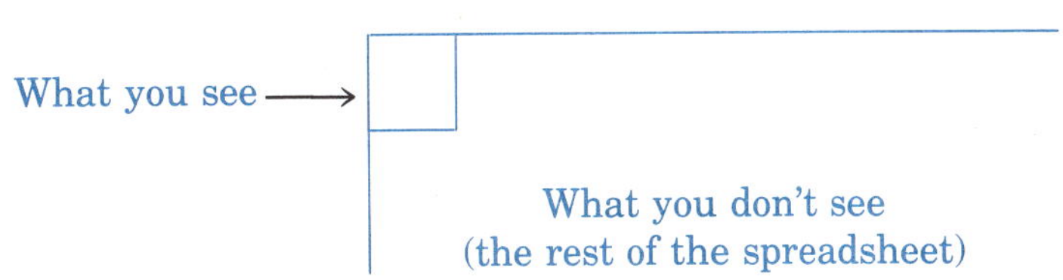

The reverse video display at cell A1 is the cell pointer.

1. Move this pointer by using the four arrowed keys to your right (Pointer Control keys).

NOTE: If instead of moving the pointer the arrowed keys cause numbers to appear at the top left of the screen, tap the Esc key, then the Num Lock key.

What happens when you keep moving the pointer to the right, or keep moving the pointer down? Notice the pointer may be used to "push" the monitor screen around on the spreadsheet.

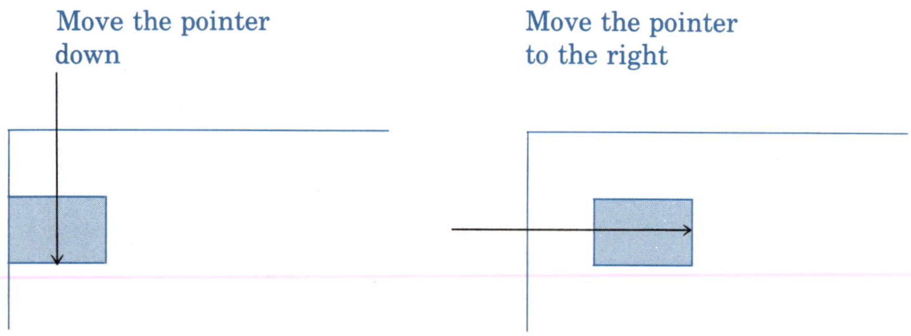

Tapping the Home key (found on the numeric keypad) will send the pointer to the A1 (top left) cell.

2. Tap the Home key.

On the far left of the keyboard are ten gray keys marked F1 through F10. These are *function keys*. Each is programmed to perform a particular operation.

1. Tap the key marked F5 and read the prompt shown at the bottom of the screen:

   `Enter destination cell: A1`

2. Now type [G57↵].

Where is the pointer located now? What column? What row? The F5 key is programmed to send the pointer wherever you want on the spreadsheet.

3. Press the Home key to return to cell A1.

EXERCISE 3: Entering Labels into a Spreadsheet

Labeling Columns

1. Move the pointer to cell B2.

In the lower left corner of the screen you will see the letter-number coordinate for the current pointer position.

2. Type [JAN] and then move the pointer to the right one cell (C2).
3. Type [FEB]. Keep going until you reach [DEC] (M2).
4. Tap the Home key.

You should have the following on your screen.

	A	B	C	D	E	F	G	H
1								
2		JAN	FEB	MAR	APR	MAY	JUN	JUL
3								
4								
5								
6								

Labeling Rows

You have just labeled the spreadsheet's columns and now you are going to label its rows. As you continue, keep a careful watch on the control panel at the bottom of the monitor screen to keep track of what VP-Planner is doing.

1. Move the pointer to A4 and type [GROSS PAY AMOUNT].
2. Move the pointer to A5 and type [TAX RATE].
3. Move the pointer to A7 (two cells down) and type [FED & STATE TAXES].

NOTE: Even with the Caps Lock toggled on, you need to use the Shift key to type upper-case special characters such as &.

4. Move the pointer to A8.

Using Label Prefixes

For your next label entry you will use one of the *label-prefixes*. The prefixes are used to format labels in their cells. The following table lists each prefix and its effect.

Character	Effect
'	Left justifies label (default)
^	Centers label
"	Right justifies label
\	Repeats label in cell

The label prefix you will use is \, the *repeating label* prefix, most useful for creating underlines in spreadsheets.

5. With the pointer on A8, type [\-↵].

NOTE: Be sure to use a backslash.

Cell A8 now should be filled with dashes.

Finishing the Row Labels

6. Enter the rest of the spreadsheet's row labels. After you have typed row labels A4 through A22 your spreadsheet should look like the one on the following page.

	A	B	C	D	E	F	G	H
1								
2		JAN	FEB	MAR	APR	MAY	JUN	JUL
3								
4	GROSS PAY AMOUNT							
5	TAX RATE							
6								
7	FED & STATE TAXES							
8	---------							
9	NET PAY AMOUNT							
10								
11	EXPENSES							
12	---------							
13	RENT							
14	UTILITIES							
15	TELEPHONE							
16	LIFE INSURANCE							
17	FOOD							
18	LEISURE							
19								
20	TOTAL EXPENSES							
21								
22	SAVINGS DEPOSITS							

EXERCISE 4: Introduction to VP-Planner Commands

Changing a Column's Width

Many of the row labels you have entered extend into column B. VP-Planner allows a label to extend into the next cell if the cell into which it is extending is blank.

Since you will be using the B column for January's data, you will need to enlarge the A column's width so it is wide enough to display all of its own labels. To widen column A you will need to use one of the spreadsheet menu commands.

Calling the Main Menu

1. Move the pointer to column A (the pointer needs to be in the column whose width you are changing).
2. Type [/].

The [/] will call VP-Planner's Main menu. In the row of submenu commands for the current Main menu command (/**W**orksheet), you should see the command **C**ol-**W**id (column width). This is the command you want to use. To access this submenu command you first must select the /**W**orksheet command of the Main menu.

```
     A          B          C          D          E          F          G          H
1
2               JAN        FEB        MAR        APR        MAY        JUN        JUL
3
4  GROSS PAY AMOUNT
5  TAX RATE

17 FOOD
18 LEISURE
19
20 TOTAL EXPENSES
 A1

2Worksheet 3Range 4Copy 5Move 6File 7Print 8Graph 9Data 0Quit
2Global 3Insert 4Delete 5Col-Wid 6Erase 7Titles 8Window 9Status 0AutoKey
```

Calling the /Worksheet Submenu

3. Type [**W**] (or ↵) to select the /**W**orksheet commands.

Now the submenu has become the menu you are choosing from and the line under the submenu gives a short explanation of the submenu command the menu pointer indicates.

4. Move the menu pointer to the command **Col-Wid** and read the message line.

```
     A          B          C          D          E          F          G          H
1
2               JAN        FEB        MAR        APR        MAY        JUN        JUL
3
4  GROSS PAY AMOUNT
5  TAX RATE

17 FOOD
18 LEISURE
19
20 TOTAL EXPENSES
 A1

2Global 3Insert 4Delete 5Col-Wid 6Erase 7Titles 8Window 9Status 0AutoKey
2Set 3Reset
```

5. Type ↵ to tell VP-Planner this is the command you want to use.

Setting the New Column Width

You now have the commands:

`2 Set` `3 Reset`

6. Select the command to **S**et and answer the next prompt

`Enter desired column width (1-72): 9`

by typing [18↵].

Column A is now twice as wide as the other columns in the spreadsheet.

EXERCISE 5: Ranges of Cells

A cell range is a rectangle defined by a starting cell address and an ending cell address (G23 . . L45). The starting address represents the upper left-hand corner of the rectangle and the ending address the lower right corner of the rectangle. These addresses must always be separated by two periods. A cell address by itself (A8) does not constitute a range. The smallest range that may be defined is a single cell (A8 . . A8). The largest is the entire spreadsheet (A1 . . IV9999). Cell ranges are used throughout VP-Planner in both commands and formulas. Therefore, a thorough understanding of them is necessary. This exercise will introduce you to range concepts by using the /Copy command.

Specifying Ranges in the /Copy Command

You now will use the second Main menu command, /Copy, meaning to put the contents of a cell, or group of cells, into another cell, or group of cells. The cells from which data are copied are referred to as the "SOURCE range" of cells; the cells to which data are copied are referred to as the "DESTINATION range" of cells.

1. Move the pointer to A8 (------------------) and type [/] to call the Main menu.
2. Now select the command Copy from this menu.

Default Specifications

When you look at the bottom of the screen you will see that VP-Planner is asking for the SOURCE range. Your object is to copy the set of dashes (in cell A8) into the rest of the cells in that row.

Since you will copy from cell A8, that single cell is the SOURCE range. VP-Planner anticipates that this may be the case and has put the range A8 . . A8 (A8 to A8) as the default answer to its own prompt.

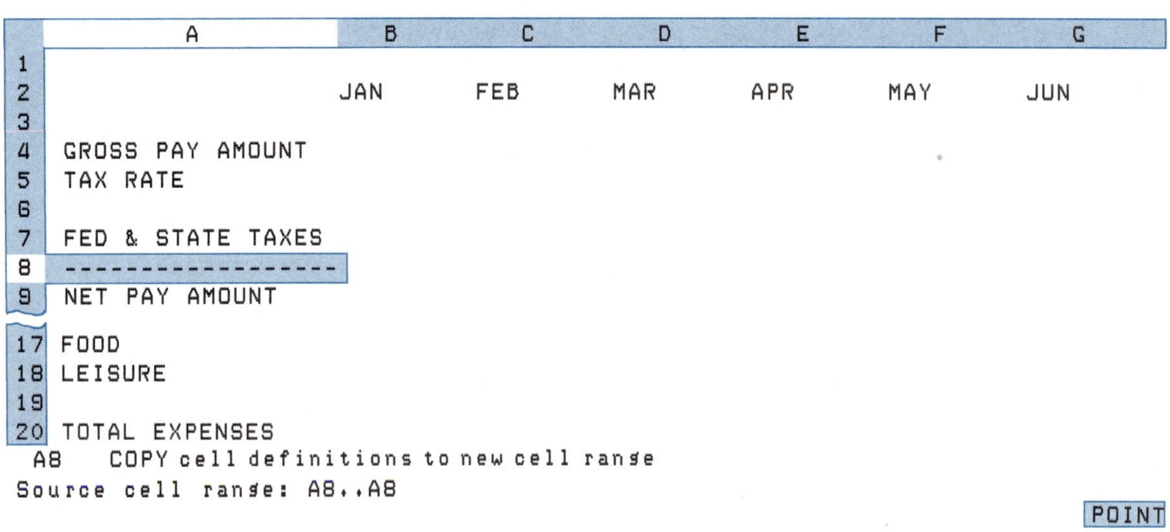

3. Type ↵ to accept A8 . . A8 as the range from which you want to copy.

Now VP-Planner wants to know the range of cells to which to copy. You are going to underline across to cell M8, so the DESTINATION range is the row of cells from B8 to M8 (B8 . . M8).

```
          A              B        C        D        E        F        G
1
2                       JAN      FEB      MAR      APR      MAY      JUN
3
4   GROSS PAY AMOUNT
5   TAX RATE
6
7   FED & STATE TAXES
8   -----------------
9   NET PAY AMOUNT

17  FOOD
18  LEISURE
19
20  TOTAL EXPENSES
  A8   COPY cell definitions to new cell range
Source cell range: A8..A8          Destination cell range: A8
                                                                POINT
```

Typing in a Range Specification

You can change the default destination address by typing the desired range.

4. Type [B8 . . M8↵]. Then make sure that this row has indeed been copied as you directed.

```
          A              B        C        D        E        F        G
1
2                       JAN      FEB      MAR      APR      MAY      JUN
3
4   GROSS PAY AMOUNT
5   TAX RATE
6
7   FED & STATE TAXES
8   -------------------  -------------------------------------------------------
9   NET PAY AMOUNT

17  FOOD
18  LEISURE
19
20  TOTAL EXPENSES
  A8
 1help 2edit 3name 4tabs 5goto 6window 7data 8table 9recalculate 0graph
277K                          16:02                                  READY
```

Pointing to a Range Specification

Another very useful way to specify a range while using a command such as /Copy is to highlight the range with the pointer. When you use the pointer to specify a range of cells, you first move the pointer to the beginning address of that range; press the period key to *anchor* that cell as the starting address; and then move the pointer to the ending address of that range and press the Enter key. You may use the Backspace key to "unanchor" the pointer at any time.

To give you experience in pointing to a range you will use the /Copy command to copy the contents of cell A12 into the rest of the cells in that row.

1. Move the pointer to cell A12 and type [/C] to call the Main menu and select the /Copy command.

The bottom of the screen should read:

```
              A             B        C        D        E        F        G
 1
 2                         JAN      FEB      MAR      APR      MAY      JUN
 3

17 FOOD
18 LEISURE
19
20 TOTAL EXPENSES
 A8   COPY cell definitions to new cell range
Source cell range: A12..A12
                                                                      POINT
```

2. Tap the Enter key to accept the default SOURCE range.
3. Now move the pointer around on the spreadsheet and watch the destination address.

The destination address changes with every move of the pointer. VP-Planner is waiting for you to move to the starting address of cells to which to copy.

4. Move to cell B12 and tap the period key.

You have just anchored the pointer so that you may now highlight to the end of the range you will specify.

5. Start moving the pointer to the right, along the twelfth row.

Notice that with each move the destination ending address changes and that the range specified is highlighted on the display.

```
      A                 B         C         D         E         F         G
1
2                   JAN       FEB       MAR       APR       MAY       JUN
3
4   GROSS PAY AMOUNT
5   TAX RATE
6
7   FED & STATE TAXES
8   ---------------------------------------------------------------------------
9   NET PAY AMOUNT
10
11   EXPENSES
12   -----------------                                                ---------
13   RENT

17  FOOD
18  LEISURE
19
20  TOTAL EXPENSES
  A12   COPY cell definitions to new cell range
 Source cell range: A12..A12        Destination cell range: B12..F12
                                                                        POINT
```

6. Move the pointer to cell M12; again look at the DESTINATION range at the bottom of the screen (B12 . . M12); and then tap the Enter key to accept the range B12 . . M12 as the appropriate destination range.

Highlighting a range rather than typing it is most useful when you are not sure how far the range goes or how large it is. When you need to see what the range includes, simply anchor the pointer to one corner of the range and then move it to the other side, the far corner. You tap the Enter key to specify the range as the area displayed in reverse video.

Naming a Specified Range

A third method of defining a range uses VP-Planner's ability to assign a name to a range of cells and later specify that range by using its name rather than typing its coordinates or highlighting it.

NOTE: When the SOURCE range is larger than one cell, the DESTINATION range may be specified as a single cell representing the upper left corner of the DESTINATION range. The SOURCE range will be copied to the DESTINATION range with the upper left cell of the SOURCE range corresponding to the upper left cell of the DESTINATION range.

The /Range Name Create Command

1. Type [/] to call the Main menu. Find the **R**ange commands and call this submenu.
2. Next call the **N**ame commands submenu, and, finally, call the command to **C**reate a range name.

The prompt "Enter name:" will appear at the bottom of the screen. VP-Planner is waiting for you to name the range you will define in the next step of using this command. Range names may be up to 15 characters long, and must not have spaces or special characters in them.

3. Name the range by typing [underline↵].

Next, VP-Planner will prompt for the range of cells you want named "underline."

4. Answer the prompt by typing in [A8 . . M8↵].

Now that you have named this range of cells (the row of underlines from A8 to M8) you may refer to it by its name in any command requesting a range specification.

Using a Named Range in a Command

5. Move the pointer to cell A19 and type [/C] to call the /Copy command.
6. This time answer the source prompt by typing [underline↵].

The DESTINATION range begins at cell A19 and goes to cell M19. Using the rule for copying more than one cell to a range, the uppermost left cell of the DESTINATION range is the cell A19. The default destination displayed is A19. If you press the period key it will change to A19 . . A19. Either A19 or A19 . . A19 will work.

7. Answer the DESTINATION prompt by typing ↵.
8. Finally, repeat this last process to underline the last row in the spreadsheet (SAVINGS DEPOSITS) by typing [/Cunderline↵A23↵].

Summary on Ranges and Using the /Copy Command

Your understanding of the concept of ranges and their use may be highly instrumental in deciding how you can best design your spreadsheets. Ranges always have the form of a rectangle. They may be defined by: a) highlighting them; b) typing in their coordinates; or 3) using the name you have previously given them. How you define them depends on the manner in which you plan to use them.

The rule of copying ranges of more than one cell into other ranges illustrates how experimentation can teach you a great deal about how VP-Planner behaves. You may be surprised if you try to copy a row of cells into a column of cells, or vice versa. Although you may not get what you expect, you will learn something that could be useful later.

EXERCISE 6: Relative vs. Absolute Cell References

Copying Formulas

When the /Copy command is used to copy formulas, a new dimension of spreadsheet design is introduced. To show you how the /Copy command affects how you enter formulas into the spreadsheet, and how those formulas later derive their values, begin to fill in the spreadsheet's numeric data.

Entering and Copying a Simple Formula

1. Move the pointer to January's gross pay amount (B4) and type [1855].
2. Now move to C4 and type [+B4↵].

```
     A                    B          C          D          E          F          G
 1
 2                       JAN        FEB        MAR        APR        MAY        JUN
 3
 4   GROSS PAY AMOUNT      1855       1855
 5   TAX RATE
 6
 7   FED & STATE TAXES
 8   ------------------------------------------------------------------------------

17   FOOD
18   LEISURE
19
20   TOTAL EXPENSES
  C4       +B4
```

This simple formula says, "Put the value found in B4 into cell C4."

3. With the pointer on C4, type [/**C**] to call the /**C**opy command.

You will copy the formula into the entire year's gross pay amounts.

4. Set this single cell (C4 . . C4) as the SOURCE range by typing [↵].

5. Set the DESTINATION range as D4 to M4, [D4 . . M4↵].

The formula will be copied into the appropriate range of cells, and all months should show a gross pay amount of 1855.

Relative References

Move the pointer along the row labeled GROSS PAY AMOUNT and watch the control panel with the current cell information at the bottom of the screen. Notice that the formula was copied in a relative fashion, i.e., each cell's formula says, "Put here the value found in the previous cell."

```
     A                    B          C          D          E          F          G
 1
 2                       JAN        FEB        MAR        APR        MAY        JUN
 3
 4   GROSS PAY AMOUNT      1855       1855       1855       1855       1855       1855
                                       ↑          ↑          ↑          ↑          ↑
                                      +B4        +C4        +D4        +E4        +F4
```

When you use a formula to compute a value for a cell to hold, that formula will usually contain cell references (VP-Planner refers to them as *cell addresses*). The single cell reference in the original formula for this example was +B4. The "+" is used to tell VP-Planner to interpret "B4" as a value instead of a label.

When that formula was copied, it was copied relative to its cell reference. As the cell into which the formula was being copied moved to the right one position, the cell referenced in the formula shifted to the right one position.

Absolute References

It often is desirable to have one or more cell references remain the same when a formula is copied. VP-Planner recognizes four cell reference modes: (1) Relative column relative row; (2) Relative column absolute row; (3) Absolute column relative row; (4) Absolute column absolute row. The cell reference mode is controlled by the presence or absence of the "$" symbol before the column or row component of the referenced cell address, as follows:

B4	Relative column relative row
B$4	Relative column absolute row
$B4	Absolute column relative row
$B$4	Absolute column absolute row

If you wanted all of the cells in the range C4 . . M4 to contain the value stored in cell B4, you would enter the formula +$B4 in cell C4 and then copy cell C4 to the range D4 . . M4. Each cell in the range C4 . . M4 then would contain the formula +$B4 and would display the value contained in cell B.

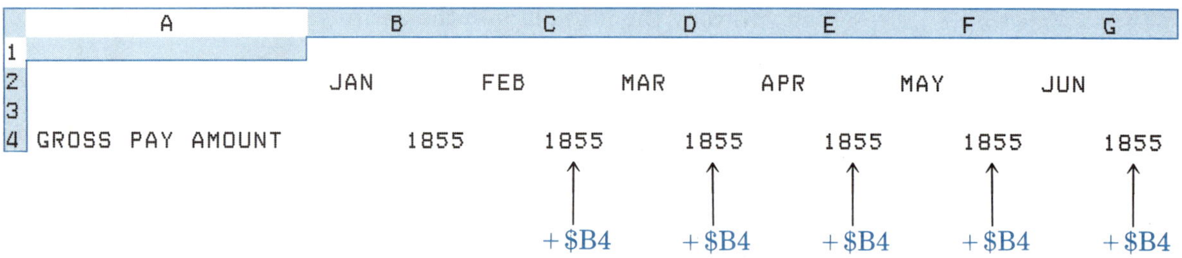

If you then were to copy the range C4 . . M4 to the range C5 . . M5, the formula in each of the cells would read $B5. Since B5 is empty, all of the cells in the range C5 . . M5 would be displayed as 0.

Rewriting the formula in cell C4 as +$B$4 and copying cell C4 to the range D4 . . M4 will produce the same result as before. However, copying cells C4 . . M4 will now result in cells C5 . . M5 containing the same values and formulas as cells C4 . . M4. This is because the formula in cell C4 was rewritten referencing absolute column B and absolute row 4 by placing the "$" in front of the address components.

The Difference between Relative and Absolute References

To demonstrate the difference between copying a formula with a relative reference and copying a formula with an absolute reference into a range of cells, assume that the year's gross pay amounts will be the same for four months. After four months you will get a raise of $200 per month.

1. If you changed the formulas in cells C4 . . M4, redo steps 2 through 5 in exercise 6.
2. Move the pointer to May's gross pay amount (F4) and type [2055↵].

What happened to the rest of the year's gross pay amounts? What would have happened if the formula copied into these cells had the cell reference +$B$4 (as absolute)? Why?

If you received a raise in May, that raise probably would stay in effect for the rest of the year. When you create an original formula to be copied into other cells, whether you enter the cell references for that formula as relative or absolute determines an important element of your spreadsheet's design.

Entering and Copying a Formula with an Absolute Reference

In the next step you will use a formula that must have one of its cell references remain absolute when it is copied into the rest of the row's cells. This formula will be used to compute the federal and state taxes for the spreadsheet.

3. Move the pointer to cell A6 and type [.23↵].

This figure represents the effective yearly tax rate you expect to pay. The formula to compute your federal and state taxes will multiply the tax rate (23%) times your gross pay amount for each month. The formula for the month of January could be typed as +A6*B4.

	A	B	C	D	E	F	G
1							
2		JAN	FEB	MAR	APR	MAY	JUN
3							
4	GROSS PAY AMOUNT	1855	1855	1855	1855	2055	2055
5	TAX RATE						
6	0.23						
7	FED & STATE TAXES	426.65					
8	------------------	----------	----------	----------	----------	----------	----------
17	FOOD						
18	LEISURE						
19							
20	TOTAL EXPENSES						

B7 +A6*B4

But if this formula is then copied into the rest of the cells in the row, the results would be:

	A	B	C	D	E	F	G
1							
2		JAN	FEB	MAR	APR	MAY	JUN
3							
4	GROSS PAY AMOUNT	1855	1855	1855	1855	2055	2055
5	TAX RATE						
6	0.23						
7	FED & STATE TAXES	426.65	0	0	0	0	0
8	------------------	----------	----------	----------	----------	----------	----------
17	FOOD						
18	LEISURE	+A6*B4	+B6*C4	+C6*D4	+D6*E4	+E6*F4	+F6*G4
19							
20	TOTAL EXPENSES						

B7 +A6*B4

The formulas are copied with both cell references relative to the cell into which the formula is being copied.

Although the formula works for January's federal and state taxes, it has not been entered to copy correctly for the rest of the cells in the row. To make each formula in the row refer to cell A6 for the tax rate that month's pay amount will be multiplied by, the original formula should be entered as either $A6*B4 or $A$6*B4. That is, the cell reference for the tax rate in this formula must be kept absolute.

4. Enter the correct formula for cell B7 and then /Copy that formula into the range of cells for the row.
5. Now move the pointer along the row and observe how the formulas differ from each other.

EXERCISE 7: Using the Pointer to Enter a Formula

When you enter a formula you can use the pointer to identify cell references for that formula. You should use this feature to reduce the chance of incorrect cell references being entered in a formula.

The formula for the net pay amount in the month of January is +B4 − B7. To enter this formula:

1. Move the pointer to B9 (the cell in which to enter the formula) and type [+].
2. Move the pointer to B4 (January's GROSS PAY AMOUNT). Look at the edit line at the bottom of the screen. It indicates the formula you are entering into cell B9.
3. Type [−] and move the pointer to B7. The finished formula should appear on the edit line as +B4 − B7.
4. Type ↵ to finish entering the formula.
5. Copy the formula into the range of cells C9 through M9.
6. Once more, move the pointer along the ninth row and look at the status line at the bottom of the screen to see how the cell references changed for each cell when the formula was copied.

	A	B	C	D	E	F	G
1							
2		JAN	FEB	MAR	APR	MAY	JUN
3							
4	GROSS PAY AMOUNT	1855	1855	1855	1855	2055	2055
5	TAX RATE						
6	0.23						
7	FED & STATE TAXES	426.65	426.65	426.65	426.65	472.65	472.65
8	-------------------------	----------	----------	----------	----------	----------	----------
9	NET PAY AMOUNT	1428.35	1428.35	1428.35	1428.35	1582.35	1582.35
		↑ +B4 − B7	↑ +C4 − C7	↑ +D4 − D7	↑ +E4 − E7	↑ +F4 − F7	↑ +G4 − G7

Both cell references were copied as relative, as they should have been.

7. Press the Home key. This is what you should see:

```
          A                 B        C        D        E        F        G
 1
 2                        JAN      FEB      MAR      APR      MAY      JUN
 3
 4  GROSS PAY AMOUNT      1855     1855     1855     1855     2055     2055
 5  TAX RATE
 6                 0.23
 7  FED & STATE TAXES   426.65   426.65   426.65   426.65   472.65   472.65
 8  ------------------------------------------------------------------------
 9  NET PAY AMOUNT     1428.35  1428.35  1428.35  1428.35  1582.35  1582.35
10
11  EXPENSES
12  ------------------------------------------------------------------------
13  RENT
14  UTILITIES
15  TELEPHONE
16  LIFE INSURANCE
17  FOOD
18  LEISURE
19  ------------------------------------------------------------------------
20  TOTAL EXPENSES
 A1

 1help 2edit 3name 4tabs 5goto 6window 7data 8table 9recalculate 0graph
276K                              14:04                                READY
```

EXERCISE 8: Rejustifying a Range of Labels

You may have noticed that the month labels are not lined up very well with the values you are entering into the spreadsheet. To demonstrate one of the /**R**ange commands and to make the spreadsheet more readable, do the following.

Using the /Range Lbl-Prefix Command (Label-Prefix)

1. Type [/**R**] to call the /**R**ange commands and select the command **Lbl**-Prefix.
2. Choose the command to **R**ight justify, and then define the range of cells to which to give this label prefix (") as B2 . . M2 (the row of month labels).

EXERCISE 9: Adding Data to the Spreadsheet

Finish the next expense amounts in the spreadsheet by entering the values in the same manner as you entered the year's gross pay amounts. For instance, for the first item, RENT, enter the number 375 into B13, the formula +B13 into cell C13, and then copy the formula into the rest of the year's rent row.

1. RENT is 375 per month all year.
2. UTILITIES are 100 per month all year.
3. TELEPHONE is 18 per month all year.
4. LIFE INSURANCE is 28.65 per month all year.

Enter the remaining expense items by using a formula to compute the amounts. For instance, the formula to enter into cell B17 (JAN's FOOD expense) is:

.30*B9

5. FOOD is 30% of NET PAY AMOUNT all year.
6. LEISURE is 15% of NET PAY AMOUNT all year.

This is what your spreadsheet should look like at this point.

	A	B	C	D	E	F	G
1							
2		JAN	FEB	MAR	APR	MAY	JUN
3							
4	GROSS PAY AMOUNT	1855	1855	1855	1855	2055	2055
5	TAX RATE						
6	0.23						
7	FED & STATE TAXES	426.65	426.65	426.65	426.65	472.65	472.65
8	------------------	----------	----------	----------	----------	----------	----------
9	NET PAY AMOUNT	1428.35	1428.35	1428.35	1428.35	1582.35	1582.35
10							
11	EXPENSES						
12	------------------	----------	----------	----------	----------	----------	----------
13	RENT	375	375	375	375	375	375
14	UTILITIES	100	100	100	100	100	100
15	TELEPHONE	18	18	18	18	18	18
16	LIFE INSURANCE	28.65	28.65	28.65	28.65	28.65	28.65
17	FOOD	428.505	428.505	428.505	428.505	474.705	474.705
18	LEISURE	214.2525	214.2525	214.2525	214.2525	237.3525	237.3525
19	------------------	----------	----------	----------	----------	----------	----------
20	TOTAL EXPENSES						

A1

1help 2edit 3name 4tabs 5goto 6window 7data 8table 9recalculate 0graph
274K 14:54 READY

EXERCISE 10: Introduction to Functions

Total expenses could be expressed in a formula as +B13+B14+B15+B16+B17+B18 for the month of January. Instead you will use one of the @ functions.

The general form of a function is **@XYZ**(argument). The @ sign tells VP-Planner that you are entering a function (which is treated as a value) into a cell. The XYZ represents the function's name, and the *argument* in the parentheses is composed of cell references, ranges, or formulas for the function to act upon.

Using the @SUM Function

1. Move the pointer to cell B20 and type [**@SUM** (B13 . . B18)↵].

The formula **@SUM**(B13 . . B18) will sum the cell contents of the cells in the range specified in the function's argument.

2. Now copy the formula into cells C20 through M20. Notice that the cell references in the function also were copied as relative.

EXERCISE 11: Finishing the Spreadsheet

Entering Savings Deposits

The label SAVINGS DEPOSITS represents money left to deposit in your bank account. Can you figure out what formula to type and how to copy it into the correct row?

1. Enter the appropriate formula into cell B22 and copy it into the rest of the cells in the spreadsheet row.

Now, your spreadsheet should look like this:

	A	B	C	D	E	F	G
1							
2		JAN	FEB	MAR	APR	MAY	JUN
3							
4	GROSS PAY AMOUNT	1855	1855	1855	1855	2055	2055
5	TAX RATE						
6	0.23						
7	FED & STATE TAXES	426.65	426.65	426.65	426.65	472.65	472.65
8	------------------	----------	----------	----------	----------	----------	----------
9	NET PAY AMOUNT	1428.35	1428.35	1428.35	1428.35	1582.35	1582.35
10							
11	EXPENSES						
12	------------------	----------	----------	----------	----------	----------	----------
13	RENT	375	375	375	375	375	375
14	UTILITIES	100	100	100	100	100	100
15	TELEPHONE	18	18	18	18	18	18
16	LIFE INSURANCE	28.65	28.65	28.65	28.65	28.65	28.65
17	FOOD	428.505	428.505	428.505	428.505	474.705	474.705
18	LEISURE	214.2525	214.2525	214.2525	214.2525	237.3525	237.3525
19	------------------	----------	----------	----------	----------	----------	----------
20	TOTAL EXPENSES	1164.407	1164.407	1164.407	1164.407	1233.707	1233.707
21							
22	SAVINGS DEPOSITS	263.9425	263.9425	263.9425	263.9425	348.6425	348.6425
23	------------------	----------	----------	----------	----------	----------	----------

A Running Savings Account Balance

You have one more row of values to add to the spreadsheet. This row will be labeled SAVINGS ACCOUNT and will reflect the total savings you expect after each month's deposit, with x amount of yearly interest, compounded monthly.

1. Move the pointer to A24 and type [SAVINGS ACCOUNT].
2. Now move to A25 and type [INTEREST RATE =].
3. Move to B25 and type [.0525] (the yearly rate of interest, 5¼%).
4. Move to A26. Type [\=↵]. Now copy this repeating label underline through to DEC (M26).
5. Move the pointer to A27 and type [BEGINNING BALANCE].
6. Then move to B27 and type in [0↵] (zero), the beginning balance for the savings account.

Entering a More Complicated Formula

You are ready to enter the formula for computing a running total of the savings account for the year. The formula will multiply the previous month's balance by one plus the monthly interest rate (add that month's interest earned), then it will add the deposit made at the end of the previous month to derive the beginning balance for the current month.

The general form of the formula for the month of FEB is +B27*(1+B25/12)+B22. The order in which the formula will be computed is:

- First—Take the yearly interest rate, B25, and divide it by 12 to determine the monthly interest rate.

  B25/12

- Second—Add one (1) to this giving the correct multiplier for determining the balance with interest added to it.

  (1+B25/12)

- Third—Take what you already have in the bank, B27, and multiply it by the multiplier to give principal plus interest earned for the month.

  +B27*(1+B25/12)

- Fourth—Finally, add the deposit you will make from the money you had (after expenses) from the month before.

  +B27*(1+B25/12)+B22

NOTE: VP-Planner evaluates formulas in the normal order of precedence. First, any operations in parentheses; second, exponentiation ^ (to the power of); third, multiplication and division (, /); and fourth, addition and subtraction (+, −).*

After entering this formula into February's beginning balance you will copy it into the appropriate cells for the rest of the year. However, one of the cell references in the formula must be copied with an absolute cell reference: all cells in the row will refer to this specific cell in their formulas.

The other two references in the formula will be relative to the particular month into which they are being copied.

Since one cell reference in the original formula must remain absolute when copied into the other cells of the row, that cell reference will need to be typed with a $ sign preceding its column letter.

To test your understanding of relative and absolute cell addresses, the following step requires that you decide which cell addresses be entered as relative and which as absolute. Refer to the previous discussions on relative and absolute cell addresses of formulas if necessary.

1. Type the correct formula for the month of FEB and copy it into the range of cells for BEGINNING BALANCE (set the DESTINATION range as D27 . . M27).

The bottom lines of your spreadsheet should look like this if you have typed the original formula correctly.

```
19  ----------------------------------------------------------------------
20  TOTAL EXPENSES     1164.407 1164.407 1164.407 1164.407 1233.707 1233.707
21
22  SAVINGS DEPOSITS   263.9425 263.9425 263.9425 263.9425 348.6425 348.6425
23  ----------------------------------------------------------------------
24  SAVINGS ACCOUNT
25  INTEREST RATE =      0.0525
26  ======================================================================
27  BEGINNING BALANCE          0 263.9425 529.0397 795.2968 1062.719 1416.011
```

Causing the Spreadsheet to Recalculate

Now that the spreadsheet is functionally complete, you can test its ability to recalculate automatically for any changes you enter into it.

If your boss gives you a $100.00 raise immediately (in January) and another $150.00 raise in May, instead of the $200.00 raise in May:

1. Change your spreadsheet to accommodate the changed salary.

Assume that taxes are cut this year and your estimated effective federal and state tax rate will drop to 18%.

2. Enter the new tax rate to see how it affects your home budget spreadsheet.

Suppose you receive a notice from your landlord informing you rent will be increased $20.00 per month beginning in March.

3. Enter the change into your spreadsheet.

Assume UTILITIES will be $125 JAN through MAR; $100 APRIL through AUGUST; $130 SEPT through DEC.

4. Change your spreadsheet to accommodate these expectations.

Your spreadsheet should look like this:

	A	B	C	D	E	F	G
1							
2		JAN	FEB	MAR	APR	MAY	JUN
3							
4	GROSS PAY AMOUNT	1955	1955	1955	1955	2105	2105
5	TAX RATE						
6	0.18						
7	FED & STATE TAXES	351.9	351.9	351.9	351.9	378.9	378.9
8	----------------------	----------	----------	----------	----------	----------	----------
9	NET PAY AMOUNT	1603.1	1603.1	1603.1	1603.1	1726.1	1726.1
10							
11	EXPENSES						
12	----------------------	----------	----------	----------	----------	----------	----------
13	RENT	375	375	395	395	395	395
14	UTILITIES	125	125	125	100	100	100
15	TELEPHONE	18	18	18	18	18	18
16	LIFE INSURANCE	28.65	28.65	28.65	28.65	28.65	28.65
17	FOOD	480.93	480.93	480.93	480.93	517.83	517.83
18	LEISURE	240.465	240.465	240.465	240.465	258.915	258.915
19	----------------------	----------	----------	----------	----------	----------	----------
20	TOTAL EXPENSES	1268.045	1268.045	1288.045	1263.045	1318.395	1318.395
21							
22	SAVINGS DEPOSITS	335.055	335.055	315.055	340.055	407.705	407.705
23	----------------------	----------	----------	----------	----------	----------	----------
24	SAVINGS ACCOUNT						
25	INTEREST RATE =	0.0525					
26	======================	==========	==========	==========	==========	==========	==========
27	BEGINNING BALANCE	0	335.055	671.5759	989.569	1333.953	1747.494

(Spreadsheet continues on the next page.)

	H	I	J	K	L	M
1						
2	JUL	AUG	SEP	OCT	NOV	DEC
3						
4	2105	2105	2105	2105	2105	2105
5						
6						
7	378.9	378.9	378.9	378.9	378.9	378.9
8	----------	----------	----------	----------	----------	----------
9	1726.1	1726.1	1726.1	1726.1	1726.1	1726.1
10						
11						
12	----------	----------	----------	----------	----------	----------
13	395	395	395	395	395	395
14	100	100	130	130	130	130
15	18	18	18	18	18	18
16	28.65	28.65	28.65	28.65	28.65	28.65
17	517.83	517.83	517.83	517.83	517.83	517.83
18	258.915	258.915	258.915	258.915	258.915	258.915
19	----------	----------	----------	----------	----------	----------
20	1318.395	1318.395	1348.395	1348.395	1348.395	1348.395
21						
22	407.705	407.705	377.705	377.705	377.705	377.705
23	----------	----------	----------	----------	----------	----------
24						
25						
26	==========	==========	==========	==========	==========	==========
27	2162.845	2580.012	2999.005	3389.83	3782.366	4176.619

EXERCISE 12: Saving the Spreadsheet

Now you will save your spreadsheet data file onto your diskette.

1. Make sure your files diskette is in the B: disk drive and that the door to the disk drive is closed.

   Your system ______________________________

   ____

2. Type [/] to call the Main menu and then select the /**F**ile command of that menu.
3. Select the **S**ave command.
4. Answer the prompt “Enter save file name:” by typing [vptut ↵]. Make sure you see the B: disk drive light go on. When the light goes off, you should see a READY prompt in the lower right corner of the monitor screen.

NOTE: "vptut" stands for "VP-Planner tutorial" and is simply a name that conforms to the rules for filenames.

EXERCISE 13: Quitting VP-Planner

Before proceeding to Part II of the tutorial, follow these instructions to quit VP-Planner and return to the DOS operating level.

1. Type [/] to call the Main menu and then select the command to **Q**uit from this menu.

VP-Planner will give you a chance to back out of this command because quitting will remove VP-Planner and your spreadsheet from RAM memory.

```
A16  You have asked to QUIT the worksheet. Are you sure? (Y/N)
```

2. Since you have saved your spreadsheet, type "Y" to complete the **Q**uit command.

Your spreadsheet will be erased from RAM memory and the VP-Planner entry menu will reappear on the screen.

3. Select the command to **Q**uit from the entry menu.

This should leave you back at the A> of the DOS operating level. If you are leaving the computer, don't forget to remove your diskette and the VP-Planner system diskette from the disk drives.

TUTORIAL EXERCISES: PART II

REQUIRED MATERIALS

1. An IBM DOS diskette
2. A VP-Planner program (system) diskette
3. Your files diskette with .WKS file from Part I
4. This manual
5. Other ____________________

Tutorial Conventions

During this tutorial you will be entering certain labels and values and using various VP-Planner menu commands on an electronic spreadsheet. The following are the conventions that this tutorial's instructions will use.

↵ When you see this symbol, press the Enter key located on the right side of the keyboard and marked with a bent arrow (↵).

[ ] Do not type brackets when the tutorial includes them in its instructions. Type only what is inside the brackets.

HOW TO GET OUT OF TROUBLE

If you want to:	*Then:*
■ Erase characters before you have entered them into a cell . . .	■ Tap the Backspace key (←) located just above the Enter key.
■ Erase the existing contents of a single spreadsheet cell . . .	■ Move the pointer to the cell and type [/**RE**↵] (**R**ange **E**rase).
■ Back up a command operation or command menu . . .	■ Tap the Esc key once. (The Esc key is located on the top row, far left side).
■ Stop any command operation and return to the READY mode . . .	■ Press and hold the Ctrl key (middle left) and then tap the Scroll Lock key (top far right).
■ Stop the tutorial and continue it later . . .	■ Type [/**FS**filename↵]. Watch the disk drive light to make sure the spreadsheet has been saved. Then type [/**QY**] to quit VP-Planner.
■ Continue the tutorial after you have stopped it . . .	■ Load VP-Planner into RAM memory and then type [/**FR**filename↵].

Getting Started

1. Insert the DOS diskette into the A: disk drive (the disk drive on the left) and close the disk drive door.
2. If the computer already is on, press and hold the Ctrl and Alt keys and then tap the Del key. If it is not on then turn on the computer and the monitor.

In a few moments DOS will be loaded automatically.

3. Answer DOS's date and time prompts.
4. When you see the A>, remove the DOS diskette from the A: disk drive.
5. Insert your "files" diskette into the B: disk drive (the disk drive on the right). Be sure to close the disk drive door.
6. Insert the VP-Planner program (system) diskette into the A: drive and close the door.
7. Type [VP↵]
8. Select the worksheet command from the entry menu and then press any key to load the VP-Planner spreadsheet into RAM.

Your system ____________________

EXERCISE 1: Loading a Spreadsheet

In Part I of the tutorial you created a spreadsheet and saved it on your diskette under the filename vptut (or you may have saved it under a name you preferred). To load the spreadsheet back into RAM memory do the following.

1. Type [/] to call the Main menu and then select its /**F**ile command.

The submenu of /**F**ile commands includes the command to **R**etrieve. The command pointer should be on this command.

```
2Retrieve 3Save 4Combine 5Xtract 6Erase 7List 8Import 9Directory 0Utility
```

2. Tap the Enter key or type [**R**] to select the /**F**ile **R**etrieve command.

VP-Planner will read through the filenames on your diskette, and place the names having a .WKS extension on the lower window line so you can select the one you want. You can either move the pointer to the spreadsheet data file you want loaded into RAM, or you may type the full filename and then tap the Enter key to load the file.

3. Select the spreadsheet you created in Part I of the tutorial and enter its filename to tell VP-Planner this is the file you want loaded into RAM.

The rest of this tutorial is designed to demonstrate the more important and/or most used spreadsheet commands. As the tutorial shows you menu lines, these commands will be underlined.

EXERCISE 2: Formatting a Spreadsheet

Formatting Ranges of Cells

On the Main menu is the command to call a set of /**R**ange commands. You used one of these commands to assign a /**R**ange **L**bl-Prefix for the row of month labels to align them more precisely with the numeric data in the spreadsheet. You also used the /**R**ange commands to name a range, then later used the name to refer to it. The /**R**ange commands include:

```
2Format 3Lbl-Prefix 4Erase 5Name 6Justify 7Protect 8Unprot 9Input 0Col-Wid
```

The first item in the /**R**ange menu is the **F**ormat command which is used for formatting ranges of cells. The submenu of /**RF** (/**R**ange **F**ormat) includes:

```
2Fixed 3Sci 4Crncy 5,(comma) 6Gen 7+/- 8Percent 9Date 0Text Reset Hide 12
```

1. Move the pointer to B25 (the yearly interest rate on savings).

You will use the /**R**ange **F**ormat commands to format this single cell to display its data in **P**ercent notation.

2. Type [/**RF**] to call the /**R**ange **F**ormat commands; find the command to format as a **P**ercent; and enter the command.

The number of decimal places will be two (2). Since 2 is the default value shown with the prompt, you can simply type ↵.

3. Tap the Enter key.

The appropriate range to format is the single cell B25; and again, the default range shown is the desired range B25 . . B25.

4. Type ↵ to enter B25 . . B25 as the appropriate range to format.

BEFORE:

```
              A                   B         C         D         E
24  SAVINGS ACCOUNT
25  INTEREST RATE =          0.0525
26  ============================================================
27  BEGINNING BALANCE               0   335.055   671.575   989.569
```

STEPS:

`/RFP` (/Range Format Percent)

```
Enter desired decimal position: 2←
Select range of cells to be altered: B25..B25←
```

AFTER:

```
              A                   B         C         D         E
24  SAVINGS ACCOUNT
25  INTEREST RATE =           5.25%
26  ============================================================
27  BEGINNING BALANCE               0   335.055   671.575   989.569
```

Notice that the value shown at the bottom of the screen,

```
B25 (P2) 0.0525
```

remains 0.0525, but for purposes of viewing the spreadsheet, the value in the cell B25 is now shown as 5.25%. The (P2) shown at the bottom of the screen with the cell's value indicates the cell is now formatted to show **Per**cent, two decimal places.

5. Now repeat the last step to format the tax rate (the 0.18 in cell A6) to display as a percent.
6. Next move the pointer to B22 (SAVINGS DEPOSITS row); call the /**RF** (/**R**ange **F**ormat) command; select **C**rncy and 2 decimal places. Set the range to format as B22 through M22.

BEFORE:

```
              A                   B         C         D         E
20  TOTAL EXPENSES       1268.045  1268.045  1288.045  1263.045
21
22  SAVINGS DEPOSITS     335.055    335.055   315.055   340.055
23  ------------------------------------------------------------
24  SAVINGS ACCOUNT
25  INTEREST RATE =           5.25%
26  ============================================================
27  BEGINNING BALANCE               0   335.055   671.575   989.569
```

STEPS:

`/RFC` (/Range Format Crncy)

```
Enter desired decimal position: 2←
Select range of cells to be altered: B22..M22 ←
```

AFTER:

```
                A                B        C        D        E
20  TOTAL EXPENSES       1268.045 1268.045 1288.045 1263.045
21
22  SAVINGS DEPOSITS      $335.06  $335.06  $315.06  $340.06
23  ------------------------------------------------------
24  SAVINGS ACCOUNT
25  INTEREST RATE =          5.25%
26  ======================================================
27  BEGINNING BALANCE            0  335.055  671.575  989.569
```

If you use the Crncy format, cells with values in them display their values in standard currency notation. The partial cents that were shown before have been rounded just for display purposes. They remain part of the value held in the cell and will be used in any formula referring to that cell.

7. Repeat the last step selecting the **T**ext command instead of the **C**rncy command for this range of cells.

BEFORE:

```
                A                B        C        D        E
22  SAVINGS DEPOSITS      $335.06  $335.06  $315.06  $340.06
23  ------------------------------------------------------
24  SAVINGS ACCOUNT
25  INTEREST RATE =          5.25%
26  ======================================================
27  BEGINNING BALANCE            0  335.055  671.575  989.569
```

STEPS:

`/RFT` (/Range Format Text)
`Select range of cells to be altered: B22..M22 ↵`

AFTER:

```
                A                B        C        D        E
22  SAVINGS DEPOSITS     +B9-B20  +C9-C20  +D9-D20  +E9-E20
23  ------------------------------------------------------
24  SAVINGS ACCOUNT
25  INTEREST RATE =          5.25%
26  ======================================================
27  BEGINNING BALANCE            0  335.055  671.575  989.569
```

This formatting command will display the formulas used in a range of cells.

8. Finally, select the /**R**ange **F**ormat **R**eset command to return the row of cells B22 . . M22 back to the default spreadsheet format (**G**eneral).

Global Formatting Commands

When the term *global* is used in computers, it generally means "in effect or affecting the entire set of data." The term *default* means "automatically in effect." For instance, the default global label-prefix for VP-Planner is ['] (left justified), and unless you specify otherwise, any label you enter into a cell will automatically be justified to the left in that cell. When you do specify otherwise, such as when you used the /**R**ange **L**bl-Prefix **R**ight command to right justify the month labels, you are "over-riding the default global setting."

VP-Planner allows you to change certain global settings through the /**W**orksheet **G**lobal commands. These commands are:

```
2Format 3Label-Prefix 4Col-Width 5Recalculation 6Protection 7Default
```

VP-Planner allows you to define a global format for the entire spreadsheet through the **/WGF** (/**W**orksheet **G**lobal **F**ormat) commands. The available formatting commands are the same as in the /**R**ange commands with the difference that the entire spreadsheet, rather than a specified range, is affected.

1. Type [/**WGF**] and select the **T**ext command.

```
              A                  B         C         D         E
20  TOTAL EXPENSES      @SUM(B13 @SUM(C13 @SUM(D13 @SUM(E13
21
22  SAVINGS DEPOSITS     +B9-B20  +C9-C20  +D9-D20  +E9-E20
23  -----------------------------------------------------------
24  SAVINGS ACCOUNT
25  INTEREST RATE =         5.25%
26  ===========================================================
27  BEGINNING BALANCE           0 +B27*(1+ +C27*(1+ +D27*(1+
```

Notice that the rates in cells A6 and B25 are the only ones unaffected by the new global format. Any cell previously formatted by a /**R**ange **F**ormat command will not be altered by a **G**lobal **F**ormat change.

2. Type [/**WGF**] and select the **C**rncy command (two decimal places).

```
              A                  B         C         D         E         F
20  TOTAL EXPENSES      *******************************************
21
22  SAVINGS DEPOSITS     $335.06  $335.06  $315.06  $340.06  $407.71
23  -----------------------------------------------------------------
24  SAVINGS ACCOUNT
25  INTEREST RATE =         5.25%
26  =================================================================
27  BEGINNING BALANCE      $0.00  $335.06  $671.58  $989.57 *********
```

Notice that when a value becomes too large to display in a cell (in this case because of the addition of $ signs and commas) VP-Planner indicates the situation by putting asterisks in the affected cell.

EXERCISE 3: Global Change of Column Widths

One solution to the problem of numeric entries that are too large to display in their cells is to enlarge the display width of the cell. One /**W**orksheet **G**lobal command allows you to change the default global column width of nine characters to any size width between one and seventy-two characters.

1. Type [/**WG**], call the **C**ol-Width command, and enter the new global column width as 12.

	A	B	C	D	E
20	TOTAL EXPENSES	$1,268.05	$1,268.05	$1,288.05	$1,263.05
21					
22	SAVINGS DEPOSITS	$335.06	$335.06	$315.06	$340.06
23	------------------------	----------	----------	----------	----------
24	SAVINGS ACCOUNT				
25	INTEREST RATE =	5.25%			
26	========================	==========	==========	==========	==========
27	BEGINNING BALANCE	$0.00	$335.06	$671.58	$989.57

EXERCISE 4: Altering the Spreadsheet

Suppose you neglected an expense item (or acquired a new one) and needed to include it in your spreadsheet.

Inserting a Spreadsheet Row or Column

1. Move the pointer to anywhere in the fourteenth row (UTILITIES) and type [/**WIR**] to set up for the /**W**orksheet **I**nsert **R**ow command.

The command to insert rows allows you to insert several rows at once by specifying a range of rows to insert. In this case, you will insert only one row, so the default range shown (x14 . . x14) is correct.

2. Type ↵ to insert the single row.
3. Now move the pointer to that month's total expense amount.

Notice that VP-Planner automatically adjusts existing cell references in its formulas and functions to accommodate an alteration (such as an inserted or deleted row) to the spreadsheet.

For instance, the formula for January's total expenses, @**SUM**(B13 . . B18), in row 21 automatically has been changed to @**SUM**(B13 . . B19) to accommodate the row inserted into the range. Similarly, the formula +B9 − B20 for January's savings deposits has been changed to +B9 − B21.

4. Move the spreadsheet pointer to A14 and label the new row PARKING since it will be the row for parking fees paid for three-month parking permits.
5. Now move to the months January, April, July, and October to enter the amount of $75.00 into these cells for the PARKING spreadsheet row.

Moving a Spreadsheet Row or Column

What if you decide parking expenses should be located under utilities rather than under rent?

1. Move the pointer to the sixteenth row, for telephone expenses, and **I**nsert a single **R**ow there.
2. Next move the pointer to A14 and type [/**M**] to call the /**M**ove command from the Main menu.
3. Enter the range to /**M**ove SOURCE as A14 . . M14 and the DESTINATION range as A16 (the uppermost left cell of the row you just inserted).

Deleting a Spreadsheet Row or Column

1. Now move the pointer back to row 14, where PARKING used to be; call the /Worksheet commands; find the Delete command; then use the command to delete that single row.

EXERCISE 5: More on Viewing the Spreadsheet

The spreadsheet you have created is so large that only a portion of it may be viewed on the screen at a time. The portion to the far left should appear as:

	A	B	C	D	E
1					
2		JAN	FEB	MAR	APR
3					
4	GROSS PAY AMOUNT	$1,955.00	$1,955.00	$1,955.00	$1,955.00
5	TAX RATE				
6	18.00%				
7	FED & STATE TAXES	$351.90	$351.90	$351.90	$351.90
8	------------------------	------------	------------	------------	------------
9	NET PAY AMOUNT	$1,603.10	$1,603.10	$1,603.10	$1,603.10
10					
11	EXPENSES				
12	------------------------	------------	------------	------------	------------
13	RENT	$375.00	$375.00	$395.00	$395.00
14	UTILITIES	$125.00	$125.00	$125.00	$100.00
15	PARKING	$75.00			$75.00
16	TELEPHONE	$18.00	$18.00	$18.00	$18.00
17	LIFE INSURANCE	$28.65	$28.65	$28.65	$28.65
18	FOOD	$480.93	$480.93	$480.93	$480.93
19	LEISURE	$240.47	$240.47	$240.47	$240.47
20	------------------------	------------	------------	------------	------------
21	TOTAL EXPENSES	$1,343.05	$1,268.05	$1,288.05	$1,338.05
22					
23	SAVINGS DEPOSITS	$260.06	$335.06	$315.06	$265.06
24	------------------------	------------	------------	------------	------------
25	SAVINGS ACCOUNT				
26	INTEREST RATE =	5.25%			
27	========================	============	============	============	============
28	BEGINNING BALANCE	$0.00	$260.06	$596.25	$913.91

To view the last eight columns of the spreadsheet you need to use the pointer to "push" the screen across (called *scrolling*). VP-Planner provides several ways in which to use the pointer to move the screen about on a large spreadsheet.

Moving Quickly About the Spreadsheet

You already have used the Function key F5 to "go to" a particular cell and the Home key to move quickly back to cell A1. To see the various other ways that you can move quickly about the spreadsheet, do the following.

1. Tap the Home key to send the pointer to A1. Next tap the PgDn key on the numeric keypad. Then tap the PgUp key found on the same keypad.

These two keys, PgDn and PgUp, move the pointer and the screen one "page" (one screen's worth of spreadsheet) up or down at a time.

2. Tap the Home key to send the pointer to A1.

Next, find the Tab key on the left side of the keyboard marked with two arrows just above the key marked Ctrl.

3. Tap the Tab key once or twice.

The lower case of this key moves the pointer and the screen one page to the right. Shift to the upper case of the key to move the pointer and screen one page to the left.

4. Tap the Home key to send the pointer to A1.
5. Now move the pointer to A8, and tap the key marked End on the numeric keypad.

Notice the indicator at the bottom of the spreadsheet showing the END mode is turned on.

6. Tap the Pointer-right key (→).
7. Tap the End key, and then tap the Pointer-left key (←).
8. Now tap the End key/Pointer-down key combination three times in a row.
9. Tap the End key/Pointer-up key combination four times in a row.

The End key turns on a mode that, when used with the pointer control keys, may be used to move the pointer rapidly through the worksheet. When you turn on the END mode and press a pointer control key, the pointer will move in the direction indicated by the pointer control key until it reaches the last nonblank cell in the spreadsheet, if the pointer was originally on a nonblank cell. The pointer will move to the cell following the last blank cell if it was originally on a blank cell.

10. Tap the End key and then the Home key.

This End key combination sends the pointer to the lowest right cell of the rectangle defined by the spreadsheet (the effective opposite of Home).

These methods of moving the pointer are extremely useful when pointing to ranges at the time they are being specified, or, when pointing to cell references in a formula at the time a formula is being created.

Freezing Titles

Another handy feature for viewing large spreadsheets is the ability to let you "freeze" rows, columns, or both. It is particularly useful when row or column labels disappear from view when the screen is pushed to another section of the spreadsheet. For instance, when you want to view the row labeled BEGINNING BALANCE, the month labels for the row disappear off the top of the screen.

1. Move the pointer to the fourth row. Type [/**W**] to call the /**W**orksheet commands and select the **T**itles command.

You want to freeze the row of month labels that is horizontal in the spreadsheet.

2. Select the **H**orizontal command of this menu.
3. Use the pointer to push the screen down the spreadsheet until the last rows appear for viewing.

Notice that the rows above the pointer's position at the time the titles were frozen do not scroll off the screen.

4. Use the pointer to push the screen to the right until the month of December is showing.

The month labels scroll with the rest of the spreadsheet, but now the row labels have disappeared.

5. Tap the Home key, move the pointer to B4, call the **T**itles command of the /**W**orksheet commands and set both horizontal and vertical title freeze.
6. Scroll the screen to the right and then down. Both the row labels and column labels now are frozen.
7. Tap the Home key.

Notice that when titles are frozen you are unable to move the pointer to them with the pointer control keys. Home now is defined as the upper left corner of the unfrozen spreadsheet. You may move the pointer into a frozen area by pressing the Function key F5 followed by the address of a cell within the frozen area.

The /**W**orksheet **T**itles **C**lear command unfreezes all title fixes.

8. Use this command to remove the title's fix on your spreadsheet.

The next portion of the tutorial introduces a concept called *modeling* and will further demonstrate techniques of dealing with large spreadsheets.

EXERCISE 6: Modeling with a Spreadsheet

Modeling allows you to ask, "What if?" and use the rapid recalculation power of the spreadsheet to obtain the answer quickly. To take you through an exercise on how you can model with the spreadsheet you will add another value to it.

Adding a Summary for Interest Earned

1. Move to the cell L30 and type [INTEREST EARNED =].

   ↑ *5 spaces*

2. Next move to N26 and type [ENDING BALANCE].
3. Now /Copy the formula in cell M28 into the cell N28.

```
(Source cell range: M28..M28    Destination cell range: N28↵ )
```

This area of the spreadsheet should now look like:

	J	K	L	M	N
18	$517.83	$517.83	$517.83	$517.83	
19	$258.92	$258.92	$258.92	$258.92	
20	----------	----------	----------	----------	
21	$1,348.40	$1,423.40	$1,348.40	$1,348.40	
22					
23	$377.71	$302.71	$377.71	$377.71	
24	----------	----------	----------	----------	
25					
26					ENDING BALANCE
27	==========	==========	==========	==========	
28	$2,770.03	$3,159.85	$3,476.38	$3,869.30	$4,263.93
29					
30			INTEREST EARNED =		

Advantages of Pointing to Enter a Formula

In cell N30 you will enter the formula that will give the total interest earned on your savings for the year. The formula will subtract the beginning balance and all deposits from the ending balance to determine its answer. Since cell references for the formula are located in several areas of the spreadsheet, you will use the pointing method to enter the formula into the appropriate spreadsheet cell. As you move about the spreadsheet to point to various cell references, try using the rapid methods of moving the pointer.

1. With the pointer on N30 type [+] to indicate that you are starting to enter a value into this cell.
2. Move the pointer to the year's ending balance amount. Look at the edit line at the bottom of the screen to see that the formula is being entered.
3. Type [−].

The pointer will return to N30 and the edit line should show +N28−.

4. Move the pointer to the beginning balance amount for January and type [−].

The pointer will return again to N30 and the formula continues to grow.

5. Now type [@**SUM**(].
6. Move the pointer to the beginning of the savings deposits values.
7. Press the period key to set the anchor for the range you are going to sum.
8. Move the pointer to the end of the savings deposits row and type [)].

The formula is complete.

+N28−B28−@**SUM**(B23 . . M23)

9. Now press the Enter key to signal that you are through entering the formula.

N30: +N28−B28−@**SUM**(B23 . . M23)

	J	K	L	M	N
18	$517.83	$517.83	$517.83	$517.83	
19	$258.92	$258.92	$258.92	$258.92	
20	----------	----------	----------	----------	
21	$1,348.40	$1,423.40	$1,348.40	$1,348.40	
22					
23	$377.71	$302.71	$377.71	$377.71	
24	----------	----------	----------	----------	
25					
26					ENDING BALANCE
27	==========	==========	==========	==========	
28	$2,770.03	$3,159.85	$3,476.38	$3,869.30	$4,263.93
29					
30			INTEREST EARNED =		$97.07

Splitting the Window on the Spreadsheet

With deposits given, two factors will affect interest earned—the interest rate and the beginning balance. You can find both values in the B column, and you can find the interest earned to the far right (out of view) in the N column. To view these columns at the same time and access them with the pointer, you may use the /**W**orksheet **W**indow set of commands.

1. Move the pointer anywhere in the C column and call the /**W**orksheet **W**indow **V**ertical command.

The Window commands **H**orizontal and **V**ertical split the screen into separate *windows* through which you can view the spreadsheet. Each window may be used to scroll the spreadsheet. VP-Planner will allow up to six windows to be defined.

The pointer can reside in only one window at any given time, but it may be moved from one window to the other by tapping the Function key marked F6.

2. Tap the Function key marked F6 several times. Then move the pointer to the window on the left.
3. Next, try moving the pointer to the right six columns.

You can scroll the spreadsheet in this window with the pointer in the same manner as you previously scrolled the spreadsheet.

4. Tap the Home key and then use the pointer to scroll up the spreadsheet until the bottom three rows are located in about the middle of the screen.

Notice that the spreadsheet on the right also scrolls. The term for such scrolling is *synchronized* and the /**W**orksheet **W**indow commands include the commands to **S**ynchronize and **U**nsynchronize the scrolling of spreadsheets being viewed through the windows.

5. Tap the F6 key to move to the right window and scroll it to the left until you can see the last three columns (L, M, and N).
6. Now move to the left window by tapping F6.

You may move the pointer in the left window to change interest rate, beginning balance, or both, and you can see the effect the changes have on interest earned for the year in the window to the right.

Test Your Understanding: Using the Spreadsheet to Model

Suppose you actually had $1500.00 in the account at the beginning of the year. Where would you enter this figure in your spreadsheet and by how much does this change affect the year's interest earned?

7. Make the change to the spreadsheet.

Assume you hear about a "sure thing" investment and are considering it as an alternative to putting your money in the Savings and Loan. The investment offers a 28% return instead of the 5.25% you currently receive. What effect would this investment have on the year's interest earned?

8. Enter the change in interest rate and observe the effect on interest earned.

Removing a Split Screen Display

1. Call the /**W**orksheet **W**indow commands and select the command to **C**lear.

The command returns the screen to one window and to its normal appearance.

EXERCISE 7: Other Yearly Summaries

To complete the spreadsheet you will add a final column of summary information of total amounts for various income and expense items.

1. Move to the cell N2 and type ["TOTALS↵].

NOTE: We've used the label prefix " to right justify label in the cell.

2. Move to cell N4 and type [@**SUM**(B4 . . M4)↵].
3. Now copy the formula into the range N5 . . N23.

Notice that several cells in this column now display $0.00. Cells containing labels are assigned a value of zero.

4. Use the /**R**ange **E**rase commands to erase the cells that tried to sum a range holding nothing but labels.

Turning Off Automatic Recalculation

You should note the increasing wait (the pointer disappears) after you make a cell entry or change a cell's content. This is because VP-Planner (by default) automatically recalculates the entire spreadsheet every time a cell's contents are changed. The larger the spreadsheet, the longer the wait becomes. To stop automatic recalculation you may use the /**W**orksheet **G**lobal **R**ecalculation **M**anual command. To turn it back on you use the /**W**orksheet **G**lobal **R**ecalculation **A**utomatic command.

While **R**ecalculation is in the **M**anual mode, you need to tap the F9 key to cause a spreadsheet recalculation.

EXERCISE 8: Printing a Spreadsheet

You now are ready to set up the spreadsheet to be printed. It is far too wide to fit on an 8″ × 10″ piece of paper; however, VP-Planner compensates by printing it on additional pieces of paper. You also can choose to condense the spreadsheet as it is printed if your printer has that feature.

1. To begin, type [/**P**] to call the /**P**rint commands of the Main menu.
2. Select the **P**rinter command.

Your first set-up operation will be to define the range of cells you want printed.

3. Select the **R**ange command and set the range for printing to be the entire year's budget spreadsheet (A1 . . O30).

Once you have specified the range to print, the specification becomes part of the spreadsheet's data (as do all of the options and specifications you select for a particular spreadsheet). So, if you save the spreadsheet after you have set your print range, you need not specify that range again in order to print the same portion of the spreadsheet later.

4. Make sure the printer is turned on, on-line, and connected to your computer (your lab may have a *shared device* control switch. You will need to adjust this switch in order to select your computer as the one currently connected to the printer.)

   Your system ______________________________

   ____

5. Advance the paper in the printer to the top of the next page.
6. Select and enter the **A**lign command of the /**P**rint **P**rinter menu to tell VP-Planner that the printer is at the top of a page.

*NOTE: Selecting **Align** does not produce a visible reaction from VP-Planner.*

7. Now select the **G**o command of the menu.

Notice that VP-Planner will print (by default) the number of columns it can fit in 72 characters across the page, then advance a page and begin printing columns where it left off. VP-Planner also will automatically "page" its printing for spreadsheets that have too many rows to fit in its default page length of 66 lines per page.

Default widths and lengths for printing (as well as several other default settings) can be changed through use of the /**P**rint **O**ptions commands.

```
2Header 3Footer 4Margins 5Borders 6Setup 7Page-Length 8Other 9Quit
```

Using Print Options

To see three very useful print **O**ptions available, do the following.

1. Select the **O**ptions commands of the /**P**rint **P**rinter menu.
2. Set the **B**orders to be "**C**olumns" A1.

With VP-Planner you may select certain columns and/or rows to be automatically included in each page of the printed spreadsheet.

3. Next select the **S**etup command.

The **S**etup command sends special control codes to the printer to alter its normal printing. One of the most useful control codes with spreadsheet applications causes the printer to print in condensed mode.

If your printer is able to print in this mode, you must send it the correct code. Since the correct codes vary from printer to printer, your answer to the Enter Setup String prompt on the screen will vary depending on the brand of printer you are using. However, with such major manufacturers as Epson, Gemini, IBM, and Okidata, the code is \015.

4. Type and enter the appropriate code for your printer.
5. Now select the **M**argins command and set the **R**ight margin to be 132.

With condensed print, the number of characters you can fit across a standard 8½″ × 11″ sheet of paper is 132. You do, however, need to extend the right margin setting to tell VP-Planner to start paging its spreadsheet at 132 characters rather than 72.

6. Select the **Q**uit command of the **O**ption commands to return you to the /**P**rint **P**rinter commands.

7. Finally, respecify the **R**ange to be printed as B1 . . O30.

The A column in the spreadsheet has been specified as a border and will be printed automatically with each page printed.

8. Now select the **A**lign command, make sure the paper is advanced to its top, and tell VP-Planner to **G**o ahead and print the spreadsheet.
9. After the printer has finished printing your spreadsheet, turn the printer off, then back on again to return it to its default print settings.
10. When you return to your computer, type [**Q**] to **Q**uit the /**P**rint **P**rinter commands.

Printing to a File

When you save your spreadsheet data, you create a *worksheet* on your diskette under the name you have given it. At the time VP-Planner saves the file it adds a .WKS extension to the name to identify it as a file it can read and use to reconstruct a spreadsheet when you later use the /**F**iles **R**etrieve command.

Another type of file VP-Planner can create is a *Print file*. Such a file is created by printing the spreadsheet as it appears on the screen to a file on the diskette instead of on paper in the printer. VP-Planner adds the extension .PRN to files created in this manner. One advantage of this feature is the ability to later use a word processing application software to edit, add to, or insert the text file into other text files.

The rest of this tutorial is designed to demonstrate how to create a Print file, to explain some of the concepts involving files, and to demonstrate some of the DOS commands that can be used to manage the files on your diskette.

1. Call the /**P**rint menu and select the **F**ile command instead of the **P**rinter command.
2. Name the file you are about to create "BUDGET."
3. Select the **O**ptions **M**argin **R**ight command and set the right margin to 72 characters.
4. Type [**Q**] to **Q**uit the **O**ptions commands and return to the /**P**rint **F**ile commands.
5. Make sure your files diskette is in the B: drive and the door is closed, and then **G**o ahead and print the spreadsheet to a file.
6. Now type [**Q**] to **Q**uit this /**P**rint **F**ile menu.

NOTE: You must complete this last step to finish the printing to a file operation.

EXERCISE 9: Resaving Your Spreadsheet

1. Now use the /**F**iles command to save your spreadsheet data file in its updated form. You will need to answer **R**eplace in order to erase the old version of "vptut" (or whatever you have named this file) on your diskette and replace it with the new one.

EXERCISE 10: Exiting VP-Planner

1. Type [/**Q**] to call the /**Q**uit command of the Main menu and answer **Y**es to the "next" prompt.
2. Select the **Q**uit command from the Entry menu.

EXERCISE 11: Back to DOS

The A> shown on the screen is DOS's prompt. When you see it on the screen, you can use DOS's commands.

Using DOS Commands to View Your Files

1. Type in the following DOS commands and read the short explanations under them.

   [B:↵]

This DOS command changes the current disk drive to B:.

   [DIR↵]

This command lists a directory of the diskette in the current drive.

   [TYPE BUDGET.PRN↵]

The DOS command TYPE will display the contents of a file on the screen. This is the file that you created with the /**P**rint **F**ile command. VP-Planner added the .PRN (Print File) extension to identify this file as a print file. The contents of the file appear on the screen just as they would on the printer's paper because the data in the file were saved in a form called ASCII (pronounced "Askey"), the American Standard Code for Information Interchange. The ASCII file format is fundamental to transferring data between application packages.

   [TYPE VPTUT.WKS↵]

This displays the contents of the worksheet file VP-Planner uses to reconstruct the spreadsheet "vptut" when you use the /**F**iles **R**etrieve command. You can see that it is not an ASCII file.

VP-PLANNER OPERATION AND COMMAND SUMMARY

VP-Planner Quick Reference Command Summary

- /Worksheet
  - Global
    - Format
      - Currency
      - , (Comma)
      - General
      - Text
    - Col-Width — Enter desired column width:
    - Recalculation
      - Natural
      - Automatic
      - Manual
  - Insert
    - Row
    - Column
  - Delete
    - Row
    - Column
  - Col-Width
    - Set
    - Reset
  - Erase
    - Yes
    - No
  - Titles
    - Both
    - Horizontal
    - Vertical
    - Clear
  - Window
    - Horizontal
    - Vertical
    - Sync
    - Unsync
  - Autokey
    - Define
    - Clear
    - Execute
    - Label>Macro
    - Macro > Label
    - Step
    - Run
    - Immedx
    - Quit
- /Range
  - Format
    - Fixed
    - Crncy
    - , (Comma)
    - Gen
    - Percent
    - Date
    - Text
  - Label-Prefix
    - Left
    - Right
    - Center
    - — Select range of cells to be altered:
  - Erase — Select range of cells to be blanked:
  - Name
    - Create
    - Delete
    - Reset
    - Show

(continued on next page)

- **/C**opy — Source cell range: — Destination cell range:
- **/M**ove — Range to move: — Destination:
- **/F**ile
  - **R**etrieve — Enter name of file to retrieve:
  - **S**ave — Enter save file name: — **C**ancel **R**eplace
  - **E**rase / **L**ist
    - **W**orksheet
    - **P**rint
    - **G**raph
    - **DBF**
    - **M**ulti-Dim
    - **B**ackup
    - **I**nterchg (DIF)
    - — Enter file name:
  - **U**tility
    - **C**opy / **R**ename — Enter source name: — Enter new name:
- **/P**rint
  - **P**rinter
    - **R**ange — Select range of cells for printing:
    - **O**ptions
      - **M**argins
      - **B**orders
      - **O**ther
    - **C**lear
    - **A**lign
    - **Q**uit
    - **S**tatus
  - **F**ile — Enter file name:

VP-PLANNER CONTROL KEYS

1 Escape key
2 Control (Ctrl) key
3 Shift key
4 Alt key
5 Slash key
6 Shift key
7 Enter (↵) key
8 Number Lock (Num Lock) key
9 Scroll Lock (Break) key
10 Del key

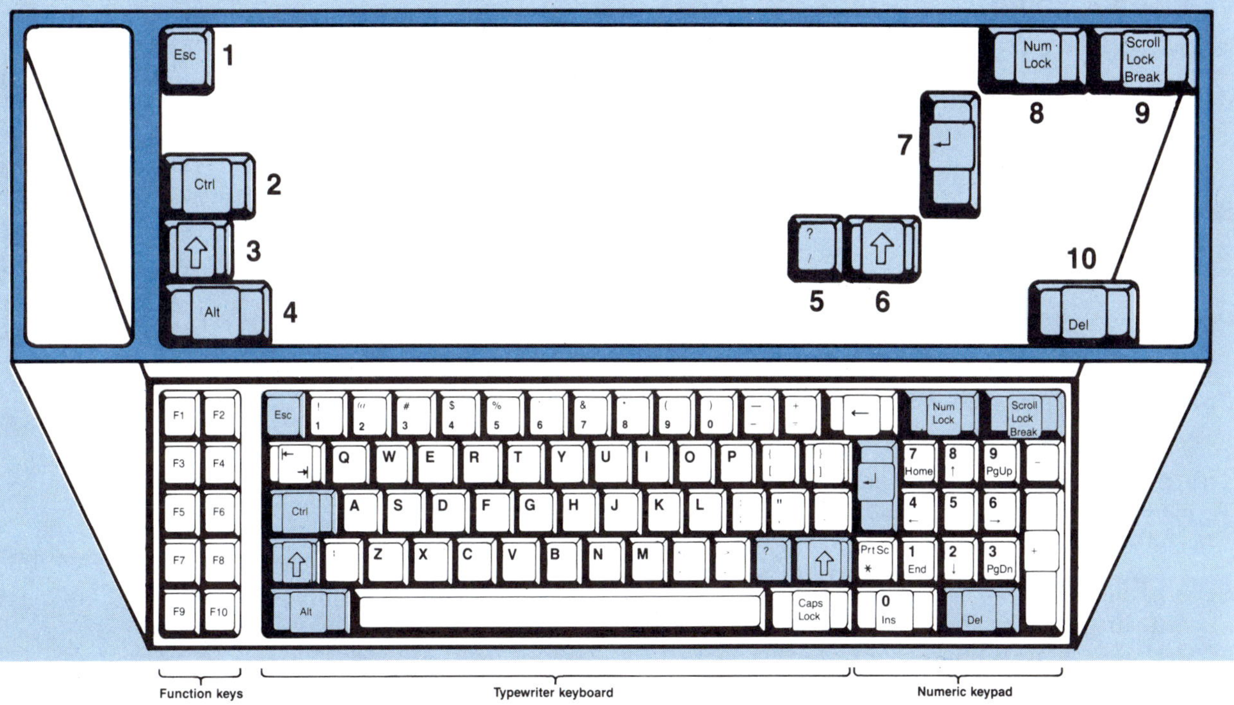

KEY COMBINATIONS

Ctrl-Break Cancels any VP-Planner command operation. Returns the spreadsheet to the READY mode.

Alt-Alpha Key Used with alphabetic keys to invoke keyboard macros.

OTHER CONTROL KEYS

Slash Key Calls VP-Planner's Main menu of commands.

Enter Key Enters the current line into memory for VP-Planner to act upon.

Escape Key Cancels current line or operation and "backs up" one step.

Num Lock Key Toggles Ten-Key Numeric to Pointer Control keys. The Shift key may be used to shift this keypad temporarily to the opposite mode.

FUNCTION KEYS 1–10

F1 HELP Accesses VP-Planner's on-line help facility. Help screens appear in context of the current operation.

F2 EDIT Allows contents of the current cell to be edited.

F3 NAME Displays the list of current range names while in the POINT mode.

F4 ABS Cycles through the four cell reference modes while pointing to a cell during formula creation.

F5 GOTO Moves the pointer to the specified cell.

F6 WINDOW Moves the pointer from one Window to the other.

F7 QUERY Repeats the last Data Query operation.

F8 TABLE Repeats the last Data Table operation.

F9 CALC Recalculates the spreadsheet.

F10 GRAPH Redraws the graph currently defined.

VP-Planner Pointer Control/Editing Keys

POINTER KEYS

Pointer Control Keys Moves the pointer one cell at a time in the direction of the pointer arrow.

Home Key Moves pointer to top left corner of spreadsheet (A1), or "to the beginning of" in modes other than READY.

PgUp Key Shifts screen and pointer one page up at a time.

PgDn Key Shifts screen and pointer one page down at a time.

Tab Key Shifts screen one page to the right (lower case), or one page to the left (upper case) at a time.

Scroll Lock Key When SCROLL is toggled on with this key, Scrolling of the spreadsheet occurs one row or column at a time.

Period Key Anchors a cell address as the starting address for a range.

POINTER KEY COMBINATIONS

End-Pointer Control Key Causes the pointer to move in the direction indicated by the pointer control key until it reaches the last nonblank cell, if the pointer was originally on a nonblank cell. The pointer will move to the cell following the last blank cell if it was originally on a blank cell.

End-Home Key Moves the pointer to the bottommost right cell in the spreadsheet's active area.

EDITING KEYS

Backspace Key Backspaces and erases the character to the left of the cursor when entering data into a cell, editing a cell, or entering a command.

Del Key Erases the character above the cursor when entering data into a cell, editing a cell, or entering a command specification.

/Worksheet Commands

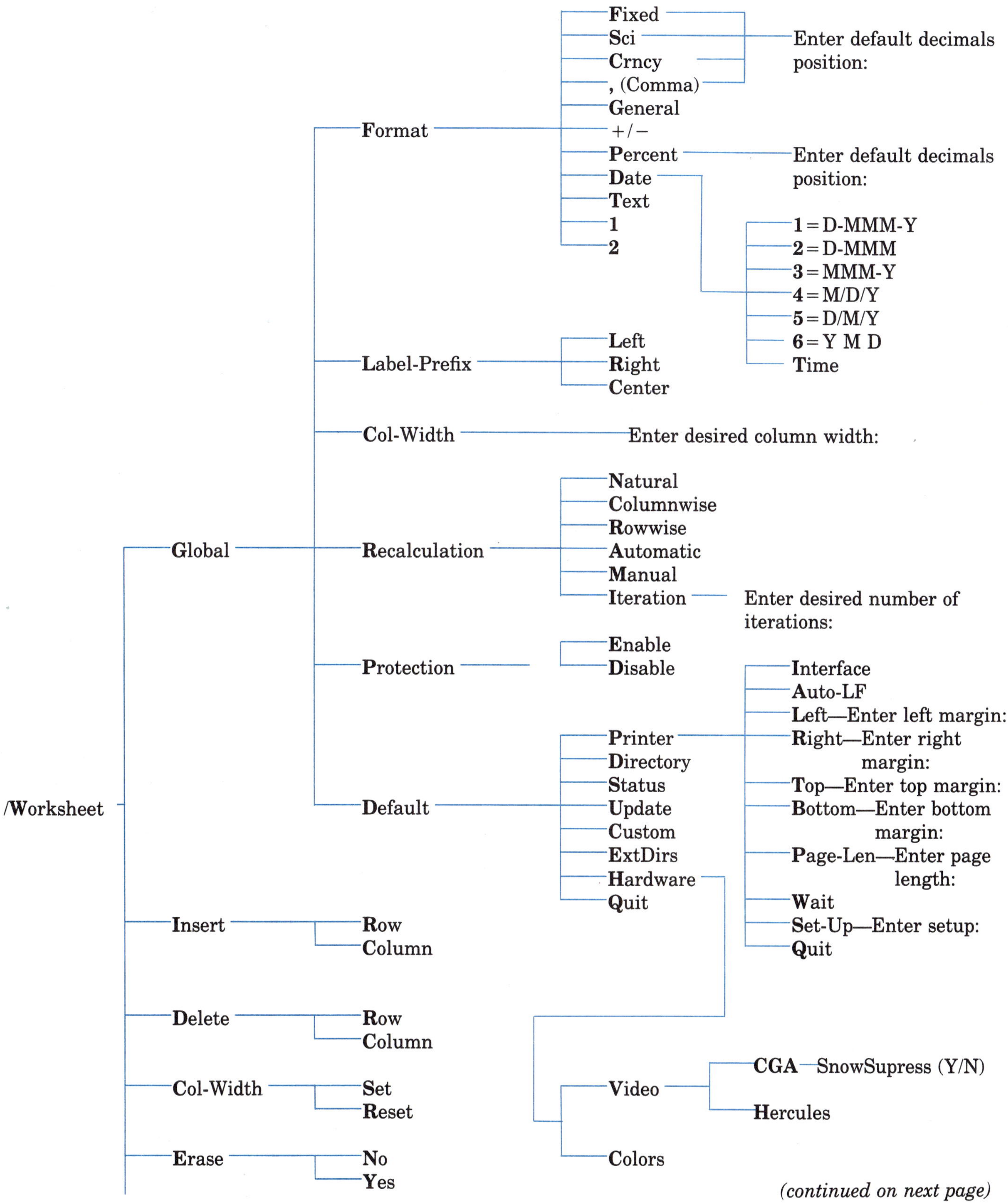

(continued on next page)

- Titles
  - Both
  - Horizontal
  - Vertical
  - Clear
- Window
  - Horizontal
  - Vertical
  - Sync
  - Unsync
  - Clear
- Status
- Autokey
  - Define
  - Clear
  - Execute
  - Label>Macro
  - Macro>Label
  - Step
  - Run
  - Immedx
  - Quit

/WGF Worksheet Global Format Fixed Sci Crncy , General +/− Percent Date Text	Sets global format for display of values. **Fixed** specifies the number of decimal places and **Sci** displays scientific notation. **Crncy** displays the $ sign and commas, with negative values in parentheses. **,** displays commas, and negatives in parentheses. **General** (default) displays values with the maximum precision allowed by the column width. **+/−** displays values in horizontal bar graph format as n number of "+" signs or "−" signs where n = value. **Percent** displays values as percentage with % sign. **Date** displays numbers as dates with the options of the following formats: D-MMM-Y, D-MMM, MMM-Y, M/D/Y, D/M/Y, Y M D, or Time. **Text** displays formulas as text in cells. **1** and **2** allow the user to define two custom formats.
/WGL Worksheet Global Label-Prefix Left Right Center	Sets global alignment of labels. **Left** (default) justifies labels from the left in cells. **Right** justifies labels from the right in cells. **Center** centers labels in cells.
/WGC Worksheet Global Col-Width	Sets global column width. Default is nine characters.

/WGR **W**orksheet **G**lobal **R**ecalculation **N**atural **C**olumnwise **R**owwise **A**utomatic **M**anual **I**teration	Sets the order of recalculation to **N**atural, **C**olumnwise, or **R**owwise. Default order is **N**atural (usually the most appropriate order for recalculation). Recalculation may be set either to **A**utomatic or **M**anual. When **M**anual is selected, **A**utomatic recalculation is turned off and the CALC Function key (F9) must be used to recalculate the spreadsheet. Default recalculation is **A**utomatic.
/WGP **W**orksheet **G**lobal **P**rotection **E**nable **D**isable	Sets global protection status of spreadsheet. Selections are **E**nable to turn protection on and **D**isable to turn it off. Default status is off. With protection on, spreadsheet cells may not be edited unless they are within an unprotected range. (See **R**ange commands /**RP** and /**RU**).
/WGD **W**orksheet **G**lobal **D**efault	May be used to redefine default printer settings, hardware settings, and default directory or disk drive. Default settings are held in a configuration file on the system diskette. By selecting **U**pdate, any changes in default settings will be saved to this file.
/WI **W**orksheet **I**nsert **R**ow **C**olumn	Inserts one or more rows or columns in the spreadsheet. Rows are inserted just above the pointer; columns are inserted just to the left of the pointer. To insert more than one row or column, define the range of rows or columns to be inserted.
/WD **W**orksheet **D**elete **R**ow **C**olumn	Deletes one or more rows or columns in the spreadsheet. A single row or column is deleted where the pointer is located. To delete more than one row or column, define the range of rows or columns to be deleted.
/WC **W**orksheet **C**ol-Width **S**et **R**eset	Sets the width of the column in which the pointer is currently located. If **R**eset is selected, the column will be set to the current **G**lobal **C**olumn-Width.
/WE **W**orksheet **E**rase **Y**es **N**o	Erases the current spreadsheet from the computer's RAM memory and displays a clean spreadsheet. Before the spreadsheet is erased, you must select Yes to the prompt. Selecting **N**o will cancel the **E**rase command. This precaution ensures that the spreadsheet is not inadvertently erased without being saved.
/WT **W**orksheet **T**itles **B**oth **H**orizontal **V**ertical **C**lear	Freezes either rows, columns, or both, as titles that will remain on the screen even if the pointer is moved to other locations on the spreadsheet. If **H**orizontal is selected, rows just above the pointer become titles. If **V**ertical is selected, columns just to the left of the pointer become titles. Selecting **B**oth will produce both title rows and columns. **C**lear will unfreeze all titles. When titles are in use, the title rows and/or columns may only be accessed when in the Point mode.

/WW **W**orksheet **W**indow **H**orizontal **V**ertical **S**ync **U**nsync **C**lear	Creates two windows on the spreadsheet by splitting the screen either horizontally or vertically, allowing two separate portions of the spreadsheet to be viewed at the same time. Either area may be accessed, and the WINDOW Function key (F6) is used to move from one window to the other. Scrolling may be **S**ynchronized or **U**nsynchronized. Different spreadsheet settings such as Formats and Titles may be defined separately in the two windows. Selecting **C**lear will return the screen to just one window; the settings from the upper or left window will be retained.
/WS **W**orksheet **S**tatus	Displays current global settings, protection status, and amount of system memory (RAM) still available.
/WA **W**orksheet **A**utokey	Records up to 255 keystrokes as an autokey macro. **D**efine assigns a macro to a function (F1 through F10). **C**lear deletes an autokey macro. **E**xecute executes an autokey macro. **L**abel>**M**acro converts label cells into autokey macros. **M**acro>**L**abel converts an autokey macro into a label cell or a range of cells. **S**tep causes a pause between the execution of autokey macro instructions. **R**un cancels the step mode and executes the macro normally. **I**mmedx executes a macro residing in the current cell.

/Range /Copy /Move Commands

- /Range
  - Format
    - Fixed / Sci / Crncy / , (Comma) — Enter decimal position: — Select range:
    - Gen / +/− — Select range:
    - Percent — Enter decimal position: — Select range:
    - Date
      - 1 = D-MMM-Y
      - 2 = D-MMM
      - 3 = MMM-Y
      - 4 = M/D/Y
      - 6 = D/M/Y
      - 7 = Y M D
      - Time
    - Text / Reset / Hide — Select range:
    - 1 / 2 — Enter decimal position: — Select range:
  - Label-Prefix
    - Left / Right / Center — Select range of cells to be altered:
  - Erase — Select range of cells to be blanked:
  - Name
    - Create / Delete — Enter name:
    - Labels
      - Right
      - Down
      - Left
      - Up
    - Reset
    - Show
  - Justify — Enter justify range:
  - Protect / Unprot — Select range to be altered:
  - Input — Enter input range:
  - Col-Width
    - Set — Select range of columns to be altered: — Enter Col-Width:
    - Reset
- /Copy — Source cell range: Destination cell range:
- /Move — Range to move: Destination:

/RF **R**ange **F**ormat **F**ixed **S**ci **C**rncy **,** **G**eneral **+**/− **P**ercent **D**ate **T**ext **R**eset	Sets format for display of values in specified range. Sets range format for display of values. **F**ixed specifies the number of decimal places and **S**ci displays scientific notation. **C**rncy displays the $ sign and commas, with negative values in parentheses. **,** displays commas, and negatives in parentheses. **G**eneral (default) displays values with the maximum precision allowed by the column width. **+**/− displays values in horizontal bar graph format as n number of "+" signs or "−" signs where n = value. **P**ercent displays values as a percentage with % sign. **D**ate displays numbers as dates with the options of the following formats: D-MMM-Y, D-MMM, MMM-Y, M/D/Y, D/M/Y, or Y M D, Time. **T**ext displays formulas as text in cells. **1** and **2** allow user to define two custom formats. **R**eset cancels all **R**ange **F**ormat commands and returns to default settings.
/RL **R**ange **L**abel-Prefix **L**eft **R**ight **C**enter	Sets alignment of labels in the specified range. **L**eft justifies labels from the left in cells. **R**ight justifies labels from the right in cells. **C**enter centers labels in cells.
/RE **R**ange **E**rase	Erases the contents of all cells in a specified range.
/RN **R**ange **N**ame **C**reate **D**elete **L**abels **R**eset **S**how	**C**reate allows a range to be named. Range names may be up to fifteen characters long. The name may then be used to specify the range in any formula or command. **D**elete is used to delete a single range name. **R**eset will delete all range names. Deleting cells at the upper left or lower right corner of a named range by deleting rows or columns (/**WD**) will cause the range name to become undefined, and any formula using that range name will show ERR. **S**how displays all defined range names.
/RP, /RU, /RI **R**ange **P**rotect **U**nprotect **I**nput	**P**rotect prevents changes to cells within the specified range when Global Protection is on. **U**nprotect allows cells to be changed. **I**nput is used to allow changes to any unprotected cells in a specified range. Pointer movement also will be restricted to these cells until the Enter key is pressed before making any change to the current cell.
/RJ **R**ange **J**ustify	Reformats a range of cells into a defined paragraph. Provides VP-Planner with limited word processing capabilities.
/C **C**opy	Copies the contents of a cell or range of cells to another cell or range of cells. Formulas should be evaluated for referencing modes before the **C**opy command is issued. The DESTINATION range is specified as the uppermost left corner of the range.

/M **M**ove	While the **C**opy command causes duplication of a cell or range, the **M**ove command is used to physically move a cell or range of cells to another location on the spreadsheet. After defining the range to be moved, place the pointer at the upper left corner of the area to which the range is to be moved. All formulas referencing cells in a moved range are changed to reflect the new positions of those cells. Formulas within the moved range change only if their references are to other cells in the range.

/File Commands

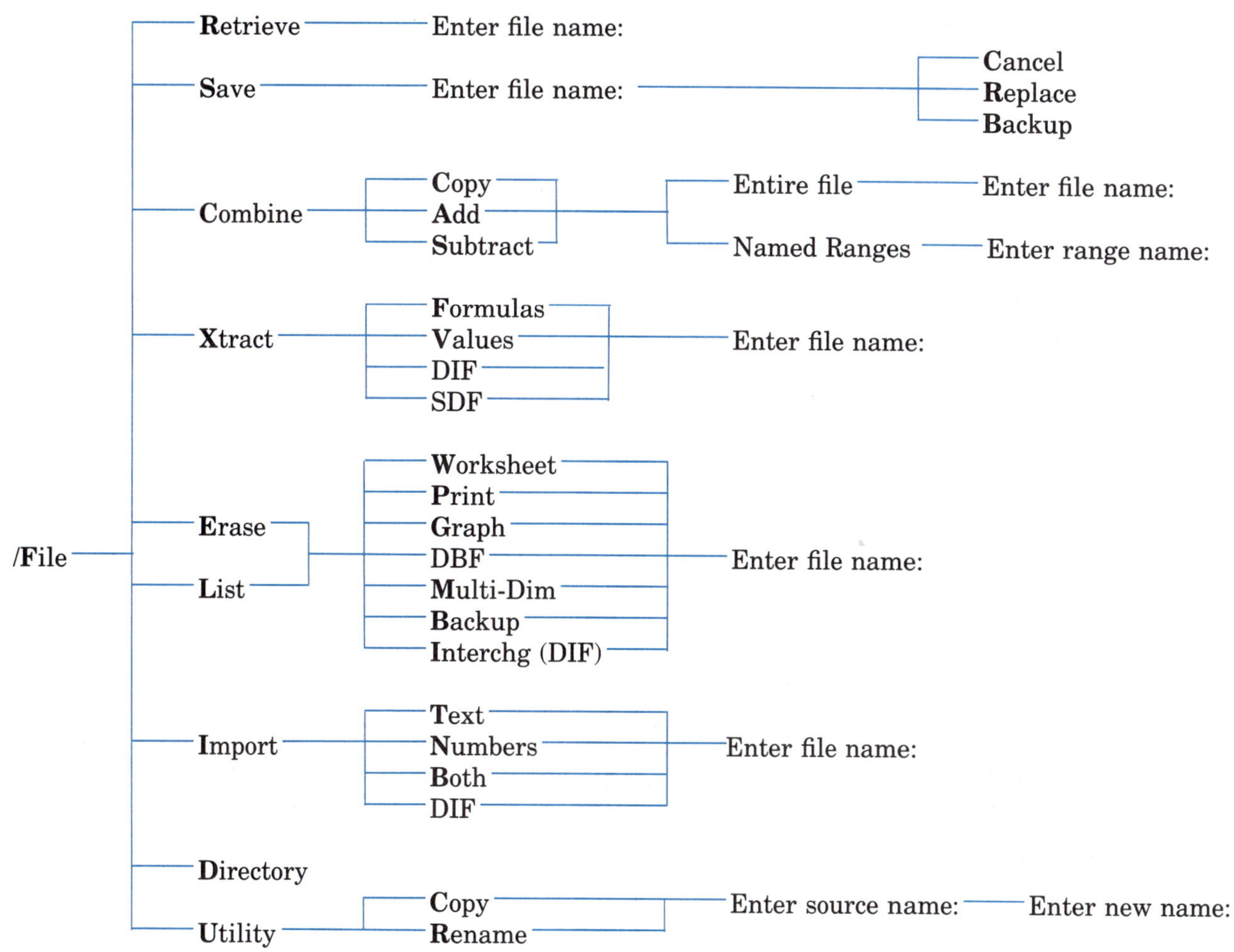

/FR **F**ile **R**etrieve	Erases the current spreadsheet and loads a new spreadsheet (.WKS) file from the diskette. Spreadsheet files on current disk or directory appear on bottom menu line. File to be loaded may be pointed to or typed in.
/FS **F**ile **S**ave	Saves the current spreadsheet on the diskette. If the spreadsheet originally was loaded into RAM memory with **/FR,** the filename used to load it will appear on the prompt line. The diskette file copy may be replaced with the current spreadsheet, a backup created a new filename may be entered, or the command cancelled.

/FC **File** **Combine** **Copy** **Add** **Subtract**	Combines all (Entire File) or part (Named Range) of a spreadsheet file on the diskette with the current spreadsheet. The position of the pointer in the current spreadsheet determines where incoming cells will be placed. Any overlayed cells below and to the right of the pointer will be replaced by the incoming cells. If the options **Add** or **Subtract** are selected, the combined spreadsheet will add to or subtract from the overlayed cells holding values.
/FX **File** **Xtract** **Formulas** **Values** **DIF** **SDF**	Writes a portion of the current spreadsheet to a diskette file. If the option **Formulas** is selected, the new spreadsheet file will retain the same formulas used in the current spreadsheet. Selecting **Values** will cause only the currently displayed values of all formulas to be saved in the new spreadsheet file as constants. **DIF** and **SDF** will create industry standard specification files that may be transported to other applications or systems.
/FE, /FL **File** **Erase** **List**	**Erase** allows VP-Planner files to be erased from the diskette without exiting from the spreadsheet program. **List** temporarily will replace the spreadsheet display with a display of files and the amount of space left on the diskette. When a "disk full" error message is encountered, these commands are helpful in recovering disk space by deleting unneeded files.
/FI **File** **Import** **Text** **Numbers** **Both** **DIF**	Reads data from any ASCII file having a .PRN extension into the current spreadsheet. If **Text** is selected, each line of the imported file will be entered into a single cell of the current spreadsheet, beginning with the current cell and moving down. If **Numbers** is selected, only values and strings delimited with legal **Label-Prefix** characters (on both sides) in the ASCII file will be read into the current spreadsheet. **Both** will bring in both text and numbers. **DIF** will import files created in DIF format.
/FD **File** **Directory** (or **Disk**)	Allows current disk drive (DOS 1.1) or directory (DOS 2.0) to be changed.
/FU **File** **Utility** **Copy** **Rename**	**File Utility Copy** and **Rename** allows files to be copied and removed from within VP-Planner without having to exit DOS.

/Print Commands

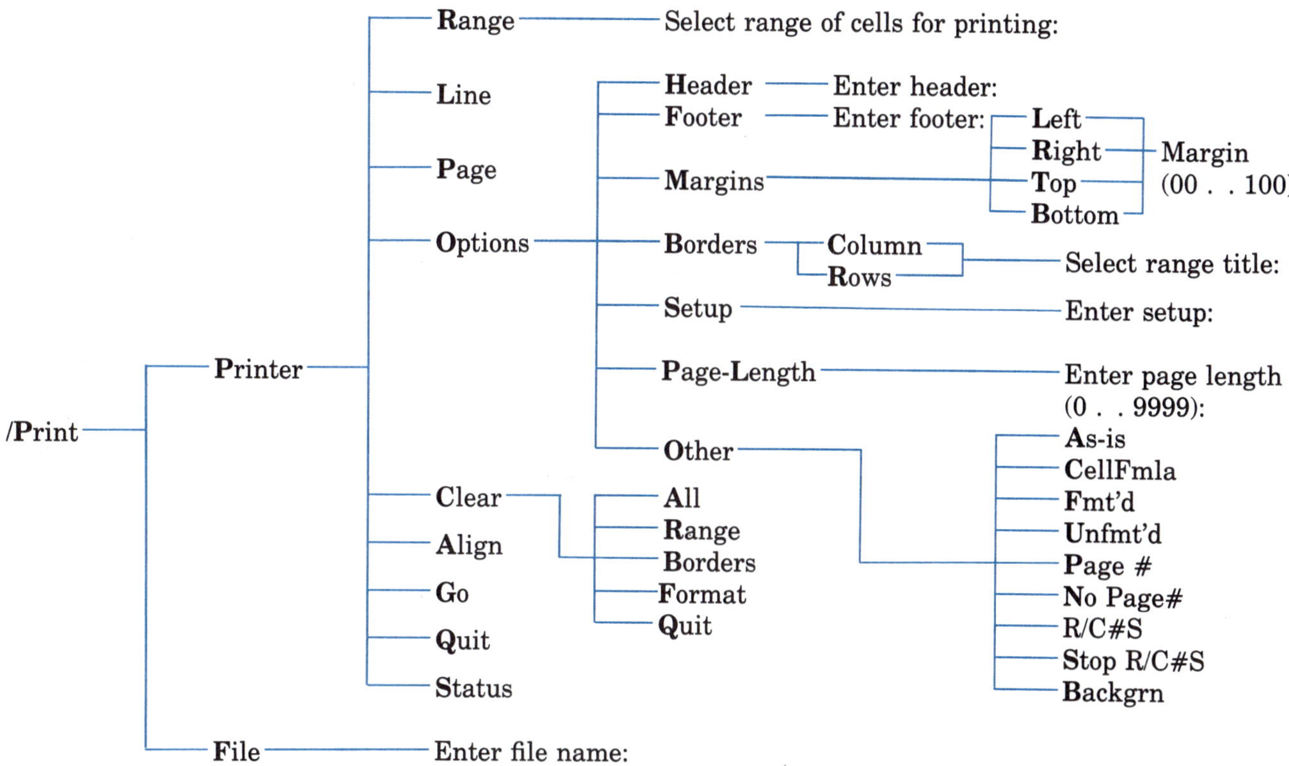

/PPR Print Printer Range	Defines the range of the current spreadsheet to be printed. If print range previously has been defined it will be displayed and may be undefined by using the Esc or Backspace keys. When the /**P**rint **G**o command is given, the currently defined range is printed.
/PPL and **/PPP** Print Printer Line Page	**L**ine advances the paper in the printer one line. **P**age advances paper one page. After printing, paper will not advance to the top of next page unless **P**age is selected.
/PPO Print Printer Options Header Footer Margins Borders Setup Page-Length Other Quit	Print **O**ptions set various print parameters. **H**eaders and **F**ooters (top and bottom page labels) may be added to each page of printed output. **M**argins may be adjusted from their default settings. **B**orders for each page of printed output may be specified as particular columns or rows from within the spreadsheet. Printer control codes used to invoke such options as condensed printing and line spacing may be sent to the printer through the **S**etup command. **P**age-Length also may be adjusted. The **O**ther command allows the spreadsheet's cell-formulas and labels to be printed one-per-line; it is useful for hard-copy documentation of a spreadsheet. **F**ormatted prints with page breaks, headers, footers, and set-up strings. **U**nformatted omits these. **P**age # causes the page number to be printed on each page. **N**o page # turns page numbering off. **R**ow/col # prints column and row labels. **S**top R/C cancels row and column printing. **B**ackground enables or disables background printing of worksheets or graphs.

/PPC **P**rint **P**rinter **C**lear	Clears all /**P**rint settings back to default values. **O**ptions to **C**lear include **A**ll, /**P**rint **R**ange, **B**orders, or **F**ormat (margins, page length, and setup string).
/PPA **P**rint **P**rinter **A**lign	**A**lign is selected to define the current printer position as the top of a page. Adjust paper in printer, and then select **A**lign.
/PPG **P**rint **P**rinter **G**o	The **G**o command begins printing, either on the printer or to a file. Before issuing the **G**o command, a /**P**rint **R**ange must be defined. When printing to a **F**ile the /**P**rint **F**ile **Q**uit command must be issued to complete the printing.
/PF **P**rint **F**ile	Printing to a **F**ile uses the same commands as printing on the printer. In this case, however, all output is sent to a text file and is given the extension '.PRN'. .PRN files may be printed at a later time using other softwares or may be used to transfer spreadsheet data to another application software.

/Graph Commands

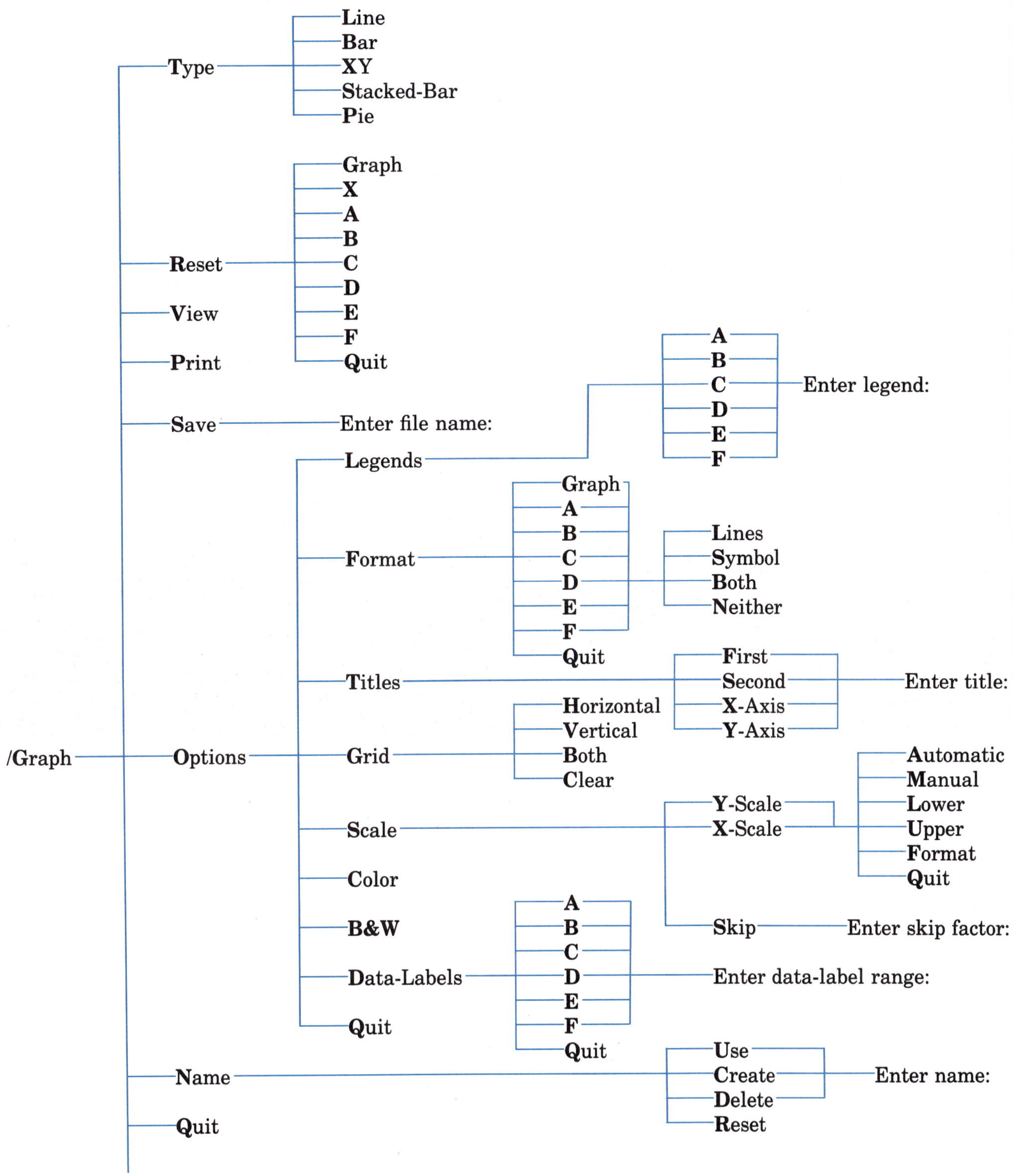

(continued on next page)

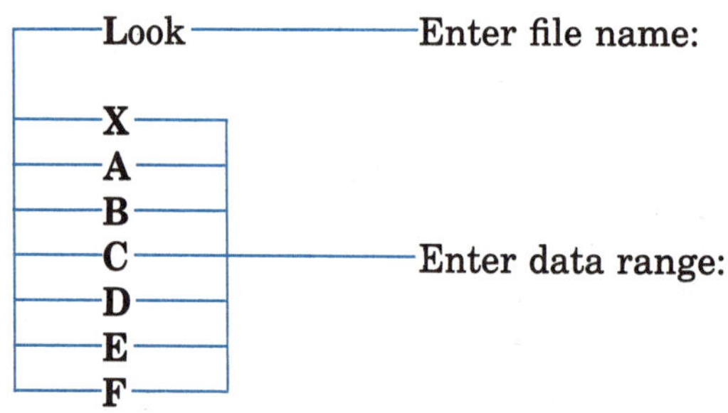

/GT Graph **T**ype **L**ine **B**ar **XY** **S**tacked-Bar **P**ie	Selects one of the five graph types: **Line** graph, **Bar** graph, **XY** graph, **Stacked-Bar** graph, or **Pie** chart. Each type requires certain definitions of spreadsheet data ranges to be used in creating the graph. The **Bar**, **Stacked-Bar**, and **Line** graphs all require at least one data range to graph and will accept up to six data ranges. These ranges are identified as the /Graph data ranges A–F. An X-range also may be defined. Values or labels in the X-range appear as labels on the graph's X-axis. The **Pie** chart accepts only one data range (**A**). An X-range may be defined and is used to label the slices of the pie. The **XY** graph is somewhat different than any of the other graph types in that the X-range must hold values. These values are scaled and placed along the X-axis. Up to six data ranges (A–F) may be used, and at least one (in addition to the X-range) is required.
/GR Graph **R**eset **G**raph **X** **A–F** **Q**uit	Cancels some or all of the currently defined graph settings. To cancel all, select Graph. Selecting each setting individually will cancel only that setting. Select **Q**uit when finished with cancelling settings.
/GV Graph **V**iew	Displays the currently defined graph on the monitor screen. If the appropriate data ranges for the graph have not been defined, the screen may be blank. Pressing any key will return the display of the spreadsheet with the /Graph commands as the current menu.
/GS Graph **S**ave	Saves the current graph in a file on the diskette as a .PIC file. These files may then be enhanced with other graphics packages.
/GP Graph **P**rint	Prints current graph.

/GO
Graph
Options
  Legend
  Format
  Titles
  Grid
  Scale
  Color
  B&W
  Data-Labels
  Quit
	Sets a number of options to enhance the display of the graph. Options include adding **T**itles, data range **L**egends, data range **D**ata-Labels, scaling the X and Y axes, and displaying the graph in **C**olor or **B**&W (Black and White).

/GN
Graph
Name
  Use
  Create
  Delete
  Reset
	This command, which is similar to using range names, allows you to give the current graph settings a name. **C**reate is used to name the settings. Selecting **U**se and entering a graph name will cause the named graph to become the current graph. **D**elete is used to delete a single graph name. **R**eset deletes all graph names. Named graph settings are saved along with the spreadsheet file.

/GX Graph X	Sets the X-range values for the **XY** graph, and labels for all other graph types.
/G(A–F) Graph A. . .F	Sets each of the six data ranges to be graphed.

/Data Commands

- **/Data**
  - **Fill** — Enter data range to fill: — Start: — Step: — Stop:
  - **Table**
    - **1–Data-Table** — Enter data-table range:
    - **2–Data-Table** — Enter data-table range:
    - **Reset**
  - **Sort**
    - **Data-Range** — Enter data range:
    - **Primary-Key** — Enter pr key address: — Enter sort order (A or D):
    - **Secondary-Key** — Enter sec key address: — Enter sort order (A or D):
    - **Reset**
    - **Go**
    - **Quit**
  - **Query**
    - **Input** — Enter input range:
    - **Criterion** — Enter criterion range:
    - **Output** — Enter output range:
    - **Find**
    - **Extract**
    - **Unique**
    - **Delete**
      - **Cancel**
      - **Delete**
    - **Reset**
    - **Quit**
  - **Distribution** — Enter value range:
  - **External**
    - **Multi-Dim** (Not available from "Worksheet." See note below.)
    - **DBF**
      - **TotRetr**
      - **AllStore**
      - **Define**
        - **Createfile**–Enter new DBF file name:
        - **Table** — Enter file name:
        - **Join** — Enter file name:
        - **OneCell** (define) — Enter file name:
      - **Browse** — Enter file name:
      - **RetrTbl/cell**
      - **StoreTbl/cell**
      - **Quit**

/Quit — Are you sure? (Y/N):

NOTE: External commands are not covered in this text. See the VP-Planner manual.

/DF **Data** **Fill**	Fills a range with values. After specifying the range to be filled, enter a starting value, an increment, and an ending value. The numbering begins in the upper left corner of the range, and continues downward and to the right until the range is filled or the ending value is reached.
/DS and **/DQ** **Data** **Sort** **Query**	Both the /**D**ata **S**ort and /**D**ata **Q**uery commands deal with ranges set up in a database format, which requires that each row in the range represent a record and each column represent a field. Names of fields are placed above each column in the database.
/DS **Data** **Sort**	Begin by specifying the **R**ange to be sorted. The order of the sort is determined by the column selected as the **P**rimary Key. A **S**econdary Key also may be selected, but is not required. **G**o is the command issued to begin sorting data. **R**eset will cancel the current sort range and keys.
/DQ **Data** **Query**	This command is used to search a database range for records meeting given criteria. Records found in the search may be highlighted (**F**ind), copied to another area of the spreadsheet (**E**xtract and **U**nique), or deleted from the spreadsheet (**D**elete). **D**elete and **F**ind require that only an **I**nput Range and a **C**riterion Range be specified. **E**xtract and **U**nique require these two ranges as well as an **O**utput Range. The field names at the top of each column must be included in these ranges. **R**eset cancels current ranges.
/DD **Data** **Distribution**	Calculates a frequency distribution for the values in a specified range.

VP-Planner Spreadsheet Functions

@ABS(value) Returns the absolute value.

@ACOS(value) Returns the arc cosine.

@ASIN(value) Returns the arc sine.

@ATAN(value,value) Returns the 2-quadrant arc tangent.

@ATAN(value x, value y) Returns the 4-quadrant arc tangent.

@AVG(list) Returns the average value of the cells in its argument.

@CHOOSE(value x,value 0,value 1, . . .value n) Returns one value from a list of values based on the index of value x. If value x = 0, value 0 is returned, if value x = 1, value 1 is returned, and so forth.

@COS(value) Returns the cosine.

@COUNT(list) Returns the number of non-blank cells in its argument.

@DATE(year,month,day) Returns the serial number for the year, month, and day.

@DAY(date) Returns the day number from a serial number.

@ERR Returns the value ERR (error).

@EXP(value) Returns the exponential.

@FALSE Returns the value 0.

@FV(payment,rate,periods) Returns the future value of an annuity with equal payments for the number of equal time periods at the given interest rate.

@HLOOKUP (value x,range,offset) Returns the value found in the same column of a table (the range) located an offset number of rows down from the first row in the table, where the columns are searched through for a value corresponding to the value x.

@IF(condition,true value,false value) Returns one of two values; the true value if the condition tested is true, or, the false value if the condition tested is false.

@INT(value) Returns the integer value.

@IRR(guess,range) Returns the internal rate of return for a range of cash flows, given the help of a guess to start the computation.

@ISERR(value) Returns 1 (TRUE) if the value is ERR, 0 if the value is not ERR.

@ISNA(value) Returns 1 (TRUE) if the value is NA, 0 if the value is not = NA.

@LN(value) Returns the log base e.

@LOG(value) Returns the log base 10.

@MAX(list) Returns the highest single value found in the cells of its argument.

@MIN(list) Returns the lowest single value found in the cells of its argument.

@MOD(value, modulo) Returns the remainder (the modulus) divided by the specified modulo.

@MONTH(date) Returns the month number from a serial number.

@NA Returns the value NA (not available).

@NOW Returns the date/time number from the system clock. (Note: No argument.)

@NPV(rate,range) Returns the net present value of a range of cash flows given a discount rate against which to compare.

@PI Returns pi (3.141592653589794).

@PMT(principal,rate,periods) Returns the periodic payment necessary for the financing of a principal amount at the given interest rate for a given number of equal time periods.

@POLY(value, range) Evaluates the polynomial for values with coefficients in the range.

@PV(payment,rate,periods) Returns the present value of an annuity with equal payments for the number of equal time periods at the given interest rate.

@RAND Generates a pseudo random number. (Note: No argument.)

@ROOT(est, range) Solves the polynomial with coefficients in the range for a value that has a polynomial value of 0 starting with est.

@ROUND(value, places) Returns the rounded value to the number of specified decimal places.

@SIN(value) Returns the sine.

@SQRT(value) Returns the square root of its argument.

@STD(list) Returns the standard deviation from the mean for the group of cells in its argument.

@STDS(list) Returns the sample standard deviation for the range list.

@SUM(list) Returns the sum of the cells found in its argument.

@TAN(value) Returns the tangent.

@TIME(hour, minute) Returns the serial number for a given hour and minute.

@TODAY Returns the serial number of DOS's system date. (Note: No argument.)

@TRUE Returns the value 1.

@VAR(list) Returns the variance of the values in the cells of its argument.

@VARS(list) Returns the sample variance for the range list.

@VLOOKUP(value x,range,offset) Returns the value found in the same row of a table (the range) located an offset number of columns to the right of the first column in the table, where the rows of the range are searched for a value corresponding to the value x.

@YEAR(date) Returns the year number from a serial number.

VP-Planner Keyboard Macro Commands

Command	Keyboard Equivalent
Function Keys	
{EDIT}	F2
{NAME}	F3
{ABS}	F4
{GOTO}	F5
{WINDOW}	F6
{QUERY}	F7
{TABLE}	F8
{CALC}	F9
{GRAPH}	F10
Pointer-Movement Keys	
{UP}	↑
{DOWN}	↓
{LEFT}	←
{RIGHT}	→
{PGUP}	PgUp
{PGDN}	PgDn
{HOME}	Home
{END}	End
Editing Keys	
{DEL}	Del
{ESC}	Esc
{BS}	←(Backspace)
~	Enter key
{GOREF}	Alt F5 (Relative GOTO)

Command	BASIC Equivalent
{?}	INPUT
/**XI**condition~	IF THEN
/**XG**location~	GOTO
/**XQ**	END
/**XC**location~	GOSUB
/**XR**~	RETURN
/**XN**message~location~	INPUT "message to user", A
/**XL**message~location~	INPUT "message to user", A$
/**XM**location~	PRINT " Print out a menu " PRINT " 1) choice " PRINT " 2) choice " PRINT " 3) choice " PRINT " Enter number of your choice" INPUT A ON A GOTO line, line, line
/**XW**n	FOR I = 1 to n I = I + 1 NEXT I (wait for n loops)

Only a few specific rules exist to help you design your spreadsheet. These suggestions may, however, prove useful in helping you design a spreadsheet that avoids the problems that beginning users are likely to experience

Separate Kinds of Data in Separate Spreadsheet Areas

The Spreadsheet's Keys

In the introductory tutorial you created a spreadsheet that incorporated elements of poor spreadsheet design. The most serious infraction was the way in which constants (real numbers) were included within the calculating body of the spreadsheet. Below, we have displayed the spreadsheet you created in the tutorial section with the contents of the cells shown. The constants are shown in color.

	A	B	C	D	E	F
1						
2		JAN	FEB	MAR	APR	MAY
3						
4	GROSS PAY AMOUNT	1955	+B4	+C4	+D4	2105
5	TAX RATE					
6	.18					
7	FED & STATE TAXES	+$A$6*B4	+$A$6*C4	+$A$6*D4	+$A$6*E4	+$A$6*F4
8	------------------	------------	------------	------------	------------	------------
9	NET PAY AMOUNT	+B4-B7	+C4-C7	+D4-D7	+E4-E7	+F4-F7
10						
11	EXPENSES					
12	------------------	------------	------------	------------	------------	------------
13	RENT	375	+B13	395	+D13	+E13
14	UTILITIES	125	+B14	+C14	100	+E14
15	PARKING	75			75	
16	TELEPHONE	18	+B16	+C16	+D16	+E16
17	LIFE INSURANCE	28.65	+B17	+C17	+D17	+E17
18	FOOD	0.3*B9	0.3*C9	0.3*D9	0.3*E9	0.3*F9
19	LEISURE	0.15*B9	0.15*C9	0.15*D9	0.15*E9	0.15*F9
20	------------------	------------	------------	------------	------------	------------
21	TOTAL EXPENSES	@SUM(B13..B	@SUM(C13..C	@SUM(D13..D	@SUM(E13..E	@SUM(F13..F
22						
23	SAVINGS DEPOSITS	+B9-B21	+C9-C21	+D9-D21	+E9-E21	+F9-F21
24	------------------	------------	------------	------------	------------	------------
25	SAVINGS ACCOUNT					
26	INTEREST RATE =	.28				
27	==================	============	============	============	============	============

Such constants are called the spreadsheet's *keys*. They are the primary source of all values displayed in the spreadsheet. If you retrace the references of the formulas you will find that they ultimately refer to a cell holding a spreadsheet key.

As you look at the spreadsheet on the screen, however, it is difficult to tell which cells are holding formulas and which are holding keys. Even using the /**W**orksheet **G**lobal **F**ormat **T**ext command will not always result in the display of a formula where a formula actually exists (such as when a cell previously has been /**R**ange **F**ormatted).

Keys in Their Own Area

It is an accepted rule of spreadsheet design that, when possible, all keys should be kept in a separate, identifiable area of the spreadsheet. The calculating area should contain either formulas referring *directly* to the keys or referring *back* to them through a series of formulas. The spreadsheet should have been initially designed in two parts.

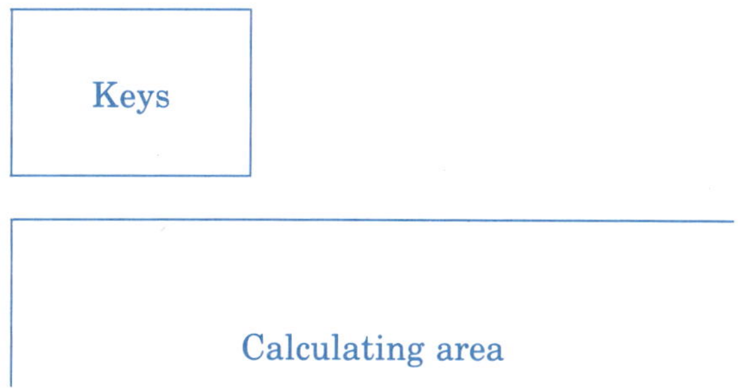

Cell references should refer directly to a given key:

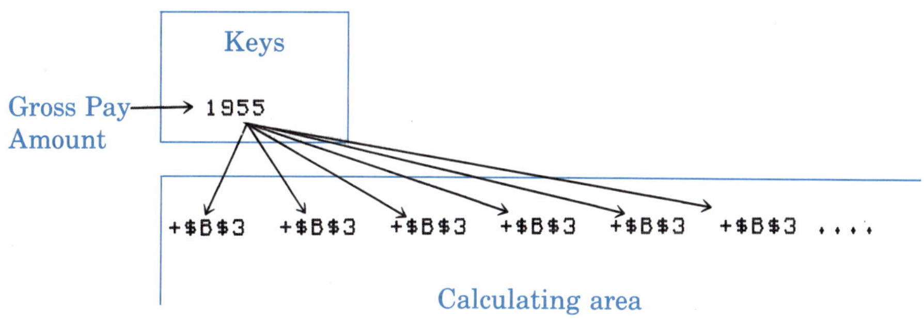

Or, they should refer to a key indirectly through a series of formulas:

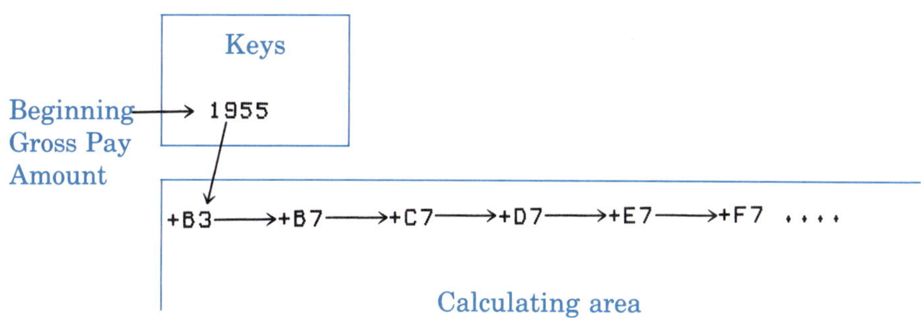

They also might use a variation:

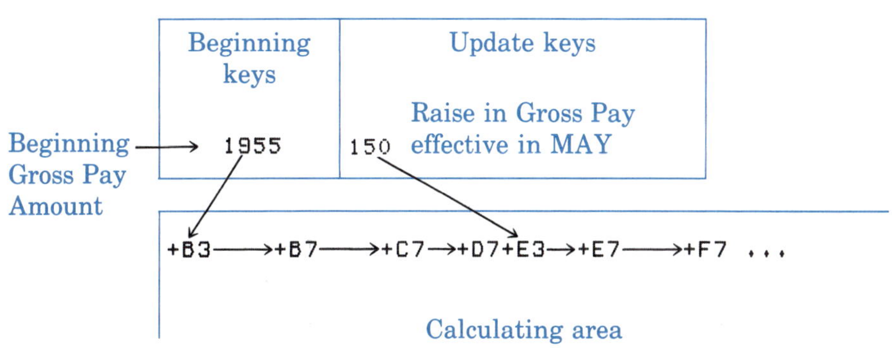

In the last example the keys have been separated into two types, beginning amounts and updates. In this spreadsheet a third type of key, percentage rates, could be included in a separate area within the spreadsheet's keys area.

Spreadsheet Documentation

Each key should have its own label to explain its use and relevance to the calculating portion of the spreadsheet. The key should be *documented.*

Along with separating the keys into their own area(s) and thoroughly documenting them, you should have an area set aside for additional documentation of the spreadsheet. This area could include things such as remarks and comments about the assumptions and relationships built into the spreadsheet, the date it was last updated, its filename, current /**P**rint **R**ange, **O**ptions, and more.

Mapping Out the Spreadsheet

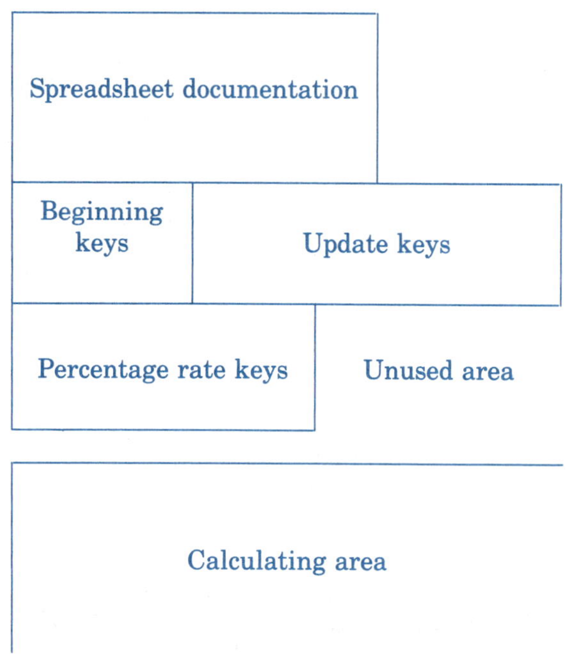

As you create more complex spreadsheets using more advanced features, you will recognize that the spreadsheet should be mapped out with a pencil and piece of paper before it is created on the computer. A question such as, "What happens to my key area if I need to use the /**W**orksheet command to insert a column or a row into my calculating area?" may lead you initially to map your spreadsheet as:

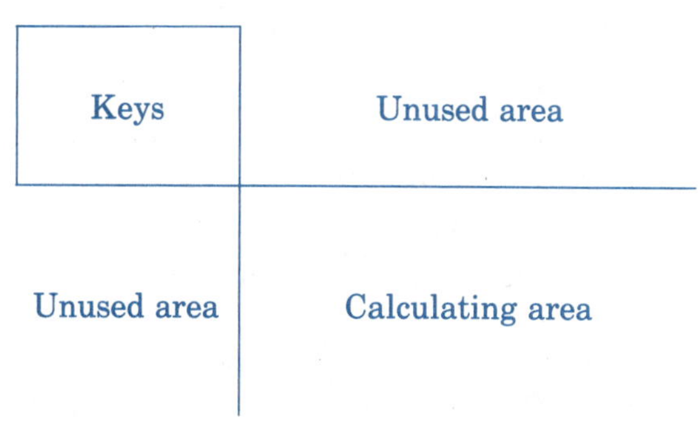

Such a plan helps you avoid potential disruption of spreadsheet areas later.

Spreadsheet Templates

You may want to use a spreadsheet that you have designed more than once. For example, a spreadsheet designed to track expenditures against a departmental budget may be needed periodically. In a case like this, you can create a spreadsheet that acts as a master copy, or in spreadsheet jargon, a *template*. The purpose of having a spreadsheet template is to avoid having to recreate the spreadsheet each time it is needed. The procedure for creating a spreadsheet template is as follows.

Once you have mapped out the spreadsheet, enter and test the labels, formulas, and keys to assure the spreadsheet is reliable in its answers. Add any necessary documentation.

After the spreadsheet is operationally complete, set all relevant keys (those constants that may change from period to period) to zero by entering zeros in the cells that contain them. Save the spreadsheet on the diskette in its template form. To save a template it is customary to use a name such as "Master" to indicate that it is the master copy.

Once you have created and saved the template, you need to: a) load that spreadsheet into RAM memory; b) enter the appropriate key values for that period; and c) save that period's finished spreadsheet on the diskette under a different name. The original template remains on the diskette in its original form for the next time it is needed.

Mixed Cell References

As discussed earlier, there are four modes for referencing cells in formulas:

Relative column relative row	B4
Absolute column absolute row	$B$4
Relative column absolute row	B$4
Absolute column relative row	$B4

The last two are known as mixed references. Although they are less frequently used, mixed references can be helpful for copying formulas into other cells.

Example of Using Mixed Cell References

To demonstrate the use of mixed addresses and their implication for spreadsheet design, consider the following situation.

	A	B	C	D	E	F	G
1							
2		JANUARY					
3							
4	COSTS		% OF SALES				
5							
6	RENT	$500.00	14.29%				
7	LABOR	$1,200.00	34.29%				
8	MATERIALS	$700.00	20.00%				
9							
10	PROFITS	$1,100.00	31.43%				
11		--------					
12	SALES	$3,500.00					

In this spreadsheet all values in the B column (the dollar figures) are spreadsheet keys. Values in the C column (percentages) are derived by formulas.

The designer of this spreadsheet intended to copy the rectangular range of labels, keys, and formulas of the spreadsheet into the area on the right side for the next month's figures.

	A	B	C	D	E	F	G
1							
2		JANUARY				JANUARY	
3							
4	COSTS		% OF SALES		COSTS		% OF SALES
5							
6	RENT	$500.00	14.29%		RENT	$500.00	14.29%
7	LABOR	$1,200.00	34.29%		LABOR	$1,200.00	34.29%
8	MATERIALS	$700.00	20.00%		MATERIALS	$700.00	20.00%
9							
10	PROFITS	$1,100.00	31.43%		PROFITS	$1,100.00	31.43%
11		--------				--------	
12	SALES	$3,500.0 0			SALES	$3,500.00	
13							

SOURCE Cell Range: DESTINATION Cell Range:

After copying the range of cells the designer can change the label JANUARY to FEBRUARY, enter new keys, and have the formulas compute the correct percent of sales figures for that month.

In constructing the original portion of the spreadsheet the formula for rent as a percent of sales would be entered and copied into the rest of the cells for that column. To be copied correctly during the first /Copy operation, the formula would need to keep the reference to sales (B12) as absolute. But, for the next /Copy operation (creating February's report) the reference for the cell must be able to shift to the right in a relative fashion (to cell F12).

The solution to the problem is to keep the reference to the SALES row absolute so it does not shift down (in a relative fashion) in the first /Copy operation, and leave the reference to SALES column as relative so it will shift to the right in the second /Copy operation.

To do this, the original formula would be entered as:

+B6/B$12

FIRST: The original formula is entered.

	A	B	C	D	E	F	G
1							
2		JANUARY					
3							
4	COSTS		% OF SALES				
5							
6	RENT	500	+B6/B$12				
7	LABOR	1200					
8	MATERIALS	700					
9							
10	PROFITS	1100					
11		--------					
12	SALES	3500					
13							

SECOND: The formula is copied into that column.

	A	B	C	D	E	F	G
1							
2		JANUARY					
3							
4	COSTS		% OF SALES				
5							
6	RENT	500	+B6/B$12				
7	LABOR	1200	+B7/B$12				
8	MATERIALS	700	+B8/B$12				
9							
10	PROFITS	1100	+B10/B$12				
11		--------					
12	SALES	3500					
13							

THIRD: The second /Copy operation is completed.

	A	B	C	D	E	F	G
1							
2		JANUARY				JANUARY	
3							
4	COSTS		% OF SALES		COSTS		% OF SALES
5							
6	RENT	500	+B6/B$12		RENT	500	+F6/F$12
7	LABOR	1200	+B7/B$12		LABOR	1200	+F7/F$12
8	MATERIALS	700	+B8/B$12		MATERIALS	700	+F8/F$12
9							
10	PROFITS	1100	+B10/B$12		PROFITS	1100	+F10/F$12
11		--------				--------	
12	SALES	3500			SALES	3500	
13							

FOURTH: The month label and keys are changed, and the spreadsheet computes the correct figures for FEBRUARY.

	A	B	C	D	E	F	G
1							
2		JANUARY				FEBRUARY	
3							
4	COSTS		% OF SALES		COSTS		% OF SALES
5							
6	RENT	$500.00	14.29%		RENT	$500.00	11.76%
7	LABOR	$1,200.00	34.29%		LABOR	$1,500.00	35.29%
8	MATERIALS	$700.00	20.00%		MATERIALS	$950.00	22.35%
9							
10	PROFITS	$1,100.00	31.43%		PROFITS	$1,300.00	30.59%
11		--------				--------	
12	SALES	$3,500.00			SALES	$4,250.00	
13							

VP-PLANNER FUNCTIONS

A spreadsheet function can be described as a shorthand method of entering a formula. Its general form is:

@XYZ(argument)

Function name ↗ (@XYZ) ↖ Function argument (argument)

When referring to a function one says that the function "returns a value from its argument" so that a function entered as **@SUM**(B13 . . B18) is said to "return the sum of the cells in its argument" (the range of cells B13 through B18). VP-Planner functions may be divided into the following basic categories, each of which is covered in subsequent discussions.

1. Mathematical and Statistical functions
2. Engineering or Scientific functions
3. Financial functions
4. Date functions
5. Logical functions

Mathematical and Statistical Functions

Mathematical Functions

@ROUND(value,places)	Returns the rounded value to the number of specified decimal places.
@INT(value)	Returns the integer value.
@MOD(value,modulo)	Returns the remainder (the modulus) divided by the specified modulo.
@SQRT(value)	Returns the square root of its argument.
@ABS(value)	Returns the absolute value.
@RAND	Generates a random number. (*NOTE*: No argument.)

Most mathematical functions are fairly straightforward; all of them deal with a single value on which to act. Their arguments do not include a range of cells from which they return a value; instead they include a single value such as a constant, a cell reference, or the computed results of a formula.

Example

	A	B	C
1			
2	-3	2	
3			
4			
5			

@ABS(-6) = 6
@ABS(A2) = 3
@ABS(A2*B2) = 6

@ROUND(value,places)

The **@ROUND** function is important for financial and other business-related spreadsheets. It is important because the values you see displayed on the monitor screen are formatted for display purposes only. All values actually are stored in RAM memory and are accurate to about 15 decimal places. The stored values are used in all of VP-Planner's computations. The results of the computations often can be confusing to beginning users who are trying to figure out why the spreadsheet does not agree with their calculators.

A solution for avoiding discrepancies in accuracy is to use the **@ROUND** function to return the rounded value (to the desired number of decimal places) for all value(s) of concern. As an example, the internal results become:

10/3 = 3.333333333333333

@ROUND(10/3,2) = 3.330000000000000

(Actually, the last two or three decimal places are undependable; however, this seldom interferes with the practical use of a spreadsheet.)

Negative "places" may be used in the **@ROUND** function to round numbers to the left of the decimal.

@ROUND(10000/3,2) = 3333.33

@ROUND(10000/3,-2) = 3300

@INT(value)

The Integer function is useful when decimal parts of a value are not desired and rounding is unnecessary, such as in some production models where a fraction of a unit will not be produced. The value returned is the true integer portion of the argument with the remainder truncated. It is not the next lowest integer value.

Example

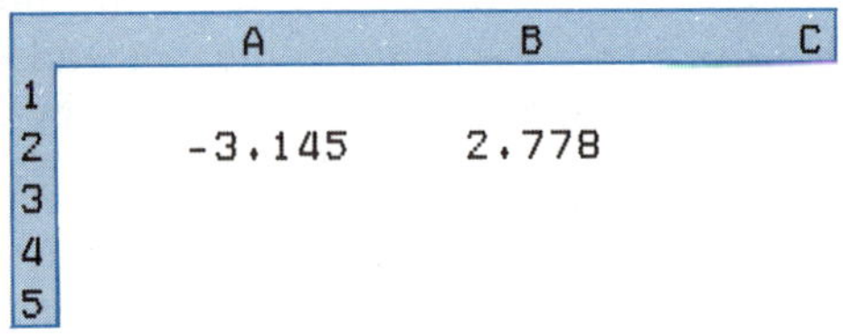

@INT(2.33) = 2
@INT(A2) = −3
@INT(A2*B2) = −8

@MOD(value,modulo)

The **@MOD** function returns the modulus of the value divided by the modulo. In longhand division it looks like this:

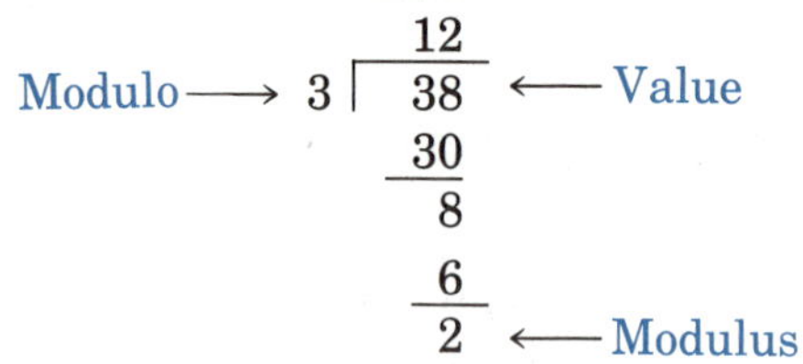

The modulus is the numerator (2) of the fractional remainder, ⅔, to the answer for this problem, 12⅔. The **@MOD** function can be useful in determining if partial batches or even/odd situations exist.

Statistical Functions

@AVG(list)	Returns the average value of the nonblank cells in its argument.
@COUNT(list)	Returns the number of nonblank cells in its argument.
@MAX(list)	Returns the highest single value found in the cells of its argument.
@MIN(list)	Returns the lowest single value found in the cells of its argument.
@STD(list)	Returns the standard deviation from the mean for the nonblank cells in its argument.
@STDS(list)	Returns the sample standard deviation for list.
@SUM(list)	Returns the sum of the cells found in its argument.
@VAR(list)	Returns the variance of the values for the nonblank cells in its argument.
@VARS(list)	Returns the sample variance for list.

Since all of these functions are important in business and are similar in form, they will be discussed as a group. The statistical functions also are fairly straightforward, but are designed to deal with several values rather than the single value used by the mathematical functions.

The values may be constants, cell references, ranges of cells, or any combination in a "list" separated by commas.

Example

	A	B	C
1			
2	2	5	7
3	4		
4	6		
5	8	12	

@SUM(6,8,1) = 15

@SUM(A2..A5,B2) = 25

@SUM(A2..A5,A2..C2,B5,10) = 56

Note that VP-Planner assigns all labels the value of 0 (zero) and uses the zeros in computing the value returned by a function. VP-Planner does not use blank cells in computing the value returned. With most of the statistical functions, cells included in the function's argument that have labels in them will result in an incorrect value being returned for the group of values of concern. Blank cells do not interfere with the results. For instance, within the range of values found in cells A1 through A6 are the values of concern 2, 4, and 6; two cells with labels in them (A3 and A5); and the blank cell A1.

Example

	A	B
1		
2	2	
3	-------	
4	4	
5	-------	
6	6	

@SUM(A1..A6)	= 12	correct
@COUNT(A1..A6)	= 5	incorrect
@AVG(A1..A6)	= 2.4	incorrect
@MAX(A1..A6)	= 6	correct
@MIN(A1..A6)	= 0	incorrect
@STD(A1..A6)	= 2.332381	incorrect
@VAR(A1..A6)	= 5.44	incorrect

To illustrate how statistical functions may be used:

Example

	A	B	C	D
1				
2	SALES	1984	1985	1986
3		----------	----------	----------
4	JAN	1250	1310	1340
5	FEB	1115	1170	1195
6	MAR	1320	1390	1420
7	APR	1405	1485	1515
8	MAY	1380	1450	1480
9	JUN	1550	1630	
10	JUL	1575	1655	
11	AUG	1525	1600	
12	SEP	1515	1590	
13	OCT	1490	1565	
14	NOV	1385	1450	
15	DEC	1320	1390	
16				

Total 1985 sales
@SUM(C4..C15) = 17685

1984 top month's sales
@MAX(B4..B15) = 1575

1985 lowest month's sales
@MIN(C4..C15) = 1170

Average January sales
@AVG(B4..D4) = 1300

Average 1st quarter sales
@AVG(B4..D6) = 1278.889

Average first and last quarter sales
@AVG(B4..D6,B13..D15) = 1340.667

Total sales entered to date
@SUM(B4..B15,C4..C15,D4..D15)
or @SUM(B4..D15) = 41465

Total data entries to date
@COUNT(B4..D15) = 29

Std dev of total monthly sales
@STD(B4..D15) = 136.6816

Variance of total monthly sales
@VAR(B4..D15) = 18681.87

Engineering and Scientific Functions

@ACOS(value)	Returns the arc cosine.
@ASIN(value)	Returns the arc sine.
@ATAN(value)	Returns the 2-quadrant arc tangent.
@ATAN2(value,value)	Returns the 4-quadrant arc tangent.
@COS(value)	Returns the cosine.
@EXP(value)	Returns the exponential.
@LN(value)	Returns the log base e.
@LOG(value)	Returns the log base 10.
@PI	Returns pi (3.141592653589794).
@ROOT(est,range)	Solves the polynomial with coefficients in range for a value that has a polynomial value of 0, starting with est.
@SIN(value)	Returns the sine.
@TAN(value)	Returns the tangent.

Engineering and scientific functions actually are mathematical functions, but they are treated separately because they are used less often in business-related spreadsheets. They, like mathematical functions, act on a single value in their argument.

Financial Functions

@IRR(guess,range)	Returns the internal rate of return for a range of cash flows, given the help of a guess to start the computation.
@NPV(rate,range)	Returns the net present value of a range of cash flows given a discount rate against which to compare.
@FV(payment,rate, periods)	Returns the future value of an annuity with equal payments for the number of equal time periods at the given interest rate.
@PV(payment,rate, periods)	Returns the present value of an annuity with equal payments for the number of equal time periods at the given interest rate.
@PMT(principal,rate, periods)	Returns the periodic payment necessary for the financing of a principal amount at the given interest rate for a given number of equal time periods.

Financial functions all are related to the time value of money and frequently are used in business. Each function requires more than one type of value in its argument in order to return the correct answer.

@IRR(guess,range)

The **@IRR** function returns an approximate internal rate of return for a series of cash flows in which IRR is defined as the rate at which those cash flows have a zero net present value. The periods are assumed to be equal in time. A guess is required as part of the function's argument to serve as a starting point for the iterative process that the computer uses to determine the IRR. If the guess is too far off the actual IRR, the computer will return an ERR message. Guesses between 0.0 and 1.0 usually will yield a calculated IRR. Sometimes there is more than one IRR possible for a series of cash flows, so different guesses may result in different values.

Example

	A	B	C	D	E	F	G
1							
2			Periodic Cash Flows				
3	-500	200	175	150	125		
4							
5	Est. rate		@IRR(0.14,A3..E3) = .1244145				
6	.14		@IRR(A6,A3..E3) = .1244145				

The guess rate is entered as a decimal and the range in the argument must be a single row or column of cells. Blank cells and cells with labels within the range are counted as cash flows of 0 for that period. Note also that the rate returned is the IRR per period. So, if the cash flows are monthly, the calculated IRR is approximately 12.44% per month. If the cash flows are yearly, the calculated IRR is approximately 12.44% per year.

@**NPV**(rate,range)

The net present value function returns the present value of a range of cash flows discounted at an opportunity cost determined at an alternate rate (called the discount rate) for the same flows. The periods are assumed to be equal in time and the rate used is a periodic discount rate. Note that with the **@NPV** function, the first cash flow in the range of cash flows is treated as occurring at the end of the first period. Subsequent cash flows are treated as occurring at the end of their periods.

Since it is usually the case (for valuation purposes) that the first cash flow is to occur at time 0 (zero), the use of the **@NPV** function often takes the following form.

First cash flow + **@NPV**(discount rate, subsequent cash flows)

Example

	A	B	C	D	E	F	G
1							
2			Periodic Cash Flows				
3	-500	200	175	150	125		
4							
5	Disc. rate	+A3+@NPV(0.0525,B3..E3) = 78.51944					
6	0.0525	+A3+@NPV(A6,B3..E3) = 78.51944					

The range in the argument must be a single row or column of cells. Blank cells and cells with labels within the range are counted as cash flows of 0 for the period. The rate used in the argument is the discount rate per period. So if the cash flows are monthly, the calculated NPV is based on a monthly discount rate of 5.25%.

@FV(payment,rate,periods) and @PV(payment,rate,periods)

The **@FV** and **@PV** functions are used to return either the future value (**@FV**) of a series of equal cash flows or the present value (**@PV**) of a series of equal cash flows at the periodic interest rate specified in the argument.

The amount of cash flow is specified as the *payment* and the number of cash flows is specified by *periods*. Again, the periods are assumed to be equal in length.

Example

	A	B	C	D	E	F	G
1							
2	Payment	125	@FV(B2,B3/12,B4) = 4862.249				
3	Interest	.0525					
4	Periods	36	@PV(B2,B3/12,B4) = 4155.133				
5							

In this example, payments of $125.00 are made monthly for 36 months with 5.25% annual interest compounded monthly. Notice how the interest rate was divided by twelve to keep the rate and period consistent.

@PMT(principal,rate,periods)

The **@PMT** function is used to determine the payments to be made, based on a principal financed, rate of interest, and length of the loan in periods.

Example

	A	B	C	D	E	F	G
1							
2	Principal	4000	@PMT(B2,B3/12,B4) = 133.8145				
3	Interest	.125					
4	Periods	36					
5							

The example assumes a $4,000 loan at 12.5% yearly interest compounded monthly for 36 months.

Date Functions

@DATE(year,month, day)	Returns the serial number for the year, month, and day.
@DAY(date)	Returns the day number from a serial number.
@MONTH(date)	Returns the month number from a serial number.
@YEAR(date)	Returns the year number from a serial number.
@TODAY	Returns the serial number of DOS's system date.

Date functions also have many business-related spreadsheet applications.

VP-Planner maintains an internal calendar that extends from January 1, 1801 to December 31, 2099. The numbers are serial: the date Jan 1, 1801 = −36157; Dec. 31, 1899 = 1; and so on up to Dec. 31, 2099 which has been assigned the number 73050. This numbering system accurately accommodates leap years.

With each date assigned a number, the computer can perform "date arithmetic."

	Date	Serial number	Arithmetic	
Date #1	86/4/17	31519	−31519	
Date #2	86/12/25	31771	+31771	
			252	Shopping days until Christmas

VP-Planner allows dates to be entered in a format to which you are accustomed, and then converts them to their serial equivalent with the **@DATE** function.

@DATE(year,month,day)

The **@DATE** function is used to return the serial number of the date in its argument.

Example

	A	B	C	D	E	F	G
1							
2	@DATE(86,4,17)	=	31519				
3							
4							

If years beyond 2000 are used in the argument, the entire year number must be specified. Once the date has been converted, the /**R**ange **F**ormat **D**ate command may be used to format the cell to display the serial date number in a standard date format.

Three options exist for date formatting.

Example

	A	B	C	D	E	F	G
1							
2	@DATE(86,4,17)	=	31519	Cell C2 is formatted General.			
3							
4	@DATE(86,4,17)	=	17-Apr-86	Cell C4 is formatted Date (DD-MMM-YY).			
5	@DATE(86,4,17)	=	17-Apr	Cell C5 is formatted Date (DD-MMM).			
6	@DATE(86,4,17)	=	Apr-86	Cell C6 is formatted Date (MMM-Y).			

Remember that the displayed contents of a cell formatted with /**R**ange **F**ormat **D**ate are not the actual contents of the cell. The cell holds, or has returned, a number that can be used in, or derived by, a formula.

Formatted as general

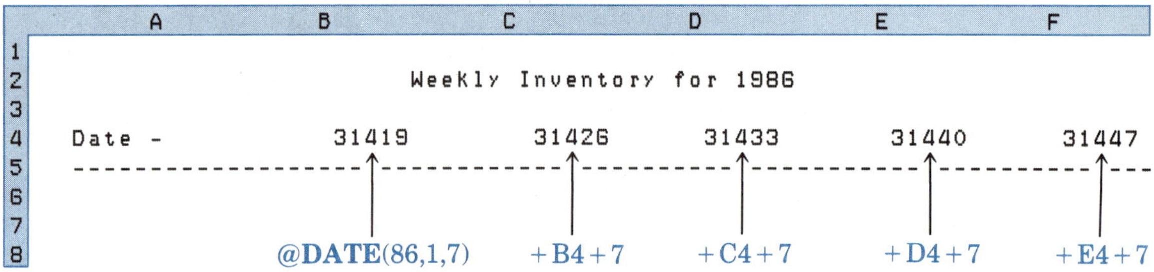

Example

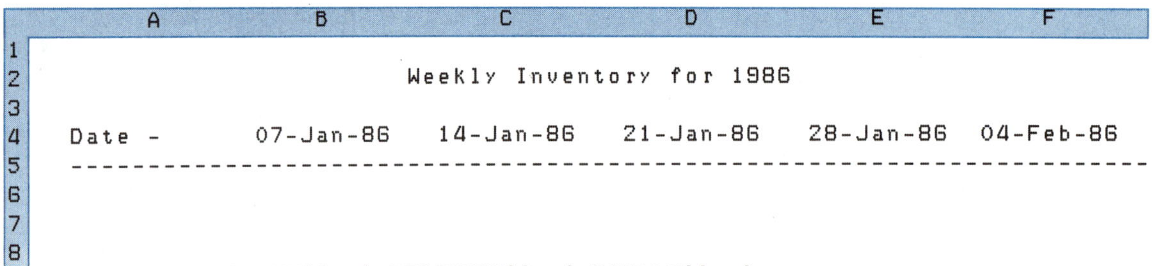

@DAY(date) @MONTH(date) @YEAR(date)

The **@DAY, @MONTH,** and **@YEAR** functions return the calendar number for the day, month, or year from a serial date number.

Example

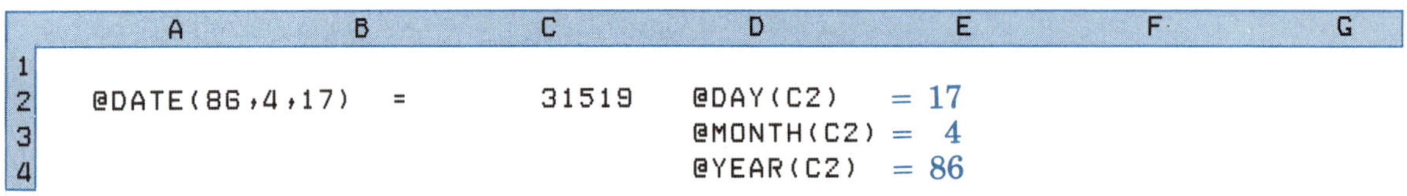

Logical Functions

@IF(condition,true value,false value)	Returns one of two values—the true value if the condition tested is true, or the false value if the condition tested is false.
@CHOOSE (value x,value 0,value 1, . . .value n)	Returns one value from a list of values based on the index of value x. If value x = 0, value 0 is returned; if value x = 1, value 1 is returned.
@VLOOKUP (value x,range, offset)	Returns the value found in the same row of a table (the range) located an offset number of columns to the right of the first column in the table, where rows are searched for a value corresponding to the value x.
@HLOOKUP (value x,range, offset)	Returns the value found in the same column of a table (the range) located an offset number of rows down from the first row in the table, where the columns are searched for a value corresponding to the value x.

@FALSE	Returns the value 0.
@TRUE	Returns the value 1.
@NA	Returns the value NA (not available).
@ERR	Returns the value ERR (error).
@ISNA(value)	Returns 1 (TRUE) if the value is = NA, 0 if the value is not = NA.
@ISERR(value)	Returns 1 (TRUE) if the value is = ERR, 0 if the value is not = ERR.

The logical functions allow the spreadsheet designer to take advantage of the computer's decision-making ability.

@IF(condition,true value,false value)

@IF is the true conditional function of VP-Planner. The first part of its argument is a logical expression using the relational operators <, >, and =. It also may include the logical operators #NOT#, #AND#, and #OR#. The computer evaluates the condition as either TRUE (equal to 1) or FALSE (equal to 0). Based on its evaluation of the **@IF** function, it returns either the true value or the false value of its argument. The following example spreadsheets demonstrate the use of the **@IF** function. Some rules of spreadsheet design will be set aside in order to help make the example easier to read and understand.

Simple Condition Single @IF

The following spreadsheet computes the gross pay for salespersons working for a firm. Each salesperson receives a base pay per month of $1200.00 and an additional 10% commission on sales greater than $10,000.

*NOTE: The dates in column A are using **@DATE**(yr,mo,day)*

Example

	A	B	C	D	E
1					
2	DATE HIRED	SALESPERSON	TERR	SALES	GROSS PAY
3					
4	05-Dec-79	Speakerman, Larry	1	15050	1705
5	15-Feb-76	Adams, Deborah	1	9050	1200
6	10-Jun-82	Edwards, Carl	1	7500	1200
7	25-Apr-84	Parsons, Shelly	2	16050	1805
8	01-Aug-67	Russell, Bob	2	14000	1600
9	31-Oct-77	Carlson, Richard	2	9050	1200
10	20-Mar-84	Hart, Nelson	3	11000	1300
11	05-May-84	Martin, Cathy	3	8750	1200
12	01-Jan-85	Hunter, Carol	3	7800	1200
13	25-Aug-78	Jackson, Steve	3	7650	1200

The formula originally entered into cell E4 (Larry Speakerman's gross pay) was:

@IF(D4>10000,1200+0.1*(D4−10000),1200)

The function says:

If the value in cell D4 is greater than 10,000
return the value 1200 + 10% of the difference
between the value in cell D4 and 10000.

Otherwise return the value 1200

The formula in cell E4 was then copied into the other cells in that column.

Simple Condition Nested @ IFs

Each salesperson is to receive a bonus based on the performance of all salespersons in their territory. Salespersons in territory #1 will receive a $50.00 bonus; those in territory #2, a $75.00 bonus; and those in territory #3, a $25.00 bonus.

	A	B	C	D	E	F
1						
2	DATE HIRED	SALESPERSON	TERR	SALES	GROSS PAY	BONUS
3						
4	05-Dec-79	Speakerman, Larry	1	15050	1705	50
5	15-Feb-76	Adams, Deborah	1	9050	1200	50
6	10-Jun-82	Edwards, Carl	1	7500	1200	50
7	25-Apr-84	Parsons, Shelly	2	16050	1805	75
8	01-Aug-67	Russell, Bob	2	14000	1600	75
9	31-Oct-77	Carlson, Richard	2	9050	1200	75
10	20-Mar-84	Hart, Nelson	3	11000	1300	25
11	05-May-84	Martin, Cathy	3	8750	1200	25
12	01-Jan-85	Hunter, Carol	3	7800	1200	25
13	25-Aug-78	Jackson, Steve	3	7650	1200	25

The formula originally entered into cell F4 (Larry Speakerman's bonus) was:

@IF(C4=1,50,**@IF**(C4=2,75,25))

In the example, the false value of the first **@IF** is another **@IF** function.

@IF(cond,true value,**@IF**(cond,true value,false value))

This total nested function says:

If the value in C4 equals 1,
return the value 50.

Otherwise,

if the value in C4 equals 2,

return the value 75.

Otherwise, return the value 25.

Complex Condition Single @IF

In the final example, complex conditions using logical operators will be used in a single **@IF** function.

In addition to receiving gross pay with commissions and the territory performance bonus, any salesperson who has worked fewer than two years with the firm and has sales greater than $10,000, or, any salesperson who has

	A	B	C	D	E	F	G
1							
2	DATE HIRED	SALESPERSON	TERR	SALES	GROSS PAY	BONUS	ADDED BONUS
3							
4	05-Dec-79	Speakerman, Larry	1	15050	1705	50	15
5	15-Feb-76	Adams, Deborah	1	9050	1200	50	0
6	10-Jun-82	Edwards, Carl	1	7500	1200	50	0
7	25-Apr-84	Parsons, Shelly	2	16050	1805	75	15
8	01-Aug-67	Russell, Bob	2	14000	1600	75	0
9	31-Oct-77	Carlson, Richard	2	9050	1200	75	0
10	20-Mar-84	Hart, Nelson	3	11000	1300	25	15
11	05-May-84	Martin, Cathy	3	8750	1200	25	0
12	01-Jan-85	Hunter, Carol	3	7800	1200	25	0
13	25-Aug-78	Jackson, Steve	3	7650	1200	25	0

worked for the firm fewer than four years and has sales greater than $12,000, or, any salesperson who has worked for the firm four years or longer and has sales greater than $15,000, will receive an additional bonus of $15.00. The company made the decision on May 1st, 1986.

The **@IF** function originally entered into G4 was:

@IF((A4>**@DATE**(84,5,1)#AND#D4>10000)#OR#(A4>**@DATE**(82,5,1)
#AND#D4>12000)#OR#A4<=**@DATE**(82,5,1)#AND#D4>15000),15,0)

Here normal order of precedence for logical operators results in a complex condition of the form:

(cond AND cond) OR (cond AND cond) OR (cond AND cond)

If the total condition is evaluated as being true, this **@IF** function will return the value 15; if false, the value 0 will be returned.

@CHOOSE(value x,value 0, value 1, . . .value n)

The **@CHOOSE** function uses an index (the integer value x) to select a value to return from a list of values (value 0 . . . value n). For example, if value x equals 0, the first value of the list is returned; if value x equals 1, the second value of the list is returned. If value x is greater than the number of values in the list, the value ERR is returned.

In the following example the **@CHOOSE** function is used to return values for a summary report for any one of three different divisions within a firm. The "Summary Report" area of the spreadsheet uses the value held in cell C3 as the index for its two **@CHOOSE** functions. To change the Summary Report, the user need only change the value in the cell C3.

Example

	A	B	C	D	E	F	G
1							
2	------------------	------------------	------------------	------------------	------------------	------------------	
3	SUMMARY REPORT	Division #	3				
4							
5	Sales/Salesperson	$9,680	← @CHOOSE(C3,@NA,B12/B14,D12/D14,F12/F14)				
6							
7	Sales/Advertising	$10.24	← @CHOOSE(C3,@NA,B12/B16,D12/D16,F12/F16)				
8	dollar						
9	==================	==================	==================	==================	==================	==================	
10		Division #1		Division #2		Division #3	
11							
12	SALES	$105,900		$135,500		$96,800	
13							
14	# Salespersons ..	12		16		10	
15							
16	Advertising cost .	$13,240		$21,275		$9,450	

Based on the value in cell C3 the **@CHOOSE** functions will return the appropriate values for Sales/Salesperson and Sales/Advertising dollar for divisions 1, 2, or 3. Notice that the **@NA** function is listed as the zero index list value. This is one method of compensating for the awkward zero index that is used in this function.

@VLOOKUP(value x,range,offset)

The **@VLOOKUP** function uses a table of values through which to search and return an appropriate value. The search is based on the value x. A classic example of the usefulness of the **@VLOOKUP** function is in looking up the appropriate tax amount for a given individual. The search through the table is based on the individual's taxable income and the value returned from the table is based on the filing status of the individual.

Using a small portion of the actual tax table that would be used, the following spreadsheet lets the user enter the taxable amount (from $24,000 to $24,500) into cell G2 and his or her filing status (1 through 4) into cell G5. The spreadsheet then uses an **@VLOOKUP** function in cell G7 to return the appropriate tax amount from the table found in range A12 . . E22.

Example

```
        A           B          C          D          E          F          G         H
1                Filing Status
2   Single ....................= 1        TAXABLE INCOME -->     24256
3   Married filing jointly ....= 2
4   Married filing separately .= 3        NUMBER FOR
5   Head of household .........= 4        FILING STATUS  -->         2
6
7                             TAX AMOUNT FROM TAX TABLE -->      3394
8                                                               ====↑====
9     Taxable   Single     Married    Married    Head of             |
20    Income                Joint     Separate    House    @VLOOKUP(G2,$TAXTABLE,G5)
11    ------    ------     ------     ------     ------
12    24,000     4,273      3,339      5,314      3,953
13    24,050     4,288      3,350      5,333      3,967
14    24,100     4,303      3,361      5,352      3,981
15    24,150     4,318      3,372      5,371      3,995
16    24,200     4,333      3,383      5,390      4,009
17    24,250     4,348      3,394      5,409      4,023
18    24,300     4,363      3,405      5,428      4,037
19    24,350     4,378      3,416      5,447      4,051
20    24,400     4,393      3,427      5,466      4,065
21    24,450     4,408      3,438      5,485      4,079
22    24,500     4,423      3,449      5,504      4,093
```

The formula in cell G7 was entered as **@VLOOKUP** (G2,$TAXTABLE,G5). Before the formula can be evaluated, the range of cells A12 . . E22 must have been named TAXTABLE. The $ sign keeps the range reference absolute if the formula is copied into other cells at a later time.

When the computer evaluates the **@VLOOKUP** function it moves to the top left cell of the range named TAXTABLE (cell A12) and compares the value there (24000) to the first element in its argument (24256). It then continues down that column, comparing each value with 24256 until it reaches a cell whose value is greater than 24256 (in this case until it reaches cell A18, 24300). It then backs up one cell (to A17) and uses the third element in its argument (in this case, 2) to move that number of columns (2) to the right. There it finds the value (3394) and returns it as the appropriate value for the function.

The values in the first column of the table (the values used to look up) must be in ascending order with no duplicates. If the first value in this column is larger than the value being looked up (first element in the argument), or if the offset (the third element in the argument) is greater than the width of the table range in columns, the result will be ERR. The offset for the first column is 0 (zero).

The **@VLOOKUP** function gets its name from the direction in which it looks up values—(V)ertically down the first column on the left side of a table. The **@HLOOKUP** function performs the same operations, but looks up its values (H)orizontally across the top row of a table, with its offset being x number of rows down from the first row.

Businesses frequently use graphics to aid in understanding data. VP-Planner has the capacity to allow you to present your spreadsheet's data in a variety of graphic forms.

VP-Planner Graphics Overview

To create a graph using VP-Planner, use the Main menu's /**G**raph commands:

```
2Type 3Reset 4View 5Print 6Save 7Options 8Name 9Quit 0Look X A B C D E F
```

Types of Graphs

You usually begin the process of creating a graph by selecting the type of graph to produce. Your options are **L**ine graph, **B**ar graph, **XY** graph, Stacked-Bar graph, and **P**ie chart.

```
2Type 3Reset 4View 5Print 6Save 7Options 8Name 9Quit 0Look X A B C D E F
  ↑
2Line   3Bar   4XY   5Stacked-Bar   6Pie
```

Specifying Data to be Graphed

After selecting the type of graph, you may select the range(s) of numeric data you want graphically represented. As many as six different ranges of data may be graphically displayed. The ranges are specified as the **A** (first), **B** (second), **C** (third), **D** (fourth), **E** (fifth), and **F** (sixth) data ranges of the /Graph commands. Sometimes an additional data range (the X range) is required to produce the graph.

```
2Type 3Reset 4View 5Print 6Save 7Options 8Name 9Quit 0Look X A B C D E F
```

A–F data ranges

X range

Viewing the Graph

After you have specified the data ranges, you may view the graph on the monitor screen by selecting the **V**iew command of the /**G**raph commands. The graph will be displayed in its basic form.

```
2Type 3Reset 4View 5Print 6Save 7Options 8Name 9Quit 0Look X A B C D E F
```

View the graph on the monitor screen

Adding Options

Typing any key will return you from viewing the graph to the /**G**raph menu of commands. There you may use the **O**ptions command to add **T**itles, **L**egends, **D**ata-Labels, **G**rids, and more to the graphics display. As you make changes or additions you may use the **V**iew command to look again at the graph.

```
2Type 3Reset 4View 5Print 6Save 7Options 8Name 9Quit 0Look X A B C D E F
```

Add labels and format the graph

Using the GRAPH (F10) Function Key

When you are satisfied with the appearance of the graph, you may exit the /Graph commands by using the /Graph **Q**uit command. You can then change the data in your spreadsheet and observe how those changes affect the graph by tapping the F10 (GRAPH) Function key. This key serves as a substitute for typing the command key sequence—/**G**raph, **V**iew, any key, **Q**uit,—that would otherwise be necessary to accomplish the same operation. After you use the F10 key to view the graph, tap any key to return you to your spreadsheet and the READY mode.

Erasing the Graph Settings

When you are ready to create another graph for the spreadsheet you may use the **R**eset command of the /**G**raph commands to erase all or some of the settings for the first graph.

```
2Type 3Reset 4View 5Print 6Save 7Options 8Name 9Quit 0Look X A B C D E F
```

Erases all or some of the graph settings

Naming a Graph

If you want to produce another graph for the same spreadsheet and do not want to lose the current graph's settings (data ranges, titles, etc.) you must use the /**G**raph **N**ame **C**reate command to name the current graph. When you name the graph, its settings are stored with the spreadsheet's data under the name you have given them. You then may make specifications for a second graph and view them as you set it up.

```
2Type 3Reset 4View 5Print 6Save 7Options 8Name 9Quit 0Look X A B C D E F
```

Makes current /Graph settings a permanent part of the spreadsheet's data

If you want to view the first graph again, you may use the /**G**raph **N**ame **U**se command. Once you do this, however, the first graph becomes the current graph. The graph settings for the second graph are lost unless the second graph also has been named for later use.

The settings you use to produce the current graph and all named graphs will be saved with the rest of the spreadsheet data when you use the /**F**ile **S**ave command, thus enabling several graphs to be created for a single spreadsheet.

Printing a Graph

VP-Planner provides two methods for printing graphs. First, you may select **Print** from the main **Graph** menu, which will send the graph directly to the printer. Second, you may save the graph as a "Picture" file by selecting **Save** and assigning a filename to the graph. VP-Planner will automatically assign the .PIC extension and then save the graph data in a binary file format that can be read and/or enhanced by several other popular graphics or presentation applications.

```
2Type 3Reset 4View 5Print 6Save 7Options 8Name 9Quit 0Look X A B C D E F
```

Prints the current graph

Saves the current graph's screen output to a separate file

Creating the Five Basic Graph Types

The following spreadsheet will be used to illustrate how each of the five basic graph types may be produced.

	A	B	C	D	E	F	G
1							
2		** Quarterly	Sales	Figures	**	Totals	Adv $/
3						1985	Sales
4	SALES REGION	#1	#2	#3	#4	-------	-------
5							
6	California	20,769	25,487	16,037	36,043	98,336	7.80%
7	Washington	18,753	23,065	19,250	29,610	90,678	5.10%
8	Oregon	19,250	22,400	17,374	28,525	87,549	4.20%
9	Idaho	14,070	19,376	14,126	25,200	72,772	2.90%
10	Alaska	13,230	14,070	10,780	14,000	52,080	2.10%

Pie Charts

In many ways, a pie chart is the simplest form of graph to produce. A pie chart uses only one data range whose sum constitutes the pie to be divided among the data elements of the range. Each slice of the pie is displayed graphically and as a computed percent of the whole. Labels describing each piece of the pie may be specified in an X range. The labels in the X range should correspond to the data elements in the A data range with the first label in the X range describing the first data element in the A data range.

	A	B	C	D	E	F	G
1							
2		** Quarterly	Sales	Figures	**	Totals	Adv $/
3						1985	Sales
4	SALES REGION	#1	#2	#3	#4	-------	-------
5							
6	California	20,769	25,487	16,037	36,043	98,336	7.80%
7	Washington	18,753	23,065	19,250	29,610	90,678	5.10%
8	Oregon	19,250	22,400	17,374	28,525	87,549	4.20%
9	Idaho	14,070	19,376	14,126	25,200	72,772	2.90%
10	Alaska	13,230	14,070	10,780	14,000	52,080	2.10%
11							

X range A6 . . A10

A data range F6 . . F10

Example

```
Type         = Pie
A data range = F6..F10
X-range      = A6..A10
View
```

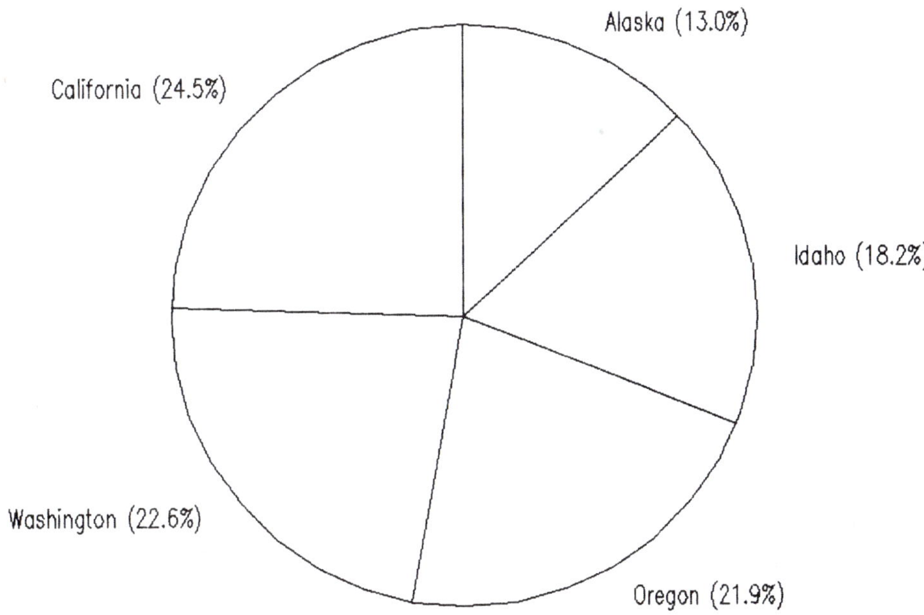

Line Graphs

Line graphs may include up to six data ranges that are plotted with the X range used to label the X axis of the graph. The first example plots quarterly sales for the California sales region.

X range → #1 #2 #3 #4 (B4..E4)

A data range → 20,769 25,487 16,037 36,043 (B6..E6)

	A	B	C	D	E	F	G
1							
2		**Quarterly Sales Figures **				Totals	Adv $/
3						1985	Sales
4		#1	#2	#3	#4	-------	-------
5							
6	California	20,769	25,487	16,037	36,043	98,336	7.80%
7	Washington	18,753	23,065	19,250	29,610	90,678	5.10%
8	Oregon	19,250	22,400	17,374	28,525	87,549	4.20%
9	Idaho	14,070	19,376	14,126	25,200	72,772	2.90%
10	Alaska	13,230	14,070	10,780	14,000	52,080	2.10%

Example

```
Type           = Line
A data range   = B6..E6
X-range        = B4..E4
View
```

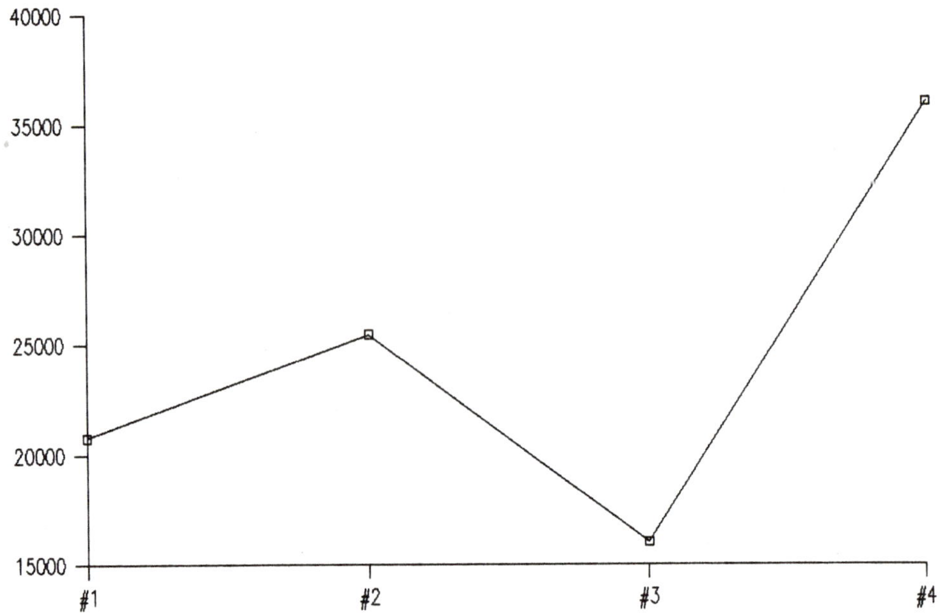

The next example uses several data ranges (A through E) to produce a line graph.

	A		B	C	D	E	F	G
1								
2				Quarterly	Sales	Figures **	Totals	Adv $/
3							1985	Sales
4		X range →	#1	#2	#3	#4	-------	-------
5								
6	Cal	A range →	20,769	25,487	16,037	36,043	98,336	7.80%
7	Was	B range →	18,753	23,065	19,250	29,610	90,678	5.10%
8	Ore	C range →	19,250	22,400	17,374	28,525	87,549	4.20%
9	Ida	D range →	14,070	19,376	14,126	25,200	72,772	2.90%
10	Ala	E range →	13,230	14,070	10,780	14,000	52,080	2.10%

Example

```
Type            = Line
A data range = B6..E6
B data range = B7..E7
C data range = B8..E8
D data range = B9..E9
E data range = B10..E10
X-range         = B4..E4
View
```

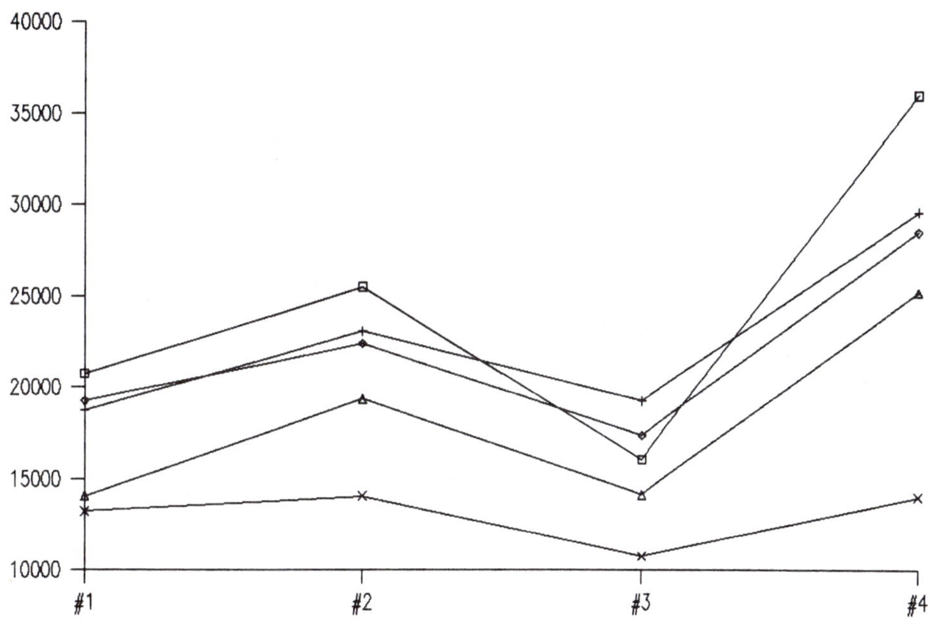

Notice that each data range (A through E) is assigned a different symbol at the data points connected by the line for that data range.

Bar Graphs

The following examples change the two preceding line graphs to bar graphs (/**G**raph **T**ype **B**ar). All other settings for the graphs remain the same.

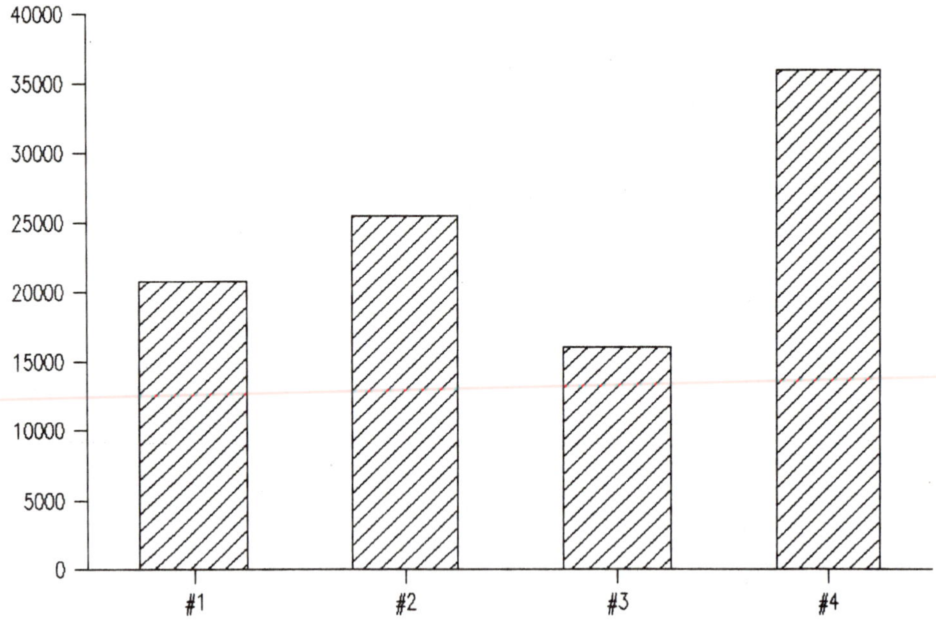

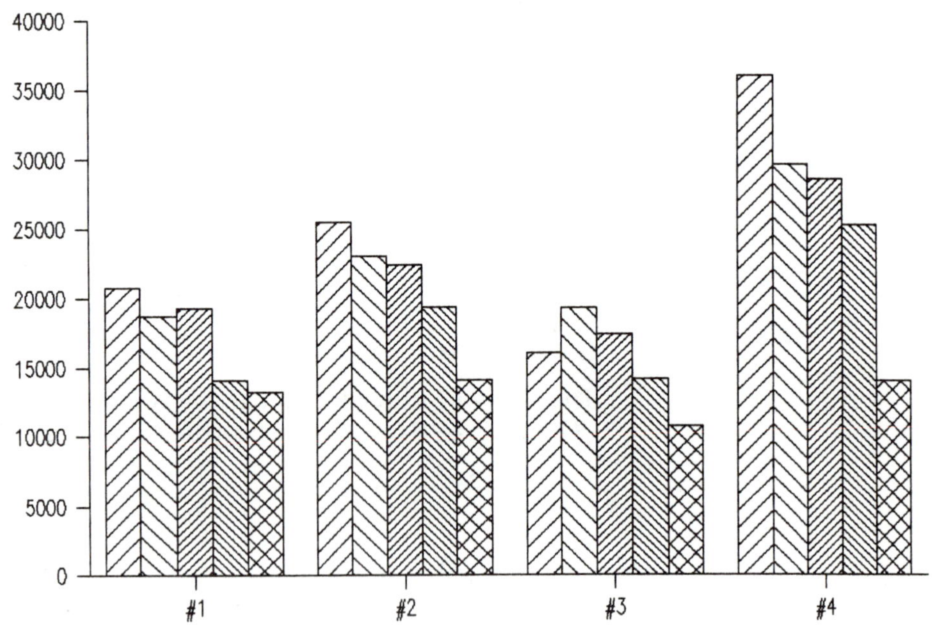

Notice that the bars for each data range are assigned a different shading.

Stacked Bar Graphs

Stacked bar graphs vary from bar graphs in that they show the elements in the data ranges as distinct contributors to the total height of a bar. All settings except **T**ype, used in the preceding bar graph, are the same for the stacked bar graph.

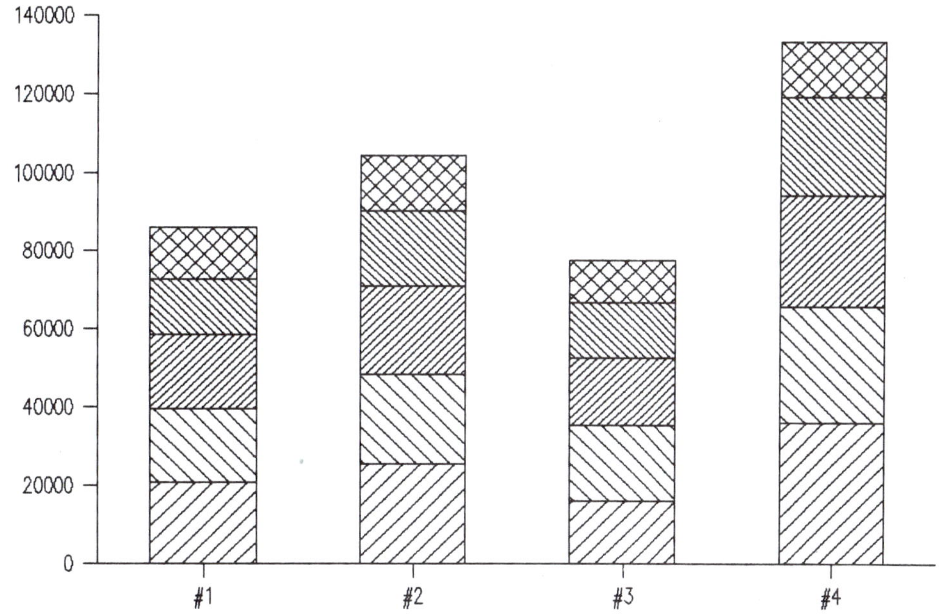

XY Graphs

XY graphs differ from the other types of graphs because they show a relationship between one or more dependent variables (data ranges A through F) and an independent variable, specified as the X range. The X range in an **XY** graph is not a range used to label the X axis or the pie slices; it is the measurement of the X axis. In the following example the X range is specified as the range of cells containing the advertising dollars to sales dollars ratio expressed as a percent. The single A data range is specified as the total yearly sales for each region. The resulting **XY** graph indicates that sales increase with an increase in advertising expenditures, but that the rate of increase diminishes as advertising expenditures continue to rise.

	A	B	C	D	E	F	G
1							
2		** Quarterly Sales Figures **				Totals	Adv $/
3						1985	Sales
4	SALES REGION	#1	#2	#3	#4	-------	-------
5							
6	California	20,769	25,487	16,037	36,043	98,336	7.80%
7	Washington	18,753	23,065	19,250	29,610	90,678	5.10%
8	Oregon	19,250	22,400	17,374	28,525	87,549	4.20%
9	Idaho	14,070	19,376	14,126	25,200	72,772	2.90%
10	Alaska	13,230	14,070	10,780	14,000	52,080	2.10%

A data range F6 . . F10
X range G6 . . G10

Example

```
Type          = XY
A data range  = FG..F10
X-range       = CG..G10
View
```

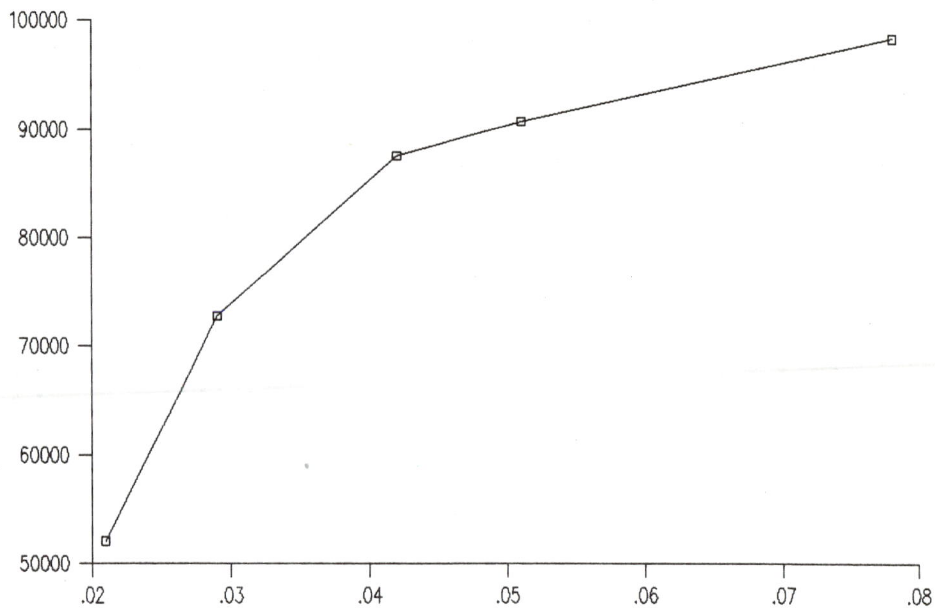

The line connecting the data points may or may not be displayed with the graph.

Adding Options to a Graph

Several **O**ption commands are available with the /**G**raph commands. They may be used to enhance and/or alter the appearance of a graph. The options tend to fall into two general categories: those used to add labels to the graph, and those used to change the display format of the graph.

Adding Labels

The **L**egend, **T**itles, and **D**ata-Labels commands of the **O**ption commands all are used to add labels to the current graph.

Legends

Legends identify the various lines on a line graph, the bars on a bar graph, or the points on an XY graph. Legends are entered as labels for the data ranges used to produce a graph. They are displayed at the bottom of the graph with the symbols, shading, or color used in the line, XY point, or bar displayed for the data range.

Titles

Titles label an entire graph with a first graph label and a second graph label. These two labels are centered and displayed at the top of the graph. Titles also may be put on the X axis and the Y axis of graphs having these two axes.

Data-Labels

Data-Labels are entered as a range of labels corresponding to the data elements in a data range. The specification of data labels is very similar to the specification of an X range used to label an X axis. Specified data labels, however, are displayed within the graph. They may be centered, left, above,

right, or below the corresponding data point in the graph. Data labels always are centered when they are used in bar graphs.
The following graph demonstrates how legends, titles, and data labels may be included in a graph.

Example

```
Type            = Bar
A data range    = B6..E6
B data range    = B7..E7
C data range    = B8..E8
D data range    = B9..E9
E data range    = B10..E10
X-range         = B4..E4
Options
    Legends
       A range =Cal
       B range =Wash
       C range =Ore
       D range =Ida
       E range =Alsk
    Titles
       First  =Comparative Quarterly Sales
       Second =California Sales Figures Displayed
       X-axis =QUARTERS
       Y-Axis =DOLLAR SALES
    Data-Labels
       A range = B6..E6
       Center
 View
```

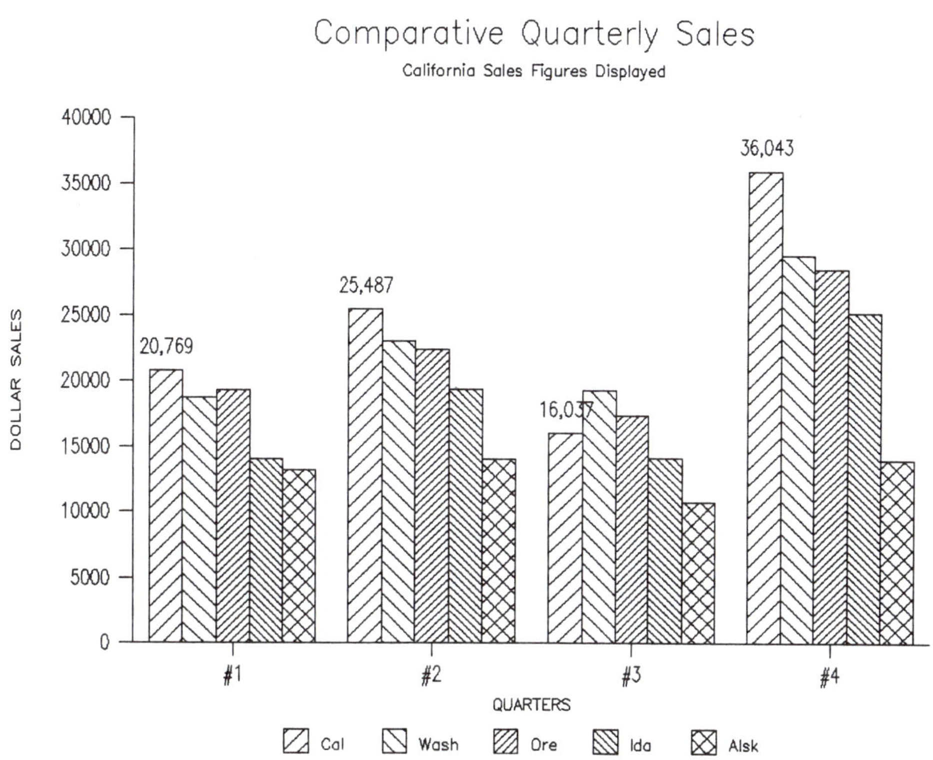

Changing Graph Formats

The **Format**, **Grid**, **Scale**, **Color** and **B&W** commands of the **Options** commands are used to format the display of the current graph.

Format Commands

The **Format** command is used for line and XY graphs. It allows the graph to display only lines; only symbols; both lines and symbols (the default setting); or neither lines nor symbols. The display can be for the entire graph or for any of the data ranges A through F.

Grid Commands

Grids within a graph may be displayed as horizontal lines corresponding to the ticks (perpendicular hash marks) on the Y axis; vertical lines corresponding to the ticks on the X axis; both (a true grid display); or cleared from the graph after having been set. The default setting is **C**lear (no grid lines).

Scale Commands

The **S**cale command may be used to override VP-Planner's automatic scaling of the Y axis, the X axis, or to skip the display of every nth label in an X range used to label the X axis. If **S**cale Y axis or **S**cale X axis is the command you select, the options become:

```
2Automatic 3Manual 4Lower 5Upper 6Format 7Quit
```

Manual turns off the automatic scaling and must be selected before you view a graph with upper and/or lower limits set with the upper or lower commands of this menu. The Automatic command returns to automatic scaling (its default setting).

If you select the **F**ormat command the next menu presented will be the same one used to format a range of cells or to globally format the spreadsheet.

```
2Fixed 3Scientific 4Currency 5,(comma) 6General 7+/- 8Percent 9Date 10Text 1 2
```

Here it is used to Format the axis scale numbers.

Color/B&W Commands

The **C**olor and **B&W** commands are mutually exclusive and have no further menus of commands attached to them. If you select the **C**olor command, the graph will be displayed in color. If you select **B&W** (the default setting), the graph will be displayed in black and white.

The bar graph with labels from page V-95 will demonstrate some of the formatting **O**ption commands. The following settings have been added to it:

Example

```
Grid        =Horizontal
Scale
   Skip     =2
   Y-Axis
     Manual
     Upper =40000
     Format=Currency / 0 decimal places
```

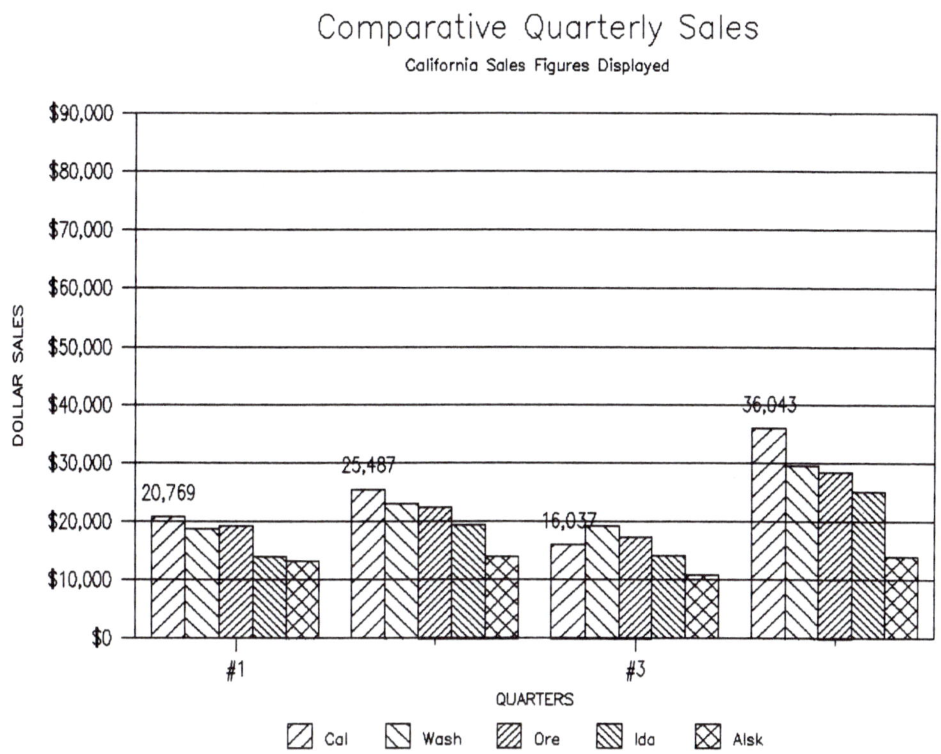

Note: VP-Planner displays the next unit above the upper limit set with scale.

VP-Planner is not a database management system (DBMS). The WORKSHEET does have commands, such as /**D**ata **S**ort and /**D**ata **Q**uery, that allow tasks normally associated with DBMSs to be performed on spreadsheet data. (VP-Planner has a Multi-Dimensional database that provides additional database management capabilities. It can also read and write dBase III files. These features, however, are not covered in this text. Please refer to the original VP-Planner manual.)

Database Structure and Terminology

The /**D**ata **S**ort commands are used to sort data and the /**D**ata **Q**uery commands are used to search through data and find cases evaluated as true for a given condition. For each command, the spreadsheet's data must be organized in a particular way.

Related data items are entered in rows across a spreadsheet. Each data item is called a *field* of data. A single row of related data is called a *record,* and the rectangular range of records is called the *database.* When you use the /**D**ata **Q**uery commands, you must have an additional row of *field names* occupying the top row of the database.

Example

	A	B	C	D	E	F	G	H	I	J
1										
2	LAST	FIRST	SEX	AGE	SALARY	← Field names				
3	Nichols	Sandy	F	40	$31,090					
4	Barons	Harold	M	21	$18,200					
5	Able	Richard	M	25	$18,450					
6	Samson	Carol	F	24	$19,380					
7	Jackson	Julie	F	32	$22,280					
8	Trember	Nick	M	33	$20,520					
9	Coneal	Rachael	F	20	$19,210	Database				
10	Brown	Scott	M	23	$18,400					
11	Sheradon	Leslie	F	22	$19,230					
12	Shackley	Suzanne	F	35	$23,850					
13	Wertz	Herbert	M	55	$31,300					
14	Ralston	Sherry	F	24	$18,170					
15	Brusky	Wayne	M	27	$20,930					
16	Austin	Chip	M	22	$18,380					
17	Drexler	Anne	F	26	$20,910					

|← Field →|

|← Record for Anne Drexler →|

The /Data Sort Commands

The /**D**ata **S**ort commands are straightforward and require only three steps to sort spreadsheet data which are organized in a database form. The menu of /**D**ata **S**ort commands consists of:

```
2Date-Range 3Primary-Key 4Secondary-Key 5Reset 6Go 7Quit
```

Setting the Data-Range to Sort

First, in sorting spreadsheet data, define the range of data to be sorted by using the **D**ata-Range command. The range includes only the actual records of the database to be sorted. Using the previous example, an appropriate range to sort would be A3 . . E17.

Example

	A	B	C	D	E	F	G	H	I	J
1										
2	LAST	FIRST	SEX	AGE	SALARY					
3	Nichols	Sandy	F	40	$31,090					
4	Barons	Harold	M	21	$18,200					
5	Able	Richard	M	25	$18,450					
6	Samson	Carol	F	24	$19,380					
7	Jackson	Julie	F	32	$22,280					
8	Trember	Nick	M	33	$20,520					
9	Coneal	Rachael	F	20	$19,210					
10	Brown	Scott	M	23	$18,400	Data-Range				
11	Sheradon	Leslie	F	22	$19,230					
12	Shackley	Suzanne	F	35	$23,850					
13	Wertz	Herbert	M	55	$31,300					
14	Ralston	Sherry	F	24	$18,170					
15	Brusky	Wayne	M	27	$20,930					
16	Austin	Chip	M	22	$18,380					
17	Drexler	Anne	F	26	$20,910					

Setting Sort Keys

The next step is to define the key(s). A key is any cell address in the column of data on which to sort the database.

Up to two fields may be specified as fields on which to sort. The Primary-Key is the field with the highest precedence for sorting. It may be the only key you specify. If you specify a Secondary-Key, the database also will be sorted on that key but it will take a lower precedence. Each key you specify provides the option of sorting in an ascending or descending sort order.

Sorting the Database

Once you have set the data-range and specified the keys on which to sort, along with their sort order, the **G**o command of the /**D**ata commands will sort the data in the data-range. The following example uses the field named SEX as the Primary-Key and the field named SALARY as the Secondary-Key in the database.

Example

```
/Data Sort
  Data-Range     - Enter Data range: A3..E17
  Primary Key    - Enter Primary Key address : C2
                         Enter Sort order (A or D): A
  Secondary Key - Enter Secondary Key address: E2
                         Enter Sort order (A or D): D
  Go
```

	A	B	C	D	E	F	G	H	I	J
1										
2	LAST	FIRST	SEX	AGE	SALARY					
3	Nichols	Sandy	F	40	$31,090					
4	Shackley	Suzanne	F	35	$23,850					
5	Jackson	Julie	F	32	$22,280					
6	Drexler	Anne	F	26	$20,910					
7	Samson	Carol	F	24	$19,380					
8	Sheradon	Leslie	F	22	$19,230					
9	Coneal	Rachael	F	20	$19,210					
10	Ralston	Sherry	F	24	$18,170					
11	Wertz	Herbert	M	55	$31,300					
12	Brusky	Wayne	M	27	$20,930					
13	Tremher	Niok	M	33	$20,520					
14	Able	Richard	M	25	$18,450					
15	Brown	Scott	M	23	$18,400					
16	Austin	Chip	M	22	$18,380					
17	Barons	Harold	M	21	$18,200					

The /Data Query Commands

The /**D**ata **Q**uery commands locate records in the database. The variation of /**D**ata **Q**uery discussed here searches the database for records that meet certain conditions (criteria). It also can copy the data in certain fields of the records to another place in the spreadsheet. This process is called *extracting data from the database.*

The Three Ranges Required to Extract Data

Three separate ranges, the Input, Criterion, and Output ranges, must be defined in order to extract data from a database.

1. The Input range includes the database and its row of field names. It is the range in which VP-Planner searches for records. You specify it by using the **I**nput command of the /**D**ata **Q**uery commands.
2. The Criterion range holds logical expressions that determine which records will be extracted from the Input range. It is usually a small range and is specified by using the **C**riterion command of the /**D**ata **Q**uery commands.
3. When a record is found that meets the Criterion range's condition(s), part or all of the record is copied to the Output range. The Output range determines which fields of the record will be copied to its area of the spreadsheet.

To use the /**D**ata **Q**uery commands effectively, you need to understand how the three ranges relate to each other and to understand how the conditions in the Criterion range work. The following example will show how the three ranges function.

An Example of Extracting Data

Using the same database as before, the task will be to extract the last names, ages, and salaries of all employees over age 30.

The first step is to define the Input range as A2 . . E17, since this range includes the row of field names and all records in the database. The field names must be included in the Input range; but if you were only interested in searching through the first ten records you could define the Input range as including the row of field names and just those ten records.

	A	B	C	D	E	F	G	H	I	J
1										
2	LAST	FIRST	SEX	AGE	SALARY					
3	Nichols	Sandy	F	40	$31,090					
4	Barons	Harold	M	21	$18,200					
5	Able	Richard	M	25	$18,450					
6	Samson	Carol	F	24	$19,380					
7	Jackson	Julie	F	32	$22,280					
8	Trember	Nick	M	33	$20,520					
9	Coneal	Rachael	F	20	$19,210					
10	Brown	Scott	M	23	$18,400					
11	Sheradon	Leslie	F	22	$19,230					
12	Shackley	Suzanne	F	35	$23,850					
13	Wertz	Herbert	M	55	$31,300					
14	Ralston	Sherry	F	24	$18,170					
15	Brusky	Wayne	M	27	$20,930					
16	Austin	Chip	M	22	$18,380					
17	Drexler	Anne	F	26	$20,910					
18										
19										

Input range

The next step is to define the Output range, the area into which the records meeting the criteria will be copied. The first row of the Output range contains the field names for the fields to be copied into the Output range. Since you want to copy into the Output range only the last names, ages, and salaries for records meeting the criteria (all employees over age 30), you next will move to another area of the spreadsheet and enter the appropriate field names into a row of cells. You then use the **O**utput command of the /**D**ata commands to define the range by its location. Here it would be H2 . . J12.

	A	B	C	D	E	F	G	H	I	J
1										
2	LAST	FIRST	SEX	AGE	SALARY			LAST	SALARY	AGE
3	Nichols	Sandy	F	40	$31,090					
4	Barons	Harold	M	21	$18,200					
5	Able	Richard	M	25	$18,450					
6	Samson	Carol	F	24	$19,380					
7	Jackson	Julie	F	32	$22,280					
8	Trember	Nick	M	33	$20,520					
9	Coneal	Rachael	F	20	$19,210					
10	Brown	Scott	M	23	$18,400					
11	Sheradon	Leslie	F	22	$19,230					
12	Shackley	Suzanne	F	35	$23,850					
13	Wertz	Herbert	M	55	$31,300					
14	Ralston	Sherry	F	24	$18,170					
15	Brusky	Wayne	M	27	$20,930					
16	Austin	Chip	M	22	$18,380					
17	Drexler	Anne	F	26	$20,910					
18										
19										

Input Range

Output Range

NOTE: The field names used in the Output range must exactly match the field names used in the Input range. Therefore, it is recommended that you copy the field name to be included in the Output range from the field names in the Input range.

The third and last range that you need to complete a /**D**ata **Q**uery **E**xtract operation is the Criterion range. In this area will be put the logical expression equivalent to "Age > 30." The minimum requirement for a Criterion range is that two cells are arranged one over the other. The top cell holds a field name and the bottom cell typically holds a logical expression. If the logical expression involves numeric data, that expression references the top cell of the appropriate field column of the database. Here an appropriate criteria would be:

AGE
+D3>30

Your next step is to move to a third area of the spreadsheet and enter the label AGE into a cell and +D3>30 into the cell below it. The two cells into which you enter the data will display:

AGE
1

The 1 displayed in the second cell is the result of the computer's evaluation of the logical expression D3>30. The value in D3 is greater than 30, so the computer evaluates it as true and displays number 1 (true). If the value in D3 were not greater than 30, the answer displayed would be 0. To make the expressions in a Criterion range readable as expressions, you usually /**R**ange **F**ormat **T**ext the range of cells holding logical expressions in a Criterion range.

Once the criteria have been entered into the cells you use the **C**riterion command of the /**D**ata commands to specify these two cells (and only these two cells) as the Criterion range.

The final step is to use the **E**xtract command of the /**D**ata **Q**uery commands to begin the operation. When this is done, the last names, salaries, and ages of every record of a person older than 30 in the Input range will be copied into the Output range.

	A	B	C	D	E	F	G	H	I	J
1										
2	LAST	FIRST	SEX	AGE	SALARY			LAST	SALARY	AGE
3	Nichols	Sandy	F	40	$31,090			Nichols	$31,090	40
4	Barons	Harold	M	21	$18,200			Jackson	$22,280	32
5	Able	Richard	M	25	$18,450			Trember	$20,520	33
6	Samson	Carol	F	24	$19,380			Shackley	$23,850	35
7	Jackson	Julie	F	32	$22,280			Wertz	$31,300	55
8	Trember	Nick	M	33	$20,520					
9	Coneal	Rachael	F	20	$19,210					
10	Brown	Scott	M	23	$18,400					
11	Sheradon	Leslie	F	22	$19,230					
12	Shackley	Suzanne	F	35	$23,850					
13	Wertz	Herbert	M	55	$31,300					
14	Ralston	Sherry	F	24	$18,170					
15	Brusky	Wayne	M	27	$20,930					
16	Austin	Chip	M	22	$18,380					
17	Drexler	Anne	F	26	$20,910					
18										
19										

Output Range

Criterion Range

AGE
+D3>30

Input Range

Criterion Range Conditions

The way that you structure your field name labels and logical expressions within a Criterion range determines the character of the records evaluated true by the criteria (conditions) in the range. To demonstrate the alternatives, several different Criterion ranges relating to this database will be discussed.

A Criterion Range with No Condition

The simplest criterion is no criterion at all. Two cells defined as the Criterion range are left blank. When they remain blank all records are evaluated as true and will have their appropriate fields copied to the Output range.

Simple Criterion Range/Simple Condition

The example used to extract records for employees older than age 30 showed a simple Criterion range (two cells) and a simple numeric condition. Another example uses a simple string condition to extract data.

When you use a simple string condition, the logical expression that makes up the condition is restricted to the relational operator = (equals), but that operator is not included in the expression. For example, in order to copy to the output fields all employees with the last name "Sheradon," the condition of the Criteria range would be entered as:

LAST
Sheradon

The result can be thought of as the expression, LAST="Sheradon." When the extraction operation using this condition is performed, all records holding the data "Sheradon" (capital "S," lower case "heradon") in the field named LAST will be copied into the Output range.

Wild Card Characters

String conditions may produce partial comparisons in a data search by including "wild card" characters in the condition. Two "wild card" characters are the asterisk (*), which means "any characters that follow," and the question mark (?), which means "any character located here." For example, the following Criterion ranges with their criteria will produce the output shown in the Output range, given the same Input and Output ranges in the preceding examples.

Criterion range

Output range

LAST
Sh*

H	I	J
LAST	SALARY	AGE
Sheradon	$19,230	35
Shackley	$23,850	22

LAST
S*

LAST	SALARY	AGE
Samson	$19,380	24
Sheradon	$19,230	22
Shackley	$23,850	35

Criterion range	
LAST	
?????1	

Output range		
LAST	SALARY	AGE
Coneal	$19,210	20

LAST	
?????1*	

LAST	SALARY	AGE
Nichols	$31,090	40
Coneal	$19,210	20
Shackley	$23,850	35

Simple Criterion Range/Complex Condition

It is possible, when using numeric-type data in a condition, to include criteria connected with the logical operators #NOT#, #AND#, #OR#. For instance, to copy all records for employees over 30 years of age and making less than $25,000, your Criterion range could be set up as follows.

LAST
+D3>30#AND#+E3<25000

Notice that, although it is required, the field name you use does not have to be at all related to a numeric-type expression. It simply needs to be an existing field name found in the Input range.

Complex Criterion Range/Simple Condition

When you need both string conditions and numeric conditions to set criteria, the Criterion range needs to be enlarged. The logical operators connecting the different types of expressions become implicit by the expressions' positioning in the Criterion range. For example, if you want to extract records for all females making less than $20,000, the appropriate logical operator is AND (SEX = "F" AND SALARY < 20000). In this case, the field names and the expressions are placed side by side in the Criterion range.

SEX	SALARY
F	+E3<20000

If, however, you want to extract records for all females or any employee making less than $20,000, the appropriate logical operator is OR (SEX="F" OR SALARY < 20000). In this case the field names are put side-by-side, but the expressions are not placed on the same line in the Criterion range.

SEX	SALARY
F	
	+E3<20000

When complex Criterion ranges are used to extract data, it is useful to think of the Criterion range as a filter through which the record must pass to reach the Output range. In the "females AND less than $20,000" example, the record begins its journey through the filter from the left and at the top of the Criterion range.

Nichols	Sandy	F	40	$31,090

SEX	SALARY
F	+E3<20000

If the expression is evaluated as true, the record keeps moving through the filter to the right. In this case the record meets another expression it must pass in order to continue its journey.

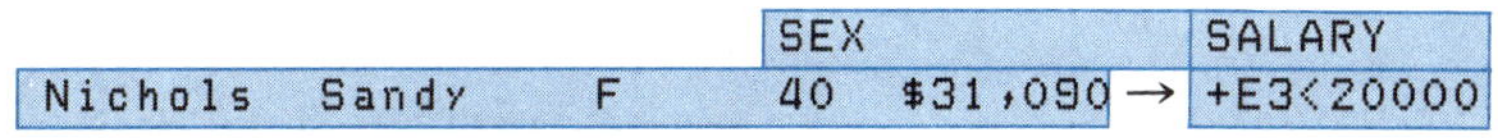

If it does not pass the condition there the record drops out of the Criterion range, and the next record in the database is tried.

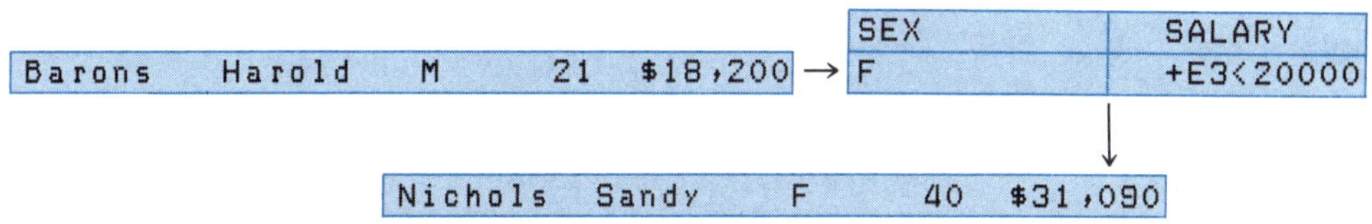

By keeping the expressions on the same line, the record is forced to pass condition AND condition before it can emerge from the right side of the Criterion range. Only when a record passes all conditions that it meets will it emerge from the right side of the Criterion range and be copied into the Output range.

In the example "female or less than $20,000," the Criterion range had its expressions located on different lines. In such a case the record approaches the filter in the same way as before.

Now, however, if the record does not pass the first condition it meets, it is able to drop down one line and still be in the Criterion range (the Criterion range is one cell deeper). It then will attempt to continue its journey through the filter along that row.

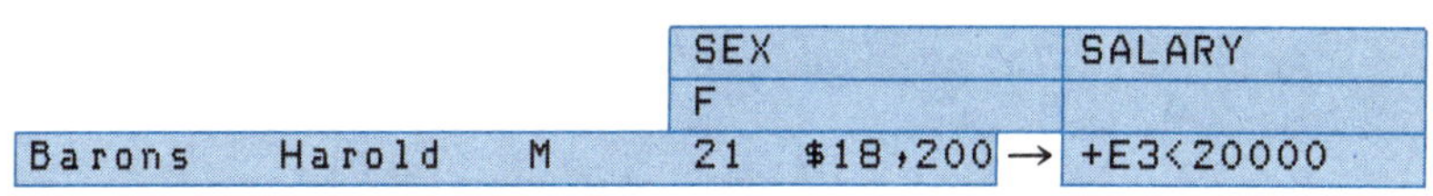

If it does not pass the next condition it reaches, the record drops out of the Criterion range and the next record is tried. If it does pass, it emerges from the right side of the Criterion range and is copied into the Output range.

By keeping the expressions on separate lines in the Criterion range, the record is given the opportunity to pass criteria OR criteria in order to be copied into the Output range.

Database Functions

The statistical functions have counterparts designed specifically for dealing with database spreadsheet data. These functions include:

@DCOUNT	**@DMIN**	**@DSTD**	**@DAVG**
@DSUM	**@DMAX**	**@DVAR**	

The purpose of database functions is to return a computed statistic, such as an average, from a range of cells, such as the column of salaries in a database, for records that meet a Criteria, such as all men in the database.

A data function's general form is:

@DFUNC(Input range, offset, Criterion range)

The first letter (**D**) of the function's name signifies that it is a database function.

The Input range in the function's argument is the same as an Input range used for the /**D**ata **Q**uery commands.

The offset in the argument is used in the same manner as the offset in the **@VLOOKUP** function: the value used for offset determines which field column of the database is used as the range of cells from which to return the function's value.

The Criterion range is the same type of range used in the /**D**ata **Q**uery commands. This range holds the conditions that determine which records the function will return values for.

Example of Using Database Functions

Like the statistical functions, the database functions are very similar to each other in form and use. To demonstrate how the data functions may be used, two **@DAVG** functions in the following example are used to return the average salaries for all males and females in the employee database.

Example

	A	B	C	D	E
1					
2	LAST	FIRST	SEX	AGE	SALARY
3	Nichols	Sandy	F	40	$31,090
4	Barons	Harold	M	21	$18,200
5	Able	Richard	M	25	$18,450
6	Samson	Carol	F	24	$19,380
7	Jackson	Julie	F	32	$22,280
8	Trember	Nick	M	33	$20,520
9	Coneal	Rachael	F	20	$19,210
10	Brown	Scott	M	23	$18,400
11	Sheradon	Leslie	F	22	$19,230
12	Shackley	Suzanne	F	35	$23,850
13	Wertz	Herbert	M	55	$31,300
14	Ralston	Sherry	F	24	$18,170
15	Brusky	Wayne	M	27	$20,930
16	Austin	Chip	M	22	$18,380
17	Drexler	Anne	F	26	$20,910
18					
19					

Input Range

Averages

Male Salaries = $20,883
@DAVG(A2 . . E17,4,G13 . . G14)

Female Salaries = $21,765
@DAVG(A2 . . E17,4,H13 . . H14)

Criterion ranges

G	H
SEX	SEX
M	F

What is a Keyboard Macro?

In its simplest form, a keyboard macro is a collection of keystrokes, entered as labels into a cell or group of cells. The cells are named by using the /**R**ange **N**ame **C**reate command. The name given the range must begin with a backslash (\) followed by a single letter of the alphabet. Once the macro has been entered and named, VP-Planner sequentially executes the keystrokes represented in it whenever the Alt key is held down and the letter of the macro's name is typed.

Creating a Simple Macro

Steps Required to Create a Macro

The following example will show the steps involved in creating a macro.

Assessing the Problem

Macros are created to solve problems or to save time. Let's suppose that you have a spreadsheet file that you have been working on for several days. Your routine is always the same. After each session you save the spreadsheet under its original name to update the file on the diskette, and then exit VP-Planner. Eight keystrokes are required to accomplish your save-and-exit routine. A macro can accomplish the task faster and in one keystroke combination.

Coding the Macro

To create a macro you record the exact sequence of keystrokes required for your regular routine. With paper and a pencil you write down the keys that you press when you complete the save-and-exit steps manually. The keystrokes and commands that you use are as follows.

Keystroke	Action
/	Call the Main menu.
F	Select the File command.
S	Select the Save command.

VP-Planner presents the prompt:

```
A1    Enter file name: ASSIGN1
```

The name shown is the one with which you loaded the file (its original name) and is the default prompt of the "Save" command.

↵ Enter Key to enter this as the right filename.

Next you see the prompt:

```
2Cancel    3Replace    4Backup
```

R To replace (update) that file.

VP-Planner returns to the READY mode.

/ To call the Main menu again.

Q To select the Quit command

Next you see the prompt:

```
A1      You have asked to QUIT the worksheet.   Are you sure?   (Y/N)
```

Y To complete the Quit operation.

After you systematically record the keystrokes as **/FS** ↵ **R/QY** on a piece of paper, you are ready to create the macro that, when executed, will complete these eight keystrokes.

Locating the Macro

Following the rules of spreadsheet design you move the pointer to an area set off from any current or foreseeable spreadsheet overlap or interference. You document the area by entering the label "Spreadsheet Macros." You are ready to type in the macro, but first you need an important piece of information. For macros, the keystroke ↵ (Enter) is represented with a tilde (~) character.

Entering the Macro

You begin entering into a cell the keystrokes you have written down for the macro. Since your keystrokes must be entered as labels, you begin your entry by typing in a label prefix (', ", or ^). When it is complete your spreadsheet keyboard macro looks like this:

```
        AA          AB          AC          AD          AE          AF          AG
1                              Spreadsheet Macros
2                              ------------------
3              /FS~R/QY
4
5
6
```

Naming a Macro

Your next step is to use the /**R**ange **N**ame **C**reate command to name the single cell AB3 . . AB3 with an appropriate macro name. You name it "D" for "Done" and you specify the range name as \D.

```
Enter name:\D
```

VP-Planner identifies a named range as one holding a keyboard macro by the backslash in its name.

Invoking a Macro

Now that the macro has been entered and named, the next time you are ready to save-and-exit you simply press and hold the Alt key then tap the D key. VP-Planner will then begin to execute in order the keystrokes in the keyboard macro named \D. The result is that the save-and-exit routine is completed with one keystroke combination rather than eight keystrokes, saving you some time.

Cautions about Macros

Although they can be useful, macros also have some drawbacks. The keystrokes in them are executed so fast that there is seldom time to stop a rampaging macro before it has done substantial damage to your spreadsheet. Even in the very simple macro used in this example, if a C or a ~ accidentally is placed where the R should be (/**FS**~R/**QY**), the macro would not replace the file on the diskette. It would then execute the /**Q**uit command causing you to lose all of the work you had completed to that point.

Safeguards against Macro Catastrophes

1. Always save your spreadsheet prior to testing a new macro.
2. The Alt-F1 key combination turns on and off (toggles) a STEP mode. When the STEP mode is on, VP-Planner executes each keystroke in the macro only after you have tapped a keyboard key. It slows down the execution of the macro and allows you to observe the results of each keystroke in it.
3. While a macro is being executed the word "macro" will appear in the left side of the screen. When the STEP mode is on, the word STEP# will appear at the left center of the screen. If you want to stop the execution of the macro before it is completed, the Ctrl-Break key combination will interrupt the execution of the macro.

Representing Special Keystrokes in a Macro

As you will recall, the tilde (~) symbol is used in macros to represent the Enter key keystroke. This is one example of how a substitute entry must be used in a macro to represent the actual keystroke used. Other special keystrokes are represented in a macro by entering the key's name or function enclosed in braces. For instance, if you wanted to create a macro to copy a single cell into the cell below it, your macro would look like /**C**~{**DOWN**}~. The macro duplicates the following steps.

1. After you have moved to the cell from which to copy you would type /**C** to call the **C**opy command.
2. The default SOURCE range shown would be that single cell, so the Enter key (~) would be pressed.
3. The default DESTINATION range next shown also would be that cell, but it can be changed by highlighting the appropriate range. To do so you would tap the "down" pointer control key. To represent the keystroke in a macro you enter {**DOWN**}.
4. The default DESTINATION range shown would then be the cell the pointer indicates (the cell below the original cell), so the Enter key (~) would be pressed.

The following table lists the special keys and keystroke counterparts used to represent them within a macro.

Macro Command	Keyboard Keystroke
Function Keys	
{EDIT}	F2
{NAME}	F3
{ABS}	F4
{GOTO}	F5
{WINDOW}	F6
{QUERY}	F7
{TABLE}	F8
{CALC}	F9
{GRAPH}	F10
Pointer-Movement Keys	
{UP}	↑
{DOWN}	↓
{LEFT}	←
{RIGHT}	→
{PGUP}	PgUp
{PGDN}	PgDn
{HOME}	Home
{END}	End
{GOREF}	Alt-F5 (Relative GOTO)
Editing Keys	
{DEL}	Del
{ESC}	Esc
{BS}	← (Backspace)
~	Enter key

Interactive Macros

{**?**} is a unique macro keystroke. It may be used to suspend the execution of a macro in order to allow the user to type in spreadsheet data, to answer command prompts, or to move the spreadsheet pointer. In the following example, a macro has been designed to /**R**ange **F**ormat any range of cells to display **C**urrency format to two decimal places.

```
/RFC2~{?}~
```

To use the macro you first move to the beginning of the range to be formatted, and then invoke the macro with the Alt-macro name key combination. The macro calls the /**R**ange **F**ormat **C**urrency (2 decimal places) command which will automatically anchor the pointer. The {?} macro keystroke then suspends the execution of the macro in order to let you move the pointer to the end of the range to format (point to it). When you are finished, tap the Enter key to signal your completion. The macro will continue executing where it left off. The final ~ in the macro is to Enter the range you have defined by pointing to it.

Building a Macro Library

The macros discussed here so far are simple, general purpose macros that could be useful in any spreadsheet. As you continue to use VP-Planner you will identify sets of keystrokes that you use often, and you may want to create a library or a collection of macros to use in each of your spreadsheets. The following procedure may be used to create a single set of general purpose macros, and then you can combine that set into any of your spreadsheets.

You begin by creating and testing your set of macros within an existing spreadsheet. In the following example, five macros have been put in a well-documented area of a spreadsheet.

```
      AA          AB           AC          AD          AE          AF          AG
1
2                              Spreadsheet Macros
3   Name        Macro          ------------------
4
5   \D          /FS~R/QY       Save/update spreadsheet and exit VP-Planner
6
7   \C          /C~{?}~        Copy current cell to any cell by pointing
8
9   \M          /RFC2~{?}~     Format $xx,xxx.xx any range beginning at current cell
10
11  \B          /RE~           Erase the current cell
12
13  \P          /PPOML10~~R132~S\027\015~Q
14                             Print macro - Set Margin Left = 10, Margin Right = 132
15                             and Setup string for condensed print (Epson printer)
```

The macro names have been entered as labels into the AA column; the actual macros are in the AB column; and a short description of each macro is in the AC column. The macros in the AB column must be separated from each other by blank cells.

Using the /File Xtract Command

Once you have entered and documented this area of the spreadsheet, it may be saved as its own file on the diskette by using the /File **X**tract command. In the example the spreadsheet macro area is saved under the name MACLIB.

```
/File Xtract
   2Formulas 3Values 4DIF 5SDF

   Enter file name: MACLIB
   Enter xtract range: AA2..AC15
```

NOTE: An Xtracted file may have its formulas converted to constants (Values) or left intact (Formulas). Since this area of the spreadsheet is all labels, it doesn't matter which option is selected.

When the Xtract operation is complete, the macro area of the spreadsheet will be saved on the diskette in its own .WKS file.

Using the /File Combine Command

When you start a new spreadsheet or when you want to have your library of macros available within an existing spreadsheet, you may use the /**F**ile **C**ombine command to read the macro library (MACLIB.WKS) into the current spreadsheet. The command will copy it into any location you desire. Here the macros are read into the current spreadsheet at the position A100.

The first step in combining a .WKS file from the diskette into a current file is to move the spreadsheet pointer to the upper left corner of the desired range location for the combined spreadsheet data. In the example the pointer will be moved to the A100 cell.

The following commands are then selected from their menus.

```
/File
   Combine
   Copy
   Entire file
   Enter file name: MACLIB
```

When the operation is complete, the MACLIB spreadsheet will be combined with the current spreadsheet and its location will extend from A100 to C113.

```
          A         B            C         D         E         F          G         H
98
99
100                              Spreadsheet Macros
101   Name      Macro            ------------------
102
103   \D        /FS~R/QY         Save/update spreadsheet and exit VP-Planner
104
105   \C        /C~{?}~          Copy current cell to any cell by pointing
106
107   \M        /RFC2~{?}~       Format $xx,xxx.xx any range beginning at current cell
108
109   \B        /RE~             Erase the current cell
110
111   \P        /PPOML10~~R132~S\027\015~Q
112                              Print macro - Set Margin Left = 10, Margin Right = 132
113                              and Setup string for condensed print (Epson printer)
```

A Macro to Name Macros

Any range names that may have existed in the file being combined no longer exist after the Combine operation. After combining your macro library into a spreadsheet you need to use the /**R**ange **N**ame **C**reate command to name each macro range in order for it to be used in the spreadsheet.

You may find it convenient to include in your macro library a macro that, when it is executed, will name each of the other macros. You will still need to name this macro before it may be executed.

Several different designs for this macro exist. The macro shown at the bottom of this macro library works if the spreadsheet pointer is on the cell indicated when it is invoked.

```
      A         B          C          D          E          F          G
98
99
100                        Spreadsheet Macros
101  Name      Macro       ------------------
102
103  \D        /FS~R/QY    Save/update spreadsheet and exit VP-Planner
104
105  \C        /C~{?}~     Copy current cell to any cell by pointing
106
107  \M        /RFC2~{?}~  Format $xx,xxx.xx any range beginning at current cell
108
109  \B        /RE~        Erase the current cell
110
111  \P        /PPOML10~~R132~S\027\015~Q
112                        Print macro - Set Margin Left = 10, Margin Right = 132
113                        and Setup string for condensed print (Epson printer)
114  pointer->  HERE
115  \S       {UP}                    Macro to /Range Name macros in Library
116           {UP}{UP}/RNC\P~~        1) Name the first cell in this macro "\S"
117           {UP}{UP}/RNC\B~~        2) Move the pointer to the cell marked HERE
118           {UP}{UP}/RNC\M~~        3) Type Alt-S
119           {UP}{UP}/RNC\C~~
120           {UP}{UP}/RNC\D~~
```

How VP-Planner Executes a Macro

Notice that the macro to name macros is several cells deep and that its range name names only the top cell of the macro. When a macro is invoked, VP-Planner begins executing from left to right the keystrokes in the cell named as the macro. When the keystrokes in the cell have all been executed, the next cell down is evaluated. If the lower cell is blank, execution of the macro stops. If the cell is holding keystrokes, those keystrokes are executed as well. An interesting design implication is that a cell within a macro can be named a different macro name and can be used to execute only the portion of the larger macro from that cell down (a macro within a macro).

A Menu of Macros—The /XMrange Command

One of the special macro commands, the /**XM**range~ (Macro menu) command, allows one macro to be made up of up to eight different macros. Any given macro can be invoked through a menu selection process almost identical to the command selection process. To demonstrate the use of the /**XM**range~ command, the macro library used so far will be redesigned and presented as a menu of macros from which to select.

The Structure of a Menu Macro

The overall design of a /**XM**range~ macro is:

/**XM**range ~

1st level	1st level	1st level	1st level
2nd level	2nd level	2nd level	2nd level
Macro 1	Macro 2	Macro 3	Macro 4

The "range" of the **/XM**range~ command is the top left cell of the 1st level, 2nd level, and macro. It must be followed by a tilde (~). The row of 1st levels consists of command names you choose for the macros below it. The row of 2nd levels is explanations for the commands found above it.

An Example of a Menu Macro

To demonstrate the basic menu macro structure, a **/XM** macro with one 1st level command name, a 2nd level explanation, and a macro will be constructed.

```
        A         B         C         D         E         F
98
99
100 /XMA101~
101 Save-Done
102 Updates saved file and exits VP-Planner
103 /FS~R/QY
104
105
```

Invoking a Menu Macro

Cell A100 is given the range name \M to identify it as a macro. When it is invoked, the first and second prompt lines of the spreadsheet will display:

```
        A         B         C         D         E         F
1
2

20
 A1
 Save-Done
Updates saved file and exits VP-Planner                          INPUT
```

If you press the Enter key (or, with Version 1A, if the first letter (S) of the "Save-Done" command is pressed), the macro (**/FS~R/QY**) under that command and the explanation in the menu macro will be executed.

Adding Menu Options

To expand the example, a macro to copy a single cell into any location will be added to the menu macro.

```
        A         B         C         D         E         F
98
99
100 /XMA101~
101 Save-Done    Copy-Cell
102 Updates saveCopies the current cell into any location
103 /FS~R/QY     /C~{?}~
104
```

Entering the 2nd level explanation for the new command stops the 2nd level explanation for the first command from extending into that cell's area. If you want to view all of both the 2nd level explanations you can set the column widths wider.

Now when the **M** macro is invoked, the first and second prompt lines of the spreadsheet will display:

```
         A         B         C         D         E         F
1
2
3
17
18
19
20
 A1
 Save-Done   Copy-Cell
Updates saved file and exits VP-Planner                       INPUT
```

If you move the command pointer to the right it will display:

```
         A         B         C         D         E         F
1
2
3
17
18
19
20
 A1
 Save-Done   Copy-Cell
Copies the current cell into any location                     INPUT
```

You can select the macro of your choice, the macro to save and exit, or the macro to copy a cell into any location, from the menu macro's menu either by pointing to it or by typing the first letter of the command shown. You will want to name your commands so that each starts with a unique letter. The Esc key may be used to back up one step, and the Ctrl-Break key combination may be used to return you to the READY mode.

To complete the example, the entire macro library will be put into this menu macro.

```
          A         B         C         D         E         F
98
99
100  /XMA101~
101  Save-Done  Copy-Cell  Format-$   Blank-Cell Printer-Set
102  Updates savCopies the Currency FoErases the Sets Margins and Setup string
103  /FS~R/QY   /C~{?}~    /RFC2~{?}~ /RE~       /PPOML10~~R132~S\027\015~Q
104
105
```

Now when the Alt-M keys are pressed, the screen displays:

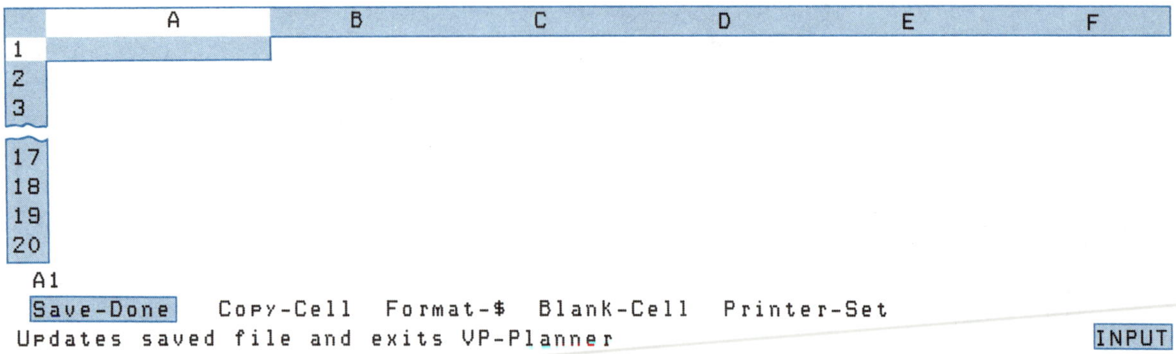

You have created your own menu complete with explanations for each command in it. It operates just like a spreadsheet menu of commands: each command shown invokes a macro you have written.

Advanced Macro Commands

If you have computer programming experience you may have noticed similarities between the macros discussed so far and writing programs using a programming language such as BASIC. In fact, macros are a type of spreadsheet programming language and the similarities become more apparent when advanced macro commands are discussed.

The following macro commands are treated as "advanced" commands since their use requires some understanding of the principals of programming. The commands will be presented by using an example macro that will be built up as new commands are discussed. An approximate equivalent of the spreadsheet macro, written as a BASIC program, will be used to help clarify the macro being discussed. Keep in mind that a BASIC program requires PRINT statements to generate output and that a spreadsheet does not. For this reason, the necessary PRINT statements have been left out of the BASIC programs.

/XQ Command

The /**XQ** command is used to stop the execution of a macro. Its BASIC counterpart is the END statement. This command will be included in the example at various points in the macro's development.

/XNmessage~range~ and /XLmessage~range~ Commands

The /**XN**message~range~ and /**XL**message~range~ commands are used to display a prompt (the "message") on the prompt line of the spreadsheet. They wait for the user to enter a response. The response is then copied into the cell defined as the "range" in the command. If the range is omitted, the response is copied into the cell where the spreadsheet pointer is located. /**XN** is used to accept a response of numeric data, and /**XL** is used to accept a response of string data (labels).

The BASIC counterparts for these commands would be variations of the INPUT command. For example:

/**XL**Enter a name~A2~ = INPUT "Enter a name"; A2$
/**XN**Enter a number~A2~ = INPUT "Enter a number"; A2

```
          A         B         C          D            E          F           G         H
 1
 2                   ------------------------------------------------
 3              ;  Purchase item =                                    ;
 4              ;  ------------------------------                     ;
 5              ;  Purchase Price    =                                ;
 6              ;                                                     ;
 7              ;  Down Payment      =                                ;
 8              ;                                                     ;
 9              ;  Terms                                              ;
10              ;  -----     Interest Rate     =                      ;
11              ;            Periods in Years =                       ;
12              ;                                                     ;
13              ;                                                     ;
14              ;            Monthly Payments   =                     ;
15              ;                                                     ;
16                 ------------------------------------------------
17
18  {HOME}
19  {GOTO}D3~/RE~{DOWN}{DOWN}/RE~
20  {DOWN}{DOWN}/RE~
21  {DOWN}{DOWN}{DOWN}{RIGHT}/RE~
22  {DOWN}/RE~
23  {DOWN}{DOWN}{DOWN}/RE~
24  {HOME}
25  /XLType in Item Description: ~D3~
26  /XNEnter Purchase price: ~D5~
27  /XNEnter Down Payment: ~D7~
28  /XNYearly Interest Rate as decimal: ~E10~
29  /XNNumber of Periods in Years: ~E11~
30  {GOTO}E14~@PMT(D5-D7,E10/12,E11*12)~
31  {HOME}
32  /XQ
```

BASIC equivalent

```
010 D3$="":D5=0
020 D7=0
030 E10=0
040 E11=0
050 E14=0
060 INPUT "Type in Item Description: ";D3$
070 INPUT "Enter Purchase price: ";D5
080 INPUT "Enter Down Payment: ";E10
090 INPUT "Yearly Interest Rate as a decimal: ";E10
100 INPUT "Number of periods in Years: ";E11
110 E14=(D5-D7)*((E10/12)/((1-(1+E10))^-(E11*12))))
120 END
```

This macro begins by erasing all of the cells it will use when it is executed, essentially the same process as initializing variables in a BASIC program. It then executes the **/XL** command and presents its prompt at the top prompt line of the spreadsheet.

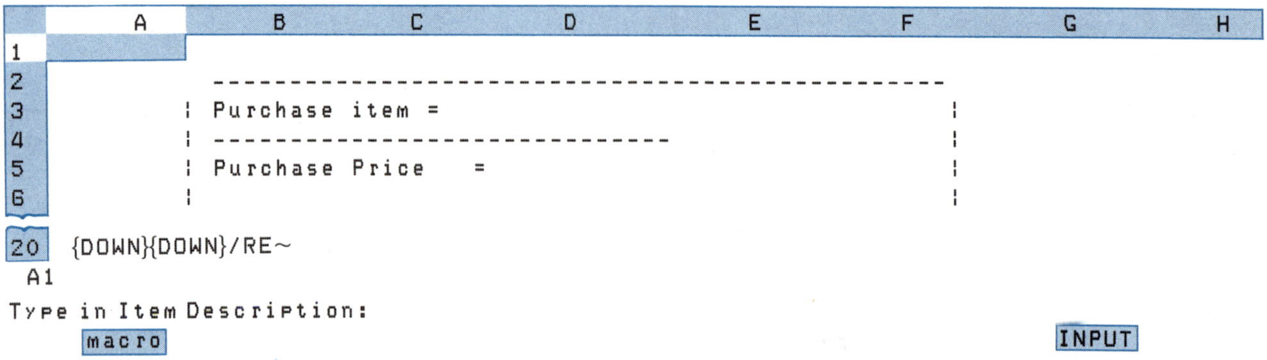

The user types in a label describing the item being considered for purchase. When the Enter key is pressed, the label is copied into the cell D3, and the next command /**XN**Enter Purchase price: ~D5~ is executed.

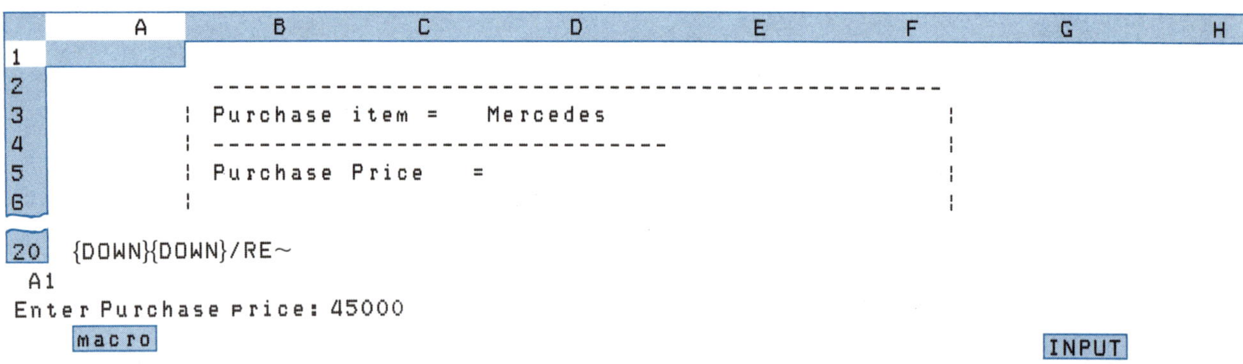

The macro continues to present prompts, accept data, and copy that data to the appropriate cells until the command {**GOTO**}E14~@**PMT**(D5–D7,E10/12,E11*12)~ is reached. This command causes the spreadsheet pointer to move to cell E14 and enter into the cell the **@PMT** function that will compute the monthly payments required, given the data provided by the user.

```
       A        B         C          D            E          F          G          H
 1
 2          ------------------------------------------
 3         ¦ Purchase item =     Mercedes                                ¦
 4         ¦ ----------------------------                                ¦
 5         ¦ Purchase Price    =  $45,000.00                             ¦
 6         ¦                                                             ¦
 7         ¦ Down Payment      =  $10,000.00                             ¦
 8         ¦                                                             ¦
 9         ¦ Terms                                                       ¦
10         ¦ -----     Interest Rate     =          18.00%               ¦
11         ¦           Periods in Years =              4                 ¦
12         ¦                                                             ¦
13         ¦                                                             ¦
14         ¦           Monthly Payments   =    $1,028.12                 ¦
15         ¦                                                             ¦
16          ------------------------------------------
```

The final command in the macro /**XQ** stops the execution of the macro.

/XIcondition~ Command

The /**XI**condition~ command is the conditional macro command. Its form is:

/**XI**condition~true action
false action

When VP-Planner encounters the /**XI**condition~ command it evaluates the numeric logical expression of the command's condition. If the condition is evaluated as true, the rest of the keystrokes, commands, etc., in the cell are executed. If the condition is not evaluated as true, execution of the macro resumes at the next cell down. The BASIC counterpart to the /**XI**condition~ command is the IF THEN command.

In the following example, the /**XI**condition~ command is used to determine if the monthly payments are in excess of $200.00. If they are, the message "EXCESSIVE PAYMENT" is displayed; execution of the macro is suspended with the /**XL** command giving the message, "Press Enter to continue;" the "EXCESSIVE PAYMENT" message is erased; and execution of the macro resumes.

The /**XI**condition~ command is inserted in the macro at cell A31. The screen that the example shows is the screen that the user views when the "Press Enter to continue" prompt of the true action has just been executed.

```
     A        B        C         D           E         F         G        H
1
2              ---------------------------------------------------
3            ¦ Purchase item =    Mercedes                        ¦
4            ¦ ------------------------------                     ¦
5            ¦ Purchase Price    =  $45,000.00                    ¦
6            ¦                                                    ¦
7            ¦ Down Payment      =  $10,000.00                    ¦
8            ¦                                                    ¦
9            ¦ Terms                                              ¦
10           ¦ -----       Interest Rate     =         18.00%     ¦
11           ¦             Periods in Years =              4      ¦
12           ¦                                                    ¦
13           ¦                                                    ¦
14           ¦             Monthly Payments   =    $1,028.12      ¦
15           ¦                                                    ¦
16             ---------------------------------------------------
17                         EXCESSIVE PAYMENT
18  {HOME}
19  {GOTO}D3~/RE~{DOWN}{DOWN}/RE~
20  {DOWN}{DOWN}/RE~
21  {DOWN}{DOWN}{DOWN}{RIGHT}/RE~
22  {DOWN}/RE~
23  {DOWN}{DOWN}{DOWN}/RE~
24  {HOME}
25  /XLType in Item Description: ~D3~
26  /XNEnter Purchase price: ~D5~
27  /XNEnter Down Payment: ~D7~
28  /XNYearly Interest Rate as decimal: ~E10~
29  /XNNumber of Periods in Years: ~E11~
30  {GOTO}E14~@PMT(D5-D7,E10/12,E11*12)~
31  /XIE14>200~{GOTO}C17~EXCESSIVE PAYMENT~/XLPress Enter to continue~A1~/RE~
32  {HOME}
33  /XQ
 C17

Press Enter to continue . . .
   macro                                                                INPUT
```

BASIC equivalent

```
010 D3$="":D5=0
020 D7=0
030 E10=0
040 E11=0
050 E14=0
060 INPUT "Type in Item Description: ";D3$
070 INPUT "Enter Purchase price: ";D5
080 INPUT "Enter Down Payment: ";D7
090 INPUT "Yearly Interest Rate as a decimal: ";E10
100 INPUT "Number of periods in Years: ";E11
110 E14=(D5-D7)*((E10/12)/((1-(1+E10))^-(E11*12)))
120 IF E14>200 THEN C17$="EXCESSIVE PAYMENT":INPUT "Press Enter to continue";A1:C17$=""
130 END
```

/XGrange~ Command

The /**XG**range~ command is used to alter the sequence of execution in a macro. Its BASIC counterpart is the GOTO command. Remember, however, that the /**XG**range~ command is completely different than the {**GOTO**} command. The {**GOTO**} command moves the spreadsheet pointer, and the /**XG**range~ command instructs VP-Planner to continue its execution of macro commands at a cell other than the one below. The cell at which to continue is specified as the "range" in the /**XG**range~ command. The term for the action performed by the /**XG**range~ command is "passing control."

The **XG**range~ command may be used with an /**XI**condition~ command to create a conditional branch within a macro or it may be used by itself to create an unconditional branch. A common use of the /**XG**range~ command takes the form:

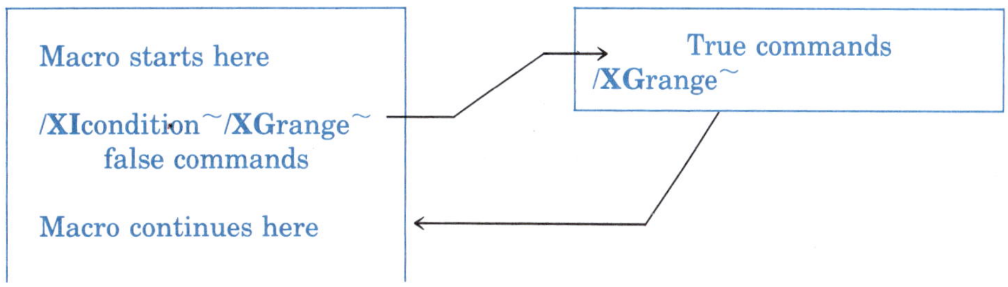

Control is conditionally passed to a set of true commands and unconditionally returned to the point following a set of false commands.

Another use of the /**XG**range~ command is to create a conditional loop in a macro. In this case the range to which to go is above the /**XG**range~ command. That causes control to circle through any commands between the /**XG**range~ command and the "range" specified in it. In the following example the user is prompted as to whether or not another set of data is desired. If the user answers "yes" the macro is repeated through a looping process. Cells A32 and A33 have been inserted to include the new commands. Note also /**RE**~ has been added to A18 to erase data temporarily held in cell A1 while the macro evaluates the user's response to the "1 = YES 2 = NO" prompt.

```
           A         B         C          D           E          F           G          H
1
2               ------------------------------------------------
3             ¦ Purchase item =    Volkswagen                            ¦
4             ¦ ------------------------------                            ¦
5             ¦ Purchase Price    =   $4,995.00                           ¦
6             ¦                                                           ¦
7             ¦ Down Payment      =     $900.00                           ¦
8             ¦                                                           ¦
9             ¦ Terms                                                     ¦
10            ¦ -----      Interest Rate     =           18.00%           ¦
11            ¦            Periods in Years =                3            ¦
12            ¦                                                           ¦
13            ¦                                                           ¦
14            ¦            Monthly Payments   =        $148.04            ¦
15            ¦                                                           ¦
16              ------------------------------------------------
17
18    {HOME}/RE~
19    {GOTO}D3~/RE~{DOWN}{DOWN}/RE~
20    {DOWN}{DOWN}/RE~
21    {DOWN}{DOWN}{DOWN}{RIGHT}/RE~
22    {DOWN}/RE~
23    {DOWN}{DOWN}{DOWN}/RE~
24    {HOME}
25    /XLType in Item Description: ~D3~
26    /XNEnter Purchase price: ~D5~
27    /XNEnter Down Payment: ~D7~
28    /XNYearly Interest Rate as decimal: ~E10~
29    /XNNumber of Periods in Years: ~E11~
30    {GOTO}E14~@PMT(D5-D7,E10/12,E11*12)~
31    /XIE14>200~{GOTO}C17~EXCESSIVE PAYMENT~/XLPress Enter to continue~A1~/RE~
32    /XNEnter another set of data? 1=YES 2=NO: ~A1~
33    /XIA1=1~/XGA18~
34    {HOME}
35    /XQ
 E14

Enter another set of DATA: 1=YES 2=NO
     macro                                                                INPUT
```

BASIC equivalent

```
010 D3$="":D5=0:A1=0
020 D7=0
030 E10=0
040 E11=0
050 E14=0
060 INPUT "Type in Item Description: ";D3$
070 INPUT "Enter Purchase price: ";D5
080 INPUT "Enter Down Payment: ";D7
090 INPUT "Yearly Interest Rate as a decimal: ";E10
100 INPUT "Number of periods in Years: ";E11
110 E14= (D5-D7)*((E10/12)/((1-(1+E10))^-(E11*12))))
120 IF E14>200 THEN C17$="EXCESSIVE PAYMENT":INPUT "Press Enter to continue";A1:C17$=""
130 INPUT "Enter another set of data? 1=YES 2=NO: ";A1
140 IF A1=1 THEN GOTO 10
150 END
```

/XCrange~—/XR~ Commands

The /**X**Crange~ and the /**XR**~ commands pass control to a range of commands, and return control to the point at which it was passed. The BASIC counterparts for these commands are the GOSUB and RETURN statements.

The general form of the /**X**Crange~ and /**XR**~ commands is:

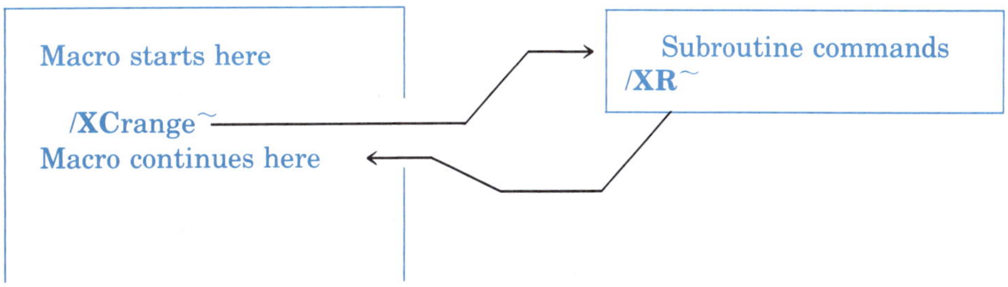

In a final addition to the example, a subroutine has been added which allows the user to get a print-out of the spreadsheet output. The subroutine prompts the user to ready the printer and then press Enter. Once the user has pressed the Enter key the subroutine defines the range to print, aligns, goes, then quits the Print Printer menu. The /**XR**~ command then returns control to the commands following the /**X**Crange~ command that passed control to the subroutine.

In the following example cells A32 and A33 and a PRINT OUT SUBROUTINE have been added to the spreadsheet in order to perform the print operation.

```
        A           B          C            D             E            F           G          H
1
2                  -----------------------------------------------
3               |  Purchase item =    Volkswagen                     |
4               |  ------------------------------                    |
5               |  Purchase Price    =    $4,995.00                  |
6               |                                                    |
7               |  Down Payment      =      $900.00                  |
8               |                                                    |
9               |  Terms                                             |
10              |  -----      Interest Rate     =          18.00%    |
11              |             Periods in Years  =              3     |
12              |                                                    |
13              |                                                    |
14              |             Monthly Payments  =        $148.04     |
15              |                                                    |
16                 -----------------------------------------------
17
18  {HOME}/RE~
19  {GOTO}D3~/RE~{DOWN}{DOWN}/RE~                  PRINT OUT SUBROUTINE
20  {DOWN}{DOWN}/RE~                               /XLReady printer then press Enter~A1~
21  {DOWN}{DOWN}{DOWN}{RIGHT}/RE~                  /PPRA1..G17~AGQ
22  {DOWN}/RE~                                     /XR~
23  {DOWN}{DOWN}{DOWN}/RE~
```

(continued on next page)

```
24  {HOME}
25  /XLType in Item Description: ~D3~
26  /XNEnter Purchase price: ~D5~
27  /XNEnter Down Payment: ~D7~
28  /XNYearly Interest Rate as decimal: ~E10~
29  /XNNumber of Periods in Years: ~E11~
30  {GOTO}E14~@PMT(D5-D7,E10/12,E11*12)~
31  /XIE14>200~{GOTO}C17~EXCESSIVE PAYMENT~/XLPress Enter to continue~A1~/RE~
32  /XNPrint out this form? 1=YES 2=NO: ~A1~
33  /XIA1=1~/XCE20~
34  /XNEnter another set of data? 1=YES 2=NO: ~A1~
35  /XIA1=1~/XGA18~
36  {HOME}
37  /XQ

Print out this form? 1=YES   2=NO
     macro                                                   INPUT
```

BASIC equivalent

```
010 D3$="":D5=0:A1=0
020 D7=0
030 E10=0
040 E11=0
050 E14=0
060 INPUT "Type in Item Description: ";D3$
070 INPUT "Enter Purchase price: ";D5
080 INPUT "Enter Down Payment: ";D7
090 INPUT "Yearly Interest Rate as a decimal: ";E10
100 INPUT "Number of periods in Years: ";E11
110 E14= (D5-D7)*((E10/12)/((1-(1+E10))^-(E11*12))))
120 IF E14>200 THEN C17$="EXCESSIVE PAYMENT":INPUT "Press Enter to continue";A1:C17$=""
130 INPUT "Print out this form? 1=YES 2=NO: ";A1
140 IF A1=1 THEN GOSUB 160
145 INPUT "Enter another set of data? 1=YES 2=NO: ";A1
148 IF A1=1 THEN GOTO 10
150 END
160 LPRINT A1$;B1$;C1$;D1$;E1$;F1$;G1$
170 LPRINT A2$;B2$;C2$;D2$;E2$;F2$;G2$
180 LPRINT A3$;B3$;C3$;D3$;E3$;F3$;G3$
190 LPRINT A4$;B4$;C4$;D4$;E4$;F4$;G4$
200 LPRINT A5$;B5$;C5$;D5;E5$;F5$;G5$
210 LPRINT A6$;B6$;C6$;D6$;E6$;F6$;G6$
220 LPRINT A7$;B7$;C7$;D7;E7$;F7$;G7$
230 LPRINT A8$;B8$;C8$;D8$;E8$;F8$;G8$
240 LPRINT A9$;B9$;C9$;D9$;E9$;F9$;G9$
250 LPRINT A10$;B10$;C10$;D10$;E10;F10$;G10$
260 LPRINT A11$;B11$;C11$;D11$;E11;F11$;G11$
270 LPRINT A12$;B12$;C12$;D12$;E12$;F12$;G12$
280 LPRINT A13$;B13$;C13$;D13$;E13$;F13$;G13$
290 LPRINT A14$;B14$;C14$;D14$;E14;F14$;G14$
300 LPRINT A15$;B15$;C15$;D15$;E15$;F15$;G15$
310 LPRINT A16$;B16$;C16$;D16$;E16$;F16$;G16$
320 LPRINT A17$;B17$;C17$;D17$;E17$;F17$;G17$
310 RETURN
```

Data Entry

Hint When you enter data into cells, watch the mode indicator at the lower right of the screen. Based on your first keystroke, VP-Planner makes an assumption about the type of data you are entering into a cell. String data beginning with a numeric character, such as 4th Street, must be entered by first typing a label prefix (',",^). Numeric data beginning with an alphabetic character, such as a cell reference, must be entered by first typing a numeric character (0 through 9, +, −,.,(,@,#,$).

Hazard If a formula displays an incorrect value that could be attributable to a cell reference value equal to zero (0), check the cells to which the formula refers to see if a number accidentally was entered as a label. If one of the cells has its data left-justified, it may well be an incorrectly entered cell. Remember that by default, values automatically are justified to the right and labels automatically are justified to the left.

Hint Use the pointing method of entering formulas for faster and more accurate results.

Hint The numeric keypad on the right side of the keyboard toggles between a ten-key or a pointer-control keypad if you tap the Num Lock key. But, it also shifts to the opposite mode if you hold down the Shift key. When you enter several cells' worth of numeric data, it is useful to leave the keypad in pointer-control mode. Shift it into its ten-key mode when you are ready to enter data into a cell. When you are done, release the Shift key and move the pointer to the next cell.

Hint You may use the F2 (EDIT) key to edit the current cell. In the EDIT mode, the cell's data are displayed at the edit line. You can use the pointer control keys (← →) to move a cursor across the data. The Home key jumps the cursor to the far left of the data; the End key jumps the cursor to the far right of the data. Pressing the Tab key jumps the cursor five characters to the right, and pressing the Shift and Tab keys jumps the cursor five characters to the left.

Any characters that you type are inserted to the left of the cursor. The Del or Backspace keys delete characters. When you are done editing, press the Enter key.

Hint Formulas and numbers may be converted to string data by inserting a label prefix as the first character in the EDIT mode.

Hint Pressing the F2 key (EDIT), and then the F9 key (CALC) converts the contents of the current cell from a formula into the constant it displays.

Hazard Beginners often find that the spreadsheet's computed answers do not agree with answers they have gotten on a calculator or by hand. The reason is that VP-Planner holds all numeric data to fifteen places of accuracy. To control the level of accuracy use the **@INT** or **@ROUND** functions. For more information refer to **@ROUND** in the "Spreadsheet Functions" and see the next Hint.

Hint The following Macro, when invoked, will edit the current cell to include the **@ROUND** function, with two decimal places of accuracy for the value that the cell computes or holds.

{**EDIT**} {**HOME**} **@ROUND** ({**END**},2)~

Hint In larger spreadsheets automatic recalculation of the entire spreadsheet will slow down data entry. You may turn off the automatic recalculation with the /**W**orksheet **G**lobal **R**ecalculation **M**anual command. When you turn it off the spreadsheet only recalculates when the F9 (CALC) key is pressed. (See next Hazard.)

Hazard When recalculation is manual, a CALC indicator at the bottom of the screen will tell you that your spreadsheet needs to be recalculated. Even so, it is an easy point to forget. To return to automatic recalculation use the /**W**orksheet **G**lobal **R**ecalculation **A**utomatic command.

Ranges

Hint When specifying a range by pointing to it, the period key may be used to shift the pointer's anchor from corner to corner. The anchor will shift each time the period key is pressed.

Hint You can use the /**R**ange **N**ame command to name areas of the spreadsheet to facilitate rapid movement about the spreadsheet with the F5 (GOTO) key. First, name a cell in a specified area of the spreadsheet with a range name. When you are ready to move to the area, press F5 and answer its "Enter address to go to:" prompt by tapping the F3 key (NAME) for a listing of your choices of named ranges; then use the menu pointer to enter the name of your choice as the answer to the prompt.

Hint The top left cell of any range is the key cell for the range. If a range has been named, and the cell is deleted with the /**W**orksheet **D**elete command, the range becomes undefined even though its name remains intact. The F5 (GOTO) key always will send the pointer to the top left cell of a named range as the address to GOTO. The top left cell is specified as the DESTINATION range for a /**C**opy or /**M**ove operation.

Cell References

Hint When pointing to cells while entering a formula, the F4 key (ABS) may be used to automatically insert dollar signs ($) into the cell reference for the cell that the pointer is currently pointing to.

Hint Moving a cell or range of cells with the /**M**ove command does not cause a change in cell references in the same manner as copying a cell or range of cells. With the /**M**ove command, all cells with references to cells within the range being moved have their references updated in a relative fashion. The updating occurs even if the references originally were entered as absolute. References within the moved range do not change unless they refer to other cells in the range.

Hint You may keep a reference to a named range absolute by inserting a dollar sign ($) in front of the range's name [for example, @**AVG**($TABLE)]. Since most named ranges are found in only one area of the spreadsheet, it is a good technique to identify them as being absolute. Otherwise, any copy operation involving a range reference will adjust the range's location in a relative fashion.

Hazard It is possible to create a cell reference that is circular. By tracking the cell references you find that they lead back to the original cell, thus forming a circle of references with every cell's displayed value dependent on that of the next. In a few esoteric applications you may do this intentionally. Usually, however, it indicates that an error has been made. Circular references are detected by VP-Planner and when one occurs, a CIRC indicator is displayed at the bottom of the screen.

Altering the Spreadsheet

Hazard Avoid using the commands /**W**orksheet **I**nsert and **D**elete **R**ows or **C**olumns to create or compact areas of the spreadsheet. Use the command /**M**ove instead to avoid accidentally inserting or deleting rows or columns important to other areas of the spreadsheet. For instance, when a row is deleted, it is deleted from the entire spreadsheet.

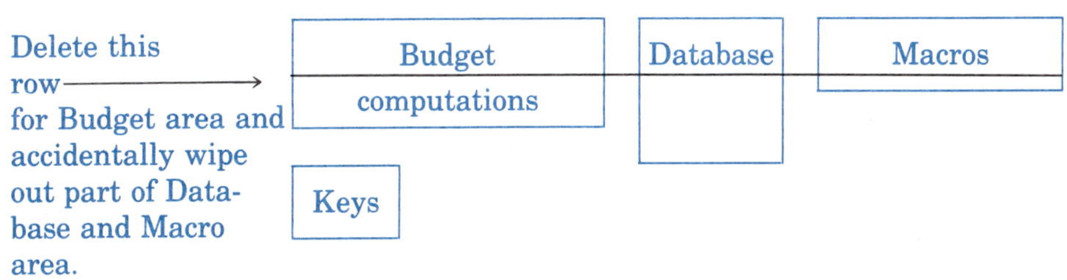

By using the /**M**ove command, you overcome the problem. Here you would /**M**ove the SOURCE range indicated to the DESTINATION range indicated.

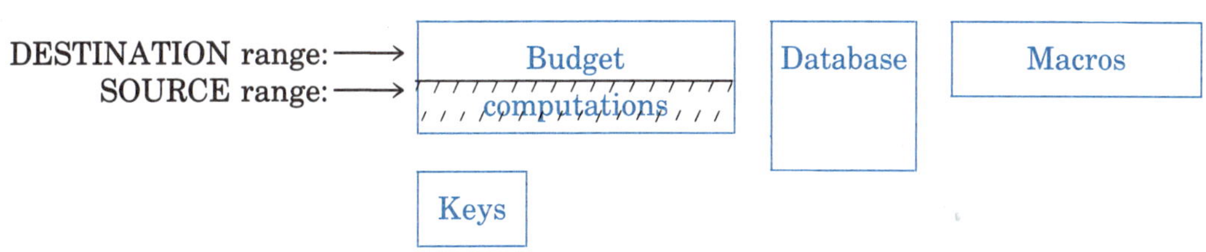

The result would be:

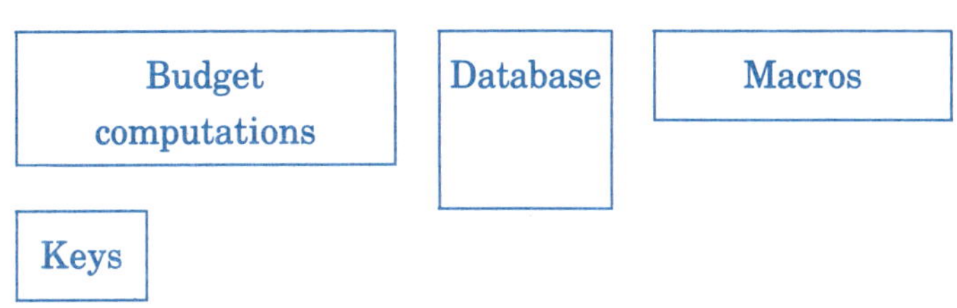

Hint Any spreadsheet data that are arranged in columns may be sorted with the /**D**ata **S**ort command. This can be useful for setting up or restructuring **@VLOOKUP** tables.

Hazard When you use the /**D**ata **S**ort commands, if one or more columns are accidentally omitted from the data range to sort, the entire set of data will probably be irreparably ruined. When several sorting operations must be done on the same data range, it is a good idea to use the /**R**ange **N**ame **C**reate command to name the range, and then use its range name to specify it after you have used the /**D**ata **S**ort **R**eset command.

Spreadsheet Design

Hint The amount of RAM memory that a spreadsheet uses is dependent on the size of its active area. The active area is defined as the rectangle large enough to contain all data entered into the cells of the spreadsheet. For example:

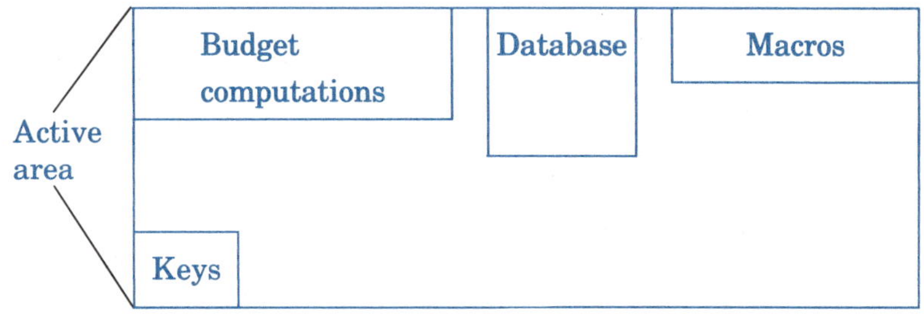

Here the active area is much larger than the area necessary to hold the spreadsheet's data, and the difference in size uses up RAM memory. You will want to consider RAM memory capacity when you map out a large spreadsheet.

Hint If you move data, delete rows and/or columns, or erase a range of cells in a spreadsheet to make available more RAM memory, the active area of the current spreadsheet remains the same and you have no immediate gain. You first must save the spreadsheet to the diskette and then retrieve it in order to realize the gain in available memory.

STUDY QUESTIONS

1. With the spreadsheet pointer on cell D2, the screen appears as:

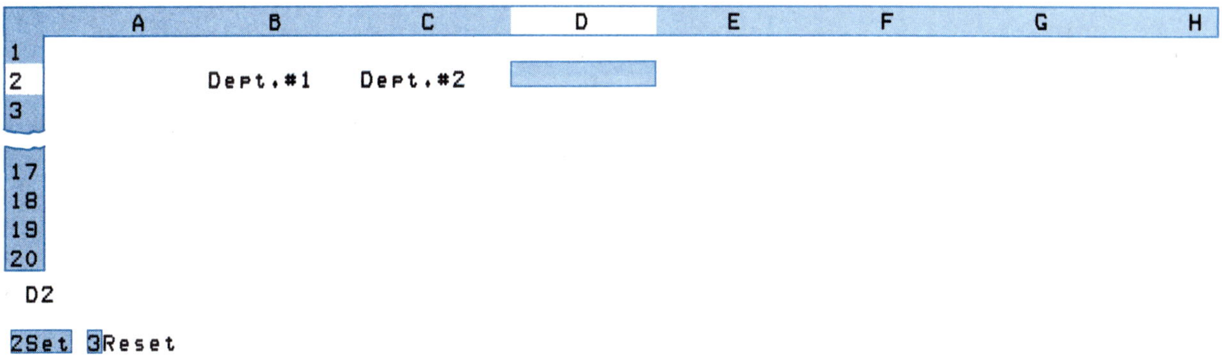

You try entering "Dept. #3" into cell D2, but instead of seeing the data being entered you hear several beeps. What is the problem?

____

____

____

2. The spreadsheet pointer is on cell B2. You are trying to enter a row of column labels. Your first label is #1 Dept. You type in the data and the screen appears as:

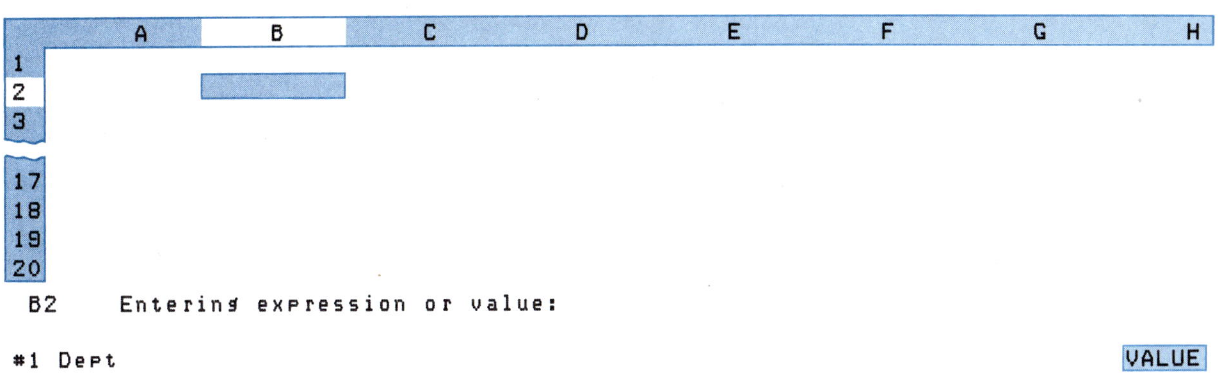

When you tap the Enter key to enter the data into B2, the computer beeps. What is the problem and how can it be solved?

____

____

____

3. The following spreadsheet is used for a simple break-even model.

	A	B	C	D	E	F	G	H
1								
2	Total Fixed Costs		=	$33,000				
3	Selling Price per Unit		=	$27				
4	Variable Costs per Unit		=	$15				
5								
6	Break-Even number of							
7	Units to Sell	=	1207					
8			=========					

a. The difference between a unit's selling price and its variable cost is the contribution margin. You determine break-even sales in units by dividing total fixed costs by a unit's contribution margin. The formula in cell C7 has been entered as +D2/D3−D4. The resulting answer of 1207, however, is wrong. The actual answer should be derived by Price − Variable cost = $12, and $33,000/$12 = 2750. What is the problem and how can it be solved?

____

____

____

b. Another way of mathematically "saying" the same thing as the formula in the last question is "the reciprocal of the contribution margin times fixed cost, or, 1/contribution margin * fixed cost." What would be an appropriate formula, using this alternate form of the equation, to enter into cell C7?

____

4. The following spreadsheet is designed to provide a simple financial forecast. The keys for the spreadsheet are: a beginning sales figure of $65,000 for the month of January; an expected growth in sales of 1.00% per month for the year; the cost of goods sold as a percent of Sales equal to 65.00%; and an expected increase of COGS amounting to .50% per month because of inflation. The cells showing percent figures hold numeric constants formatted with the /**R**ange **F**ormat **P**ercent command. All other cells holding numeric data have been formatted with the /**R**ange **F**ormat **C**urrency command (0 decimal places).

```
      A            B            C            D            E            F            G            H
1
2    198x   FINANCIAL FORECAST
3
4    January Sales    .    $65,000            COGS/SALES           =      65.00%
5    Sales Growth Rate=      1.00%            Inflation Rate       =       0.50%
6
7
8                  SALES      COGS        NET
9
10   JAN
11   FEB
12   MAR
13   APR
14   MAY
15   JUN
16   JUL
17   AUG
18   SEP
19   OCT
20   NOV
21   DEC
22
23  TOTALS
24                ------     ------     ------
```

a. The first formula you enter will be the formula to display January's sales figure. What would be an appropriate formula to enter into cell B10?

____

b. You will enter the next formula into B11. It will be the formula to display February's sales figure. The formula will be copied into the rest of the month cells in column B (B12 . . B21) with the /Copy command. What would be an appropriate formula to enter into cell B11?

____

```
      A          B          C          D          E               F        G        H
 1
 2  198x   FINANCIAL FORECAST
 3
 4  January Sales        $65,000              COGS/SALES       =       65.00%
 5  Sales Growth Rate=     1.00%              Inflation Rate   =        0.50%
 6
 7
 8              SALES      COGS       NET
 9
10  JAN        $65,000
11  FEB        $65,650
12  MAR        $66,307
13  APR        $66,970
14  MAY        $67,639
15  JUN        $68,316
16  JUL        $68,999
17  AUG        $69,689
18  SEP        $70,386
19  OCT        $71,090
20  NOV        $71,800
21  DEC        $72,518
22
23 TOTALS
24             ------     ------     ------
```

c. Next enter the formula to total the B column into cell B23. Use a spreadsheet function. Once you enter the function it will be copied into the two cells in row 23 (C23 and D23). What would be an appropriate entry for cell B23?

____

d. Next enter the formula for January's COGS into C10. The formula will be copied into the remaining cells in the column (C11 . . C21). What would be an appropriate formula to enter into cell C10?

____

e. NET is the difference between SALES and COGS for each month. The next steps in creating this forecasting spreadsheet are to enter a formula into January's NET (D10) and to copy that formula into the rest of the month's NET cells (D11 . . D21). What would be an appropriate formula to enter into D10?

____

f. Checking the spreadsheet with your calculator you find the SALES TOTALS (B23) to be off by a dollar. Why the discrepancy? How can it be remedied?

____

____

5. The next five questions refer to the following spreadsheet. The constants and formulas that are entered are shown here documented to the right on the same row in which they occur.

```
     A         B         C          D          E          F          G        H
 1
 2  Invoice Discount =    15.00%    <——0.15
 3
 4  Product #1
 5  ---------
 6  Quantity Ordered =        30    <——30
 7  Suggested Retail =    $21.95    <——21.95
 8
 9  Invoice Total     = $658.50     <——+C6*C7
10  Less Discount         $98.78    <——+$C$2*C9
11
12  Invoice Billing   = $559.73     <——+C9−C10
```

a. If a single row is inserted while the pointer is on the seventh row, how will the insertion affect the formulas in cells C9, C10, and C12? The row will be inserted just above the pointer.

```
     A         B         C          D          E          F          G        H
 1
 2  Invoice Discount =    15.00%
 3
 4  Product #1
 5  ---------
 6  Quantity Ordered =        30
 7  Suggested Retail =    $21.95
 8
 9  Invoice Total     = $658.50 <—__________
10  Less Discount         $98.78 <—__________
11
12  Invoice Billing   = $559.73 <—__________
13 ------------------------------------------------------------------------------
```

____

b. If the formula in cell C10 is copied into the second cell to its right, E10, what would be the formula in cell E10?

____

```
     A         B         C          D          E          F          G        H
 1
 2  Invoice Discount =    15.00%
 3
 4  Product #1
 5  ---------
 6  Quantity Ordered =        30
 7  Suggested Retail =    $21.95
 8
 9  Invoice Total     = $658.50
10  Less Discount         $98.78 <—— +$C$2*C9 ————————<—————————
11
12  Invoice Billing   = $559.73
 ------------------------------------------------------------------------------
```

____

c. If the formula in cell C12 is copied into cell C14 what would be the formula in cell C14?

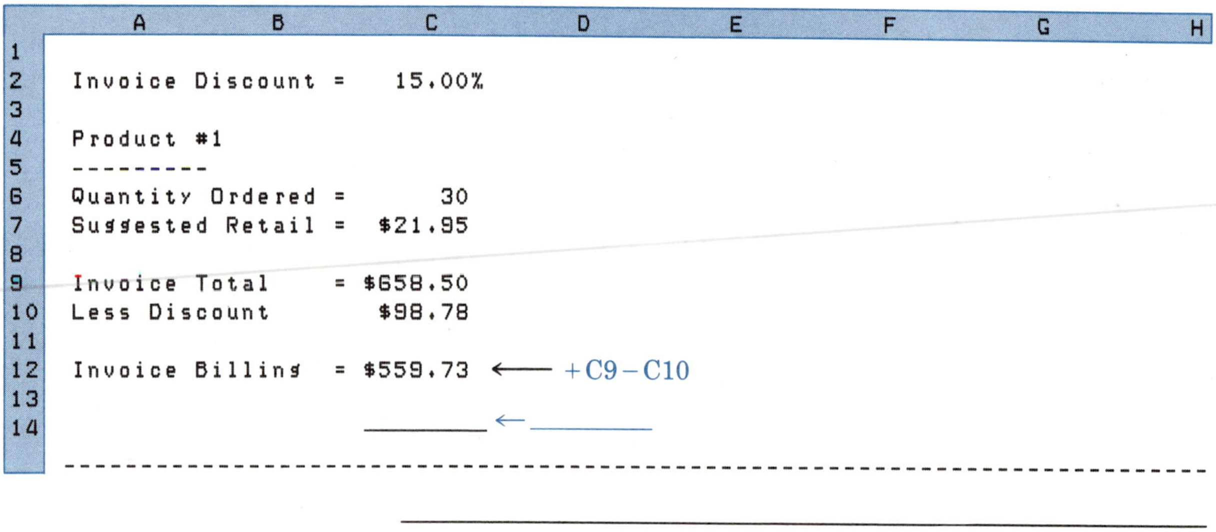

d. If the formula in cell C12 is copied into cell E9, what would be the formula in cell E9?

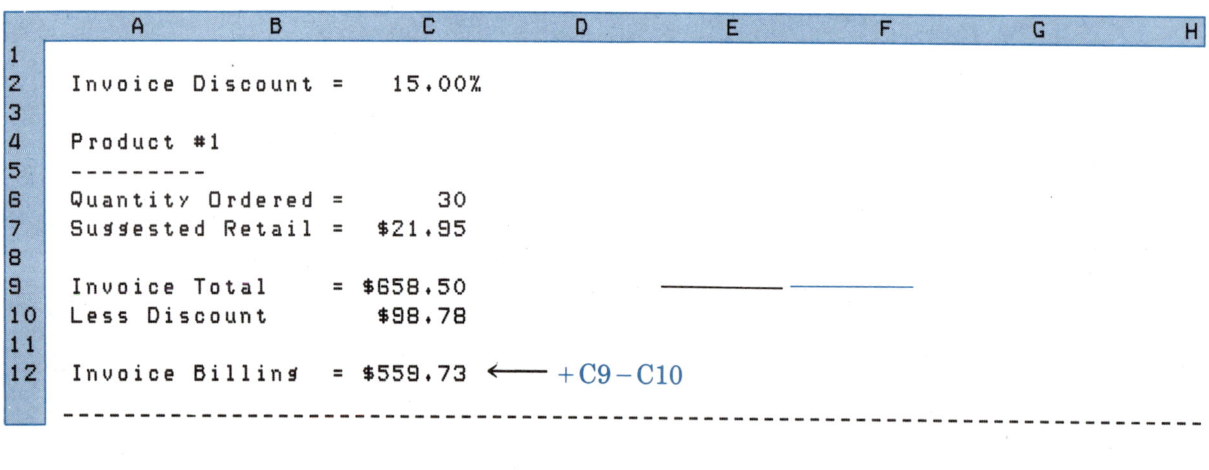

e. If the formula in cell C9 is moved to the right two cells (to E9) how does this change the formulas in cells E9, C10 and C12?

```
     A        B         C         D         E         F         G         H
1
2  Invoice Discount =    15.00%
3
4  Product #1
5  ---------
6  Quantity Ordered =        30
7  Suggested Retail =    $21.95
8
9  Invoice Total    =   $658.50
10 Less Discount         $98.78
11
12 Invoice Billing  =   $559.73
   ---------------------------------------------------------------------------
```

6. The default global column width for a spreadsheet is nine characters. If you use the /**W**orksheet **C**ol-Width **S**et command to set column C to be 12 characters wide, and then use the /**W**orksheet **G**lobal **C**ol-Width command to set the spreadsheet's cells one character wider (ten characters each), what is the effect on column C?

7. A range of cells is formatted to display currency format with zero (0) decimal places with the /**R**ange **F**ormat **C**rncy command. The spreadsheet is then global formatted to display currency format with two decimal places with the /**W**orksheet **G**lobal **F**ormat **C**rncy command. What is the effect on the previously formatted range?

8. The following spreadsheet is designed to provide budget information for a monthly period. Projected sales are compared to actual sales. A budgeted labor cost based on 17.5% of actual sales is compared to an actual labor cost, and a budgeted cost of goods sold based on 55% of actual sales is compared against actual COGS. The formulas and constants used in the spreadsheet are documented on the same line in which they occur. How might the spreadsheet have been better designed?

```
     A        B         C         D         E         F         G         H
1
2  Monthly Report    DECEMBER              1986
3  ---------------------------------------------
4  Projected Sales          =   4,500  <--- 4500
5  Actual Sales             =   5,200  <--- 5200
6  Over (Under) Projected   =     700  <--- +D5-D4
7  Budgeted Labor cost      =     910  <--- 0.175*D5
8  Actual Labor Cost        =   1,200  <--- 1200
9  Over (Under) Budget      =     290  <--- +D8-D7
10 Budgeted COGS            =   2,860  <--- 0.55*D5
11 Actual COGS              =   2,750  <--- 2750
12 Over  (Under) Budget     =   (110)  <--- +D11-D10
```

9. Describe the steps involved in making the preceding example a spreadsheet template to be used each month.

____

____

10. Use the following Inventory spreadsheet for the next six questions:

	A	B	C	D	E	F	G	H
1								
2	Item Part	Quant	Per Unit		Extensions			
3	Number	On Hand	Cost	Price	Cost	Price		
4								
5	19165	35	$1.21	$1.65	$42.35	$57.75		
6	19166	46	$ .35	$ .49	$16.10	$22.54		
7	19167	89	$3.55	$4.80	$315.95	$427.20		
8	19168	12	$2.67	$3.60	$32.04	$43.20		
9	19169	53	$2.25	$3.00	$119.25	$159.00		
10	19170	6	$1.95	$2.65	$11.70	$15.90		
11	19171	22	$1.55	$2.10	$34.10	$46.20		
12	19172	31	$5.50	$7.45	$170.50	$230.95		
13	19173	100	$3.95	$5.35	$395.00	$535.00		
14	19174	19	$4.25	$5.75	$80.75	$109.25		
15	19175	77	$ .65	$ .85	$50.05	$65.45		
16	19176	33	$1.19	$1.60	$39.27	$52.80		
17								
18	INVENTORY LEVELS							
19		Maximum Quantity =		100				
20		Minimum Quantity =		6				
21		Average Quantity =		44				
22								
23	INVENTORY COSTING AND PRICING							
24	Total Dollars/Cost Basis			=$1,307.06				
25	Avg. per Item/Cost Basis			= $108.92				
26	Average Margin Per Unit			= $ .85				

a. In cell D19 a formula using a spreadsheet function has been entered. It returns the highest value found in its argument and is used here to indicate the greatest number of quantity on hand in inventory for a single item. What is an appropriate form for the function entered into cell D19?

____

b. A similar formula has been entered into cell D20. It returns the lowest value found in its argument and is used here to indicate the item with the least number of quantity on hand in inventory. What is an appropriate form for the function entered into cell D20?

____

c. The next cell entry (D21) is a formula using a function to return the mean (average) quantity on hand. This value (43.583333) has, in turn, been rounded by another function in the formula to return the final value of 44. What is an appropriate form for the function entered in cell D21?

____

d. The extensions shown are dollar values of inventory based on per unit cost or selling price times quantity on hand. Cell D24, under the label INVENTORY COSTING AND PRICING, contains a function returning the total inventory dollar amount of the cost extensions. What would be an appropriate formula for cell D24?

____

e. The next formula, in cell D25, computes the average inventory value per item inventoried. The formula can be written using two functions to arrive at its value. What would be an appropriate formula to enter into cell D25?

____

f. The final formula computes the average per unit margin. Margin is the difference between a unit's cost and its price. What would be an appropriate formula to enter into cell D26?

____

11. Use the same Inventory Spreadsheet with some modifications for the last three questions:

	A	B	C	D	E	F	G	H
1						Min. Stock	level =	30
2	Item Part	Quant	Per	Unit	Order	Max. Stock	level =	100
3	Number	On Hand	Cost	Price	Quantity	Max. Order	Cost =	$80.00
4						Min. Order	Quant =	50
5	19165	35	$1.21	$1.65	65			
6	19166	46	$ .35	$ .49	54			
7	19167	89	$3.55	$4.80	0			
8	19168	12	$2.67	$3.60	88			
9	19169	53	$2.25	$3.00	0			
10	19170	6	$1.95	$2.65	94			
11	19171	22	$1.55	$2.10	78			
12	19172	31	$5.50	$7.45	0			
13	19173	100	$3.95	$5.35	0			
14	19174	19	$4.25	$5.75	81			
15	19175	77	$ .65	$ .85	0			
16	19176	33	$1.19	$1.60	67			
17	----------	----------	----------	----------	----------	----------	----------	
18								
19	PRICE LOOK UP		Item Part Number =		19169			
20	================|					>USER INPUT		
21			Quantity Ordered =		65			
22								
23	Unit Price	=	$2.25					
24	Back Order	=	12					
25	----------	----------	----------	----------	----------	----------	----------	

a. The column on the right (Order Quantity) has had a formula entered and copied into it. The formula uses a logical function with logical operators to display the number of items to order from the manufacturer. The function in effect says, "If the quantity on hand is less than 30, then display an order quantity of 100 minus the quantity on hand for the item (to bring the stock level up to 100 units of the item). If the cost of the item times the quantity needed to bring its stock level up to 100 is less than $80.00, and the quantity to order is greater than 50, display the quantity to order as 100 – (quantity on hand for the item). If condition one and condition two are not true, display the value zero."

The keys for the formula are held in cells H1 through H4 and are referenced by the original formula entered into cell E5. What would be an appropriate formula, suitable for copying into the rest of the cells in the column, to enter into cell E5?

____

b. At the bottom of the spreadsheet is an area designed to look up prices in the inventory part of the spreadsheet. Cells E19 and E21 are set aside for the user to enter in the sales order part number and quantity for any item inventoried.

The formula in C23 uses the data entered into the cell E19 to search for, then display, the unit price for the item with that part number. What would be an appropriate formula to enter into cell C23?

____

c. The final formula in the spreadsheet (in cell C24) performs the following action: if the quantity ordered is greater than the quantity on hand then the difference is displayed with the label "Back Order"; otherwise, the value zero is displayed there. What would be an appropriate formula to enter into cell C24?

____

VP-PLANNER KEY TERM GLOSSARY

Anchoring The process of establishing the starting cell address of a range by pressing the period key.

Cell The intersection of a column and a row on a spreadsheet.

Cell Addresses The letter and number identification of a spreadsheet cell.

Command Pointer The reverse video that appears around a VP-Planner command. The command pointer can be moved across the screen with the pointer control keys. Pressing the enter key while the command pointer is on a particular command executes that command.

Control Panel Bottom four window lines comprised of the Status Line, Edit Line, Menu Line, and Message Line.

Database A collection of related data kept in the form of records.

Database Management Systems An application software that manages the storage, access, maintenance, and updating of a database.

Font A style of print.

Freeze A feature that prevents rows or columns from scrolling off the screen.

Function Precoded routines that perform a series of operations or calculations quickly; functions are often shortcuts to accomplish what would otherwise require a long numeric expression.

Global Affecting an entire set of data.

Keyboard Macro A collection of keystrokes entered as labels into a cell or a group of cells. Macros are used as shortcuts to accomplish a routine with a single keystroke.

Label A string expression entered into a cell.

Label Prefix A prefix that precedes a label and formats the label in its cells (' " ^ \).

Legend An explanatory text that identifies what various parts of a graph represent.

Modeling A process of testing various scenarios. The process allows you to ask "What if . . ." and receive a prompt answer through the rapid recalculation of the spreadsheet.

Range of Cells Specified rectangular block of cells.

Scroll The vertical or horizontal movement of data on a monitor screen.

Spreadsheet Data File The data of a spreadsheet that is saved to a file on a diskette with the extension .WKS.

Spreadsheet Text File The output of a spreadsheet printed to a file with the extension .PRN.

Synchronize To scroll two separate spreadsheets as they appear in two different windows.

Template A master copy of a spreadsheet, parts of which can be updated, so that the initial spreadsheet design can be used more than once.

Tree diagram A command summary that details progressively more specific layers of commands.

Value A number or formula that is entered into a cell.

Window A split screen which allows the user to view two separate portions of the spreadsheet simultaneously.

Window Lines Four lines that appear at the bottom of the monitor screen that is used by VP-Planner to display information about current operations.

MODULE OUTLINE

INTRODUCTION

WordPerfect Basics

TUTORIAL EXERCISES

EXERCISE 1: Creating a Document File | EXERCISE 2: WordPerfect's Basic Editing Operations | EXERCISE 3: Practice Revisions | EXERCISE 4: Formatting Text | EXERCISE 5: Practice Reformatting the Document | EXERCISE 6: Saving a Document | EXERCISE 7: Printing a Document | EXERCISE 8: The Concept of Boiler Plating

WORDPERFECT OPERATION AND COMMAND SUMMARY

WordPerfect Quick Reference Command Index | WordPerfect Control Keys | WordPerfect Full Command Index | WordPerfect Command Summary | WordPerfect Codes

Learning WordPerfect

WordPerfect is an application software designed to do word processing. It allows the user to create text by typing characters on the computer's keyboard. As the text is typed, it is entered into RAM (random access memory). The computer then can be used to manipulate the data. Manipulating text data is the primary function of word processing software. When the text has been manipulated into its finished form, the word processing software's commands can be used to print the text on the printer.

This module begins with a brief discussion of WordPerfect basics and file handling. It continues with tutorial exercises that present the operations used to create, edit, format, and print a text file. The tutorial exercises then present the commands and techniques used in a timesaving procedure called *boiler plating*. Here the exercises provide you with the opportunity to practice the word processing operations covered in the tutorial.

The tutorial is followed by a WordPerfect operation and command summary, which briefly describes WordPerfect's full range of commands and control key operations. Here you also will find a convenient WordPerfect quick reference command index that gives the most commonly used WordPerfect commands.

As you progress through the material, you may notice slight differences between the menus and commands presented here and those shown on your monitor screen. These differences occur because of minor changes made to different versions of WordPerfect.

WordPerfect Basics

Typing on Electronic Pages

WordPerfect is designed primarily to process string data. When you type the data on the keyboard, your words, sentences, and paragraphs appear on the monitor screen much as they would appear on a piece of paper in a typewriter. A small blinking cursor on the screen indicates where the next character that you type will appear.

As you continue to type, the lines of text begin to scroll on the monitor screen in the same way that paper feeds through a typewriter when the carriage return is pressed. When one screen's worth of text is complete, the text at the top of the screen scrolls up and disappears to make room at the bottom of the screen for new lines of text. Although the text disappears from view, the computer continues to hold it as part of the data in the file. You may use various WordPerfect commands to scroll text back and forth to review text that is not currently displayed on the screen.

When you have typed a printed page worth of text (default of 55 lines), WordPerfect displays a line of dashes across the screen (called a *page break*) to indicate that a new page is about to begin. The "electronic pages" of text are connected as new pages are added for every 55 lines of text typed.

WordPerfect refers to the text files you create in this manner as *documents,* or *document files.*

Manipulating String Data

As you enter text, you may move the cursor to edit any previously entered word, sentence, or paragraph. *Editing* a document involves either revising data by changing the written content of the text or formatting data by changing the appearance of the text. *Revisions* include operations such as deleting words, inserting words, moving paragraphs, and correcting misspellings. *Formatting* includes such operations as centering text, changing line spacing and margins, boldfacing, and underlining. WordPerfect's commands enable you to perform such data manipulations.

WordPerfect Command Structure

WordPerfect provides menu commands to accomplish the revision and formatting operations. The command mode of WordPerfect is entered by typing certain keystrokes and keystroke combinations. The first keystroke in a keystroke combination will be the Ctrl, Shift, or Alt key. The second keystroke in a keystroke combination will be a Function key (see WordPerfect Control Keys, page W–36, for information on the location of the keys on the keyboard).

The Keyboard Command Template

WordPerfect provides a keyboard template to place over the Function keys on the keyboard. The template is essential to a beginning WordPerfect user because it lists the 40 main commands of WordPerfect—essentially it can be thought of as WordPerfect's main menu of commands. There are four such commands for each of the 10 Function keys. The four commands for each Function key are color coded to describe the keystroke or keystroke combination used to execute them, where

Red = Ctrl

Green = Shift

Blue = Alt

Black = Function key

To execute a command shown in red, green, or blue, you first press and hold the appropriate control key (Ctrl, Shift, or Alt), and then press the Function key. To execute a command shown in black, you simply press the Function key.

WordPerfect Menus

When many of the WordPerfect commands are executed, they present menus of additional commands. The additional commands are selected by typing their number or letter. For instance, on the keyboard template next to Function key 1, the command Super/Subscript is shown in green. If you press and hold the Shift key and then type the F1 key, the following menu will be displayed on the screen:

```
1 Superscript; 2 Subscript; 3 Overstrike; 4 Adv Up; 5 Adv Dn; 6 Adv Ln: 0
```

If your intention is to superscript text in the document, you would press 1.

Command Conventions

In this module, the keystrokes used to execute a command are shown with a dash (-) to indicate keystroke combinations. Commas are used to separate the keystrokes. For instance, in the last example the keystrokes used to superscript text would be shown in the manual as **Shift-F1, 1.**

WordPerfect's File Handling

WordPerfect, with all of its features, is a large software that could consume a considerable amount of RAM. In addition, as document files become several pages long, they rapidly use up RAM. WordPerfect circumvents the memory's size limits by keeping in RAM only the data currently needed. The rest of the data is maintained on disks and are brought into RAM as necessary.

How WordPerfect is Loaded into RAM

To use the full extent of its commands, the WordPerfect software requires that four diskettes be available during editing. The diskettes are labeled "WordPerfect," "Speller," "Thesaurus," and "Learning."

The basic word processing software of WordPerfect is kept on the WordPerfect diskette. During normal editing operations, the WordPerfect diskette must be kept in the disk drive. Software comprising other features of WordPerfect, such as its spelling checker, thesaurus, and on-line help facility (found on the Learning diskette), are kept individually on the other three diskettes. To use the other features of WordPerfect, the other diskettes must be inserted into the disk drive when needed.

Because of its total size, WordPerfect is best suited for computers having a hard disk. By copying all of the data comprising WordPerfect onto the hard disk, you eliminate the need to change disks each time you use a special feature of the software.

How Document Files are Loaded and Saved

When you first load WordPerfect into RAM, the software allows you to immediately begin entering text to create a document file. As you type, the data you enter begins to use up memory. When the memory of the computer becomes full, WordPerfect begins to save parts (blocks) of the document onto temporary files on the WordPerfect disk. Once a block of data is copied onto a diskette file, the space it has occupied in RAM may be erased to make room for new data.

If you move backwards in the text to correct errors or add data, and the section on which you want to work is not in RAM, WordPerfect copies what is in RAM onto the diskette file. It then reads the section on which you want to work into the memory space that was freed up. A current file being moved between RAM and disk storage in this fashion is called an *open* file.

When you are through creating and editing a document, you must use the appropriate WordPerfect commands to *close* the file. Closing a file causes all data in the document to be saved to your disk. The document will be saved under the name you give it at the time you save it.

Learning WordPerfect

WordPerfect is best learned by using it. Although you may be able to learn the fundamentals of creating and editing standard document files in just a few hours, the full set of WordPerfect commands and operations may take months to learn.

Getting Help

One WordPerfect command, Help, provides an extensive on-line summary of information on the various commands of WordPerfect. To use the Help facility, you type **F3** (Help) and then follow the instructions shown to access various command topics. The data used to provide the Help facility are on the WordPerfect diskette labeled "Learning." You may need to insert the Learning diskette into the disk drive as instructed to use the Help command. When finished with the Help facility, you press the Space or ↵ key to return to the editing mode.

REQUIRED MATERIALS

1. An IBM DOS Diskette
2. A WordPerfect program diskette
3. Your files diskette
4. A WordPerfect keyboard template
5. This manual
6. Other ______________________________

Tutorial Conventions

During the WordPerfect tutorial, you will create several small text files using various WordPerfect commands. The conventions used in the tutorial's instructions are:

↵	The bent arrow means to press the Enter key located on the right side of the keyboard.
key-key	Press and hold the first key, then type the next key shown.
key, key	Type the first key, then type the second key.
[ ]	Do not type the brackets; type only what is inside them.

HOW TO GET OUT OF TROUBLE

If you want to:	*Then:*
■ Backspace and erase characters to the left of the cursor . . .	■ Tap the Backspace key located on the far right side of the top row.
■ Erase a line of text . . .	■ Move the cursor to the line to be erased and press the Home key, the Cursor left key, and then type **Ctrl-End.**
■ Stop a command operation and return to editing the document . . .	■ Type **F1** (Cancel).
■ Stop the tutorial to continue later . . .	■ Type **F7, Y,** B:WPTUT↵, Y.
■ Continue with the tutorial after stopping . . .	■ After loading WordPerfect into RAM, type **Shift-F10,** B:WPTUT↵.

Getting Started

1. Insert the DOS diskette into the A: disk drive (the disk drive on the left) and close the disk drive door.
2. Insert your files diskette into the B: disk drive (the disk drive on the right) and close the disk drive door.
3. If the computer already is on, press and hold the Ctrl and Alt keys and then tap the Del key. Otherwise, turn on the computer and the monitor.

In a few moments, DOS will be loaded automatically.

4. Answer DOS's date and time prompts.
5. When you see the A> on the screen, remove the DOS diskette from the

A: disk drive and insert the WordPerfect program diskette into the disk drive.

6. Put the WordPerfect keyboard template over the Function keys on the keyboard.
7. Type [WP↵].

If you are using the Training Version of WordPerfect or your WordPerfect diskette has not been installed for a printer, WordPerfect will pause and display one or two screens of information. After reading the screens, type ↵ to continue.

Your system ______________________________

____

____

____

EXERCISE 1: Creating a Document File

When WordPerfect is first loaded, you are presented with a blank screen onto which you may enter text. A blinking cursor should appear on the first position of the first line on the screen. At the bottom of the screen, a "status line" appears, which is used to display various messages about current editing operations. This is where many of WordPerfect's menus of commands will appear.

Entering Text

You are going to type part of a form letter prepared for prospective renters inquiring about units in a townhouse complex. As you enter the following text, be certain to type ↵ (Enter) only when the tutorial indicates that you are to do so. To correct typing errors as you go, use the Backspace key (top row, right side of keyboard) to backspace and erase characters you have typed.

1. Type [↵↵ Thank you for your interest in Vista Ridge Townhouses. We feel that our one and two bedroom deluxe townhouse apartments offer adult living at its finest.↵↵ Each large unit has wall to wall carpeting, drapes, private patio and sun deck with a breath-taking view. In addition you will find the townhouse of your choice equipped with self-defrosting refrigerator, self-cleaning oven, dishwasher and garbage disposal unit.↵ ↵]

At this point the screen should appear as:

```

Thank you for your interest in Vista Ridge Townhouses.  We feel
that our one and two bedroom deluxe townhouse apartments offer
adult living at its finest.

Each large unit has wall to wall carpeting, drapes, private patio
and sun deck with a breath-taking view.  In addition you will
find the townhouse of your choice equipped with self-defrosting
refrigerator, self-cleaning oven, dishwasher and garbage disposal
unit.

_

                                    Doc 1  Pg 1  Ln 13     Pos 10
```

How WordPerfect Manipulates String Data as It Is Entered

As you enter text, the *word wrap* feature of WordPerfect automatically begins a new line when the right margin of the current line is reached. If you want to begin a new line of text before you have reached the end of the previous line (such as when you want to begin a new paragraph), you must press the Enter key. Pressing the Enter key stops the word wrap and moves the cursor forward to the next line.

Hard and Soft Returns

When a line is automatically wrapped to the next line by WordPerfect, the line is ended with what is known as a *soft return*. Groups of lines having soft return endings are considered by WordPerfect to be paragraphs of words. When a line is ended by typing ↵ (Enter), the line is ended by what is known as a *hard return*. A hard return separates paragraphs in WordPerfect.

Adding Text to a File

You will now finish the body of the text of the form letter.

1. Enter the text necessary to bring this document to the form shown in the following screen.

```
Thank you for your interest in Vista Ridge Townhouses.  We feel
that our one and two bedroom deluxe townhouse apartments offer
adult living at its finest.

Each large unit has wall to wall carpeting, drapes, private patio
and sun deck with a breath-taking view.  In addition you will
find the townhouse of your choice equipped with self-defrosting
refrigerator, self-cleaning oven, dishwasher and garbage disposal
unit.

Every tenant enjoys year round swimming and sauna plus use of our
recreation room and tennis courts.

We are located in the South West Heights area, close to shopping,
city parks and University campus.  For an appointment to view one
of our fine townhouse apartments and a tour of the grounds,
please call Mr. Smith at (503) 244-7163.



                                      Doc 1  Pg 1  Ln 20     Pos 10
```

EXERCISE 2: WordPerfect's Basic Editing Operations

The basic editing operations of WordPerfect are revisional by nature. They allow you to change the content of the text by deleting and inserting characters, words, and larger units of text. To perform such operations, certain keystrokes are used. The general steps involved are:

1. Move the cursor to the location where the change is to be made.
2. Use the appropriate keystrokes to make the change.

Moving the Cursor through a Document

The right side of the keyboard has a numeric keypad that contains four keys with arrows on them. These keys (cursor control keys) may be used to move the cursor one character (Pos) to the left or right and one line (Ln) up or down by typing the key with the appropriate directional arrow on it.

1. Use the cursor control keys to move the cursor under the *c* in *city* by following the path indicated in the following text.

```
We are located in the South West Heights area, close to shopping,
city parks and University campus.  For an appointment to view one
of our fine townhouse apartments and a tour of the grounds,
please call Mr. Smith at (503) 244-7163.
_
```

2. Watch the cursor move as you tap the cursor left key (←) three or four times. Now tap the cursor right key (→) five or six times.

Notice that when you attempt to move the cursor past the left or right margins of text, the cursor follows the word wrap path (either backwards or forwards) that was set when you entered the text.

Where the Cursor May Not Be Moved

The various cursor movement commands of WordPerfect may be used to move the cursor anywhere on the screen where characters of text exist. The cursor may not be moved to areas where there are no text characters. To demonstrate, do the following.

1. Move the cursor to under the *r* in *our* in the third paragraph.

```
Every tenant enjoys year round swimming and sauna plus use of our
recreation room and tennis courts.

We are located in the South West Heights area, close to shopping,
```

2. Tap the Cursor Down key. Then tap it again.

Notice that the cursor jumped to the last character entered in the line to which it was being moved.

3. Now, with the cursor on line 15 (the status line displays the cursor's current line (Ln) location), try to move the cursor to the right.

Since no characters are entered into line 15, the cursor moves to the next line down following the word wrap.

When you want to move the cursor to an area of the screen where no characters exist, you may use the Space bar or Tab key to enter spaces or tabs (which are characters) into a line of text to move the cursor to the desired character position (displayed as Pos on the status line).

WordPerfect Cursor Control Keys

There are several keystrokes and keystroke combinations used to move the cursor around in a document. While the WordPerfect keyboard template summarizes some of them, it is best to memorize the full list in order to use the word processing software most efficiently. To gain experience in some of the cursor control key operations, do the following.

4. Read the following table and practice the cursor control keystrokes shown in color.

Cursor Movement	Keystroke
Character Left	Left
Character Right	Right
Line Up	Up
Line Down	Down
Word Left	Ctrl-Left
Word Right	Ctrl-Right
Forward to Character a	Ctrl-Home a
Beginning of Line	Home, Left
End of Line	Home, Right
Top of File	Home, Home, Up
Bottom of File	Home, Home, Down
To Page nn	Ctrl-Home, nn
Screen Up	− (Numeric Keypad)
Screen Down	+ (Numeric Keypad)
Page Up	PgUp
Page Down	PgDn
Previous Position	Ctrl-Home, Ctrl-Home
Column Left	Ctrl-Home, Left
Column Right	Ctrl-Home, Right

Revising a Paragraph of Text

Now that you are able to move the cursor throughout your document, you are ready to learn the basic word processing commands that allow you to revise text by inserting, deleting, or typing over characters, words, or lines of text.

Insert or Typeover Text

At the bottom of the numeric keypad (the cursor control keys), there is a key marked "Ins" for Insert. The Ins key is used to switch WordPerfect between one of two editing modes, Insert and Typeover. The default mode is Insert.

1. If you see a Typeover message displayed on the left side of the status line, type the Ins key to switch WordPerfect back to the Insert mode.
2. Move the cursor to the first line of the second paragraph, and then to under the *u* in *unit.*

```
Each large unit has wall to wall carpeting, drapes, private patio
and sun deck with a breath-taking view.  In addition you will
find the townhouse of your choice equipped with self-defrosting
refrigerator, self-cleaning oven, dishwasher and garbage disposal
unit.
```

3. Now type [apartment].

The paragraph now should appear as:

```
Each large apartment unit has wall to wall carpeting, drapes, private patio
and sun deck with a breath-taking view.  In addition you will
find the townhouse of your choice equipped with self-defrosting
refrigerator, self-cleaning oven, dishwasher and garbage disposal
unit.
```

When the Insert mode is on, any characters that you type will be inserted into the text to the left of the cursor.

4. Now move the cursor with one of the cursor control keys.

```
Each large apartment unit has wall to wall carpeting, drapes,
private patio and sun deck with a breath-taking view.  In
addition you will find the townhouse of your choice equipped with
self-defrosting refrigerator, self-cleaning oven, dishwasher and
garbage disposal unit.
```

Notice that WordPerfect automatically rewraps the lines in a paragraph when revisions are made to it. This is referred to by WordPerfect as its "screen rewrite" feature.

5. Press the Ins key once.

Notice that the Typeover message appears on the left side of the status line.

6. Now move the cursor under the *a* in *apartment* and type [townhouse].

The paragraph now should appear as:

```
Each large townhouse unit has wall to wall carpeting, drapes,
private patio and sun deck with a breath-taking view.  In
addition you will find the townhouse of your choice equipped with
self-defrosting refrigerator, self-cleaning oven, dishwasher and
garbage disposal unit.
```

When the Typeover mode is on, any characters that you type will type over (overwrite) existing characters of text.

Deleting Text

There are several keystrokes and keystroke combinations that may be used to delete text from a document. The following table describes many of them:

Delete Operation	Keystroke
Current Character	Del
Previous Character	Backspace
Current Word	Ctrl-Backspace
Current Word Left	Home, Backspace
Current Word Right	Home, Del
End of Line	Ctrl-End
End of Page	Ctrl-PgDn

Deleting Characters

1. Move the cursor down one line and under the *w* in *with.*

```
Each large townhouse unit has wall to wall carpeting, drapes,
private patio and sun deck with a breath-taking view.  In
addition you will find the townhouse of your choice equipped with
self-defrosting refrigerator, self-cleaning oven, dishwasher and
garbage disposal unit.
```

The Del key found on the numeric keypad may be used to delete the character above the cursor.

2. Tap the Del key three times.

The Backspace key is used to delete the character to the immediate left of the cursor. If the Typeover mode is on, the characters are replaced with spaces. If the Insert mode is on, the characters are deleted from the text and the space is closed up.

3. Move the cursor four characters to the right (under the *b* in the word *breath-taking*). Use the Ins key to make sure the Insert mode is on, and then tap the Backspace key four times.

Deleting Words

Another delete operation uses the keystroke combination Ctrl-Backspace to delete the word at the cursor location. A word is defined by WordPerfect to be a group of characters separated from other groups by spaces, or the group of spaces to the right of the cursor.

4. Move the cursor to under any letter in the word *breath-taking* and type Ctrl-Backspace.

Deleting Lines of Text

The final delete operation to be discussed here is one which deletes the line to the right of the cursor. The keystroke combination used is Ctrl-End. Although these exercises do not include a demonstration of the operation, you will find the keystroke combination to be very useful when you need to delete small sections of text.

The Cancel Command—WordPerfect's Panic Button

One of the first commands one should become familiar with is WordPerfect's Cancel command (**F1**). The Cancel command may be used to abort or exit from WordPerfect commands. The Cancel key also may be used to recover any or all of the last three text deletions or Typeover text.

Recovering Deleted Text

To recover text, you move the cursor to the position where you want the recovered text to appear and then type **F1.** The most recent deletion will appear on the screen at the cursor location. The "(**2**) Show Previous Deletion" command may be used to continuously scroll through the last three deletions, with each deletion appearing on the screen in order. When the appropriate deletion is displayed on the screen, you type **1** to recover it, or type Cancel (**F1**) to abort the recovery operation.

EXERCISE 3: Practice Revisions

1. Use the methods of your choice to insert, overwrite, and/or delete the words in the paragraph so that it appears as follows.

```
Each large townhouse unit has wall to wall carpeting, drapes,
private patio and sun deck.  You will also find the townhouse of
your choice equipped with a modern self-defrosting refrigerator,
self-cleaning oven, dishwasher and garbage disposal unit.
```

EXERCISE 4: Formatting Text

WordPerfect Format Codes

When WordPerfect commands and keystrokes are used to format text, codes are imbedded into the document. The codes that format text tend to fall into three general categories: hard and soft codes; format forward codes; and start and stop codes. The following discusses each category as it presents the more important or most used formatting commands and keystrokes in WordPerfect.

Hard and Soft Codes

Soft codes are, for the most part, codes which WordPerfect generates and automatically inserts into a document. *Hard codes* are generated by the user. For instance, you learned earlier that WordPerfect inserts soft returns at the ends of lines when it wraps text, and that typing the Enter key produces a hard return at the end of a line. The soft return is flexible; it can be (and is) moved when a paragraph is rewritten. A hard return is inflexible;

WordPerfect will not automatically move or remove it from the end of a line.

Deleting Unwanted Codes—The Reveal Codes Command

The WordPerfect command Reveal Codes is designed to allow you to see and, if desired, delete imbedded codes from the document. It may be used by typing **Alt-F3.**

1. Move the cursor to under the *E* in *Every* (first letter, third paragraph) and type **Alt-F3.**

The screen will appear:

```
your choice equipped with a modern self-defrosting refrigerator,
self-cleaning oven, dishwasher and garbage disposal unit.

Every tenant enjoys year round swimming and sauna plus use of our
recreation room and tennis courts.

We are located in the South West Heights area, close to shopping,
                                             Doc 1  Pg 1  Ln 12     Pos 10
{    ▲    ▲    ▲    ▲    ▲    ▲    ▲    ▲    ▲    ▲    ▲    ▲   ]▲    ▲    ▲
your choice equipped with a modern self[-]defrosting refrigerator,[SRt]
self[-]cleaning oven, dishwasher and garbage disposal unit.[HRt]
[HRt]
Every tenant enjoys year round swimming and sauna plus use of our[SRt]
recreation room and tennis courts.[HRt]
[HRt]
We are located in the South West Heights area, close to shopping,[SRt]
```

The top portion of the screen displays your document as it appears during editing. The bottom portion of the screen displays the same text with its imbedded codes. Codes appearing in the text will be highlighted and enclosed in brackets. The code [SRt] indicates a soft return, and the code [HRt] indicates a hard return. The code [-] indicates a hard hyphen has been entered. (Refer to the WordPerfect Operation and Command Summary under Format Line, Hyphenation, for a discussion of hard and soft hyphens.)

The cursors appearing in the top and bottom portions of the screen may be moved at the same time using the cursor control keys. This feature allows you to move about and scroll through the text without leaving the Reveal Codes screen.

2. Watch the bottom portion of the screen and move the cursor to the left two characters.

The bottom cursor should now be between the period and the [HRt] code at the end of line 10 (see the status line now located in the middle of the screen to determine the current cursor line).

The Del and Backspace keys may be used to delete codes from a document while in the Reveal Codes screen.

3. Tap the Del key once. Then tap it again.

Notice that when the Del key is typed in the Reveal Codes screen, it deletes the character or code to the immediate right of the bottom cursor.

4. Type **F1** (Cancel) to exit the Reveal Codes screen.
5. Now tap the Space bar twice to insert spaces between the last two sentences of the second paragraph.

By removing the hard returns that separate them, you are able to combine paragraphs.

Other Hard and Soft Codes

Hard and Soft Page Breaks

WordPerfect generates soft page breaks [SPg] every 55 lines of text. You can force a page break to occur by typing Ctrl-↵. A [HPg] code will be inserted into the text.

Hard Spaces

If you do not want two or more words to be separated from each other when WordPerfect wraps a line in a paragraph, you can insert hard spaces between the words. To produce a hard space, you type Home, Space. A [ ] code will be inserted into the text.

All of the hard codes can be directly deleted with the Backspace or Del keys without using the Reveal Codes screen. The same is not true for other types of codes.

Format Forward Codes

Many of the codes imbedded into a document by WordPerfect are "Format forward" in nature. To demonstrate how such codes work, you will use a command to imbed a code into the document that changes the left and right margins.

Changing Left and Right Margins

1. Move the cursor to the beginning of paragraph two, under the *E* in *Each*.
2. Type **Shift-F8** (Format Line).

The Format Line command presents a menu of commands. At the bottom of the screen, you should see the menu:

```
1 2 Tabs; 3 Margins; 4 Spacing; 5 Hyphenation; 6 Align Char:0
```

The command to select from the menu is **3**, Margins.

3. Type [**3**].

The prompt "[Margin Set] 10 74 to Left =" indicates that the current (default) margins are left = 10 and right = 74, and that you are to enter the new margin settings.

4. Type [5↵80↵] to set the left margin to 5 characters and the right margin to 80 characters.

The screen will now appear as:

```
     Thank you for your interest in Vista Ridge Townhouses.  We feel
     that our one and two bedroom deluxe townhouse apartments offer
     adult living at its finest.

Each large townhouse unit has wall to wall carpeting, drapes, private patio
and sun deck. You will also find the townhouse of your choice equipped with
a modern self-defrosting refrigerator, self-cleaning oven, dishwasher and
garbage disposal unit.  Every tenant enjoys year round swimming and sauna
plus use of our recreation room and tennis courts.

We are located in the South West Heights area, close to shopping, city parks
and University campus.  For an appointment to view one of our fine townhouse
apartments and a tour of the grounds, please call Mr. Smith at (503) 244-
7163.

                                              Doc 1  Pg 1  Ln 7      Pos 5
```

When the Margins command was executed, WordPerfect inserted a [Margin Set:5,80] code into the document at the cursor location.

5. Type **Alt-F3** (Reveal Codes) to see the imbedded code. When finished, type **F1** (Cancel) to return to the editing screen.

Notice that all of the text following the [Margin Set:] code was rewritten to fit the new left and right margins. A format forward code affects all of the following text up to the end of the document, or until another similar code is encountered.

6. Move the cursor to under the *W* in *We* in the last paragraph and repeat the previous steps to set the margins Left = 20, Right = 55. Next, tap the cursor left key to view the text centered on the screen.

Deleting Format Forward Codes

You may use the Reveal Codes screen to delete codes that affect the document in a format forward manner, or you may often delete them using the Backspace or Del keys without entering the Reveal Codes screen.

1. Move the cursor under the *E* in *Each* in the second paragraph and type the Backspace key.

Notice the message "Delete [Margin Set]? (Y/N)" at the bottom of the screen. If you now type Y, the code will be deleted from the document. If you type any other key, the code will not be deleted.

2. Use the method of your choice to delete the two [Margin Set:] codes that are in the document.
3. Now move to the top row on the screen (at the beginning of the file) and use the Format Line, Margins command to set the left margin to 8 and the right margin to 70.

Changing Line Spacing

Another useful formatting command is the Format Line, Spacing command. This command is presented on the same menu as the Margins command.

1. With the cursor at the top of the document type **Shift-F8, 4** (Format Line, Spacing).
2. Answer the prompt by typing [**2**↵].
3. Next use the Reveal Codes command to view the [Spacing Set:] code now imbedded in the text.

Start and Stop Codes

In general, the start and stop codes imbed two codes into the document. The text between the two codes is the segment affected by the command's format.

Centering Text

WordPerfect's Center command (**Shift-F6**) inserts start and stop codes to center text between them. To give you experience in using this command, do the following.

1. Move the cursor to the top of the screen (line 1) and type [↵] to insert two blank lines there.
2. Next type **Shift-F6** (Center) to begin the Center command.
3. Now type [Vista Ridge Townhouses↵].

Typing ↵ ends the Center command.

4. Next use the Reveal Codes command to view the codes [C] and [c] inserted into the document by the Center command. The text between these commands should be centered.

Bold Type and Underline

Two other WordPerfect commands that insert start and stop codes into the document in the same manner as the Center command are **F6** (Bold), which is used to print text darker than normal, and **F8** (Underline), which is used to underline text when it is printed. To boldface or underline text, you may type, respectively, the **F6** or **F8** keys (Bold or Underline) to begin the command, enter the text to be bolded or underlined, and then type the **F6** or **F8** keys (Bold or Underline) again to stop the command.

Deleting Start and Stop Codes

You may delete start and stop codes in the same manner as you delete format forward codes, with or without the Reveal Codes screen. However, with start and stop codes only one of the two codes need be deleted; the other will automatically be deleted.

EXERCISE 5: Practice Reformatting the Document

1. Use the commands and operations discussed so far to:
   - **a.** Set the left margin to 6 and the right margin to 72 for the entire document.
   - **b.** Complete the letterhead, as shown, using the Center command.

```
         Vista Ridge Townhouses
         ~~~~~~~~~~~~~~~~~~~~~~

    1800 S.W. Sunset View Avenue
          Portland, OR 97207
```

   - **c.** Set the line spacing to 1 for the letterhead and 2 for the rest of the document.
   - **d.** Underline the phone number. Note that the underlined text will appear highlighted on the screen and will print underlined.
   - **e.** Delete all unnecessary codes from your document.

The finished document appears on the following page.

Vista Ridge Townhouses

1800 S.W. Sunset View Avenue
Portland, OR 97207

Thank you for your interest in Vista Ridge Townhouses. We feel that our one and two bedroom deluxe townhouse apartments offer adult living at its finest.

Each large townhouse unit has wall to wall carpeting, drapes, private patio and sun deck. You will also find the townhouse of your choice equipped with a modern self-defrosting refrigerator, self-cleaning oven, dishwasher and garbage disposal unit. Every tenant enjoys year round swimming and sauna plus use of our recreation room and tennis courts.

We are located in the South West Heights area, close to shopping, city parks and University campus. For an appointment to view one of our fine townhouse apartments and a tour of the grounds, please call Mr. Smith at (503) 244-7163.

EXERCISE 6: Saving a Document

You may save a document file onto your diskette by using the Save (**F10**) command.

1. Type **F10** (Save) to begin the save operation.

The message "Document to be Saved:" will appear at the bottom of the screen on the status line.

NOTE: Be sure to specify the drive where your files diskette resides in the next step—A: for the A: drive, B: for the B: drive, etc.

2. Type [B:WPTUT↵].

The B: specifies that the file is to be saved on the diskette in the B: disk drive. WPTUT stands for WordPerfect tutorial and is simply a filename that conforms to the rules for filenames.

Notice that the filename now appears on the left side of the status line. If you save the document again, the procedure will be slightly different. After typing **F10** (Save) the computer will respond with the prompt "Document to be Saved:B:\WPTUT." If you type ↵, the document will be saved again under its original name. You may, however, enter another name under which to save the document. The next prompt shown "Replace B:\WPTUT? (Y/N)" is a cautionary step designed to prevent you from accidentally replacing the file on the diskette with the file in memory. You must type "Y" to complete the resave operation.

While you create and edit your documents it is highly recommended that you use the Save command about every 15 minutes or so.

EXERCISE 7: Printing a Document

You are now ready to print the letter. To print a document currently in memory, the Print command (**Shift-F7**) is used.

1. Make sure the printer is on, on-line, and connected to your computer. (Your lab may have a shared device control switch. You will need to select your computer as the one currently connected to the printer.)
2. Advance the paper in the printer to the top of the next page.
3. Now type **Shift-F7** (Print).

The following menu will appear at the bottom of the screen:

```
1 Full Text; 2 Page; 3 Options; 4 Printer Control; 5 Type-thru; 6 Preview 0
```

4. Type [1] to select the Full Text command.

The printer should respond by printing the document complete with margins, centered text, and underlining. Notice that the printed text is left and right justified to the margins. To print text with a ragged right margin, the type of justification you see on the screen, you must turn justification off with the Format Print, Right Justification Turn off command (**Ctrl-F8,3**).

Vista Ridge Townhouses
~~~~~~~~~~~~~~~~~~~~~~

1800 S.W. Sunset View Avenue
Portland, OR 97207

Thank you for your interest in Vista Ridge Townhouses. We feel that our one and two bedroom deluxe townhouse apartments offer adult living at its finest.

Each large townhouse unit has wall to wall carpeting, drapes, private patio and sun deck. You will also find the townhouse of your choice equipped with a modern self-defrosting refrigerator, self-cleaning oven, dishwasher and garbage disposal unit. Every tenant enjoys year round swimming and sauna plus use of our recreation room and tennis courts.

We are located in the South West Heights area, close to shopping, city parks and University campus. For an appointment to view one of our fine townhouse apartments and a tour of the grounds, please call Mr. Smith at <u>(503) 244-7163</u>.
~~~~~~~~~~~~~~~~~~~~~~

The Exit Command

The WordPerfect Exit command (**F7**) is used to properly exit from many WordPerfect menu commands, erase your document file from memory, and return to DOS (erase your document and WordPerfect from memory).

You are first going to use the Exit command to erase your document from memory.

1. Type **F7** (Exit).
2. Answer the next prompt "Save Document? (Y/N)" by typing [N]. You have already just saved the document with the Save command.
3. Answer the next prompt "Exit WP? (Y/N)" by typing [N] or [↵].

The screen should now be clear to continue with the tutorial.

EXERCISE 8: The Concept of Boiler Plating

Many situations exist where a standard form or document (general text) needs to be "filled in" with specific information. When this is the case, it is possible to automatically merge the specific information into the general text to produce the desired finished document.

The term *boiler plating* describes a concept of design in which similar parts (plates) are used to construct different finished products (boilers). To demonstrate this concept, and an important set of word processing operations called "block" operations, the rest of the tutorial deals with the following example.

One responsibility included in the property management of a townhouse development might be the task of typing up rental agreements for new tenants to sign. The terms of such agreements could vary with the property being rented and other miscellaneous items such as pet deposits, parking arrangements, and locker rental.

You are first going to create a rental agreement form. This document will be the standard form into which certain specific information later will be merged. The standard file is called the *primary* file. You next will create several smaller files that contain the specific information. These files are called *secondary* files.

As you create the rental agreement you will be introduced to uses of the Block command. Also, you will enter codes called Merge codes into the rental agreement. The codes later will be used by WordPerfect to merge the desired secondary files into the primary file (the specific information files into the rental agreement).

Creating the Primary File

You will begin to create the rental agreement by entering a centered heading. This time, however, you are going to center the heading after it has been typed. To do this, you will use the Block command.

Formatting Blocks of Text

The Block command is used to define a portion of text to be subsequently affected by a command. To block a portion of text, you move the cursor to the beginning of the text and type **Alt-F4** (Block). A blinking "Block on" message will appear at the bottom of the screen. You then move the cursor to the end of the text. The text being blocked will be displayed on the screen in reverse video. If you decide to abort the block operation, you may type **F1** (Cancel) to turn off the block. The last step is to type the command keystroke or keystroke combination to affect the block of text. Commands that may be used to format a block of text include those listed in the following table.

Command	Description	Menu	Keystrokes
Bold	Print block in bold type	Bold	F6
Center	Center block in document	Center	Shift-F6
Change Case	Convert UPPER/lower cases	Switch	Shift-F3
Delete	Delete a block of text		Backspace
Flush Right	Align block flush to right margin	Flush Right	Alt-F6
Subscript	Print block as subscript	Super/Subscript	Shift-F1
Superscript	Print block as superscript	Super/Subscript	Shift-F1
Underline	Print block as underlined	Underline	F8

1. With the cursor at line 1, position (Pos) 10, type:

```
[←┘
Vista Ridge Townhouses←┘
Rental Agreement←┘
======================←┘]
```

2. Now move the cursor to under the *V* in *Vista* and type **Alt-F4** (Block).

Notice the blinking Block on message at the bottom of the screen.

3. Move the cursor to the right five or six characters.

Notice that the text being blocked is displayed in reverse video.

4. Now tap the cursor down key three times.

The text to be centered should now be completely blocked.

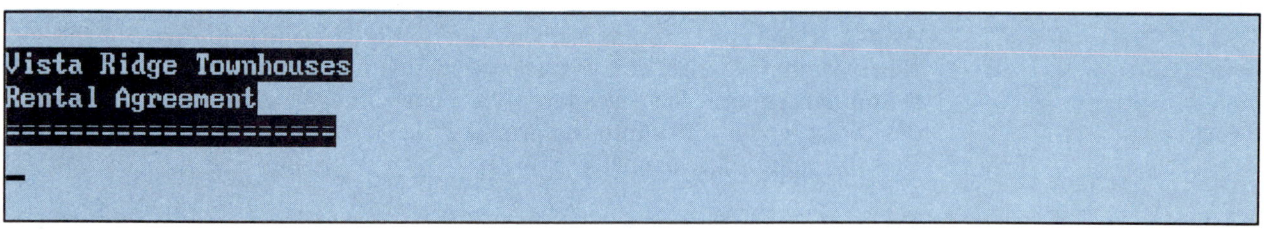

5. Now type **Shift-F6** (Center).

At the bottom of the screen the message "[Center]? (Y/N)" will appear.

6. Type [Y] to center the document heading.

Since most people prefer to format their text after it has been entered, the ability to block existing text to center, underline, or boldface the text is a useful feature.

Introduction to Merge Codes

You are now going to enter the terms of the rental agreement into the document. As you do this, you will enter Merge codes into the document which will later affect the manner in which the merge operation is performed.

The Merge codes are generated within the document by holding down the Ctrl key and then typing a letter key. The codes are not imbedded into the document like other WordPerfect codes; instead, they are displayed on the screen as the code letter with a ˆ preceding it. The Reveal Codes screen will display a properly entered Merge code as highlighted.

The first merge codes you will use are the following.

Ctrl-C ˆC

The ˆC code pauses the merge to allow text to be entered from the keyboard. It may be used to customize certain portions of a document or in conjunction with other codes to direct the merge process. After entering the text from the keyboard during the merge operation, type **F9** (Merge R) to continue the merge.

Ctrl-O (ˆOmessageˆO)

The ˆO merge code is generally used with other merge codes in the primary file. It displays a message on the status line at the bottom of the screen.

1. Enter the first few lines of the rental agreement, as shown below. Be sure to use the Ctrl-letter keystroke combination to generate the codes shown.

```
                    Vista Ridge Townhouses
                       Rental Agreement
                    =====================

This rental agreement made and entered into this ^C day of ^C
1988, by and between Vista Ridge Townhouses hereinafter called
the lessor, and ^OEnter lessee's first and last names^O^C
hereinafter called the lessee,
```

The first two ˆC codes in the document will pause the merge operation for you to enter the date of the contract. The two ˆO codes will display the message between them (Enter lessee's first and last names) on the status line and the ˆC code immediately following will pause the merge to allow you to enter the first and last names. When entering data from the keyboard while the merge operation is in progress, you will need to type **F9** (Merge R) to continue after each pause (each ˆC code).

The next paragraph in the rental agreement contains the standard terms of the contract.

2. Enter the paragraph as shown here.

```
                    Vista Ridge Townhouses
                       Rental Agreement
                     ====================

This rental agreement made and entered into this ^C day of ^C
1988, by and between Vista Ridge Townhouses hereinafter called
the lessor, and ^OEnter lessor's first and last names^O^C
hereinafter called the lessee,

In consideration of the covenants and stipulations herein
contained on the part of the lessee to be paid, kept and
faithfully performed, the lessor does hereby lease, demise and
let unto said lessee those certain premises, for the stated
payments in lawful money, known and described as follows:
```

Later in the tutorial you will create several small files having contract clauses in them. The smaller files are the secondary files for the merge operation. They will be merged into the rental agreement document. The smaller files will have similar names such as SIZE1, SIZE2 and CLEAN1, CLEAN2.

Ctrl-P (^Pfilename^P)

The next Merge code you will enter into the rental agreement is ^P. The ^P merge code is used to insert a document file into the text. The code is most useful when used in conjunction with a ^C merge code (^P^C^P) to allow the filename to be entered from the keyboard during the merge.

Nested Merge Codes

It is possible to put Merge codes within Merge codes to effect the merge operation. For instance, the Merge code

```
^PSIZE1^P
```

will cause the file named "SIZE1" to be merged into the primary file. The Merge codes

```
^P^C^P
```

will pause the merge operation between the ^P codes to let you enter the filename from the keyboard. The Merge codes

```
^PSIZE^C^P
```

will pause to let you enter the last part of the filename. If you type [1], **F9** during the pause, the file named SIZE1 will be merged into the text. Finally, the Merge codes

```
^OEnter the size: 1 Small, 2 Large ^PSIZE^C^P^O
```

places (nests) the last example into a ^Omessage^O Merge code that will display its message at the bottom of the screen while the Merge operation pauses for you to enter the last part of the filename.

3. Now complete the rental agreement as shown. Be sure to use the Ctrl key to generate the Merge codes, and note that the dollar signs in the text occur at the screen position (Pos) 60.

```
let unto said lessee those certain premises, for the stated
payments in lawful money, known and described as follows:

^OEnter apartment size: 1 Small, 2 Large ^PSIZE^C^P^O

Additional monthly fees:
^OLocker Storage? (Y/N) ^PLOCK^C^P^O

                              Total Monthly Rent $

Deposits:
^OCleaning fee: 1 Small, 2 Large ^PCLEAN^C^P^O
^OPet Deposit? (Y/N) ^PPET^C^P^O

                                  Total Deposits $

                                Payment Received $

Signed: ______________________ Lessor

        ______________________ Lessee
```

NOTE: Be sure to specify the drive where your files diskette resides in the next step: A: for the A: drive, B: for the B: drive, etc.

4. Now use the Save command to save the rental agreement under the name "B:RA" (RA stands for Rental Agreement).

Changing the Default Disk Drive

The default disk drive (the drive to which WordPerfect will automatically look to for document files) is the drive that was current at the time WordPerfect was loaded into RAM. In the tutorial, that drive was the A: drive. So far you have specified the B: drive with the filename during the save operations. The next steps in the tutorial will change the default drive to B: so that you will no longer need to specify the drive during save operations.

NOTE: If your Getting Started steps of the tutorial were different than those stated in the manual, the following may need to be changed to set the right default drive: enter A: for the A: drive, B: for the B:, etc.

The List Files Command

The List Files command (**F5**) may be used to change the default disk drive and perform several file management operations from within WordPerfect. The screen presented by the List Files command displays the files on the current diskette.

1. Type **F5** (List Files).

At the bottom of the screen you will see the message:

`Dir A:\*.*` (Type = to change default Dir)

2. Type = and then type [B:↵] to specify the B: drive as the default drive.

The screen should now display

`Dir B:\*.*` (Type = to change default Dir)

3. Type [↵] to continue with the List Files command.

Listing Files on the Screen

The List Files command will next present a screen containing the filenames of the files on the current drive. The filenames WPTUT and RA should be displayed on the screen.

1. Type **F1** (Cancel) to exit from the List Files screen.
2. Next clear the document screen with the Exit command by typing **F7**,N,↵.

Creating the Secondary Files

The next steps in the tutorial involve creating the secondary files that will be merged with the primary file to produce the finished contract. In this portion of the tutorial you will gain additional experience with block operations.

Assume the development includes two basic styles of townhouses. You will start by typing a description for the first of these styles.

1. Starting on line 1, position (Pos) 10, enter the following text. Note that a ^C Merge code is entered after "Address:", and that the dollar sign occurs at the screen position (Pos) 60.

```
Townhouse apartment, 750 sq. ft. living area, one bedroom, one
bath.  Includes drapes, carpets, kitchen appliances.

Address: ^C S.W. Sunset View Avenue  Portland, OR 97207


Rental Fee .................................. $325.00/month
```

2. Now move the cursor to the beginning of the text and block the apartment description by typing **Alt-F4** and then moving the cursor to the end of the text.

```
Townhouse apartment, 750 sq. ft. living area, one bedroom, one
bath.  Includes drapes, carpets, kitchen appliances.

Address: ^C S.W. Sunset View Avenue  Portland, OR 97207


Rental Fee .................................... $325.00/month
```

Cut-and-Paste Operations

The term "cut and paste" refers to your ability to move, copy, or delete blocks of text using WordPerfect's Move command (**Ctrl-F4**). As you perform cut-and-paste operations, WordPerfect makes a copy of the blocked text and stores it in RAM in what is known as the "Move file buffer." The copy then is treated by WordPerfect as a separate file.

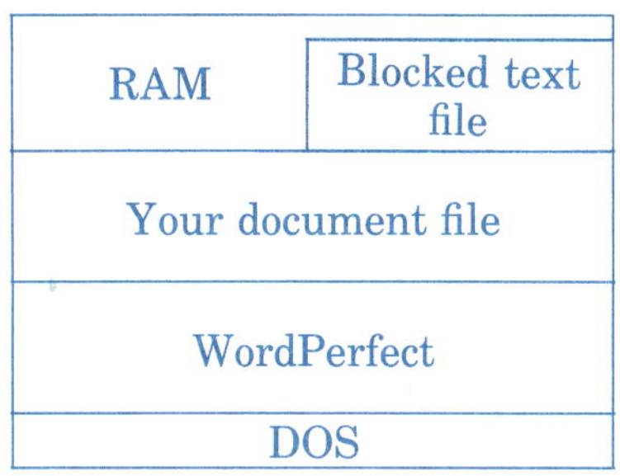

By creating a separate file, WordPerfect can move or copy a block of text to another location in the document or save a block of text onto the diskette under its own name. When you delete a block of text, it is copied into a different file buffer, the Undelete buffer, in case you want to later retrieve it with the Cancel command.

Copying a Block of Text

1. With the description blocked, type **Ctrl-F4** (Move).

The following menu will appear on the screen

```
1 Cut Block; 2 Copy Block; 3 Append; 4 Cut/Copy Column 5 Cut/Copy Rectangle:0
```

2. Type **2** (Copy Block).

The screen will return to its normal appearance; however, a copy of the block now exists in the Move file buffer.

3. Move the cursor two lines below the text on the screen and type **Ctrl-F4** (Move) again.

The Move menu now appears as

```
Move 1 Sentence; 2 Paragraph; 3 Page; Retrieve 4 Column; 5 Text; 6 Rectangle:0
```

The Move menu is composed of two parts: the first consists of three Move commands (Sentence, Paragraph, and Page) and the second consists of three

Retrieve commands (Column, Text, and Rectangle). To complete the copy operation, you need to use the Retrieve Text command of this menu.

4. Type **5** (Retrieve Text).

There are many variations of cut-and-paste operations that may be performed with the Move command. For a discussion of each, you will need to refer to the WordPerfect command summary. There are, however, three basic cut-and-paste operations that will work in most situations.

Block/Copy Block the text and then type **Ctrl-F4, 2** (Move, Copy Block). Move the cursor to where the copied block is to appear and type **Ctrl-F4, 5** (Move, Retrieve Text).

Block/Move Block the text and then type **Ctrl-F4, 1** (Move, Cut Block). Move the cursor to where the moved block is to appear and type **Ctrl-F4, 5** (Move, Retrieve Text).

Block/Delete Block the text and then type the Backspace key. The prompt "Delete Block? (Y/N)" will appear at the bottom of the screen. Type Y.

Saving a Block onto the Diskette

The last important block operation is one in which a block of text is saved onto the diskette under its own filename.

1. Use the basic editing keystrokes to edit the copied block of text to reflect that the second style of townhouse has 1,250 square feet, two bedrooms, and one and a half baths. It rents for $375.00 per month.

```
Townhouse apartment, 750 sq. ft. living area, one bedroom, one
bath.  Includes drapes, carpets, kitchen appliances.

Address: ^C S.W. Sunset View Avenue  Portland, OR 97207


Rental Fee ................................. $325.00/month

Townhouse apartment, 1,250 sq. ft. living area, two bedrooms, one
1/2 bath.  Includes drapes, carpets, kitchen appliances.

Address: ^C S.W. Sunset View Avenue  Portland, OR 97207


Rental Fee ................................. $375.00/month
```

Now that you have written the two descriptions, you will create two separate document files on your diskette, each containing one of the descriptions. The two files will have the same filename beginning—SIZE.

2. Block the first description (lines 1 through 7) and then type **F10** (Save). Answer the prompt at the bottom of the screen "Block Name:" by typing

[SIZE1↵]. Next, type **F1** (Cancel) to turn the block off for the first description.

3. Repeat the last steps used to save the second description under the filename SIZE2.
4. Now use the List Files command to be sure the files were saved onto the diskette and then clear the document screen with the Exit command (**F7**,N,↵).

Finishing the Secondary Files

1. Continue the tutorial by creating four more document files in the same manner as you created the two townhouse description files. Each line of text will be a separate file. The names under which to save the files are CLEAN1, CLEAN2, PETY, and LOCKY in the order that they appear on the screen from top to bottom. Notice again that the dollar signs occur in position (Pos) 60.

```
Cleaning Fee Non-refundable ..................... $ 35.00

Cleaning Fee Non-refundable ..................... $ 55.00

Pet Deposit ..................................... $ 50.00/pet

Locker Storage .................................. $ 25.00/month
```

For the Merge operation to work correctly, WordPerfect must find all secondary files to be merged with the primary file. Two of the Merge codes used in the primary file prompt for (Y/N) answers. The Y or the N then is used as the last character of the filename for the secondary file to merge. You have created the PETY and LOCKY files, the files that will be merged if the answer is "Y" to the prompts.

You must now create the PETN and LOCKN files. These files, however, will contain only one space character. This is done so that if there are no pets or lockers in the contract (i.e., the answer is "N" to either of the prompts), only one space will be merged with the primary file.

2. Type **F7, N,** ↵ to clear the document screen.
3. Tap the Space bar once and then type **F10,** [PETN↵] to create the PETN file using the Save command.
4. Next type **F10,** [LOCKN↵] to create the LOCKN file from the same document screen.

Merging Text

The final steps of the tutorial will be to create and print a rental agreement for the following situation. The date is July 29th. The renters are John and Lisa Leighstone. They will be renting the 1,250 square foot apartment (large unit) located at the address 9110 S.W. Sunset View Avenue. They have a Siamese cat and will need locker storage for their belongings.

The Merge/Sort command will be used to complete the Merge operation.

1. Make sure the document screen is cleared by typing **F7,** N, ↵.
2. Next type **Ctrl-F9, 1** (Merge/Sort, Merge).
3. Answer the Primary file: prompt by typing [RA↵].
4. Answer the Secondary file: prompt by typing [↵].

When the secondary files are specified from within the primary file, they need not be specified here.

The Merge operation will begin. A copy of RA, the primary file, will appear on the screen and the merge operation will be paused to allow you to enter the day, 29th.

```
                      Vista Ridge Townhouses
                         Rental Agreement
                      ====================

This rental agreement made and entered into this_day of ^C
1988, by and between Vista Ridge Townhouses hereinafter called
the lessor, and ^OEnter lessee's first and last names^O^C
hereinafter called the lessee,

In consideration of the covenants and stipulations herein
contained on the part of the lessee to be paid, kept and
faithfully performed, the lessor does hereby lease, demise and
let unto said lessee those certain premises, for the stated
payments in lawful money, known and described as follows:

^OEnter apartment size: 1 Small, 2 Large ^PSIZE^C^P^O

Additional monthly fees:
^OLocker Storage? (Y/N) ^PLOCK^C^P^O

                               Total Monthly Rent $

Deposits:
* Merging *                                          Doc 1  Pg 1  Ln 6        Pos 59
```

During the merge operation you will need to type the F9 key (Merge R) after each time you have entered data.

5. Type [29th], **F9.** Next type [July], **F9.**

The Merge should now be paused for you to enter the lessee's names. Notice the message "Enter lessee's first and last names" at the bottom of the screen.

6. Type [John and Lisa Leighstone], **F9.**

The next pause is caused by the Merge Codes line in the primary file

```
^OEnter apartment size: 1 Small, 2 Large ^PSIZE^C^P^O
```

Notice that the message and the first part of the filename appear at the bottom of the screen. The Leighstones will be renting a large unit.

7. Type **2, F9.**
8. At the next pause (at the ^C code in the SIZE2 secondary file) enter the address by typing [9110], **F9.**

The rest of the pauses during the Merge operation will be for you to specify the secondary files to be merged. The Leighstones need locker storage, the cleaning fee will be for a large unit, and they will need to pay a pet deposit.

9. Answer these Merge prompts appropriately.
10. When the merge operation is completed, fill in the total amounts and print the file with the **Shift-F7,1** (Print, Full Text) command.

The finished contract will look like the example on the following page.

11. To conclude the tutorial, save the finished contract under the name WPTUT2, and then exit WordPerfect by typing **F7,** N, Y.

Vista Ridge Townhouses
Rental Agreement
=====================

This rental agreement made and entered into this 29th day of July 1988, by and between Vista Ridge Townhouses hereinafter called the lessor, and John and Lisa Leighstone hereinafter called the lessee,

In consideration of the covenants and stipulations herein contained on the part of the lessee to be paid, kept and faithfully performed, the lessor does hereby lease, demise and let unto said lessee those certain premises, for the stated payments in lawful money, known and described as follows:

Townhouse apartment, 1,250 sq. ft. living area, two bedrooms, one 1/2 bath. Includes drapes, carpets, kitchen appliances.

Address: 9110 S.W. Sunset View Avenue Portland, OR 97207

Rental Fee $375.00/month

Additional monthly fees:
Locker Storage .... $ 25.00/month

Total Monthly Rent $400.00

Deposits:
Cleaning Fee Non-refundable .... $ 55.00

Pet Deposit .... $ 50.00/pet

Total Deposits $105.00

Payment Received $505.00

Signed: ______________________ Lessor

______________________ Lessee

WordPerfect Quick Reference Command Index

Command	Description	Command Menu	Keystroke
Block/Bold	Print block in bold type	Bold	F6
Block/Center	Center block in document	Center	Shift-F6
Block/Copy	Copy block	Move	Ctrl-F4
Block/Move	Move a block	Move	Ctrl-F4
Block/Print	Print a block of text	Print	Shift-F7
Block/Save	Save a block of text to disk	Save	F10
Block/Underline	Print block as underlined	Underline	F8
Bold	Print text in boldface type	Bold	F6
Cancel	Cancel command or message	Cancel	F1
Center	Center text between margins	Center	Shift-F6
Change Directory	Set current drive/directory	List Files	F5
Copy Pg. Para. Sent.	Copy a page, paragraph, or sentence	Move	Ctrl-F4
Delete Pg. Para. Sent.	Delete a page, paragraph, or sentence	Move	Ctrl-F4
Fonts	Change printer character fonts	Format Printer	Ctrl-F8
Footnote	Print footnotes	Footnote	Ctrl-F7
Headers/Footers	Create headers and footers	Format Page	Alt-F8
Help	On-line documentation	Help	F3
▶Indent	Indent paragraph from left	▶Indent	F4
▶Indent◀	Indent paragraph left and right	▶Indent◀	Shift-F4
Line Spacing	Set spacing between lines	Format Line	Shift-F8
Margin Bottom	Change number of lines per page	Format Page	Alt-F8
Margin Top	Set the top page margin	Format Page	Alt-F8
Margins Left/Right	Set left and right margins	Format Line	Shift-F8
Move Pg. Para. Sent.	Move a page, paragraph, or sentence	Move	Ctrl-F4
Outline	Automatic outline feature	Mark Text	Alt-F5
Page # Change	Change page number	Format Page	Alt-F8
Page # Off/On	Page numbers on/off	Format Page	Alt-F8
Page # Position	Specify page number position	Format Page	Alt-F8
Pitch	Change printer character pitch	Format Printer	Ctrl-F8
Print Cancel	Abort printing	Print	Shift-F7
Print Continue	Resume printing	Print	Shift-F7
Print Disk Page	Print certain pages from disk	Print	Shift-F7
Print Text	Print the current document	Print	Shift-F7
Print Stop	Stop printing a document	Print	Shift-F7
Retrieve File	Retrieve a document	Retrieve	Shift-F10
Right Justify On/Off	Print text justified	Format Printer	Ctrl-F8
Save File	Save a document	Save	F10
Search and Replace	Global search and replace feature	Replace	Alt-F2
Search Backward	Search backward for word pattern	◀Search	Shift-F2
Search Forward	Search forward for word pattern	▶Search	F2
Spell	Use the spelling check feature	Spell	Ctrl-F2
Subscript	Print text as subscript	Super/Subscript	Shift-F1
Superscript	Print text as superscript	Super/Subscript	Shift-F1
Switch	Edit two files concurrently	Switch	Shift-F3
Tab Stops	Set tab stops for document	Format Line	Shift-F8
Undelete	Recover deleted text	Cancel	F1
Underline	Underline text	Underline	F8

WordPerfect Control Keys

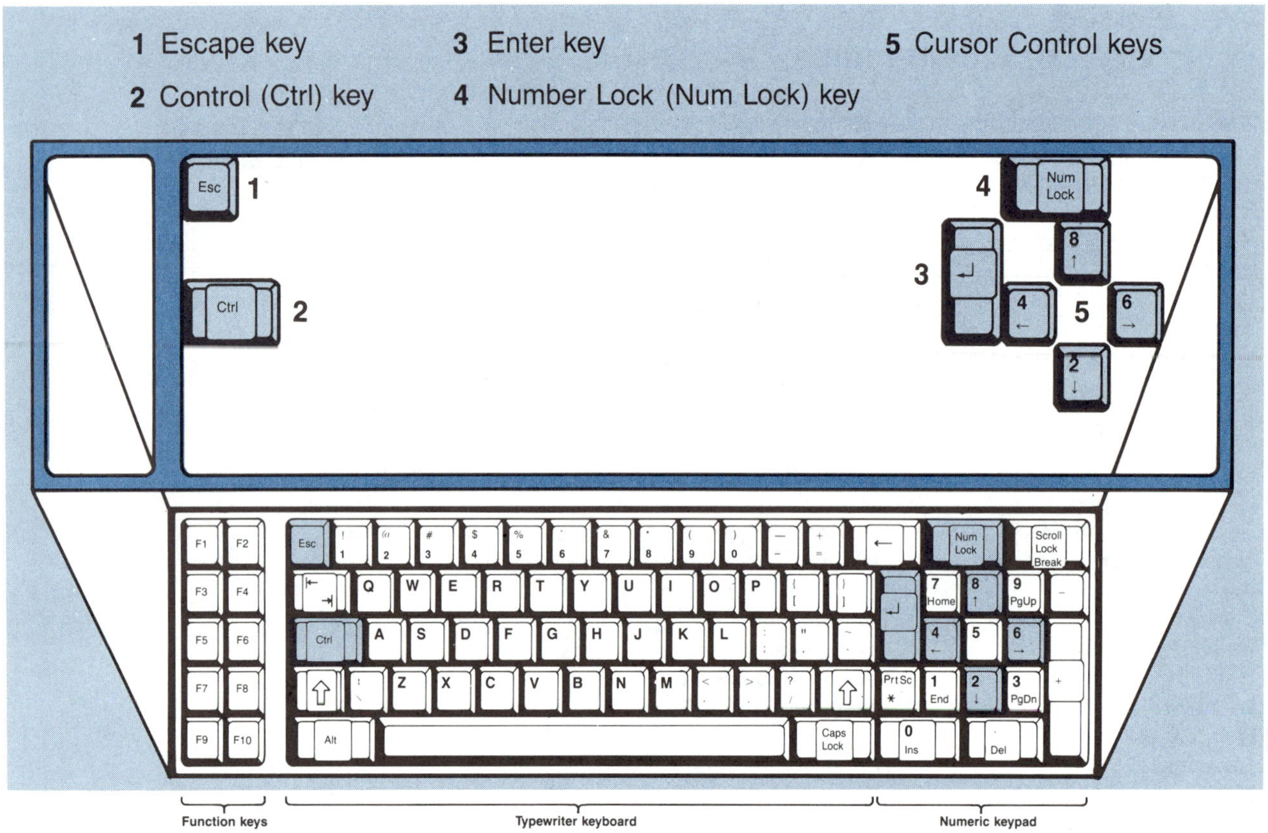

CONTROL KEYS

Alt-letter key Executes a keystroke macro named with the Alt key.

Ctrl-Enter Inserts a hard page break [HPg] into the document.

Ctrl-letter key May be used to insert Merge codes into a document.

Enter key Inserts a hard return [HRt] into the document.

Esc key May be used to execute the following keystroke n number of times. Type Esc, a number, and then type the keystroke or keystroke combination to repeat.

Home, Space Inserts a hard space [ ] into the document.

Ins key Toggles between Insert and Typeover editing modes.

Num Lock key Toggles ten-key numeric keypad to cursor control keys. The shift key may be used to temporarily shift this keypad to the opposite mode.

Tab key Inserts a [TAB] code into the document and tabs the cursor to the next tab stop.

WordPerfect Cursor Control Keys

To Move	Press
Character Left	Cursor Left (Left)
Character Right	Cursor Right (Right)
Line Up	Cursor Up (Up)
Line Down	Cursor Down (Down)
Word Left	Ctrl-Left
Word Right	Ctrl-Right
Forward to Character *a*	Ctrl-Home *a*
Beginning of Line	Home, Left
End of Line	Home, Right (or End)
Top of File	Home, Home, Up
Bottom of File	Home, Home, Down
To Page *nn*	Ctrl-Home, *nn*
Screen Up	− (Numeric Keypad)
Screen Down	+ (Numeric Keypad)
Page Up	PgUp
Page Down	PgDn
Previous Position	Ctrl-Home, Ctrl-Home
Column Left	Ctrl-Home, Left
Column Right	Ctrl-Home, Right
Margin Release	Shift-Tab

WordPerfect Delete Keys

To Delete	Press
Current Character	Del
Previous Character	Backspace
Current Word	Ctrl-Backspace
Current Word Left	Home, Backspace
Current Word Right	Home, Del
End of Line	Ctrl-End
n Number of Lines	Esc, *n*, Ctrl-End
End of Page	Ctrl-PgDn
Block	Block, Backspace

WordPerfect Full Command Index

Command	Description	Command Menu	Keystroke
Advance Down	Print text below normal line	Super/Subscript	Shift-F1
Advance to Line	Printer advance to line *nn*	Super/Subscript	Shift-F1
Advance Up	Print text above normal line	Super/Subscript	Shift-F1
Align Char	Change Align Character	Format Line	Shift-F8
Alt/Ctrl Keys	Assign graphic characters	Screen	Ctrl-F3
Block Text	Blocked text operations	Block	Alt-F4
Block/Append	Append a block to a disk file	Move	Ctrl-F4
Block/Bold	Print block in bold type	Bold	F6
Block/Center	Center block in document	Center	Shift-F6
Block/Copy	Copy block	Move	Ctrl-F4
Block/Flush Right	Align block flush to right margin	Flush Right	Alt-F6
Block/List	Mark text for list	Mark Text	Alt-F5
Block/Move	Move a block	Move	Ctrl-F4
Block/Print	Print a block of text	Print	Shift-F7
Block/Protect	Protect block from soft page breaks	Format Page	Alt-F8
Block/Redline	Mark text for addition	Mark Text	Alt-F5
Block/Replace	Search and replace word in block	Replace	Alt-F2
Block/Save	Save a block of text to disk	Save	F10
Block/Sort	Sort text in block	Merge/Sort	Ctrl-F9
Block/Spell	Spell feature on block	Spell	Ctrl-F2
Block/Strikeout	Mark text for deletion	Mark Text	Alt-F5
Block/Subscript	Print block as subscript	Super/Subscript	Shift-F1
Block/Superscript	Print block as superscript	Super/Subscript	Shift-F1
Block/ToC	Mark text for table of contents	Mark Text	Alt-F5
Block/Underline	Print block as underlined	Underline	F8
Bold	Print text in boldface type	Bold	F6
Cancel	Cancel command or message	Cancel	F1
Center	Center text between margins	Center	Shift-F6
Center Page	Center page top to bottom	Format Page	Alt-F8
Change Case	Convert UPPER/lower cases	Switch	Shift-F3
Change Directory	Set current drive/directory	List Files	F5
Colors	Change screen attributes	Screen	Ctrl-F3
Columnar Text	Use text columns feature	Math/Columns	Alt-F7
Comments	Document text internally	Text In/Out	Ctrl-F5
Cond End Of Page	Protect lines from soft page breaks	Format Page	Alt-F8
Copy File	Copy a file	List Files	F5
Copy Page	Copy a page	Move	Ctrl-F4
Copy Paragraph	Copy a paragraph	Move	Ctrl-F4
Copy Sentence	Copy a sentence	Move	Ctrl-F4
Cut/Copy/Dele Column	Cut and paste a column	Move	Ctrl-F4
Cut/Copy/Dele Rectangle	Cut and paste a rectangle	Move	Ctrl-F4
Date	Insert DOS system date	Date	Shift-F5
Date Function	Automatic date/time	Date	Shift-F5
Delete File	Delete a file	List Files	F5
Delete Page	Delete a page	Move	Ctrl-F4
Delete Paragraph	Delete a paragraph	Move	Ctrl-F4
Delete Sentence	Delete a sentence	Move	Ctrl-F4
Endnote	Print endnotes on last page	Footnote	Ctrl-F7
Flush Right	Align text flush to right margin	Flush Right	Alt-F6
Fonts	Change printer character fonts	Format Printer	Ctrl-F8
Footnote	Print footnotes	Footnote	Ctrl-F7
Headers/Footers	Create headers and footers	Format Page	Alt-F8
Help	On-line documentation	Help	F3

Command	Description	Command Menu	Keystroke
Hyphenation	Automatic hyphenation feature	Format Line	Shift-F8
▶Indent	Indent paragraph from left	▶Indent	F4
▶Indent◀	Indent paragraph left and right	▶Indent◀	Shift-F4
Line Draw	Draw screen boxes and lines	Screen	Ctrl-F3
Line Numbers	Automatic line numbers	Format Printer	Ctrl-F8
Line Spacing	Set spacing between lines	Format Line	Shift-F8
Lines per Inch	Change printer lines per inch	Format Printer	Ctrl-F8
Lock Document	Protect with password	Text In/Out	Ctrl-F5
Look at File	View a disk file	List Files	F5
Macro Create	Create a keystroke macro	Macro Def	Ctrl-F10
Macro Retrieve	Load and execute a keystroke macro	Macro	Alt-F10
Mail Merge	Merge addresses, salutations	Merge/Sort	Ctrl-F9
Margin Bottom	Change number of lines per page	Format Page	Alt-F8
Margin Top	Set the top page margin	Format Page	Alt-F8
Margins Left/Right	Set left and right margins	Format Line	Shift-F8
Math	Use math feature	Math/Columns	Alt-F7
Merge Operations	Merge feature	Merge/Sort	Ctrl-F9
Move Page	Move a page	Move	Ctrl-F4
Move Paragraph	Move a paragraph	Move	Ctrl-F4
Move Sentence	Move a sentence	Move	Ctrl-F4
Outline	Automatic outline feature	Mark Text	Alt-F5
Overstrike	Print text overstrike	Super/Subscript	Shift-F1
Page Length	Specify page length	Format Page	Alt-F8
Page # Change	Change page number	Format Page	Alt-F8
Page # Off/On	Page numbers on/off	Format Page	Alt-F8
Page # Position	Specify page number position	Format Page	Alt-F8
Page # Position Change	Page Number Column Positions	Format Page	Alt-F8
Para#	Automatic paragraph numbers	Mark Text	Alt-F5
Pitch	Change printer character pitch	Format Printer	Ctrl-F8
Preview Print	View printed document on screen	Print	Shift-F7
Print Cancel	Abort printing	Print	Shift-F7
Print Continue	Resume printing	Print	Shift-F7
Print Disk Page	Print certain pages from disk	Print	Shift-F7
Print from Disk	Print a file from disk	List Files	F5
Print from Disk	Print from a disk file	Print	Shift-F7
Print Full Text	Print the current document	Print	Shift-F7
Print Options	Printer, copies, bind width	Print	Shift-F7
Print Page	Print the current page	Print	Shift-F7
Print Stop	Stop printing a document	Print	Shift-F7
Print to Disk	Print to a disk file (ASCII)	Print	Shift-F7
Printer Commands	Insert printer control codes	Format Printer	Ctrl-F8
Printer Install	Define printer(s) for use	Print	Shift-F7
Redline	Mark text for addition	Mark Text	Alt-F5
Rename	Rename a file	List Files	F5
Retrieve File	Retrieve a document	Retrieve	Shift-F10
Retrieve File	Retrieve a document	List Files	F5
Rewrite	Reformat text manually	Screen	Ctrl-F3
Right Justify On/Off	Print text justified	Format Printer	Ctrl-F8
Save File	Save a document	Save	F10
Save in ASCII	Save in DOS text file format	Text In/Out	Ctrl-F5
Search and Replace	Global search and replace feature	Replace	Alt-F2
Search Backward	Search backward for word pattern	◀Search	Shift-F2
Search Forward	Search forward for word pattern	▶Search	F2
Select Operations	Extract records by condition	Merge/Sort	Ctrl-F9

Command	Description	Command Menu	Keystroke
Shell	Return temporarily to DOS	Shell	Ctrl-F1
Sort Merge Files	Sort secondary merge files	Merge/Sort	Ctrl-F9
Sort Operations	Sort records feature	Merge/Sort	Ctrl-F9
Spell	Use the spelling check feature	Spell	Ctrl-F2
Subscript	Print text as subscript	Super/Subscript	Shift-F1
Summary	Document text internally	Text In/Out	Ctrl-F5
Superscript	Print text as superscript	Super/Subscript	Shift-F1
Suppress Format	Suppress page formatting	Format Page	Alt-F8
Suppress Format, Page	Suppress formatting for a page	Format Page	Alt-F8
Switch	Edit two files concurrently	Switch	Shift-F3
Tab Align	Align text to tab stops	Tab Align	Ctrl-F6
Tab Stops	Set tab stops for document	Format Line	Shift-F8
Text In	Retrieve an ASCII file	List Files	F5
Text In/Out	Foreign file transfer	Text In/Out	Ctrl-F5
Thesaurus	Use thesaurus feature	Thesaurus	Alt-F1
Type-thru	Use printer as typewriter	Print	Shift-F7
Undelete	Recover deleted text	Cancel	F1
Underline	Underline text	Underline	F8
Underline Style	Change style of underlining	Format Printer	Ctrl-F8
Widow/Orphan	Protect lines from soft page breaks	Format Page	Alt-F8
Window	Split screen for viewing	Screen	Ctrl-F3
Word Search File	Search files for word pattern	List Files	F5

WordPerfect Command Summary

Block — Alt-F4 — Code = [Block]

The Block command is used to define a portion of text to be subsequently affected by a command. To block a portion of text, move the cursor to the beginning of the text to be blocked and type **Alt-F4** (Block). A blinking "Block on" message will appear at the bottom of the screen. Next, move the cursor to the end of the text. Note that while Block is on, typing a character will automatically move the cursor forward to the character and typing ↵ will move the cursor forward to the next hard return [HRt]. The blocked text will be displayed on the screen in reverse video.

Once a portion of text has been blocked, any of the following commands may be executed:

Command	Description	Menu	Keystrokes
Append	Append a block to a disk file	Move	Ctrl-F4,3
Bold	Print block in bold type	Bold	F6
Center	Center block in document	Center	Shift-F6
Change Case	Convert UPPER/lower cases	Switch	Shift-F3
Copy	Copy block	Move	Ctrl-F4,2
Cut	Cut block from text	Move	Ctrl-F4,1
Cut/Copy Column	Cut or copy a column	Move	Ctrl-F4,4
Cut/Copy Rectangle	Cut or copy a rectangle	Move	Ctrl-F4,5
Delete	Delete a block of text		Backspace
Flush Right	Align block flush to right margin	Flush Right	Alt-F6
Index	Mark text for index	Mark Text	Alt-F5
List	Mark text for list	Mark Text	Alt-F5
Print	Print a block of text	Print	Shift-F7
Protect	Protect a block from page breaks	Format Page	Alt-F8
Redline	Mark text for addition	Mark Text	Alt-F5,3
Replace	Search and replace word in block	Replace	Alt-F2
Save	Save a block of text to disk	Save	F10
Sort	Sort text in block	Merge/Sort	Ctrl-F9
Spell	Spell feature on block	Spell	Ctrl-F2
Strikeout	Mark text for deletion	Mark Text	Alt-F5,4
Subscript	Print block as subscript	Super/Subscript	Shift-F1
Superscript	Print block as superscript	Super/Subscript	Shift-F1
ToC	Mark text for table of contents	Mark Text	Alt-F5
Underline	Print block as underlined	Underline	F8

For more information on the Block command operations, refer to the appropriate command menu.

To turn a Block off, type **F1** (Cancel) or **Alt-F4** (Block).

Bold — F6 — Code = [B] bold text [b]

The Bold command is used to print text in boldface type (darker than normal). Typing **F6** (Bold) inserts [B] and [b] codes into the text. Text typed afterwards is entered between the codes and is displayed on the screen in highlight. To stop bolding text, type **F6** (Bold) again.

Block/Bold

To boldface existing text, block the text and then type **F6** (Bold).

Cancel — F1

Exits a WordPerfect menu or message and recovers up to three levels of deleted text from the Undelete buffer.

The Cancel key (**F1**) may be used to abort most WordPerfect menu or command operations. The Cancel command also may be used to recover any or all of the last three text deletions. To recover text, move the cursor to the position where you want the recovered text to appear and then type **F1** (Cancel). The most recent deletion will appear on the screen at the cursor location. The "(2) Show Previous Deletion" command may by used to continuously scroll through the last three deletions, with each deletion appearing on the screen in order. When the appropriate deletion is displayed on the screen, type **1** to recover it. Type Cancel (**F1**) to abort the recovery operation.

Center — Shift-F6 — Code = [C] centered text [c]

The Center command is used to center text between the current left and right margins. To assure proper centering, move the cursor to the left margin before using the Center command. Typing **Shift-F6** (Center) inserts [C] and [c] codes into the text. Text typed afterwards is entered between the codes and appears centered as it is typed. Centering of text is stopped when the ↵ (Enter) key is typed.

You can center an existing line of text by moving the cursor to the left margin on the line and typing **Shift-F6,** Down (Center, Cursor Down).

Block/Center

To center two or more lines of existing text, block the text and then type **Shift-F6** (Center).

Date — Shift-F5

Date: 1 Insert Text; 2 Format; 3 Insert Function: 0

The Date command may be used to insert, with a variety of formats, the current DOS system date and/or time into a document. Dates or times may be inserted either as text or as functions which automatically update each time the file is opened for editing.

(1) Insert Text

Inserts the current date/time as text at the cursor location.

(2) Format

Allows the date/time format to be changed. The menu of options is self-explanatory.

(3) Insert Function — Code = [Date: date format specifications]

Inserts the date/time as a code function. The code function will display the current DOS date and/or time each time the document is opened for editing or printing. The display will be in the current date format.

Exit — F7

The Exit command is used to save the current document and exit WordPerfect. It also is used to exit many WordPerfect commands or operations.

In order to assure that your documents are saved correctly, you should always quit WordPerfect with the Exit command. Type **F7** (Exit), and then either save or do not save your file (Y or N, respectively). Next type Y in answer to the "Exit WP? (Y/N)" prompt.

If you are editing two documents (see the Switch command), you will need to exit from each before returning to DOS.

Flush Right — Alt-F6 — Code = [A] justified text [a]

The Flush Right command is used to align text flush against the right margin. Typing **Alt-F6** (Flush Right) inserts [A] and [a] codes into the text and causes the cursor to jump to the right margin. Text typed afterwards is entered between the codes and appears right justified as it is typed. Right justifying of text is stopped when the ↵ (Enter) key is typed. (To right justify text at tab stops, see the Tab Align command.)

Block/Flush Right

To right justify two or more lines of existing text, block the text and then type **Alt-F6** (Flush Right).

Footnote — Ctrl-F7

1 Create; 2 Edit; 3 New #; 4 Options; 5 Create Endnote; 6 Edit Endnote: 0

WordPerfect provides for footnotes and endnotes to be included in a document in a variety of standard formats. The numbering of the notes is maintained automatically by WordPerfect.

The procedure for creating footnotes or endnotes is straightforward. You move the cursor to the word, sentence, or paragraph that the footnote will reference, and where you want the note number to appear in the text. You then type **Ctrl-F7** (Footnote) and select either the Create (footnote) or the Create Endnote command from the menu. You next enter the note on a blank screen provided by the command. When finished, you type **F7** (Exit) and a note number appears on the document screen at the cursor position.

Footnotes will be printed at the bottom of the page containing the text they reference, while endnotes will be printed on the last page of the document. **Alt-F3** (Reveal Codes) may be used to view the first 50 characters of a note imbedded in a document.

(1) Create — Code = [Note:Foot,#;[Note #] note text]

The Create command is used to create footnotes. Move the cursor to the place where the footnote number is to appear and type **Ctrl-F7,1** (Footnote, Create). Next, enter the text for the footnote on the blank screen provided by the command and then type **F7** (Exit).

(2) Edit

The Edit command is used to edit footnotes. Type **Ctrl-F7, 2** (Footnote, Edit) and then enter the number of the footnote you want to edit. Type **F7** (Exit) when done.

(3) New # — Code = [Set Note#:n]

The New # command is most useful when one document is divided into two or more files. To resume proper footnote numbering in the next file, move the cursor to the left of the first note number in the file and type **Ctrl-F7, 3**

(Footnote, New #). Then, enter the appropriate starting number for the footnotes in the file. All subsequent footnotes in the file will be automatically renumbered.

(4) Options Code = [FmtOpt]

The Options command provides several alternate formatting styles for footnotes and endnotes. When a default format setting is changed with the Options command, the code [FmtOpt] is inserted into the text at the cursor location. The formatting change then affects the remaining text.

The following are brief descriptions of format styles and their default values:

1 Spacing within notes — Default = 1
Set the line spacing for notes, 1, 1.5, 2 lines, etc . . .

2 Spacing between notes — Default = 1
Set the number of lines between notes, 1, 1.5, 2 lines, etc . . .

3 Lines to keep together — Default = 3
Forces WordPerfect to keep *n* number of lines within a note together if the note needs to be split onto two pages.

4 Start footnote numbers each page — Default = *N*
Y causes footnote numbers to start at 1 for each page.

5 Footnote numbering mode — Default = 0
Options include 0 = Numbers (1, 2, 3, etc.)
1 = Characters (*, **, ***, etc.)
2 = Letters (a, b, c, etc.)

6 Endnote numbering mode — Default = 0
Same as footnote numbering mode.

7 Line separating text and footnotes — Default = 1
Before printing footnotes on a page, WordPerfect prints a solid line to separate them from the text. This option is used to define what type of line will be printed. The choices are

0 = No line
1 = 2 inch line on left
2 = Full length line across page
3 = 2 inch line with a (Continued . . .) message for split footnote.

8 Footnotes at bottom of page — Default = Y
N causes footnotes to immediately follow the text on a page.

9 Characters for notes — Default = *
When the number mode for footnotes or endnotes is specified as characters, WordPerfect uses the asterisk. This option allows you to change the character.

The last four options of the Options command allow you to redefine the manner in which the footnote or endnote number appears in the text, or with the footnote or endnote. Type **Ctrl-F7, 4** (Footnote, Options) and then the letter of your choice, A through D.

A	String for footnotes in text	Default = Superscript, Note #
B	String for endnotes in text	Default = Superscript, Note #
C	String for footnotes in note	Default = Subscript, Note #
D	String for endnotes in note	Default = Note #

You may redefine the display of a number by including characters, an underline, and/or a superscript. Codes necessary for the new display are obtained from typing command keys. For instance, to add parentheses and underline a footnote number appearing in the text you would type **Ctrl-F7, 4** (Footnote, Options) and then **A** (String for footnotes in text). The message "Replace with: [SuperScrpt][Note]" appears on the screen. You then type **Shift-F1, 1** (Super/Subscript, Superscript), (, **F8** (Underline to begin underlining), **Ctrl-F7, 1** (Footnote, Footnote/Endnote), **F8** (Underline, to end underlining),)↵.

When done, the string for footnotes in text appears as [Suprscrpt]([Undrline][Note][u]) and the number appearing in the text for a footnote will be displayed as $^{\underline{(1)}}$.

Format Line   Shift-F8

1 2 Tabs; 3 Margins; 4 Spacing; 5 Hyphenation; 6 Align Char: 0

(1) or (2) Tabs   Code = [Tab Set: tab stops]

The Tabs command is used to set tab stops within a document. When tab stops are set with the Tabs command, a [Tab Set:] code is inserted into the text, and it stays in effect for the rest of the document or until another [Tab Set:] code is encountered.

When the Tabs command is executed the following lines appear at the bottom of the screen:

```
..L....L....L....L....L....L....L....L....L....L....L....L....L....L....L....L.
89012345678901234567890123456789012345678901234567890123456789012345678901234556
 10        20        30        40        50        60        70        80
Delete EOL (clear tabs); Enter number (set tab); Del (clear tab);
Left; Center; Right; Decimal; .= Dot leader; Press EXIT when done.
```

The top line indicates the tab positions of the current tab stops. By default, WordPerfect automatically sets L (Left justified) tabs every five positions. A cursor will be displayed on the line. The cursor may be moved left and right with the cursor control keys.

Types of Tab Stops

There are seven different types of tab stops you may specify with the Tabs command. Each type affects the manner in which data will be oriented to the tab stop when it is typed after the Tab key or Indent commands are used to move the cursor to the tab stop. The following describes the tab stop types and provides examples of how they affect text.

		Examples
		Tab | Stop
L	Left justify	|Left justify
R	Right justify	Right justify|
D	Decimal align	123.00
C	Center	Center text
L.	Left justify w/dot leader	. . . . .Left w/leader
R.	Right justify w/dot leader	. . . . . . .Right w/leader|
D.	Decimal align w/dot leader	. . . . 123.00

Deleting Tab Stops

To delete an existing tab stop, you may move the cursor to the tab position and type the Del key. To delete all tab stops, you may move the cursor to the left margin and type Ctrl-End.

Setting Tab Stops

There are two ways in which you may set new tab stops. One is to enter the position number for the tab stop. When a number is typed and entered, WordPerfect automatically puts an L (Left tab stop) at the position number. You also may set multiple tab stops in this way by typing the first tab stop position, a comma, and then the interval between tab stops that you desire. For instance, 0,5↵ will return the tabs to WordPerfect's default tab setting of L's occurring every five positions.

The other method of setting tab stops is to move the cursor to the appropriate place on the tab line and enter the letter of the type of tab stop you want to occur there. If you want the tab stop to have a preceding dot leader you type the letter and then a period (.).

When finished specifying tab stops, you type Exit to quit the Tabs command.

(3) Margins — Code = [Margin Set:margin settings]

The Margins command is used to set the left and right margins within a document. When the Margins command is executed, a [Margin Set:] code is inserted into the document and the margins will stay in effect for the rest of the document or until another [Margin Set:] code is encountered. To change margins, type **Shift-F8, 3** (Format Line, Margins) and then enter the new left and right margins.

(4) Spacing — Code = [Spacing Set:n.n lines]

The Spacing command is used to set the spacing between lines in the document. When the Spacing command is executed, a [Spacing Set:] code is inserted into the document. Line spacing then will stay in effect for the rest of the document or until another [Spacing Set:] code is encountered.

Spacing may be set at line and half-line intervals. For instance, 2 specifies double spacing and 1.5 specifies 1 ½ lines between text lines. The screen will display the nearest whole number of line spaces for the current line spacing.

To change line spacing in a document, type **Shift-F8, 4** (Format Line, Spacing) and then enter the appropriate number.

(5) Hyphenation Code = [Hyph on], [Hyph off], [H-Zone Set:], [-], -, / [HZone Set] 7,0 Off Aided 1 On; 2 Off; 3 Set H-Zone; 4 Aided; 5 Auto:0

Word wrapping occurs in a paragraph when the last word of a line is wrapped to the next line in the document. By default, if a word begins before the right margin and ends after the right margin, the entire word is automatically wrapped to the next line.

The Hyphenation command may be used to cause WordPerfect to either automatically hyphenate a word, or pause and allow you to hyphenate a word, before wrapping the hyphenated portion to the next line. The hyphenation feature only hyphenates words that meet certain criteria. The criteria for such words may be changed with the Set H-Zone command.

The H-Zone is an area measured in characters to the left and right from the right margin. The default H-Zone used by WordPerfect is 7 characters to the left and 0 characters to the right of the right margin. The setting causes the hyphenation feature to stop on words which begin 7 or less characters before the right margin and extend 0 or more characters to the right of the margin.

Hyphens inserted into a word by the Hyphenation feature are soft hyphens, hyphens that will only be displayed or printed when they occur at the end of a line. Undisplayed soft hyphens may be viewed with the Reveal Codes command. You may enter soft hyphens into a document without the Hyphenation feature by typing **Ctrl, -.**

To use the Hyphenation feature, type **Shift-F8, 5** (Format Line, Hyphenation). If you want to change the current H-Zone settings, type **3** (Set H-Zone) and enter the new left and right settings. If you want WordPerfect to automatically hyphenate words according to its internal set of rules, type **5** (Auto). If you want to hyphenate each word yourself type **4** (Aided) and then type **1** (On) to turn on the Hyphenation feature. If you later want to turn off the Hyphenation feature, type **Shift-F8, 5, 2** (Line Format, Hyphenation, Off).

The **1** On, **2** Off, and **3** Set H-Zone commands all insert codes into the document that affect the remaining text.

If Auto hyphenation is in effect and WordPerfect encounters a word not covered by its internal rules, it will shift to Aided hyphenation temporarily.

(6) Align Char Code = [Align Char:a]

The Align Char command is used to change the character that WordPerfect uses to align text at tab stops. The default Align Char character is the period (.). The Align Char command inserts an [Align Char:] code into the document that affects the remaining text.

Format Page Alt-F8

The Format Page command is used to specify various formatting options for a document.

(1) Page Number Position Code = [Pos Pg#:n]

The Page Number Position command may be used to turn on/off automatic page numbering or position the page number in one of eight different locations. The page number positions include top left of every page; top center of every page; top right of every page; top alternating left and right; bottom left of every page; bottom center of every page; bottom right of every page; and bottom alternating left and right.

Page numbers are present to print in column 10 (Left), column 42 (Center), and column 74 (Right). See Format Page, Page Number Column Positions for information on how to change the page number column settings.

To include a page number in a header or footer, enter **Ctrl-B** (^B) into the header or footer at the location where the page number is to be printed.

(2) New Page Number Code = [Pg#:n]

The New Page Number command may be used to set a new beginning page number within a document. Type **Alt-F8, 2** (Format Page, New Page Number) and answer the "New Page #:" prompt by entering the beginning page number. Page numbers may be printed in Arabic (1,2,3, . . .) or Roman (I,II,III, . . .) number style.

(3) Center Page Top to Bottom Code = [Center Pg]

The Center Page Top to Bottom command is used to vertically center a page of text. Move the cursor to the top of the page (before any imbedded codes) and type **Alt-F8, 3** (Format Print, Center Page Top to Bottom).

(4) Page Length Code = [Pg Lnth:n,n]

The Page Length command is used to specify various paper lengths and lines of text on a printed page. The default settings are for 8½″ × 11″ paper, 66 lines long with 54 lines of text. You may adjust the bottom margin for pages in a document by changing the number of lines of text with the Page Length command. Move the cursor to the top of the page before any codes and type **Alt-F8, 4, 3** (Format Page, Page Length, Other). Then, change the Number of Single Spaced Text Lines:.

(5) Top Margin Code = [Top Mar:n]

The top margin is preset to 1 inch (12 half lines). To change the top margin, move the cursor to the beginning of the page before any codes and type **Alt-F8, 5** (Format Page, Top Margin). Then, enter the new margin setting in half lines. Changing the top margin does not change the number of single-spaced text lines on a page (the determinant of the bottom margin). To adjust the number of lines for the desired bottom margin, use the Format Page, Page Length command.

(6) Headers or Footers Code = [Hdr/Ftr:header/footer text]

Headers or footers may be included in a document with the Headers or Footers command. Up to two headers (A and B) and two footers (A and B) may be included in the text. To create a header or footer, move the cursor to the beginning of the page and type **Alt-F8, 6** (Format-Page, Headers or Footers). Next, select the header or footer you want to create (A or B). Then, specify the pages upon which you want the header or footer to appear. Your choices are Every Page, Odd Pages, or Even Pages. After selecting the page display format, the screen will clear for you to enter the header or footer text. When finished, type Exit to save the data and return to the Format Page menu.

A [Hdr/Ftr:header/footer text] code will be inserted into the text. To edit a header or footer, move the cursor past the location of the code and type **Alt-F8, 6** (Format Page, Headers or Footers) and then enter the number of the appropriate header or footer to edit. Next type **4** (Edit).

You may include a page number in a header or footer by typing **Ctrl-B** at the location within the header or footer where you want the page number to occur.

(7) Page Number Column Positions — Code = [Pg#Col:left,center,right]

Page numbers are preset to print in column 10 (Left), Column 42 (Center), or column 74 (Right). The default locations may be changed with the Page Number Column Positions command.

(8) Suppress for Current page only — Code = [Suppress:]

The Suppress for Current page only command may be used to suppress various page format options for the current page. The command is self-explanatory.

(9) Conditional End of Page — Code = [CndlEOP:n]

The Conditional End of Page command is used to keep a certain number of lines in a document from being separated by a soft page break.

Move the cursor to the line above the first line in the document to be protected and type **Alt-F8, 9** (Format Page, Conditional End of Page) and then enter the number of lines to protect.

(A) Widow/Orphan — Code = [W/O On] [W/O Off]

A widow is the first line of a paragraph appearing on the last line of a page and an orphan is the last line of a paragraph appearing on the first line of a page. To prevent such last and first lines from being separated from their paragraphs, type **Alt-F8, A** (Format Page, Widow/Orphan). A [W/O On] code will be inserted at the cursor location and the following text will be protected against widows and orphans. To turn off widow/orphan protection, move the cursor to where protection is to end and type **Alt-F8, A** (Format Page, Widow/Orphan) again.

Block/Protect — Code = [BlockPro:On] [BlockPro:Off]

To protect a block of text from being separated by soft page breaks, first block the text to be protected and then type **Alt-F8** (Format Page).

Format Print — Ctrl-F8

(1) Pitch/Font — Code = [Font Change:n,n]

Pitch refers to the number of characters per inch that will be printed on a line. Font refers to the style of character that will be printed. Pitch and font often are related. For instance, Elite font is usually set to 12 pitch (12 characters per inch) and Courier font is usually set to 10 pitch.

Most printers are able to print in more than one pitch or font; however, each type of printer is different in the pitches and fonts it may print.

WordPerfect supplies eight different font settings for a printer. To change a font setting, you first move the cursor to where the change is to occur and then type **Ctrl-F8, 1** (Format Printer, Pitch/Font). You then enter the desired pitch and the number (1 through 8) for the desired font. The code [Font Change:n,n] is imbedded, which affects the following text.

To determine which of your printer's fonts are invoked with each of WordPerfect's eight font settings, it is recommended that you create a small test file. With the imbedded codes included, the test file may look like the following.

[Font Change:10,1]	This is a test of font 1
[Font Change:10,2]	This is a test of font 2
[Font Change:10,3]	This is a test of font 3
[Font Change:10,4]	This is a test of font 4

.

.

.

and so on

Once the file is printed, the font styles for each line will be apparent and you will be able to tell if the pitch for the font needs to be changed. For instance, if the characters are too far apart, you will raise the pitch for the font.

(2) Lines per Inch — Code = [LPI:n]

The Lines per Inch command is used to change the number of lines printed in a vertical inch on the page. The two possible settings are 6 and 8 lines per inch. The default is 6 lines per inch. Changing the lines per inch to 8 may cause problems with some printers.

Right Justification — Code = [Rt Just On] [Rt Just Off]
(3) Turn off (4) Turn on

Text may be justified to both the left and right margins when it is printed. To view such text on the screen, you must use the Print, Preview command.

To stop left/right justification, move the cursor to where you want the justification to end and type **Ctrl-F8, 3** (Format Print, Turn off Right Justification). A [Rt Just Off] code will be imbedded in the text.

To begin left and right justification of text, move the cursor to the place where left/right justification is to begin and type **Ctrl-F8, 4** (Format Print, Turn on Right Justification). A [Rt Just On] code will be imbedded in the document and will affect the following text.

Underline Style — Code = [Undrl Style:n]

Four commands affect the way in which underlining is done by the printer. "Continuous" underlines tabs, indents, flush rights, while "Non-Continuous" does not. Both Continuous and Non-Continuous underline spaces. "Single" or "Double" underlining may be selected; however, not all printers support double underlining.

(9) Sheet Feeder Bin Number — Code = [Bin#:n]

The Sheet Feeder Bin Number command is used with printers having more than one sheet feeder bin.

(A) Insert Printer Command — Code = [Cmnd:]

The Insert Printer Command command is used to insert a printer control code into a document. Control codes must be obtained from the printer's manual. When entering the control code into a document, characters less than ASCII 32 or greater than ASCII 126 must be entered as decimal numbers in angle brackets (for example <27> = Esc). All keyboard characters may be entered as decimal numbers in angle brackets (for example, M or <77>).

(B) Line Numbering — Code = [LnNum:On] [LnNum:Off]

The Line Numbering command is used to automatically number each line in a document. Move the cursor to where you want line numbering to begin and then type **Ctrl-F8, B, 2** (Format Print, Line Numbering, Turn on). A small, self-explanatory menu concerning ways of numbering will be presented on the screen. To turn off line numbering, move the cursor to the place where numbering is to end and type **Ctrl-F8, B, 1** (Format Print, Line Numbering, Turn off).

Help — F3

The Help command provides on-line documentation for the user. The documentation is kept on a separate diskette. If you are using a computer with two floppy disk drives, you will need to insert the Learning diskette into the B: drive to use the Help command. If you have a hard disk drive, the Learning disk should be copied onto the same subdirectory as WordPerfect.

To exit the Help screens, type the Space bar or ↵.

▶Indent — F4 — Code = [->Indent]

The ▶Indent command indents a paragraph from the left to the next tab stop. See Format Line, Tabs for information on setting tab stops.

To create a "hanging paragraph," one which is indented to the right of a heading, type the heading, **F4** (Indent), and then enter the paragraph.

▶Indent◀ — Shift-F4 — Code = [->Indent<-]

The ▶Indent◀ command indents a paragraph from the left and right to the next tab stop. See Format Line, Tabs for information on setting tab stops.

List Files — F5

1 Retrieve; 2 Delete; 3 Rename; 4 Print; 5 Text In; 6 Look; 7 Change Directory; 8 Copy; 9 Word Search; 0 Exit: 6

The List Files command provides commands to change the default disk drive, perform basic file maintenance operations, and search through files for word pattern occurrences.

Changing the Default Disk Drive

When the F5 key is first pressed, a message:

`Dir A:\*.*` (Type = to change default Dir)

appears on the screen. The A:*.* part of the message indicates which drive is the current drive. To cause WordPerfect to automatically look to another drive or directory for your word processing files type = ↵ and then enter the drive device name and/or path for the appropriate subdirectory.

The List Files Screen

When the correct directory is displayed, type ↵ to cause WordPerfect to display the List Files screen. The screen will appear similar to the following.

```
04/03/88  09:15              Directory B:\*.*
Document Size:    27292                            Free Disk Space:   198656

. <CURRENT>       <DIR>              | .. <PARENT>     <DIR>
ACCT334B.         25485  01/30/88 12:35 | ACCT344A.      23288  02/01/88 08:55
BIBLO    .         4266  03/17/88 10:06 | DRAWS    .      2026  02/15/88 16:00
INDEX    .         2854  03/09/88 10:07 | MEMO1    .       829  03/19/88 10:02
MEMO2    .          263  02/25/88 11:55 | MEMO3    .       791  01/07/88 14:30
MEMO4    .          791  03/19/88 14:30 | MGMT431A.      26313  03/11/88 10:04
MGMT431B.         26557  03/07/88 10:05 | NOTE1    .       323  01/17/88 13:30
RESUME   .         2348  03/09/88 14:00

1 Retrieve; 2 Delete; 3 Rename; 4 Print; 5 Text In;
6 Look; 7 Change Directory; 8 Copy; 9 Word Search; 0 Exit: 6
```

The top of the screen displays a header with information about the DOS system date and time, the size of the document currently being edited, the current directory, and disk space available.

The first eight commands on the List Files screen are commands associated with file maintenance. The inverted screen appearing at the top of the list of filenames is a cursor. The cursor may be moved to any one of the files displayed on the screen. To execute the file maintenance commands, you first move the cursor to the appropriate filename and then type the number of the command you wish to execute.

The cursor control, PgUp, and PgDn keys may be used to move the cursor. Also, if you begin to type the filename of a file, the cursor will jump to the first filename with matching characters for the keystrokes you type (a feature called "Name Search").

(1) Retrieve

The Retrieve command loads a document into memory for editing or printing. The retrieved document will be inserted at the editing cursor location into any document that may already be in memory. Type **F5↵** (List Files), move the List Files cursor to the file to be retrieved, and then type **1** (Retrieve).

(2) Delete

Erases a file from the disk. Type **F5↵** (List Files), move the List Files cursor to the file to be deleted, and then type **2** (Delete). The message "Delete filename? (Y/N) N" will appear at the bottom of the screen. Type Y to complete the file deletion operation. When a file is deleted, it is permanently erased from the disk.

(3) Rename

Renames a file. Type **F5↵** (List Files), move the List Files cursor to the file to be renamed, and then type **3** (Rename). Then enter the new filename.

(4) Print

Prints a file from the disk. Type **F5↵** (List Files), move the List Files cursor to the file to be printed, and type **4** (Print). To cancel a print operation type **Shift-F7, 4, C** (Print, Printer Control, Cancel). To print one or more specific pages from a file on a disk see Print, Printer Control.

(5) Text In

Text In may be used to retrieve an ASCII file. Such ASCII files may include Lotus or VP Planner .PRN files, or dBase III .TXT, .FMT, or .PRG files.

(6) Look

The Look command allows you to view a file on the diskette without retrieving it. Look is the default command of the List Files command. If you move the List Files cursor to a filename and type ↵, the contents of the file will be displayed on the screen, but the file will not be retrieved.

(7) Change Directory

The Change Directory command may be used to change the current disk drive and/or subdirectory without leaving the List Files screen.

(8) Copy

The Copy command is used to make a copy of a file. Type **F5↵** (List Files), move the List Files cursor to the file to be copied, and then type **8** (Copy). Then enter the file specification for the copied file.

(9) Word Search

The Word Search command is designed to search for occurrences of a word pattern in the files of the current disk and/or subdirectory. The size of the word pattern is limited to 20 characters. When the search is completed, the List Files screen will display only those files having the specified word pattern within them. It is recommended that you enclose the word pattern to be searched for with quotes. Upper- and lower-case characters are treated the same when a word search is performed.

The wild card characters ? and * may be used in the word pattern. The ? (question mark) has the effect of saying "accept any character here." For example, if the word pattern to search for is entered as

```
"April ?, 1988"
```

all files with dates entered as text that match the word pattern, except for the middle character, will be displayed on the List Files screen. That is, files dated "April 2, 1988", "April 3, 1988", and so on, will be displayed.

The * (asterisk) has the effect of saying "accept any remaining characters here." For example, if the word pattern to search for is entered as

```
"Water*"
```

all files having words such as "Waterville", "Waterdale", and so on, will be displayed.

Logical operators may be affected with the ; (semicolon) for AND and , (comma) for OR. The order of logical operator execution is from left to right. For example,

```
"Bill";"product review"
```

will display all files with the word patterns "Bill" and "product review" within them.

```
"Bill","Larry";"product review"
```

will display all files with the word patterns "Bill" or "Larry" that also have the pattern "product review"—that is, ("Bill" OR "Larry") AND "product review".

Marking Files

You can Delete, Print, Copy or Word Search multiple files by marking the files with an asterisk. Move the cursor to the files you want to erase, copy, print, or search. Then type an * (asterisk). You then select the command you want executed from the List Files menu.

Macro

Alt-F10

The Macro command is used to load and execute a keystroke macro that was named with ↵ or characters at the time it was created. See Macro Def for more information on creating, saving, and executing keystroke macros.

Macro Def

Ctrl-F10

When using WordPerfect, you type three basic types of keystrokes: character keystrokes, which enter text into the document; keystroke commands, which perform certain operations (such as Ctrl-End to delete the line right); and menu keystrokes, which invoke WordPerfect's command mode.

A macro is a collection of keystrokes, saved by WordPerfect, that may be executed (automatically retyped) at any time. The keystrokes in the macro may be character, keystroke command, or menu in nature. Macros are a means-to-save-time feature of WordPerfect.

To explain how keystroke macros may be created, suppose that you have created a document within which there are several key words you now wish to italicize. The font number (see Format Print, Fonts, page W–49) for italics on your printer is #2. To italicize the words in the document you have been using the steps:

1. Move the cursor to the beginning of the word.
2. Type **Ctrl-F8, 1, Down, 2,** ↵, ↵. (The set of keystrokes used to insert the [Font Change:] code for font #2, then exit the command.)

3. Type Ctrl-Right (to jump the cursor to the other side of the word).
4. Type **Ctrl-F8, 1, Down, 1, ↵**, ↵. (The set of keystrokes used to insert the [Font Change:] code for font #1, then exit the command.)

Notice that, except for the keystrokes used to move the cursor to the word in step 1, all other keystrokes are exactly the same for any word you may want to italicize. That is, the remaining keystrokes are systematic. Large groups of systematic keystrokes are prime candidates for becoming keystroke macros.

Steps in Creating and Using Keystroke Macros

There are four basic steps required to create a keystroke macro:

1. Begin defining the macro by typing **Ctrl-F10** (Macro Def).
2. Enter a name for the macro.
3. Type the keystrokes you want saved in the macro.
4. End defining the macro by typing **Ctrl-F10** (Macro Def) again.

How you may execute a macro (cause WordPerfect to automatically retype the keystrokes within it) depends on the name you give the macro in step 2 of steps required to create a macro.

Naming and Using a Macro

Two to Eight Characters If you enter a name consisting of two to eight characters, the macro is saved on the disk with a .MAC filename extension. The macro is then available for use with any document on the disk—it is permanent in nature. To execute the macro you type **Alt-F10** (Macro) and then enter the name of the macro.

Alt-letter If you name the macro by holding down the Alt key and typing a letter key (A to Z), the macro is saved on the disk under the filename ALT(letter) with a .MAC extension. The macro then is available for use with any document on the disk—it is permanent in nature. To execute the macro you type Alt-letter. That is, if you named the macro Alt-A, you would later type **Alt-A** to execute it.

Enter Key If you name the macro by typing ↵, the macro is kept in RAM but is not saved on the disk—it is temporary in nature. Only one such macro may be in memory at one time. To execute the macro, you type **Alt-F10** and then ↵.

Single Letter If you name the macro by typing a single letter (A to Z), the macro is kept in RAM, but is not saved on the disk—it is temporary in nature. Several temporary macros may be created in this manner. To execute a macro given a single character name, type **Alt-F10** (Macro) and then enter the single character name.

Repeating a Macro

A macro can be caused to repeat itself *n* number of times by using the Esc key. For instance, assume the example macro was named Alt-I when it was created. To italicize the next five words you could type **Esc, 5, Alt-I.**

Pausing a Macro

You can cause a macro to pause so you may enter text from the keyboard while it is executing. To insert a pause into a macro type **Ctrl-PgUp,** ↵, ↵ at the point where you want the macro to pause when you create the macro.

Mark Text Alt-F5

1 Outline; 2 Para #; 3 Redline; 4 Short Form; 5 Index; 6 Other Options: 0

Block/Mark Text

Mark for: 1 ToC; 2 List; 3 Redline; 4 Strikeout; 5 Index; 6 ToA: 0

The Mark Text command provides three basic functions: to generate automatic outline and paragraph numbering; to mark text for copy editing; and to generate tables of content, lists, and indexes. The Block/Mark Text command is related to the operations of the Mark Text command. The following discusses the Mark Text and Block/Mark Text commands by functional area.

Outline and Paragraph Numbering

(1) Outline — Code = [Par#:Auto]

WordPerfect provides a feature which automatically inserts and maintains outline numbers. The numbers are generated by code functions that are inserted into the text when the Outline feature is on and the Enter key is typed.

The nature of the number displayed by a code function depends on the function's position on the screen. It changes according to the tab stop (see Format-Line, Tabs) upon which it occurs or follows.

It is generally easier to insert [TAB]s or [->Indent]s before a code function to ensure that it is moved to a current tab stop. The following shows the various default number type displays and the [TAB]s required to generate them.

I.	No [TAB]s
[TAB] A.	1 [TAB]
[TAB][TAB] 1.	2 [TAB]s
[TAB][TAB][TAB] a.	3 [TAB]s
[TAB][TAB][TAB][TAB] (1)	4 [TAB]s
[TAB][TAB][TAB][TAB][TAB] (a)	5 [TAB]s
[TAB][TAB][TAB][TAB][TAB][TAB] (i)	6 [TAB]s

To start automatic outlining, type **Alt-F5, 1** (Mark Text, Outline). Each time you strike the Enter key, an outline number will appear on the screen. It is recommended that you first generate several outline code functions by typing Enter, Space, Enter, Space, Enter, and so on, until the screen appears:

I.
II.
III.
IV.
V.
VI.
VII.
VIII.
IX.
X.
XI.
XII.
XIII.

You then may edit the text into your outline format using the Tab key or Indent command (**F4**) to insert [TAB]s or [->Indent]s before the outline code functions on the screen. Renumbering of the displayed numbers will be automatic. The following is an example of how the text will appear after editing.

I. Introduction
  A. History of Company
    1. Founding Father
    2. Beginning Era
      a. First Product Line
      b. Number of Employees
      c. Community Response
    3. The Expansion Years
      a. New Product Lines
      b. New Markets
        (1) Foreign Sales
          (a) Japan
          (b) England
      c. Growth in Earnings
II.

To turn off the generation of code functions by the Outline feature, type **Alt-F5, 1** (Mark Text, Outline) again.

To begin another outline in the same document, you type **Alt-F5, 6, 1, 2** (Mark Text, Other Options, Define Paragraph/Outline Numbering, Outline Numbering). Then type **1** in answer to the "Starting Paragraph Number (in Legal Style):" prompt.

(2) Para# — Code = [Par#:Auto] (Automatic) [Par#:n] (Fixed level)

The Para# command is very similar to the Mark Text, Outline command. The differences are that only one code function is inserted into the text each time the command is typed and you are able to defeat the automatic level number type.

To fix the displayed level number type, you may enter the desired level when you see the "Paragraph Level (ENTER for automatic)" prompt. For instance, if you type **2** when you see the message, the paragraph number will appear in the default form A. And, it will not change its form when it is indented or tabbed to the right on the screen. It will change its value, however, if preceding code functions of the same level are deleted or inserted (i.e., renumbering stays in effect).

To insert an automatic code function when the Para# command is given, type ↵ in answer to the "Paragraph Level (ENTER for automatic)" prompt.

Mark Text for Copy Edit

(3) Redline — Code = [RedLn] [r]

When two or more people are involved in revising text, it is often desirable to "call out" or identify certain segments of text as being proposed changes. The Redline command is designed to help identify text being suggested for addition to a document.

Redlining causes text to be marked with vertical bars in the far left column when printed. To redline text, type **Alt-F5, 3** (Mark Text, Redline) to begin redlining, type the text you want redlined, and then type **Alt-F5, 3** (Mark text, Redline) again to stop redlining.

Block/Redline To redline a block of existing text, block the text to be redlined then type **Alt-F5, 3** (Mark Text, Redline).

To remove all redline codes from a document, type **Alt-F5, 6, 6** (Mark Text, Other Options, Remove all Redline Markings and all Strikeout text from document).

(4) Block/Strikeout — Code = [StrkOut] [s]

The Block/Strikeout command is designed to help identify text being suggested for deletion from a document.

Block/Strikeout causes text to be overstruck with dashes when printed. To strikeout a block of text, first block the text to be struck out and then type **Alt-F5, 4** (Mark Text, Strikeout).

To remove all struck out text from a document, type **Alt-F5, 6, 6** (Mark Text, Other Options, Remove all Redline Markings and all Strikeout text from document).

Tables of Content, Lists, Indexes

Each of the operations here produce a table of references, with or without associated page numbers. The table is either alphabetized by reference (as in an index) or ordered by appearance (as in a table of contents). The sorting and generated page numbers (if any) are both done automatically by WordPerfect. The overall process for producing any of the tables is:

1. Mark the words, phrases, or topics within the document to which the table will refer.
2. Select the position and format for the table.
3. Generate the table.

The following discusses the various table types and how you may mark text to be included in them. For information on how to position, format and generate the various tables, refer to the last Mark Text command, **6** Other Options.

(4) Short Form

The Short Form command is used to mark text for a Table of Authorities. A Table of Authorities is a list of citations for a legal brief. See the WordPerfect manual or Help screens for more information on the subject.

(1) Block/ToC — Code = [Mark: ToC,n] heading text [EndMark:ToC,n]

The Block ToC command is used to mark text to be included in a table of contents. To mark the text, block the topic heading to be included in the table of contents and type **Alt-F5, 1** (Mark Text, ToC).

Up to five levels of headings may be included in a table of contents. When you mark a portion of text to be included in a table of contents, you must specify which level (1 to 5) the heading is to be included as. The headings in the finished table of contents will appear indented to their appropriate level:

First level . . . . nn
    Second level . . . . nn
    Second level . . . . nn
    Second level . . . . nn
        Third level . . . . nn
        Third level . . . . nn
    Second level . . . . nn
First level . . . . nn

Block/List — Code = [Mark:List,n] list text [EndMark:List,n]

The Block List command is used to mark text to be included in a list. To mark the text, block the word, phrase, or heading and then type **Alt-F5, 2** (Mark Text, List).

Up to five lists (1 to 5) may be generated per document. When you mark a block of text to be included in a list, you must specify which list (1 to 5) the text is to be included in. For instance, if you are producing a list of graphs found in a document, you may move to the heading for each graph and mark it to be included in list number 1. If you also intend to produce a list of tables for the document, you may move to the heading for each table and mark it to be included in list number 2.

(5) Index — Code = [Index:heading]

There are several ways in which you may mark words or phrases to be included in an index. The general procedure is to move the cursor to the location in the text where the desired subject for the index occurs. You next type **Alt-F5, 5** (Mark Text, Index). At this point you will be prompted to enter a heading.

Index Headings Items marked for inclusion in an index may have one or two headings (a heading and/or a subheading). If only a heading is entered, the item appears in the index by itself. If a heading and a subheading are entered, all items having the same heading will appear under the heading with their own subheading. For example:

Almond 15
Apples
    Crab 23
    Delicious 34
    Gravenstein 5
    McIntosh 12
    Newton 16
Artichoke 36

Here, the subjects Almond and Artichoke were marked in the text with only a heading. The varieties of apples were all marked with the heading "Apples" and the appropriate variety type subheading.

Methods of Entering Headings To enter the index heading(s) for a subject you do one of the following:

1. Move the cursor to a key word in the text and type **Alt-F5, 5** (Mark Text, Index). The word at the cursor location will be displayed with the heading prompt, and typing ↵ will cause the word to become the heading. If the word does not appear how you want the heading to appear, you may type and enter a different heading.

2. Block the word or phrase in the text and type **Alt-F5, 5** (Mark Text, Index). The blocked text will be displayed with the heading prompt and typing ↵ will cause it to become the heading.
3. Create a Concordance file. A Concordance file may be used to save time when an index reference is made to a subject that occurs in several places.

A Concordance file is simply a WordPerfect document that you create that contains a list of words or phrases separated by hard returns [HRt]s. It is used by WordPerfect to search the document for the words and phrases and generate index references for them. The words and phrases within a Concordance file may be used with the words or phrases that are marked throughout the text to generate the index. The generation of an index will take less time if the words and phrases within the Concordance file are sorted.

(6) Other Options

The Other Options command is used to define paragraph and outline numbering format; determine the location and format for tables; remove all redline markings and Strikeout text from the document; and generate a table of contents, lists, and an index for the document.

(1) Define Paragraph/Outline Numbering To change the style and punctuation used in automatic paragraph and outline numbering, the Define Paragraph/Outline Numbering command may be used. At the top of the screen presented by the command, there are three predefined numbering styles that you may select. To create your own style type **4** (Other) and then edit the matrix of Levels, Number style, and Punctuation numbers to reflect your choices from the menu below.

(2) (3) (5) Define Table of Contents, List, Index The next three commands to be discussed are all used to determine the position and format of tables that subsequently will be generated. (See Mark Text, Tables of Content, Lists, Indexes for information on WordPerfect tables.) The commands used to position and define the formats for the various tables differ only slightly in their form. The Define Table of Contents command will prompt for the number of heading levels you desire, the Define List command will prompt for the number (1 to 5) of the list you are currently defining, and the Define Index command will prompt you for a Concordance file filename (if any).

To define a table of contents, list, or index, you first move the cursor to the page and location where you want the table to appear when it is generated. You next type **Alt-F5, 6** (Mark Text, Other Options) and select the number for the type of table you are generating. After answering the initial prompts, you must specify the format for the table. Your options and examples of each follow.

(1)	No Page Numbers	Example	
(2)	Page Numbers Follow Entries	Example	47
(3)	(Page Numbers) Follow Entries	Example	(47)
(4)	Flush Right Page Numbers	Example	47
(5)	Flush Right Numbers with Leaders	Example	47

After defining the table, you will be returned to the editing mode and a [DefMark:ToC], [DefMark:List], or [DefMark:Index] code will be inserted into the document at the cursor location. If you later wish to reposition, redefine, or regenerate a table, you should remove the existing [DefMark] code from the document first.

(6) Remove all Redline Markings and all Strikeout text from document This command removes all [RedLn] [r] codes from the document and deletes all text currently marked with Strikeout. See Mark Text, Mark Text for Copy Edit for more information.

(8) Generate Tables and Index The last command of the Other Options command, Generate Tables and Index, is used to generate the table of contents, lists, and/or index for the [MarkDef] codes within the document. When done, the command inserts an [EndDef] code at the bottom of the table.

Math/Columns Alt-F7

1 Math On; 2 Math Def; 3 Column On/Off; 4 Column Def; 5 Column Display: 0

1 Math Off; 2 Calculate

The Math/Columns command is used to deal with two separate types of operations: inserting math functions into a document with the math feature of WordPerfect and typing columnar text to produce text in a newsprint or table format with WordPerfect's text columns feature.

Math Feature

WordPerfect provides a math feature for doing automatic calculations within a document. There are several steps involved in preparing a document to have math calculations within it. When the steps are completed, the document will include a portion of text that has been structured for doing math calculations. The structured portion of text may be represented as:

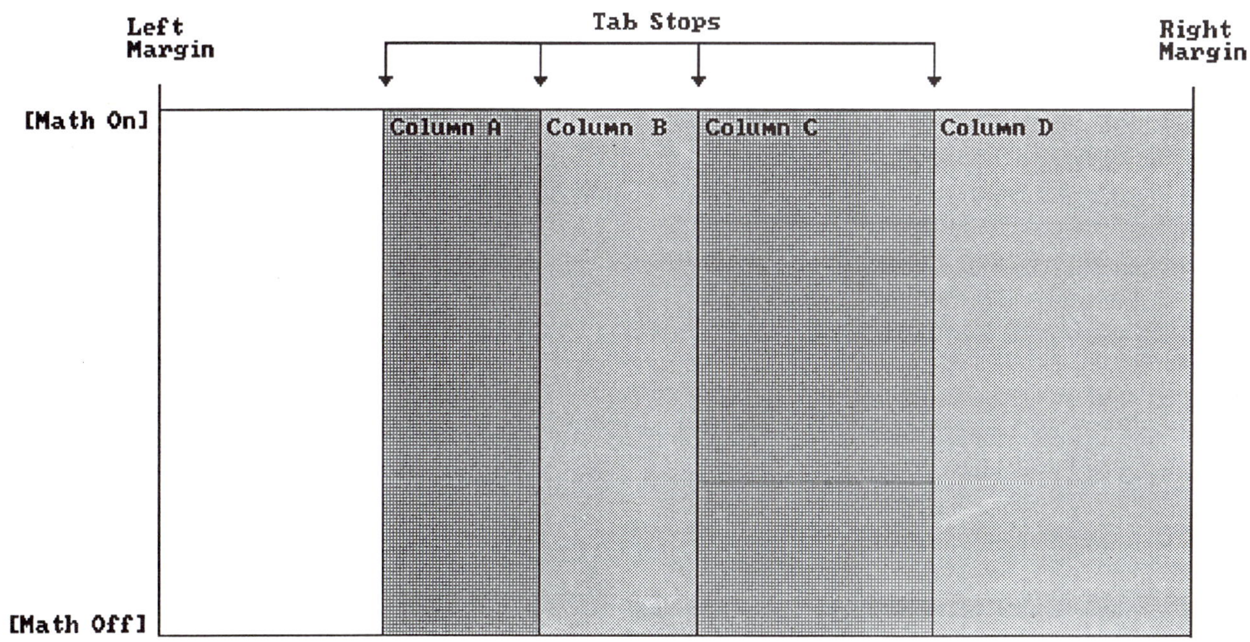

The text defined for math operations is set apart with [Math On] and [Math Off] codes imbedded into the text. Within the math portion of text, various columns are defined by the current tab stops (see Format Line, Tabs for information on setting tab stops).

The area between the left margin and the first tab stop to the right of the left margin may be used to enter text. The columns labeled A, B, C, and so on, may be defined for one of four different data types. If you want the column to contain Subtotals, Totals, and Grand totals, you specify the column to be Numeric. Numeric is the default definition of all columns. If you want the column to contain text, you specify the column to be Text. If you want the column to display totals obtained from the column to the immediate left, you specify the column to be Total. Finally, if you want the column to display the results of formulas referring to values obtained from other columns, you specify the column to be Calculation.

Steps in Creating a Math Document

There are five basic steps in creating a math portion within a document.

1. Set the appropriate tab stops.
2. Define the columns for math data type.
3. Turn Math On.
4. Enter the math data.
5. Calculate.

The following discusses the various Math commands in conjunction with other steps required to create such a document.

Set the Tab Stops The first step in creating a math area within a document is to set tab stops for the math portion that coincide with the planned format. Note that a [Tab Set:Ln,Ln...] code will be imbedded in the text at the current cursor location and will affect only the text following it.

Define the Columns

(2) Math Def **Code: [Math Def]**

The next step is to define the columns for the particular type data they will contain. When the Math Def command is executed, the screen appears as follows.

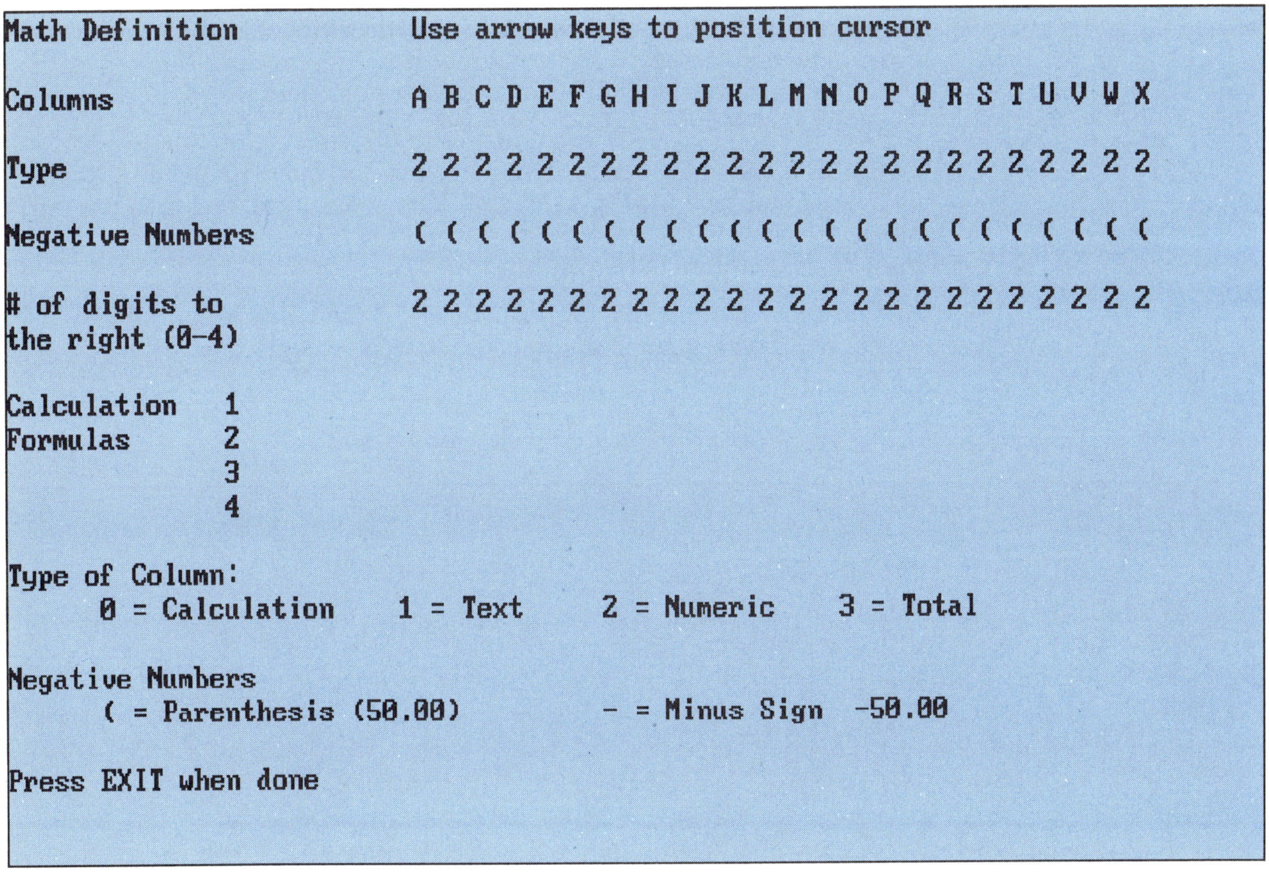

The various columns (A through X) are displayed at the top of the screen. A corresponds to the first tab stop, B to the second, and so on. Beneath each column letter are three specifications that can be changed for the column using the Math Def screen: the column type; how negative numbers will be displayed (in parentheses or with negative signs); and how many digits to the right of the decimal place will be displayed. Initially, all columns are set to Numeric type, negatives in parentheses, and a display of two digits to the right of the decimal. The following briefly discusses the different column types available and the operations associated with them.

(1) Text Defining a column for text allows you to enter labels, headings, descriptions, and so on, into the column. The area from the left margin to the first tab stop is always "Text" in nature. Columns after the first tab stop should be defined for text if they are to contain text.

(2) Numeric Columns defined as Numeric are designed to contain numbers and WordPerfect operators for subtotals, extra subtotals, totals, extra totals, and grand totals. The following describes the operators used by WordPerfect and the order in which they should appear within a column.

Order	Operator	Meaning
1st	+	Subtotal (totals the numbers up to the last subtotal above it)
2nd	t	Extra subtotal (used for a single entry subtotal)
3rd	=	Total (totals the subtotals up to the last total above it)
4th	T	Extra total (used for a single entry total)
5th	*	Grand total (totals the totals up to the last grand total above it)

A sixth operator, N, may be used in conjunction with the other operators listed to produce a negative subtotal. For instance, the operator N+ will produce a Subtotal that will be subtracted, rather than added, in a subsequent Total or Grand total.

To generate one of the totals listed here, you first move to the top of the math area and type **Alt-F7, 1** (Math/Columns, Math On) and then use the tab key to move to the appropriate place in the Numeric column and type the correct operator.

A typical math portion having one Numeric column and using the area between the left margin and first tab stop for labels might appears as:

```
April 1988
                             Sales
Purchases
   Item A                    100.00
   Item B                    200.00
   Item C                    300.00
      Subtotal                  +

   Item 1                     50.00
   Item 2                    100.00
   Item 3                    150.00
      Subtotal                  +

   Other                    t200.00

Returns
   Item A                     10.00
   Item B                     20.00
   Item C                     30.00
      Subtotal                  N+


Month End Total                 =
```

When the Math/Columns, Calculate command is executed (the last step in creating a math document), the operators in the Numeric column will cause the screen to display:

```
April 1988
                        Sales
Purchases
   Item A               100.00
   Item B               200.00
   Item C               300.00
      Subtotal          600.00+

   Item 1                50.00
   Item 2               100.00
   Item 3               150.00
      Subtotal          300.00+

   Other               t200.00

Returns
   Item A                10.00
   Item B                20.00
   Item C                30.00
      Subtotal          N60.00+


Month End Total       1,040.00=
```

The screen displays the WordPerfect operators next to the calculated values; however, they will not be printed.

(3) Total Columns defined as Total are most often used to display totals obtained from the column to the immediate left. The operators used in Total columns are the same as those used in Numeric columns.

It is important to note that subtotals, totals, and grand totals in a Total column will obtain their displayed values from both the column to the left and from the same column. That is, a Total (=) entered into a Total column will display the sum amount for all subtotals occurring above it in both the Total column and in the column to the left.

(0) Calculation A column defined as Calculation may be used to enter formulas into the document. A maximum of four columns may be defined as Calculation in nature. One formula may be entered into a Calculation column. The formula then is used to compute values from numbers found across the rows in the math area. When you tab the cursor to a Calculation column, WordPerfect displays an ! (exclamation point) at the cursor location. The ! indicates that the formula will be used to compute a value for that row (line).

You enter a Calculation formula into the Math Def screen at the time you specify the column to be (**0,** Calculation). An example of a formula designed to display 20% of the value found on the same line in the A column would be A*.2. Totals across rows in the A, B, and C columns could be obtained with the formula A+B+C.

All formulas are evaluated from left to right (there is no operator precedence), and nested parentheses are not allowed.

Four WordPerfect specific operators are available; however, they must be used independently from one another and other formulas. The operators are:

+	Add numbers in the Numeric columns.
+/	Average numbers in the Numeric columns.
=	Add numbers in the Total columns.
=/	Average numbers in the Total columns.

Turn Math On

(1) Math On **Code: [Math On]**

The next step is to insert the [Math On] code into the document at the point where the math column tab stops occur. Move the cursor to the top of the math portion and type **Alt-F7, 1** (Math/Columns, Math On).

Executing the Math On command inserts a [Math On] code into the document. When the cursor is moved past a [Math On] code, the message "Math" appears in the bottom lefthand corner of the screen. While the message appears on the screen, the Math/Columns command menu changes. Math On becomes Math Off, and Math Def becomes Calculate.

Enter the Math Data

The next step is to enter the labels, numbers, and operators into the math portion of the screen. Use the tab key to place the cursor in the appropriate column before you enter the data.

Numbers will align flush right to the tab stop with the period (.) key used for alignment. Numbers that overlap into the previous column will cause incorrect calculations. Reset the tab stops for the math portion to widen the column if this problem occurs.

When finished entering data, move the cursor to the bottom of the math area and type **Alt-F7, 1** (Math/Columns, Math Off). The command will insert a [Math Off] code into the document, which completes the partitioning of the math portion from the rest of the document.

Calculate

(2) Calculate

The final step in creating a math document is to calculate the math area. Calculations or recalculation may only be done while the "Math" message is displayed at the bottom of the screen. Therefore, the cursor must be somewhere between the imbedded [Math On] codes. Type **Alt-F7, 2** (Math/Columns, Calculate) to calculate the math area.

Once a math portion of a document has been created, you may move the cursor to the area and change the numbers within it. Care must be taken to maintain the original alignment of numbers to their tab stops. It is generally easier to delete a number and its preceding [TAB] code with the Backspace key and then to retab to the column and enter a new number. You then must use the Math/Columns Calculate command to recalculate the area for the new values.

Text Columns Feature

The Text Columns feature is used to produce text that is columnar in format. The two basic styles of columnar text include "Newspaper," where text continuously runs through columns on a page, and "Parallel," where text is table-like in nature.

Steps in Creating Text Columns

There are four basic steps in creating a document with columnar text.

1. Define the style and left and right margins for each column.
2. Turn Columns On.
3. Enter the text.
4. Turn Columns Off.

The following discusses the various Column commands in conjunction with other steps required to create text columns.

Define Columns

(4) Column Def Code = [Col Def:margin settings]

The Column Def command is used to define the style and margins for text columns. When the Columns Def command is executed, the following screen appears:

```
Text Column Definition

     Do you wish to have evenly spaced columns? (Y/N) N
     If yes, number of spaces between columns:
     Type of columns: 1
          1 - Newspaper
          2 - Parallel with Block Protect

     Number of text columns (2-24): 0

     Column     Left       Right      Column     Left       Right
      1:                               13:
      2:                               14:
      3:                               15:
      4:                               16:
      5:                               17:
      6:                               18:
      7:                               19:
      8:                               20:
      9:                               21:
     10:                               22:
     11:                               23:
     12:                               24:
```

Your answers to the first two prompts, "evenly spaced columns?" and "spaces between columns:", are used by WordPerfect when it later sets automatic left and right margins for each column. The margins may, however, be changed after they are generated.

The next prompt, "Type of Columns:", is used to specify either Newspaper or Parallel style columns.

(1) Newspaper style produces columns through which text flows. The following screen shows an example of Newspaper style:

Vista Ridge News

- Rec Room Remodeled -
The recreation room in Harris Commons will be closed for remodeling until July 17th.

When completed, the newly remodeled facility will provide a large toddlers area, a new indoor propane gas bar-b-que (with all the accessories) and a spacious cedar sun deck facing the pool.

To reserve rental time for your late summer social events, see Mr. Smith in the manager's office, Building A.

- Welcome Newcomers -
Vista Ridge welcomes two new families this month.

Parallel style produces columns into which text is entered in a horizontal fashion. It is used when the text is record-like in structure and where items within the records have varying line lengths. The following screen shows an example of Parallel style:

Vista Ridge Cleaning/Occupancy Journal

Unit	Style	Comments
Apartment 1A	3 bedroom, 2 floors, 1 1/2 baths.	Available for occupancy August 23rd. Replace living room carpet, paint throughout.
Apartment 3F	1 bedroom, studio	Vacant. Repaper walls in kitchen, repair front steps.

The "Number of text columns (2-24):" prompt is answered with the number of columns you want to appear on a page. In the examples above, 3 columns were specified.

The last specifications made to define columns are the left and right margins for each column. WordPerfect will compute a set of margins and allow you to edit them. When the margins are all correctly specified, type **F7** (Exit) to exit the Column Def screen.

When the Column Def screen is exited, a [Col Def:] code is inserted into the text at the cursor location. The style and margins for columns stay in effect for the rest of the document or until another [Col Def:] code is encountered.

Turn Column On

(3) Column On/Off — Code = [Col on] [Col off]

The next step in creating text columns is to turn Column On. To do so, move the cursor to where columnar text is to begin and type **Alt-F7, 3** (Math/Columns, Column On/Off). The command inserts a [Col on] code into the text.

Enter the Text

Newspaper Style If the style of columns is newspaper, you simply enter the text as you would during normal editing. When the first column on a page is filled (the bottom of the page is reached), WordPerfect will move to the top of the second column for you to continue entering text.

If you want to begin the next column before the bottom of the page is reached, you may do so by entering a hard page (Ctrl-↵) on the line that you want the current column to end.

Parallel Style If the style of columns is Parallel, you begin by entering the text for the first record item into the first column. When done, you type Ctrl-↵ (Hard Page) to move the cursor to the second column to enter the second item for the record.

The Hard Page keystroke in Parallel column text mode causes [BlockPro:Off/On] and [Col off/on] codes to be imbedded in the document. The codes are used by WordPerfect to maintain the horizontal structure of the record type data. Care must be taken to avoid deleting these codes.

Editing in Columnar Text Modes

To move quickly from one column to the next, the following keystrokes may be used:

Ctrl-Home, Right	Jump one column right.
Ctrl-Home, Left	Jump one column left.
Ctrl-Home, Home, Right	Jump to last column.
Ctrl-Home, Home, Left	Jump to first column.

You must block text to cut or copy it within a column.

Faster Editing

(5) Column Display

You may speed up scrolling and screen rewriting by using the Column Display command to display each column on a separate page while editing.

Turn Column Off

(3) Column On/Off — Code = [Col on] [Col off]

The final step in creating text columns is to turn Column Off. To do so, move the cursor to where columnar text is to end and type **Alt-F7, 3** (Math/Columns, Column On/Off). The command inserts a [Col off] code into the text.

Merge Codes — Alt-F9

The Merge Codes command provides a menu of merge codes used in merge text operations. To select a code from the menu, type **Alt-F9** (Merge Codes) and then enter the letter for the merge code you wish to insert into the document. An alternate method of inserting merge codes is to press and hold the Ctrl key and then type the letter for the code. For instance, the keystroke **Ctrl-R** inserts a ^R into the text.

The following is a brief description of the various merge codes. (For more information on merge text operations see Merge/Sort, Merge Operation, page W–71.)

Ctrl-C	^C	Pauses the merge to allow text to be entered from the keyboard. Type **F9** (Merge R) to continue the merge.
Ctrl-D	^D	Inserts the current DOS system date into the text.
Ctrl-E	^E	Marks the end of a record in a secondary file.
Ctrl-Fn^	^F	Selects field n from the secondary file for merging into the primary file.
Ctrl-G	^G	Begins execution of a macro (^Gmacro name^G) at the end of the merge.
Ctrl-N	^N	Advances one record in the secondary file. Ends the merge if End Of File is reached.
Ctrl-O	^O	Displays a message (^Omessage^O) on the status line at the bottom of the screen.
Ctrl-P	^P	Inserts a document file (^Pfilename^P) into the text.
Ctrl-Q	^Q	Stops the merge.
Ctrl-R	^R	Marks the end of a field in a secondary file.
Ctrl-S	^S	Changes the secondary file in use (^Sfilename^S).
Ctrl-T	^T	Sends all previously merged text to the printer.
Ctrl-U	^U	Rewrites the screen.
Ctrl-V	^V	Allows for the transfer of merge codes into the document being created.

Merge E

Shift-F9

The Merge E command inserts a ^E merge code and a hard return [HRt] into a document. The command may be used to separate records in a secondary merge file. (For more information on merge text operations see Merge/Sort, Merge Operations, page W–71.)

Merge R

F9

The Merge R command inserts a ^R merge code and a hard return [HRt] into a document. The command may be used to separate fields within records in a secondary merge file. (For more information on merge text operations see Merge/Sort, Merge Operations, page W–71.)

Merge/Sort

Ctrl-F9

The Merge/Sort command provides two WordPerfect features that are similar to those found in Data Base Management System software. The merge feature includes operations which combine text from two or more files to produce form letters, mailing labels, contracts, and so on. The sort operations may be used to sort text within a document and conditionally select and extract text from a document.

Merge Operations

(1) Merge

Certain situations exist where a standard form or document (general text) needs to be "filled in" with specific information. When this is the case, it is possible to automatically merge the specific information into the general text to produce the desired finished document.

All merge operations require a primary file (the file containing the general text) and a secondary file (the file containing the specific information). Merge codes are placed into the primary file. They cause WordPerfect to look to the secondary file for the specific information. When a merge is completed, the appropriate specific information will be merged with the general text and the finished document(s) will be ready to print.

The following discusses the steps and merge codes involved in completing a merge operation. It begins with an example of a simple merge used to create a form letter.

Simple Merges

The most common use of merge operations is to provide inside addresses and salutations for form letters. Here, the general text is the letter itself and the specific information is the name and address of the particular person to be included in the letter.

Creating a Secondary File

In the example, the first step will be to create the file containing the specific information (i.e, the secondary file). The information in the secondary file will include the first name, last name, phone number, and complete address for three different people.

The information in the secondary file is organized like data in a database. Together, the separate information items for each person constitute a record of data. Records in a secondary file are separated from each other with a ^R merge code and a hard return [HRt]. The ^R merge codes may be generated by typing **F9** (Merge R). The **F9** keystroke generates the ^R code and a hard return. You may generate ^R codes without the hard return (to insert them before existing hard returns) by typing a Ctrl-R keystroke.

The separate information items for each record (first name, last name, phone number, etc.) are entered into fields within the record and are separated from each other with a ^E merge code and a hard return [HRt] . The ^E merge codes may be generated by typing **Shift-F9** (Merge E). The **Shift-F9** keystroke generates the ^E code and a hard return [HRt]. You may generate ^E codes without the hard return (to insert them before existing hard returns) by typing a Ctrl-E keystroke.

The finished secondary file has the form:

```
Mr.^R                          <——Field #1
David^R                        <——Field #2
Cupra^R                        <——Field #3
(503) 229-3767^R               <——Field #4
9100 S.W. Alder Street^R       <——Field #5
Portland, OR 97221^R           <——Field #6
^E                         <——————End of record #1
Ms.^R                          <——Field #1
Sharon^R                       <——Field #2
Colson^R                       <——Field #3
^R                             <——Field #4
8766 N.W. Everett^R            <——Field #5
Portland, OR 97207^R           <——Field #6
^E                         <——————End of record #2
Dr.^R                          <——Field #1
Michael^R                      <——Field #2
Jerich^R                       <——Field #3
(503) 244-7163^R               <——Field #4
178 S.W. 4th Ave               <——Field #5
Apartment 27G^R
Portland, OR 97001^R           <——Field #6
^E                         <——————End of record #3
```

The fields in the secondary file are referred to by their number. Notice that Field #3 is the field that holds the last name for every person (each record) in the file. The Field#/item relationship must be maintained in the secondary file. If an information item is not available for a given record such as Ms. Colson's phone number (Field #4, record #2), an empty field must be entered there. However, the fields may be variable in length, such as the address (Field #5) for Dr. Jerich (record #3).

The next step in the example is to save the file under the filename "PROSPECTS" and clear the document from RAM with the Exit command.

Creating a Primary File

The primary file in the example will be the form letter into which the names and addresses of the secondary file will be merged. Fields of data from the secondary file are inserted into the primary file at the locations where ^Fn^ merge codes appear. The ^F indicates Field and the n^ indicates the Field number. For instance, putting the merge code ^F3^ into the primary file will cause the last names in the example secondary file to be inserted at the position where the ^F3^ merge code occurs.

The ^Fn^ codes may be generated by moving the cursor to the appropriate location in the primary file and typing **Alt-F9, F** (Merge Codes, ^F). You then answer the "Field Number?" prompt by entering the appropriate Field number. Another method is to move the cursor to the appropriate location and type **Ctrl-F,n,**^ where "n" is the Field number.

If you want to avoid blank lines in the finished document caused by empty fields in the secondary file, you may enter the ^F code as ^Fn?^.

When the primary file is finished it appears as:

```
                    Vista Ridge Townhouses

}F1} }F2} }F3}
}F5}
}F6}

Dear }F2}:

Thank you, }F2}, for your recent visit and tour of the
grounds at Vista Ridge Townhouses.

We have reviewed your references and are pleased to
inform you that we are able to offer any of our
available units for your immediate occupancy.

We appreciate your patience and look forward to meeting
you again. If you have any questions we can answer at
this time, please call me.

Sincerely,



Jerome Smith
Manager
```

Once the primary file is created, it is saved onto the disk (under the filename ACCEPTED in this example) and the document screen is cleared with the Exit command.

The final step in completing the simple merge is to type **Ctrl-F9, 1** (Merge/Sort, Merge) and then answer the "Primary file:" prompt by entering ACCEPTED and the "Secondary file:" prompt by entering PROSPECTS.

When the merge operation is completed, a document will appear on the screen consisting of three form letters, each separated by hard page codes automatically inserted by the merge feature. Each letter will have a different inside address and salutation. The first such letter appears as on the following page.

Vista Ridge Townhouses

Mr. David Cupra
9100 S.W. Alder Street
Portland, OR 97221

Dear David:

Thank you, David, for your recent visit and tour of the grounds at Vista Ridge Townhouses.

We have reviewed your references and are pleased to inform you that we are able to offer any of our available units for your immediate occupancy.

We appreciate your patience and look forward to meeting you again. If you have any questions we can answer at this time, please call me.

Sincerely,

Jerome Smith
Manager

The file may then be printed.

Other Merge Codes

There are several merge codes available with WordPerfect. (For a complete list and brief description of merge codes, see Merge Codes, page W–69.) The following discusses some of the more important merge codes and how they may be used.

Ctrl-C ˆC

The ˆC code pauses the merge to allow text to be entered from the keyboard. It may be used to customize certain portions of a document or, in conjunction with other codes, to direct the merge process. After entering the text from the keyboard, type **F9** (Merge R) to continue the merge.

Ctrl-D ˆD

The ˆD merge code may be placed in the primary file to automatically insert the current DOS system date into the text. The date will be inserted as text in the current Date Format (see Date, Format for information on setting date formats).

Ctrl-O ˆOmessageˆO

The ˆO merge code is generally used with other merge codes in the primary file. It displays a message on the status line at the bottom of the screen. Examples of how ˆO may be used with other codes include:

^O Enter tenant's name ^O^C Displays the "Enter tenant's name" message at the bottom of the screen and then pauses the merge at the position of the ^C merge code to allow text to be entered from the keyboard.

^O Enter filename to merge ^P^C^P^O Displays the "Enter filename to merge" message at the bottom of the screen and then pauses between two ^P codes for the filename to be entered from the keyboard.

Ctrl-P (^Pfilename^P)

The ^P Merge code is used to insert a document file into the text. The code is most useful when used in conjunction with a ^C merge code (^P^C^P) to allow the filename to be entered from the keyboard during the merge.

Ctrl-Q ^Q

The ^Q merge code stops the merge at the point where the code occurs. A ^Q code may be placed in the primary or secondary files.

Ctrl-S (^Sfilename^S)

Placed in a primary file, the ^S merge code may be used to switch to a different secondary file during the merge.

Ctrl-T ^T

Used in the primary file, the ^T merge code sends all previously merged text to the printer.

Sort/Select Operations

(2) Sort

The Merge/Sort command may be used to sort text or conditionally extract (Select) text from a document. When text is sorted, it appears ascending or descending in alphabetical or numeric order. When text is selected, only certain text (text which passes a condition) will appear.

Input/Output Files When sorting or selecting text, WordPerfect uses an

input file ⟶ process ⟶ output file

approach. The text to be sorted or selected from exists in the Input file. During the sort or select operation, a copy of the data in the Input file is made first. The copy then is sorted or selected (processed), and the processed data next are written to the Output file. If the Output file is specified as being the same as the Input file, the original data in the Input file will be overwritten by the processed data.

When the date to be processed exists as a portion of text within a larger document, the procedure to follow is as follows: Retrieve the file; Block the portion of text to be processed; type **Ctrl-F9, 2** (Merge/Sort, Sort) to begin the sort or select operation. The block of text is treated as both the Input and Output file by the Sort command.

Because of their overwriting nature, it is highly recommended that you save or backup your files before attempting to complete a sort or select operation.

Sort/Select Keys

Keys are the data items upon which WordPerfect sorts text, or they are the data items used in logical expressions upon which WordPerfect selects text.

Keys are specified by their location in the text and by their data type, string or numeric (WordPerfect refers to string data as being "alphanumeric").

There are three different text formats that may be sorted or selected: line, merge, or paragraph. In each case, the text is organized into records (the units of text which will be sorted or selected). The keys are found within the records. Each format varies in how its keys are defined.

Line Format In Line format the records to sort or select are arranged on lines with fields of data (data items) occurring at tab stops (see Format Line, Tabs for information on setting tab stops). Each line of data is considered to be a record, and each data item is considered to be a field of data. The data items are entered by using the Tab or Indent (**F4**) keys to separate them from each other.

```
Field 1          Field 2      Field   Field 4         Field 5     Field 6
                               3
   ↓                ↓          ↓        ↓                ↓           ↓

Pratt John       225-1234     M   06/22/82        1949.00     200.00
Smoler Ellen     225-3212     F   09/15/83        1650.00     300.00
Jones David      292-3832     M   06/15/82        1550.00      25.00
Sill Sally       224-4321     F   02/15/84        1507.00       0.00
                 ^            ^   ^                   ^           ^
                 L            L   L                   D           D
```

In the example above, Left and Decimal tab stops were set and the data items for name, phone, gender, date, salary, and account were entered with the Tab key used to align the data items at the appropriate tab stops.

The keys for Line format text are defined by data type (string or numeric), the field number where they occur, and the word number within the field where they occur. For instance, if you wanted to sort or select the example text by salary, you would define the appropriate key as numeric, field #5, word #1. If you wanted to sort or select the text by first names, you would specify the key as alphanumeric, field #1, word #2.

Merge Format With Merge format, records exist in a secondary file and are separated by ^E merge codes. Fields are separated by ^R merge codes. See Merge/Sort, Merge Operations for more information on secondary Merge files.

```
Mr.^R                          ←——Field #1
David^R                        ←——Field #2
Cupra^R                        ←——Field #3
(503) 229-3767^R               ←——Field #4
9100 S.W. Alder Street^R       ←——Field #5
Portland, OR 97221^R           ←——Field #6
^E                         ←————————End of record #1
Ms.^R                          ←——Field #1
Sharon^R                       ←——Field #2
Colson^R                       ←——Field #3
^R                             ←——Field #4
8766 N.W. Everet^R             ←——Field #5
Portland, OR 97207^R           ←——Field #6
^E                         ←————————End of record #2
```

The keys for Merge format text are defined by data type (string or numeric), the field number where they occur, and the word number within the field where they occur. For instance, if you wanted to sort or select the example merge text by last name, you would define the appropriate key as alphanumeric, field #3, word #1. If you wanted to sort or select the text by ZIP codes, you would specify the key as alphanumeric, field #6, word #3.

Paragraph Format In Paragraph format, the record is considered to be the text occurring between two or more hard returns [HRt]s. The keys used to sort or select paragraphs are defined by the line in which they occur, the field in which they occur (if Tabs or Indents are used they define fields such as Field #1 at [TAB] or [Indent] #1 and so on), and the word number in the line or field of the paragraph where they occur. For instance, if you wanted to sort or select paragraphs by the first word of the first line in each paragraph, and the first line of each paragraph is indented, you would specify the key as alphanumeric, line #1, field #2, word #1.

Sorting/Selecting Text

You begin to sort or select text by making sure that there are current backup copies of the text available. You next decide if the text needs to be blocked. If so, you block the text. You then type **Ctrl-F9** (Merge/Sort). If text is blocked, the Sort command menu screen will appear next.

If text is not blocked, you will need to type **2** (Sort) and then answer the Input file/Output file prompts by entering the filenames or typing ↵ for (Screen). Selecting (Screen) is the same as specifying the current document as the Input and/or Output file. After completing the steps, the Sort command menu screen will appear. In the following examples, a line format blocked portion of text will be used. The Sort menu screen appears as follows.

```
Smoler Ellen     225-3212  F   09/15/83   1650.00   300.00
Pratt John       225-1234  M   06/22/82   1949.00   200.00
Jones David      292-3832  M   06/15/82   1550.00    25.00
Sill Sally       224-4321  F   02/15/84   1507.00     0.00
Knat Michael     221-1235  M   09/15/80   1800.00   125.00
Smith Paul       223-8251  M   11/15/81   1700.00   350.00
Martins Mary     222-2123  F   11/01/85   1600.00   200.50
Beam Sandy       225-6912  F   02/15/86   1450.00   175.00
Johnson Frank    223-7928  M   03/20/86   1500.00     0.00

                                    Doc 3  Pg 1  Ln 1      Pos 10
[               ▲     ▲  ▲          ▲      ▲    ]
---------------------------- Sort by Line ----------------------------

Key Typ Field Word         Key Typ Field Word        Key Typ Field Word
 1   a    1    1            2                         3
 4                          5                         6
 7                          8                         9
Select


Action                     Order                     Type of Sort
Sort                       Descending                Line Sort

1 Perform Action; 2 View; 3 Keys; 4 Select; 5 Action; 6 Order; 7 Type: 0
```

A portion of the blocked text is displayed at the top of the screen. The Sort menu screen begins with a ruler line which displays the current tab stops. Beneath the ruler line is an area used to define keys, and four descriptions of current Sort screen settings: Select, Action, Order, and Type of Sort. At the bottom of the screen appears the Sort command menu.

(1) Perform Action

The Perform Action command is used to execute the sort or select operation after all of the appropriate sort/select settings have been made.

(2) View

The View command may be used to scroll through the text at the top of the screen without leaving the Sort menu screen.

(3) Keys

The Keys command is used to define the keys to be used in a sort or select operation. When the Keys command is executed, the cursor jumps to the key definition area of the Sort menu screen and you are allowed to edit the key definition displayed there. The first Sort key is defined by default as alphanumeric, field #1, word #1.

There are nine key definitions available. If the action for which the keys are being defined is Sort, the sort order will be primary sort on key #1, secondary sort on key #2, and so on. In the example here, if you wanted the records to be sorted first by Male/Female and then by salary amounts within those two categories, you would set key #1 to a, 3, 1 (alphanumeric, field #3, word #1) and key #2 to n, 5, 1 (numeric, field #5, word #1).

(4) Select

The Select command is used to extract records of text that meet certain criteria. When the select process is over, only those records meeting the criteria will appear in the Output file or on the screen. To select records, you must first define all keys that will be used in the criteria. You then type **4** (Select) and enter the logical expression to be used as the select criteria. The WordPerfect operators for such expressions include:

Relational		Logical	
=	Equal	+	OR
<	Less than	*	AND
>	Greater than		
<=	Less than or equal to		
>=	Greater than or equal to		
<>	Not equal to		

In the example, if you wanted to extract those records for men with salaries greater than or equal to $1650.00, you would first define the two keys for gender and salary. Here, key #8 will be defined for gender as a, 3, 1 (alphanumeric, field #3, word #1) and key #9 will be defined for salary as n, 5, 1 (numeric, field #5, word #1).

You then may type **4** (Select) and the cursor will jump to the Select description area on the screen for you to enter the criteria. The criteria is entered in the form:

```
Key8=M * Key9>=1650
```

Once the Select command has been used to enter a criterion, the action to perform automatically becomes Select rather than Sort. To return to sorting, you must type **4** (Select) and delete the criteria shown on the screen (use the Del, Backspace key, or Ctrl-End keys).

(5) Action

When a select criteria exists, the Action command may be used to (**1**) Select and Sort or (**2**) Select Only. With Select and Sort, the extracted records are sorted on the currently defined keys. With Select Only, they are only extracted.

(6) Order

The Order command may be used to set the sort order to (**1**) Ascending or (**2**) Descending.

(7) Type

The Type command is used to specify the format type, (**1**) Merge, (**2**) Line, or (**3**) Paragraph, for the data being sorted or selected. The current type is displayed under the ruler line of the Sort menu screen.

Move Ctrl-F4

Move 1 Sentence; 2 Paragraph; 3 Page; Retrieve 4 Column; 5 Text; 6 Rectangle:0

Block/Move

1 Cut Block; 2 Copy Block; 3 Append; 4 Cut/Copy Column; 5 Cut/Copy Rectangle:0

The Move command is used to perform the "cut-and-paste" operations of WordPerfect. The operations include moving a section of text to another location, copying a section of text to another location, and deleting a section of text from the document.

The text being moved, copied, or deleted is temporarily held during and after the operation in what is called a "file buffer." If the text is being moved or copied, it is placed in the Move file buffer. When text is deleted, it is held in the Undelete file buffer. Once a cut-and-paste operation is completed, a copy of the text remains in the file buffer. The copy of text in the file buffer will be replaced by a subsequent Move or Delete operation.

The Move and Block/Move commands are related. Both are designed to facilitate the cutting and pasting of various sizes and shapes of text. The following discusses each of the commands and the type of text for which they are designed.

Move (1) Sentence (2) Paragraph (3) Page

The Move Sentence, Paragraph and Page commands are used to: (**1**) cut a portion of text to be moved to another location; (**2**) make a copy of a portion of text to be copied to another location; or (**3**) delete a portion of text from the document.

The three commands differ only in the lines of text they are designed to cut, copy, or delete. A sentence is defined by WordPerfect to be that text which occurs between periods and/or hard returns. A paragraph is defined by WordPerfect to be that text which occurs between hard returns. A page is defined by WordPerfect to be that text which occurs between soft or hard page breaks.

To move lines of text, position the cursor on the sentence, paragraph, or page to be affected and type **Ctrl-F4** (Move). Next select the appropriate text definition, sentence, paragraph, or page, by entering **1, 2,** or **3,** respectively. The sentence, paragraph, or page of text will become highlighted on the screen. Next answer the menu prompt (**1** Cut; **2** Copy; **3** Delete:) by typing **1** (Cut). The highlighted text will be removed from the screen and placed into the Move file buffer. To complete the move operation, position the cursor at the location where you want the text to appear and type **Ctrl-F4, 5** (Move, Retrieve text).

To copy the text, position the cursor on the text and type **Ctrl-F4** (Move). Next select the appropriate text definition and answer the menu prompt (**1** Cut; **2** Copy; **3** Delete:) by typing **2** (Copy). The highlighted text will be copied, and the copy will be placed into the Move file buffer. To complete the copy operation, position the cursor at the location where you want the copied text to appear and type **Ctrl-F4, 5** (Move, Retrieve text).

To delete the text, position the cursor on the text and type **Ctrl-F4** (Move). Next, select the appropriate text definition and answer the menu prompt (**1** Cut; **2** Copy; **3** Delete:) by typing **3** (Delete). The highlighted text will be erased from the document. It will, however, be placed in the Undelete buffer and can be retrieved with the Cancel command, if necessary.

Retrieve (4) Column (5) Text (6) Rectangle

The Retrieve Column, Text, and Rectangle commands are used to retrieve text from the Move file buffer and place it at the current cursor location. Each command is designed for the way in which the text was initially placed in the Move file buffer. To retrieve text, move the cursor to the location where you want the retrieved text to appear and type **Ctrl-F4** (Move). Then enter the appropriate Retrieve command: Column, Text, or Rectangle. Retrieving copied text does not erase it from the Move file buffer—it may be retrieved again if desired.

The Retrieve Column command retrieves text placed in the Move file buffer by the Block/Move, Cut/Copy Column command. The Retrieve Text command retrieves text placed in the Move file buffer by the Move Sentence, Paragraph and Page commands, as well as the Block/Move, Cut Block, and Copy Block commands. The Retrieve Rectangle command retrieves text placed in the Move file buffer by the Cut/Copy Rectangle command.

See the appropriate commands for more information on placing text into the Move file buffer.

Block/Move (1) Cut Block

The Block/Move, Cut Block command is used to place a block of text into the Move file buffer in order to move the block to another location in the document. To move a block of text, block the text to be moved and type **Ctrl-F4, 1** (Move, Cut Block). The highlighted (blocked) text will be removed from the screen and placed into the Move file buffer. To complete the move operation, position the cursor at the location where you want the text to appear and type **Ctrl-F4, 5** (Move, Retrieve Text).

Block/Move (2) Copy Block

The Block/Move, Copy Block command is used to place a copy of a block into the Move file buffer in order to copy the block to another location in the document. Block the text to be copied and then type **Ctrl-F4, 2** (Move, Copy Block). The highlighted text will be copied and placed into the Move file buffer. To complete the copy operation, position the cursor at the location where you want the copied text to appear and type **Ctrl-F4, 5** (Move, Retrieve Text). Retrieving copied text does not erase it from the Move file buffer—it may be retrieved again if desired.

Block/Move (3) Append

The Block/Move, Append command is used to append a blocked portion of text to the bottom of a disk file. To use the command, block the text and then type **Ctrl-F4, 3** (Move, Append). Next enter the name of the file to which the block of text is to be appended.

Block/Move (4) Cut/Copy Column

The Block/Move, Cut/Copy Column command is used to move, copy, or delete a column of text defined by tabs, tab aligns, indents, or hard returns. Move the cursor to the top of the column of text you want to move, copy, or delete and then turn Block on by typing **Alt-F4** (Block). Next move the cursor to the bottom of the column. The entire block will be highlighted at this point. Then type **Ctrl-F4, 4** (Move, Cut/Copy Column). Now only the column in which the cursor is located will be highlighted. Next select (**1**) Cut, (**2**) Copy, or (**3**) Delete to move, copy, or delete the text in the column. Finally, if the operation is to move or copy the column of text, move the cursor to where you want the column of text to appear and type **Ctrl-F4, 4** (Move, Retrieve Column).

Block/Move (5) Cut/Copy Rectangle

The Block Move, Cut/Copy Rectangle command is used to move, copy, or delete a rectangular segment of text. Move the cursor to the top left corner of the rectangle of text you want to move, copy, or delete and then turn Block on by typing **Alt-F4** (Block). Next move the cursor to the bottom right corner of the rectangle. The entire block will be highlighted at this point. Then type **Ctrl-F4, 5** (Move, Cut/Copy Rectangle). Now only the rectangle described by its top left and bottom right corners will be highlighted. Next select (**1**) Cut, (**2**) Copy, or (**3**) Delete to move, copy, or delete the text in the rectangle. Finally, if the operation is to move or copy the rectangle of text, move the cursor to where you want the text to appear and type **Ctrl-F4, 6** (Move, Retrieve Rectangle).

Print — Shift-F7

1 Full Text; 2 Page; 3 Options; 4 Printer Control; 5 Type thru; 6 Preview

The Print command is used to print the current document either in full or by page, change certain options and printer controls, print directly from the keyboard, and preview on the screen what the printed text will look like.

(1) Full Text

Type **Shift-F7, 1** (Print, Full Text) to print the entire current document. To print a document from the disk, see List Files, Print (page W–53). To cancel a print operation, type **Shift-F7, 4, C** (Print, Printer Control, Cancel).

(2) Page

Type **Shift-F7, 2** (Print, Page) to print the current page (the page upon which the cursor is located). To print a page from a document on a disk, see Print, Printer Control (bottom of page).

Block/Print

To print a block of text, block the text to be printed and then type **Shift-F7** (Print). To cancel a print operation, type **Shift-F7, 4, C** (Print, Printer Control, Cancel).

(3) Options

The Options command provides three print control features. Once a feature has been changed with the Options command, you are returned to the Print commands to complete the printing operation. When you exit the Print commands, the Options return to their default values. See Printer Control for changing these options in a more permanent manner.

1 Printer Number You may select another printer definition for WordPerfect to use by entering the numbers 1 through 6 on this menu option. Type **Shift-F7, 3, 1** (Print, Options, Printer Number) and then enter the number for the appropriate printer definition. See Print, Printer Control for more information.

Unless printer #6 has been redefined by a user, it will have the definition of "DOS Text Printer." Specifying a Printer Number 6 will cause WordPerfect to print the document, page, or block of text onto a disk file under the name DOS.TXT. The .TXT file will be ASCII and its text format will be preserved with padded spaces. To cancel a print to file operation, type **Shift-F7, 4, C** (Print, Printer Control, Cancel).

2 Number of Copies Prints, in sequential order, n number of copies of the document.

3 Binding Width (1/10 in.) Offsets printing n 1/10's of an inch on odd and even pages for binding two-sided copies. Text is shifted to the right on odd-numbered pages and to the left on even-numbered pages.

(4) Printer Control

The Printer Control command is used to define the various printers that may be used to print documents as well as to monitor and control ongoing print operations. The Printer Control screen appears as follows.

```
Printer Control
                                        C - Cancel Print Job(s)
1 - Select Print Options                D - Display All Print Jobs
2 - Display Printers and Fonts          G - "Go" (Resume Printing)
3 - Select Printers                     P - Print a Document
                                        R - Rush Print Job
Selection: 0                            S - Stop Printing


Current Job

Job Number: n/a                         Page Number:  n/a
Job Status: n/a                         Current Copy: n/a
Message:    The print queue is empty

Job List

Job  Document           Destination          Forms and Print Options



Additional jobs not shown: 0
```

Several menu selections appear at the top of the screen. Displayed below the menu selections are various messages about printing operations that may be occurring. The three menu options to the left (1 through 3) deal with defining printer specifications. The six menu options on the right (C, D, G, P, R, S) deal with controlling print operations.

1 Select Print Options This command is the same as **Shift-F7, 3** (Print, Options) except that any changes made to Printer Number, Number of Copies, and Binding Width will stay in effect until you exit WordPerfect. See Print, Options (page W–83) for more information.

Printer Install

Printers vary in what they can do and in the control codes that cause them to do what they do. Therefore, WordPerfect needs to know what printer(s) it will be using. Once specified, however, the printer information is saved with the software and need not be specified again.

In an overview, WordPerfect may have up to six different printers defined for it at one time. WordPerfect refers to the printer definitions as being for printer number 1, printer number 2, and so on. The Print, Options (**Shift-F7, 3**) or Print, Printer Control, Select Print Options (**Shift-F7, 4, 1**) commands may be used to tell WordPerfect to use a particular printer by its number to print a document.

The default printer number is always printer number 1. Therefore, if you have predefined printer number 1 as being an Epson FX 80 (one brand and model of printer), WordPerfect will conform its data to the requirements of that printer each time it prints.

If you have another printer, for instance, a Laser Jet 500+ (another brand and model of printer), you may define it as being printer number 2. However, if you want to print with the Laser Jet, you will need to use the Print, Options or Print, Printer Control, Select Print Options commands to specify printer number 2 as being the printer definition for WordPerfect to use.

2 Display Printers and Fonts Displays the six printer numbers and the brand/model of printer for which each number is currently defined.

3 Select Printers The Select Printers command is the command used to assign a printer definition to a printer number. Type **Shift-F7, 4, 3** (Print, Printer Control, Select Printers) to begin the assignment operation.

The top of the screen will show the definitions currently in use. The bottom of the screen will show which of those definitions is currently being used for printer number 1. Typing the Cursor Up or Cursor Down keys will continuously scroll through the six printer numbers showing the definitions in use for each.

Continue typing Cursor Up or Cursor Down until the desired printer number appears. To change the definition for the printer number, you may either enter one of the numbers displayed next to the definitions at the top of the screen or type PgDn to produce an extensive list of printer models from which to choose. If you type PgDn, you will find the list of printers is much too large to fit on one screen. Use the PgDn and PgUp keys to scan through the list. When you find the printer definition you desire, enter its number.

When you are finished, type **F7** (Exit) to save the definitions or **F1** (Cancel) to abort the printer number assignment operation.

C Cancel Print Job(s) The Cancel Print Job(s) command is used to abort the printing of one or more documents.

D Display All Print Jobs Displays a list of all documents waiting to be printed.

G "Go" (Resume Printing) Resumes printing a document after the printer has been stopped.

P Print a Document Prints a document from the disk. WordPerfect will prompt for the filename of the document. It next prompts Page(s): (All). If you type ↵, the full document will be printed. You may, however, specify that only certain pages be printed. To specify certain pages you may enter one of the following:

N	Print page number N
N-	Print from page number N to end of document
N-n	Print pages N through n inclusive
-N	Print from beginning of document through page N

Page numbers must be entered in the way you have assigned them to the document.

R Rush Print Job Moves a document waiting to be printed to the head of the printing queue.

S Stop Printing Suspends printing until the Go (Resume Printing) or Cancel Print Job(s) command is given.

(5) Type thru

The Type thru command allows the printer to be used as a typewriter. Options include sending each character to the printer as it is typed or sending a line of text to the printer after it has been typed and edited on the screen.

(6) Preview

The Preview command creates a temporary file for you to view on the screen. The file is designed to most closely resemble the document when it is printed. The Preview command is useful for discovering formatting problems caused by errant codes.

To preview a document, type **Shift-F7, 6** (Print, Preview) and then answer the prompt to preview the entire document or the current page. In a few moments the screen will display the document as it will appear when printed. You cannot edit the Preview screen; however, if you find a formatting error in the Preview screen, you may use the Switch command (**Shift-F3**) to return to your WordPerfect document and make changes to it. When you are finished with the preview file, type **F7** (Exit).

Replace

Alt-F2

The Replace command is used to search the document for occurrences of specific words, phrases, or WordPerfect codes and replace them with another word, phrase, or code. To use the Replace command, type **Alt-F2** (Replace).

The prompt "w/Confirm? (Y/N)" will appear on the screen. If you type "Y," WordPerfect will stop on each word pattern for which it is searching and will prompt "Confirm? (Y/N)." You then answer "Y" to replace the word pattern and "N" to skip and continue searching. If you type "N" to the "w/Confirm (Y/N)" prompt, WordPerfect will automatically replace all of the occurrences of the word pattern with the replacement word pattern.

The next prompt displayed by the Replace command is ->Srch. At this point, you type the word pattern for which to search. You may type any keyboard characters or specify WordPerfect codes by typing the keystroke combinations that would normally generate the codes. When finished typing the search word pattern, type **Alt-F2** (Replace) again.

The next prompt "Replace with:" is answered by typing the word pattern you want the search word pattern to be replaced with. You may answer this prompt in the same manner as you answer the ->Srch prompt.

When you have finished typing the replace word pattern, type **Alt-F2** (Replace) again and the search and replace operation will commence.

The Replace command only searches forward from the current cursor position. Lower-case search characters will match upper- and lower-case characters in the document; upper-case search characters will only match upper-case characters. An extended search, one in which headers, footers, footnotes, and endnotes are also searched, may be done by typing the Home key before typing **Alt-F2** (Replace).

Block/Replace

The Replace operation may be done on a block of text by blocking the text to be searched before typing **Alt-F2** (Replace).

Retrieve

Shift-F8

The Retrieve command may be used to retrieve a document file onto a clear screen or into a current document at the cursor location. Type **Shift-F10** (Retrieve) and then enter the filename of the file you wish to retrieve.

Reveal Codes

Alt-F3

Splits the screen and reveals imbedded WordPerfect codes. Cursor control keys synchronously move top and bottom cursors (cursors in the text and code screens). The Del or Backspace keys may be used to delete codes or text. Typing any other key returns the screen to the normal editing mode.

Save

F10

The Save command may be used to save a document without clearing the screen or returning to DOS. It is recommended that you use the Save command frequently while you are editing. Type **F10** (Save). If the document is one that has not been previously saved, you must next enter a filename under which to save it. If the file has been previously saved, WordPerfect will display the original filename as the default answer to the "Document to be Saved:" prompt. Type ↵ if you want to save the document under the same name (replace the copy on the disk). Type a new name if you do not want to replace the file on the disk. If you use an existing filename, WordPerfect will pause and prompt "Replace file (Y/N)." Type Y to replace the file on the disk and type N or ↵ to abort the Save operation.

Block/Save

You may save a block of text by blocking the text before you type **F10** (Save).

Screen

Ctrl-F3

0 Rewrite; 1 Window; 2 Line Draw; 3 Ctrl/Alt keys; 4 Colors; 5 Auto Rewrite: 0

(0) Rewrite

The Rewrite command is used to rewrite the screen once the Auto Rewrite feature has been turned off. Type **Ctrl-F3,↵**.

(1) Window

The Window command may be used to split the screen horizontally to view documents 1 and 2 at the same time (see Switch, page W–92). Type **Ctrl-F3, 1** and then enter the number of screen lines to be displayed for the current document. Typing 11 will split the screen in half (two equal windows). Typing 24 will return the screen to the normal one-screen mode. Screens may not be split into windows of less than two lines.

Use the Switch command (**Shift-F3**) to move the cursor from one window to the other.

(2) Line Draw

The Line Draw command is used for drawing boxes and lines in the current text file. It provides screen graphic characters and commands that allow shapes to be drawn on the screen by using the cursor control keys. However, many printers do not support the screen graphics characters used by the Line Draw command, and printing a file with such characters in it may lead to unpredictable results.

The Line Draw command is composed of two menus. The relationship of the menus may be graphically represented as follows.

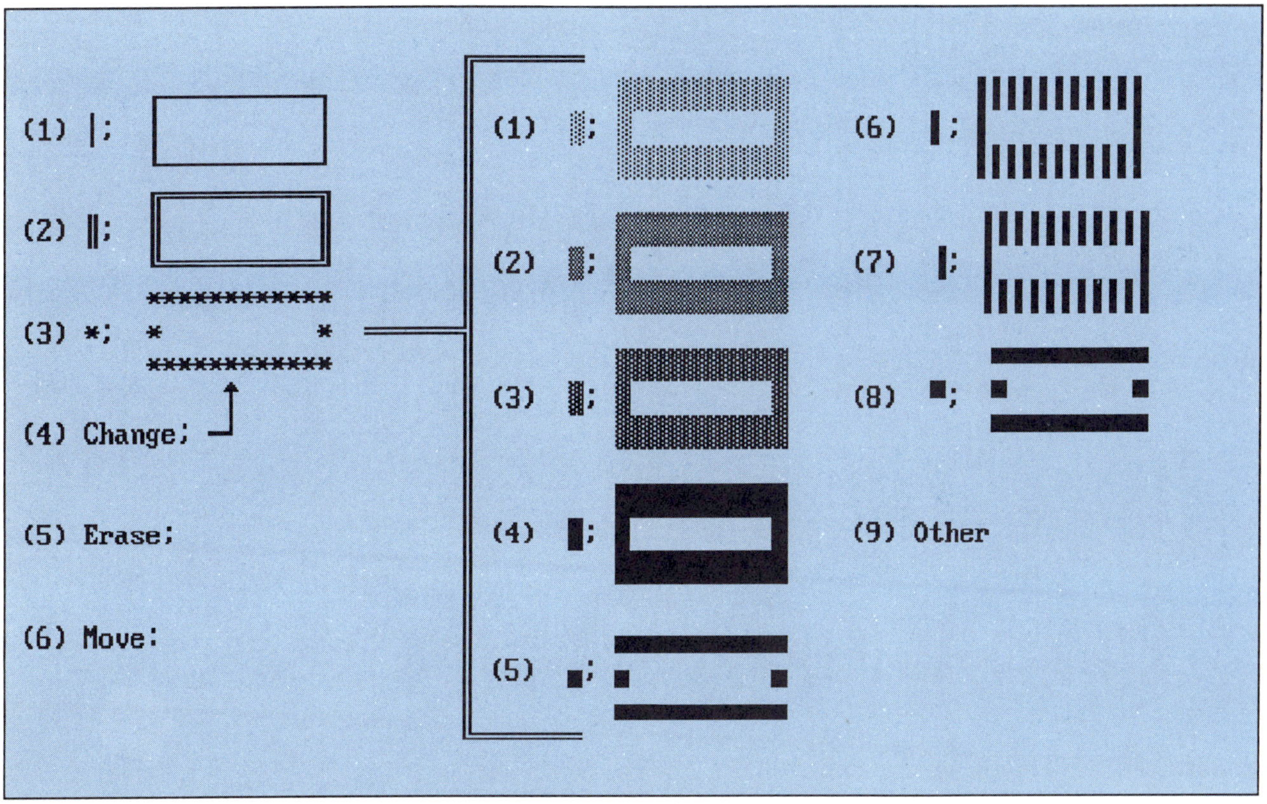

The first menu presented (far left) has six options. Options **(1)** through **(3)** are different graphics characters with which boxes and lines may be drawn. The third character (*) can be changed with the next option, Change. The last two options are Erase and Move.

To draw a line or box, first move the cursor to the point at which drawing is to begin. Next type **Ctrl-F3, 2** (Screen, Line Draw) and enter the number **1, 2** or **3** to specify the graphics character of your choice. You may now draw lines composed of the selected character by using the cursor control keys to move in the appropriate draw direction.

To stop drawing and move the cursor to a new location, type **6** (Move). To erase characters on the screen, type **5** (Erase) and then move the cursor under the characters you wish to erase.

The third graphics character shown on the Line Draw menu, *, can be changed to any one of the characters shown on the right (**1** through **8**). Type **4** (Change) and then select and enter the number of the desired graphics character from the second Line Draw menu. **9** (Other) may be used to define a keyboard character to use in drawing lines.

(3) Ctrl/Alt keys

Screen graphics characters may be assigned to Ctrl-key and Alt-key combination keystrokes. However, many printers do not support the screen graphics characters used by the Ctrl/Alt keys command, and printing a file with such characters in it may lead to unpredictable results.

To assign a graphics character to a keystroke combination, type **Ctrl-F3, 3** (Screen, Ctrl/Alt keys). WordPerfect will display the following.

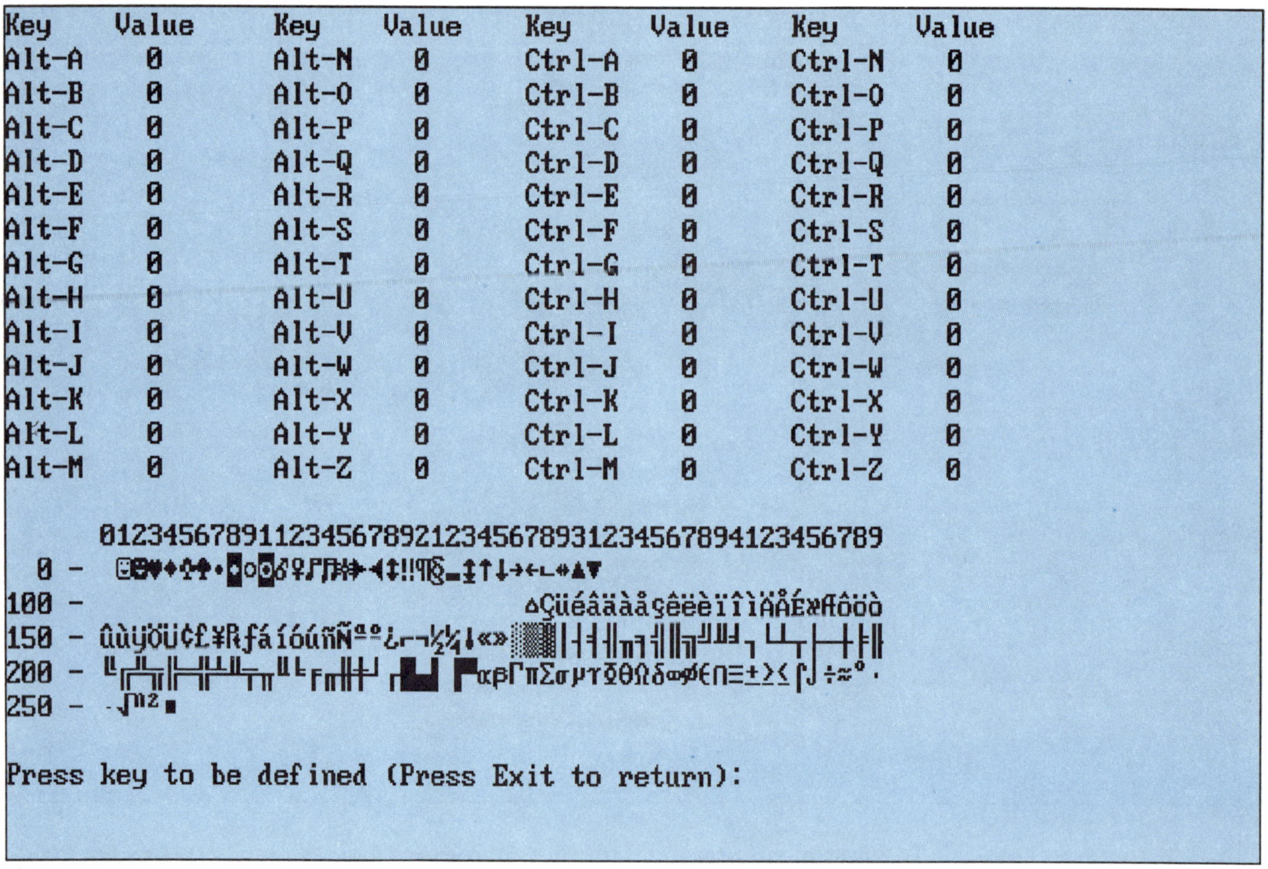

Key	Value	Key	Value	Key	Value	Key	Value
Alt-A	0	Alt-N	0	Ctrl-A	0	Ctrl-N	0
Alt-B	0	Alt-O	0	Ctrl-B	0	Ctrl-O	0
Alt-C	0	Alt-P	0	Ctrl-C	0	Ctrl-P	0
Alt-D	0	Alt-Q	0	Ctrl-D	0	Ctrl-Q	0
Alt-E	0	Alt-R	0	Ctrl-E	0	Ctrl-R	0
Alt-F	0	Alt-S	0	Ctrl-F	0	Ctrl-S	0
Alt-G	0	Alt-T	0	Ctrl-G	0	Ctrl-T	0
Alt-H	0	Alt-U	0	Ctrl-H	0	Ctrl-U	0
Alt-I	0	Alt-V	0	Ctrl-I	0	Ctrl-V	0
Alt-J	0	Alt-W	0	Ctrl-J	0	Ctrl-W	0
Alt-K	0	Alt-X	0	Ctrl-K	0	Ctrl-X	0
Alt-L	0	Alt-Y	0	Ctrl-L	0	Ctrl-Y	0
Alt-M	0	Alt-Z	0	Ctrl-M	0	Ctrl-Z	0

Press key to be defined (Press Exit to return):

The table shown at the bottom of the screen represents the various graphics characters you may assign to combination keystrokes. The numbers bordering the table are used to determine a character's code number. For instance, the one-half sign (½) found roughly in the middle of the table has the code number 150 + 10 + 10 + 1 = 171. To assign the ½ to the keystroke Alt-H, type Alt-H and then enter the number 171.

Once a combination keystroke has been assigned a graphics character, typing the keystroke will generate the character in your text.

(4) Colors

The Colors command is used to change the screen attributes for color, monochrome, or black-and-white monitors. The command is largely self-explanatory.

The command affects only the current document screen. To change the screen attributes for both document screens, the Colors command must be executed from both documents. Screen attributes are saved onto the WordPerfect software and remain in effect until later changed with the Colors command.

(5) Auto Rewrite

Turns off the automatic reformatting of text. Once the command is issued it stays in effect until WordPerfect is exited. To reformat text with Auto Rewrite off, type **Ctrl-F3, 0** (Screen, Rewrite)

Shell

Ctrl-F1

The Shell command allows you to temporarily exit WordPerfect to DOS if the computer has enough RAM to accommodate the operation. To return to WordPerfect from DOS, type EXIT↵.

If you choose to return to DOS through the Shell command, you should always return to WordPerfect and exit by typing **F7** (Exit) before turning off the computer.

▶Search

F2

The ▶Search command is used to move the cursor forward to occurrences of specific words, phrases, or WordPerfect codes. To use the ▶Search command, type **F2** (▶Search).

The prompt "->Srch" will be displayed on the screen by the Search command. At this point you type the word pattern for which to search. You may type any keyboard characters or specify WordPerfect codes by typing the keystroke combinations that would normally generate the codes. When you have finished typing the search word pattern, type **F2** (▶Search) again and the search operation will commence. When the specified word pattern is found, the search will halt and the cursor will be moved to the location where the word pattern occurs in the document. To continue the search for the same word pattern, type **F2, F2** (▶Search, ▶Search).

Lower-case search characters will match upper- and lower-case characters in the document. Upper-case search characters will only match upper-case characters. An extended search, one in which headers, footers, footnotes, and endnotes also are searched, may be done by typing the Home key before typing **F2** (▶Search).

◀Search

Shift-F2

The ◀Search command is used to move the cursor backwards to occurrences of specific words, phrases, or WordPerfect codes. The ◀Search command works in the same manner as the ▶Search command. See ▶Search for more information on the Search operation.

Spell

Ctrl-F2

Check 1 Word; 2 Page; 3 Document; 4 Change Dictionary; 5 Look Up; Count

WordPerfect comes with a spell checking feature that will search a document for words not found in its 115,000+ word dictionary. The dictionary data are kept on a separate diskette. If you are using a computer with two floppy disk drives, you will need to insert the Speller diskette into the B: drive each time it is needed. If you have a hard-disk drive, the Speller diskette may be copied onto the same subdirectory as WordPerfect.

Check (1) Word (2) Page (3) Document

The spelling feature may be used to check the current word, page, or document. Each is similar in how WordPerfect checks for spelling errors.

WordPerfect will move to the start of the word, page, or document and begin comparing the word(s) found there with the words in its dictionary. When it finds a word not listed in its dictionary it stops and presents a screen similar to the following.

```
Each large townhouse unit has wall to wall carpeting, drapes,

privite patio and sun deck. You will also find the townhouse of

your choice equipped with a modern self-defrosting refrigerator,

self-cleaning oven, dishwasher and garbage disposal unit.  Every

tenant enjoys year round swimming and sauna plus use of our

================================================================================

  A. primite                  B. private                  C. privity
  D. previewed                E. privata                  F. privati
  G. privet                   H. proved                   I. provide




Not Found!  Select Word or Menu Option (0=Continue): 0
1 Skip Once; 2 Skip; 3 Add Word; 4 Edit; 5 Look Up; 6 Phonetic
```

At the top of the screen is the portion of the document where WordPerfect found the unknown word. Beneath is a list of words WordPerfect did find in its dictionary that may be the correct spelling for the unknown word. At the bottom of the screen is the Spell menu of commands.

Select Word or Menu Option (0 = Continue):

If the correct spelling for the word appears in the middle of the screen, you may type the letter preceding it (A., B., etc.) to cause WordPerfect to replace the unknown word with the correct spelling. WordPerfect will automatically capitalize the word if it occurs in the document as capitalized.

(1) Skip Once

If you type **1** (Skip Once), WordPerfect will continue its search and, if it finds the word again, it will stop for you to correct it.

(2) Skip

If you type **2** (Skip), WordPerfect will continue its search and ignore the word if it occurs again.

(3) Add Word

You may use the Add Word command to cause WordPerfect to add the word to its dictionary.

(4) Edit

You may use the Edit command to edit the word. When you have finished, type the Enter key. If the edited word is not found in the dictionary, WordPerfect will not continue.

(5) Look Up (6) Phonetic

You may use the Look Up and Phonetic commands to look up words. If Look Up is used, you type the word to be looked up and if it is found, it is displayed on the screen. With Phonetic, WordPerfect will look up and display all words which phonetically approximate the current misspelled word.

Double Word

During its search, WordPerfect will also stop on occurrences of double words. You are given the options Skip, Delete the 2nd word, Edit, or Disable double-word checking.

Words Containing Numbers

If WordPerfect finds a word containing a number, you are given the options Skip, Ignore words containing numbers, or Edit.

Word Count

When it has finished checking the document, WordPerfect will display the total number of words it checked during the Spell operation.

Super/Subscript — Shift-F1

1 Superscript; 2 Subscript; 3 Overstrike; 4 Adv Up; 5 Adv Dn; 6 Adv Ln: 0

(1) Superscript — Code = [SuprScrpt]

Causes one character of text to be printed above the normal line. Move the cursor beneath the character to be superscripted and type **Shift-F1, 1.**

Block/Superscript To superscript more than one character, block the text to be superscripted and then type **Shift-F1, 1.**

(2) Subscript — Code = [SubScrpt]

Causes one character of text to be printed below the normal line. Move the cursor beneath the character to be subscripted and type **Shift-F1, 2.**

Block/Subscript To subscript more than one character, block the text to be subscripted and then type **Shift-F1, 2.**

(3) Overstrike — Code = [Ovrstk]

Causes one character to be overstruck by the preceding character. Move the cursor under the character to be overstruck and type **Shift-F1, 3.** For instance, to produce a not equal sign type /**Shift-F1,3**=. The screen will display only the =; however, the printer will print ≠.

(4) Adv Up

Code = [Adv▲]

Causes all following characters to be printed above the normal line. Move the cursor under the character where the elevated text is to begin and type **Shift-F1, 4.** Use Adv Dn (**Shift-F1, 5**) to return text to normal line height. (*Note:* Many printers do not support this feature.)

(5) Adv Dn

Code = [Adv▼]

Causes all following characters to be printed below the normal line. Move the cursor under the character where the dropped text is to begin and type **Shift-F1, 5.** Use Adv Up (**Shift-F1, 4**) to return text to normal line height. (*Note:* Many printers do not support this feature.)

(6) Adv Ln

Code = [AdvLn:nn]

Causes the printer to advance the paper to line nn before it resumes printing. Move the cursor to the point at which advancement is to begin and type **Shift-F1, 6.** Then enter the line number at which printing is to resume. The printed line number for the current cursor position may be found on the status line at the bottom of the screen.

Switch

Shift-F3

WordPerfect allows editing of two text files at the same time. When WordPerfect is first loaded, the default file for editing is Document 1 (displayed as Doc 1 on the status line). To begin editing Document 2, type **Shift-F3.**

All editing and file operations are treated as separate operations between the two documents. You must exit both documents before exiting WordPerfect.

You may copy text from one file to the other. First, block the text to be copied and then type **Ctrl-F4, 2** (Move, Copy Block). Next, type **Shift-F3** (Switch), move the cursor to where you want the copied text to appear, and then type **Ctrl-F4, 5** (Move, Retrieve Text).

You may view both Document 1 and Document 2 at the same time by using the Window command (see Screen **Ctrl-F3**).

Block/Switch

You may use Switch to convert case type for text. To convert lower case to upper case, block the text to be converted and type **Shift-F3** (Switch). Next type **1** (Uppercase). To convert upper case to lower case, block the text to be converted and type **Shift-F3** (Switch). Next type **2** (Lowercase).

Tab Align

Ctrl-F6

Code = [A] [a]

The Tab Align command is used to tab the cursor to the next tab stop and align the text typed afterwards flush right to the tab stop. See Format Line, Tabs for information on setting tab stops. The text typed after the Tab Align command is entered between [A] and [a] codes imbedded in the text. The Enter, Tab, or Align Character keys, or the Tab Align command will stop the flush right formatting of the text.

The Enter key may be used to produce right aligned columns of text. In the following example, the Tab Align Command was used to move the cursor to the tab stop, the name was typed, and then the Enter key was pressed.

```
                 tab stop
                    |
        Richard Alden
           Kathey Dole
          Jerry Calvin
               Jo Hays
```

The Tab key may be used to produce right and left justified columns of text. In the following example, the Tab Align command was used to move the cursor to the first tab stop, the name was entered, and then the Tab key was used to move the cursor to the second tab stop where the role was entered. The Enter key was used to move to the next line.

```
            tab stop    tab stop
                   |    |
     Richard Alden      Leading Man
       Kathey Dole      Leading Woman
      Jerry Calvin      Actor 1
           Jo Hays      Actor 2
```

The default Align Character is the period (.). The Align Character may be changed with the Format Line, Align Char command. With the Align Character key, the text is right justified until the current Align Character is typed, and then the text entered becomes left justified. The feature is most useful for entering dollar amounts. Here the Tab Align command was used to move the cursor to the tab stop. The dollar amounts were typed and then the period key (the current Align Character key) was typed. Finally the cent amount was entered and the Enter key was typed to move to the next line.

```
          tab stop
              |
      $1,250.73
         $15.00
          $0.00
    $116,000.35
```

Text In/Out

Ctrl-F5

The Text In/Out command is used to convert file formats for transfer between software, protect files from being viewed or printed by others, and to create or edit text summaries and comments. The Text In/Out command presents the screen menu on the following page.

```
Document Conversion, Summary and Comments

     DOS Text File Format
          1 - Save
          2 - Retrieve  (CR/LF becomes [HRt])
          3 - Retrieve  (CR/LF in H-Zone becomes [SRt])

     Locked Document Format
          4 - Save
          5 - Retrieve

     Other Word Processor Formats
          6 - Save in a generic word processor format
          7 - Save in WordPerfect 4.1 format

     Document Summary and Comments
          A - Create/Edit Summary
          B - Create Comment
          C - Edit Comment
          D - Display Summary and Comments



Selection: 0
```

The following discusses various file format conversion operations for file transfer between software. The discussion of operations is done in a slightly different order than they appear on the screen.

Foreign File Transfer

(1) Save (DOS Text File Format)

The Save (DOS Text File Format) command saves the current document in ASCII format and removes all imbedded WordPerfect codes from within it. All soft returns, [SRt]s, are converted to hard returns. CHR(13)s and Tabs, [TAB]s, are converted to spaces, CHR(32)s. Spaces are used to pad Center, Indent, and Flush Right text. See Print, Options (page W–82) for information on creating a similar DOS file.

Save (Other Word Processor Formats)

(6) Save in a generic word processor format

Saving the current document in a generic word processor format removes all imbedded WordPerfect codes from within the file and replaces soft returns, [SRt]s, with spaces, CHR(32)s. Spaces are used to pad Center, Indent, and Flush Right text.

(7) Save in WordPerfect 4.1 format

Removes all control codes specific to WordPerfect's Version 4.2.

Retrieve (DOS Text File Format)

(2) Retrieve (CR/LF becomes [HRt])

Hard returns in the file become hard returns in WordPerfect.

(3) Retrieve (CR/LF in H-Zone becomes [SRt])

Hard returns in the file become soft returns in WordPerfect if they occur between the current left and right margins. Two or more sequential hard returns in the file become hard returns in WordPerfect.

Locked Document Format

WordPerfect allows a document to be locked with a password. However, if you forget the password, you will not be able to retrieve the file.

To lock the current text file, type **Ctrl-F5, 4** (Text In/Out, Save Locked Document). WordPerfect will respond with the message:

```
Enter Password:
```

The password you type will not be displayed on the screen. Instead, WordPerfect will prompt you to:

```
Re-Enter Password:
```

so it may check for correct duplication of keystrokes. A password may be up to 75 characters in length.

Once the password has been verified, you may save the document. From that point on, the password will be needed to retrieve or save the file.

To unlock a locked document, it is necessary to use the Text In/Out command. Type **Ctrl-F5, 5** (Text In/Out, Retrieve Locked Document). Next type **F10** (Save), ↵ (to save it under the same name), answer the "Enter Password:" prompt by typing ↵, and then type "Y" to replace the file on the disk.

Document Summary and Comments

WordPerfect provides a means to document your documents. That is, you are able to insert text into a document that will not be printed. Such "internal" documentation is done through the Summary and Comments commands of the Text In/Out command.

(A) Create/Edit Summary — Code = [Smry/Cmnt ... text ....]

One Summary may be created for each document. While it may be created from anywhere within the text, it will be placed at the beginning of the file by WordPerfect. The Create/Edit Summary command produces the following screen.

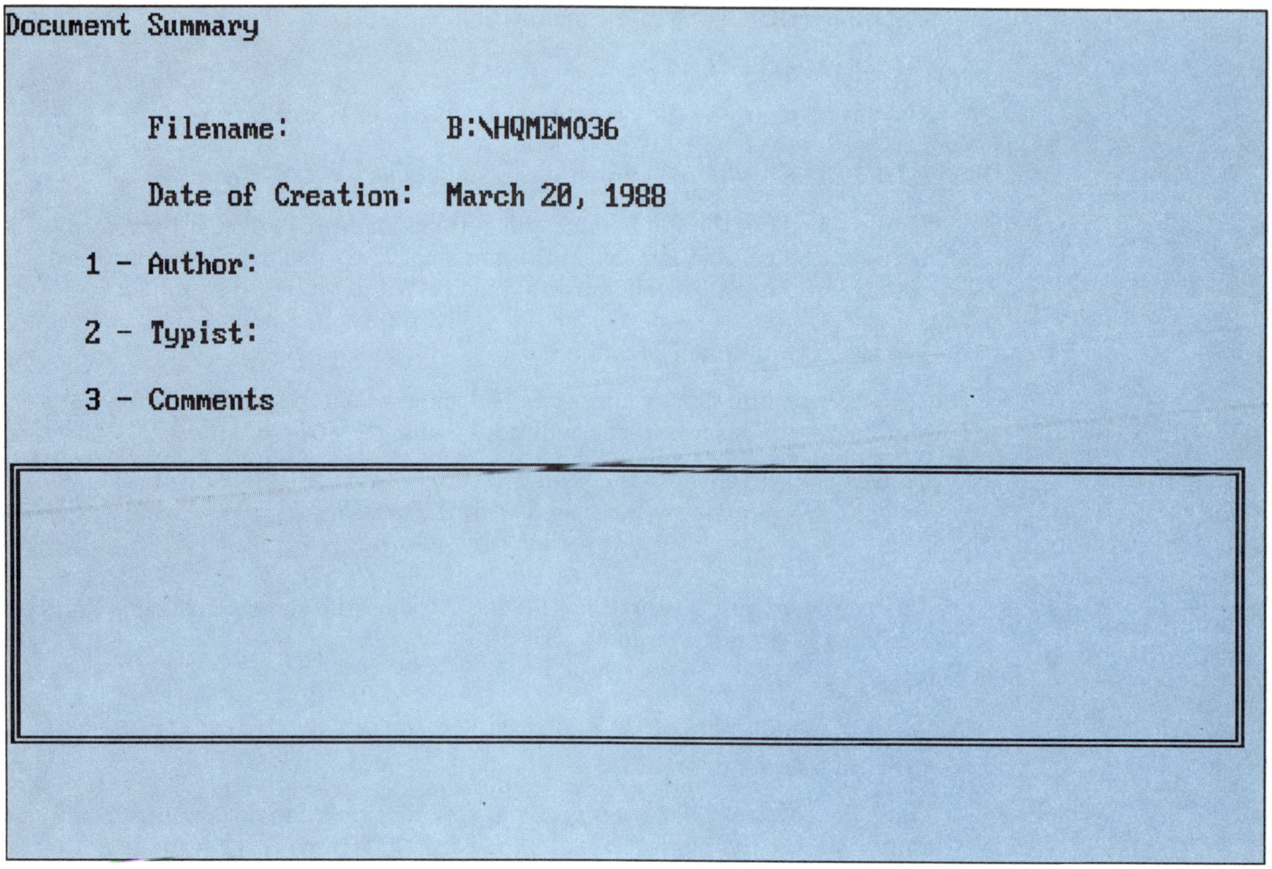

The Date of Creation is obtained by WordPerfect from the current DOS system date and the filename will be the same name under which the file is saved.

Author and Typist may be entered by the user, up to 40 characters each, and Comments about the file may be entered up to 880 characters. Text formatting within the Summary screen is limited.

To display the Summary on the screen, use the Display Summary and Comments command. To delete a summary, move to the top of the file and use Reveal Codes to find the imbedded text. Then, use the Backspace or Del key to erase it.

(B) Create Comment — Code = [Smry/Cmnt ... text ....]

The Create Comment command provides room for 1,024 characters to be entered into the text at the current cursor location. Text formatting within the Comments screen is limited.

To display comments on the screen, use the Display Summary and Comments command. To delete a comment, move the cursor to the place where the comment occurs and use Reveal Codes to find the imbedded text. Then, use the Backspace or Del key to erase it.

(C) Edit Comment

The Edit Comment may be used to change an existing comment. Type **Ctrl-F5, C** (Text In/Out, Edit Comment) to begin editing. WordPerfect will find the comment for editing by searching backwards in the file. Therefore, if there is more than one comment in the file, you must move the cursor past the comment you wish to edit and then enter the Edit Comment command.

(D) Display Summary and Comments

Turns on or off the display of summaries and comments within the document.

Thesaurus Alt-F1

1 Replace Word; 2 View Doc; 3 Look Up Word; 4 Clear Column:0

WordPerfect comes with a thesaurus feature which displays synonyms for words. The data through which WordPerfect searches to find such synonyms are kept on a separate diskette. If you are using a computer with two floppy disk drives, you will need to insert the Thesaurus diskette into the B: drive each time it is needed. If you have a hard disk drive, the Thesaurus diskette may be copied onto the same subdirectory as WordPerfect.

To cause WordPerfect to display synonyms for a word existing in your text, move the cursor under the word and then type **Alt-F1**. If the word is a "headword," a word that can be looked up by WordPerfect, the screen will appear similar to the following.

```
We are located in the South West Heights area, close to shopping,
city parks and University campus.  For an appointment to view one
of our fine townhouse apartments and a tour of the grounds,
please call Mr. Smith at (503) 244-7163.

fine=(a)
 1 A ·choice          5    ·keen              fine-(v)
   B ·splendid             ·precise            9    ·charge
   C ·superb               ·sharp                   ·penalize
   D ·superior                                      ·tax
                      6    ·elegant
 2 E ·average              ·exquisite         fine-(ant)
   F ·fair                 ·refined           10   ·inferior
   G ·mediocre                                      ·terrible
                      7    ·minute                  ·thick
 3 H ·fragile              ·small                   ·coarse
   I ·narrow               ·subtle                  ·blunt
   J ·slender                                       ·crude
   K ·thin            fine-(n)                      ·obvious
                      8    ·assessment
 4 L ·delicate             ·charge            11   ·reward
   M ·gossamer             ·fee
   N silky                 ·forfeit
                           ·penalty
1 Replace Word; 2 View Doc; 3 Look Up Word; 4 Clear Column: 0
```

The word shown in reverse video located in the text at the top of the screen is the headword for which the search was made.

Beneath the text are displayed synonyms organized into subgroups according to connotation. The subgroups are organized into word-type categories:

adjective (a), noun (n), verb (v), and antonym (ant). The synonyms displayed with a bullet (small dot to the left) are themselves headwords upon which a search may be made.

There may be more synonyms found than can be displayed on the screen. If this is the case, the Cursor Up and Cursor Down keys (also PgUp and PgDn keys) may be used to scroll through them.

All synonyms found for a word constitute a "Column" of synonyms. There may be more than one word's synonyms displayed on the screen and, if there are, the synonyms are displayed in separate columns.

(1) Replace Word

A synonym may be selected to replace the headword in the text. To do so, you type **1** and then the letter displayed to the left of the appropriate synonym. If a letter is not displayed next to the synonym of your choice, you may move one there by typing the Cursor Left or Cursor Right keys before entering the Replace Word command.

(2) View Doc

The View Doc command allows you to move the cursor through the text at the top of the screen without leaving the Thesaurus command. You may not edit the text; however, you may scroll through it to view text not currently displayed.

If you wish to select another headword from the text, you may move the cursor under it and type **Alt-F1** (Thesaurus) again. If you do not want to select another headword, you may type **F7** (Exit) to return to the Thesaurus.

(3) Look Up Word

The Look Up Word command allows you to directly type in a headword for which WordPerfect will search.

(4) Clear Column

The Clear Column command erases the last column of synonyms from the screen.

Underline — F8 — Code = [U][u]

The Underline command is used to print text as underlined. Typing **F8** (Underline) inserts [U] and [u] codes into the text. Text typed afterwards is entered between the codes and is displayed on the screen in highlight. To stop underlining text, type **F8** (Underline) again.

Block/Underline

To underline a block of text, block the text and then type **F8** (Underline).

WordPerfect Codes

_(blinking)	Cursor Position
[ ]	Hard Space
[-]	Hyphen
-	Soft Hyphen
/	Cancel Hyphenation
[A][a]	Tab Align or Flush Right (begin and end)
[Adv▲]	Advance Up ½ Line
[Adv▼]	Advance Down ½ Line
[AdvLn:n]	Advance to Specific Line Number
[AlignChar:]	Alignment Character
[B][b]	Bold (begin and end)
[Bin#:n]	Sheet Feeder Bin Number
[Block]	Beginning of Block
[BlockPro:Off]	Block Protection off
[BlockPro:On]	Block Protection on
[C][c]	Centering (begin and end)
[Center Pg]	Center Current Page Top to Bottom
[Cmnd:]	Imbedded Printer Command
[CndlEOP:n]	Conditional End of Page (n = number of lines)
[Col Def:]	Column Definition
[Col Off]	End of Text Columns
[Col On]	Beginning of Text Columns
[Date:n]	Date/Time function (format)
[DefMark:Index,n]	Index Definition (n = format)
[DefMark:List,n]	List Definition (n = List Number)
[DefMark:ToC,n]	Table of Contents Definition (n = ToC Level)
[EndDef]	End of Index, List, or ToC
[EndMark:List,n]	End Marked Text (n = List Number)
[EndMark:ToC,n]	End Marked Text (n = ToC Level)
[Font Change:n,n]	Specify New Font or Print Wheel (n = pitch,font)
[FtnOpt]	Footnote/Endnote Options
[Hdr/Ftr:n,n;text]	Header or Footer Definition (n = type,occurrence)
[HPg]	Hard Page
[HRt]	Hard Return
[Hyph on]	Hyphenation on
[Hyph off]	Hyphenation off
[HZone Set:n,n]	Reset Size of Hyphenation Zone (n = left,right)
[->Indent]	Beginning of Indent
[->Indent<-]	Beginning of Left/Right Indent
[Index:heading; subheading]	Index mark
[LnNum:Off]	End of Line Numbering
[LnNum:On]	Beginning of Line Numbering
[LPI:n]	Lines per Inch
[<-Mar Rel:n]	Left Margin Release (n = positions moved)
[Margin Set:n,n]	Left and Right Margin Reset
[Mark:List,n]	Begin Marked Text for List (n = List Number)
[Mark:ToC,n]	Begin Marked Text for ToC (n = ToC Level)
[Math Def]	Definition of Math Columns
[Math Off]	End of Math

[Math On]	Beginning of Math
!	Formula Calculation
t	Subtotal Entry
+	Do Subtotal
T	Total Entry
=	Do Total
*	Do Grand Total
[Note:End,n;[note#]text]	Endnote (n = Endnote Number)
[Note:Foot,n;[note#]text]	Footnote (n = Footnote Number)
[Ovrstk]	Overstrike Preceding Character
[Par#:Auto]	Automatic Paragraph/Outline Number
[Par#:n]	Fixed Paragraph Number (n = level number)
[Par#:Def]	Paragraph Numbering Definition
[Pg#:n]	New Page Number
[Pg#Col:n,n,n]	Column Position for Page Numbers (n = left,center,right)
[PgLnth:n,n]	Set Page Length (n = form lines, text lines)
[PosPg#:n]	Set Position for Page Numbers
[RedLn][r]	Redline (begin and end)
[RtJustOff]	Right Justification off
[RtJustOn]	Right Justification on
[SetFtn#:n]	New Footnote Number
[Smry/Cmnt:n]	Document Summary/Comment (n = first 100 characters of summary or comment)
[SpacingSet:n]	Spacing Set
[SPg]	Soft New Page
[SRt]	Soft Return
[StrkOut][s]	Strikeout (begin and end)
[SubScrpt]	Subscript
[SuprScrpt]	Superscript
[Suppress:n]	Suppress Page Format Options (n = format(s))
[TAB]	Move to Next Tab Stop
[TabSet:]	Tab Reset
[ToA:n;[short form];	Mark Table of Authorities with
[<Full Form>]	Full Form (n = section number)
[ToA:;[short form];]	Mark Table of Authorities with Short Form
[TopMar:n]	Set Top Margin in Half-Lines
[U][u]	Underlining (begin and end)
[Undrl Style:n]	Underline Style
[W/O Off]	Widow/Orphan Off
[W/O On]	Widow/Orphan On

File Operations

Hazard Be careful of your keystrokes when saving your documents. You could easily miss a keystroke, which would result in saving a file named "Y" onto your diskette. The keystrokes used to resave a file with the Save command are **F10,** ↵ Y. The keystrokes used to resave a file during an exit from WordPerfect with the Exit command are **F7,** ↵, ↵, Y. To avoid confusion, it is suggested that you use the Save command liberally while editing and just prior to exiting WordPerfect. You should not use the Exit command to resave your file.

Hazard Much literature about WordPerfect suggests that you use the space allocated to the filename extension for part of the name you give the document. For instance, you might name a memo "ACCT1887. MEM" to indicate that it is a memo concerning account #1887. This is poor advice because doing this might lead to a variety of complex problems. It is best not to use the extension space. Restrict your filenames to eight characters or less, begin the filename with a letter and include no special characters or spaces in the filename.

Hint To create a print file, one in which the text is written to a file in ASCII with columns, centered text, headers, footers, and so on, preserved, use the Print, Printer Control command (**Shift-F7, 4**) to specify the current printer (**1** Select Printer) as the DOS Text Printer (Printer #6 by default) and then print the document. A print file will be created on the diskette under the name DOS.TXT.

Hint Files can be merged by simply retrieving one file into another. When a file is retrieved, it will be inserted into any existing text at the location of the editing cursor.

Block Operations

Hint If you are careful not to inadvertently delete or typeover text while doing so, most of the basic cut-and-paste operations can be done using the Undelete file buffer instead of the Move buffer. Under certain circumstances the Undelete buffer is preferable to the Move buffer because it is able to hold three blocks of text at a time instead of one. In a large document, where several blocks of text are being moved or copied to locations throughout the document, the Undelete buffer may be used to save time. (Together the Move and Undelete buffers are able to hold up to four blocks of text.)

Hint If you accidentally unblock a block of text, you can immediately restore it by typing **Alt-F4, Ctrl-Home, Ctrl-Home** (Block, Previous position). The technique will not work correctly if the cursor has been moved after the unblocking event.

Hazard There is only one Undelete buffer and one Move buffer. If you are editing two documents concurrently (see the Switch command), they share the buffers.

Hint Blocks of text can be copied or moved between Doc 1 and Doc 2 (see the Switch command for information on editing two files concurrently). If you want to copy a block of text from a file on the diskette into the current file, use the Switch command to go to the other document screen, retrieve the diskette file, block the text, and then use either the Move command or Backspace key to put the block into a buffer. Then use the Switch command to return to the original document and retrieve the block from the buffer with **Ctrl-F4, 5** (Move, Retrieve Text) or **F1** (Undelete).

Editing Text

Hint The first step toward the efficient use of WordPerfect is to quickly memorize all of the editing and cursor control keys and key combinations, and then use them. The next step is to memorize the most used and important WordPerfect commands. (An index of the commands can be found in the WordPerfect Quick Reference Command Index of this manual.) The last step is to read through all of the Command Summary provided here. By familiarizing yourself with each WordPerfect feature, you will know if the software is designed to deal with certain types of problems when they arise.

Hint To produce a hanging paragraph, one in which the text resides offset to the right of a heading (as the paragraph here resides offset from the heading "Hint"), type the heading and then type **F4** or **Shift-F4** (->Indent or ->Indent<-) and then enter the text.

Hazard The default answer to the Replace command's "w/confirm" prompt is "N" for no. This is surprising since experience shows that global replace operations without confirmation can often have unanticipated and difficult to rectify results. If using a text editor's Replace command is new to you, be sure to specify "Y" for yes when the "w/confirm" prompt appears.

Hint When working on a large document over a period of time, it is often desirable to return to where you left off editing when you later retrieve a file. To do so, you may invent a place marker by using keyboard characters (such as the marker "-=-") and place it in the file at the location to which you want to return. Then you save the file. When you later retrieve the file, you can use the ▶Search command to find the marker.

Hint To view the current tab stops on the screen while editing, type **Ctrl-F3, 1,** Up, ↵ (Screen, Window, Cursor Up, Enter). To turn off the tab stop display, type **Ctrl-F3, 1,** Down, ↵ (Screen, Window, Cursor Down, Enter).

Hint The Esc key may be used to repeat a keystroke or keystroke combination *n* number of times. For instance, to produce a row of asterisks across the document (64 asterisks), move the cursor to the left margin and type Esc, 64, *.

WordPerfect Codes

Hazard Be sure to develop the habit of deleting unnecessary codes from your document. Forgetting that a code is in place can lead to a document becoming cluttered with difficult to read codes.

Hint You can quickly locate imbedded codes in your document with the ▶Search and ◀Search commands. Type **F2** or **Shift-F2** (Search forward or Search backward) and then type the initial keystroke combinations that created the code for which you are searching.

The screen will display a menu of commands that generate imbedded codes. Select the appropriate command from the menu and then type **F2** or **Shift-F2** again.

Hint You can quickly delete all occurrences of a particular code with the Replace command. Move the cursor to the top of the document and type **Alt-F2** (Replace). Answer "Y" to the "w/confirm" prompt and answer the ->Srch prompt by typing the initial keystroke combination that created the code. The screen will display a menu of commands that generate imbedded codes. Select the appropriate command from the menu and then type **Alt-F2** again. Answer the "Replace with:" prompt by typing **Alt-F2** once more.

Hint Be systematic about where you place your codes. If you often change line spacing or margins for paragraphs, consistently put the codes in the same place (just above the paragraph, just before the first letter, etc.) for each paragraph you reformat. If you have a favorite format of margins, line spacing, page numbering, and so on, create a small file of the necessary codes and save it under a filename like "HEADER". Then when you are ready to create a new document, you can simply retrieve HEADER as the first step in creating the document.

Hazard Some of the Format forward codes can cause unexpected results if they are misentered or not completely thought out before being entered. As a precaution, if you intend to imbed a Format forward code that is meant to affect a segment of text (such as a paragraph), first move forward to the end of the segment and enter the code that will restore the original format. Then move back in the text and enter the code to affect the segment.

Hazard Some codes must occur at the top of a page in order to have the desired effect. Codes that set new page numbers, change headers or footers, or affect the top margin are some examples. You may want to place a hard page break in your document above such codes to keep them from being forced down on a page by rewrites occurring above them.

Printing Files

Hint There are several ways in which you may print a file or portion of a file. To Print the current page of the current document or the current document, use **Shift-F7** (Print). To print a block of text, block the text and then type **Shift-7** (Print). To print all of a file that is on the diskette, use the List Files, Print command (**F5, 4**). To print only certain pages of a file that is on the diskette, use **Shift-F7, 4, P** (Print, Printer Control, Print Document) command.

Hint Many printers have a "print buffer" which accepts data from the computer and stores it to be printed later. When you cancel a print operation with the Print, Printer Control, Cancel Print Job(s) command (**Shift-F7, 4, C**), or stop a print operation with Print, Printer Control, Stop Printing (**Shift-F7, 4, S**), WordPerfect stops its output of data to the printer; however, it does not erase the printer's print buffer. If your printer does not stop printing after you have issued the commands to do so, turn the printer off to erase the print buffer and then turn the printer back on again.

Special Features

Hint You can greatly speed up a spell check operation by not waiting for WordPerfect to display all of its dictionary found words when it stops on an unknown word. For instance, if you can see on the screen that the word is one which you want to skip, type **1** or **2** as soon as WordPerfect stops on the word. WordPerfect will immediately continue its search for unknown words.

Hazard When you use WordPerfect to automatically generate tables of contents, lists, and indexes, the tables it produces are heavily formatted with [->Indent], [<-Margin Rel:] and [A] (Flush Right) format codes. While the coded text can be edited, it can be quite confusing to try to do so.

If you must edit a table after it has been generated, you may block and save the table, use the Switch command to change documents, retrieve the table, and resave it in DOS Text File Format with the Text In/Out command. The Text In/Out, Save DOS Text File Format command will leave the table intact and strip the WordPerfect codes from it. You may then use the Switch command to return to the original document and retrieve the table into the current document for editing.

Hint If you decide to insert a portion of newspaper-style columnar text into an existing document, first create the portion as a separate file and make sure it ends with a [Col Off:] code. Then retrieve it into the document.

Hazard The WordPerfect Math feature uses [A] [a] (Flush Right) codes to align numbers at tab stops. The codes are generated when the Tab or Indent keys are used to move the cursor to a tab stop when the math data is entered. If you later edit the math portion of the document, you must be careful to keep the numbers properly aligned to their tab stops. It is usually easier to delete the original [TAB] and number and then retab to the appropriate place to reenter the number.

STUDY QUESTIONS

1. What is the main difference between word processing and typing? What is the resulting advantage for word processing?

2. There are places in a document where the cursor may not be moved with the cursor control keys. Describe the areas and the method that one might use to move the cursor to them.

3. If the Cursor Left key is tapped again and again, what path will the cursor follow?

4. How does WordPerfect define a paragraph?

5. Name the three general categories of format codes.

6. To which of the three categories of format codes do the codes generated by the **F6** (Bold) command belong?

7. To which of the three categories of format codes do the codes generated by WordPerfect to produce a page break after 55 lines belong?

8. To which of the three categories of format codes do the codes generated by the **Shift-F8, 4** (Format Page, Spacing) belong?

9. To which of the three categories of format codes do the codes generated by the **F4** (▶Indent) command belong?

10. Describe two differences between hard returns and soft returns.

11. What keystrokes can be used to delete a soft return?

12. What is a hard page and when would you want to use one in your document?

13. How can you keep WordPerfect from separating two or more words at the end of a line when it rewrites a paragraph?

14. If the Format forward code [Margin Set:] is entered at the top of a document, will it stop affecting text when it reaches the Format forward code [Spacing Set:]?

____

15. How can you prevent a Format forward code from affecting the rest of your document?

____

16. What can be done to underline, boldface, or center text after it has been entered?

____

17. The term "cut and paste" refers to your ability to perform three basic operations on a block of text. Name the three operations.

____

18. How does WordPerfect treat text held in its editing buffers, such as the Move and Undelete buffers?

____

19. How many blocks of text can be held in the Move buffer at one time?

____

20. How many blocks of text can be held in the Undelete buffer at one time?

____

21. If a block of text is undeleted with the Cancel command, does a copy of the block remain in the Undelete buffer?

____

22. In the following table, the top line was entered and then copied to the next four lines. Would the Move or Undelete buffer require the fewest keystrokes to complete the table.

____

Day __________ / Time: __________ Phone # __________
Day __________ / Time: __________ Phone # __________
Day __________ / Time: __________ Phone # __________
Day __________ / Time: __________ Phone # __________
Day __________ / Time: __________ Phone # __________

The following questions concern the commands listed on the Function keyboard template.

23. Which command is used to generate a table of contents, lists, and/or indexes for a document?

____

24. Which command may be used to produce automatic outline numbers?

____

25. Which Function key provides commands that are primarily like those in a database management system?

____

26. Which three Function keys provide most of the formatting commands of WordPerfect?

____

27. Which Function key provides commands that are primarily spreadsheet in nature?

____

28. Which command may be used to generate columnar text?

____

29. Which command provides the means to transfer data between different software?

____

Boiler Plating Using similar parts to create a unique product.

Closing The act that copies all text data from RAM to a permanent form on a diskette. Equivalent to *saving*.

Document or Document Files A text file with electronic page breaks.

Editing In WordPerfect, revising data by changing the written content of the text.

Formatting In WordPerfect, making changes that deal with the appearance of the text—condensing the text, changing line spacing and margins, boldfacing, and underlining.

Hard Code Codes generated by the user rather than by WordPerfect.

Hard Return A hard return separates lines of text in WordPerfect.

Justify To align characters to the left or to the right of a page.

Menu Commands WordPerfect commands that accomplish all editing and most formatting.

Opening In WordPerfect, the act that allows the user to enter or edit data in the file while it is held in RAM memory. Equivalent to *loading*.

Page Break A line of dashes that WordPerfect displays on the screen to indicate that the user has typed in a full page of printed text and a new page is about to begin.

Primary File A standard WordPerfect file

Revising In WordPerfect, changing text that has been entered by deleting words, inserting words, moving paragraphs, formatting text, or correcting misspellings.

Scroll The vertical movement of lines of type on a monitor. In WordPerfect, when one screen's worth of text is complete, the text at the top of the page disappears from view to make room at the bottom of the screen for new lines of text.

Secondary File Smaller WordPerfect files which contain specific information.

Soft Code A code WordPerfect generates and automatically inserts into a document.

Soft Return A line automatically wrapped to the next line. Groups of lines ending with soft returns are considered paragraphs by WordPerfect.

Word Wrap A feature of WordPerfect that automatically begins a new line when the right margin of the current line is reached.

MODULE OUTLINE

Learning dBase III

INTRODUCTION

dBase III® is a database management system (DBMS) software, the type of application software that allows the user to create, maintain, and manipulate records of data.

You may use dBase III commands in two separate ways. You can use one command at a time in a direct mode in which dBase executes each command as it is entered; or you may use several (a batch of) commands, held in a file that you create, and that dBase will execute as a group when you type the appropriate command.

The following section begins with a brief discussion of dBase basics and dBase III's file handling. It continues with tutorial exercises designed for use with dBase III or dBase III Plus. These exercises focus on the fundamentals of using dBase commands in the direct mode. In the tutorial you will create a database of records; learn how to edit, append, and delete records from the database; sort and index records; search for particular records in the database; and produce dBase reports.

The tutorial is followed by a dBase III operation and command summary that briefly describes the full range of commands and control key operations available with dBase III. Included in this section is a summary of changes made and new commands found in Ashton Tate's later version, *dBase III PLUS™*.

Following the operation and command summary is an extended discussion about how dBase commands may be assembled in a file, and then executed as a group. Here you will find several examples sequenced in a step-by-step manner as they present new dBase III commands and concepts. The examples here use the database created in the dBase III tutorial.

Database Basics

The term *database* describes data organized in a manner to make it possible to access specific information. In many computer applications, data in a database are organized in records with fields holding related data. When the data are arranged in this manner, the database is known as a *relational database*. In the following example, checkbook data is shown arranged as a small relational database.

```
2160 03/03/86 Payless Drug Store            13.60  Medicine
2161 03/05/86 Vista Ridge Properties       325.00  Rent
2162 03/05/86 AT&T                          13.50  Phone
2163 03/11/86 Albertson's Food              35.15  Grocery
2164 03/15/86 First Federal                160.00  Car payment
```

In this example, each record contains data on a check written against a personal checking account. The five fields of each record hold a check number, date, payee, amount, and purchase description, as shown respectively.

Record Structure

Before data such as these may be entered into computer format, the structure of the records for the database must be defined. The structure describes each field with a field name, the type of data it will hold, and the length of the field in characters. Once the record structure has been defined, all records entered or later added to the database will have the same number of fields with the same lengths, and each field will hold the same type data for that record.

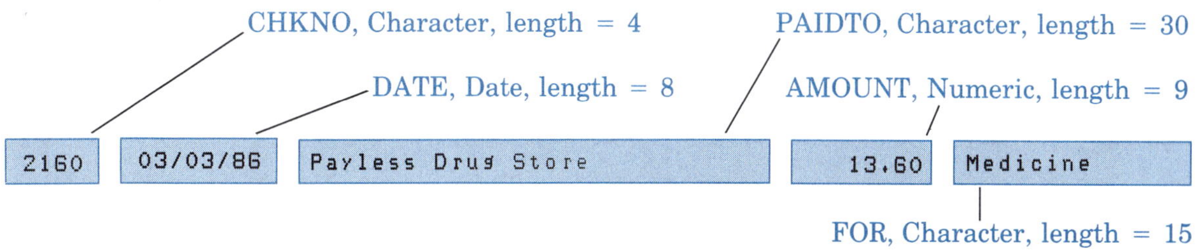

Here each field has been given a name and has been described by data type and length.

dBase III Data Types

In addition to the standard data types, string and numeric, dBase III allows date and logical data types to be entered into its variables and fields.

Date-Type Data

Date-type data are either entered into record fields whose structure has been prespecified to hold date-type data, or into variables by converting string-type data into date-type data with a dBase function. All fields or variables holding date-type data are automatically eight characters long, and the default order of date data held in them is month/day/year.

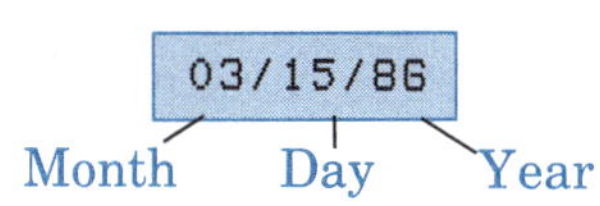

Logical-Type Data

Fields or variables holding logical-type data are automatically one character long. They hold a logical True or a logical False value. These can be directly entered into fields as T, t, Y, or y for True and F, f, N, or n for False, or entered indirectly into fields or variables as .T. or .t. for True and .F. or .f. for False. Once a logical field or variable has had data assigned to it, it may (as a single item) be used as a condition in an expression.

dBase III Command Structure

Command Driven Software

dBase III may be used as a menu driven or command driven software. Menu driven software provide menus of commands from which you select your choice(s). Command driven software respond to command words which you type and enter. In the following tutorial you will be given the steps to assure you are left in a command mode, the primary use mode of dBase III. Entering the command word **ASSIST** will put you into dBase's menu driven mode. While dBase III's menu driven mode may help beginning users learn command syntax, its slow speed and limited uses make dBase III's command mode preferable.

Using dBase's command mode requires that you memorize the dBase command words. Fortunately, consistencies between dBase commands make them relatively easy to memorize, and they tend to resemble standard English terminology. For instance, to display all checks written to First Federal in this example database you could type:

```
DISPLAY ALL FOR paidto = "First Federal"
```

To display only the amounts of the checks written to First Federal you could type:

```
DISPLAY ALL amount FOR paidto = "First Federal"
```

dBase III's File Handling

dBase III is a relatively large software which in its entirety would use up a considerable amount of RAM memory. In addition, as databases become several hundred records long, they would use up RAM memory rapidly. dBase circumvents the RAM size limitations by keeping only data currently needed in RAM there at any time. It maintains the rest of the data on the diskette and brings it into RAM as necessary.

How dBase is Loaded into RAM Memory

The set of instructions that makes up the dBase III software is kept in several separate program files. Using certain dBase commands causes the disk drive holding the dBase diskette to activate because such commands are not covered by the instructions currently in RAM, and the program file to execute the command needs to be read into RAM memory.

Through software segmentation dBase is able to use less RAM space to accomplish its database operations. However, you must keep the diskette with dBase on it in the disk drive at all times while you are working with it.

How a Database is Loaded and Saved

The first step in creating a database is to name the diskette file that will hold the records of data. dBase then creates a file on the diskette, leaving it empty but in a state where data may be saved (copied) to it. A file left in this condition is said to be *open*.

dBase then provides space in RAM memory to hold database record data. When you enter the data it uses up the available RAM. When the space fills, dBase begins to save parts (blocks) of the data into the file on the diskette. Once a block of data is copied to the diskette, the space it occupies in RAM may be erased to make room for new records to be entered.

When dBase needs to process database data stored on the diskette, the data are read into RAM memory, processed, and then written back out onto the diskette file in processed form.

When you are done using dBase, you type and enter dBase's **QUIT** command, which causes any data left in RAM to be copied onto the diskette file so that all data are saved. **QUIT** is always the last command you type when you use dBase.

dBase's Other Files

dBase is able to create and maintain several other types of files in addition to database files which are given a .DBF filename extension, and dBase III may have several different files loaded into RAM memory or open at the same time. The other types of files typically are used by dBase to modify or support its processing of data in a database. The following briefly describes the types of files dBase III can create and provides the filename extension that dBase gives them.

.DBF *Database files* are created in an editing mode. They hold the records and the record structure of a database.

.DBT *Database memo files* are created as auxiliary files, and are used in conjunction with a database (.DBF) file when the database file has memo field(s) specified as part of its record structure. A memo field in a database record automatically has a ten-character length. The data of a memo field are used to access up to 4,000 characters of text held in a .DBT file for that field.

.FMT *Format files* are created in an editing mode. They contain dBase commands used to set a screen format for displaying data.

.FRM *Report form files* are created by the **MODIFY REPORT** command. A report form file holds specifications entered in an editing mode, which are later used by the **REPORT FORM** command to format a dBase report.

.LBL *Label form files* are created by the **MODIFY LABEL** command. A label form file holds specifications entered in an editing mode, which are later used by the **LABEL FORM** command to format mailing or identification labels.

.MEM *Memory variable files* are created with the **SAVE TO** command. They hold the variable names and contents of all variables current at the time that the command was executed.

.NDX *Index files* are created by the **INDEX** command. .NDX files are used concurrently with a database (.DBF) file to treat the database as though its records are sorted.

.PRG *Program files* (called *command files*) are created in an editing mode and hold dBase commands to be executed in sequence when the **DO** command is given. A dBase III .PRG file is very similar to a program written in a programming language.

.TXT *Text files* may be created by several dBase III commands. They are ASCII data format files that can be processed by other software.

If you are using dBase III Plus you will want to refer to the "Changes Summary for dBase III Plus" for information on new file types and minor changes made to existing file types.

Learning dBase III

The dBase III commands for direct creation, maintenance, and processing of a database are fairly straightforward; however, the full range of commands available in dBase make it closer to being a programming language than an applications software. A knowledge of another programming language such as BASIC, COBOL or Pascal is perhaps the greatest aid in learning to use dBase III to its fullest extent.

As you progress through the material in this manual, you may notice slight differences between the screens displayed here and those on your monitor. These are due to minor changes made to the different versions of dBase III.

If you are using dBase III Plus you will want to read the section marked "The **HISTORY** Buffer" (page D-101) before beginning the tutorial exercises. The **HISTORY** buffer feature of dBase III Plus may save you considerable time in completing the tutorial.

Getting Help

dBase has a command, **HELP,** which will present information about specific dBase commands and operations. To use the command, you type the command word **HELP,** followed by a space, then the command or operation on which you want information. If dBase has the information, it will display it on the monitor screen for you to read.

REQUIRED MATERIALS

1. An IBM DOS diskette
2. The dBase III System diskette(s)
3. Your files diskette
4. This manual
5. Other ______________________________

Tutorial Conventions

During the tutorial you first will create a small database and then you will use various dBase III commands to manipulate and display records in it. Here are the conventions used for the tutorial's instructions.

↵	When you see this symbol, press the Enter key located on the right side of the keyboard and marked with a bent arrow (↵).
^	This character means press and hold the Ctrl key and then tap the next key shown.
{ }	If braces are used, do not type them but only what is inside them.

HOW TO GET OUT OF TROUBLE

If you want to:	*Then:*
Erase characters being entered as a dBase III command or data . . .	Tap the Backspace key (←) located just above the Enter key.
Stop any command operation and return to the dot prompt . . .	Tap the Esc key, located on the top far left side of keyboard.
Stop any editing operation and return to the dot prompt . . .	Press and hold the Ctrl key and then tap the End key (convention is ^End).
Stop the tutorial and continue it later . . .	At the dot (.) prompt type {**QUIT↵**}.
Continue with the tutorial after you have stopped it . . .	After loading dBase III into RAM memory type {**SET DEFAULT TO B:↵ USE** empfile↵}.

Getting Started

1. Insert the DOS diskette into the A: disk drive (the disk drive on the left) and close the disk drive door.
2. If the computer is on already, press and hold the Ctrl and Alt keys, and then tap the Del key. If the computer is not on, turn on the computer and the monitor.

In a few moments DOS will be loaded automatically.

3. Answer DOS's date and time prompts.
4. When you see the A>, remove the DOS diskette from the A: disk drive.

5. Insert the dBase III System diskette #1 into the A: drive and close the disk drive door.
6. Type {DBASE↵}
7. When you see the message "Insert System Disk 2 and press ENTER", take #1 out and insert the dBase III System diskette #2 into the A: drive, close the disk drive door, and tap the Enter key.

In a few moments dBase III will load into RAM memory. You will know dBase is loaded when you see an extended copyright notice appear on the screen. At the bottom of the screen a dot (.) prompt appears next to a blinking cursor.

8. a. If you are using dBase III and do not see the dot (.) prompt as described, tap the Esc key.
   b. If you are using dBase III Plus, tap the Esc key, and then type:

   {**SET STATUS OFF** ↵}

   {**SET MENUS OFF** ↵}

9. Insert your files diskette into the B: disk drive and be sure to close the disk drive door.
10. Now type {**SET DEFAULT TO** B: ↵}

This dBase command causes dBase to automatically address the B: drive for any file to which you later refer.

Your system ____

____

____

____

____

____

dBase III's Dot (.) Prompt Command Mode

The dot (.) appearing on the screen indicates that you are in dBase's command mode. When the dot appears with the cursor next to it, anything that you type and enter is evaluated as a command by dBase III.

Syntax Errors

If you type an incorrect form of a dBase command while you are in the command mode, dBase will display either a "syntax error" message, or, if the mistake is in the first word of the command, an "*** unrecognized command verb" message.

Recovering from Syntax Errors

When dBase III detects a syntax error, it displays its error message and the command it was evaluating at the time on the screen with a question mark over the area where it stopped evaluating the command. For example, if in the last step of Getting Started you had typed:

```
. SET DFEAULT TO B:
```

dBase would respond:

```
Syntax error
             ?
SET DFEAULT TO B:
Do you want some help? (Y/N)
```

To recover from a command with a syntax error, first tap any key except "Y" to answer the "Do you want some help?" message, then type the command again, making sure the word DEFAULT (and all other words) are spelled correctly.

EXERCISE 1: Creating a Database

To begin the tutorial you will create a small database of records. Each record's data concern an employee of a small retail shop where policy allows personal store purchases to be charged against the employee's store account.

Using the CREATE Command

To begin to build the database, you use the **CREATE** command. This command has the form **CREATE** [<filename>]. The filename you specify is used to name the database (.DBF) file.

1. Type {**CREATE** empfile↵}. (Empfile stands for employee file.)

The **CREATE** command causes dBase to leave the dot (.) prompt mode and enter one of its editing (or data entry) modes. You can tell that you are in one of dBase's editing modes when the area of the screen at the cursor location is displayed in reverse video (black on white). When you are in one of dBase's editing modes, you do not enter dBase commands since all characters that you type will be treated as data by dBase. To save the data you have entered and exit from dBase's editing modes (return to the dot (.) prompt command mode), you may type {^End}.

Specifying a Database Record Structure

The following will appear on the screen:

```
B:empfile.dbf                                        Bytes remaining:   4000
                                                     Fields defined:       0

   field name  type      width  dec          field name  type      width  dec
   ==========================================    ==========================================
 1             Char/text

Names start with a letter; the remainder may be letters, digits, or underscore
```

Each field of the record structure needs to be specified with a field name; the type of data (Character, Numeric, or Date) it will hold; how many characters in width it will be; and finally, if the field is numeric, how many decimal places will be displayed.

2. Begin to specify the record structure by typing {employee↵} into the area under "field name."

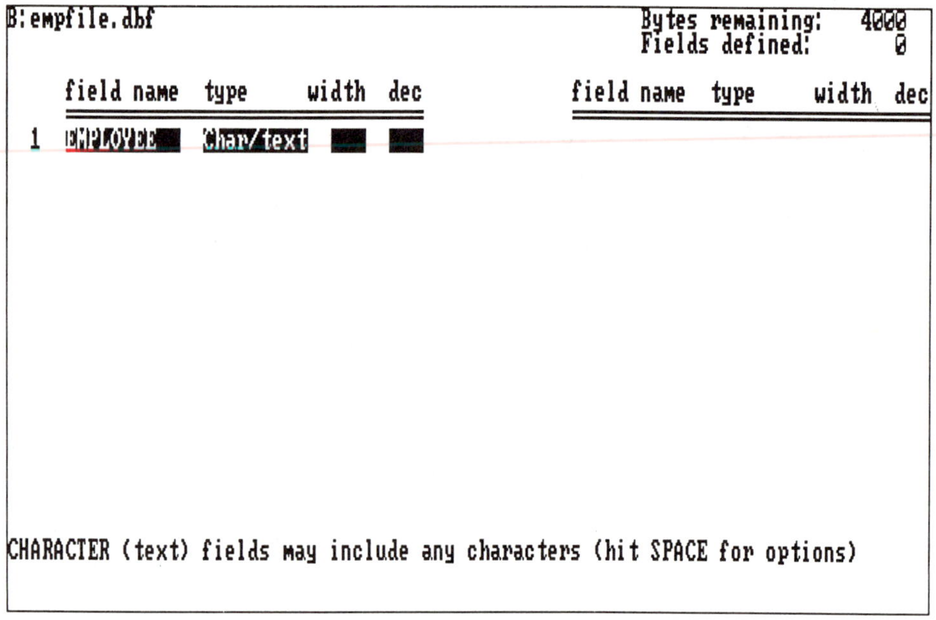

Next you will enter the data type for the field named employee. There are a total of five data types available, three of which are used in the tutorial. To select a data type for a field, you may either enter the first letter of the data type description (C = Char/text, N = Numeric, D = Date) or you may tap the space bar to cause dBase to display different data types in the area, and then tap the Enter key when the appropriate type is displayed.

3. Tap the space bar several times to see the different types displayed, and then type {C} to specify Char/text data.
4. Next type {20↵} into the area under "width" to specify that the field named employee is to be 20 characters wide.

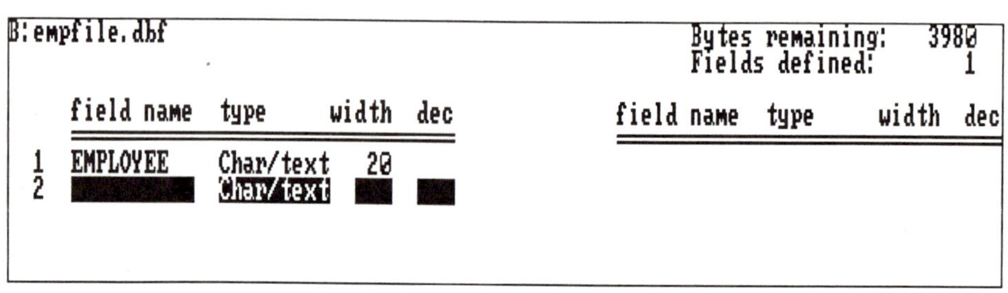

Notice that dBase skipped over the decimal places ("dec"), and the areas to specify the next field are presented. Two rules of field specification to remember are (1) only numeric fields have their decimal places specified, and (2) all date fields have a width of eight characters.

In the next steps you will finish specifying the record structure for the database empfile. Take care to enter all data exactly as shown. If you make an error in entering data, tap the Esc key twice to abort, and then start over by typing {**CREATE** empfile↵}.

5. Now finish specifying the record structure by entering the following data:

```
B:empfile.dbf                                              Bytes remaining:   3947
                                                           Fields defined:       6

    field name  type      width  dec                 field name  type      width  dec
    ==============================                   ==============================
 1  EMPLOYEE    Char/text   20
 2  TELEPHONE   Char/text    8
 3  SEX         Char/text    1
 4  EMPLOYED    Date         8
 5  SALARY      Numeric      8    2
 6  ACCOUNT     Numeric      8    2
 7              Char/text
```

6. When dBase presents field 7, press the Enter key or type {^End}.

Typing ↵ when the last field is presented, or typing {^End}, signals dBase that you are ready to end specifying the record structure. The message

```
Hit RETURN to confirm--any other key to resume
```

will appear at the bottom of the screen.

7. Tap the Enter key.

Each Record's Structure

The record structure you have defined for the database named "empfile" includes six fields, three of which will hold characters, two of which will hold numeric data, and one of which will hold date-type data. Each field's length has been specified, so the total length of each record is known.

Example Record

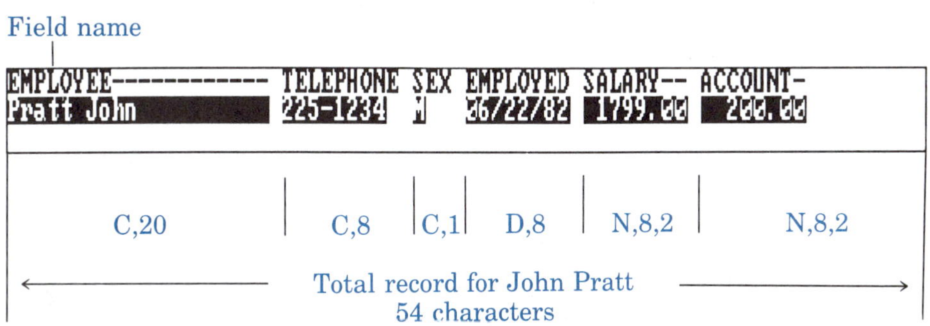

EXERCISE 2: Entering Records into a Database

Your next steps involve entering data into the records of the database. As you enter data into records you will be in another dBase editing (or data entry) mode. On the screen you should see the prompt:

```
Input data records now? (Y/N)
```

1. Type {Y}.

dBase will begin by displaying the first record (Record No. 1) with empty fields (shown in reverse video) into which you can now enter data.

```
Record No.        1
EMPLOYEE
TELEPHONE
SEX
EMPLOYED         /  /
SALARY                .
ACCOUNT               .
```

Each field's name is displayed to the left of the field. A cursor will be located at the first character of the first field to indicate where the data typed will be entered.

On the right side of the keyboard is a numeric keypad with four keys having arrows on them (see illustration). The arrowed keys (*cursor control keys*) may be used to move the cursor from field to field (up and down keys), or from character to character within a field (left and right keys). If an attempt is made to move the cursor past the top field of the current record, the previous record is displayed.

dBase presents the next record for data entry once the last field of the previous record has had data entered into it, or once an attempt has been made to move the cursor past the last field of the previous record.

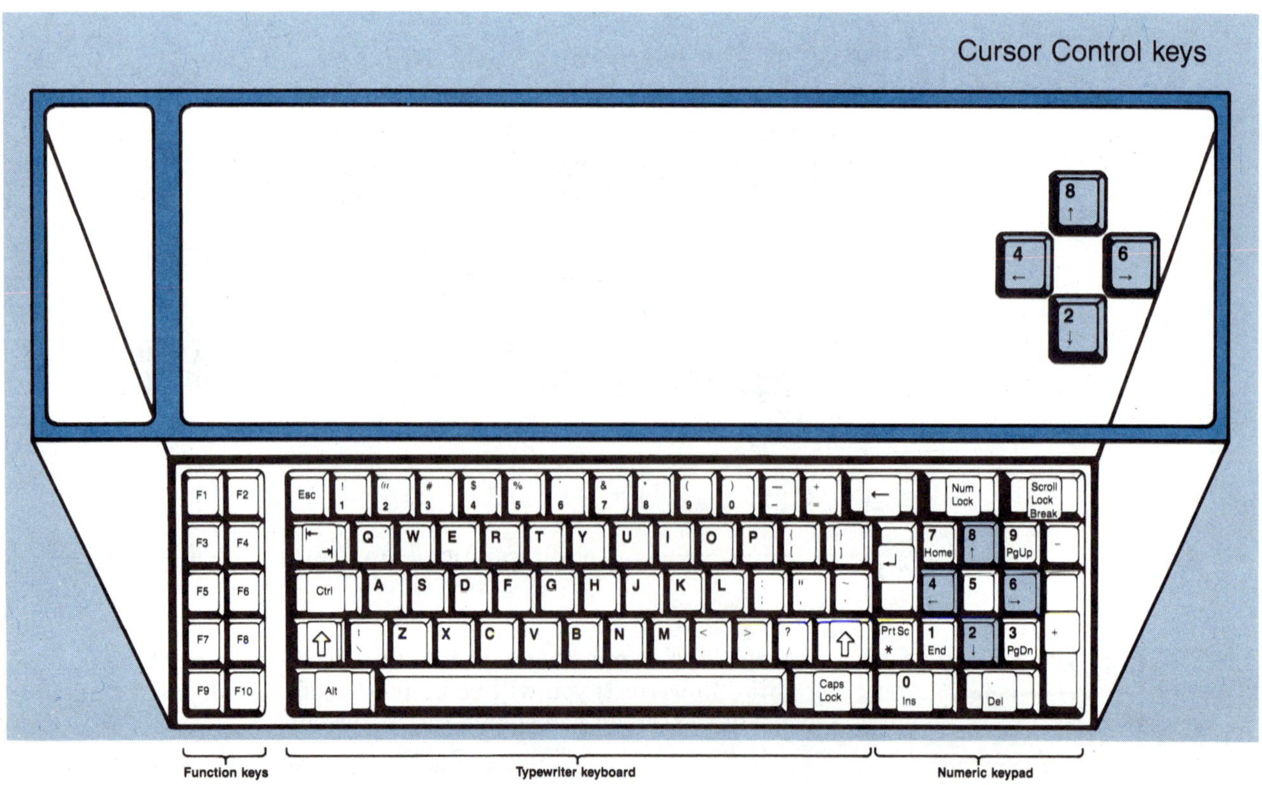

Entering Records

2. Enter the following data into each field of each record, 1 through 8, after you have read the following notations.

NOTE: (1) Make sure that you enter the upper-case/lower-case characters for the data, exactly as shown. (2) Type {**USE** empfile↵**APPEND**↵} if you accidentally return to the dot (.) prompt before you are finished entering the record data. (3) If you make an error when you are entering data, don't worry. You will see later how to edit records, delete records, and make other changes.

Record No.	1	Record No.	2
EMPLOYEE	Pratt John	EMPLOYEE	Smoler Ellen
TELEPHONE	225-1234	TELEPHONE	225-3212
SEX	M	SEX	F
EMPLOYED	06/22/82	EMPLOYED	09/15/83
SALARY	1799.00	SALARY	1650.00
ACCOUNT	200.00	ACCOUNT	300.00

Record No.	3	Record No.	4
EMPLOYEE	Jones David	EMPLOYEE	Phields Sally
TELEPHONE	222-7690	TELEPHONE	224-4321
SEX	M	SEX	F
EMPLOYED	06/15/82	EMPLOYED	02/15/84
SALARY	1550.00	SALARY	1507.50
ACCOUNT	225.00	ACCOUNT	150.00

Record No.	5	Record No.	6
EMPLOYEE	Knat Michael	EMPLOYEE	Smith Paul
TELEPHONE	221-1235	TELEPHONE	223-8251
SEX	M	SEX	M
EMPLOYED	09/15/80	EMPLOYED	11/15/81
SALARY	1800.00	SALARY	1700.00
ACCOUNT	125.00	ACCOUNT	350.00

Record No.	7	Record No.	8
EMPLOYEE	Martins Mary	EMPLOYEE	Beam Sandy
TELEPHONE	222-2123	TELEPHONE	225-6912
SEX	F	SEX	F
EMPLOYED	11/01/85	EMPLOYED	02/15/86
SALARY	1600.00	SALARY	1450.00
ACCOUNT	200.50	ACCOUNT	175.00

Ending Data Entry

3. When you are done entering the data, type {^End} (or ↵ on the first field of the next blank record presented) to save the data and return to dBase's dot (.) prompt.

EXERCISE 3: Putting a Database in Use

The USE Command

Before you can process the records in a database with dBase's commands you first must specify the database file to use by typing the **USE** command.

1. Type {**USE** empfile↵} to cause dBase to access (open) the database file you have created.

When a database is in use, the data in it are not constantly displayed on the screen as are other types of data with other applications software. Nonetheless the entire database is present in RAM memory (or on the diskette) and is accessible to you through the commands of dBase III.

EXERCISE 4: Altering the Database

The **EDIT** and **BROWSE** Commands

To edit records in a database you may use either the **EDIT** command or the **BROWSE** command of dBase III. Both commands cause dBase to enter an editing mode where you can move to different fields of different records to change the data in them.

The two commands (**EDIT** and **BROWSE**) differ only in the way that they present the records on the screen for viewing. **EDIT** presents the records one at a time in the same format as records are entered into a database.

```
Record No.        1
EMPLOYEE        Pratt John
TELEPHONE       225-1234
SEX             M
EMPLOYED        06/22/82
SALARY           1799.00
ACCOUNT           200.00
```

BROWSE presents the records horizontally in groups (one screen's worth at a time), in a form much closer to how you can visualize them represented in memory while dBase is working with them.

```
Record No.          1     empfile
EMPLOYEE------------ TELEPHONE SEX EMPLOYED SALARY-- ACCOUNT-
Pratt John           225-1234  M   06/22/82 1799.00   200.00
Smoler Ellen         225-3212  F   09/15/83 1650.00   300.00
Jones David          222-7690  M   06/15/82 1550.00   225.00
Phields Sally        224-4321  F   02/15/84 1507.50   150.00
Knat Michael         221-1235  M   09/15/80 1800.00   125.00
Smith Paul           223-8251  M   11/15/81 1700.00   350.00
Martins Mary         222-2123  F   11/01/85 1600.00   200.50
Beam Sandy           225-6912  F   02/15/86 1450.00   175.00
```

Editing Keystroke Commands

In either editing mode, you may use commands for such things as moving the cursor, scrolling the database, or deleting a record. The commands are executed by tapping keys found on the numeric keypad or by typing Ctrl-keystroke combinations. Here is a brief summary of the keystrokes to which you may refer while you complete the following steps.

BROWSE Editing Keystroke Commands

Action Desired	Keys
Move right within a field	Cursor-right
Move left within a field	Cursor-left
Move to the next field	End
Move back one field	Home
Move to the next record	Cursor-down
Move back one record	Cursor-up
Scroll 18 lines up in the database	PgUp
Scroll 18 lines down in the database	PgDn
Delete a character	Del
Delete all characters in a field	^Y
Insert mode on/off	Ins
Delete current record	^U
Save updates and exit	^End

Using BROWSE to Edit Records

1. Type {**BROWSE**↵}

dBase will display the small database on the screen. Notice that the first record in the database is displayed in reverse video.

Moving from One Record to Another—The ^C and ^R Commands

2. Tap the cursor-down key several times, and then tap the cursor-up key several times.

The cursor up and down keystroke commands move the reverse video display from one record to another. They demonstrate an important fundamental of database operations when they are used to move the reverse video display up and down through the database.

Introduction to the Database Record Pointer

While a database is in use, an unseen *record pointer* exists at all times. At any given moment the record pointer points to one particular record in the database, called the *current record*.

While in the browse editing mode, the command keys cursor-down and cursor-up move the record pointer one record down or up, and dBase displays the current record in reverse video. In the command dot (.) prompt mode there are commands that move the record pointer from one record to another, but it is seldom visually apparent that the pointer in fact has been moved.

Other Editing Keystroke Commands

Once you have moved the record pointer to the record to edit, you may move the cursor to the field to edit by typing the End key (forward one field) or Home key (back one field) keystroke commands.

When you have reached the field of concern, the cursor-left and cursor-right keys may be used to move the cursor within the field. Any characters that you type will be written over the characters that exist in the field unless the Ins keystroke command is used to turn on an insert mode. When the insert mode is on, any characters that you type will be inserted into the field. The Del key may be used to delete the character above the cursor.

Updating the Records

3. Use the editing features of the **BROWSE** mode to modify the database to reflect the following changes:
   a. David Jones has moved and his new phone number is 292-3832.
   b. Sally Phields is now married and her new last name is Sill.
   c. John Pratt has received a raise of $150.00 per month to bring his monthly salary to 1949.00
4. Correct any incorrect data that may have been entered when you created the database.

When you are finished the database should appear as:

```
Record No.          1     empfile
EMPLOYEE------------ TELEPHONE SEX EMPLOYED SALARY-- ACCOUNT-
Pratt John           225-1234  M   06/22/82  1949.00  200.00
Smoler Ellen         225-3212  F   09/15/83 1650.00   300.00
Jones David           292-3832 M   06/15/82 1550.00   225.00
 SillSally           224-4321  F   02/15/84 1507.50   150.00
Knat Michael         221-1235  M   09/15/80 1800.00   125.00
Smith Paul           223-8251  M   11/15/81 1700.00   350.00
Martins Mary         222-2123  F   11/01/85 1600.00   200.50
Beam Sandy           225-6912  F   02/15/86 1450.00   175.00
```

Marking a Record for Deletion

In order to delete a record from the database you must complete two steps. First, you mark the record for deletion. Then you execute the dot (.) prompt command **PACK.** The **PACK** command physically removes the record from the database.

You may mark a record for deletion either in an editing mode or in the command dot (.) prompt mode. To execute the **PACK** command you must be in the dot (.) prompt mode.

When you are in an editing mode, you mark a record for deletion by moving the record pointer to the appropriate record and typing {^**U**}. The record still appears on the screen, but the message "*DEL*" is displayed at the top of the screen whenever that record becomes the current record. You may "un-mark" such a record by moving the record pointer to it and typing {^**U**} again.

Finishing the Editing Session

5. If you have any unwanted records in the database, mark them for deletion now.
6. Type {^End} to save the changes made; end the editing session; and return to the dot (.) prompt command mode.

7. If you marked any records for deletion, type {**PACK**←┘} to physically erase them from the database.

Adding Records to the Database

When you need to add records to an existing database, you use the dBase III **APPEND** command. After you type **APPEND,** dBase puts you in the same editing mode you were in when you last entered records. The **APPEND** command lets you add records, starting at the next available record number, until you execute the ^End (save and exit) keystroke command.

Setting the Editing Menus On

dBase has several editing modes, and the append mode is one. To help you remember the different editing keystroke commands, dBase provides brief summaries at the top of the screen while in an editing mode if you have previously entered the **SET MENU ON** command from the dot (.) prompt mode.

1. Type {**SET MENU ON** ←┘}.
2. Type {**APPEND**←┘} and add the following information into the blank record that dBase will present:

EMPLOYEE	Johnson Frank
TELEPHONE	223-7928
SEX	M
EMPLOYED	03/20/86
SALARY	1500.00
ACCOUNT	0.00

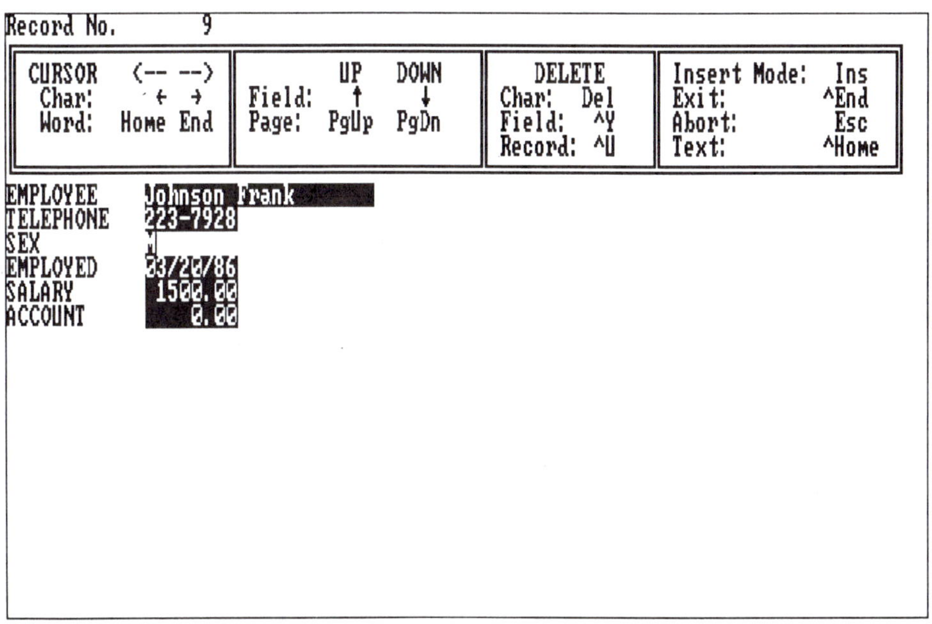

3. Type {^End} to quit appending records when you are done.

EXERCISE 5: dBase III Dot (.) Prompt Command Fundamentals

dBase III Command Conventions and Terminology

When you refer to the dBase Operation and Command Summary in this manual or to the dBase user's manual published by the software's developer, Ashton Tate, you often will see the commands described in a form:

COMMAND [<scope>] [<expression list>] [**FOR** <condition>]

Commands in Upper Case

When commands are presented in the form shown above, the word(s) shown in upper case are dBase command word(s). Although the convention uses upper case to indicate the word is a dBase command, you may type the command in upper or lower case when you are using it.

Command Parameters

The items following the command word(s) are called *command parameters*. Parameters may be defined as additions to a command that affect the way in which the command will be executed. The types of parameters that are allowed for any particular command are described with the lower-case words such as "scope." The <. . .>s surrounding a parameter indicate that the data entered are user supplied. When a command's parameters are shown in brackets, e.g., [<scope>], they are optional—the command will work without them.

Using the DISPLAY Command to Explain Command Terminology

The next several steps are designed to illustrate the most important points of the command descriptions and the fundamentals of processing data using dBase III commands.

The Purpose and Form of the DISPLAY Command

The **DISPLAY** command may be used to display records of the database in a variety of ways. When you see the command listed in a reference, its form will be similar to:

DISPLAY [<scope>] [<expression list>] [**FOR** <condition>]

Using the DISPLAY Command with No Parameters

1. Type {**DISPLAY**↵}.

dBase will respond by displaying a single record of the database:

```
Record#  EMPLOYEE                  TELEPHONE SEX EMPLOYED   SALARY  ACCOUNT
      9  Johnson Frank             223-7928  M   03/20/86  1500.00     0.00
```

When the **DISPLAY** command is used with no parameters it displays all of the fields of data for a single record. The record displayed will be the one to which the record pointer is pointing at the moment.

More on the Database Record Pointer

The **APPEND** command that you executed previously moved the record pointer to the last record in the database so that you could enter data into the record. Since then the record pointer has not been moved. It can be considered as existing alongside the records in the database:

	Record No.	EMPLOYEE	TELEPHONE	SEX	EMPLOYED	SALARY	ACCOUNT
	1	Pratt John	225-1234	M	06/22/82	1949.00	200.00
	2	Smoler Ellen	225-3212	F	09/15/83	1650.00	300.00
	3	Jones David	292-3832	M	06/15/82	1550.00	225.00
	4	Sill Sally	224-4321	F	02/15/84	1507.50	150.00
	5	Knat Michael	221-1235	M	09/15/80	1800.00	125.00
	6	Smith Paul	223-8251	M	11/15/81	1700.00	350.00
	7	Martins Mary	222-2123	F	11/01/85	1600.00	200.50
record	8	Beam Sandy	225-6912	F	02/15/86	1450.00	175.00
pointer →	9	Johnson Frank	223-7928	M	03/20/86	1500.00	0.00

Moving the Record Pointer

Several dBase commands move the record pointer when they are executed, and some commands are designed specifically to move the pointer. The dBase commands **SKIP** [n], **GO TOP, GO BOTTOM,** and **GOTO** <n>, (where "n" is the number of records to **SKIP** or the record number to **GOTO**) are used to move the record pointer.

Type in the following commands (shown in color). See how the record pointer is moved as you view the record displayed (shown in normal type) by the **DISPLAY** command.

NOTE: dBase commands may be typed in upper or lower case. You need only to type the first four letters of a dBase command. For example, disp↵ works as well as **DISPLAY**↵.

1. Type

```
. GO TOP↵
. DISPLAY↵
Record#  EMPLOYEE          TELEPHONE  SEX  EMPLOYED   SALARY  ACCOUNT
      1  Pratt John        225-1234   M    06/22/82  1949.00   200.00
. SKIP↵
Record no.       2
. DISPLAY↵
Record#  EMPLOYEE          TELEPHONE  SEX  EMPLOYED   SALARY  ACCOUNT
      2  Smoler Ellen      225-3212   F    09/15/83  1650.00   300.00
. SKIP 3↵
Record no.       5
. DISPLAY↵
Record#  EMPLOYEE          TELEPHONE  SEX  EMPLOYED   SALARY  ACCOUNT
      5  Knat Michael      221-1235   M    09/15/80  1800.00   125.00
. GO BOTTOM↵
. DISPLAY↵
Record#  EMPLOYEE          TELEPHONE  SEX  EMPLOYED   SALARY  ACCOUNT
      9  Johnson Frank     223-7928   M    03/20/86  1500.00     0.00
. GOTO 3↵
. DISPLAY↵
Record#  EMPLOYEE          TELEPHONE  SEX  EMPLOYED   SALARY  ACCOUNT
      3  Jones David       292-3832   M    06/15/82  1550.00   225.00
```

Using the **DISPLAY** Command with the <scope> Parameter

The Three Possible Scopes

The first listed user-supplied parameter of the **DISPLAY** command is <scope>. The parameter is found in several dBase commands and it affects the record pointer when it is used. The three possible <scope>s are **ALL, NEXT**<n>, and **RECORD**<n>. "n" describes a record number that you supply.

A Scope of **ALL**

1. Type {**DISPLAY ALL**↵}.

dBase will respond by displaying:

Record#	EMPLOYEE	TELEPHONE	SEX	EMPLOYED	SALARY	ACCOUNT
1	Pratt John	225-1234	M	06/22/82	1949.00	200.00
2	Smoler Ellen	225-3212	F	09/15/83	1650.00	300.00
3	Jones David	292-3832	M	06/15/82	1550.00	225.00
4	Sill Sally	224-4321	F	02/15/84	1507.50	150.00
5	Knat Michael	221-1235	M	09/15/80	1800.00	125.00
6	Smith Paul	223-8251	M	11/15/81	1700.00	350.00
7	Martins Mary	222-2123	F	11/01/85	1600.00	200.50
8	Beam Sandy	225-6912	F	02/15/86	1450.00	175.00
9	Johnson Frank	223-7928	M	03/20/86	1500.00	0.00

A <scope> of **ALL** changes the way in which the **DISPLAY** command is executed. It has the same effect as typing **GO TOP, DISPLAY, SKIP, DISPLAY, SKIP, DISPLAY,** continuing until you reach the end of the database.

2. Now type {**DISPLAY**↵}.

dBase will display:

```
Record#  EMPLOYEE                TELEPHONE  SEX  EMPLOYED   SALARY  ACCOUNT
```

The fact that no record data are displayed (including Record#) indicates that the record pointer currently resides past the bottom of the database.

A Scope of **RECORD**<n>

3. Type {**DISPLAY RECORD** 2↵}.

dBase will display:

Record#	EMPLOYEE	TELEPHONE	SEX	EMPLOYED	SALARY	ACCOUNT
2	Smoler Ellen	225-3212	F	09/15/83	1650.00	300.00

The <scope> **RECORD**<n> has the same effect as typing **GOTO** 2, **DISPLAY.**

A Scope of NEXT<n>

4. Now type {**DISPLAY NEXT** 3↵}.

dBase will respond by displaying:

```
Record#  EMPLOYEE                TELEPHONE SEX EMPLOYED   SALARY  ACCOUNT
      2  Smoler Ellen            225-3212  F   09/15/83  1650.00   300.00
      3  Jones David             292-3832  M   06/15/82  1550.00   225.00
      4  Sill Sally              224-4321  F   02/15/84  1507.50   150.00
```

The <scope> **NEXT**<n> has the same effect as **DISPLAY, SKIP, DISPLAY**. . .<n> number of times.

Using the DISPLAY Command with the <expression list> Parameter

The second optional parameter of the **DISPLAY** command is <expression list>. An <expression> (<exp> for short) is an item, or group of items with operators whose value can be determined by dBase III. An expression list is one or more expressions separated by commas.

The items in an expression may include constants, dBase functions, and/or variable names such as the names used to describe the fields holding database data. The operators used in an expression may include the mathematical operators (^, *, /, +, −), the relational operators (<, >, =), and the logical operators (.NOT.,.AND.,.OR.). When an expression contains relational operators, dBase will evaluate the expression as being either .T. for true or .F. for false.

To give you experience in using expression lists, do the following:

1. Type {**CLEAR**↵}.

CLEAR is the dBase III command to clear the screen.

2. Next type {**DISPLAY** employee↵}.

NOTE: "employee" is a field name so it must be typed in its entirety. It may, however, be typed in upper or lower case.

dBase will display the record number and contents of the single field, employee, for the current record. Notice that the field label over the employee's name appears exactly as typed in the expression list of the **DISPLAY** command.

3. Continue by typing {**DISPLAY ALL** employee,telephone↵}.

dBase will respond by displaying:

```
Record#  employee                telephone
      1   Pratt John              225-1234
      2   Smoler Ellen            225-3212
      3   Jones David             292-3832
      4   Sill Sally              224-4321
      5   Knat Michael            221-1235
      6   Smith Paul              223-8251
      7   Martins Mary            222-2123
      8   Beam Sandy              225-6912
      9   Johnson Frank           223-7928
```

"employee, telephone" is an example of an expression list containing two fields (variables) separated by commas.

To make the following examples more sensible, assume that management prefers its employees to keep their account amounts less than 15 percent of their monthly salaries.

4. Type {**DISPLAY ALL** employee,"Limit =",.15* salary↵}.

dBase will display:

```
Record#  employee          "Limit =",.15  * salary
      1  Pratt John         Limit  =      292.3500
      2  Smoler Ellen       Limit  =      247.5000
      3  Jones David        Limit  =      232.5000
      4  Sill Sally         Limit  =      226.1250
      5  Knat Michael       Limit  =      270.0000
      6  Smith Paul         Limit  =      255.0000
      7  Martins Mary       Limit  =      240.0000
      8  Beam Sandy         Limit  =      217.5000
      9  Johnson Frank      Limit  =      225.0000
```

"employee, "Limit =", .15 * salary" is an example of an expression list consisting of a field, a constant, an expression with two items, and an operator whose value can be determined.

5. Next type

{DISPLAY ALL employee,INT(.15 * salary),INT(.15 * salary - account) OFF↵}

dBase will display.:

```
employee         INT(.15 * salary)  INT(.15 * salary - account)
Pratt John                     292                           92
Smoler Ellen                   247                          -52
Jones David                    232                            7
Sill Sally                     226                           76
Knat Michael                   270                          145
Smith Paul                     255                          -95
Martins Mary                   240                           39
Beam Sandy                     217                           42
Johnson Frank                  225                          225
```

In this example, the **INT** function is used to remove trailing cents and zeros from the limit amount (**INT**(.15 * salary)) and from the amount the employee is currently under/over(−) that limit (**INT**(.15 * salary − account)).

Notice that a previously unmentioned **DISPLAY** parameter, **OFF,** may be used to stop the display of each record's record number. It also is possible to stop the display of the expression labels (first row of output) by typing the command **SET HEADING OFF.** To reestablish the display of expression labels you type **SET HEADING ON.**

6. Now type {**DISPLAY ALL** employee,.15 * salary − account > 0 ↵}.

dBase will display:

```
Record#  employee                .15 * salary - account > 0
      1  Pratt John              .T.
      2  Smoler Ellen            .F.
      3  Jones David             .T.
      4  Sill Sally              .T.
      5  Knat Michael            .T.
      6  Smith Paul              .F.
      7  Martins Mary            .T.
      8  Beam Sandy              .T.
      9  Johnson Frank           .T.
```

Here the use of an expression containing a relational operator results in dBase evaluating the expression as being either .T. for true or .F. for false for each record. This is a special form of expression referred to by dBase as a "condition."

Using the **DISPLAY** Command with the **FOR**<condition> Parameter

Using Conditions within a dBase Command

The third parameter is [**FOR**<condition>], which allows selective execution of the command with which it is used.

A <condition> is an expression that includes relational operators causing dBase to evaluate it as either .T. for true or .F. for false. The items in the condition may include constants, dBase functions, and/or variable names such as the names for the fields used to hold database data. The operators used in a condition may include the mathematical operators (^, *, /, +, −), the relational operators (<, >, =), and the logical operators (.NOT., .AND., .OR.).

A Change in Scope

When the [**FOR**<condition>] parameter is used with a command, the default <scope> of the command becomes **ALL** records. The change in scope causes the record pointer to move to the top of the database, where the first record is evaluated for the fields of concern included in the **FOR**<condition>.

.T. and .F.

The record at the top of the database will be evaluated as either .T. for true or .F. for false. If the value determined for the condition is .F.alse, the command will not be executed for the record; dBase will move the pointer to the next record and evaluate it.

Using Simple Conditions

1. Type the following commands (printed in color) to see how the optional parameter [**FOR**<condition>] affects the **DISPLAY** command's response (shown in normal print).

```
. CLEAR←
. DISPLAY FOR sex = "M"←
Record#  EMPLOYEE                TELEPHONE SEX EMPLOYED   SALARY  ACCOUNT
      1  Pratt John              225-1234  M   06/22/82  1949.00   200.00
      3  Jones David             292-3832  M   06/15/82  1550.00   225.00
      5  Knat Michael            221-1235  M   09/15/80  1800.00   125.00
      6  Smith Paul              223-8251  M   11/15/81  1700.00   350.00
      9  Johnson Frank           223-7928  M   03/20/86  1500.00     0.00
. DISPLAY employee,telephone FOR sex = "F"←
Record#  employee                telephone
      2  Smoler Ellen            225-3212
      4  Sill Sally              224-4321
      7  Martins Mary            222-2123
      8  Beam Sandy              225-6912
. DISPLAY FOR sex = "f"←
Record#  EMPLOYEE                TELEPHONE SEX EMPLOYED   SALARY  ACCOUNT
```

No records will be displayed since you entered the record data characters "M" or "F" (upper case) into the fields named sex. The "M" and "F" used in the command's [**FOR**<condition>] parameter are references to data items in your database. You must refer to such items precisely, and in the same case as they exist in their fields.

2. Continue by typing

```
. DISPLAY FOR employee = "Smith Paul"←
Record#  EMPLOYEE                TELEPHONE SEX EMPLOYED   SALARY  ACCOUNT
      6  Smith Paul              223-8251  M   11/15/81  1700.00   350.00
. DISPLAY FOR employee = "Smi"←
Record#  EMPLOYEE                TELEPHONE SEX EMPLOYED   SALARY  ACCOUNT
      6  Smith Paul              223-8251  M   11/15/81  1700.00   350.00
. DISPLAY FOR employee = "Sm"←
Record#  EMPLOYEE                TELEPHONE SEX EMPLOYED   SALARY  ACCOUNT
      2  Smoler Ellen            225-3212  F   09/15/83  1650.00   300.00
      6  Smith Paul              223-8251  M   11/15/81  1700.00   350.00
. DISPLAY FOR employee = "S"←
Record#  EMPLOYEE                TELEPHONE SEX EMPLOYED   SALARY  ACCOUNT
      2  Smoler Ellen            225-3212  F   09/15/83  1650.00   300.00
      4  Sill Sally              224-4321  F   02/15/84  1507.50   150.00
      6  Smith Paul              223-8251  M   11/15/81  1700.00   350.00
```

Although you must refer to the data items precisely, you may refer to character items in part, as long as the segment ("Smi" for instance) is meant to evaluate as .T.rue from the far left of the data field. In other words, the segment must begin at the beginning.

3. Type

```
. DISPLAY FOR employee < "K"←
Record#  EMPLOYEE                TELEPHONE SEX EMPLOYED   SALARY  ACCOUNT
      3  Jones David             292-3832  M   06/15/82  1550.00   225.00
      8  Beam Sandy              225-6912  F   02/15/86  1450.00   175.00
      9  Johnson Frank           223-7928  M   03/20/86  1500.00     0.00
```

Character data inequalities also may be used in a condition.

```
. DISPLAY FOR salary * 12 <= 18000←┘
Record#  EMPLOYEE              TELEPHONE SEX EMPLOYED   SALARY  ACCOUNT
      8  Beam Sandy            225-6912  F   02/15/86  1450.00   175.00
      9  Johnson Frank         223-7928  M   03/20/86  1500.00     0.00
```

You may use numeric expressions with mathematical operators as items in a condition.

Converting Data Types

The data items used within a simple condition must be of the same data type. You often may need to convert one data item into another data type for use in the **FOR**<condition> parameter. Data type conversion is accomplished through using dBase functions. Two such functions are the DTOC (Date to Character) and CTOD (Character to Date) functions. To give you experience in converting data types, do the following.

1. Type

```
. DISPLAY FOR employed > CTOD("01/01/84")←┘
Record#  EMPLOYEE              TELEPHONE SEX EMPLOYED   SALARY  ACCOUNT
      4  Sill Sally            224-4321  F   02/15/84  1507.50   150.00
      7  Martins Mary          222-2123  F   11/01/85  1600.00   200.50
      8  Beam Sandy            225-6912  F   02/15/86  1450.00   175.00
      9  Johnson Frank         223-7928  M   03/20/86  1500.00     0.00
```

Here the character data "01/01/84" needs to be converted to date-type data with the CTOD (Character to Date) function in order to compare it with the data in the date field "employed."

Using Complex Conditions

Logical operators may be used with relational operators to test for more than one condition at a time.

1. Type

```
. CLEAR←┘
. DISPLAY ALL←┘
Record#  EMPLOYEE              TELEPHONE SEX EMPLOYED   SALARY  ACCOUNT
      1  Pratt John            225-1234  M   06/22/82  1949.00   200.00
      2  Smoler Ellen          225-3212  F   09/15/83  1650.00   300.00
      3  Jones David           292-3832  M   06/15/82  1550.00   225.00
      4  Sill Sally            224-4321  F   02/15/84  1507.50   150.00
      5  Knat Michael          221-1235  M   09/15/80  1800.00   125.00
      6  Smith Paul            223-8251  M   11/15/81  1700.00   350.00
      7  Martins Mary          222-2123  F   11/01/85  1600.00   200.50
      8  Beam Sandy            225-6912  F   02/15/86  1450.00   175.00
      9  Johnson Frank         223-7928  M   03/20/86  1500.00     0.00
. DISPLAY FOR salary < 1600 .AND. sex = "F"←┘
Record#  EMPLOYEE              TELEPHONE SEX EMPLOYED   SALARY  ACCOUNT
      4  Sill Sally            224-4321  F   02/15/84  1507.50   150.00
      8  Beam Sandy            225-6912  F   02/15/86  1450.00   175.00
```

```
. DISPLAY employee,salary FOR salary < 1600 .OR. salary > 1800↵
Record#  employee               salary
      1  Pratt John            1949.00
      3  Jones David           1550.00
      4  Sill Sally            1507.50
      8  Beam Sandy            1450.00
      9  Johnson Frank         1500.00
```

Displaying Certain Data with DISPLAY

Use the **DISPLAY** command and its parameters to display the described information from the database.

1. Display all fields of the second record.

```
Record#  EMPLOYEE               TELEPHONE SEX EMPLOYED    SALARY  ACCOUNT
      2  Smoler Ellen           225-3212  F   09/15/83   1650.00   300.00
```

2. Display only the employee's name and salary for all records.

```
Record#  employee               salary
      1  Pratt John            1949.00
      2  Smoler Ellen          1650.00
      3  Jones David           1550.00
      4  Sill Sally            1507.50
      5  Knat Michael          1800.00
      6  Smith Paul            1700.00
      7  Martins Mary          1600.00
      8  Beam Sandy            1450.00
      9  Johnson Frank         1500.00
```

3. Display the name, gender, and date hired for all employees who make $1600.00 or more per month.

```
Record#  employee               sex employed
      1  Pratt John             M   06/22/82
      2  Smoler Ellen           F   09/15/83
      5  Knat Michael           M   09/15/80
      6  Smith Paul             M   11/15/81
      7  Martins Mary           F   11/01/85
```

4. Display the name, date hired, and salary of all employees who were hired before May 30, 1984.

```
Record#  employee               employed   salary
      1  Pratt John             06/22/82  1949.00
      2  Smoler Ellen           09/15/83  1650.00
      3  Jones David            06/15/82  1550.00
      4  Sill Sally             02/15/84  1507.50
      5  Knat Michael           09/15/80  1800.00
      6  Smith Paul             11/15/81  1700.00
```

5. Display the name, date hired, and salary of all men who were hired on or before June 15, 1982.

```
Record#  employee               employed   salary
      3  Jones David            06/15/82  1550.00
      5  Knat Michael           09/15/80  1800.00
      6  Smith Paul             11/15/81  1700.00
```

EXERCISE 6: Other Important dBase Dot (.) Prompt Commands

The DELETE and RECALL Commands

Marking and Unmarking Records for Deletion

The **DELETE** command may be used to mark a record for deletion when you are in the dot (.) prompt command mode. The form of the **DELETE** command is

DELETE [<scope>] [**FOR** <condition>]

To unmark a record marked for deletion, the **RECALL** command may be used. Its form is:

RECALL [<scope>] [**FOR** <condition>]

1. To demonstrate using the two commands, type the following:

```
. GO TOP↵
. DELETE↵
       1  record deleted
. DISPLAY NEXT 3↵
Record#  EMPLOYEE              TELEPHONE SEX EMPLOYED   SALARY  ACCOUNT
      1 *Pratt John            225-1234  M   06/22/82  1949.00   200.00
      2  Smoler Ellen          225-3212  F   09/15/83  1650.00   300.00
      3  Jones David           292-3832  M   06/15/82  1550.00   225.00
```

Notice that record #1 still appears, but there is an asterisk next to it. The asterisk indicates that the **DELETE** command marked the record for deletion, but did not physically remove it from the database. To unmark this record, you may use the **RECALL** command.

2. Continue by typing

```
. GOTO 1↵
. RECALL↵
       1  record recalled
. DISPLAY NEXT 3↵
Record#  EMPLOYEE              TELEPHONE SEX EMPLOYED   SALARY  ACCOUNT
      1  Pratt John            225-1234  M   06/22/82  1949.00   200.00
      2  Smoler Ellen          225-3212  F   09/15/83  1650.00   300.00
      3  Jones David           292-3832  M   06/15/82  1550.00   225.00
```

3. Next type

```
. GOTO 1↵
. DELETE FOR employee = "Jones Da"↵
       1  record deleted
. DISPLAY↵
Record#  EMPLOYEE              TELEPHONE SEX EMPLOYED   SALARY  ACCOUNT
```

(The record pointer is left at the bottom of the database.)

```
. GO TOP↵
. DISPLAY NEXT 3↵
Record#  EMPLOYEE              TELEPHONE SEX EMPLOYED   SALARY  ACCOUNT
      1  Pratt John            225-1234  M   06/22/82  1949.00   200.00
      2  Smoler Ellen          225-3212  F   09/15/83  1650.00   300.00
      3 *Jones David           292-3832  M   06/15/82  1550.00   225.00
. DELETE FOR salary > 1600↵
      4 records deleted
```

```
. DISPLAY ALL←┘
Record#  EMPLOYEE                  TELEPHONE SEX EMPLOYED    SALARY  ACCOUNT
      1  *Pratt John               225-1234  M   06/22/82   1949.00   200.00
      2  *Smoler Ellen             225-3212  F   09/15/83   1650.00   300.00
      3  *Jones David              292-3832  M   06/15/82   1550.00   225.00
      4   Sill Sally               224-4321  F   02/15/84   1507.50   150.00
      5  *Knat Michael             221-1235  M   09/15/80   1800.00   125.00
      6  *Smith Paul               223-8251  M   11/15/81   1700.00   350.00
      7   Martins Mary             222-2123  F   11/01/85   1600.00   200.50
      8   Beam Sandy               225-6912  F   02/15/86   1450.00   175.00
      9   Johnson Frank            223-7928  M   03/20/86   1500.00     0.00
. RECALL ALL←┘
      5 records recalled
. DISPLAY ALL←┘
Record#  EMPLOYEE                  TELEPHONE SEX EMPLOYED    SALARY  ACCOUNT
      1   Pratt John               225-1234  M   06/22/82   1949.00   200.00
      2   Smoler Ellen             225-3212  F   09/15/83   1650.00   300.00
      3   Jones David              292-3832  M   06/15/82   1550.00   225.00
      4   Sill Sally               224-4321  F   02/15/84   1507.50   150.00
      5   Knat Michael             221-1235  M   09/15/80   1800.00   125.00
      6   Smith Paul               223-8251  M   11/15/81   1700.00   350.00
      7   Martins Mary             222-2123  F   11/01/85   1600.00   200.50
      8   Beam Sandy               225-6912  F   02/15/86   1450.00   175.00
      9   Johnson Frank            223-7928  M   03/20/86   1500.00     0.00
```

The PACK Command

To physically delete all records marked for deletion you use the **PACK** command. The **PACK** command has no parameters, its form is simply **PACK.** Once it is executed, all records marked for deletion are permanently erased from the database.

The COUNT, SUM, and AVERAGE Commands

The **COUNT, SUM,** and **AVERAGE** commands are used to provide summary data for the database. Their forms are

COUNT [**FOR**<condition>] [**TO**<memvar>]

SUM <expression list> [**FOR**<condition>] [**TO**<memvar>]

AVERAGE<expression list> [**FOR**<condition>] [**TO**<memvar>]

Notice the introduction of a new type of command parameter, [**TO**<memvar>].

Memory Variables

When the **COUNT, SUM,** and **AVERAGE** commands are executed, dBase will display a number on the monitor screen. For instance, typing {**SUM** account←┘} with empfile in use causes dBase to display:

```
. SUM account
      9 records summed
   account
   1725.50
```

The number 1725.50 represents the sum of all account fields in the database. The [**TO**<memvar>] parameter of the three commands causes dBase not only to display the number, but also to store the number in a memory location (variable) for later reference. You can consider a memory variable a single field with its own unique name, independent of the database, and able to hold either character, numeric, or date-type data. The variable's name is supplied by the user when the variable is created. Several dBase commands use <memvar>s in their parameters.

The **STORE TO** and = Commands

The **STORE** command places data directly into a memory variable. Its form is

STORE<expression> **TO**<memvar>

dBase's **STORE** command is comparable to the **LET** command in BASIC.

dBase Commands	BASIC Commands
STORE 5 **TO** A	**LET** A = 5
STORE 10 **TO** B	**LET** B = 10
STORE A+B **TO** C	**LET** C = A+B
STORE "Hello There" **TO** D	**LET** D$ = "Hello There"

Another method of directly placing data into a dBase memory variable is to use the equal (=) sign. The dBase commands above would then take the form:

```
A = 5
B = 10
C = A+B
D = "Hello There"
```

Memory variable names must start with a letter and may be up to ten characters long. The additional characters can be letters or numbers, but no special characters or spaces should be included in the names.

The ? Command

The **?** command is used to display the contents of a memory variable, the contents of a field in the current record, an expression, and/or a string or numeric constant. It is comparable to BASIC's **PRINT** command. As an example of how the **?** command works, assume the record pointer is on the first record of this database, and you type the following:

```
A = 5
B = 10
? "Hello There",A,A*B,employee
```

dBase will respond to the last command (the **?** command) by displaying:

```
Hello There          5                    50 Pratt John
```

The **DISPLAY MEMORY** Command

The **DISPLAY MEMORY** command displays the name, type of data, and the contents of all memory variables currently defined. With dBase III, 256 memory variables may be currently defined.

Using the COUNT and SUM Commands

1. Type

```
. COUNT FOR sex = "M" TO x←
      5 records
. COUNT FOR sex = "F" TO y←
      4 records
. ? "Total men =",x←
Total men =          5
. ? "Total women =",y←
Total women =          4
. DISPLAY MEMORY←
X           pub   N          5  (          5.00000000)
Y           pub   N          4  (          4.00000000)
    2 variables defined,      18 bytes used
  254 variables available,   5982 bytes available
.CLEAR←
```

2. Continue by typing

```
. SUM salary FOR sex = "M" TO xpay←
      5 records summed
     salary
    8499.00
. SUM salary FOR sex = "F" TO ypay←
      4 records summed
     salary
    6207.50
. ? "Total male salaries = ",xpay←
Total male salaries =        8499.00
. ? "Total female salaries = ",ypay←
Total female salaries =        6207.50

. AVERAGE salary FOR sex = "M" TO xavg←
      5 records averaged
  salary
 1699.80
. AVERAGE salary FOR sex = "F" TO yavg←
      4 records averaged
  salary
 1551.88
. xprint = "Average male salary ="←
Average male salary =
. yprint = "Average female salary ="←
Average female salary =
. ? xprint,xavg←
Average male salary =        1699.80
. ? yprint,yavg←
Average female salary =        1551.88
```

```
. DISPLAY MEMORY↵
X              pub    N            5   (          5.00000000)
Y              pub    N            4   (          4.00000000)
XPAY           pub    N      8499.00    (      8499.00000000)
YPAY           pub    N      6207.50    (      6207.50000000)
XAVG           pub    N      1699.80    (      1699.80000000)
YAVG           pub    N      1551.88    (      1551.87500000)
XPRINT         pub    C   "Average male salary ="
YPRINT         pub    C   "Average female salary ="
    8 variables defined,      102 bytes used
  248 variables available,   5898 bytes available
. CLEAR↵
```

The **REPLACE** Command

One highly useful dBase command is **REPLACE,** whose form is:

REPLACE [<scope>] <field> **WITH** <expression> [**FOR** <condition>]

The **REPLACE** command is most useful for making the same change to several records meeting a certain condition. For instance, to give all women in the database a 10 percent increase in salary, the command

REPLACE salary **WITH** salary + (salary * .10) **FOR** sex = "F"

could be entered. When executed, each of the female employees would receive a pay raise of 10 percent. The command says, in effect, "For each record, replace what is in the field named salary, with what is there plus 10 percent of what is there, if "F" is found in the field named sex for that record."

The default <scope> is **ALL** since the **FOR** parameter is used; the <field> to replace is salary; the <expression> to replace the field salary with is "salary + (salary * .10)"; and the <condition> of the **FOR** parameter is "sex = "F".

1. Type the following to see how dBase's **REPLACE** command works.

```
. CLEAR↵
. DISPLAY RECORD 6↵
Record#  EMPLOYEE               TELEPHONE SEX EMPLOYED   SALARY  ACCOUNT
      6  Smith Paul             223-8251  M   11/15/81  1700.00   350.00
. REPLACE telephone WITH "244-1010"↵
      1  record replaced
. DISPLAY↵
Record#  EMPLOYEE               TELEPHONE SEX EMPLOYED   SALARY  ACCOUNT
      6  Smith Paul             244-1010  M   11/15/81  1700.00   350.00
. CLEAR↵
. REPLACE account WITH account + 50.75 FOR employee = "Jones Da"↵
      1  record replaced
. DISPLAY RECORD 3↵
Record#  EMPLOYEE               TELEPHONE SEX EMPLOYED   SALARY  ACCOUNT
      3  Jones David            292-3832  M   06/15/82  1550.00   275.75
```

NOTE: The account amount was $225.00 before the change.

```
. CLEAR↵

. REPLACE employee WITH "Nichols Sandy",telephone WITH "229-1111" FOR employee =
 "Beam Sa"↵
      1  record replaced
. DISPLAY RECORD 8↵
Record#  EMPLOYEE                TELEPHONE SEX EMPLOYED   SALARY  ACCOUNT
      8  Nichols Sandy           229-1111  F   02/15/86  1450.00   175.00
```

Notice that when a command is longer than the screen line of 80 characters, dBase automatically wraps it around to the next line. The maximum length of a dBase III command is 254 characters.

The **LOCATE** Command

The **LOCATE** command is used to move the record pointer to the first record in the database whose data evaluate as .T.rue for the command's **FOR** <condition>. The form of the **LOCATE** command is:

LOCATE [<scope>] **FOR** <condition>

If the [<scope>] is omitted or is specified as **ALL,** the search for record(s) evaluating .T.rue begins at the top of the database and continues down, record after record (sequentially) until a record that satisfies the **FOR** condition is found, or until the bottom of the database is reached. If a record that satisfies the **FOR** <condition> is found, dBase stops the record pointer on it, making it the current record, and displays its record number on the screen.

The **CONTINUE** Command

Once the **LOCATE** command has found a record that satisfies its **FOR** <condition>, another dBase command, **CONTINUE,** may be used to locate the next record in the database that satisfies the same **FOR** <condition>. The **CONTINUE** command has no parameters.

EXERCISE 7: Sorting a Database

The **SORT** Command

Two different methods exist for sorting the records in a dBase III database. One method uses the **SORT** command with the form:

SORT TO <new file> **ON** <field list>

When the **SORT** command is executed, dBase creates a second database file on the diskette, using the records and record structure from the current database file. You then have two database files from which to choose when you enter the **USE** command.

For example, if you type {**SORT TO** payfile **ON** salary↵} while "empfile" is in use, a second database (.DBF) file will be created under the name "payfile". If you then type {**USE** payfile↵**DISPLAY ALL**↵} the database would be displayed as it exists, sorted according to salary with the records of the database renumbered.

```
. SORT TO payfile ON salary↵
  100% Sorted            9 Records sorted
. USE payfile↵
. DISPLAY ALL↵
Record#  EMPLOYEE                TELEPHONE SEX EMPLOYED  SALARY   ACCOUNT
      1  Nichols Sandy           229-1111  F   02/15/86  1450.00   175.00
      2  Johnson Frank           223-7928  M   03/20/86  1500.00     0.00
      3  Sill Sally              224-4321  F   02/15/84  1507.50   150.00
      4  Jones David             292-3832  M   06/15/82  1550.00   275.75
      5  Martins Mary            222-2123  F   11/01/85  1600.00   200.50
      6  Smoler Ellen            225-3212  F   09/15/83  1650.00   300.00
      7  Smith Paul              244-1010  M   11/15/81  1700.00   350.00
      8  Knat Michael            221-1235  M   09/15/80  1800.00   125.00
      9  Pratt John              225-1234  M   06/22/82  1949.00   200.00
```

The INDEX Command

The other method of sorting records is with the **INDEX** command:

INDEX ON <expression> **TO** <index file>

The **INDEX** command, however, does not actually sort the records in the database nor does it create an entire new database file. Instead, it creates a smaller index file which is given an .NDX file extension when it is saved onto the diskette.

An index file is able to reside in RAM memory with its related database and is copied into RAM memory when the **USE** command is given with its **INDEX** parameter. For instance, if you type {**INDEX ON** salary **TO** paydex ↵}, an index (.NDX) file named paydex will be created on the diskette.

If you then type {**USE** empfile **INDEX** paydex↵}, both the database (empfile.DBF) and index (paydex.NDX) file will be read into RAM memory.

An Index File in RAM Memory

Using the model of computer RAM memory, an index file in use with a database can be thought of as:

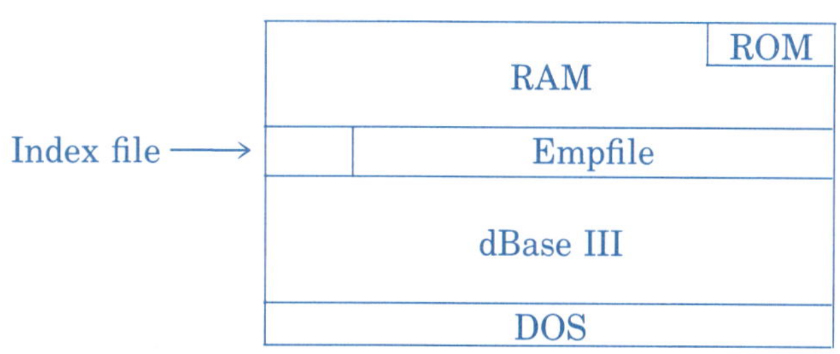

The index file is used with the database to treat the database as if it were sorted. Continuing with the example, if you then type {**DISPLAY ALL**↵} the screen will display:

```
. INDEX ON salary TO paydex↵
       9 records indexed
. USE empfile INDEX paydex↵
. DISPLAY ALL↵
Record#  EMPLOYEE                TELEPHONE SEX EMPLOYED    SALARY   ACCOUNT
      8  Nichols Sandy           229-1111  F   02/15/86   1450.00    175.00
      9  Johnson Frank           223-7928  M   03/20/86   1500.00      0.00
      4  Sill Sally              224-4321  F   02/15/84   1507.50    150.00
      3  Jones David             292-3832  M   06/15/82   1550.00    275.75
      7  Martins Mary            222-2123  F   11/01/85   1600.00    200.50
      2  Smoler Ellen            225-3212  F   09/15/83   1650.00    300.00
      6  Smith Paul              244-1010  M   11/15/81   1700.00    350.00
      5  Knat Michael            221-1235  M   09/15/80   1800.00    125.00
      1  Pratt John              225-1234  M   06/22/82   1949.00    200.00
```

Notice the record numbers have not changed. They are still in their original order in the database file, "empfile".

How an Index File Affects the Record Pointer

1. Type

```
. CLEAR↵
. INDEX ON employee TO namedex↵
       9 records indexed
. USE empfile INDEX namedex↵
. DISPLAY ALL↵
Record#  EMPLOYEE                TELEPHONE SEX EMPLOYED    SALARY   ACCOUNT
      9  Johnson Frank           223-7928  M   03/20/86   1500.00      0.00
      3  Jones David             292-3832  M   06/15/82   1550.00    275.75
      5  Knat Michael            221-1235  M   09/15/80   1800.00    125.00
      7  Martins Mary            222-2123  F   11/01/85   1600.00    200.50
      8  Nichols Sandy           229-1111  F   02/15/86   1450.00    175.00
      1  Pratt John              225-1234  M   06/22/82   1949.00    200.00
      4  Sill Sally              224-4321  F   02/15/84   1507.50    150.00
      6  Smith Paul              244-1010  M   11/15/81   1700.00    350.00
      2  Smoler Ellen            225-3212  F   09/15/83   1650.00    300.00
```

When you create an index file you usually **INDEX ON** a <field>. This field becomes the index file's key. The keys in the index file are sorted and used with their corresponding record numbers to direct the record pointer to the database. It is useful to consider the record pointer as residing next to the index file, not next to the database, and the index file as being made up of a sorted list of key data with their associated record numbers.

Index File		Database File						
→ Johnson Frank	9	1	Pratt John	225-1234	M	06/22/82	1949.00	200.00
Jones David	3	2	Smoler Ellen	225-3212	F	08/15/83	1650.00	300.00
Knat Michael	5	3	Jones David	292-3832	M	06/15/82	1550.00	275.75
Martins Mary	7	4	Sill Sally	224-4321	F	02/15/84	1507.50	150.00
Nichols Sandy	8	5	Knat Michael	221-1235	M	09/15/80	1800.00	125.00
Pratt John	1	6	Smith Paul	244-1010	M	11/15/81	1700.00	350.00
Sill Sally	4	7	Martins Mary	222-2123	F	11/01/85	1600.00	200.50
Smith Paul	6	8	Nichols Sandy	229-1111	F	02/15/86	1450.00	175.00
Smoler Ellen	2	9	Johnson Frank	223-7928	M	03/20/86	1500.00	0.00

With an index file in use with a database, a command such as **GO TOP** sends the record pointer to the top of the index file rather than to the top of the database. dBase then uses the record number located there to determine which record to make the current record. So if a command such as **DISPLAY** is executed while the record pointer is at the top of the index file, record 9 of the database file in the example will be displayed.

The result of using a command such as **DISPLAY ALL** is that the pointer goes to the top of the index file, dBase **DISPLAYS** the record for the record number located there, **SKIPS** the record pointer in the index file, and **DISPLAYS** the database record for the next record number found there.

Index File		Database File						
→Johnson Frank	9	1	Pratt John	225-1234	M	06/22/82	1949.00	200.00
Jones David	3	2	Smoler Ellen	225-3212	F	08/15/83	1650.00	300.00
Knat Michael	5	→3	Jones David	292-3832	M	06/15/82	1550.00	275.75
Martins Mary	7	4	Sill Sally	224-4321	F	02/15/84	1507.50	150.00
Nichols Sandy	8	5	Knat Michael	221-1235	M	09/15/80	1800.00	125.00
Pratt John	1	6	Smith Paul	244-1010	M	11/15/81	1700.00	350.00
Sill Sally	4	7	Martins Mary	222-2123	F	11/01/85	1600.00	200.50
Smith Paul	6	8	Nichols Sandy	229-1111	F	02/15/86	1450.00	175.00
Smoler Ellen	2	9	Johnson Frank	223-7928	M	03/20/86	1500.00	0.00

The process continues until the pointer reaches the bottom of the index file, and the database records appear on the screen as if they are sorted by employee name.

Indexing on More than One Field

You may create key data for an index file based on more than one field of record data, as long as the data being used are characters or converted to characters. To do this you type **INDEX ON** <field> + <field> **TO** <index file>.

2. To demonstrate type

```
. INDEX ON sex+employee TO empdex←
      9 records indexed
. USE empfile INDEX empdex←
. DISPLAY ALL←
Record#  EMPLOYEE            TELEPHONE SEX EMPLOYED   SALARY  ACCOUNT
      7  Martins Mary        222-2123  F   11/01/85  1600.00   200.50
      8  Nichols Sandy       229-1111  F   02/15/86  1450.00   175.00
      4  Sill Sally          224-4321  F   02/15/84  1507.50   150.00
      2  Smoler Ellen        225-3212  F   09/15/83  1650.00   300.00
      9  Johnson Frank       223-7928  M   03/20/86  1500.00     0.00
      3  Jones David         292-3832  M   06/15/82  1550.00   275.75
      5  Knat Michael        221-1235  M   09/15/80  1800.00   125.00
      1  Pratt John          225-1234  M   06/22/82  1949.00   200.00
      6  Smith Paul          244-1010  M   11/15/81  1700.00   350.00
```

Indexing on more than one field creates an index file with its key data sorted on characters found in the first field (in this case an "M" or "F") followed by characters found in the second field (employee's name here).

Index File

→FMartins Mary	7
FNichols Sandy	8
FSill Sally	4
FSmoler Ellen	2
MJohnson Frank	9
MJones David	3
MKnat Michael	5
MPratt John	1
MSmith Paul	6

Advantages of Indexing

Automatic Updating

Indexing a database is typically the more efficient method of sorting records in a database. One of its advantages is that an index file automatically is updated for records added, deleted, or edited when it is in use with its database.

Several index files may be put into use with the database by entering their names into a list, with each name separated by commas, when you type the **USE** command:

USE empfile **INDEX** paydex,namedex, ...

All index files in use will be updated for changes made to the database; and the first index file listed is the one where the record pointer will reside.

Faster Record Search/The SEEK Command

When the commands discussed so far cause dBase to search through the database for records, the search is conducted sequentially from the top of the database to the bottom, with each record evaluated to see if it is .T.rue for the **FOR** <condition>. In large databases the sequential process of searching can take considerable time.

When a database is in use with an index file, dBase can find a record very rapidly if the data item for which it is searching is key data for the index. The faster search is done with the **SEEK** command:

SEEK <key expression>

For instance, using an index file with employee names as key data in use with the database "empfile" you could move the pointer to Sandy Nichols' record by typing the command:

SEEK "Nicho"

The reason that **SEEK** is so much faster at locating a record is because the data through which it is searching (the index file's key data) are sorted. With sorted data the search does not have to begin at the top of the data. It can begin anywhere in the list of key data items. If the first key data item evaluated is less than the one for which dBase is searching, dBase can jump the pointer down several data items to make another evaluation. If the record pointer overshoots (if the second key data item is greater than the one for which dBase is searching) the bounds have been set for finding the sought after key data item, and the search continues in the same up and down manner until dBase finds the data item.

The result is that fewer evaluations need to be made in order to find the key data item and its record number.

Index File

```
                          -------------------
                          Johnson Frank      9
                          Jones David        3
1st  guess       ------>  Knat Michael       5  (Lower)
 |                        Martins Mary       7
 |    3rd guess  ------>  Nichols Sandy      8  (Hit)
 |        |               Pratt John         1
2nd guess        ------>  Sill Sally         4  (Higher)
                          Smith Paul         6
                          Smoler Ellen       2
                          -------------------
```

NOTE: ***If you are using dBase III Plus, move to the "dBase III Plus Tutorial Exercises Supplement" to complete the tutorial (page D-51).***

EXERCISE 8: Creating a dBase III Report

The REPORT Command

One of the most powerful single commands of dBase is its **REPORT** command:

> **REPORT FORM** [<form file>] [<scope>] [**FOR** <expression>] [**HEADING**<character string>] [**TO PRINT**]

The default <scope> of the **REPORT** command is **ALL.** When executed, the **REPORT** command produces a report similar to the following:

Employee Full Report
====================

Employee Name	Phone #	Hire Date	Current Salary	Account Balance
Johnson Frank	223-7928	03/20/86	1500.00	0.00
Jones David	292-3832	06/15/82	1550.00	275.75
Knat Michael	221-1235	09/15/80	1800.00	125.00
Martins Mary	222-2123	11/01/85	1600.00	200.50
Nichols Sandy	229-1111	02/15/86	1450.00	175.00
Pratt John	225-1234	06/22/82	1949.00	200.00
Sill Sally	224-4321	02/15/84	1507.50	150.00
Smith Paul	244-1010	11/15/81	1700.00	350.00
Smoler Ellen	225-3212	09/15/83	1650.00	300.00

The report is columnar with each column containing the evaluated results of an expression. The columns have column labels and the report has a report title. Totals and subtotals may or may not be included in the report. To produce such a report, the **REPORT** command requires that several specifications be made. A report's specifications are entered while in a dBase editing mode, and are automatically saved in a [<form file>] (given a (.FRM) extension by dBase) when editing mode is exited by typing {^End}.

Creating a Report Form File—The MODIFY REPORT Command

The **MODIFY REPORT** command is used to enter the editing mode in which you make a report's specifications. The command's form is

MODIFY REPORT <form file>

To give you experience in creating report form files for the **REPORT** command to use, you will first create the form file which produces the example report shown previously.

1. Type {**USE** empfile **INDEX** namedex↵}.

The database(s) whose data will be referred to in the report specifications must be in use prior to executing the **MODIFY REPORT** command.

2. Type {**SET MENU OFF**↵}.

The editing menu of **MODIFY REPORT** prevents the display of useful information. Refer to the editing keystrokes provided here as you complete the following steps.

Action Desired	Keys
Move right on a line	Cursor-right
Move left on a line	Cursor-left
Move to the next line	Cursor-down
Move back one line	Cursor-up
Move to the next screen	PgDn
Move back one screen	PgUp
Delete character over cursor	Del
Delete all characters right of cursor	^Y
Insert mode on/off	Ins
Delete current column specifications	^U
Insert new column specifications	^N
Save specifications and exit	^End

3. Now type {**MODIFY REPORT** fullrepo↵}.

"fullrepo" will be the filename of the form file for this report. The following will appear on the screen. The record structure and filename for empfile are displayed at the top of the screen. The large reverse video area at the location of the cursor is the area into which you may enter the report title (page heading).

```
Structure of file B:empfile.dbf
==========================================================
EMPLOYEE   C  20 | SALARY     N  8  2 |          |
TELEPHONE  C   8 | ACCOUNT    N  8  2 |          |
SEX        C   1 |                    |          |
EMPLOYED   D   8 |                    |          |
==========================================================

                    Page heading:



          Page width (# chars):          80
          Left margin (# chars):          8
          Right margin (# chars):         0
          # lines/page:                  58
          Double space report? (Y/N):     N
```

4. Enter the report title as shown:

```
                    Page heading:
  Employee Full Report
  ====================
```

5. When done, tap the Cursor down key until the cursor moves to the area labeled "Page width (# chars)" and change the default answer of 80 to 72 by typing over the characters found there.

The screen should now appear as:

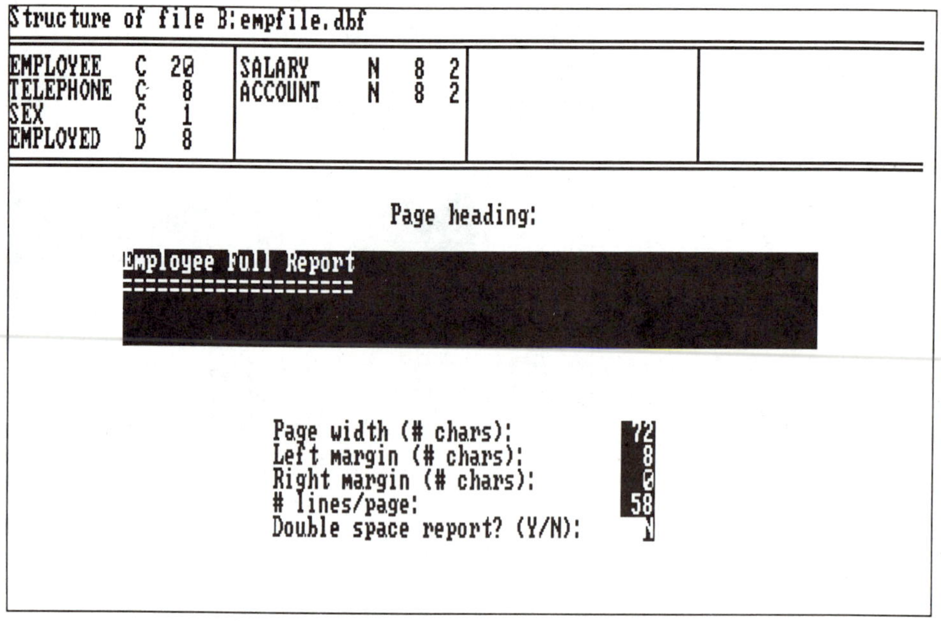

6. Now tap the PgDn key to move to the next screen.

The next screen presented is for use when report subtotals are desired. The report for which you are making specifications has no subtotals.

7. Tap the PgDn key again.

The next screen presented is for the first column of data in the report. Here you specify the contents of the column (Field contents) and the column label to be used in the report (Field header).

8. Enter this information as shown:

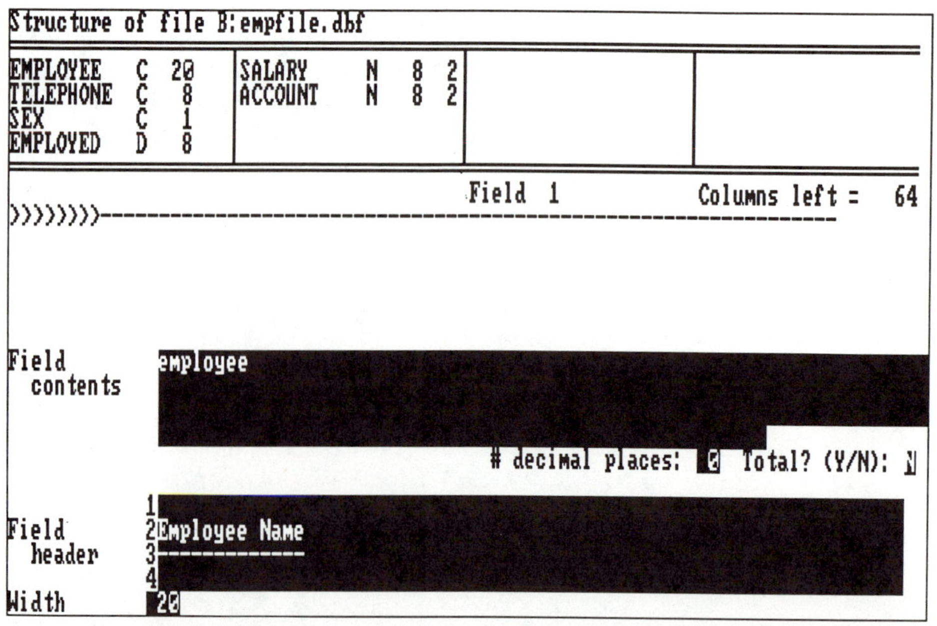

9. When done, tap the PgDn key to move to the next screen, and then use it to complete the next column's specifications as shown:

```
Structure of file B:empfile.dbf

EMPLOYEE   C  20  SALARY    N  8  2
TELEPHONE  C   8  ACCOUNT   N  8  2
SEX        C   1
EMPLOYED   D   8

                                  Field  2          Columns left =   43
>>>>>>>>
        Employee Name
        -------------

        XXXXXXXXXXXXXXXXXXXX

Field         telephone
  contents

                                       # decimal places: 0  Total? (Y/N): N

             1
Field        2Phone #
  header     3-------
             4
Width         8
```

10. Tap the PgDn key to move to the screen for the third column's specifications.

Before continuing, notice the area between the display of empfile's record structure and the area into which you are entering data.

```
                                  Field  3          Columns left =   34
>>>>>>>>
        Employee Name        Phone #
        -------------        -------

        XXXXXXXXXXXXXXXXXXXX XXXXXXXX
```

At the top right of this area is information about the field you are currently on (Field 3) and the number of characters (columns) remaining before the right-hand margin (now set at 72) will be reached according to the widths of the columns already specified (in this example, 34).

Beneath the field and columns information is an emerging picture of what the finished report will look like. Shown here are the characters used by the left margin (>>>>>>>>), the specified column labels, and a mask for the characters of data included in the column.

The default width of each column in the report is based on the width of the field (or expression) specified as the contents of the column, or the width of the column heading, whichever is larger. The default value can be changed by entering a different value into the area labeled "Width." Within the printed report column, character or date data will be automatically left justified, while numeric data will be right justified.

11. Finish specifying the report's column contents with the following data.

Field 3:

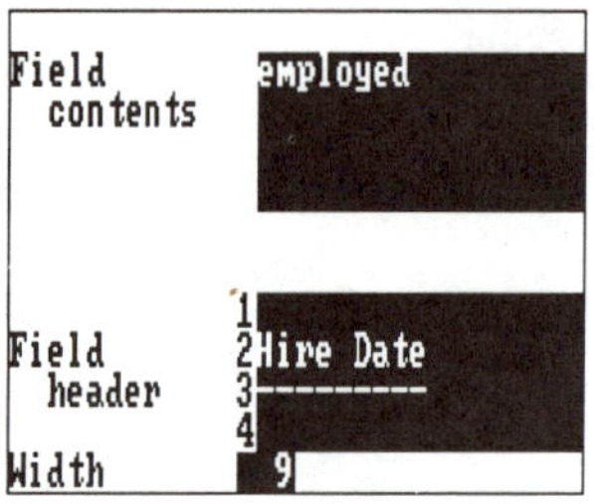

Field 4:

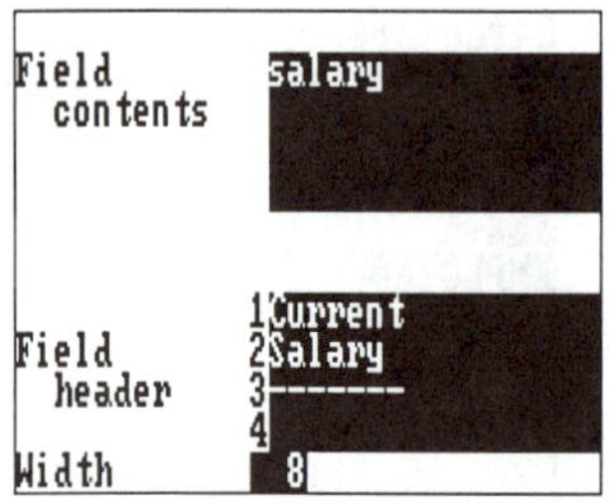

Field 5:

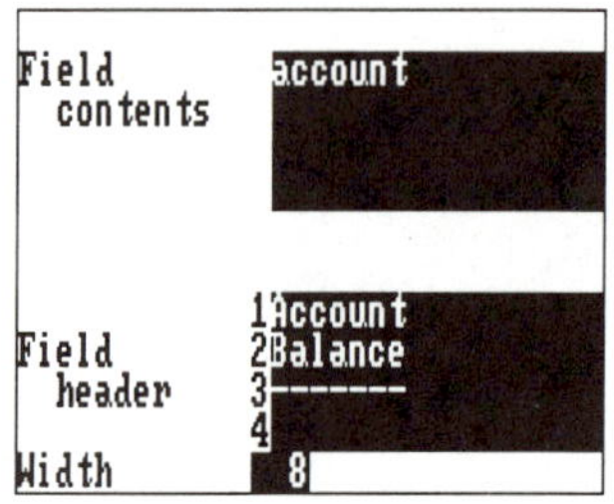

When finished entering the data for field 5, the screen should appear as:

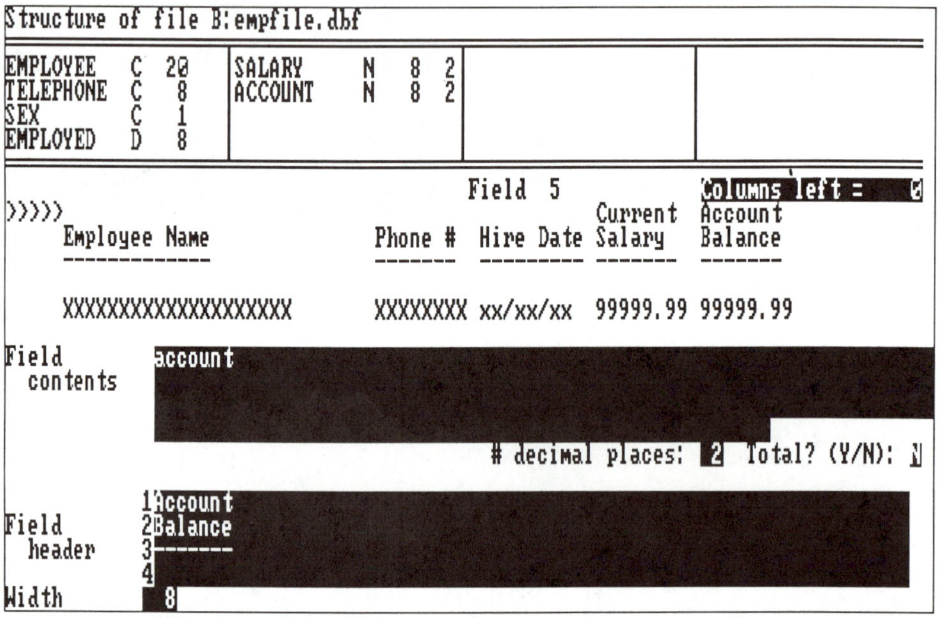

12. Now type {^End} to save the report data and exit to the dot (.) prompt.

Running Reports

With the report specifications entered and saved in a form file, you are now able to produce the report using the **REPORT** command.

1. Type {**REPORT FORM** fullrepo↵}.

```
. REPORT FORM fullrepo

Page No.      1
01/01/86
                          Employee Full Report
                          ====================
                                                   Current   Account
Employee Name         Phone #   Hire Date   Salary   Balance
-------------         -------   ---------   -------  -------
Johnson Frank         223-7928 03/20/86    1500.00     0.00
Jones David           292-3832 06/15/82    1550.00   275.75
Knat Michael          221-1235 09/15/80    1800.00   125.00
Martins Mary          222-2123 11/01/85    1600.00   200.50
Nichols Sandy         229-1111 02/15/86    1450.00   175.00
Pratt John            225-1234 06/22/82    1949.00   200.00
Sill Sally            224-4321 02/15/84    1507.50   150.00
Smith Paul            244-1010 11/15/81    1700.00   350.00
Smoler Ellen          225-3212 09/15/83    1650.00   300.00
```

Later you will see how to print a report on the printer.

Changing a Report's Specifications

A report's specifications may be altered by using the **MODIFY REPORT** command. To give you experience in using this command and the editing mode it provides do the following:

1. Type {**MODIFY REPORT** fullrepo↵}.

Refer to the **MODIFY REPORT** editing keystrokes (*see table, page D–38*) to assist you in making the following changes.

2. **a.** Change the report's "Left margin (# chars):" to 4.
   b. Reduce the width of the column containing employee names (field 1) from 20 to 16.
   c. Increase the width of the telephone column (field 2) to 10.
   d. Move to the account column (field 5) and insert a new column into the report (type ^**N** to do this).
   e. Enter the following data into the new field 5.

```
Field contents   = INT(salary*.15)
# decimal places = 2
Field header     = Account
                   Limit
                   ------
Width            = 9
```

```
Field       INT(salary*.15)
 contents

                       # decimal places: 2  Total? (Y/N): N

           1Account
Field      2Limit
 header    3------
           4
Width       9
```

3. Type {^End} to exit the **MODIFY REPORT** editing mode, then type

```
{REPORT FORM fullrepo↵ }
```

The report produced should have the form:

```
Page No.      1
01/01/86
                                Employee Full Report
                                ====================
                                             Current    Account   Account
Employee Name      Phone #     Hire Date     Salary      Limit    Balance
-------------      -------     ----------    -------    -------   -------
Johnson Frank      223-7928    03/20/86     1500.00     225.00      0.00
Jones David        292-3832    06/15/82     1550.00     232.00    275.75
Knat Michael       221-1235    09/15/80     1800.00     270.00    125.00
Martins Mary       222-2123    11/01/85     1600.00     240.00    200.50
Nichols Sandy      229-1111    02/15/86     1450.00     217.00    175.00
Pratt John         225-1234    06/22/82     1949.00     292.00    200.00
Sill Sally         224-4321    02/15/84     1507.50     226.00    150.00
Smith Paul         244-1010    11/15/81     1700.00     255.00    350.00
Smoler Ellen       225-3212    09/15/83     1650.00     247.00    300.00
```

Running Selective Reports

dBase's **REPORT** command lets you be selective with your reports through the use of the **FOR** condition parameter of the command. Type the following:

```
. REPORT FORM fullrepo FOR sex = "F"↵
Page No.      1
01/01/86
                                Employee Full Report
                                ====================
                                             Current    Account   Account
Employee Name      Phone #     Hire Date     Salary      Limit    Balance
-------------      -------     ----------    -------    -------   -------
Martins Mary       222-2123    11/01/85     1600.00     240.00    200.50
Nichols Sandy      229-1111    02/15/86     1450.00     217.00    175.00
Sill Sally         224-4321    02/15/84     1507.50     226.00    150.00
Smoler Ellen       225-3212    09/15/83     1650.00     247.00    300.00
. REPORT FORM fullrepo FOR employed < CTOD("01/01/83")↵
Page No.      1
01/01/86
                                Employee Full Report
                                ====================
                                             Current    Account   Account
Employee Name      Phone #     Hire Date     Salary      Limit    Balance
-------------      -------     ----------    -------    -------   -------
Jones David        292-3832    06/15/82     1550.00     232.00    275.75
Knat Michael       221-1235    09/15/80     1800.00     270.00    125.00
Pratt John         225-1234    06/22/82     1949.00     292.00    200.00
Smith Paul         244-1010    11/15/81     1700.00     255.00    350.00
```

Adding a Report Heading

Another **REPORT** command parameter, **HEADING,** may be used to further describe the report being produced.

1. Type

```
. REPORT FORM fullrepo FOR account > .15 * salary HEADING "Employees Currently O
  ver Limit"
    Page No.      1     Employees Currently Over Limit
    01/01/86

                          Employee Full Report
                          ====================
                                                 Current      Account    Account
    Employee Name     Phone #     Hire Date       Salary        Limit    Balance
    -------------     -------     ---------      -------      -------    -------
    Jones David       292-3832    06/15/82       1550.00       232.00     275.75
    Smith Paul        244-1010    11/15/81       1700.00       255.00     350.00
    Smoler Ellen      225-3212    09/15/83       1650.00       247.00     300.00
```

Totals in a Report

dBase's **REPORT** command also allows totals to be included in a report if they are specified in the form file. Create a new (.FRM) file by following the next steps.

1. Type {**MODIFY REPORT** salaries↵}.
2. Complete the first screen presented by entering the following data:

```
Page heading              = Salary Summary Report
                            ============================
Page width (# chars)      = 55
Left margin (# chars)     = 20
```

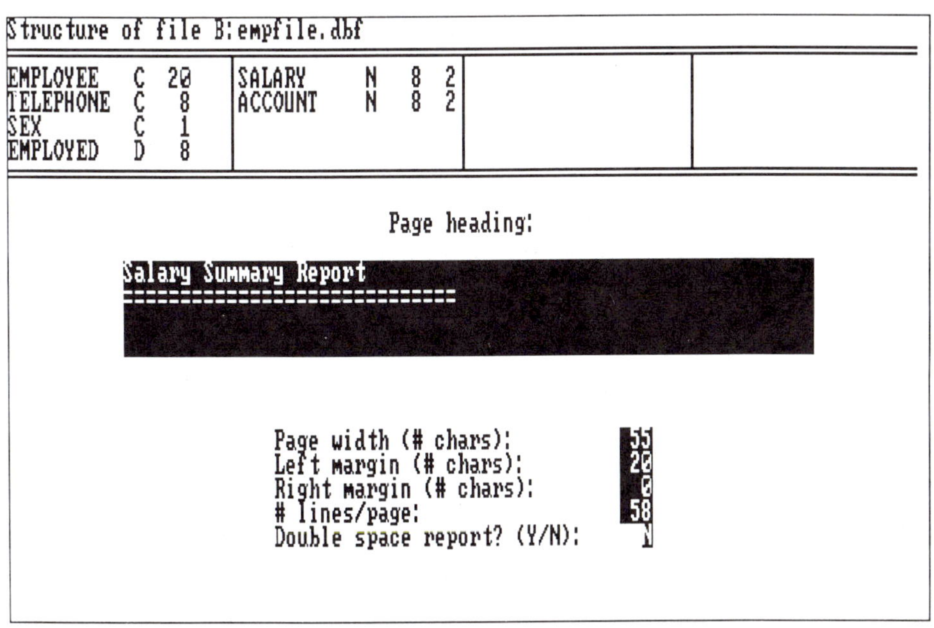

3. Type {PgDn} to move to the next screen.

The next screen presented is for use when report subtotals are desired. It is not used when reports include only totals.

4. Type {PgDn} again to move to the first column's data screen. Complete this screen with the following data:

```
Field contents  = employee
Field header    = Employee Name
                  -------------
```

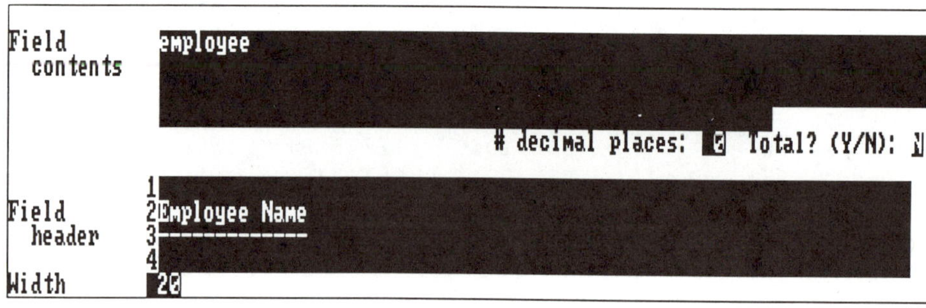

5. Type {PgDn} to move to Field 2. Enter this field's data:

```
Field contents  = "$"
```

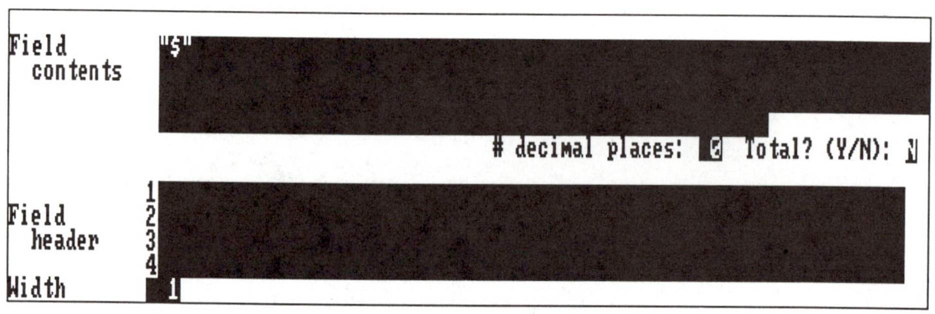

6. Type {PgDn} to move to Field 3.

The last column of the report will have a total printed.

7. Enter this column's data as:

```
Field contents  = salary
Field header    = Salary
                 ------
Total (Y/N)     = Y
```

```
Field          salary
  contents

                                   # decimal places: 2  Total? (Y/N): Y

              1
Field         2Salary
  header      3------
              4
Width          8
```

8. Type {^End} to exit the **MODIFY REPORT** editing mode, then type

REPORT FORM salaries↵

dBase will display:

```
. REPORT FORM salaries
                     Page No.     1
                     01/01/86
                            Salary Summary Report
                        =============================

                     Employee Name           Salary
                     -------------           ------
                     Johnson Frank        $  1500.00
                     Jones David          $  1550.00
                     Knat Michael         $  1800.00
                     Martins Mary         $  1600.00
                     Nichols Sandy        $  1450.00
                     Pratt John           $  1949.00
                     Sill Sally           $  1507.50
                     Smith Paul           $  1700.00
                     Smoler Ellen         $  1650.00
                    *** Total ***
                                            14706.50
```

Subtotals in Reports

You can subtotal groups of data with the **REPORT** command if the database in use is currently indexed or sorted on the field(s) by which you wish to subtotal and the appropriate specifications have been made in the **MODIFY REPORT** editing mode. To give you experience in report subtotals, complete the following steps:

1. Type {**USE** empfile **INDEX** empdex↵ **MODIFY REPORT** acctrepo↵}.
2. Complete the first screen presented by entering the following data:

```
Page heading:         = Salaries & Accounts By Gender
                        * Personnel Department *
Page width (# chars)  = 65
Left margin (# chars) = 15
```

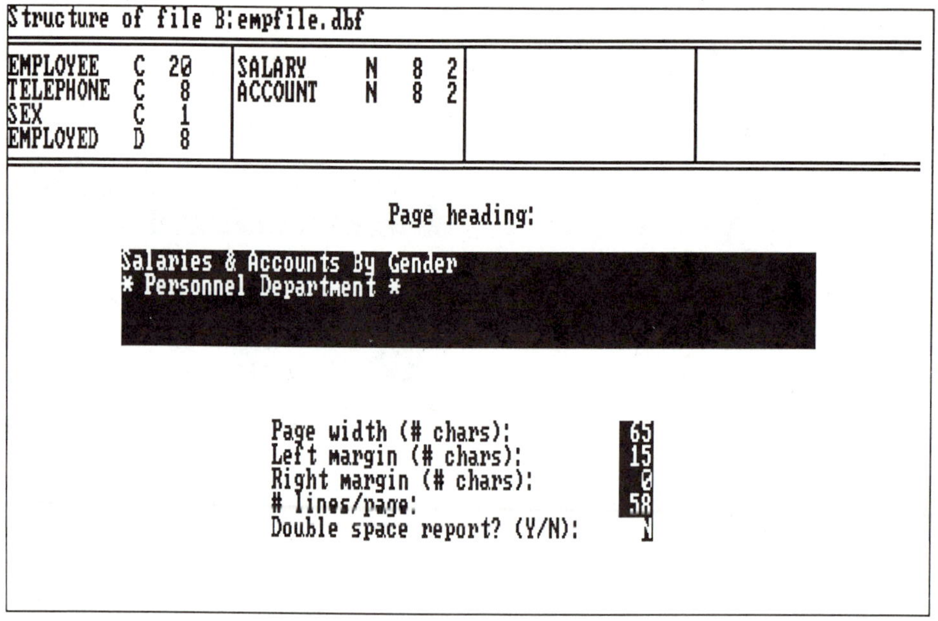

3. Type {PgDn} to move to the next screen.
4. Complete this screen by entering the following data.

```
Group/subtotal on       = sex
Group/subtotal heading  = Gender =
```

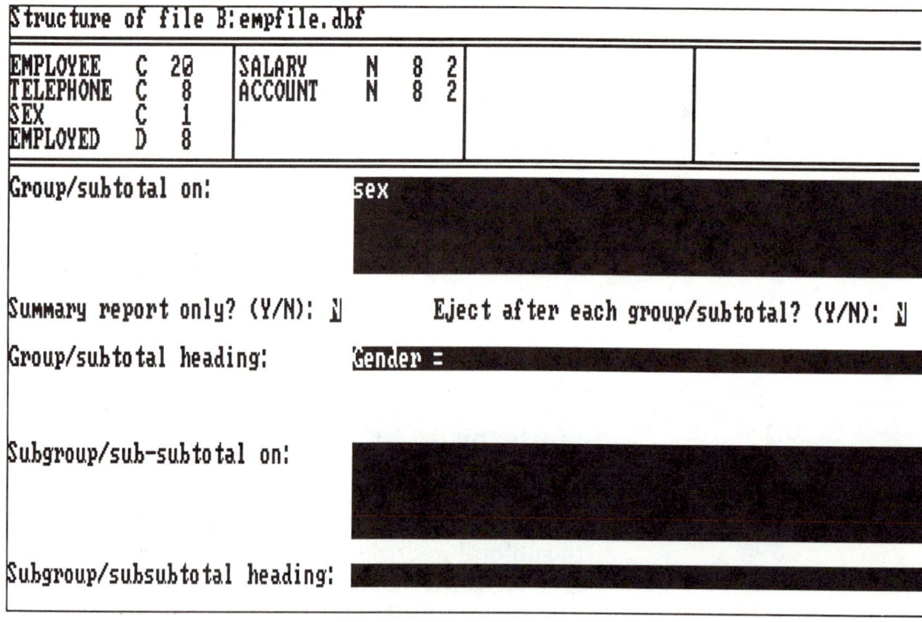

5. Now complete the following screens as shown. Make sure to change the "Total? (Y/N)" default answer "N" to "Y" in the columns for salary and account.

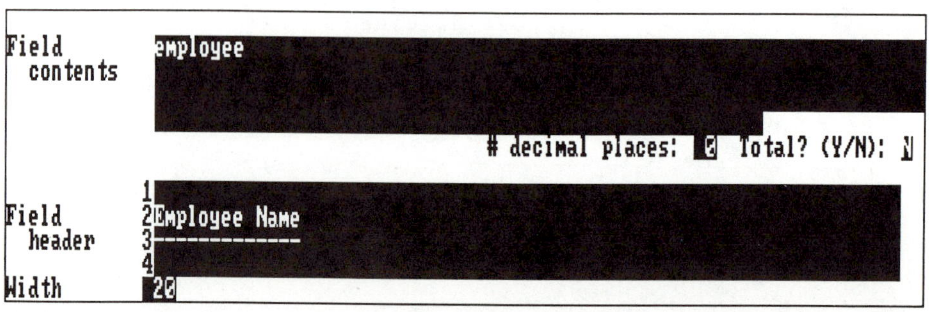

```
Field          salary
  contents

                                 # decimal places: 2  Total? (Y/N): Y

              1
Field         2Salary
  header      3------
              4
Width          8
```

```
Field          account
  contents

                                 # decimal places: 2  Total? (Y/N): Y

              1
Field         2Account
  header      3-------
              4
Width          8
```

6. Now type {^End} to exit the **MODIFY REPORT** editing mode, then type {**REPORT FORM** acctrepo↵} to produce the following report:

```
. REPORT FORM acctrepo
 Page No.     1
 01/01/86
            Salaries & Accounts By Gender
               * Personnel Department *
 Employee Name            Salary  Account
 -------------            ------  -------
** Gender = F
 Martins Mary            1600.00   200.50
 Nichols Sandy           1450.00   175.00
 Sill Sally              1507.50   150.00
 Smoler Ellen            1650.00   300.00
** Subtotal **
                         6207.50   825.50
** Gender = M
 Johnson Frank           1500.00     0.00
 Jones David             1550.00   275.75
 Knat Michael            1800.00   125.00
 Pratt John              1949.00   200.00
 Smith Paul              1700.00   350.00
** Subtotal **
                         8499.00   950.75
*** Total ***
                        14706.50  1776.25
```

Printing Out a Report

The **REPORT** command will print a report when you include the **TO PRINT** parameter in it.

1. Make sure the printer is turned on, on-line, and connected to your computer. (Your lab may have a shared device control switch. You will need to select your computer as the one currently connected to the printer.)

Your system ____

____

____

____

____

____

____

____

2. Type in the following **REPORT** commands.

```
REPORT FORM fullrepo TO PRINT
REPORT FORM salaries TO PRINT FOR employed < CTOD("01/01/84")
REPORT FORM acctrepo TO PRINT
REPORT FORM fullrepo TO PRINT FOR sex= "M" .AND. employed > CTOD("01/01/82")
    HEADING "All Male Employees Hired After 1981"
```

EXERCISE 9: Quitting dBase III

To quit dBase and return to the DOS operating level (A>) you use the **QUIT** command. The **QUIT** command is very important since it saves all new file data that may have been created during the session. It then closes all dBase files that may be open at the time before returning to DOS.

QUIT is always the last command you enter when you use dBase III.

1. Type {**QUIT**↵} to end this dBase session.

This section is designed for those completing the tutorial using dBase III Plus. Its purpose is to provide experience in producing dBase reports, and in using dBase III's new "friendlier user interface"—a full-screen, menu-driven mode used for executing dBase operations. The full-screen, menu-driven mode is available with many dBase III Plus commands.

EXERCISE 8: Creating a dBase III Report

The REPORT Command

The **REPORT** command is one of the most powerful single commands of dBase.

> **REPORT FORM** [<form file>] [<scope>] [**FOR** <expression>]
> [**HEADING**<character string>] [**TO PRINT**]

The default <scope> of the **REPORT** command is **ALL.** When executed, the **REPORT** command produces a report similar to the following:

```
                         Employee Full Report
                         ====================
                                                     Current   Account
 Employee Name             Phone #   Hire Date       Salary    Balance
 -------------             -------   ---------       -------   -------
 Johnson Frank             223-7928  03/20/86        1500.00      0.00
 Jones David               292-3832  06/15/82        1550.00    275.75
 Knat Michael              221-1235  09/15/80        1800.00    125.00
 Martins Mary              222-2123  11/01/85        1600.00    200.50
 Nichols Sandy             229-1111  02/15/86        1450.00    175.00
 Pratt John                225-1234  06/22/82        1949.00    200.00
 Sill Sally                224-4321  02/15/84        1507.50    150.00
 Smith Paul                244-1010  11/15/81        1700.00    350.00
 Smoler Ellen              225-3212  09/15/83        1650.00    300.00
*** Total ***
                                                    14706.50   1776.25
```

The report is columnar, with each column containing the evaluated results of an expression. The columns have column labels and the report has a report title. Totals and subtotals may or may not be included in the report. To produce such a report, the **REPORT** command requires that several specifications be made. A report's specifications are entered while in a dBase full-screen, menu-driven mode, and are automatically saved in a [<form file>] (given a (.FRM) extension by dBase) when the mode is exited by selecting the Exit menu option.

Creating a Report Form File—The MODIFY REPORT Command

The **MODIFY REPORT** command is used to enter the mode in which you make a report's specifications. The command's form is:

> **MODIFY REPORT** <form file>

To give you experience in creating report form files for the **REPORT** command to use, you will first create the form file which produces the example report shown previously.

1. Type {**USE** empfile **INDEX** namedex↵}.

The database(s) whose data will be referred to in the report specifications must be in use prior to executing the **MODIFY REPORT** command.

2. Now type {**MODIFY REPORT** fullrepo↵}.

"fullrepo" will be the filename of the form file for this report. The following will appear on the screen:

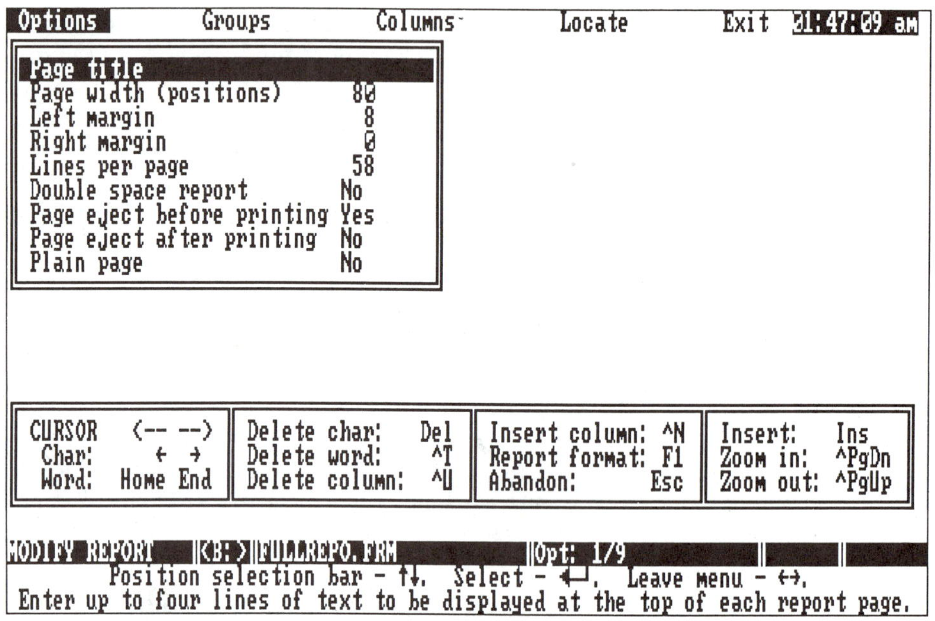

Navigating through dBase III Menus

Across the top of the screen appears a single line of menu options: Options; Groups; Columns; Locate; and Exit. This line is referred to as the *menu bar*. You will see one of the options highlighted with a reverse video display.

1. Press the cursor-right key two or three times.

Notice that as the highlight moves across the menu bar, dBase presents a new screen below the highlighted option. The screen appearing below the menu bar option is called a *pull down* menu, and is the current menu from which you may select.

To make a selection from a pull down menu, the cursor-down or cursor-up keys may be used to move the highlight of the pull down menu down or up. When the desired menu item is highlighted, the Enter key is pressed to invoke that menu operation. When a menu operation is invoked, you are often left in an editing mode for data entry. The following table of editing keystrokes may be referred to as you complete the next tutorial steps.

MODIFY REPORT Editing Keystrokes

Action Desired	Keys
Move right on a line	Cursor-right
Move left on a line	Cursor-left
Move to the next line	Cursor-down
Move back one line	Cursor-up
Delete character over cursor	Del
Delete all characters right of cursor	^Y
Insert mode on/off	Ins
Save and exit editing mode	^End
Columns Menu Bar Option Only	
Move to the next column	PgDn
Move back one column	PgUp
Delete current column specifications	^U
Insert new column specifications	^N

Making Report Specifications

1. Move the menu bar highlight to Options, then select "Page title" from the pull down menu by typing ↵.

Selecting "Page title" causes dBase to provide an area on the screen into which you may enter the report title.

2. Enter the report title as shown.

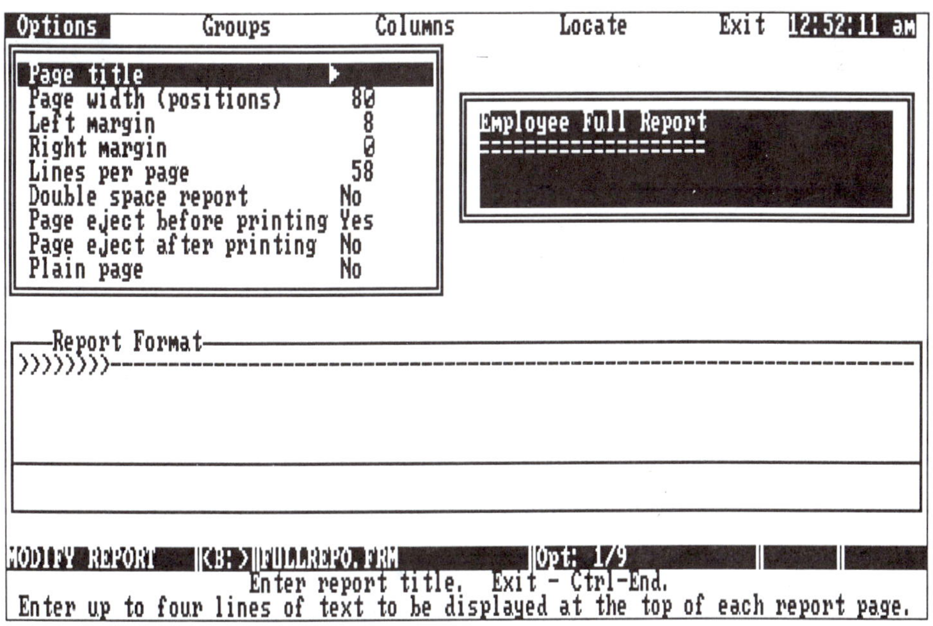

3. When done, type {^End} to save and exit the editing mode.
4. Next move the pull down highlight to the menu item marked "Page width (positions)" and select this item by typing ↵. Change the default answer of 80 characters to 72 characters by typing {72↵}.

You are now ready to specify the contents of the report's columns. To do so you will use the pull down menu provided by the Columns option of the menu bar.

5. Move the menu bar highlight to "Columns."

The pull down menu presented is for the first column of data in the report. Here you specify the contents of the column (Contents) and the column label to be used in the report (Heading).

6. Select the Contents menu item by typing ↵, and then enter the column contents of the first column by typing {employee↵}.

Notice that the default value for "Width" changed from 0 to 20. Twenty characters is the field width of the field named "employee" in empfile.

When you enter the contents of a report column, dBase checks to see if it is in the form of an expression it can evaluate. If field names are used, they must be fields found in the active database(s). If the expression is made up of a single field name, dBase will automatically set the default width of the report column to the same width as the field to which it refers.

7. Next select the Heading item of the pull down menu and enter the column heading as shown:

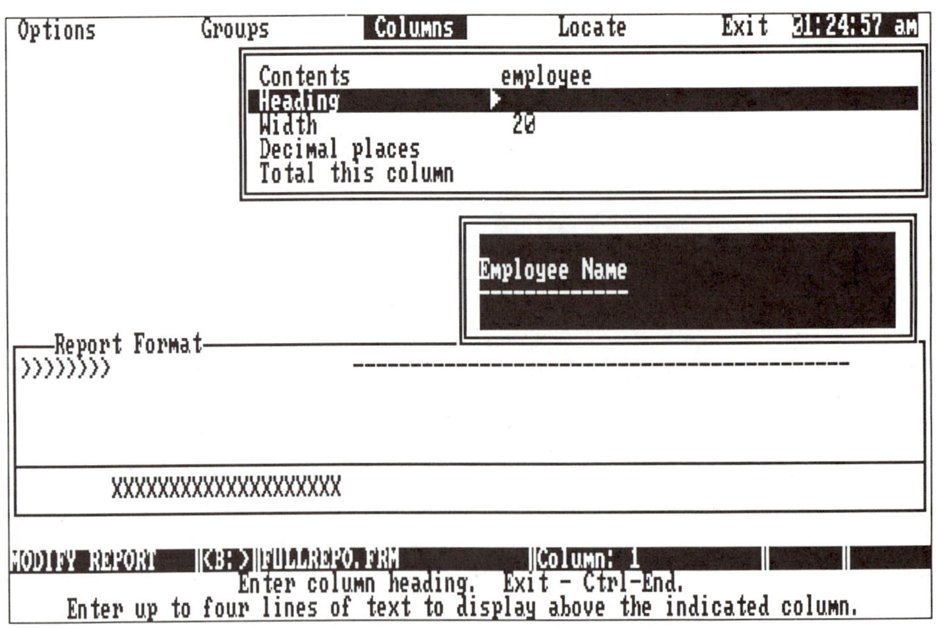

8. When done, type {^End}.

When specifying the contents and headings of report columns, the PgDn key may be used to move to the next column and the PgUp key is used to move a previous column.

9. Tap the PgDn key and complete the next column's specifications as shown. (Remember that you must select a menu item by typing ↵ before you enter the data.)

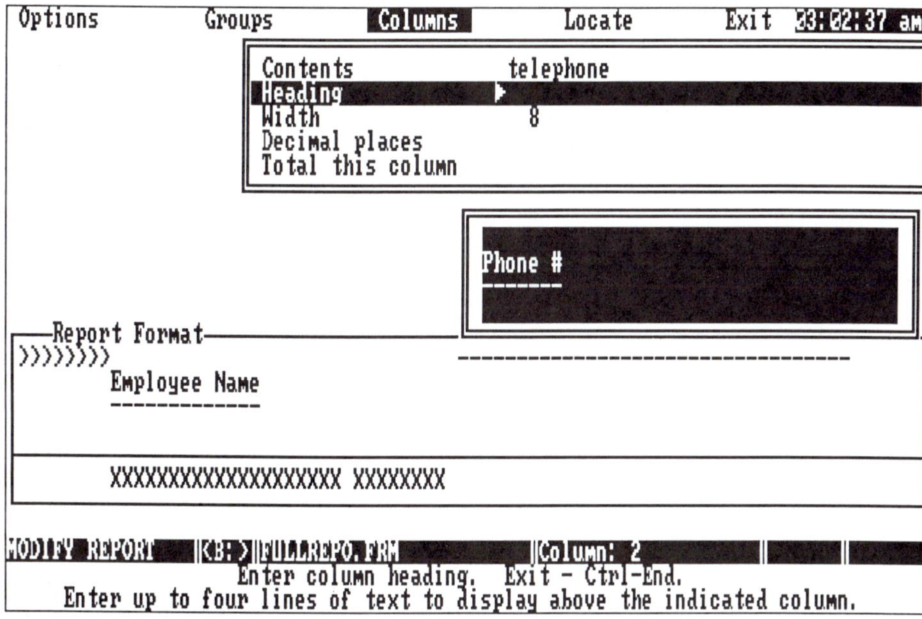

10. After entering the column heading, tap the PgDn key to move to the third column's specifications.

Before continuing, notice the area in the bottom half of the screen.

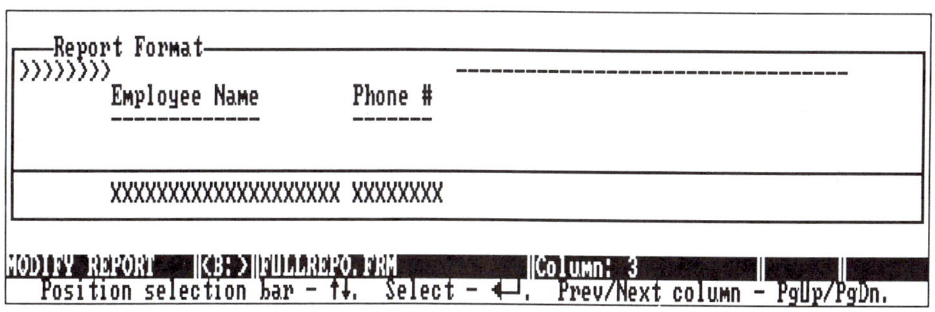

At the bottom of this area is a highlighted line (called the *status bar*) having information about the report you are creating, fullrepo, and the column you are currently on, Column 3.

Over the status bar is an emerging picture representing what the finished report will look like. Shown here are the characters used by the left margin (>>>>>>>>), the specified column labels, and a mask for the characters of data included in the column.

The default width of each column in the report is based on the width of the field (or expression) specified as the contents of the column, or the width of the column heading, whichever is larger. The default value can be changed by entering a different value using the Width menu item. Within the printed report column contents of character or date data will be automatically left justified, while contents of numeric data will be right justified.

11. Finish specifying the report's column contents with the following data.

Column 3:

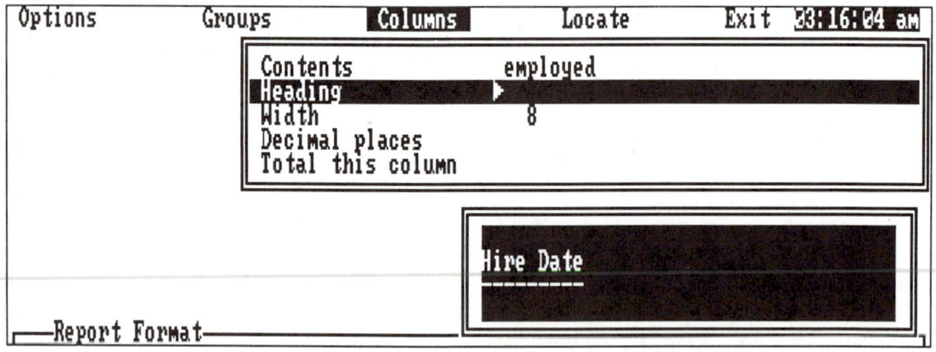

Column 4:

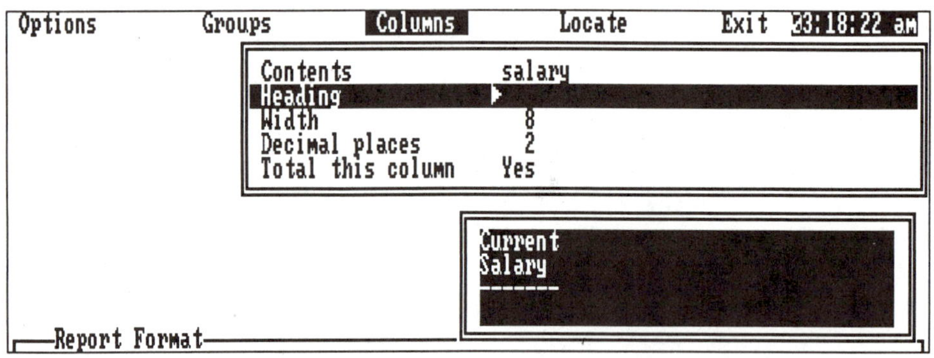

Column 5:

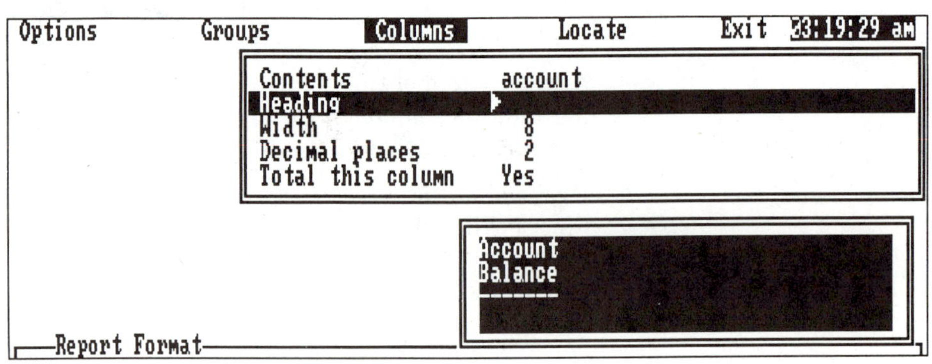

When finished entering the data for field 5 the screen should appear as:

```
Options            Groups        Columns        Locate       Exit  03:20:30 am
                         Contents                 account
                         Heading                  Account;Balance;-------
                         Width                    8
                         Decimal places           2
                         Total this column        Yes

 Report Format
                                     Current  Account   ------
oyee Name        Phone #  Hire Date  Salary   Balance
---------        -------  ---------  -------  -------

XXXXXXXXXXXXXXXX XXXXXXXX mm/dd/yy   #####.## #####.##

MODIFY REPORT  <B:> FULLREPO.FRM        Column: 5          Ins
   Position selection bar - ↑↓.  Select - ↵.  Prev/Next column - PgUp/PgDn.
     Enter up to four lines of text to display above the indicated column.
```

12. Now move the menu bar highlight to Exit and select the Save option to save the report data and exit to the dot (.) prompt.

Running Reports

With the report specifications entered and saved in a form file you are now able to produce the report using the **REPORT** command.

1. Type {**REPORT FORM** fullrepo↵}.

```
. REPORT FORM fullrepo
        Page No.      1
        01/01/80
                         Employee Full Report
                         ====================
                                                   Current   Account
        Employee Name     Phone  #   Hire Date    Salary    Balance
        -------------     --------   ---------    -------   -------
        Johnson Frank     223-7928   03/20/86     1500.00      0.00
        Jones David       292-3832   06/15/82     1550.00    275.75
        Knat Michael      221-1235   09/15/80     1800.00    125.00
        Martins Mary      222-2123   11/01/85     1600.00    200.50
        Nichols Sandy     229-1111   02/15/86     1450.00    175.00
        Pratt John        225-1234   06/22/82     1949.00    200.00
        Sill Sally        224-4321   02/15/84     1507.50    150.00
        Smith Paul        244-1010   11/15/81     1700.00    350.00
        Smoler Ellen      225-3212   09/15/83     1650.00    300.00
       *** Total ***
                                                 14706.50   1776.25
```

Later you will see how to print a report on the printer.

Changing a Report's Specifications

A report's specifications may be altered by using the **MODIFY REPORT** command. To give you experience in using this command as well as the full-screen, menu-driven mode it provides, do the following:

1. Type {**MODIFY REPORT** fullrepo↵}.

Refer to the **MODIFY REPORT** editing keystrokes (see table, page D–53) to assist you in making the following changes.

2. a. Change the report's "Options" / "Left margin" to 4.
   b. Reduce the Width of the column containing employee names (Column 1) from 20 to 16.
   c. Increase the Width of the telephone column (Column 2) to 10.
   d. Move to the account column (Column 5) and insert a new column into the report (type ^**N** to do this).
   e. Enter the following data into the new Column 5.

```
Contents        = INT(salary*.15)
Heading         = Account
                  Limit
                  -------
Width           = 9
Decimal places  = 2
```

```
Options          Groups        Columns         Locate        Exit  12:34:47 am
                          Contents                 INT(salary*.15)
                          Heading                  Account;Limit;--------
                          Width                      9
                          Decimal places             2
                          Total this column        Yes

 Report Format
                                          Current  Account   Account   --
ployee Name     Phone #      Hire Date Salary   Limit     Balance
-----------     -------      --------- -------  --------  -------

XXXXXXXXXXXXXX XXXXXXXX   mm/dd/yy  #####.## ######.## #####.##

MODIFY REPORT   |<B:>|FULLREPO.FRM          |Column: 5
   Position selection bar - ↑↓.  Select - ↵.  Prev/Next column - PgUp/PgDn.
         Enter the number of decimal places to display for this column.
```

3. Select the Save menu item of the Exit menu bar option to exit the **MODIFY REPORT** mode, and then type:

```
{REPORT FORM fullrepo↵}
```

The report produced should have the form:

```
Page No.       1
01/01/86
                          Employee Full Report
                          ====================
                                                  Current   Account   Account
Employee Name        Phone #    Hire Date          Salary     Limit   Balance
-------------        -------    ----------        -------   -------   -------
Johnson Frank        223-7928   03/20/86          1500.00    225.00      0.00
Jones David          292-3832   06/15/82          1550.00    232.00    275.75
Knat Michael         221-1235   09/15/80          1800.00    270.00    125.00
Martins Mary         222-2123   11/01/85          1600.00    240.00    200.50
Nichols Sandy        229-1111   02/15/86          1450.00    217.00    175.00
Pratt John           225-1234   06/22/82          1949.00    292.00    200.00
Sill Sally           224-4321   02/15/84          1507.50    226.00    150.00
Smith Paul           244-1010   11/15/81          1700.00    255.00    350.00
Smoler Ellen         225-3212   09/15/83          1650.00    247.00    300.00
*** Total ***
                                                 14706.50   2204.00   1776.25
```

Running Selective Reports

dBase's **REPORT** command lets you be selective with your reports through the use of the **FOR** condition parameter of the command.

1. Type the following:

```
. REPORT FORM fullrepo FOR sex = "F"↵
Page No.       1
01/01/86
                          Employee Full Report
                          ====================
                                                  Current   Account   Account
Employee Name        Phone #    Hire Date          Salary     Limit   Balance
-------------        -------    ----------        -------   -------   -------
Martins Mary         222-2123   11/01/85          1600.00    240.00    200.50
Nichols Sandy        229-1111   02/15/86          1450.00    217.00    175.00
Sill Sally           224-4321   02/15/84          1507.50    226.00    150.00
Smoler Ellen         225-3212   09/15/83          1650.00    247.00    300.00
*** Total ***
                                                  6207.50    930.00    825.50
```

```
. REPORT FORM fullrepo FOR employed < CTOD("01/01/83")↵
Page No.       1
01/01/86
                          Employee Full Report
                          ====================
                                                  Current   Account   Account
Employee Name        Phone #    Hire Date          Salary     Limit   Balance
-------------        -------    ----------        -------   -------   -------
Jones David          292-3832   06/15/82          1550.00    232.00    275.75
Knat Michael         221-1235   09/15/80          1800.00    270.00    125.00
Pratt John           225-1234   06/22/82          1949.00    292.00    200.00
Smith Paul           244-1010   11/15/81          1700.00    255.00    350.00
*** Total ***
                                                  6999.00   1049.00    950.75
```

Adding a Report Heading

Another **REPORT** command parameter, **HEADING,** may be used to further describe the report being produced.

1. Type

```
. REPORT FORM fullrepo FOR account > .15 * salary HEADING "Employees Currently O
ver Limit"
     Page No.       1     Employees Currently Over Limit
     01/01/86
                               Employee Full Report
                               ====================
                                              Current    Account   Account
     Employee Name       Phone #    Hire Date   Salary      Limit   Balance
     -------------       -------    ---------   -------    -------   -------
     Jones David         292-3832   06/15/82   1550.00     232.00    275.75
     Smith Paul          244-1010   11/15/81   1700.00     255.00    350.00
     Smoler Ellen        225-3212   09/15/83   1650.00     247.00    300.00
    *** Total ***
                                               4900.00     734.00    925.75
```

Report Totals

When a column's contents are specified as numeric data, dBase's **MODIFY REPORT** command defaults the column's "Total this column" menu item answer to "Yes." To remove report totals, you must move the pull down menu highlight to the "Total this column" menu item and type ↵. When this is done, the answer toggles to "No" and report totals will not be printed for that column. Repeating the process will toggle the "Total this column" answer back to "Yes."

Subtotals in Reports

You can subtotal groups of data with the **REPORT** command if the database in use is currently indexed or sorted on the field(s) by which you wish to subtotal and the appropriate specifications have been made in the **MODIFY REPORT** editing mode. To give you experience in report subtotals, complete the following steps:

1. Type {**USE** empfile **INDEX** empdex↵ **MODIFY REPORT** acctrepo↵}.
2. Use the Options menu bar option to enter the following report data:

```
Page title               = Salaries & Accounts By Gender
                           * Personnel Department *
Page width (positions)= 65
Left margin (# chars) = 15
```

```
 Options         Groups          Columns         Locate        Exit  01:54:10 am

 Page title                  ▸Salaries
 Page width (positions)        65         Salaries & Accounts By Gender
 Left margin                   15         * Personnel Department *
 Right margin                   0
 Lines per page                58
 Double space report           No
 Page eject before printing    Yes
 Page eject after printing     No
 Plain page                    No
```

3. Move to the Groups option of the menu bar.
4. Complete this pull down menu screen by entering the following data.

```
Group on expression     = sex
Group heading           = Gender =
```

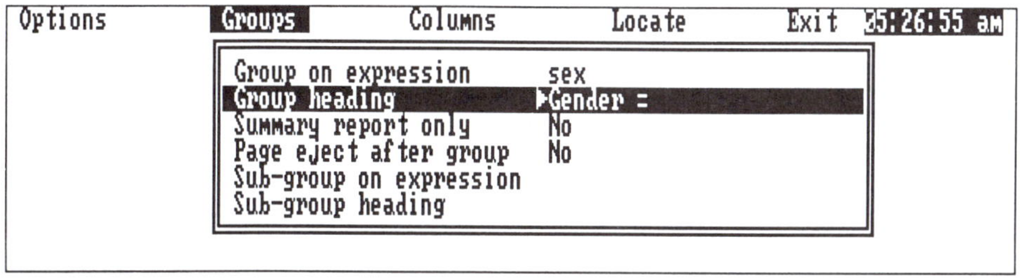

5. Now move the menu bar highlight to Columns and complete the following column specifications as shown.

Column 1:

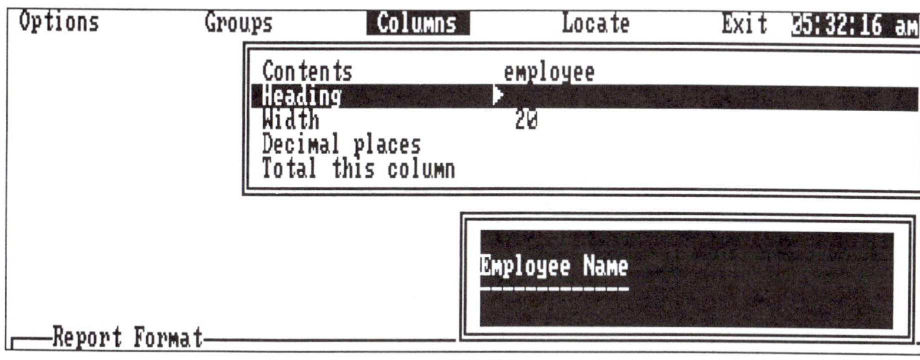

Column 2:

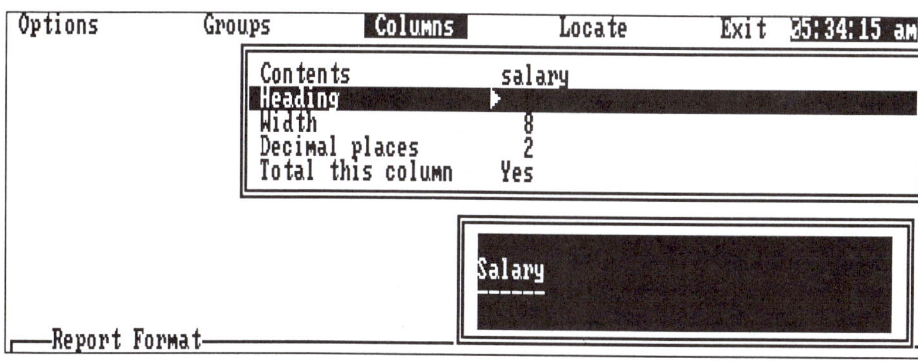

Column 3:

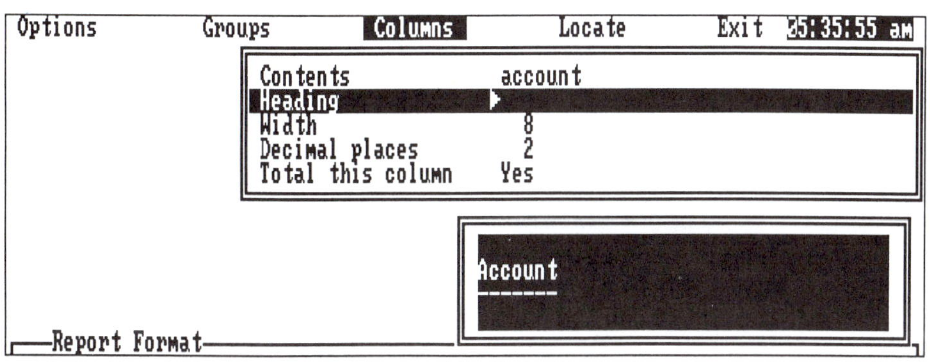

6. Save and exit the **MODIFY REPORT** mode, and then type {**REPORT FORM** acctrepo↵} to produce the following report:

```
. REPORT FORM acctrepo

                Page No.     1
                01/01/86
                           Salaries & Accounts By Gender
                              * Personnel Department *

                Employee Name             Salary   Account
                -------------             ------   -------
               ** Gender = F
                Martins Mary             1600.00    200.50
                Nichols Sandy            1450.00    175.00
                Sill Sally               1507.50    150.00
                Smoler Ellen             1650.00    300.00
               ** Subtotal **
                                         6207.50    825.50

               ** Gender = M
                Johnson Frank            1500.00      0.00
                Jones David              1550.00    275.75
                Knat Michael             1800.00    125.00
                Pratt John               1949.00    200.00
                Smith Paul               1700.00    350.00
               ** Subtotal **
                                         8499.00    950.75
               *** Total ***
                                        14706.50   1776.25
```

More on Column Contents

It is important to note that the contents of a report column can be any expression that dBase is able to evaluate. In order to create such expressions, it is often necessary to convert data types within them through the use of dBase functions.

Data Type Conversion Functions

You have already used the CTOD function to convert character-type data to date-type data in the tutorial. This was done so that a comparison of like data types could be made in a condition. Other dBase functions used to convert data types include the following.

DTOC(<date variable>)

Date To Character Function   Converts date-type data to character type data.

```
. DISPLAY
Record#  EMPLOYEE             TELEPHONE SEX EMPLOYED   SALARY  ACCOUNT
      7  Martins Mary         222-2123  F   11/01/85  1600.00   200.50

. ? DTOC(employed) = "11-01-85"
.F.

. ? DTOC(employed) = "11/01/85"
.T.
```

STR(<numeric data> [,<length>] [,<decimals>])

Numeric to String Function Returns a character string converted from a numeric expression. Most useful for deleting leading spaces in output of numeric data and/or forcing the display of desired decimal places.

```
. DISPLAY
Record#  EMPLOYEE                TELEPHONE SEX EMPLOYED   SALARY  ACCOUNT
      7  Martins Mary            222-2123  F   11/01/85  1600.00   200.50
. ? employee," / Limit =",salary*.15
Martins Mary         / Limit =      240.0000
. ? employee," / Limit =",STR(salary*.15,6,2)
Martins Mary        / Limit = 240.00
```

VAL(<character data>)

Character to Value Function Returns the numeric value of numbers held as strings beginning at the first character of <character data>.

```
. ? VAL("7312 S.W. Fulton Park Blvd.")
                        7312.00
. ? VAL("P.O. Box 7312")
             0.00
```

The Immediate If Function

A useful function now available with dBase III Plus is the Immediate If function. Its form is:

IIF(<condition>,<true expression>,<false expression>)

The Immediate If function returns its <true expression> if its <condition> evaluates .T.rue and its <false expression> if its <condition> evaluates .F.alse. It is most useful for including conditional column output in a dBase III Plus report.

With the **IIF** function, the <true expression> and <false expression> may be character-, numeric-, or date-type data. However both expressions must be of the same data type.

Producing Reports with More Complex Column Contents

To give you experience in using more complex expressions in report column contents, complete the following steps.

1. Type {**USE** empfile **INDEX** namedex↵}.
2. Next type {**AVERAGE** salary **TO** salavg↵}.
3. Type {date = CTOD("01/01/87")↵}.

   You may enter today's date here. Use the format mm/dd/yy.

The last two steps create two memory variables: one numeric variable named "salavg," holding the average salary and one date-type variable named "date," holding today's date. They are variables to which the finished report specifications will refer.

4. Type {**MODIFY REPORT** salaries↵}.

5. Complete the reports "Options" as shown:

```
Page title              = Salary Summary Report
                          =============================
Page width (positions) = 77
Left margin             =  3
```

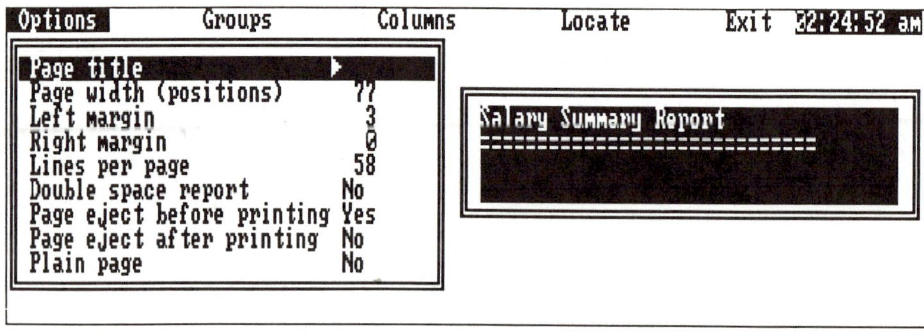

6. Move to the Columns option of the menu bar and enter the first column's data as:

```
Contents    = employee
Heading     = Employee Name
              -------------
Width       = 16
```

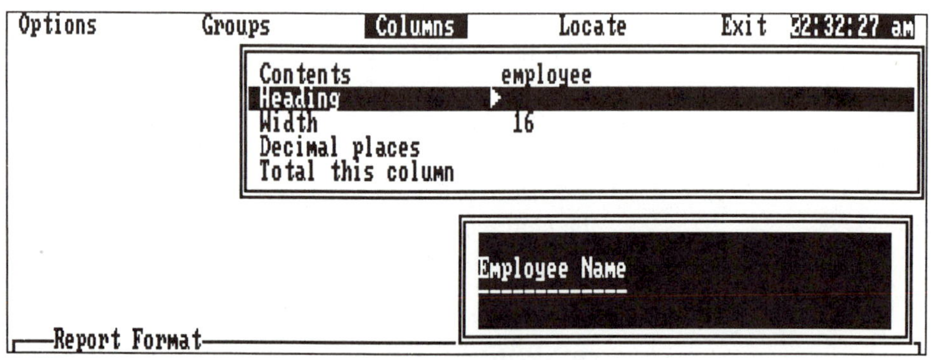

7. Type {PgDn} to move to the next column.

The next column's contents will be salary. This time, however, you are going to precede the displayed dollar amount (numeric data) with a dollar sign ($) (character data) in the column. To do so you will use the **STR** function to convert salary into character data, then concatenate (add) it to the string, "$."

8. Complete this column's data as shown:

```
Contents    = "$"+STR(salary,8,2)
Heading     = Monthly
              Salary
              -------
Width       = 9
```

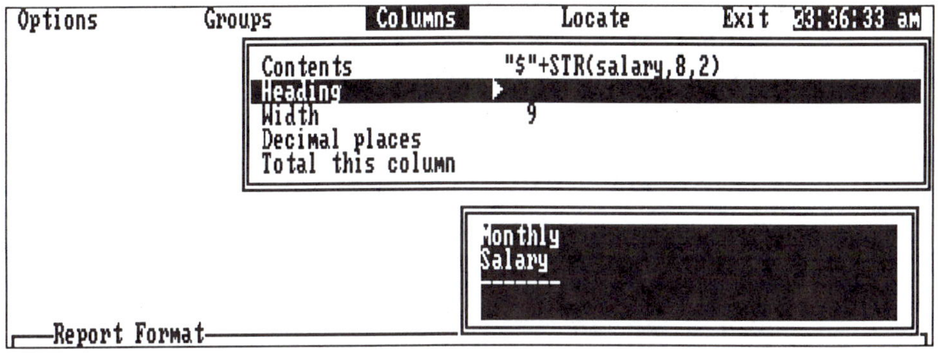

9. Type {PgDn} to move to the next column.

In this column (Column 3) you will enter the contents which will display the number of years each employee has worked for the company. To arrive at the final expression used, you must know that date-type data may be used in certain mathematical operations. The following are some examples of "date arithmetic."

`. date1 = CTOD("06/15/87")` `06/15/87`	Place the date-type data for June 15, 1987 into the variable "date1."
`. ? date1 + 90` `09/13/87`	Print datel + 90. September 13, 1987 occurs 90 days after June 15, 1987.
`. date2 = CTOD("08/14/87")` `06/15/87`	Place the date-type data for August 14, 1987 into the variable "date2."
`? date2 - date1` `60`	Print date2 minus date1. There are 60 days between June 15 and August 14, 1987.

By using the memory variable "date," which is holding today's date and the date field "employed," which holds the hire date for each employee along with some date arithmetic and display formatting using the **STR** function, you are able to enter the contents for the Column 3.

10. Enter the column data as shown.

```
Contents    = STR((date-employed)/365,5,1)
Heading     = Years
              Employed
              --------
Width       = 8
```

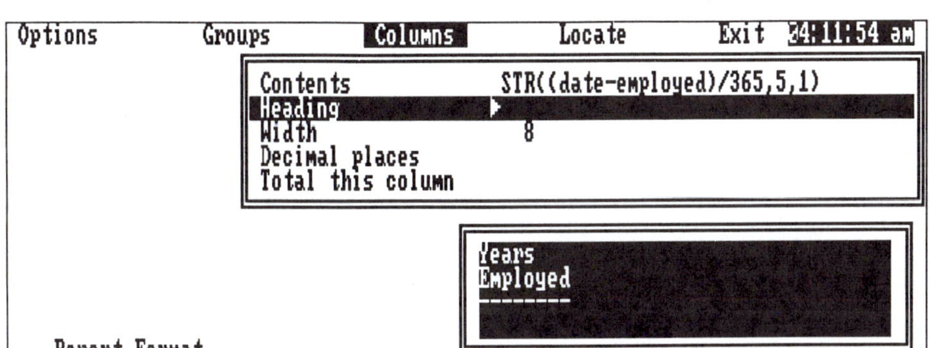

11. Type {PgDn} to move to Column 4.

Into this column you will enter a simple expression for column contents. Its purpose is to provide a vertical line through the report.

12. Enter the column contents as shown.

```
Contents       = "|"
Width          = 1
```

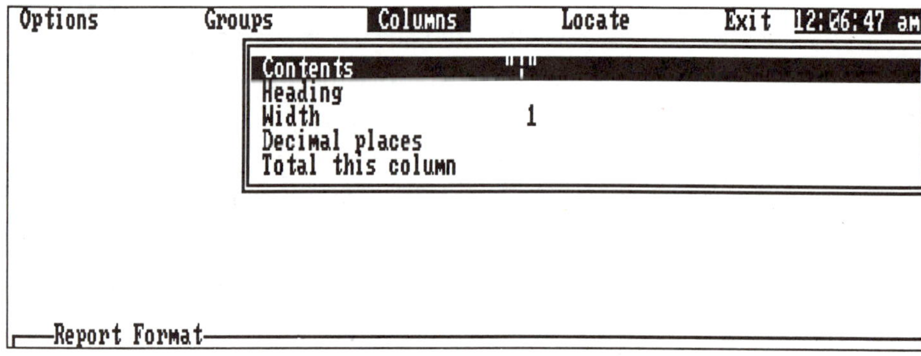

13. Type {PgDn} to move to the final column of the report, Column 5.

This column will have the heading "Comments" and its contents will produce the following: If the employee's salary is above or equal to the average salary, no data will be displayed in the column for that employee. However, if the employee's salary is below the average, the message "Under average salary" will be displayed in the column for that employee. The only way to produce such a column of data in a report is through using the **IIF** function.

14. Enter Column 5's data as shown.

```
Contents       = IIF(salary >= salavg, "","Under average salary")
Heading        = Comments
                 --------
Width          = 20
```

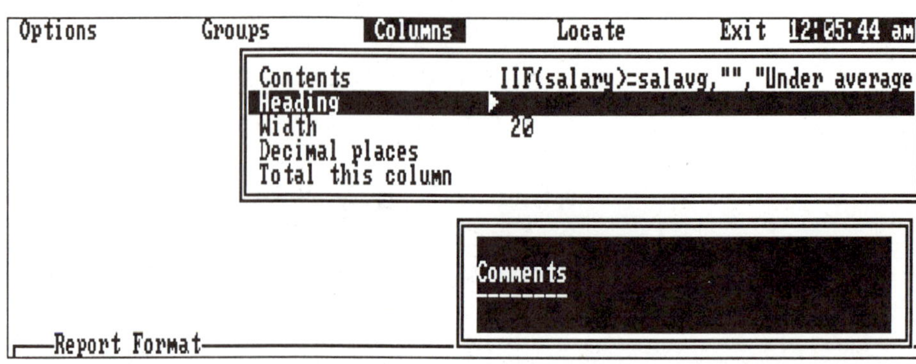

15. Save and exit the **MODIFY REPORT** mode, and then type {**REPORT FORM** salaries↵} to produce the following report:

```
. REPORT FORM salaries
  Page No.     1
  01/01/80
                                   Salary Summary Report
                               =============================
                           Monthly   Years
  Employee Name             Salary    Employed    Comments
  -------------             -------   --------    --------
  Johnson Frank            $ 1500.00    0.8     ; Under average salary
  Jones David              $ 1550.00    4.6     ; Under average salary
  Knat Michael             $ 1800.00    6.3     ;
  Martins Mary             $ 1600.00    1.2     ; Under average salary
  Nichols Sandy            $ 1450.00    0.9     ; Under average salary
  Pratt John               $ 1949.00    4.5     ;
  Sill Sally               $ 1507.50    2.9     ; Under average salary
  Smith Paul               $ 1700.00    5.1     ;
  Smoler Ellen             $ 1650.00    3.3     ;
```

Printing Out a Report

The **REPORT** command will print a report on the printer when you include the **TO PRINT** parameter in it.

1. Make sure the printer is turned on, on-line, and connected to your computer. (Your lab may have a shared device control switch. You will need to select your computer as the one currently connected to the printer.)

Your system ____

____

____

____

____

____

____

____

2. Type in the following **REPORT** commands.

```
REPORT FORM fullrepo TO PRINT
REPORT FORM salaries TO PRINT FOR employed < CTOD("01/01/84")
REPORT FORM acctrepo TO PRINT
REPORT FORM fullrepo TO PRINT FOR sex= "M" .AND. employed >= CTOD("01/01/82")
    HEADING "All Male Employees Hired After 1981"
```

EXERCISE 9: Quitting dBase III

To quit dBase and return to the DOS operating level (A>) you use the **QUIT** command. The **QUIT** command is very important since it saves all new file data that may have been created during the session. It then closes all dBase files that may be open at the time before returning to DOS.

QUIT is always the last command you enter when you use dBase III.

1. Type {**QUIT**↵} to end this dBase session.

dBase III Quick Reference Command Summary

dBase III Commands

? ["literal"],[<field>],[<expression>]

@ <x,y> [**SAY** <exp>] [**GET** <variable>]

ACCEPT ["<string prompt>"] **TO** <memvar>

APPEND

APPEND BLANK

APPEND FROM <file> [**FOR** <condition>] [**SDF**]

ASSIST

AVERAGE <expression list> [<scope>] [**FOR/WHILE** <condition>] [**TO** <memvar list>]

BROWSE [**FIELDS** <field list>]

CANCEL

CHANGE [<scope>] [**FIELDS** <field list>] [**FOR/WHILE** <condition>]

CLEAR

CLEAR ALL

CLEAR GETS

CLEAR MEMORY

CLOSE [**DATABASES**][**,FORMAT**] [**,INDEX**] [**,PROCEDURE**] [**,ALTERNATE**]

CONTINUE

COPY TO <file> [<scope>] [**FIELDS** <field list>] [**FOR/WHILE** <condition>] [**SDF**]

COPY FILE [<drive>] <filename.ext> **TO** [<drive>] <filename.ext>

COUNT [<scope>] [**FOR/WHILE** <condition>] [**TO** <memvar>]

CREATE <filename>

CREATE LABEL <filename>

CREATE REPORT <filename>

DELETE [<scope>] [**FOR/WHILE** <condition>]

DIR [<drive:>] [<skeleton>]

DISPLAY [<scope>] [<expression list>] [**FOR/WHILE** <condition>] [**OFF**] [**TO PRINT**]

DISPLAY MEMORY

DISPLAY STATUS [**TO PRINT**]

DISPLAY STRUCTURE

DO <filename> [**WITH** <expression list>]

DO CASE
  CASE <condition>
    any commands
  [**CASE** <condition>]
    any commands
  [**CASE** <condition>]
    any commands
  [**OTHERWISE**]
    any commands
ENDCASE

DO WHILE <condition>
    any commands
  [**LOOP**]
  [**EXIT**]
    any commands
ENDDO

EDIT [<n>]

EJECT

ERASE <filename.extension>

FIND <cstring>

GO <n> or **GOTO** <n>

GO [**TOP**]/[**BOTTOM**]

HELP [<key word>]

IF <condition>
    <any statements>
  [**ELSE**]
    <any statements>
ENDIF

INDEX ON <expression> **TO** <index file>

INPUT [<"string prompt">] **TO** <memvar>

INSERT [**BEFORE**] [**BLANK**]

JOIN WITH <alias> **TO** <filename> **FOR** <condition> [**FIELDS** <field list>]

LABEL FORM <label filename> [<scope>] [**SAMPLE**] [**TO PRINT**] [**FOR/WHILE** <condition>] [**TO FILE** <filename>]

LIST [<scope>] [<expression list>] [**FOR/WHILE**<condition>] [**OFF**] [**TO PRINT**]

LIST MEMORY

LIST STATUS

LIST STRUCTURE

LOCATE [<scope>] **FOR** <condition>

MODIFY COMMAND <file>

MODIFY LABEL <label form filename>

MODIFY REPORT <report form filename>

MODIFY STRUCTURE

NOTE or *

PACK

PARAMETERS <expression list>

PRIVATE [<memvar list>], or [**ALL** [**LIKE/ EXCEPT**] <skeleton>]

PROCEDURE <procedure name>

PUBLIC <memory variable list>

QUIT

READ

RECALL [<scope>] [**FOR/WHILE** <condition>]

REINDEX

RELEASE [<memvar list>], or [**ALL** [**LIKE/ EXCEPT**] <skeleton>]

RENAME <filename.ext> **TO** <new filename.ext>

REPLACE [<scope>] <field> **WITH** <exp> [,<field2> **WITH** <exp2>] [**FOR/WHILE** <condition>]

REPORT [**FORM** <form file>] [<scope>] [**FOR** <condition>] [**PLAIN**] [**HEADING** <cstring>] [**NO EJECT**] [**TO PRINT**] [**TO FILE** <filename>]

RESTORE FROM <filename> [**ADDITIVE**]

RETURN [**TO MASTER**]

RUN <command>

SAVE TO <filename> [**ALL** [**LIKE/EXCEPT**] <skeleton>]

SEEK <expression>

SELECT <Work Area/Alias>

SET ALTERNATE on/OFF

SET ALTERNATE TO <filename>

SET BELL ON/off

SET CARRY on/OFF

SET COLOR TO <standard> [,<enhanced>] [,border]

SET CONFIRM on/OFF

SET CONSOLE ON/off

SET DEBUG on/OFF

SET DECIMALS TO <n>

SET DEFAULT TO <drive>

SET DELETED on/OFF

SET DELIMITER on/OFF

SET DELIMITER TO <character string> [**DEFAULT**]

SET DEVICE TO <PRINT/SCREEN>

SET ECHO on/OFF

SET ESCAPE ON/off

SET EXACT on/OFF

SET FILTER TO [<condition>]

SET FIXED on/OFF

SET FORMAT TO [<format file>]

SET FUNCTION <n> **TO** <"character expression">

SET HEADING ON/off

SET HELP ON/off

SET INDEX TO <index file list>

SET INTENSITY ON/off

SET MARGIN TO <n>

SET MENUS on/OFF

SET PATH TO <path list>

SET PROCEDURE TO <filename>

SET PRINT on/OFF

SET RELATION [**TO** <key expression> /numeric expression **INTO** <alias>]

SET SAFETY ON/off

SET STEP on/OFF

SET TALK ON/off

SET UNIQUE on/OFF

SKIP [-] [<n>]

SORT TO <new file> **ON** <field> [**/A**] [**/D**] [,<field> [**/A**] [**/D**]] .. [**FOR** <condition>]

STORE <expression> **TO** <memvar list>

SUM <expression list> [<scope>] [**FOR/ WHILE** <condition>] [**TO** <memvar list>]

TEXT
any data.
ENDTEXT

TOTAL ON <key field> **TO** <file> [**FIELDS** <field list>] [**FOR/WHILE** <condition>]

TYPE <filename.ext> [**TO PRINT**]

UPDATE ON <key field> **FROM** <alias> **REPLACE** <field> **WITH** <field> ... [**RANDOM**]

USE <file> [**INDEX** <index file list>]

WAIT [string prompt] [**TO** <memvar>]

ZAP

dBase III Functions

&<character variable> Macro Function

ASC(<character data>) ASCII Code Function

AT(<cstring1>,<cstring2>) Substring Search Function

BOF( ) Beginning-of-File Function

CDOW(<date variable>) Character Day of Week Function

CHR(<numeric exp>) Character String Function

CMONTH(<date variable>) Character Month Function

COL( ) Column Function
CTOD(<character data>) Character to Date Function
DATE( ) Date Function
DAY(<date variable>) Day Function
DELETED( ) Deleted Record Function
DOW(<date variable>) Day of Week Function
DTOC(<date variable>) Date to Character Function
EOF( ) End-of-File Function
EXP(<numeric data>) Exponential Function
FILE([<drive:>]<filename.ext>] File Existence Function
INT(<numeric data>] Integer Function
LEN(<character data>] Length Function
LOG(<numeric data>) Logarithm Function
LOWER(<character data>) Lower-case Function
MONTH(<date variable>) Month Function
PCOL( ) Printer Column Function
PROW( ) Printer Row Function
RECNO( ) Record Number Function
ROUND(<numeric data>,<n>) Round Function
ROW( ) Row Function
SPACE(<numeric data>) Space Function
SQRT(<numeric data>) Square Root Function
STR(<numeric data> [,<length>] [,<decimals>]) Numeric to String Function
SUBSTR(<character data>,<start>,<length>) Substring Function
TIME( ) Time Function
TRIM(<character data>) Trim Function
TYPE("<expression>") Data Type Function
UPPER(<character data>) Upper-case Function
VAL(<character data>) Character to Value Function
YEAR(<date variable>) Year Function

Important dBase III Keys

Control Keys (Dot (.) Prompt Mode)

Esc key	Erases the current command line, or aborts a current operation.
^P	Toggles the printer ON and OFF.
^Num Lock	Pauses operations; any key continues.
← (Backspace key)	Backspaces and deletes characters on the current line.

Editing Keystroke Commands

APPEND, CHANGE and EDIT Modes

Cursor-right key	Moves cursor right one character.
Cursor-left key	Moves cursor left one character.
Cursor-down key	Moves cursor to the next field.
Cursor-up key	Moves cursor to the previous field.
PgDn	Saves current record and advances to next record.
PgUp	Saves current record and backs to previous record.
Ins	Toggles between overwrite and **INSERT** modes.
Del	Deletes character over cursor.
← (Backspace key)	Deletes character left of cursor
^T	Erases word to right of cursor
^Y	Erases field to right of cursor.
^PgDn	Enter the dBase word processor to edit a memo field.

^PgUp	Exit editing a memo field.
^U	Toggles the record *DEL* mark on and off.
^End	Saves changes and returns to dot (.) prompt.
Esc	Aborts editing of current record and returns to dot (.) prompt.

BROWSE Mode

Cursor-right key	Moves cursor right one character.
Cursor-left key	Moves cursor left one character.
Home key	Moves cursor to the previous field.
End key	Moves cursor to the next field.
Cursor-down key	Saves current record and advances to next record.
Cursor-up key	Saves current record and backs to previous record.
PgUp key	Scrolls the screen up 17 lines.
PgDn key	Scrolls the screen down 17 lines.
^Cursor-right key	Pans the screen right one field.
^Cursor-left key	Pans the screen left one field.
Ins	Toggles between overwrite and **INSERT** modes.
Del	Deletes character over cursor.
← (Backspace key)	Deletes character left of cursor.
^T	Erases word to right of cursor
^Y	Erases field to right of cursor.
^U	Toggles the record *DEL* mark on and off.
^End	Saves changes and returns to dot (.) prompt.
Esc	Aborts editing of current record and returns to dot (.) prompt.

MODIFY LABEL and MODIFY REPORT Modes

Cursor-right key	Moves cursor right one character.
Cursor-left key	Moves cursor left one character.
Cursor-down key	Moves cursor to the next line.
Cursor-up key	Moves cursor to the previous line.
PgDn key	Saves current screen and advances to next screen.
PgUp key	Saves current screen and backs to previous screen.
Ins	Toggles between overwrite and **INSERT** modes.
Del	Deletes character over cursor.
← (Backspace key)	Deletes character to left of cursor.
^T	Erases word to right of cursor.
^Y	Erases field or line to right of cursor.
^U	Deletes current column or line specification.
^N	Inserts new column or line for specification.
^End	Saves changes and returns to dot (.) prompt.
Esc	Aborts all changes made and returns to dot (.) prompt.

MODIFY COMMAND and MEMO Field—dBase Word Processor

Cursor-right key	Moves cursor right one character.
Cursor-left key	Moves cursor left one character.
Home key	Moves cursor one word to the left.
End key	Moves cursor one word to the right.
Cursor-down key	Moves cursor to the next line.
Cursor-up key	Moves cursor to the previous line.
PgUp key	Scrolls the screen up 17 lines.
PgDn	Scrolls the screen down 17 lines.
Ins	Toggles between overwrite and **INSERT** modes.
↵ (Enter key)	Terminates current line. With **INSERT** on, inserts a line below the current line.
Del	Deletes character over cursor.
← (Backspace key)	Deletes character to left of cursor.
^T	Erases word to right of cursor.
^Y	Erases current line.
^KR	Reads and inserts another file into the current file.
^End	Saves changes and returns to dot (.) prompt.
Esc	Aborts all changes made and returns to dot (.) prompt.

Conventions and Terminology

Conventions

UPPER CASE	=	dBase III command or statement
lower case	=	User supplied information
[........]	=	Optional portions
<.......>	=	User supplied names or expressions
/	=	Choice of commands

Example

```
DISPLAY [<scope>] [<expression list>] [FOR/WHILE<condition>] [OFF]
```

dBase command

Optional user supplied information

Optional choice of dBase commands

User supplied information for optional command

Optional command

Terminology

<cstring> or <literal>	Character string(s). In most cases must be delimited with single quotes (' '), double quotes (" "), or brackets ([ ]).
<exp> or <expression>	An item or group of items and operators whose value can be determined.

<condition>	A logical expression resulting in a .T.rue or .F.alse evaluation. Operators in conditions may include:

Relational:	<	(less than)
	>	(greater than)
	=	(equal to)
	<=	(less than or equal to)
	>=	(greater than or equal to)
	< >	(not equal to)
Logical:	.NOT.	
	.AND.	
	.OR.	

<field list>	A list of field names delimited with commas.
<file>	Name of file you wish to create or access.
<key>	List of field(s) used to create index files or sorted database.
<memvar>	The name of a memory variable.
<n>	A number.
<scope>	Specifies range of records for executing the command. <scope> has three possible values: **ALL** records in file, **NEXT** <n> records in file, and **RECORD** <n>.

dBase III Commands

? ["literal"],[<field>],[<expression>]

Displays the evaluation of expressions. Can be used without an expression to space down a line. Similar to the BASIC statement **PRINT.**

<exp>
```
. ? 500-account
   300.00
```
<literal>
```
. ? "employee"
employee
```
<field>
```
. ? employee
Pratt John
```
combination
```
. ? employee, "Account = ", account, account<500
Pratt John          Account =      200.00 .T.
```

@ <x,y> [**SAY** <exp>] [**GET** <variable>]

Displays data on screen or printer at specified coordinates. Usually used only in command files.

x and y are numeric expressions designating the screen row (x = 0 to 24) and column (y = 0 to 80) coordinate where data are to be displayed. The @ **GET** (at get) command is used with the **READ** command to allow direct access to a field or memory variable for editing.

```
                1               2               3               4               5               6               7
     01234567890123456789012345678901234567890123456789012345678901234567890

 4.  @ 5,30 SAY employee
 5                                         Pratt John
 6
 7.  STORE "                               " TO name
 8.  @ 11,35 SAY "Enter name" GET name
 9
10
11                                                 Enter name [                    ]
12.  STORE 11 TO row
13.  @ row+2,35 SAY "Account limit"        Account limit        292.3500
14.  @ row+2,50 SAY salary * .15
15
16.  READ
```

When the **READ** command is executed, the cursor jumps to the first field or variable placed on the screen by an @ **GET** command. The user then may edit the data there with all the keystroke commands of an editing mode. When finished, the edited data replace any previous data that may have been in the field or variable.

ACCEPT ["<string prompt>"] **TO** <memvar>

Used in command files, this command is designed to prompt for character string data and then to place the user's response into a memory variable.

```
. ACCEPT "Enter employee's name:" TO name
Enter employee's name:Martin
. ? name
Martin
. LOCATE FOR employee = name
Record =          7
```

APPEND

Appends a blank record and enters the record addition (**APPEND**) editing mode.

APPEND BLANK

Appends a blank record to the bottom of the file in use.

APPEND FROM <file> [**FOR** <condition>] [**SDF**]

Appends data from a database (.DBF) or ASCII file to the database in use. If the **FROM** file is a .DBF file, any records marked for deletion in the **FROM** <file> will not be appended and only data in fields with like field names will be appended to the file in use.

```
. CREATE deptmail
```

```
B:deptmail.dbf                                          Bytes remaining:   3975
                                                        Fields defined:       2

    field name  type        width  dec          field name  type       width  dec
    ==================================          ==================================
  1 EMPLOYEE    Char/text    20
  2 DEPT        Char/text     5
```

```
Input data records now? (Y/N) No
. USE deptmail
. APPEND FROM empfile
      9 records added
. EDIT 1
```

```
Record No.       1
EMPLOYEE      Pratt John
DEPT
```

SDF (System Data Format) parameter allows ASCII files to be appended from.

```
. APPEND FROM lotus.prn SDF
```

ASSIST

Provides a menu-driven mode for execution of dBase III operations.

AVERAGE <expression list> [<scope>] [**FOR/WHILE** <condition>] [**TO** <memvar list>]

Computes the averages of the expressions in its <expression list> for the records evaluated .T.rue by the **FOR/WHILE** <condition> and stores them to the memory variables in its <memvar list>. Default scope is **ALL.**

```
. AVERAGE salary,account FOR sex = "F" TO fsal,facct
      4 records averaged
  salary   account
 1551.88   206.38
```

BROWSE [**FIELDS** <field list>]

Enters the **BROWSE** editing mode. The optional parameter of [**FIELDS** <field list>] causes dBase to display only the fields listed for editing. The fields in the <field list> must be separated by commas.

CANCEL

Used in a command file, stops command execution and returns to the dBase dot (.) prompt mode.

CHANGE [<scope>] [**FIELDS** <field list>] [**FOR/WHILE** <condition>]

Allows editing of specified fields of data for records .T.rue for the **FOR/WHILE** <condition>. Editing of records is done in the same screen format as **EDIT** and **APPEND.**

```
. CHANGE FIELDS employee,account FOR account > 0
```

```
Record No.       1
EMPLOYEE      Pratt John
ACCOUNT         200.00
```

CLEAR

Clears the screen and releases any @ **GET**s that may have been active.

CLEAR ALL

Closes all databases in use, releases all memory variables, and selects work area 1. (See **USE, RELEASE,** and **SELECT** commands).

CLEAR GETS

Releases all active **GET** commands without erasing the screen.

CLEAR MEMORY

Releases all memory variables.

CLOSE <file type list>

Closes all files of the <file type list>. File types may be **ALTERNATE, DATABASES, FORMAT, INDEX** or **PROCEDURE.**

CONTINUE

Resumes a search initiated with a **LOCATE** command. (See **LOCATE,** page D–81.)

COPY TO <file> [<scope>] [**FIELDS** <field list>] [**FOR/WHILE** <condition>]

Copies the database in use to another .DBF file which it creates at the time the command is executed.

COPY TO <file> [**SDF**] [**DELIMITED** [**WITH** <delimiter>]] [**FOR/WHILE** <condition>]

[**SDF**] (System Data Format) parameter allows an ASCII file copy of the database in use to be created.

```
COPY TO lotus.prn SDF
```

COPY FILE [<drive>] <filename.ext> **TO** [<drive>] <filename.ext>

Makes a copy from the specified file to the specified file.

COPY STRUCTURE TO [<drive>] <filename>

Creates a .DBF file with the specified <filename>, whose record structure is the same as the current database. No records are copied to the new file.

COUNT [<scope>] [**FOR/WHILE** <condition>] [**TO** <memvar>]

Counts the number of records in the database in use which are .T.rue for the command's **FOR/WHILE** <condition>. Default scope is **ALL** records.

CREATE <filename>

Creates the record structure for a new database (given a .DBF filename extension). User enters the record structure in a dBase editing mode.

CREATE LABEL <filename>

Identical to **MODIFY LABEL.** (See **MODIFY LABEL,** page D–81.)

CREATE REPORT <filename>

Identical to **MODIFY REPORT.** See **MODIFY REPORT,** page D–82.)

DELETE [<scope>] [**FOR/WHILE** <condition>]

Marks record(s) for deletion. Records marked for deletion will not be physically removed from the database until the **PACK** command is executed. Records also may be marked for deletion with ^**U** while in edit modes.

DIR [<drive:>] [<skeleton>]

Lists filenames of files. **DIR** with no parameters displays the names of all .DBF files on the default drive. The <drive:> parameter may be used to specify another disk drive. The <skeleton> parameter is used to display other types of files.

<skeleton>s are made up of filename characters and masking characters that act as "wild cards." The asterisk (*) indicates "Accept any other characters," while the question mark (?) means, "Accept any single character in this position."

```
. DIR *.FRM
FULLREPO.FRM         SALARIES.FRM          ACCTREPO.FRM
   5970 bytes in       3 files
 352256 bytes remaining on drive.
. DIR report?.PRG
REPORT1.PRG           REPORT2.PRG
    2048 bytes in       2 files
  352256 bytes remaining on drive.
```

```
. DIR *.*
```
(Will display all files on the disk drive.)

DISPLAY [<scope>] [<expression list>] [**FOR/WHILE** <condition>] [**OFF**] [**TO PRINT**]

Displays records of database in use on the monitor screen. [**TO PRINT**] parameter echoes screen output to the printer.

DISPLAY MEMORY

Displays names, types, and contents of all current memory variables.

DISPLAY STATUS [TO PRINT]

Lists files that are open, with information about their relationships, **SET** command settings, Function key assignments, and other current environment information. [**TO PRINT**] parameter echoes screen output to the printer.

DISPLAY STRUCTURE

Displays field names, types, widths, and decimals (the record structure) of the database in use.

DO <filename> [**WITH** <expression list>]

Opens and begins execution of the commands in the specified command file. **WITH** parameter is used to pass expressions between command files. See **PARAMETERS, PRIVATE,** and **PUBLIC** commands.

DO CASE
  CASE <condition>
    any commands
  [**CASE** <condition>]
    any commands
  [**CASE** <condition>]
    any commands
  [**OTHERWISE**]
    any commands
ENDCASE

Used in command files, this command structure is used to select a single set of commands to execute. It is useful when the criteria for command executions are mutually exclusive. The [**OTHERWISE**] parameter is optional and is executed when no **CASE** is .T.rue. **ENDCASE** is needed to complete the command structure.

EXAMPLE—dBase Command File

```
USE empfile
? "              MENU OPTIONS            "
? "        A.  Add a Record              "
? "        B.  Delete a Record           "
? "        C.  Edit Records              "
ACCEPT "Enter Menu letter of your choice?" TO choice
choice = UPPER(choice)
DO CASE
  CASE choice = "A"
    APPEND
  CASE choice = "B"
    INPUT "Record number of record to delete ? " TO n
    GOTO n
    DISPLAY employee
    ACCEPT "Correct record ? (Y/N)" TO confirm
    IF UPPER(confirm) = "Y"
      DELETE
      PACK
    ENDIF
  CASE choice = "C"
    BROWSE
  OTHERWISE
    ? "No Menu letter ",choice," exists"
ENDCASE
RETURN
```

DO WHILE <condition>
any commands
[**LOOP**]
[**EXIT**]
any commands
ENDDO

Used in command files, the **DO WHILE ENDDO** command structure creates a program loop. Commands between the **DO WHILE** and its **ENDO** are executed repeatedly until the **DO WHILE**'s <condition> is no longer .T.rue. The **LOOP** command causes command execution to jump back to the **DO WHILE** command. The **EXIT** command causes command execution to jump to the command immediately following the **ENDDO** command.

EXAMPLE—dBase Command File

```
USE empfile
SET TALK OFF
SET PRINT ON
```

```
DO WHILE .NOT. EOF
  IF account > .15 * salary
    ? "To:",employee
    ? "From:  Accounting"
    ?
    ? "You have exceeded your personal account limit by"
    ? account - .15 * salary, ".  Please make arrangements"
    EJECT
    SKIP
    LOOP
  ENDIF
  ? "To:",employee
  ? "From:  Accounting"
  ?
  ? "The amount on your personal account as of", DATE()
  ? "is", account
  EJECT
  SKIP
ENDDO

SET PRINT OFF
SET TALK ON
RETURN
```

EDIT [<n>]

Allows editing of database in use, starting at record number <n>.

EJECT

Causes printer to form feed (page eject) if **SET PRINT ON** or **SET DEVICE TO PRINT** commands are active.

ERASE <filename.extension>

Erases a file from the diskette. **ERASE** may not be used to erase an open file.

EXIT

See **DO WHILE** command (page D–78).

FIND <cstring>

Used with index files, **FIND** positions the record pointer to first database record indexed by <cstring>. If **FIND** <memvar> is used, the memory variable must be preceded by an ampersand (&). (See **SEEK,** page D–85.)

```
. USE empfile INDEX namedex
. FIND Smith P
. DISPLAY
Record#  EMPLOYEE                          TELEPHONE SEX EMPLOYED    SALARY  ACCOUNT
      6  Smith Paul                        244-1010   M  11/15/81   1700.00   350.00
. STORE "Johns" TO z
Johns
. FIND &z
. DISPLAY
Record#  EMPLOYEE                          TELEPHONE SEX EMPLOYED    SALARY  ACCOUNT
      9  Johnson Frank                     223-7928   M  03/20/86   1500.00     0.00
```

GO <n> or **GOTO** <n>

Moves the record pointer to the record with the record number <n>.

GO [**TOP**]/[**BOTTOM**]

Moves the record pointer to the top or the bottom of the database in use.

HELP [<key word>]

HELP invokes a menu-driven, on-line facility that provides information on various dBase III commands and operations. If a command or function is specified in the <key word> parameter, **HELP** provides a screen of summary information on that command or function.

IF <condition>
    <any statements>
  [**ELSE**]
    <any statements>
ENDIF

Used in command files, the **IF ENDIF** command structure permits conditional execution of commands. The [**ELSE**] clause is optional. If the <condition> evaluates .T.rue, the commands that follow the **IF** command up to the [**ELSE**] command or **ENDIF** command are executed. Otherwise the commands following the [**ELSE**] or **ENDIF** command are executed. Each **IF** command used must have a matching **ENDIF.**

INDEX ON <expression> **TO** <index file>

Creates an index file for the database in use. The index file is based on key field(s) specified in the <expression>.

INPUT [<"string prompt">] **TO** <memvar>

Used in command files, **INPUT** is used to prompt for numeric data, while **TO** places the user's response into a memory variable.

```
. INPUT "Enter employee's salary:" TO pay
Enter employee's salary:1600
. ? pay
      1600
. LOCATE FOR salary = pay
Record =         7
```

INSERT [**BEFORE**] [**BLANK**]

Inserts a record into the database in use immediately after or before (with [**BEFORE**] parameter) the current record. If [**BLANK**] parameter is omitted, **INSERT** enters an editing mode for the record inserted.

JOIN WITH <alias> **TO** <filename> **FOR** <condition> [**FIELDS** <field list>]

Creates a new database by combining the records of the .DBF files in use in the two database areas. Records are added to a third database (specified by **TO** <filename>). Combined records are created when the **FOR** <condition> evaluates .T.rue for the current record of the current database as it is compared to each record of the <alias> database. That is, each record of the current database is compared to all records of the <alias> database.

LABEL FORM <label filename> [<scope>] [**SAMPLE**] [**TO PRINT**] [**FOR/WHILE** <condition>] [**TO FILE** <filename>]

Produces labels from the specifications within a label (.LBL) file. Label files are created with the **MODIFY LABEL** command.

The [**SAMPLE**] parameter may be used to print test labels to assure proper label registration. [**TO FILE** <filename>] parameter may be used to print labels in ASCII format to a diskette file.

LIST

The following **LIST** commands are identical to the **DISPLAY** commands except that there are no periodic pauses and the default <scope> is **ALL** when there is a <scope>.

LIST [<scope>] [<expression list>] [**FOR/WHILE** <condition>] [**OFF**] [**TO PRINT**]

LIST MEMORY

LIST STATUS

LIST STRUCTURE

LOCATE [<scope>] **FOR** <condition>

Moves the record pointer to the first record in the database for which the **FOR** <condition> evaluates as .T.rue. **CONTINUE** command finds next such record.

```
. LOCATE FOR salary <= 1600
Record =        3
. CONTINUE
Record =        4
. CONTINUE
Record =        7
```

LOOP

See **DO WHILE** command (page D–78).

MODIFY COMMAND <file>

Enters dBase's Word Processor editing mode to create or edit ASCII files. Normally used to edit command (.PRG) files, the **MODIFY COMMAND** mode also may be used to edit .TXT and .FMT files. The maximum file size that **MODIFY COMMAND** can edit is 4,096 bytes.

MODIFY LABEL <label form filename>

The **MODIFY LABEL** command is used to create or edit a label form file to hold label specifications for use by the **LABEL FORM** command. The label specifications are entered in a dBase editing mode similar to the **MODIFY REPORT** mode, and the file created is given a .LBL file extension by dBase.

The **MODIFY LABEL** and **LABEL FORM** commands are primarily designed to produce mailing or identification labels on tractor-fed label stock paper. To produce such labels, the width and height of the labels, left print margin, lines and spaces between labels, and number of labels across a page must be specified. These specifications are made in the first screen the **MODIFY LABEL** command presents. An area for remarks which will not be printed with the labels is also provided.

```
Structure of file B:empfile.dbf                INSERT
=====================================================
EMPLOYEE    C  20  | SALARY     N   8  2 |
TELEPHONE   C   8  | ACCOUNT    N   8  2 |
SEX         C   1  |                     |
EMPLOYED    D   8  |                     |
=====================================================

              Width of label:            35
              Height of label:            5
              Left margin:                0
              Lines between labels:       1
              Spaces between labels:      0
              Number of labels across:    1

Remarks:
```

The next screen presented is for the specifications of the label contents.

```
Structure of file B:empfile.dbf                INSERT
=====================================================
EMPLOYEE    C  20  | SALARY     N   8  2 |
TELEPHONE   C   8  | ACCOUNT    N   8  2 |
SEX         C   1  |                     |
EMPLOYED    D   8  |                     |
=====================================================

                       Label contents:
         1
         2
         3
         4
         5
```

Only character-type data may be specified as label contents. Therefore, date-type data must be converted with the **DTOC** function and numeric-type data must be converted with the **STR** function.

MODIFY REPORT <report form filename>

The **MODIFY REPORT** command is used to create or edit a report form (.FRM) file to hold report specifications for use by the **REPORT FORM** command. See "Producing dBase Reports," dBase III Tutorial Exercises, for further information.

MODIFY STRUCTURE

Alters the record structure of the database in use. The **MODIFY STRUCTURE** command may be used to add new fields or delete fields from the record structure. It also may be used to rename fields or change their lengths. The modifications, however, should be done according to the following procedures.

First, use **MODIFY STRUCTURE,** to add or delete any fields necessary. Fields may be inserted with {^**N**} or deleted with {^**U**}. Once field additions or deletions are complete, type {^End} to exit the **MODIFY STRUCTURE** editing mode.

Next, use **MODIFY STRUCTURE** to change any field names necessary. Editing keystrokes are the same as in the **BROWSE** editing mode. Once field names have been changed, type {^End} to exit the **MODIFY STRUCTURE** editing mode.

Finally, use **MODIFY STRUCTURE** to change any field widths necessary. Once the new field widths are specified, type {^End} to exit the **MODIFY STRUCTURE** editing mode.

NOTE or *

Used in command files, this command allows comments to be placed into a command file. Comparable to the **REM** statement of BASIC.

PACK

Erases all records marked for deletion in the database in use.

PARAMETERS <expression list>

Used in command files, receives expressions passed with the [**WITH** <expressions list>] parameter of a **DO** <filename> [**WITH** <expression list>] command. **PARAMETERS** must be the first executable command in the receiving program.

PRIVATE [<memvar list>], or [**ALL** [**LIKE/EXCEPT**] <skeleton>]

Usually used in command files, **PRIVATE** permits the use of memory variables that have the same names as variables created outside the command file.

PROCEDURE <procedure name>

Identifies the beginning of each procedure in a procedure file. A procedure file is a command (.PRG) file that has been declared and opened as a procedure file with the **SET PROCEDURE TO** <filename> command.

Short program subroutines called procedures typically are found within a procedure file. Each subroutine starts with a **PROCEDURE** <procedure name> command and ends with a **RETURN** command. There may be up to 32 separate procedures in a procedure file.

Procedures are executed with the **DO** command in the same manner as command (.PRG) files are executed. Procedures having the same <procedure name> as an existing command (.PRG) files' <filename> will take execution precedence.

PUBLIC <memory variable list>

Declares memory variables as global, allowing them to be used by any program at any level. Memory variables must be declared **PUBLIC** before data are assigned to them.

QUIT

Ends a dBase session and returns to DOS. **QUIT** closes all files and must be typed at the end of each dBase session.

READ

Allows editing of field or memory variable contents placed on the screen with the @ **GET** command. See @ command for example and explanation (p. D–73).

RECALL [<scope>] [**FOR/WHILE** <condition>]

Recalls record(s) marked for deletion ("unmarks" them).

REINDEX

Updates (rebuilds) all active files.

RELEASE [<memvar list>], or [**ALL** [**LIKE/EXCEPT**] <skeleton>]

Erases memory variables from RAM memory. <skeleton>s are made up of variable name characters and masking characters that act as "wild cards." The asterisk (*) indicates, "Accept all remaining characters", while the question mark (?) means, "Accept any single character in this position."

```
. DISPLAY MEMORY
MALES        pub   N          5  (          5.00000000)
MPAY         pub   N    8499.00  (       8499.00000000)
MACCT        pub   N     950.75  (        950.75000000)
FEMALES      pub   N          4  (          4.00000000)
FPAY         pub   N    6207.50  (       6207.50000000)
FACCT        pub   N     825.50  (        825.50000000)
    6 variables defined,       54 bytes used
  250 variables available,   5946 bytes available

. RELEASE ALL LIKE M*          <- MALES, MPAY, and MACCT will be released.
. RELEASE ALL LIKE MA*         <- MALES and MACCT will be released.
. RELEASE ALL LIKE ?PAY        <- MPAY and FPAY will be released.
. RELEASE ALL EXCEPT F????     <- ALL but FPAY and FACCT will be released.

. RELEASE ALL                  <- Erases all variables from RAM memory.
```

RENAME <filename.ext> **TO** <new filename.ext>

Renames a file on the diskette from dBase. Filename extensions must be included.

```
. RENAME fullrepo.FRM TO report.FRM
```

REPLACE [<scope>] <field> **WITH** <exp> [,<field2> **WITH** <exp2>] [**FOR/WHILE** <condition>]

Replaces the contents of specified fields with the evaluation of the **WITH** <expression> for the records of the database in use.

REPORT [<**FORM** file>] [<scope>] [**FOR** <condition>] [**PLAIN**] [**HEADING** <cstring>] [**NO EJECT**] [**TO PRINT**] [**TO FILE** <filename>]

Creates a dBase report from a report form (.FRM) file. [**PLAIN**] omits page numbers and dates; [**TO FILE** <filename>] produces an ASCII text file.

RESTORE FROM <filename> [**ADDITIVE**]

Reads memory variables and their contents into RAM memory after they have been saved to a .MEM file with the **SAVE** command. The **ADDITIVE** parameter keeps current variables intact; otherwise they are lost.

RETURN [**TO MASTER**]

Used in command files, the **RETURN** command returns control to the command file which called it or to the dBase dot (.) prompt. [**TO MASTER**] returns control to the highest calling level command file.

RUN <command>

Runs a designated .COM or .EXE file from within dBase.

SAVE TO <filename> [**ALL** [**LIKE/EXCEPT**] <skeleton>]

Saves current memory variables in a file given an .MEM extension. <skeleton>s are made up of variable name characters and masking characters that act as "wild cards." The asterisk (*) indicates, "Accept all remaining characters," while the question mark (?) means, "Accept any single character in this position."

```
. DISPLAY MEMORY
MALES        pub   N          5  (         5.00000000)
MPAY         pub   N    8499.00  (      8499.00000000)
MACCT        pub   N     950.75  (       950.75000000)
FEMALES      pub   N          4  (         4.00000000)
FPAY         pub   N    6207.50  (      6207.50000000)
FACCT        pub   N     825.50  (       825.50000000)
    6 variables defined,      54 bytes used
  250 variables available,  5946 bytes available

. SAVE TO vfile ALL LIKE M*         ←MALES, MPAY, and MACCT will be saved.
. SAVE TO vfile ALL LIKE MA*        ←MALES and MACCT will be saved.
. SAVE TO vfile ALL LIKE ?PAY       ←MPAY and FPAY will be saved.
. SAVE TO vfile ALL EXCEPT F????    ←ALL but FPAY and FACCT will be saved.

. SAVE ALL                          ←Saves all current variables in the specified file.
```

The **RESTORE** command is used to read the variables and their contents from a .MEM file into RAM memory.

SEEK <expression>

Used with index files, **SEEK** positions the record pointer to the first database record indexed by the <expression>. **SEEK** is similar to **FIND,** but also is able to search for numeric indexed keys.

```
. USE empfile INDEX namedex
. SEEK "Smith P"
. DISPLAY

Record#  EMPLOYEE              TELEPHONE SEX EMPLOYED   SALARY  ACCOUNT
      6  Smith Paul            244-1010  M   11/15/81  1700.00   350.00
. STORE "Johns" TO z
Johns
. SEEK z
. DISPLAY

Record#  EMPLOYEE              TELEPHONE SEX EMPLOYED   SALARY  ACCOUNT
      9  Johnson Frank         223-7928  M   03/20/86  1500.00     0.00
. INDEX ON salary TO saldex
      9 records indexed
. USE empfile INDEX saldex

. SEEK 1600
. DISPLAY

Record#  EMPLOYEE              TELEPHONE SEX EMPLOYED   SALARY  ACCOUNT
      7  Martins Mary          222-2123  F   11/01/85  1600.00   200.50
```

SELECT <Work Area/Alias>

dBase III allows up to ten databases to be used at the same time. When multiple databases are in use they can be thought of as existing in separate areas of RAM memory called "Work Areas." Work Area 1 is the default area for a database in **USE.** To bring a second database into use, you first must execute the **SELECT** <Work Area> command, and then the **USE** command.

Each Work Area maintains a separate database record pointer. Commands affecting the record pointer must be executed from the Work Area in which the intended database for the command resides.

Field data from the current record in any Work Area may be read into the current Work Area by specifying an "alias" as part of the field name.

```
. USE empfile
. SELECT 2
. USE deptmail

. DISPLAY ALL
Record#  EMPLOYEE             DEPT
      1  Pratt John           Acct.
      2  Smoler Ellen         Sales
      3  Jones David          Sales
      4  Sill Sally           Acct.
      5  Knat Michael         Pers.
      6  Smith Paul           Acct.
      7  Martins Mary         Sctry
      8  Nichols Sandy        Sctry
      9  Johnson Frank        Sales

. GOTO 2
. DISPLAY

Record#  EMPLOYEE             DEPT
      2  Smoler Ellen         Sales
. SELECT 1
. DISPLAY
Record#  EMPLOYEE             TELEPHONE SEX EMPLOYED    SALARY  ACCOUNT
      1  Pratt John           225-1234  M   06/22/82   1949.00   200.00
. SKIP 5
Record no.       6
. DISPLAY
Record#  EMPLOYEE             TELEPHONE SEX EMPLOYED    SALARY  ACCOUNT
      6  Smith Paul           244-1010  M   11/15/81   1700.00   350.00
. DISPLAY deptmail->employee, deptmail->dept

Record#  deptmail->employee   deptmail->dept
      6  Smoler Ellen         Sales
```

SET

dBase has an extensive set of operating features that can be turned on or off, or changed in other ways with **SET** commands. The **SET** commands have two general forms:

SET <parameter> [ON or OFF]

or

SET <parameter> **TO** <option>

The [ON or OFF] **SET** commands are shown here with the normal default setting of each indicated in upper-case characters.

SET BELL ON/off—default setting is normally **ON.**

SET ALTERNATE on/OFF

ON sends all screen output (except full-screen output such as @ **SAY,** @ **GET,** and output of the editing modes) in ASCII format to a file on the diskette. The **SET ALTERNATE ON** command must be preceded by the **SET ALTERNATE TO** <file> command. OFF stops output to the diskette file.

SET ALTERNATE TO <filename>

Creates a disk file given a .TXT extension. The file is used for saving screen output (in ASCII format) when the **SET ALTERNATE ON** command is given. **SET ALTERNATE TO** with no filename specified closes the .TXT file.

SET BELL ON/off

dBase rings a bell at various points during data entry. OFF stops the ringing.

SET CARRY on/OFF

The **SET CARRY** command is used when adding records to a database in the **APPEND** or **INSERT** editing modes. When **CARRY** is **SET ON,** data in the fields of the previous record automatically will be copied into like fields of the next record presented. OFF leaves all fields of the next record blank.

SET COLOR TO <standard> [,<enhanced>] [,border]

Three screen attributes may be altered with the **SET COLOR** command: the display of the normal <standard> screen may be changed from its default colors of white on black; the reverse video display <enhanced> of the editing modes may be changed from its default colors of black on white; and the area around the screen <border> may be changed from its default color of black.

<standard> and <enhanced> color specifications are made in color pairs, foreground/background. Numbers may be used to specify colors.

Color	Number Code	Color	Number Code
Black	0	Red	4
Blue	1	Magenta	5
Green	2	Yellow	6
Cyan	3	White	7

An asterisk (*) may be used to cause a blinking color, and a plus sign (+) may be used to cause a high intensity color. The following command may be entered to set a <standard> screen of white on blue, <enhanced> screen of bright white on red, and a magenta border:

```
SET COLOR TO 7/1,7+/4,5
```

If variables are used to set screen colors, they must be preceded with an ampersand (&).

```
SET COLOR TO &color1/&color2
```

SET CONFIRM on/OFF

In editing modes, when a field or variable has been filled with data, dBase automatically moves the cursor to the next field or variable for editing. The **SET CONFIRM ON** command disables automatic skipping to the next field, and the Enter key must be pressed to proceed.

SET CONSOLE ON/off

ON sends output to screen. OFF stops all output to screen.

SET DEBUG on/OFF

ON sends output created by the **SET ECHO ON** command to the printer. OFF sends the output to the screen.

SET DECIMALS TO <n>

Determines the minimum number of decimal places that will be displayed as a result of certain functions and calculations. Applies only to the operation of division and the functions **SQRT, LOG,** and **EXP.**

SET DEFAULT TO <drive>

Makes the specified drive the default drive.

SET DELETED on/OFF

ON stops dBase from processing records that are marked for deletion during execution of commands which allow a <scope> parameter, unless the scope is specified as **RECORD** <n> or **NEXT** <n> and the first record of the scope is deleted.

SET DELIMITER on/OFF

ON causes fields displayed in the editing modes to be delimited by a character string previously specified with the **SET DELIMITER TO** command, or to colons (:) if no **SET DELIMITER TO** command has been made.

SET DELIMITER TO <character string> [**DEFAULT**]

Assigns a character string for use in delimiting fields displayed in the editing modes. To change delimiters, the **SET DELIMITER TO** <character string> and **SET DELIMITER ON** commands are used. To return to the default delimiter of colons (:) the [**DEFAULT**] parameter may be used.

SET DEVICE TO <**PRINT/SCREEN**>

Determines if output from @ **SAY** and @ **GET** commands will be sent to the screen (default device) or to the printer. If sent to the printer, @ **GET** commands are ignored, and any command that would cause the printer to backup causes a page eject.

SET ECHO on/OFF

ON displays on the screen the command currently being executed. Used during execution of command files, **SET ECHO ON** allows you to trace the execution of commands in the file. See **SET DEBUG** on/OFF, **SET STEP** on/OFF.

SET ESCAPE ON/off

ON allows user to abort execution of a command file or dot (.) prompt command by tapping the Esc key. OFF disables this feature.

SET EXACT on/OFF

dBase allows partial matches of items in a <condition>. For instance, **DISPLAY FOR** employee = "Smit" will cause dBase to display the record for Paul Smith in the database "empfile." ON requires exact matches in any comparison of character strings in a **FOR** <condition>, **FIND** commands, or other string comparison operations. With **EXACT ON** only **DISPLAY FOR** employee = "Smith Paul" will display the record. (Notice, however, the spaces padded to the right and existing in the field "employee" do not have to be included in the item.)

SET FILTER TO [<condition>]

Causes the current database to appear as if it contains only certain records. **SET FILTER TO** with no condition turns off the filter.

```
. SET FILTER TO sex = "M"
. DISPLAY ALL

Record#  EMPLOYEE                     TELEPHONE SEX EMPLOYED    SALARY  ACCOUNT
      1  Pratt John                   225-1234  M   06/22/82   1949.00   200.00
      3  Jones David                  292-3832  M   06/15/82   1550.00   275.75
      5  Knat Michael                 221-1235  M   09/15/81   1800.00   125.00
      6  Smith Paul                   244-1010  M   11/15/81   1700.00   350.00
      9  Johnson Frank                223-7928  M   03/20/86   1500.00     0.00
```

SET FIXED on/OFF

When **SET FIXED** is ON, all displays of numeric data contain the exact number of decimal places specified by the **SET DECIMALS** command, or two decimal places if the **SET DECIMALS** command has not been executed.

SET FORMAT TO [<format file>]

Opens a format (.FMT) file which dBase will use to format the screen for **APPEND, CHANGE, EDIT,** and **INSERT** commands. .FMT files are command files renamed using the **RENAME** command of dBase or DOS to have the .FMT file extension and whose commands are made up of @ **SAY**s and @ **GET**s only. **SET FORMAT TO** closes any open .FMT file.

SET FUNCTION <n> **TO** <"character expression">

Stores the specified "string" into the Function key <n>. For example, **SET FUNCTION 2 TO** "Columbus Ohio" stores the string into the Function key #2. Each time F2 is tapped, the string 'Columbus Ohio' will appear on the monitor screen at the location of the cursor just as if you had typed it. Type **DISPLAY STATUS** for default Function key values.

SET HEADING ON/off

OFF removes the column headings for the **DISPLAY, LIST, AVERAGE,** and **SUM** commands.

SET HELP ON/off

OFF disables the "Do you want some help? (Y/N)" message generated by syntax errors.

SET INDEX TO <index file list>

Reads index (.NDX) files into memory for use with the current database file. Essentially the same as **USE** <database> **INDEX** <index file list>.

SET INTENSITY ON/off

OFF stops the reverse video display of data when in the editing modes.

SET MARGIN TO <n>

Sets left margin of printer to <n> columns.

SET MENUS on/OFF

ON causes the display of keystroke command menus when in an editing mode.

SET PATH TO <path list>

Defines an alternate path for existing files referred to but not found in the current directory.

SET PROCEDURE TO <filename>

Declares and opens a command (.PRG) file as a procedure file. Only one procedure file per work area may be open at one time. (See **PROCEDURE,** page D–83.)

SET PRINT on/OFF

ON sends all output not formatted with @ **SAY,** @ **GET,** or presented in editing modes to the printer. OFF stops such output to the printer.

SET RELATION [**TO** <key expression>/<numeric expression> **INTO** <alias>]

Links the movement of the record pointer in the current database to the movement of the pointer in an open database of another work area. The second database is identified by its <alias>. If a <key expression> is used, it must be contained in both databases with the second database indexed on the key expression. If a numeric expression is used, pointer movement is based on record numbers and the second database must not be indexed. Only one relation may be set from any work area. Using **SET RELATION TO** with no parameters unlinks pointer movement. The following example uses a key expression to set a relationship.

Work Area 1 B:deptmail			Work Area 2 B:mailrout indexed on area			
Record#	EMPLOYEE	DEPT	Record#	MANAGER	AREA	MAILCODE
1	Pratt John	Acct.	4	Evans Claire	Acct.	106
2	Smoler Ellen	Sales	1	Jacobs, William	Pers.	103
3	Jones David	Sales	2	Butler John	Sales	107
4	Sill Sally	Acct.	3	Branden Julie	Sctry	101
5	Knat Michael	Pers.				
6	Smith Paul	Acct.				
7	Martins Mary	Sctry				
8	Nichols Sandy	Sctry				
9	Johnson Frank	Sales				

```
. SELECT 1
. SET RELATION TO dept INTO mailrout
. LOCATE FOR employee = "Smith P"
Record =       6
. ? mailrout->manager, mailrout->mailcode,"ATTN.",employee
Evans Claire            106 ATTN. Smith Paul
. LOCATE FOR employee = "Johnso"
Record =       9
. ? mailrout->manager, mailrout->mailcode,"ATTN.",employee
Butler John             107 ATTN. Johnson Frank
```

To make the record pointer in the second database point to the same record number as the record pointer in the current database, the **SET RELATION TO** command would have the form:

```
SET RELATION TO RECNO() INTO <alias>
```

SET SAFETY ON/off

OFF disables the "<filename> already exists, overwrite it? (Y/N)" message.

SET STEP on/OFF

ON aids debugging of a command file by causing dBase to pause after it executes each command in the file.

SET TALK ON/off

dBase displays various messages associated with the execution of certain commands. **SET TALK OFF** stops display of the messages.

SET UNIQUE on/OFF

Used in conjunction with an index (.NDX) file, **SET UNIQUE ON** eliminates the chance of records with duplicate field data being processed by dBase III commands.

SKIP [-] [<n>]

Moves record pointer up or down <n> records in the current database. Default value is +1.

SORT TO <new file> **ON** <field> [/**A**] [/**D**] [,<field>] [/**A**] [/**D**] .. [**FOR** <condition>]

Creates a copy of the database in use with all records arranged in order of the data held in the <field>(s) specified. Sorting is done in ascending order unless otherwise specified with the [/**D**] (descending) parameter.

STORE <expression> **TO** <memvar list>

Stores the value of an expression to a memory variable.

SUM <expression list> [<scope>] [**FOR/WHILE** <condition>] [**TO** <memvar list>]

Computes the sum of the expressions in its expression list for the records evaluated .T.rue by the **FOR/WHILE** <condition>, and stores the sums to the memory variables in its memvar list. Default scope is **ALL** records.

```
. SUM salary,account FOR sex = "F" TO fsal,facct
      4 records summed
     salary       account
    6207.50        825.50
```

TEXT
  any data
ENDTEXT

Used in command files, allows text to be included without the use of the @ **SAY** or **?** commands. dBase treats all data between the **TEXT** and **ENDTEXT** commands as text to be output.

TOTAL ON <key field> **TO** <file> [**FIELDS** <field list>] [**FOR/WHILE** <condition>]

Creates a database (.DBF) file by copying only those records with a unique <key field> from the database in use to it. The database in use must be in use with an index file having the same <key> or be presorted by the same <key> specified in the **TOTAL** command. Records with the same keys are not copied to the **TO** <file>, but can have their numeric fields totaled in the **TO** database by using the **FIELDS** <field list> parameter.

TYPE <filename.ext> [**TO PRINT**]

TYPE displays the contents of an unopened file. The [**TO PRINT**] parameter echoes screen output to the printer.

UPDATE ON <key field> **FROM** <alias> **REPLACE** <field> **WITH** <field> ... [**RANDOM**]

Allows batch update of a presorted or indexed database.

USE <file> [**INDEX** <index file list>]

Specifies the database for command operation processing. **USE** closes the previous file in use and sets the record pointer to the first record. **USE** with no parameters closes the current database.

WAIT [string prompt] [**TO** <memvar>]

Used in command files, the **WAIT TO** command pauses execution of the commands in the file until a single keyboard character is typed. The character typed (if printable) is stored in the specified variable.

ZAP

Removes all records from the current database. Same as **DELETE ALL**↵ and **PACK**↵

dBase III Functions

&<character variables>

Macro Function The **&** function is used with memory variables holding character data. It causes dBase not to treat the memory variable name literally.

```
. STORE "employee,'Limit -',salary*.15" TO limit
employee,'Limit -',salary*.15
. DISPLAY ALL &limit
Record#  employee          'Limit -'   salary*.15
      1  Pratt John         Limit -      292.3500
      2  Smoler Ellen       Limit -      247.5000
      3  Jones David        Limit -      232.5000
      4  Sill Sally         Limit -      226.1250
      5  Knat Michael       Limit -      270.0000
      6  Smith Paul         Limit -      255.0000
      7  Martins Mary       Limit -      240.0000
      8  Nichols Sandy      Limit -      217.5000
      9  Johnson Frank      Limit -      225.0000
```

ASC(<character data>)

ASCII Code Function Returns the ASCII code number of the left-most character in the <character data>. See ASCII Character Codes in the appendix for character code numbers.

```
. DISPLAY
Record#  EMPLOYEE                TELEPHONE SEX EMPLOYED   SALARY  ACCOUNT
      1  Pratt John              225-1234  M   06/22/82  1949.00   200.00
. ? ASC(employee)
  80                   ← The ASCII code for "P" is 80.
. ? ASC(sex)
  77                   ← The ASCII code for "M" is 77.
. ? CHR(ASC(sex)+32)
m                      ← The ASCII code for any capital letter is 32 less
                         than its lower-case equivalent.
```

AT(<cstring1>,<cstring2>)

Substring Search Function Returns an integer equal to the character place number in <cstring2> where a substring identical to <cstring1> occurs.

```
. GOTO 7
. DISPLAY
Record#  EMPLOYEE                TELEPHONE SEX EMPLOYED   SALARY  ACCOUNT
      7  Martins Mary            222-2123  F   11/01/85  1600.00   200.50
. ? AT("Mary",employee)
    9
```

BOF()

Beginning-of-File Function Returns .T.rue if an attempt has been made to go before the first record in a database.

```
. DISPLAY
Record#  EMPLOYEE                TELEPHONE SEX EMPLOYED   SALARY  ACCOUNT
      7  Martins Mary            222-2123  F   11/01/85  1600.00   200.50
```

```
. ? BOF()
.F.
. GO TOP
. ? BOF()
.F.
. SKIP -1
Record no.       1
. ? BOF()
.T.
```

CDOW(<date variable>)

Character Day of Week Function Returns the name of the day for a date from a date memory variable or field.

```
. DISPLAY
Record#  EMPLOYEE                 TELEPHONE SEX EMPLOYED   SALARY  ACCOUNT
      1  Pratt John               225-1234  M   06/22/82  1949.00   200.00
. ? CDOW(employed)
Tuesday
```

CHR(<numeric exp>)

Character String Function Returns the ASCII character equivalent of the <numeric exp>.

```
. ? CHR(65)
A
. ? CHR(65+32)
a
```

CMONTH(<date variable>)

Character Month Function Returns the name of the month from a date variable or field.

```
. DISPLAY
Record#  EMPLOYEE                 TELEPHONE SEX EMPLOYED   SALARY  ACCOUNT
      1  Pratt John               225-1234  M   06/22/82  1949.00   200.00
. ? CMONTH(employed)
June
```

COL( )

Column Function Returns the current column position of the cursor.

CTOD(<character data>)

Character-to-Date Function Converts character-type data to date-type data. The character data must be in the order mm/dd/yy, but any character can separate the numbers used.

```
. DISPLAY
Record#  EMPLOYEE                 TELEPHONE SEX EMPLOYED   SALARY  ACCOUNT
      1  Pratt John               225-1234  M   06/22/82  1949.00   200.00
. ? employed = CTOD("06 22 82")
.T.
. ? employed < CTOD("01-01-84")
.T.
```

DATE( )

Date Function Returns the DOS system date in a format mm/dd/yy.

```
. ? DATE()
1/01/80
```

DAY(<date variable>)

Day Function Returns the day number from a date variable or field.

```
. DISPLAY
Record#  EMPLOYEE                 TELEPHONE SEX EMPLOYED   SALARY  ACCOUNT
      1  Pratt John               225-1234  M   06/22/82  1949.00   200.00
. ? DAY(employed)
 22
```

DELETED( )

Deleted Record Function Returns .T. if the current record is marked for deletion.

```
. GOTO 7
. DISPLAY
Record#  EMPLOYEE                 TELEPHONE SEX EMPLOYED   SALARY  ACCOUNT
      7  Martins Mary             222-2123  F   11/01/85  1600.00   200.50
. ? DELETED()
.F.
```

DOW(<date variable>)

Day-of-Week Function Returns the day number of the date from a date variable or field. Numbers begin with Sunday = 1 and end with Saturday = 7.

```
. DISPLAY
Record#  EMPLOYEE                 TELEPHONE SEX EMPLOYED   SALARY  ACCOUNT
      7  Martins Mary             222-2123  F   11/01/85  1600.00   200.50
. ? DOW(employed)
 6
```

DTOC(<date variable>)

Date-to-Character Function Converts date-type data to character-type data.

```
. DISPLAY
Record#  EMPLOYEE                 TELEPHONE SEX EMPLOYED   SALARY  ACCOUNT
      7  Martins Mary             222-2123  F   11/01/85  1600.00   200.50
. ? DTOC(employed) = "11-01-85"
.F.
. ? DTOC(employed) = "11/01/85"
.T.
```

EOF( )

End-of-File Function Returns .T.rue if an attempt is made to go past the last record in a database.

```
. DISPLAY
Record#  EMPLOYEE                 TELEPHONE SEX EMPLOYED   SALARY  ACCOUNT
      7  Martins Mary             222-2123  F   11/01/85  1600.00   200.50
. ? EOF()
.F.
. GO BOTTOM
. ? EOF()
.F.
```

```
. SKIP
Record no.       10
. ? EOF()
.T.
```

EXP(<numeric data>)

Exponential Function Returns the value of e^x.

```
. ? EXP(1.000)
2.718
```

FILE(<"[drive:]filename.ext">)

File Existence Function Returns .T.rue if the file exists on the specified drive. (Default drive if not specified).

```
. ? FILE("B:fullrepo.FRM")
.T.
```

INT(<numeric data>)

Integer Function Returns the integer value.

```
. ? 3.333333333
3.333333333
. ? INT(3.333333333)
          3
. ? INT(-4.3678)
    -4
```

LEN(<character data>)

Length Function Returns the number of characters in <character data>.

```
. ? LEN("Hello")
         5
. DISPLAY
Record#  EMPLOYEE                 TELEPHONE SEX EMPLOYED   SALARY  ACCOUNT
      7  Martins Mary             222-2123  F   11/01/85  1600.00   200.50
. ? LEN(employee)
        20
. ? LEN(TRIM(employee))
        12
```

LOG(<numeric data>)

Logarithm Function Returns the natural logarithm.

```
. ? LOG(2.71828)
  1.00000
```

LOWER(<character data>)

Lower-Case Function Returns the lower-case equivalent of its <character data>.

```
. ? LOWER("HELLO")
hello
. DISPLAY
Record#  EMPLOYEE                 TELEPHONE SEX EMPLOYED   SALARY  ACCOUNT
      7  Martins Mary             222-2123  F   11/01/85  1600.00   200.50
. ? LOWER(employee)
martins mary
```

MONTH(<date variable>)

Month Function Returns the month number from a date variable or field.

```
. DISPLAY
Record#  EMPLOYEE                  TELEPHONE SEX EMPLOYED    SALARY  ACCOUNT
      1  Pratt John                225-1234  M   06/22/82   1949.00   200.00
. ? MONTH(employed)
  6
```

PCOL( )

Printer Column Function Returns the current column position of the printer.

PROW( )

Printer Row Function Returns the current row position of the printer.

RECNO( )

Record Number Function Returns the integer value equal to the current record number.

```
. GOTO 7
. DISPLAY
Record#  EMPLOYEE                  TELEPHONE SEX EMPLOYED    SALARY  ACCOUNT
      7  Martins Mary              222-2123  F   11/01/85   1600.00   200.50
. ? RECNO()
         7
```

ROUND(<numeric data>,<n>)

Round Function Rounds off numbers <n> decimal places to the right of the decimal, or rounds numbers to the left of the decimal if <n> is negative.

```
. DISPLAY
Record#  EMPLOYEE                  TELEPHONE SEX EMPLOYED    SALARY  ACCOUNT
      7  Martins Mary              222-2123  F   11/01/85   1600.00   200.50
. ? ROUND(account,0)
   201.00
. ? ROUND (17566.10,-2)
 17600.00
```

ROW( )

Row Function Returns the current row position of the cursor.

SPACE(<numeric data>)

Space Function Returns a string of spaces equal in length to the evaluation of <numeric data>.

```
. ? SPACE(10*2),employee
                     Martins Mary
```

SQRT(<numeric data>)

Square Root Function Returns the square root of <numeric data>.

STR(<numeric data> [,<length>] [,<decimals>])

Numeric to String Function Returns a character string converted from a numeric expression. Most useful for deleting leading spaces in output of numeric data and/or forcing the display of desired decimal places.

```
. DISPLAY
Record#  EMPLOYEE                TELEPHONE SEX EMPLOYED   SALARY  ACCOUNT
      7  Martins Mary            222-2123  F   11/01/85  1600.00   200.50
. ? employee," / Limit =",salary*.15
Martins Mary           / Limit =     240.0000
. ? TRIM(employee)," / Limit =",STR(salary*.15,6,2)
Martins Mary  / Limit = 240.00
```

SUBSTR(<character data>,<start>,<length>)

Substring Function Returns the portion of <character data> from a specified beginning location and for a specified length.

```
. DISPLAY
Record#  EMPLOYEE                TELEPHONE SEX EMPLOYED   SALARY  ACCOUNT
      7  Martins Mary            222-2123  F   11/01/85  1600.00   200.50
. ? SUBSTR(employee,9,4)
Mary
```

TIME( )

Time Function Returns the system time in the format hh:mm:ss.

TRIM(<character data>)

Trim Function Removes trailing spaces from <character data>.

```
. DISPLAY
Record#  EMPLOYEE                TELEPHONE SEX EMPLOYED   SALARY  ACCOUNT
      7  Martins Mary            222-2123  F   11/01/85  1600.00   200.50
. ? employee,telephone
Martins Mary          222-2123
. ? TRIM(employee),telephone
Martins Mary 222-2123
```

TYPE("<expression>")

Data-Type Function Returns a one-character evaluation 'C', 'N', 'L', 'M', or 'U' for the <expression> data type—character, numeric, logical, memo, or undefined, respectively. The <expression> must be enclosed in either single or double quotes.

```
. ? TYPE("employee")
C
. ? TYPE("salary")
N
. ? TYPE("account<.15*salary")
L
. STORE 550 TO a
550
. ? TYPE("a")
N
. RELEASE a
. ? TYPE("a")
U
```

UPPER(<character data>)

Upper-Case Function Returns the upper-case equivalent of its <character data>.

```
. ? UPPER("hello")
HELLO
. DISPLAY
Record#  EMPLOYEE                    TELEPHONE SEX EMPLOYED   SALARY  ACCOUNT
      7  Martins Mary                222-2123  F   11/01/85  1600.00   200.50
. ? UPPER(employee)
MARTINS MARY
```

VAL(<character data>)

Character-to-Value Function Returns the numeric value of numbers held as strings beginning at the first character of <character data>.

```
. ? VAL("7312 S.W. Fulton Park Blvd.")
                         7312.00
. ? VAL("P.O. Box 7312")
           0.00
```

YEAR(<date variable>)

Year Function Returns the year number of a date from the <date variable>.

```
. DISPLAY
Record#  EMPLOYEE                    TELEPHONE SEX EMPLOYED   SALARY  ACCOUNT
      7  Martins Mary                222-2123  F   11/01/85  1600.00   200.50
. ? YEAR(employed)
 1985
```

New File Types

.CAT

Catalog files are created with the **SET CATALOG TO** <filename> command. .CAT files are used to group related files. Once the **SET CATALOG TO** <filename> command has been executed, the specified catalog file becomes active. Any command entered after this opens or creates a dBase III Plus file (with the exception of .MEM, .PRG, and .TXT files) causes the opened or created file to become listed in the active .CAT file.

While a .CAT file is active, dBase recognizes only the files listed in it when the **CATALOG QUERY (?)** parameter is used in a dBase III Plus command. The **?** parameter may be used in any command having a filename as part of its syntax. When the parameter is used, dBase presents a menu of cataloged files (recognized by dBase as being an appropriate file type by their filename extensions) from which you may select to complete the command.

Catalog files are actually database files (normally given a .DBF filename extension) that are automatically given a .CAT extension at the time they are created. When a catalog file is activated with **SET CATALOG TO** it becomes an open database file in work area 10. To stop the appending of filenames to an active catalog without closing the catalog file you may type **SET CATALOG OFF.** To continue adding filenames, type **SET CATALOG ON.** To close an active catalog file, type **SET CATALOG ON** with no <filename> specified.

.QRY

Query files are created with the **CREATE QUERY** <filename> or **MODIFY QUERY** <filename> commands. They contain conditions which act as record filters for dBase to use in processing a database.

The user enters the conditions in a .QRY file in a menu driven mode. To activate a query file the command **SET FILTER TO FILE** <filename> is used. See **MODIFY QUERY** (page D–105) for more information on database filters.

.SCR

Screen files are created with the **CREATE SCREEN** <filename> or **MODIFY SCREEN** <filename> commands. They serve as source files used by dBase to generate format (.FMT) files, which are files containing @ **SAY** and @ **GET** commands used to format screen displays.

When creating a screen file, the user selects the database(s) and fields to be used from "Set Up" menus provided by dBase. The fields then may be positioned on the screen through editing keystrokes, and accompanying screen text may be entered. Fields may be specified to be displayed with @ **GET** or @ **SAY** commands, and **PICTURE** parameters for display of fields may be established through a menu selection process. When finished, dBase saves the .SCR file, and generates a format (.FMT) file (having the same filename) from it. .FMT files are activated and display their screens with **SET FORMAT TO** <filename>, followed by an **APPEND, CHANGE, EDIT, INSERT,** or **READ** command.

.VUE

View files are created with the **CREATE VIEW** <filename> or **MODIFY VIEW** <filename> commands. They are used to hold a set of working relationships between dBase III files. When the **CREATE VIEW** <filename>, **MODIFY VIEW** <filename>, or the **CREATE VIEW** <filename> **FROM ENVIRONMENT** commands are executed, a view file with the specified filename is created with data from the current environment. The view file contains a listing of all active databases; their indexes in use; the work areas in which the databases are located; any relations between the databases that may exist (see **SET RELATION TO**); and the active field list, .FMT file, and/or filter (if any) for each database in use.

The view file then may be edited with the **MODIFY VIEW** or **CREATE VIEW** commands. Once a view file has been created, it may be used to reinstate the environment recorded within it through the **SET VIEW TO** <filename> command.

The HISTORY Buffer

dBase III Plus sets aside a small portion of RAM memory (a buffer) called HISTORY, into which it stores previously executed commands. The default number of commands stored in HISTORY is 20 commands. The buffer allows the user to back up, edit, and then reenter a previous command.

To display a previous command entered from the dot (.) prompt mode, the cursor-up key is typed. Each time the key is typed, dBase displays the next previous command (scrolls back through the commands in HISTORY). To scroll forward, the cursor-down key is typed. When the desired command is displayed, the following keystrokes may be used to edit the command.

HISTORY Editing Keystrokes

Keystroke	Action
Cursor-right key	Moves cursor right one character
Cursor-left key	Moves cursor left one character.
Home key	Moves cursor one word to the left.
End key	Moves cursor one word to the right.
Ins key	Toggles between overwrite and **INSERT** modes.
Del key	Deletes character over cursor.
← (Backspace key)	Deletes character to left of cursor.
^T	Erases word to right of cursor.
^Y	Erases line to right of cursor.
Esc	Aborts all changes made and moves cursor to the beginning of the command line.

When editing is completed, the ↵ (Enter key) may be typed to re-enter the command.

To change the number of command lines stored in HISTORY the **SET HISTORY TO** <n> command is used. To cause commands executed from within a command (.PRG) file to be stored in HISTORY, the **SET DOHISTORY ON** command is used.

Changes Made to Existing dBase III Commands in dBase III Plus

General Changes

<scope>

A new <scope>, **REST,** has been added to dBase III Plus. **REST** causes dBase command processing to begin on the current record and continue to the end of the database.

FOR/WHILE <condition>

The **FOR/WHILE** <condition> parameter no longer requires **FOR/WHILE** to be mutually exclusive. All commands allowing a **FOR/WHILE** <condition> parameter now allow both a **FOR** <condition> and a **WHILE** <condition> parameter to be used. **WHILE** has precedence over **FOR.**

Specific Changes

@ <x1,y1> **[CLEAR] TO** <x2,y2> **[DOUBLE]**

The @ command has new parameters in dBase III Plus that may be used to draw a box on the screen. <x1,y1> describe the upper left corner of the box with x = screen row, y = screen column. <x2,y2> describe the lower right corner of the box, and the [**DOUBLE**] parameter may be added to draw a double line for the box. If the optional [**CLEAR**] parameter is used, the screen is erased in the rectangle described by <x1,y1> and <x2,y2>.

APPEND FROM <file> [**FOR** <condition>] [**TYPE** <file type>]

With dBase III Plus, records marked for deletion in the **FROM** <file> will be appended and become unmarked in the file appended to.

The [**SDF**] parameter has been replaced in dBase III Plus with the [**TYPE** <file type>] parameter. The options for <file type> include:

SDF	System Data Format files. ASCII files.
DIF	A VisiCalc file format.
SYLK	Multiplan spreadsheet format.
WKS	Lotus 1-2-3 spreadsheet format.

BROWSE [**FIELDS** <field list>] [**LOCK** <n>] [**FREEZE** <field>] [**NOFOLLOW**] [**NOMENU**] [**WIDTH** <n>] [**NOAPPEND**]

The dBase III Plus **BROWSE** command has several new parameters, most of which may be specified in the dot (.) prompt mode when entering the **BROWSE** command, or selected from a menu bar while in the **BROWSE** mode. The menu bar is toggled on/OFF with the F10 key.

[**LOCK** <n>]	Prevents the scrolling of the <n> left-most fields when ^cursor-left or ^cursor-right is used to pan the screen across the database.
[**FREEZE** <field>]	Allows only editing of the specified field. All other fields are displayed normally.
[**NOFOLLOW**]	Prevents the record pointer from moving with an indexed record when a key field of the record is edited.
[**NOMENU**]	Prevents access to the menu bar.
[**WIDTH** <n>]	Limits the display of any field to a maximum of <n> characters in length.

[**NOAPPEND**] Prevents appending of records in the **BROWSE** mode.

COPY TO <file> [<scope>] [**FIELDS** <field list>] [**DELIMITED** [**WITH** <delimiter>]] [**FOR** <condition>] [**WHILE** <condition>] [**TYPE** <file type>]

The [**SDF**] parameter has been replaced with the [**TYPE** <file type>] parameter. The options for <file type> include:

SDF System Data Format files. ASCII files.
DIF A VisiCalc file format.
SYLK Multiplan spreadsheet format.
WKS Lotus 1-2-3 spreadsheet format.

EDIT [<scope>] [**FIELDS** <field list>] [**WHILE** <condition>] [**FOR** <condition>]

The changes made to the **EDIT** command make it identical to the dBase III **CHANGE** command. (See **CHANGE** page D–75.)

INDEX ON <expression> **TO** <index file> [**UNIQUE**]

In dBase III Plus, a new parameter, [**UNIQUE**] causes only the first record of several records having the same key <expression> to be indexed in the .NDX file.

MODIFY LABEL, MODIFY REPORT

In dBase III Plus, both commands use the full-screen, menu-driven mode for data entry.

NOTE, *, or **&&**

Another form of the comment command (**&&**) allows comments to be placed at the end of a line on which another command exists.

READ [**SAVE**]

In dBase III Plus, a new parameter, [**SAVE**], prevents the **READ** command from clearing (deactivating) the screen's @ **GET**s when editing is finished.

Also, with dBase III Plus, multiple screens containing @ **GET**s may be produced which allow the user to page back and forth among the screens by typing the PgUp and PgDn keys. The multiple-page screens must be generated from a .FMT file with **READ** commands inserted at the desired page breaks.

REPORT [**FORM** <form file>] [<scope>] [**FOR** <condition>] [**PLAIN**] [**HEADING** <cstring>] [**NO EJECT**] [**TO PRINT**] [**TO FILE** <filename>] [**SUMMARY**]

In dBase III Plus, a new parameter [**SUMMARY**] produces the same type of report as specifying "Summary report only" as "Yes" when the report form was created.

SET

In addition to executing dBase **SET** commands from the dot (.) prompt mode or from within a command file, dBase III Plus provides a full-screen, menu-driven mode for executing many of the **SET** commands. This mode is entered by typing {**SET**}.

SET COLOR TO <standard> [,<enhanced>] [,border]

The screen color attributes may no longer be specified by color number in dBase III Plus, but instead must be specified by color letter(s). The letters used to specify colors are:

Color	*Letter Code*	*Color*	*Letter Code*
Black	N	Red	R
Blue	B	Magenta	RB
Green	G	Brown	GR
Cyan	BG	White	W
Blank	X		

SET CONSOLE ON/off

SET CONSOLE OFF only works from within command files with dBase III Plus. The console (screen) is always ON in the dot (.) prompt mode.

SET FUNCTION <n> **TO** <"character expression">

Function key F1 cannot be changed with the **SET FUNCTION** command using dBase III Plus.

SET UNIQUE on/OFF

SET UNIQUE is used only to configure an index (.NDX) file at the time the index file is created with dBase III Plus.

New dBase III Plus Commands

CALL <module name> [**WITH** <expression>]

Executes a binary file placed in memory with the **LOAD** command.

CLEAR FIELDS

Resets the display of fields to all fields and performs a **SET FIELDS OFF.** (See **SET FIELDS TO** page D–111.)

CLEAR TYPEAHEAD

Erases all characters currently in the keyboard buffer.

CREATE VIEW FROM ENVIRONMENT

Creates a view (.VUE) file from the files currently open. See .VUE *View files* (page D–100.)

DISPLAY HISTORY [LAST <n>] **[TO PRINT]**

Displays the commands currently in the HISTORY buffer. Default is all commands. [**LAST** <n>] parameter may be used to display the last <n> number of commands. **[TO PRINT]** parameter may be used to echo output to the printer.

EXPORT <filename.> **TYPE PFS**

Copies the current dBase III database and its open .FMT file (if any) to a single file named <filename> in the database format used by PFS:FILE.

IMPORT FROM <filename> **TYPE PFS**

Creates a dBase III database (.DBF) file and a format (.FMT) file, both having the same filename, from a PFS:FILE database file named <filename>. At the time a file is imported, dBase creates a view (.VUE) file which relates the .DBF and .FMT files.

LIST HISTORY [LAST <n>] [**TO PRINT**]

Same as **DISPLAY HISTORY.** See **DISPLAY HISTORY** (above).

LOAD <filename> [.<ext>]

Loads a binary file into memory where it may be executed with the **CALL** command.

MODIFY QUERY <filename>

The **MODIFY QUERY** is used to create or change a query (.QRY) file used by the **SET FILTER TO FILE** <filename> command. The **MODIFY QUERY** command uses a full-screen, menu-driven mode for data entry.

To set a filter condition equivalent to all men with salaries greater than $1,600 for the database empfile.DBF, you would first put empfile into use, and then type the **MODIFY QUERY** <filename> command.

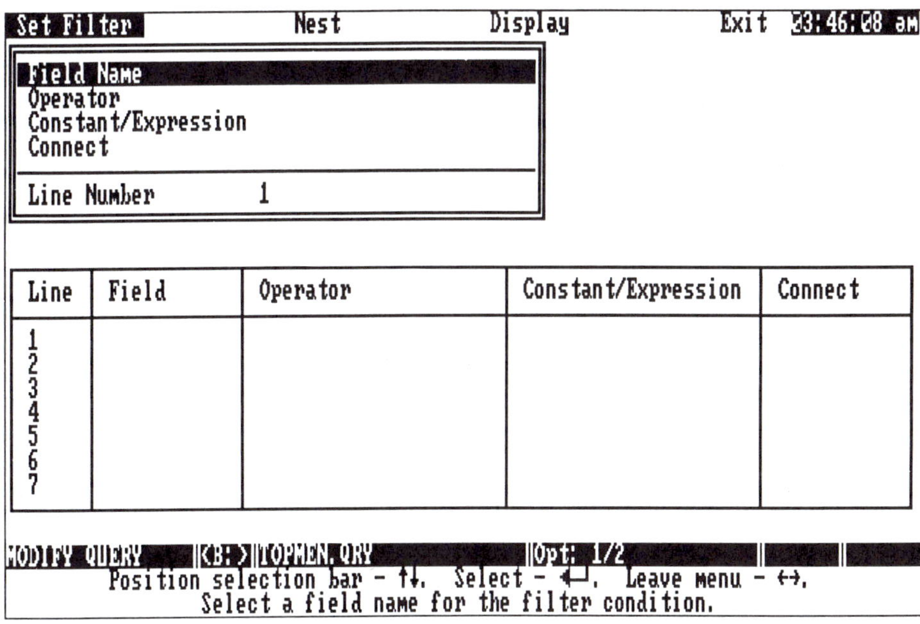

The Set Filter option of the menu bar is used to select fields, relational operators, expressions, and logical operators to form the filter condition. Each item and operator of the condition are selected from a menu.

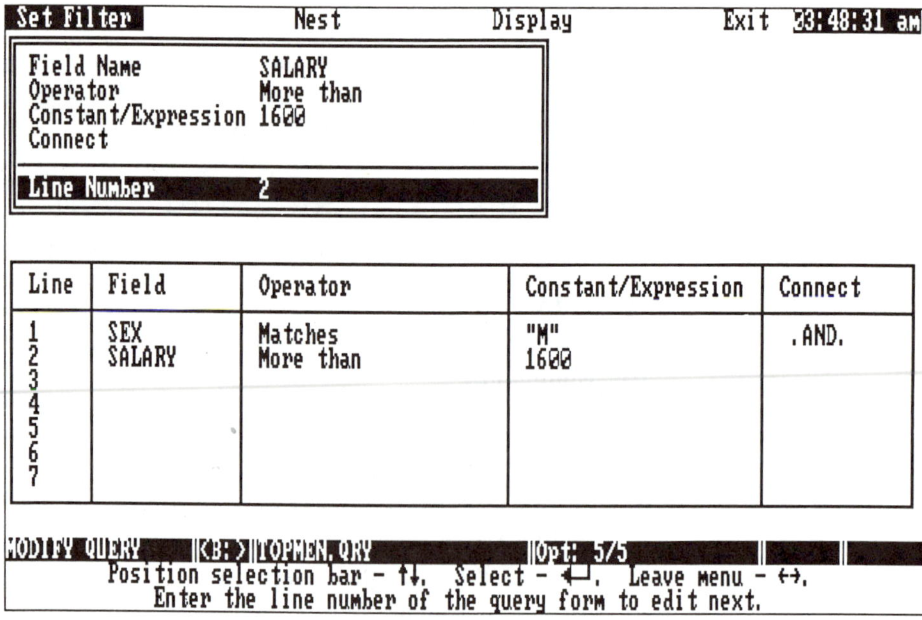

When finished, the condition(s) specified are described on lines one through seven.

The next option of the menu bar, Nest, is used to add parentheses to a total condition composed of more than two conditions connected with logical operators. Here the positions for parentheses are entered as starting or stopping on a condition, with the start or stop position entered as the condition number by the order it appears in the total condition (1st, 2nd, 3rd, etc.).

The Display option of the **MODIFY QUERY** menu bar displays the records of the current database that pass the condition filter currently defined. The Exit option is used to save the .QRY file and return to the dot (.) prompt mode.

Once a .QRY file has been created, the **SET FILTER TO FILE** <filename> is used to activate the filter condition(s) in it. While the filter is active, only those records passing it will be processed by dBase. To deactivate a filter, the **SET FILTER TO** command is used.

MODIFY SCREEN <filename>

The **MODIFY SCREEN** command serves as a dBase III program generator. The programs it generates are .FMT files created from screen (.SCR) files. .FMT files are composed of @ **SAY** and @ **GET** commands—commands used to format screens for data input and output.

MODIFY SCREEN uses a full-screen, menu-driven mode for data entry and provides a blank screen (called the *blackboard*) on which the input/output screen is created by the user. The menus and blackboard are mutually-exclusive data entry modes, toggled between by typing the F10 key.

The **MODIFY SCREEN** menu bar provides a Set Up option for selecting the fields of data to be displayed on the finished screen. First, a database is selected from a menu of available databases (or created if necessary), and then the fields to be included in the screen are selected from a menu generated by the Load Fields menu command.

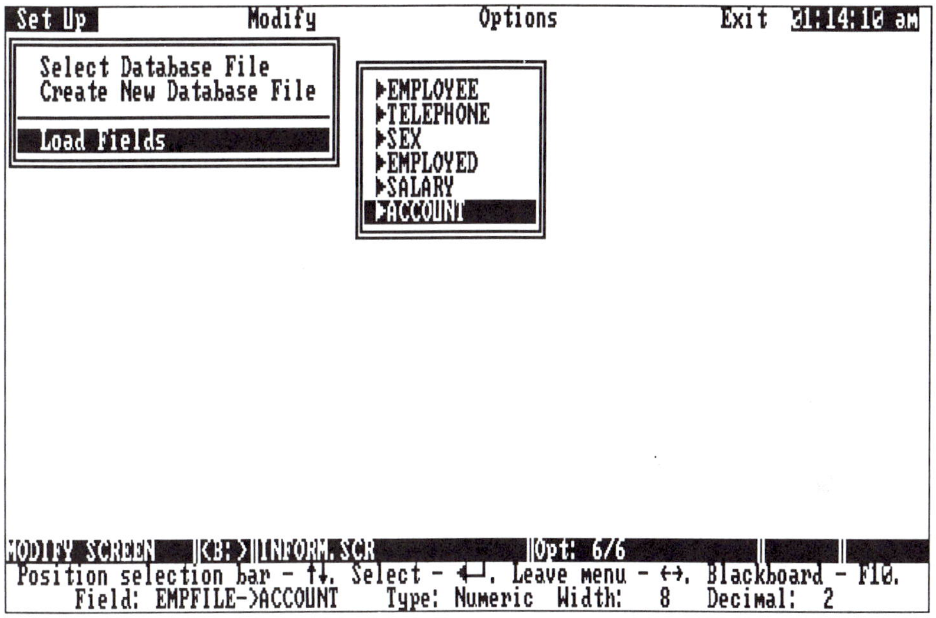

The selected fields are placed on the blackboard, displayed in reverse video next to their field names. The user then is left in the blackboard mode.

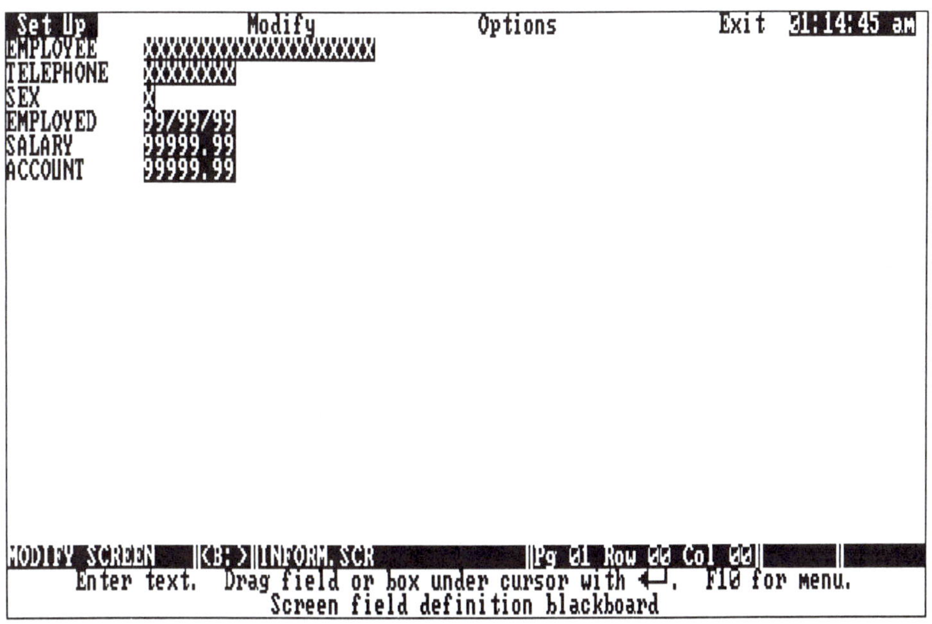

While in the blackboard mode, editing keystrokes similar to those of **MODIFY COMMAND** allow the user to enter screen text. To relocate a field currently displayed on the blackboard, the user moves the cursor to the first character of the field, presses the Enter key, moves the cursor to the new position, and presses the Enter key again.

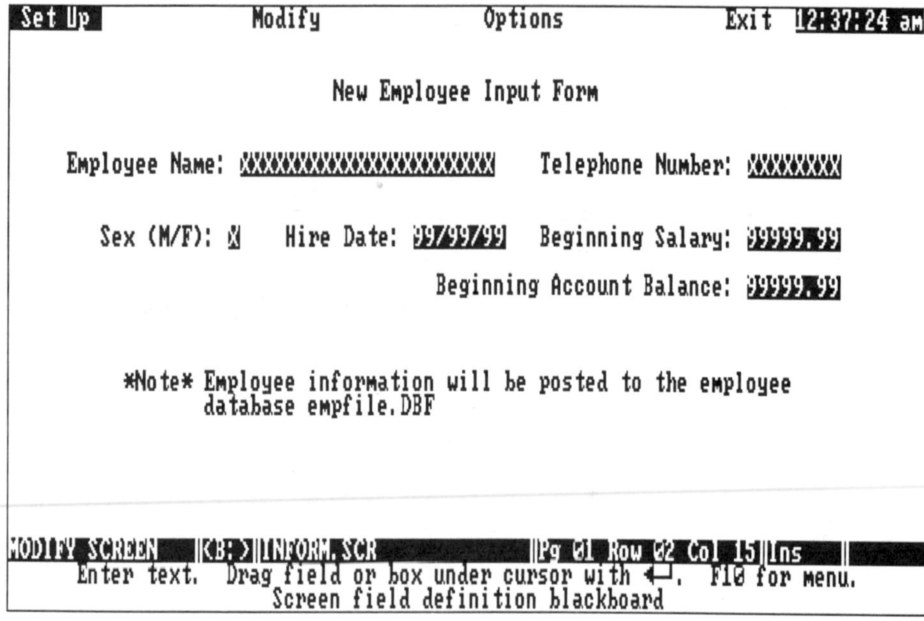

The Modify option of the menu bar is used to determine if a field will be placed on the screen with an @ **SAY** or an @ **GET** command. All fields initially placed on the blackboard are placed there as @ **GET**s. Modify also allows **PICTURE** clauses to be established for the field, as well as permits field contents, type, width, and decimals to be altered. To modify a field, the user moves the cursor to the first character of the field while in the blackboard mode, and then toggles to the menu mode by typing F10 and selects the Modify option of the menu bar.

The Options menu bar option may be used to draw a line or a box with single or double bars on the blackboard screen. To draw a line or box, the user toggles to the menu mode, selects Options, and selects single or double bars. Then the user toggles to the blackboard mode, moves the cursor to one corner of the area to be boxed or lined, presses the Enter key, moves the cursor to the opposite diagonal corner of the area to be boxed or lined, and types the Enter key again.

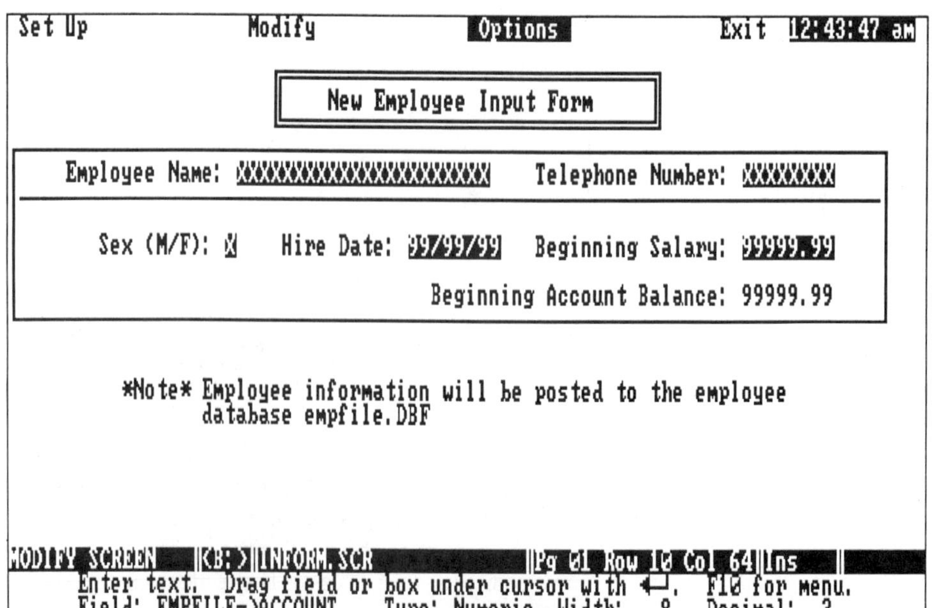

When the blackboard is finished, the Exit option of the menu bar is used to save the .SCR file and generate the .FMT file from it. Both files have the same filename. Later if the .SCR file is altered with **MODIFY SCREEN,** a new .FMT file is produced when the Exit operation is completed. The following is a listing of the .FMT file created in this example:

```
@  2, 28  SAY "New Employee Input Form"
@  5,  5  SAY "Employee Name:"
@  5, 20  GET  EMPFILE->EMPLOYEE
@  5, 46  SAY "Telephone Number:"
@  5, 64  GET  EMPFILE->TELEPHONE
@  8,  8  SAY "Sex (M/F):"
@  8, 19  GET  EMPFILE->SEX
@  8, 24  SAY "Hire Date:"
@  8, 35  GET  EMPFILE->EMPLOYED
@  8, 46  SAY "Beginning Salary:"
@  8, 64  GET  EMPFILE->SALARY
@ 10, 37  SAY "Beginning Account Balance:"
@ 10, 64  SAY  EMPFILE->ACCOUNT
@ 14, 10  SAY "*Note* Employee information will be posted to the employee"
@ 15, 17  SAY "database empfile.DBF"
@  1, 23  TO  3, 56    DOUBLE
@  6,  0  TO  6, 76
@  4,  0  TO 11, 76
```

A format (.FMT) file is activated with the **SET FORMAT TO** <filename> command. Once activated, it affects the screen displays for the **APPEND, CHANGE, EDIT, INSERT** and **READ** commands. For instance, to add a new employee to the database "empfile. DBF" using the screen display created in the example, you could type the following:

```
USE empfile
SET FORMAT TO inform
APPEND
```

The **APPEND** mode screen would appear as:

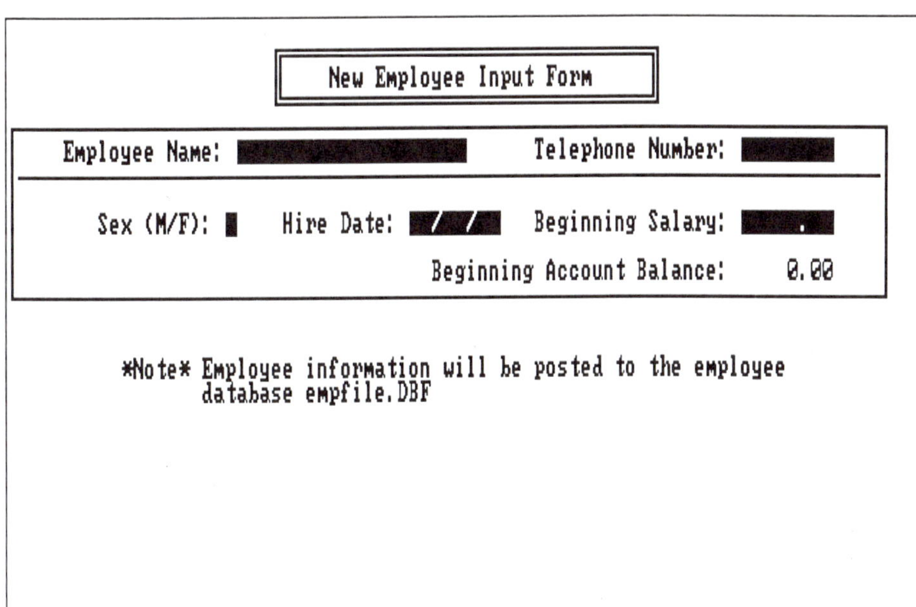

MODIFY VIEW <filename>

The **MODIFY VIEW** command uses a full-screen, menu-driven mode for data entry. The resulting file contains a listing of the databases; their active indexes; the work areas in which the databases are located; any relations between the databases that may exist (see **SET RELATION TO**); and the active field list, .FMT file, and/or filter (if any) for each database in use.

Once a view file has been created, it may be used to reinstate the environment recorded within it through the **SET VIEW TO** <filename> command.

ON <event type> [<command>]

Used in command files, the **ON** command is an event-trapping command. <event type>s are **ERROR** (a dBase error is generated); **ESCAPE** (the user has typed the Esc key); or **KEY** (any key is typed). **ON** is used to branch program execution when the specified event occurs. It activates a type of global condition that causes dBase to return to the **ON** command's <command> parameter and execute it if the specified event occurs. To turn off the global condition, the **ON** <event type> command is used with no <command> parameter specified.

RELEASE MODULE

Releases a binary file placed in memory with the **LOAD** command.

RESUME

Resumes program execution after it has been interrupted with the **SUSPEND** command.

RETRY

Similar to the **RETURN** command, **RETRY** returns control to the calling line (rather than the next line) of a calling program. It is most useful when used for error recovery within a program or procedure to return control to an **ON** <event type> [<command>] command.

SET CATALOG ON/off

OFF may be used to suspend updating of the current .CAT file for dBase files being opened or created. ON resumes updating of the .CAT file.

SET CATALOG TO [<filename>]

SET CATALOG TO <filename> may be used to create or open an existing .CAT file. To close the current .CAT file **SET CATALOG TO** with no <filename> is used. (See .CAT Catalog files page D–100.)

SET CENTURY on/OFF

ON causes the display of date-type data to show all four characters for the year.

SET COLOR ON/off

SET COLOR ON/off is used to switch between color and monochrome displays for systems having both.

SET DATE [AMERICAN/ANSI/BRITISH/ITALIAN/FRENCH/GERMAN]

SET DATE is used to alter the format display for date-type data. The display is normally set to **AMERICAN.** For purposes of data transfer the **ANSI** (American National Standards Institute) display format is quite useful. With this format it becomes possible to convert dBase III date-type data into character-type data (using the DTOC function), and then transfer the data with an order of characters more usable to other software. The various formats for date-type data display are:

AMERICAN	mm/dd/yy	**ITALIAN**	dd-mm-yy
ANSI	yy.mm.dd	**FRENCH**	dd/mm/yy
BRITISH	dd/mm/yy	**GERMAN**	dd.mm.yy

SET DOHISTORY on/OFF

ON causes commands executed from within a command (.PRG) file to be stored in the HISTORY buffer.

SET FIELDS on/OFF

ON activates the field filter created by a **SET FIELDS TO** <field list> command. OFF deactivates the field filter.

SET FIELDS TO [<field list>/**ALL**]

SET FIELDS TO <field list> is used to create a field filter. A field filter prevents many dBase commands from processing fields not listed in the <field list>. The **[ALL]** parameter may be used to include all fields of the current database in the field list. **SET FIELDS TO** with no parameters removes all fields from the field list. The field filter may be turned on and off with the **SET FIELD** on/OFF command. Several precautionary notes are listed in the dBase III Plus manual about this command.

SET FILTER TO FILE <filename>

Opens and activates the specified query (.QRY) file. (See **MODIFY QUERY** page D–105.)

SET HISTORY TO <n>

Sets the number of commands held in the HISTORY buffer to <n>. Default is 20 commands. If <n> is smaller than the current number of commands, all commands in the buffer are erased.

SET MEMOWIDTH TO <n>

Adjusts the output width of memo field data to <n> characters. The default memo output width is 50 characters.

SET MESSAGE TO [<character string>]

Causes the specified <character string> to be displayed at the bottom line of the monitor screen. **SET MESSAGE TO** with no parameter removes the display of user-defined messages.

SET ORDER TO [<n>]

Establishes the controlling index file from the <index file list> of the **USE** <filename> **INDEX** <index file list> command. The <n>th index file in the <index file list> becomes the controlling index when **SET ORDER TO** <n> is executed. If <n> is specified as 0, or **SET ORDER TO** with no <n> is used, the database is processed as being unindexed. **SET ORDER TO** does not close active index files.

SET STATUS ON/off

Toggles ON/off the status bar displayed on line 22 of the monitor screen.

SET TITLE ON/off

Toggles ON/off the catalog file title prompt.

SET TYPEAHEAD TO <n>

Sets the number of characters held in the keyboard buffer. Normally 20 characters are held.

SET VIEW TO <filename>

Opens a view (.VUE) file and reinstates the environment specified in it.

SUSPEND

Used in command (.PRG) files, **SUSPEND** is a debugging command used to temporarily halt the execution of a dBase program. **RESUME** may be used to continue program execution.

New dBase III Plus Functions

ABS(<numeric data>)

Absolute Value Function The ABS function returns the absolute value of its argument and may be used to find the difference between two numbers without determining first which number is larger.

```
. ? ABS(45 - 55)
 10
```

DBF( )

Database Function Returns the name of the current database.

```
. ? DBF()
B:empfile.dbf
```

DISKSPACE( )

Disk Space Function Returns the number of bytes (characters) of available disk space on the current drive.

```
. ? DISKSPACE()
    279552
```

ERROR( )

Error Number Function Returns the dBase III Plus error number corresponding to the error trapped with an **ON ERROR** command.

FIELD(<n>)

Field Name Function Returns the field name for the <n>th field of the record structure for the current database.

```
. ? FIELD(4)
EMPLOYED
```

FKLABEL(<n>) and **FKMAX**( )

Function Key Label and Function Key Maximum Functions Return the labels and maximum number of programmable keys of the current system, respectively.

FOUND( )

Found Function Returns a logical .T.rue if the previous search operation, **FIND, SEEK, LOCATE,** or **CONTINUE,** was successful.

GETNV(<"operating system variable">)

Get Environmental Variable Function Returns the contents of the specified operating system variable as a string.

IIF(<condition>,<true expression>,<false expression>)

Immediate IF Function Returns its <true expression> or its <false expression> based on the evaluation of its <condition>. Most useful for including conditional field output in dBase III Plus **REPORT**s and **LABEL**s, the **IIF** function performs the same type of operation as an **IF ELSE ENDIF** structure. With the **IIF** function, the <true expression> and <false expression> may be character-, numeric-, or date-type data. However, both expressions must be of the same data type.

You may nest **IIF** functions to create extended conditional tests. An example might be:

IFF(<condition>,<true exp.>,**IIF**(<condition>,<true exp.>,<false exp.>))

Here, the <false exp.> of the first IIF function is another IIF function. This form of nested function works in the same manner as the following **IF** structure:

```
IF condition
  true expression
ELSE
  IF condition
    true expression
  ELSE
    false expression
  ENDIF
ENDIF
```

In the next example the database empfile.DBF is used. The **IIF** function is one that could be included in a REPORT column to produce the following results: if the account amount is less than 12 percent of salary, output nothing; if the account amount is between 12 percent and 15 percent, output "Near Limit"; if the account amount is over 15 percent of salary, output "Over Limit by " x amount. Notice the **STR** function is used to convert the second **IIF** function's false expression into the same data type as all other expressions used.

IIF(account<.12*salary," ",**IIF**(account> = .12*salary**.AND.**account<.15*salary, "Near Limit","Over Limit by " + **STR**(account – .15*salary,5,2)))

INKEY( )

Inkey Function Returns an integer (the ASCII value) representing the last key typed by a user. This function is used in command files to trap user keystrokes and branch program execution accordingly.

ISALPHA(<character data>)

Is Alphabetic Function Returns a logical .T.rue if the character data begins with any upper- or lower-case letter A through Z.

ISCOLOR( )

Is Color Mode Function Returns a logical .T.rue if dBase is running in a color mode.

ISLOWER(<character data>)

Is Lower-Case Function Returns a logical .T.rue if the first character in the <character data> is lower case.

ISUPPER(<character data>)

Is Upper-Case Function Returns a logical .T.rue if the first character in the <character data> is upper case.

LEFT(<character data>,<n>)

Left Substring Function Returns the left-most <n> number of characters from its <character data>.

```
. ? LEFT("This is a test",4)
This
```

LTRIM(<character data>)

Left Trim Function Removes leading spaces from its <character data>.

LUPDATE( )

Last Update Function Returns the system date recorded for the last time the current database was updated.

MAX(<numeric data1>, <numeric data2>)

Maximum Function Returns the higher value, numeric data1 or numeric data2.

MESSAGE( )

Error Message Function Returns the error message as character data.

```
. ON ERROR STORE MESSAGE() TO z
. sdsad
*** Unrecognized command verb.
. ? z
*** Unrecognized command verb.
```

MIN(<numeric data1>, <numeric data2>)

Minimum Function Returns the lower value, numeric data1 or numeric data2.

MOD(<numeric data1>, <numeric data2>)

Modulus Function Returns the remainder resulting from dividing numeric data1 by numeric data2.

NDX(<n>)

Index File Function Returns the name of the <n>th active index file in the current work area.

OS( )

Operating System Function Returns the name of the current operating system.

READKEY( )

Read Key Function Returns an integer (the ASCII value) for the last keystroke typed while in a full screen editing mode.

RECCOUNT( )

Record Count Function Returns the number of records in the current database.

RECSIZE( )

Record Size Function Returns the record size for the records in the current database.

REPLICATE(<character data>, <n>)

Replicate Function Returns its character data <n> number of times.

```
. ? REPLICATE("<>",25)
<><><><><><><><><><><><><><><><><><><><><><><><><>
```

RIGHT(<character data>, <n>)

Right Substring Function Returns the right-most <n> number of characters from its <character data>.

```
. ? RIGHT("This is a test",4)
test
```

RTRIM(<character data>)

Right Trim Function Removes trailing spaces from its <character data>, the same as the **TRIM** function.

STUFF(<character data1>, <start position n>, <replace length n>, <character data2>)

Substring Replace Function Replaces or inserts its <character data2) into its <character data1>, starting at the location in <character data1> equal to <start position n> after removing the number of characters equal to <replace length n> from <character data1>.

```
. ? STUFF("This is a test",9,0,"ANOTHER ")
This is ANOTHER a test
. ? STUFF("This is ANOTHER test",9,7,"NOT a")
This is NOT a test
```

TRANSFORM(<expression>,<**PICTURE** format string>)

Transform Function Establishes a display format for data.

VERSION( )

Version Function Returns the version of dBase III currently in use.

An Overview of Command Files

In the dBase tutorial you used a number of dBase commands to manipulate the data in the database empfile.DBF. You displayed records, replaced data in fields, used memory variables to store totals, created report forms, and more. dBase executed all of the commands immediately after you entered them.

The direct mode of entering commands can be quite useful for extracting needed information or performing various operations quickly. However, as the commands to perform an operation become longer and more complex, or when certain commands or sets of commands are used repeatedly, typing and entering each command becomes a cumbersome way to accomplish tasks. At such times you may want to consider saving the command(s) in a command file.

A command file is similar to a program written in BASIC or other programming language. It contains dBase commands which dBase will execute, one after another. All of the commands you have used may be included in a command file, and several dBase commands and command structures are normally used only in command files.

Creating a dBase III Command File

Command files are created in the Modify editing mode. To enter the Modify mode from the dot (.) prompt mode you use the **MODIFY COMMAND** command whose form is:

MODIFY COMMAND <filename>

Command files that you create in this editing mode are stored on your diskette under a filename that you supply. dBase adds a .PRG file extension to the name to identify it as a dBase program.

When you type the **MODIFY COMMAND** command, dBase first looks to the default drive for a .PRG file with the same <filename> you specified. If one does not exist, it allocates space on the diskette for a new file under the name specified. If it does find a .PRG file with the specified name, it copies the file into RAM memory for you to edit.

Entering dBase Commands into a Command File

When a new .PRG file is specified in the **MODIFY COMMAND** command, a blank screen is presented to the user. Each command in the command file is typed on a single line and the Enter key is used to advance forward (down the screen) to enter the next command. Since you are in an editing mode, dBase will not execute the commands when you enter them.

Previous lines may be edited using keystroke commands similar to the keystroke commands used in dBase's other editing modes (**EDIT** or **BROWSE,** for example.)

Saving a Command File

As with all of dBase's editing modes the keystroke command ^End is used to save the .PRG file onto the diskette and return you to the dot (.) prompt mode.

Executing the Commands in a Command File

dBase will open the command file and begin to execute the commands in it when the **DO** command is typed from the dot (.) prompt mode. The **DO** command has the basic form:

DO <filename>

When the **DO** command is entered, commands in the specified file will be executed in the order that they appear, top to bottom, until the last command is completed. dBase then will return to the dot (.) prompt mode.

The Steps for Creating a Command File

In summary, the basic steps in creating a command file are:

1. Type {**MODIFY COMMAND** <filename>} to begin editing.
2. Type each command on a separate line.
3. Type {^End} to save the file.
4. Type {**DO** <filename>} to execute the commands in the file.

Correcting the Commands in a Command File

If you have made mistakes, you may easily edit your command file by repeating steps 1 through 3 above and using the editing keystroke commands while in the editing mode to make the necessary changes.

MODIFY COMMAND Editing Keystroke Commands

Keystroke	Action
Cursor-right key	Moves cursor right one character.
Cursor-left key	Moves cursor left one character.
Home key	Moves cursor one word to the left.
End key	Moves cursor one word to the right.
Cursor-down key	Moves cursor to the next line.
Cursor-up key	Moves cursor to the previous line.
PgUp key	Scrolls the screen up 17 lines.
PgDn key	Scrolls the screen down 17 lines.
Ins key	Toggles between overwrite and **INSERT** modes.
↵ (Enter key)	Terminates current line. With **INSERT** on, inserts a line below the current line.
Del key	Deletes character over cursor.
← (Backspace key)	Deletes character to left of cursor.
^T	Erases word to right of cursor.
^Y	Erases current line.
^KR	Reads and inserts another file into the current file.
^End	Saves changes and returns to dot (.) prompt.
Esc key	Aborts all changes made and returns to dot (.) prompt.

dBase III Example Command Files

The following discussion will provide a general idea of how command files may be used in conjunction with databases. It will introduce you to some of the most often used programming commands and structures through a set of example programs.

Databases and Other Files Used

The first six sample programs are written to be used with the database empfile.DBF created in the dBase tutorial. Here is the structure of empfile.DBF and a listing of its records:

```
Structure for database : B:empfile.dbf
Number of data records :        9
Date of last update    : 01/01/86
Field  Field name   Type        Width    Dec
    1  EMPLOYEE     Character      20
    2  TELEPHONE    Character       8
    3  SEX          Character       1
    4  EMPLOYED     Date            8
    5  SALARY       Numeric         8      2
    6  ACCOUNT      Numeric         8      2
** Total **                        54
```

Record#	EMPLOYEE	TELEPHONE	SEX	EMPLOYED	SALARY	ACCOUNT
1	Pratt John	225-1234	M	06/22/82	1949.00	200.00
2	Smoler Ellen	225-3212	F	08/15/83	1650.00	300.00
3	Jones David	292-3832	M	06/15/82	1550.00	275.75
4	Sill Sally	224-4321	F	02/15/84	1507.50	150.00
5	Knat Michael	221-1235	M	09/15/80	1800.00	125.00
6	Smith Paul	244-1010	M	11/15/81	1700.00	350.00
7	Martins Mary	222-2123	F	11/01/85	1600.00	200.50
8	Nichols Sandy	229-1111	F	02/15/86	1450.00	175.00
9	Johnson Frank	223-7928	M	03/20/86	1500.00	0.00

One sample program, program #6 raises.PRG, requires that another database be created and have data appended into it from empfile.DBF. The steps for creating this second database are:

1. Type {**CREATE** history↵}.
2. Enter the structure as shown:

```
B:history.dbf                                        Bytes remaining:   3964
                                                     Fields defined:       3

     field name  type       width  dec          field name  type       width  dec
     ==============================            ==============================
  1  EMPLOYEE    Char/text    20
  2  DATEINCR    Date          8
  3  SALARY      Numeric       8    2
```

3. Type {**USE** history↵}.
4. Type {**APPEND FROM** empfile↵}.
5. Type {**REPLACE ALL** dateincr **WITH** CTOD("01/01/80")↵}.
6. Type {**DISPLAY ALL**↵}.

For a more complete explanation see **APPEND,** dBase III Operation and Command Summary (page D–74.)

The database history.DBF should appear as:

Record#	EMPLOYEE	DATEINCR	SALARY
1	Pratt John	01/01/80	1949.00
2	Smoler Ellen	01/01/80	1650.00
3	Jones David	01/01/80	1550.00
4	Sill Sally	01/01/80	1507.50
5	Knat Michael	01/01/80	1800.00
6	Smith Paul	01/01/80	1700.00
7	Martins Mary	01/01/80	1600.00
8	Nichols Sandy	01/01/80	1450.00
9	Johnson Frank	01/01/80	1500.00

Other files referred to and used in the sample programs also are products of completing the dBase tutorial. They include:

acctrepo.FRM
empdex.NDX
fullrepo.FRM
salaries.FRM

Sample Program Formats

Each sample program is presented in five parts:

1. A *program description* of the task that the program is designed to perform.
2. A listing with summary explanations of the *new commands* used in the particular program.
3. A *program listing* of the command file.
4. Any *preliminary commands* required to execute the program successfully.
5. A *sample execution* showing what the output of that program may be.

The description prefacing each program includes an algorithm for the program. An algorithm is a step-by-step outline of the program's operation. Each step is described in words close to those used in everyday communication.

Sample Program #1—payment.PRG

Program Description

The first sample program is designed to let the user post payment to an employee's personal account. The intended database in use is empfile.DBF.

The general algorithm for the program is:

1. Present the user with the employee's name for the current record.
2. Ask the user for the amount of payment.
3. Replace the current record's "account" field with what is there minus the payment.
4. Prompt the user to indicate when he/she is done.

New Commands Used

* <comment> dBase considers anything following an asterisk (*) on a line a comment and will ignore it. Comments must be placed on lines separate from other commands. See **NOTE,** dBase III Command Summary, page D–83.

CLEAR The **CLEAR** command clears the screen at any point in a command file.

? <field>,"<literal>",<memvar> The **?** command displays "the value of" current fields, memory variables, and/or constants on the monitor screen. If more than one item follows the **?** command, the items must be separated by commas.

? "<literal>" + <field> The + sign may be used to combine data items when the data are character type.

INPUT <string prompt> **TO** <memvar> **INPUT** pauses execution of the program after it displays its <string prompt>. The user is then allowed to type and enter a response to the prompt. The response is held in the <memvar>. The **INPUT** command must be used for numeric-type data responses.

ACCEPT <string prompt> **TO** <memvar> **ACCEPT** is the counterpart of **INPUT.** It is used for character string-type data. The response will be held in the <memvar> as character string data.

REPLACE <field> **WITH** <expression> Replaces the contents of the specified <field> with the value of the <expression>.

RETURN Signals the end of the command file and returns control to the dot (.) prompt or program from which the program was called.

Program Listing

```
*  PROGRAM:  Payment.PRG  -  to post payment to employee's account

CLEAR

?
? "        *  *  *  Payment to Employee Account  *  *  *  "
?
? "             Employee:  " + employee
? "             Acct Bal = ",account
?

INPUT "            Enter amount of payment  " TO pmt
REPLACE account WITH account - pmt

?
?
? "             New Balance = ",account
?
ACCEPT "When finished viewing screen, press return key " TO dummy
CLEAR
RETURN
```

Preliminary Commands

```
USE empfile
SET TALK OFF
LOCATE FOR employee = "Jones"
DO payment
```

Sample Execution

```
  *   *   *  Payment to Employee Account  *   *   *

        Employee:  Jones David
        Acct Bal =    275.75

        Enter amount of payment  125.00


        New Balance =    150.75

        When finished viewing screen, press return key
```

Sample Program #2—purchase.PRG

Program Description

The second sample program lets the user post a purchase to an employee's personal account. The intended database in use is empfile.DBF.

The second program differs from the first in that it includes **IF ELSE ENDIF** structures to check certain conditions before it posts any changes to the database. The general algorithm is:

1. Present the user with the employee's name and account balance for the current record.
2. Ask the user for the amount of purchase.
3. If the purchase plus the balance on the account is more than 15 percent of that employee's salary
   - **A.** Ask the user if the purchase is authorized.

   Otherwise,
   - **B.** Replace the current record's field "account" with what is there plus the purchase amount.

   End if.
4. If the user answered "Yes" to the purchase authorized question,
   - **A.** Replace the current record's field "account" with what is there plus the purchase amount.

   Otherwise,
   - **B.** Inform the user that the purchase is over limit and will not be posted to the account.

   End if.
5. Prompt the user to indicate when he/she is done.

New Commands Used

IF <condition>
(any statements)
ELSE
(any statements)
ENDIF

The <condition> is made up of items and operators whose .T.rue or .F.alse value can be determined. If the <condition> evaluates .T.rue, the commands following the **IF** command up to the **ELSE** (or **ENDIF** if no **ELSE** command is included) will be executed. If the <condition> evaluates .F.alse, the commands following the **ENDIF** command (or **ELSE** command if included) will be executed. Every **IF** command must have a corresponding **ENDIF** command to signal the end of that command structure. The **ELSE** portion of the structure and the commands following it are optional.

STORE <expression> **TO** <memvar> Places the value of the <expression> into a memory variable <memvar>. The <memvar> will be either of character-, numeric-, or date-type depending on what is stored to it.

UPPER (<character data>) The **UPPER** (<character data>) function returns the upper-case equivalent of its character string argument. It is often useful for comparisons of character strings input by a user.

Program Listing

```
*  PROGRAM:  purchase.PRG  - to post employee purchases to database
CLEAR
?
?
? "           *  *  *  Employee Purchase on Account  *  *  * "
?
? "             Employee:  " + employee
? "             Acct Bal =  ",account
?
INPUT "             Enter Amount of Desired Purchase  " TO amt
IF account + amt > salary * .15
  ?
  ?  "Employee's account will exceed 15% of salary with this purchase"
  ?  "OK from Credit Manager required "
  ?
  ACCEPT "   OK received  (y/n) ?  " TO ok
ELSE
  REPLACE account WITH account + amt
ENDIF
IF UPPER(ok) = "Y"
  REPLACE account WITH account + amt
  ?
  ? "             New Balance = ",account
ELSE
  ? " Approval Denied  -  Purchase not Posted  "
ENDIF
```

```
?
?
ACCEPT "When finished viewing screen, press return  " TO dummy
CLEAR
RETURN
```

Preliminary Commands

```
USE empfile
SET TALK OFF
GOTO 6
DO purchase
```

Sample Execution

```
         *  *  *  Employee Purchase on Account  *  *  *

           Employee:  Smith Paul
           Acct Bal =     350.00

           Enter Amount of Desired Purchase 700

Employee's account will exceed 15% of salary with this purchase
OK from Credit Manager required

   OK received  (y/n) ? y

             New Balance =   1050.00

When finished viewing screen, press return
```

Sample Program #3—transact.PRG

Program Description

Sample program #3 is known as a calling program. It is designed to allow the user to access either program #1 "payment.PRG" or program #2 "purchase.PRG" through its execution. A graphic representation of the relationship might be:

```
                      payment.PRG
transact.PRG  —<
                      purchase.PRG
```

Within transact.PRG the user is asked if the transaction to be posted is a payment or a purchase. Depending on the response, the command **DO** payment is executed or **DO** purchase is executed. When either **DO** command is executed, dBase starts executing the command file specified in it. When dBase is finished with the called command file, it returns to executing transact.PRG where it left off. Sample program #3 also introduces the idea of initializing, in which the preliminary commands necessary with the first two programs become part of this calling program.

Finally, transact.PRG incorporates a loop in which the posting of amounts to accounts is repeated until the user chooses to quit.

The general algorithm for program #3 "transact.PRG" is:

1. Initialize by setting **TALK OFF** and selecting empfile.DBF for use.
2. Present the user with documentation of the program.
3. Set a <memvar> flag as true.
4. Continue executing the following loop instructions until the flag is no longer true.
    - **A.** Present the user with the data in the database.
    - **B.** Ask the user for the name of the employee of concern.
    - **C.** Move the record pointer to that employee's record.
    - **D.** If the end of file is encountered (the name cannot be found),
        - **a.** Ask the user if a retry is desired.

      Otherwise (if the end of file is not encountered),
        - **b.** Clear the screen and present a menu, choice 1 = Post purchases, choice 2 = Post payments.
        - **c.** If user answers choice 1,
            - **c1.** Execute purchase.PRG.

          Otherwise,
            - **c2.** If user answers choice 2,
                - **c2a.** Execute payment.PRG.

              End if.

          End if.
        - **d.** Ask the user if more transactions are desired.

      End if.
    - **E.** If user answered "no" either to "Retry" or "More transactions,"
        - **a.** Change the <memvar> flag to no longer true.

      End if.
5. End of the loop instructions.

New Commands Used

SET TALK OFF One of several **SET** commands that allows you to set dBase features on or off. You will want to place this command at the beginning of your program to prevent dBase's "talk" from cluttering up the screen.

USE <file> Most programs will use a specific database. Placing the appropriate **USE** command at the beginning of your command file ensures that the proper database is in use.

TEXT
<any data>
ENDTEXT

This command structure allows you to print several lines of text without having to use a **?** command on each line.

DO WHILE <condition>
(any commands)
ENDDO

This structure is used for creating loops. As long as the <condition> evaluates .T.rue, the commands between the **DO WHILE** and **ENDDO** will be done repeatedly, with the condition checked at the beginning of each iteration.

To end the execution of the loop, one or more items used in the <condition> must change to make the <condition> .F.alse. When this occurs, the next time the **DO WHILE** evaluates its <condition> it resumes execution of the program at the command following the loop's **ENDDO** command.

GO TOP **GO TOP** restores the record pointer to the top of your database, and may be used liberally to ensure that all records will be processed by commands.

LOCATE FOR <condition> The **LOCATE** command moves the record pointer to the first or next record which satisfies the condition of the **FOR** <condition>.

EOF( ) End-of-file (EOF) is a dBase function whose returned value is .F.alse until an attempt is made to move the record pointer past the bottom of the database. Its returned value then becomes .T.rue until the record pointer is moved up.

TRIM <character data> The **TRIM** function removes trailing blank spaces from the character data of its argument.

DO <file> **DO** may be used to call another program from the current program. When a **RETURN** is encountered in the called program, the calling program resumes execution at the command following the **DO** <file> command.

Program Listing

```
*  PROGRAM:  transact.PRG  - calling program for purchase and payment programs
SET TALK OFF
USE empfile
CLEAR
TEXT
   This program is for updating employees' personal accounts.  After
   entering the employee's name, you will be able to process either
   purchases on account or payments made to the account.

   Following is a list of employees in the database:
ENDTEXT

STORE 1 TO more
DO WHILE more = 1
   ?
   DISPLAY ALL employee OFF
   ?
   ACCEPT "Enter Name of Employee  " TO name
   GO TOP
   LOCATE FOR UPPER(employee) = UPPER(name)
   IF EOF()
      ?
      ? "No employee " + TRIM(name) + " found. "
      ?
      ACCEPT "   Retry (y/n) ?  " TO ans
   ELSE
      CLEAR
      ?
      ? "                          Transactions Menu "
      ?
      ? "                          1 - Post Purchases "
      ? "                          2 - Post Payments  "
      ?
      ACCEPT "                            select  1 or 2  " TO choice
      IF choice = "1"
         DO purchase
      ELSE
         IF choice = "2"
            DO payment
         ENDIF
      ENDIF
      ?
      ?
      ACCEPT "    More transactions to process  (y/n)  ? " TO ans
   ENDIF
   IF UPPER(ans) = "N"
      STORE 0 TO more
   ENDIF
ENDDO
RETURN
```

Preliminary Commands

```
DO transact
```

Sample Execution

```
   This program is for updating employees' personal accounts.  After
   entering the employee's name, you will be able to process either
   purchases on account or payments made to the account.

   Following is a list of employees in the database:

 employee
 Pratt John
 Smoler Ellen
 Jones David
 Sill Sally
 Knat Michael
 Smith Paul
 Martins Mary
 Nichols Sandy
 Johnson Frank

Enter Name of Employee  Johnson

                           Transactions Menu

                           1 - Post Purchases
                           2 - Post Payments

                             select  1 or 2  1



          *  *  *  Employee Purchase on Account  *  *  *

             Employee:  Johnson Frank
             Acct Bal =       0.00

             Enter Amount of Desired Purchase  800.00


Employee's account will exceed 15% of salary with this purchase
OK from Credit Manager required

   OK received  (y/n) ?  n

 Approval Denied  -  Purchase not Posted

When finished viewing screen, press return

                                 <<new screen>>

     More transactions to process  (y/n)  ? n
```

Sample Programs #4 and #5—reports1.PRG and reports2.PRG

Program Description

The next two sample programs also are connected to each other. Program #4, reports1.PRG, is the calling program, and program #5, reports2.PRG, is the program being called. Their relationship might be graphically depicted as:

reports1.PRG ——— reports2.PRG

Sample program #4, reports1.PRG, allows the user to select the way in which a report will be displayed or output, and to select the report to be produced. It then conditionally initializes the appropriate output devices and calls reports2.PRG to produce the desired report. Both programs use the **DO CASE** structure, which is similar to the **IF ELSE** structure.

The general algorithm for sample program #4, reports1.PRG, is:

1. Initialize by setting **TALK OFF** and selecting empfile.DBF with its index file empdex.NDX as the database for use.
2. Present the user with a menu numbered 1 through 3 with the options: 1) displayed on screen, 2) sent to printer, 3) written to a file.
3. Instruct the user to enter his/her answer.
4. Clear the screen and present to the user a second menu numbered 1 through 4 with the options: 1) Salary Summary Report, 2) Salaries & Accounts by Gender, 3) Employee Full Report, 4) All of the above.
5. Instruct the user to enter his/her answer.
6. Determine the Case.
   - **A.** Case: if the user answered, "sent to printer,"
     - **a.** initialize the printer,
     - **b.** Do reports2.PRG,
     - **c.** un-initialize the printer.
   - **B.** Case: If the user answered "written to a file,"
     - **a.** initialize a .TXT file,
     - **b.** Do reports2.PRG,
     - **c.** un-initialize the file.
   - **C.** Otherwise,
     - **a.** Do reports2.PRG. The output automatically will be sent to the screen.

   End Case.

The general algorithm for sample program #5, reports2.PRG, is:

1. Determine the Case.
   - A. Case: If the user selected "Salary Summary Report,"
     - a. produce the report using the salaries.FRM file.
   - B. Case: If the user selected "Salaries & Accounts by Gender,"
     - a. produce the report using the acctrepo.FRM file.
   - C. Case: If the user selected "Employee Full Report,"
     - a. produce the report using the fullrepo.FRM file.
   - D. Otherwise,
     - a. produce the report using the salaries.FRM file, and then prompt to continue,
     - b. produce the report using the acctrepo.FRM file, and then prompt to continue,
     - c. produce the report using the fullrepo.FRM file, and then prompt to continue.

   End Case.
2. Return to report1.PRG

New Commands Used

USE <file> **INDEX** <filename> The **INDEX** <filename> parameter causes processing of records according to a previously created index file.

DO CASE
  CASE <condition>
    (any commands)
  CASE <condition>
    (any commands)
  OTHERWISE
    (any commands)
ENDCASE

The **DO CASE** command is useful when the <condition>s used are mutually exclusive. As soon as <condition> is evaluated as .T.rue, the commands following it will be executed. Afterward, execution resumes with the command following **ENDCASE.**

The OTHERWISE is optional. If it is used, commands following **OTHERWISE** will be executed when none of the previous **CASE** <condition>s are .T.rue.

PARAMETERS <expression list> **PARAMETERS** is the command used to accept memory variables being passed by a calling program. It is the receiving command for the **WITH** <expression list> parameter of the **DO** command. **PARAMETERS** must be the first executable command in the program being called.

SET PRINT ON This **SET** command sends the screen output to the printer. **SET PRINT OFF** is the reverse of this command.

SET ALTERNATE TO <filename> **SET ALTERNATE ON** is used to send screen output to a text file on the diskette, which is given the extension .TXT. The text file later may be edited with a word processing software such as WordStar.

To change the alternate file, use the command **SET ALTERNATE TO** <new filename>. To close the alternate file, use the command without a <filename> specified.

SET ALTERNATE ON Alternate must be set on before screen output will be sent to the alternate file. **SET ALTERNATE OFF** will suspend sending output to the current text file.

NOTE: The program reports1.PRG (program #4) calls the program reports2.PRG (program #5). See reports2.PRG for further explanation.

Program Listing

```
*  PROGRAM:  reports1.PRG  - to print report forms

SET TALK OFF
USE empfile INDEX empdex
CLEAR
?
? "     This program allows you to print a number of reports  "
?
? "                 These reports may be:        "
?
? "            1 -  Displayed on the screen only   "
?
? "            2 -  Sent to the printer            "
?
? "            3 -  Written to a text file         "
?
?
ACCEPT "         Select  1, 2, or 3 " TO mode
CLEAR
?
? "  Which of the following reports would you like to use ?   "
?
? "            1 -  Salary Summary Report  "
?
? "            2 -  Salaries & Accounts by Gender "
?
? "            3 -  Employee Full Report   "
?
? "            4 -  All of the above       "
?
?
ACCEPT   "         Select one of the above " TO choice
CLEAR

DO CASE
   CASE mode = "2"
      SET PRINT ON
      DO reports2 WITH choice
      SET PRINT OFF
   CASE mode = "3"
      SET ALTERNATE TO reports.txt
      SET ALTERNATE ON
      DO reports2 WITH choice
      SET ALTERNATE OFF
      SET ALTERNATE TO
   OTHERWISE
      DO reports2 WITH choice
ENDCASE
RETURN
```

New Commands Used

Reports2.PRG uses no new commands. It provides an example of a procedure that only would be called from another program in which the value of the memory variable "choice" has been defined.

The commands in this program could have been included in reports1, but they would need to have been listed three times. In this case, it is more efficient to place the commands in their own file, reports2, and call this program from three places in reports1 with the single command, **DO** reports2.

Program Listing

```
*  PROGRAM:  reports2.PRG  - called from reports1.PRG

PARAMETERS choice
DO CASE
   CASE choice = "1"
      REPORT FORM salaries
   CASE choice = "2"
      REPORT FORM acctrepo
   CASE choice = "3"
      REPORT FORM fullrepo
   OTHERWISE
      REPORT FORM salaries
      ACCEPT "Press return for next report " TO dummy
      REPORT FORM acctrepo
      ACCEPT "Press return for next report " TO dummy
      REPORT FORM fullrepo
      ACCEPT "Press return to continue     " TO dummy
ENDCASE
RETURN
```

Preliminary Commands

```
DO reports1
```

Sample Execution

```
     This program allows you to print a number of reports

                   These reports may be:

              1 -  Displayed on the screen only

              2 -  Sent to the printer

              3 -  Written to a text file

           Select  1, 2, or 3 1

                                      <<new screen>>

Which of the following reports would you like to use ?

              1 -  Salary Summary Report

              2 -  Salaries & Accounts by Gender

              3 -  Employee Full Report

              4 -  All of the above

          Select one of the above 3

                                      <<new screen>>

   Page No.      1
   01/01/86
                               Employee Full Report
                               ====================

                                                Current    Account   Account
   Employee Name    Phone #    Hire Date        Salary      Limit    Balance
   -------------    -------    ---------        -------    -------   -------

   Martins Mary     222-2123   11/01/85         1600.00     240.00    200.50
   Nichols Sandy    229-1111   02/15/86         1450.00     217.00    175.00
   Sill Sally       224-4321   02/15/84         1507.50     226.00    150.00
   Smoler Ellen     225-3212   08/15/83         1650.00     247.00    300.00
   Johnson Frank    223-7928   03/20/86         1500.00     225.00      0.00
   Jones David      292-3832   06/15/82         1550.00     232.00    150.75
   Knat Michael     221-1235   09/15/80         1800.00     270.00    125.00
   Pratt John       225-1234   06/22/82         1949.00     292.00    200.00
   Smith Paul       244-1010   11/15/81         1700.00     255.00   1050.00
```

Sample Program #6—Raises.PRG

Program Description

This sample program is designed to maintain a second database, history.DBF, which is used to keep records of each employee's raises over a period of time.

Raises.PRG introduces the idea of presenting screens, using the @ **SAY** and @ **GET** commands. It allows the user to enter data through screens by using the **READ** command. Also included in Raises.PRG are the commands and parameters used when more than one database are put into use at the same time.

The general algorithm for the sample program #6, raises.PRG, is:

1. Initialize by setting **TALK OFF** and setting a flag to "Y."
2. Select work area #1 and put empfile.DBF into use in that area.
3. Select work area #2 and put history.DBF into use there.
4. Continue executing the following loop instructions until the flag is no longer = "Y."
   - **A.** Select work area #1.
   - **B.** Initialize the memory variables to be used and display a program description.
   - **C.** Ask the user to enter the name of the emplyee of concern.
   - **D.** Move empfile's record pointer to the employee's record.
   - **E.** If the end of file is encountered (the name cannot be found),
     - **a.** Ask the user if a retry is desired
   - **F.** Otherwise
     - **a.** Present a screen for the user to input the date of the raise and the percent increase.
     - **b.** Compute the new salary and replace the current record's salary field with the new salary.
     - **c.** Display the new salary on the screen for the user to view.
     - **d.** Select work area #2.
     - **e.** Move history's record pointer to the first record whose field "employee" matches the field "employee" of the current record in empfile.
     - **f.** Insert a blank record immediately before the current record in history.
     - **g.** Fill the fields in the blank record with the appropriate data.
     - **h.** Display all data in history for that employee.
     - **i.** Ask the user if he/she has more salary increases to enter.

     End If.
   - **G.** If the user did not answer "Y"es to retry or more message,
     - **a.** change the flag to "N."

     End If.

End of the loop instructions.

New Commands Used

SELECT <Work Area> Ten separate work areas, each capable of holding one database, are available. To put more than one database into use, first select the desired work area with the **SELECT** command, and then enter the **USE** command for that database. Independent record pointers are maintained for each database in use. Field data may be read across work areas by using aliases.

CTOD (<character data>) The Character-to-Date Function is used to convert character-type data to date-type data. In raises.PRG the **CTOD** function is used to store a date to a memory variable.

UPPER(TRIM(<memvar>)) This is an example of using one function within another. In the sample program it is used so that the upper case of the <memvar>, without any trailing blank spaces, can be compared to a <field>. When functions are nested, the innermost function will be evaluated first.

@ x,y SAY <expression> This command prints the contents of an <expression> starting at a specific location on the screen. The x-coordinate is the row number; the y-coordinate is the column number. The <expression> in the command normally will be a <field>, a <memvar>, or a "<character string>".

@ x,y GET <variable> Similar to the @ **SAY,** the @ **GET** command is used to input or edit the contents of a <field> or <memvar>, placing it on the screen at the specified row and column. If a <memvar> is used, it must have been previously defined with a **STORE** command.

READ The @ **GET** commands may be followed by a **READ** command. When the **READ** is encountered, the contents of all @ **GET**s on the screen are stored to the <field> or <memvar>.

INSERT [BLANK] [BEFORE] The **INSERT BLANK** command adds a blank record to the database in use at the current position of the record pointer. This is usually done so that a subsequent **REPLACE** command can be used to store data in the new record. The [**BEFORE**] parameter is used to place the blank record immediately before the record being pointed to.

Program Listing

```
*  PROGRAM:  raises.PRG  - to keep records of previous salary levels
SET TALK OFF
CLEAR
SELECT 1
USE empfile
SELECT 2
USE history
STORE "Y" TO more

DO WHILE more = "Y"
  SELECT 1
  STORE CTOD("  /  /  ") TO effdate
  STORE "                    " TO name
  STORE "   " TO increase
  CLEAR
  @ 5,10 SAY "*   *   *   Entering Salary Increases   *   *   *  "
  @ 10,10 SAY "Name of employee (Last First) " GET name
  READ
  LOCATE FOR UPPER(employee) = UPPER(TRIM(name))
  IF EOF()
    ?
    ? "No Employee " + TRIM(name) + " found. "
    ?
    ACCEPT "Retry (Y/N) ? " TO ans
  ELSE
    CLEAR
    @ 8,15 SAY "EMPLOYEE"
    @ 8,45 SAY "CURRENT SALARY"
    @ 10,15 SAY employee
    @ 10,50 SAY salary
    @ 15,15 SAY "Enter Date (mm/dd/yy)  "
    @ 15,40 GET effdate
    @ 17,15 SAY "Enter % increase as decimal "
    @ 17,45 GET increase
    READ
    REPLACE salary WITH salary + (salary * VAL(increase))
    CLEAR
    @ 5,20 SAY "New Salary =  "
    @ 5,35 SAY salary

    SELECT 2
    LOCATE FOR employee = empfile->employee
    INSERT BLANK BEFORE
    REPLACE employee WITH empfile->employee, dateincr WITH effdate,
       salary WITH empfile->salary

    @ 10,15 SAY "SALARY HISTORY"
    ?
    DISPLAY FOR employee = empfile->employee OFF
    ?
    ?
    ACCEPT "   More Salary Increases to enter (Y/N) ? " TO ans
  ENDIF
  IF UPPER(ans) <> "Y"
    STORE "N" TO more
  ENDIF
ENDDO
RETURN
```

Preliminary Commands

```
DO raises
```

Sample Execution

```
         *   *   *  Entering Salary Increases   *   *   *

         Name of employee (Last First) Sill

                            <<new screen>>

             EMPLOYEE                        CURRENT SALARY

             Sill Sally                             1507.50

             Enter Date (mm/dd/yy)    06/15/86

             Enter % increase as decimal  .10

                            <<new screen>>

                   New Salary =    1658.25

              SALARY HISTORY

 EMPLOYEE                DATEINCR     SALARY
 Sill Sally              06/15/86    1658.25
 Sill Sally              01/01/80    1507.50

 More Salary Increases to enter (Y/N) ?  n
```

Sample Program #7—menu.PRG

Program Description

The final sample program, menu.PRG, has no new commands, structures, or functions to explain. It is the main calling program designed to allow the user to select which of the six previous sample programs he/she would like to access. It is the program that ties the other six into a system—a database management system—of programs. With it the system can be graphically displayed as:

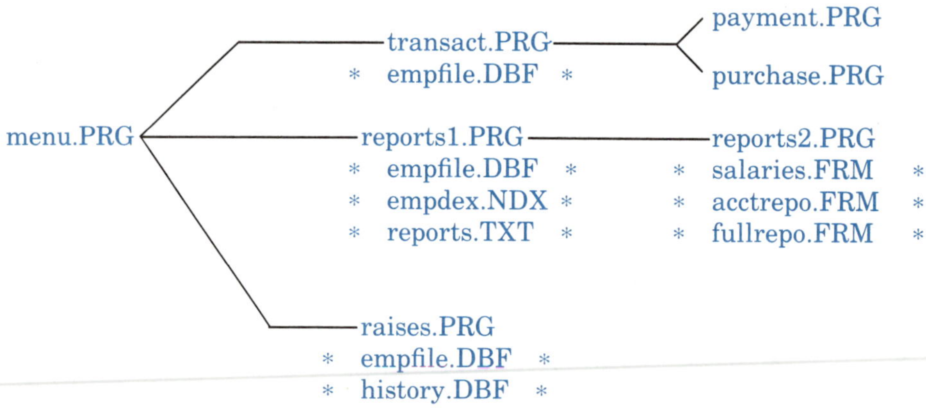

Program Listing

```
*  PROGRAM:  menu.PRG  - main menu to call programs
SET TALK OFF
STORE 1 TO true
DO WHILE true = 1
   CLEAR
   ?
   ? "                    * * * * *  MAIN MENU * * * * *     "
   ?
   ? "                 1  -  Employee Account Transactions "
   ?
   ? "                 2  -  Reports    "
   ?
   ? "                 3  -  Salary Increases  "
   ?
   ? "                 4  -  Quit     "
   ?
   ACCEPT "                        ENTER SELECTION   " TO select
   DO CASE
      CASE select = "1"
         DO transact
      CASE select = "2"
         DO reports1
      CASE select = "3"
         DO raises
      OTHERWISE
         STORE 0 TO true
   ENDCASE
ENDDO
CLEAR
SET TALK ON
RETURN
```

Preliminary Commands

```
DO menu
```

Sample Execution

```
    * * * * *  MAIN MENU * * * * *

1  -   Employee Account Transactions

2  -   Reports

3  -   Salary Increases

4  -   Quit

       ENTER SELECTION
```

Programming Tips

1. If you have a command that is too long to fit on one line (80 characters), dBase will automatically wrap the command down to the next line as you type it in. When dBase wraps a command, the far right side of the Modify mode screen will display a missing "<." This indicates that there is no Enter key character at the end of the line. dBase stops evaluating a command when it encounters an Enter key character. To remove an Enter key character that is accidentally included in an extended command, move the cursor to the end of the line and type **^T.** Then type spaces until dBase rewraps the line. dBase command lines may be up to 254 characters long.
2. You may want to leave blank lines in your program to improve readability. Blank lines will not affect how the program runs; neither will indenting program lines. The practice of indenting command structures is invaluable to program debugging and readability, as demonstrated in the example dBase command files.
3. dBase command files may be up to 4,096 bytes (characters) long. Files approaching this limit begin to show considerable delays in editing operations. Commands entered beyond this limit will be truncated from the file by dBase.

   dBase is a procedural language, designed for creating interrelated programs to accomplish a processing task. The separate programs (procedures) are connected through structures of program calls and returns. This fundamental difference between dBase and other programming languages, such as BASIC, requires that the programmer design systems that are subroutine in nature.
4. When dBase encounters a syntax error in your program, it may display a message similar to:

```
Syntax error
          ?
SET TALK TO OFF
Called from - B:transact.prg
Terminate command file? (Y/N)
```

Normally you will want to type {**N**} or ↵ to halt execution of the command file, note the command that caused the error message, and then use the **MODIFY COMMAND** command to edit that program line.

Two dBase commands useful for debugging command files are **SET ECHO** on/OFF and **SET STEP** on/OFF.

File Handling

Hint The following commands may be used for file maintenance operations when in dBase's dot (.) prompt mode.

To obtain a listing of all files on the default drive diskette, use the commands:

```
DIR *.*     or     DISPLAY FILE LIKE *.*
```

To erase a file on the diskette use the commands:

```
ERASE <filename.ext>     or     DELETE FILE <filename.ext>
```

To rename a file, use the command:

```
RENAME <filename.ext> TO <new filename.ext>
```

To make a copy of a file, use the command:

```
COPY [drive:]<filename.ext> TO [drive:]<filename.ext>
```

To display the contents of a file without opening it, use the command:

```
TYPE <filename.ext>
```

To produce a hard-copy of the contents of a file without opening it use the command:

```
TYPE <filename.ext> TO PRINT
```

Hazard Files that are currently open may not be erased, renamed, copied, or typed with the preceding commands.

Hazard Do not name a database (.DBF) file with the single letter A through J. These letters are reserved as database alias names.

Hazard dBase III allows up to 15 files (10 of which may be database files) to be open at once. However, DOS does not automatically allow that many files to be open. To use at dBase its full capacity, the DOS diskette used to load DOS must have the following ASCII file on it.

```
FILES = 20
BUFFERS = 24
```

and, the ASCII file must have the name CONFIG.SYS. You can create such a file with a word processor, dBase's **MODIFY COMMAND** mode, or in the same manner as the .BAT file was created in the introductory Hints and Hazards.

Hint The following commands open/load and close/save the various dBase file types.

.DBF *Database files.* The **USE** <filename> command opens a database file. To close the file, type **USE** with no <filename> specified.

.FMT *Format files.* Format files are command files with only @ **SAY** and @ **GET** commands in them. They may be created and saved in the **MODIFY COMMAND** mode, in which case they need to have their extensions specified in the **MODIFY COMMAND** command as <file-

name.FMT> (or be renamed later to have the .FMT extension). .FMT files may also be generated from .SCR files by the **MODIFY SCREEN** command.

A .FMT file is opened with the **SET FORMAT TO** <filename> command. Once opened, all commands which invoke full-screen editing of the database in use or current variables will use the screen display format of the .FMT file. Only one .FMT file may be open at a time in a given work area. To close an opened .FMT file, use the **SET FORMAT TO** command with no filename specified.

.FRM *Form files*. The **REPORT FORM** command automatically opens and closes form files. Form files are created with the **MODIFY REPORT** command.

.LBL *Label files*. The **LABEL FORM** command automatically opens and closes label files. Label files are created with the **MODIFY LABEL** command.

.MEM *Memory variable files*. The **SAVE TO** <filename> creates .MEM files. They are loaded into RAM with the **RESTORE FROM** <filename> command. They may be erased from RAM with the **RELEASE** or **CLEAR MEMORY** commands.

.NDX *Index files*. The **INDEX ON** <expression> **TO** <filename> command creates index files. They then are loaded into RAM with the **USE** command with its **INDEX** parameter (**USE** <filename> **INDEX** <filename>). The **USE** <filename> command without the **INDEX** parameter can be used to erase an index file from RAM.

.PRG *Program or command files*. Command files are created and saved in the modify mode (**MODIFY COMMAND** <filename>) or with a word processing software. They are ASCII data format files. A command file is loaded into RAM and executed with the **DO** <filename> command. A command file may be automatically loaded and executed when dBase is loaded by typing {dBase <filename>↵} from DOS's A> operating level.

.TXT *Text files*. Text files are ASCII data format files and may be created several ways. The **COPY TO** <filename> **SDF** command creates a .TXT file copy of the database in use. The **SET ALTERNATE TO** <filename> and **SET ALTERNATE ON** commands create a .TXT file copy of all screen output (except editing mode output) generated after the **SET ALTERNATE ON** command is executed. **SET ALTERNATE OFF** stops the echo of screen output to the .TXT file; **SET ALTERNATE TO** with no filename specified closes the .TXT file. Both the **LABEL FORM** and **REPORT FORM** command will create ASCII .TXT files when the [**TO FILE** <filename>] parameter is used with them.

Hint The **CLOSE ALL** command closes/saves/erases all files currently in RAM.

Hazard Do not remove your files diskette from the disk drive before you type {**QUIT↵**} to save all data and close all files. Not doing so may result in lost data and/or files that will be destroyed.

Data Processing

Hint The data held in fields and Memory variables are constants. You may not, for instance, **EDIT** a numeric field

```
ACCOUNT: 75+1200.00
```

to add 75.00 to what is there.

Expressions may be used, however, to put constants into fields or variables using dBase commands. For instance {**STORE** account+75 **TO** macct} or {**REPLACE** account **WITH** account+75} are examples of dBase commands that use expressions to put a constant into a memory variable or field.

Hint Memo fields do not hold record data, but instead hold an address used to access text data which is kept in a memo field (.DBT) file for each record having memo data. dBase uses the .DBT file in conjunction with a database file when the database file has a record structure that includes Memo fields.

Hazard Since the data in Memo fields are not actually part of their associated record they cannot be processed by dBase commands. It is not possible, for instance, to search memo data for occurrences of strings; sort or index records on Memo field contents; or perform batch replacement operations on Memo data.

Hint Certain mathematical operations may be performed with date-type data. The following are some examples of "date arithmetic."

`. date1 = CTOD("06/15/87")` `06/15/87`	Place the date-type data for June 15, 1987 into the variable "date1."
`. ? date1 + 90` `09/13/87`	Print date1 + 90. September 13, 1987 occurs ninety days after June 15, 1987.
`. date2 = CTOD("08/14/87")` `06/15/87`	Place the date-type data for August 14, 1987 into the variable "date2."
`? date2 - date1` `60`	Print date2 minus date1. There are 60 days between June 15, 1987 and August 14, 1987.

Hint String comparisons in expressions must be the same case as well as use the same characters in order for a condition to evaluate as .T.rue. The upper-case function (**UPPER**(character data)) or lower-case function (**LOWER**(character data)) may be used to ensure that a field or variable's string data are compared in the same case. For example:

```
LOCATE FOR UPPER(employee)="MARTINS MARY"
```

Hazard Fields holding string data automatically are padded with spaces (**CHR**(32)'s) which are evaluated as such in expressions. To remove trailing spaces, use the **TRIM** function. With dBase III Plus you can remove leading spaces with the **LTRIM** function.

Hazard Memory variables holding numeric data, hold their data to several decimal places of accuracy (varies between versions of dBase) regardless of the number of places displayed on the screen. Fields hold numeric data to the number of places of accuracy specified when the record structure for the database was entered. Read through the following commands and their results:

```
. ? 10/3
  3.33
. STORE 10/3 TO test
  3.33
. ? test
          3.33
. ? 3.33 = test
.F.
. ? STR(test,19,15)
  3.333333333333333
. ? 3.333333333333333 = test
.T.
. REPLACE account WITH test
      1 record replaced
. DISP account
Record#    account
      9       3.33
. ? STR(account,19,15)
  3.330000000000000
```

Hint You can control the number of decimal places of accuracy for numeric data held in memory variables by using the **ROUND** function.

```
. STORE ROUND(10/3,2) TO test
.  3.33
. ? STR(test,19,15)
  3.330000000000000
```

Hint People with programming backgrounds often are initially confused by the dBase commands used primarily in the dot (.) prompt mode (e.g., **DISPLAY, REPLACE, LOCATE,** and so on) and their parameters of <scope>, <field list>, and **FOR** <expression>. The commands are complete subroutines with all the fundamental processing operations (assignment, condition, iteration) which are called by the command when it is entered.

dBase III Features

Hint The bell that rings during data entry can be annoying. To turn off the bell from the dot (.) prompt mode, type {**SET BELL OFF↵**}. To turn it back on, type {**SET BELL ON↵**}.

Hint The error message "Do you want some help? (Y/N)" can also be annoying. To stop the display of this message, type {**SET HELP OFF↵**} and to turn it back on, type {**SET HELP ON↵**}.

Hint The gray Function keys on the left side of the keyboard are programmed by dBase to hold the following strings:

F1	**HELP**	F6	**DISPLAY STATUS**
F2	**ASSIST**	F7	**DISPLAY MEMORY**
F3	**LIST**	F8	**DISPLAY**
F4	**DIR**	F9	**APPEND**
F5	**DISPLAY STRUCTURE**	F10	**EDIT**

Tapping one of these keys causes the command shown to be typed, displayed on the screen, and entered.

You may change the strings by using the **SET FUNCTION** <n> **TO** <string> command. For example, **SET FUNCTION** 2 **TO** "San Diego, CAL" will store that city and state in the F2 key. If you want to include an Enter key character (**CHR**(13)) at the end of the string, add a semicolon at the end (**SET** F2 **TO** "San Diego, CAL;".

The Function key F1 is not programmable with the **SET FUNCTION** command.

Limits and Constraints

Hint The following are some limits and constraints to various dBase III data processing operations:

Maximum filename length—8 characters

Maximum field name length—10 characters

Maximum memory variable name length—10 characters

Maximum characters in a field, memory variable, command file line, report heading or <cstring>—254 characters

Maximum fields to a record—128 fields

Maximum characters to a record—4,000 characters

Maximum current memory variables or @ **GET**s—256

Maximum .PRG file size—4,096 bytes

dBase III Output

Hint To obtain a hard copy listing of a command file, use the **TYPE** <filename.PRG> **TO PRINT** command.

Hint To obtain hard copy of screen output generated from the dot (.) prompt mode, use dBase III's output-generating commands (**DISPLAY, LIST, REPORT FORM, LABEL FORM, TYPE,** etc.) that include the [**TO PRINT**] parameter which causes an echo of screen output to the printer. For commands not having the [**TO PRINT**] parameter, follow these steps:

1. Make sure your computer is connected and on-line to a printer that is turned on.
2. Either press and hold the Ctrl key and then tap the P key, or type {**SET PRINT ON**↵} to toggle on the printer echo.
3. Enter the appropriate commands to generate the desired output.
4. Either press and hold the Ctrl key and then tap the P key again, or type {**SET PRINT OFF**↵} to toggle off the printer echo.

Hint To obtain hard copy of one screen's worth of data while in an editing mode, press and hold a shift key and then tap the key marked PrtSc.

Hazard If the computer's connection to the printer is not complete or the printer is not turned on, the preceding steps to obtain hard copy may result in the computer locking up until the connection is complete or the printer is turned on.

Hint When you use the **?** command to print field data on the screen, fields holding string data will be displayed with their padded spaces. To eliminate the spaces, use the **TRIM** function.

Hint When you use the **?** command to print memory variables holding numeric data, the data will be displayed with a default length of 11 characters and an accuracy of two decimal places. To control length and displayed accuracy, use the **STR** function. To control just the displayed accuracy use the **SET DECIMALS TO** command.

Hint The .TXT ASCII files produced by the **SET ALTERNATE** commands and the [**TO FILE** <filename>] parameter of the **REPORT FORM** and **LABEL FORM** commands are accessible by word processing software. When text format is important and the text is a one-time product, it usually is more efficient to create a .TXT file with the essential data in it and then use a word processing software to edit it into finished form.

STUDY QUESTIONS

1. Individual data items of a relational database are held in ________.

2. Related data items of a relational database are held in ________.

3. To create a database, the ________________ must be defined before any data are entered into the database.

4. Each field of the records in a database is prespecified with a unique ____________, a fixed ____________, and a certain data ____________.

5. If the length of the first field in the first record is known, is the length of the first field in the second record known? Why? ____________

 ____

6. If the length of the data held in the first field of the first record is known, is the length of the data in the first field of the second record known? Why? ________________________________

 ____

7. Is it possible for one record in a database to have an extra field? Why?

 ____

 ____

8. dBase III has two modes. Direct access to data in fields or memory variables is done in one of the ____________ modes, and commands are executed from the ____________ mode.

9. What event indicates that you are in a mode that allows direct access to data in fields or memory variables? ________________

10. What will be the result of entering 75/100 into a numeric field of a record when you are in an editing mode? Why? ____________

 ____

11. With a database in use, what will be the result of typing {**DISPLAY↵**}?

 ____

12. What are the three possible <scope>s and how do they affect the record pointer? ________________________________

 ____

 ____

13. Where is the record pointer left after executing a command using the <scope> **ALL**?

 ____

14. What command parameter specifies the individual data items in each record for the command to act upon?

 ____

15. What is the default <scope> for any command using the **FOR** <expression> parameter? ____________________

Given the following database, list the record numbers of the records that will be acted on by the **DISPLAY** commands shown.

Record#	EMPLOYEE	TELEPHONE	SEX	EMPLOYED	SALARY	ACCOUNT
1	Pratt John	225-1234	M	06/22/82	1949.00	200.00
2	Smoler Ellen	225-3212	F	09/15/83	1650.00	300.00
3	Jones David	292-3832	M	06/15/82	1550.00	275.75
4	Sill Sally	224-4321	F	02/15/84	1507.50	150.00
5	Knat Michael	221-1235	M	09/15/80	1800.00	125.00
6	Smith Paul	244-1010	M	11/15/81	1700.00	350.00
7	Martins Mary	222-2123	F	11/01/85	1600.00	200.50
8	Nichols Sandy	229-1111	F	02/15/86	1450.00	175.00
9	Johnson Frank	223-7928	M	03/20/86	1500.00	0.00

16. **DISPLAY FOR** employed < **CTOD**("01/01/84") **.AND.** salary < 1600

____

17. **DISPLAY FOR DTOC**(employed) < "01/01/84" **.AND.** salary < 1600

____

18. **DISPLAY FOR** account < 200 **.AND.** account >= 300

____

19. **DISPLAY FOR** account >= 200 **.AND.** account <= 300

____

20. **DISPLAY FOR** salary < 1550 **.OR.** account > 300

____

21. **DISPLAY FOR** SEX = "F" **.AND.** salary < 1550 **.OR.** account > 300

____

22. **DISPLAY FOR** SEX = "F" **.AND.** (salary <1550 **.OR.** account > 300)

____

23. **DISPLAY FOR** 1=1

____

24. Describe the differences between the **SORT ON** <field> **TO** <filename> command and the **INDEX ON** <expression> **TO** <filename> command.

____

____

____

____

____

25. Describe the differences between the **LOCATE** command and the **FIND** command.

____

____

____

MODULE OUTLINE

Learning BASICA

Why a Programming Language?

Unlike most other software covered in this manual, BASICA is considered a true programming language. This means the software BASICA requires that the user have a knowledge of programming theory in order to use the computer as a tool.

It is becoming accepted that with applications software the need for knowledge of programming theory is unnecessary. While it is true that the applications software available today may be used in a productive way without it, it is also true that when you begin to take the applications software to the limits of their capabilities, you inevitably find that you need to understand the principles of programming theory. The macros of Lotus 1-2-3, command files of dBase II, and the Mail Merge utility used with WordStar are examples of application areas where the user must understand elements of programming theory.

BASIC—A Language Developed to Teach Programming Theory

BASIC is the acronym for "Beginners All Symbolic Instruction Code." It is the name for a programming language developed at Dartmouth College under the direction of professors John G. Kemeny and Thomas E. Kurtz during the academic year 1963–1964. BASIC was developed to teach beginning students the constructs of programming theory and is one of the easiest high-level languages to learn.

While it may be possible to teach programming theory by using applications software rather than a programming language, BASIC has been used to teach programming for a longer period of time, so that several excellent books, teaching techniques, and assignments on the subject have evolved. The same is not true for applications software.

Versions of BASIC

Today, more than twenty years after its conception, more than 50 versions of BASIC have been developed for use on a variety of hardware systems. While they each conform to a standard called ANSI Minimal BASIC, they often exceed the requirements of the standard in scope of commands and operations. Systematic differences between versions of BASIC often are associated with the hardware on which they are designed to be used.

The Nature of the BASICA Section

This section differs from other sections of the manual that deal with applications packages because it is assumed here that you either have previous exposure to BASIC or can refer to one of the many good texts on the subject for programming concepts.

The BASICA tutorial exercises focus on the systematic differences between BASICA on the IBM PC and other versions of BASIC that you may have used or to which a text might refer. The syntax of essential commands, file handling, and editing operations are the primary focuses of the tutorial.

The operation and command summary of this section does not attempt to cover all the commands and operations of the language. You will need to refer to an IBM BASIC manual if you intend to pursue more intense programming endeavors.

One of the best sources of information for the beginning or intermediate programmer can be example programs. This section of the manual has more than 40 examples of BASIC programs, shown with their output. Careful study of the programs will provide insights to programming style and techniques, as well as to BASICA statement syntax.

Sequential and random access data files also are introduced in this section. The knowledge that you gain by using BASICA to create, maintain, and query these two types of data files is directly applicable to your understanding of many of the features and operations of the applications software.

BASIC for the IBM PC

Three versions of BASIC have been developed by MicroSoft Corporation for the IBM PC. BASICA is the "advanced" version, and the other two versions, Cassette BASIC and Disk BASIC, are subsets of BASICA.

Cassette BASIC

Cassette BASIC is not software, but *firmware*. It is called firmware because the instruction set for Cassette BASIC is imbedded in a ROM memory chip inside the computer. If you turn on the computer with no diskette in the A: drive and the door open, the computer will default to this version of BASIC. It is called "Cassette BASIC" because you need a cassette player and interface cord to save your BASIC programs. The computer has not read DOS into memory and so does not have the instruction set that it needs to save data to a diskette.

Disk BASIC

Disk BASIC is software found on the DOS diskette (usually purchased with the computer) under the name BASIC.COM. Disk BASIC has all of the operations and commands of Cassette BASIC plus commands and operations for accessing and storing data on diskettes.

Advanced BASIC

The third version of BASIC is called Advanced BASIC. It also is found on the DOS diskette under the filename BASICA.COM. Advanced BASIC has all the operations and commands of Disk BASIC, plus advanced graphics and music commands. Advanced BASIC, or BASICA, is the version of BASIC used in the tutorial exercises and other topics of this section.

REQUIRED MATERIALS

1. An IBM DOS diskette
2. Your files diskette
3. This manual
4. Other ______________________________

Tutorial Conventions

During this tutorial you will create BASICA programs and use various BASICA commands and operations. Here are the conventions used for the tutorial's instructions.

↵ When you see this symbol, press the Enter key located on the right side of the keyboard and marked with a bent arrow (↵).

^ This character means press and hold the Ctrl key, and then tap the next key shown.

[ ] If brackets are used, do not type them, but only what is inside them.

HOW TO GET OUT OF TROUBLE

If you want to:	*Then:*
■ Erase characters being entered as a BASICA command or program line. . .	■ Tap the Backspace key (←) located just above the Enter key.
■ Stop any command operation and return to the Ok prompt. . .	■ Press and hold the Ctrl key and then tap the Scroll Lock (Break) key.
■ Stop the tutorial to continue later. . .	■ Type [SAVE"filename↵]. Watch the disk drive light to make sure the program has been saved, and then type [SYSTEM↵] to return to DOS.
■ Continue with the tutorial after you have stopped. . .	■ Type [LOAD"filename↵] after loading BASICA into RAM memory and inserting your files diskette into the A: drive.

Getting Started

1. Insert the DOS diskette into the A: disk drive (the disk drive on the left) and close the disk drive door.
2. If the computer already is on, press and hold the Ctrl and Alt keys and then tap the Del key. Otherwise, turn on the computer and the monitor.

In a few moments DOS will be automatically loaded.

3. Answer DOS's date and time prompts.
4. When you see the A>, type [BASICA↵].

The programming language BASICA is provided on the DOS Master diskette.

5. If you see the Version message:

```
The IBM Personal Computer Basic
Version C1.10 Copyright IBM Corp 1981
```

you do not have the correct version of BASIC loaded into memory. Repeat steps 1 through 4.

6. Remove the DOS diskette from the A: drive and then insert your files diskette into that drive. Be sure to close the disk drive door.

Your system ____

EXERCISE 1: BASICA Basics

Inherent BASICA Editing Operations

The following editing operations are almost universal for the different versions of BASIC, and they hold true for IBM's BASICA. The operations are based on the fact that each line in a BASIC program must have a line number, and that no two lines may have the same number. In addition, the computer automatically will arrange program lines by their numbers, not by the order in which they are typed.

- *Inserting a line.* Give the new program line a line number between the two line numbers of the lines above and below where it is to be inserted.
- *Deleting a line.* Type the line number of the line to be deleted and then press the Enter key.
- *Replacing a line.* Type the new line with the same line number of the line to be replaced.

Writing a BASICA Program

You will create a short BASICA program. Be sure to include all spaces, commas, quotes, etc., exactly as they are shown. If you make a mistake before you type ↵ (enter the line), use the Backspace key (←) located just above the Enter key to backspace and erase the error, and then continue typing the line correctly. If you make a mistake after typing ↵, refer to the "Inherent Editing Commands" for procedures to correct it.

1. Now, enter the BASIC program:

```
10 REM Example Program #1←┘
20 PRINT "This is a simple example"←┘
30 PRINT←┘
40 INPUT "Enter a number ",A←┘
50 INPUT "Enter another number ",B←┘
60 PRINT←┘
70 PRINT A;" times ";B;" equals ";A*B←┘
```

Viewing a BASICA Program

Clearing the Screen with ^Home

The Home key is located on the upper right side of the keyboard. When used with the Ctrl key the Home key clears the screen and leaves the cursor in the upper left corner (home position) of the screen.

1. Type [^Home].

Listing a Program on the Monitor Screen

1. Now type [**LIST**←┘] to list the following program on monitor screen:

```
LIST
10 REM Example Program #1
20 PRINT "This is a simple example"
30 PRINT
40 INPUT "Enter a number ",A
50 INPUT "Enter another number ",B
60 PRINT
70 PRINT A;" times ";B;" equals ";A*B
Ok
```

2. Check once more to make certain the program is entered correctly.

Listing a Program on the Printer

To list a BASICA program on the printer you may use the **LLIST** (**LIST** with an extra *L*) command.

1. Make sure the printer is turned on, on-line, and connected to your computer. (Your lab may have a shared device control switch. You will need to select your computer as the one currently connected to the printer.)
2. Now type [**LLIST**←┘].

   Your system ____

   ____

   ____

   ____

   ____

Listing Portions of a BASICA Program

With either the **LIST** or the **LLIST** command you can list only certain lines of a program by specifying their line numbers. To demonstrate how to specify particular lines in the **LIST** command, do the following.

1. Type [**LIST** 20←] (list a single line).

```
LIST 20
20 PRINT "This is a simple example"
Ok
```

2. Type [**LIST** 20–50←] (list a section of lines).

```
LIST 20-50
20 PRINT "This is a simple example"
30 PRINT
40 INPUT "Enter a number ",A
50 INPUT "Enter another number ",B
Ok
```

3. Type [**LIST** 30–←] (list from a line on).

```
LIST 30-
30 PRINT
40 INPUT "Enter a number ",A
50 INPUT "Enter another number ",B
60 PRINT
70 PRINT A;" times ";B;" equals ";A*B
Ok
```

4. Type [**LIST** –40←] (list up to a line).

```
LIST -40
10 REM Example Program #1
20 PRINT "This is a simple example"
30 PRINT
40 INPUT "Enter a number ",A
Ok
```

Executing a BASICA Program

As with most versions of BASIC, the **RUN** command is used to execute a BASICA program. The output of a BASICA program may be displayed on the screen, the printer, or simultaneously on both the screen and the printer.

Running a Program on the Monitor Screen

1. Type [^Home] to clear the screen.
2. Type [**RUN**←].
3. Answer the program's INPUT statement prompts by entering the numbers 25 and 4.

The output that should appear on the screen is:

```
RUN
This is a simple example

Enter a number 25
Enter another number 4

 25  times  4  equals  100
Ok
```

Running a Program on the Printer

To cause the output of a BASICA program to be sent to the printer rather than to the screen, the command **LPRINT** may be used in place of the **PRINT** command. INPUT prompts must be duplicated with **LPRINT** statements within the body of the program. For instance, to cause all of the output of the program to be printed on the printer, the program would have to be changed to the following.

```
10 REM Example Program #1
20 LPRINT "This is a simple example"
30 LPRINT
40 INPUT "Enter a number ",A
45 LPRINT "Enter a number ",A
50 INPUT "Enter another number ",B
55 LPRINT "Enter another number ",B
60 LPRINT
70 LPRINT A;" times ";B;" equals ";A*B
```

Running a Program on the Screen and the Printer

With versions of BASICA numbered 2.0 or higher it is possible to use a Ctrl-key combination to toggle on an echo of all screen output to the printer. You press and hold the Ctrl key and then tap the key marked "PrtSc." Once toggled on, all output that appears on the screen also is sent to the printer. Output to the printer may be stopped by typing ^PrtSc again (toggle off).

If you are using a version of BASICA 2.0 +, do the following.

1. Repeat the procedure to prepare for printer output.
2. Type [^PrtSc] to toggle on the printer.
3. Type [**RUN**↵].
4. Answer the program's INPUT statement prompts with two numbers of your choice.
5. Type [^PrtSc] to toggle off the printer.

EXERCISE 2: BASICA File Operation Commands

Saving a BASICA Program—The SAVE Command

The **SAVE** command is used to save a copy of the BASICA program in RAM memory onto the diskette. This command is entered with a filename (which you specify) under which the program is saved. If a file with that name already exists on the diskette, it will be replaced by the file being saved. The computer will not hesitate or give you any message that the previous diskette file will be or has been erased.

1. Type [**SAVE**"exone↵].

If your files diskette is in the B: drive, the command syntax to save the program is [**SAVE**"B:exone↵].

2. Now type [^Home] [**LIST**↵].

```
LIST
10 REM Example Program #1
20 PRINT "This is a simple example"
30 PRINT
40 INPUT "Enter a number ",A
50 INPUT "Enter another number ",B
60 PRINT
70 PRINT A;" times ";B;" equals ";A*B
Ok
```

Notice that saving a program does not erase it from memory. It simply saves a copy of the program on the diskette.

Erasing a BASICA Program from RAM Memory—The **NEW** Command

To erase a program from RAM you may use the **NEW** command.

1. Type

```
[NEW↵ ]
[LIST↵ ]
```

Unless you have saved the program on a diskette, it will be lost when the **NEW** command is executed.

Loading a BASICA Program—The **LOAD** Command

The **LOAD** command is used to copy a BASICA program from the diskette into RAM memory.

1. Type [^Home] to clear the screen and continue with the following.

```
[LOAD"exone↵ ]
[LIST↵ ]
```

If your files diskette is in the B: drive, the command syntax to load the program is [**LOAD**"B:exone↵].

Listing the Files on a Diskette—The **FILES** Command

The **FILES** command is used to display the filenames and extensions of files on a diskette.

1. Type [**FILES**↵].

Erasing a Diskette File—The **KILL** Command

The **KILL** command is used to erase a file from the diskette. The file's name and extension must be specified when you use the **KILL** command.

1. Type [**KILL**"exone.BAS↵]. Then type [**FILES**↵].

The file "exone.BAS" should not appear in the listing of files given by the **FILES** command.

2. Type [**SAVE**"exone↵] to make another diskette copy of the program now in RAM memory.

Renaming a Diskette File—The NAME Command

The **NAME** file **AS** file command is used to rename a diskette file from BASICA. Like the **KILL** command, this command requires filenames and extensions.

1. Type [**NAME**"exone.BAS" **AS** "progone.BAS"].
2. Now type [**FILES**↵] to see that the file has been renamed.

Combining BASICA Programs—The MERGE Command

A special BASICA file handling command, **MERGE,** may be used to combine a BASICA program from the diskette with a BASICA program in RAM (the current program). The program being merged (the one on the diskette) must have been last saved in ASCII data format, which is a standard format for data. (For more information on ASCII see Module 6: Data Transfer between Applications.

To save a program file in ASCII you add a ",A after the filename when you use the **SAVE** command.

When two BASICA programs are merged, the line numbers determine how the computer will merge them together. The effect is the same as typing the program being merged from the diskette while the current program is in memory. Lines of the merged program that have the same line numbers (as lines) of the current program will replace lines in the current program. Other lines will be placed into the current program based on their line numbers.

Creating a Heading File for Merging

To gain experience in using the **MERGE** command, you will create a small BASICA program consisting of REM statements that may be merged into the beginning of any BASICA program you later create.

1. Make sure you have the file "progone" saved on your diskette, and then type [**NEW**↵] to erase that program from RAM memory.
2. Create the following BASICA program, keeping the line numbers the same as shown and filling in your particular information where appropriate.

```
3 REM ****************************************
4 REM Assignment # nn
5 REM Program Name -
6 REM
7 REM Prepared for: Course name/number/section
8 REM By          : your name
9 REM Date        : mm/dd/yy
10 REM **************************************
```

3. Save the program by typing [**SAVE**"header",**A**↵].
4. Next load the program "progone" into memory and list it on the monitor screen.

Notice that loading a BASICA program automatically erases any program that may have been in RAM memory.

5. Finally, type [**MERGE**"header↵] and then [**LIST**↵].

```
MERGE"header
Ok
LIST
3 REM ****************************************
4 REM Assignment # nn
5 REM Program Name -
6 REM
7 REM Prepared for: Course name/number/section
8 REM By          : your name
9 REM Date        : mm/dd/yy
10 REM ***************************************
20 PRINT "This is a simple example"
30 PRINT
40 INPUT "Enter a number ",A
50 INPUT "Enter another number ",B
60 PRINT
70 PRINT A;" times ";B;" equals ";A*B
```

Notice that line 10 of the program being merged, "header," replaced line 10 of the current program, "progone," and that all other lines occur in sequence, according to line number.

EXERCISE 3: Current File Operations

Renumbering BASICA Program Lines—The RENUM Command

There will be occasions when it will be necessary or desirable to renumber the program lines in your BASICA program. The **RENUM** command is used to perform this operation.

This BASICA command has the form:

Line number to start numbering at

Beginning number — Amount to increment

```
RENUM n,n,n
```

The default "beginning number" is 10; the "default line number to start numbering at" is the first line; and the "amount to increment" is 10.

To use the **RENUM** command do the following.

1. Type [**LIST**↵**RENUM**↵**LIST**↵].

```
LIST
3 REM ****************************************
4 REM Assignment # nn
5 REM Program Name -
6 REM
7 REM Prepared for: Course name/number/section
8 REM By            : your name
9 REM Date          : mm/dd/yy
10 REM ***************************************
20 PRINT "This is a simple example"
30 PRINT
40 INPUT "Enter a number ",A
50 INPUT "Enter another number ",B
60 PRINT
70 PRINT A;" times ";B;" equals ";A*B
OK
RENUM
OK
LIST
10 REM ****************************************
20 REM Assignment # nn
30 REM Program Name -
40 REM
50 REM Prepared for: Course name/number/section
60 REM By            : your name
70 REM Date          : mm/dd/yy
80 REM ***************************************
90 PRINT "This is a simple example"
100 PRINT
110 INPUT "Enter a number ",A
120 INPUT "Enter another number ",B
130 PRINT
140 PRINT A;" times ";B;" equals ";A*B
```

2. Type [**RENUM** ,, 1↵**LIST**↵].

```
RENUM ,,1
OK
LIST
10 REM ****************************************
11 REM Assignment # nn
12 REM Program Name -
13 REM
14 REM Prepared for: Course name/number/section
15 REM By            : your name
16 REM Date          : mm/dd/yy
17 REM ***************************************
18 PRINT "This is a simple example"
19 PRINT
20 INPUT "Enter a number ",A
21 INPUT "Enter another number ",B
22 PRINT
23 PRINT A;" times ";B;" equals ";A*B
```

Notice that if a single option number is used to affect the **RENUM** command, as in this case, where the number to increment was specified as 1, commas must be used to satisfy any preceding options in the command.

3. Type [**RENUM** 18,100,20↵**LIST**↵].

```
RENUM 100,18,20
OK
LIST
10 REM ****************************************
11 REM Assignment # nn
12 REM Program Name -
13 REM
14 REM Prepared for: Course name/number/section
15 REM By          : your name
16 REM Date        : mm/dd/yy
17 REM ***************************************
100 PRINT "This is a simple example"
120 PRINT
140 INPUT "Enter a number ",A
160 INPUT "Enter another number ",B
180 PRINT
200 PRINT A;" times ";B;" equals ";A*B
```

Deleting Sections of a Program—The DELETE Command

The **DELETE** command may be used to delete lines of a BASICA program. Its syntax is similar to that of the **LIST** command.

`DELETE 20`	Deletes the single line 20
`DELETE 20-50`	Deletes the lines 20 through 50
`DELETE -30`	Deleted the lines up to 30
`DELETE 50-`	Deletes the lines 50 on

Full-Screen Editing

In addition to the inherent editing found in most versions of BASIC, IBM's BASICA has full-screen editing available for you to use.

The Full-Screen Editing Keys

The next steps of the tutorial demonstrate several control key combinations and operations you will find useful when you edit your BASICA programs. Many of the keys it references may be found on the right side of the keyboard on (or around) the numeric keypad (see page B–14).

Principles of Full-Screen Editing

With BASICA's full-screen editing the monitor screen acts as an "electronic message board." When you type a command or program line, you are typing a message for the computer. When you press the Enter key, you are sending that message to the computer for it to act on as a command, or to accept as a BASIC program line.

As you type, the message will begin to clutter up the message board. You already have seen how to erase the board with ^Home. But, as long as a message is still on the board, you can move the cursor back to the message and send it to the computer again by pressing the Enter key.

Four keys on the right side of the keyboard (on the numeric keypad) marked with arrows are called cursor control keys. They allow you to move the cursor anywhere on the screen.

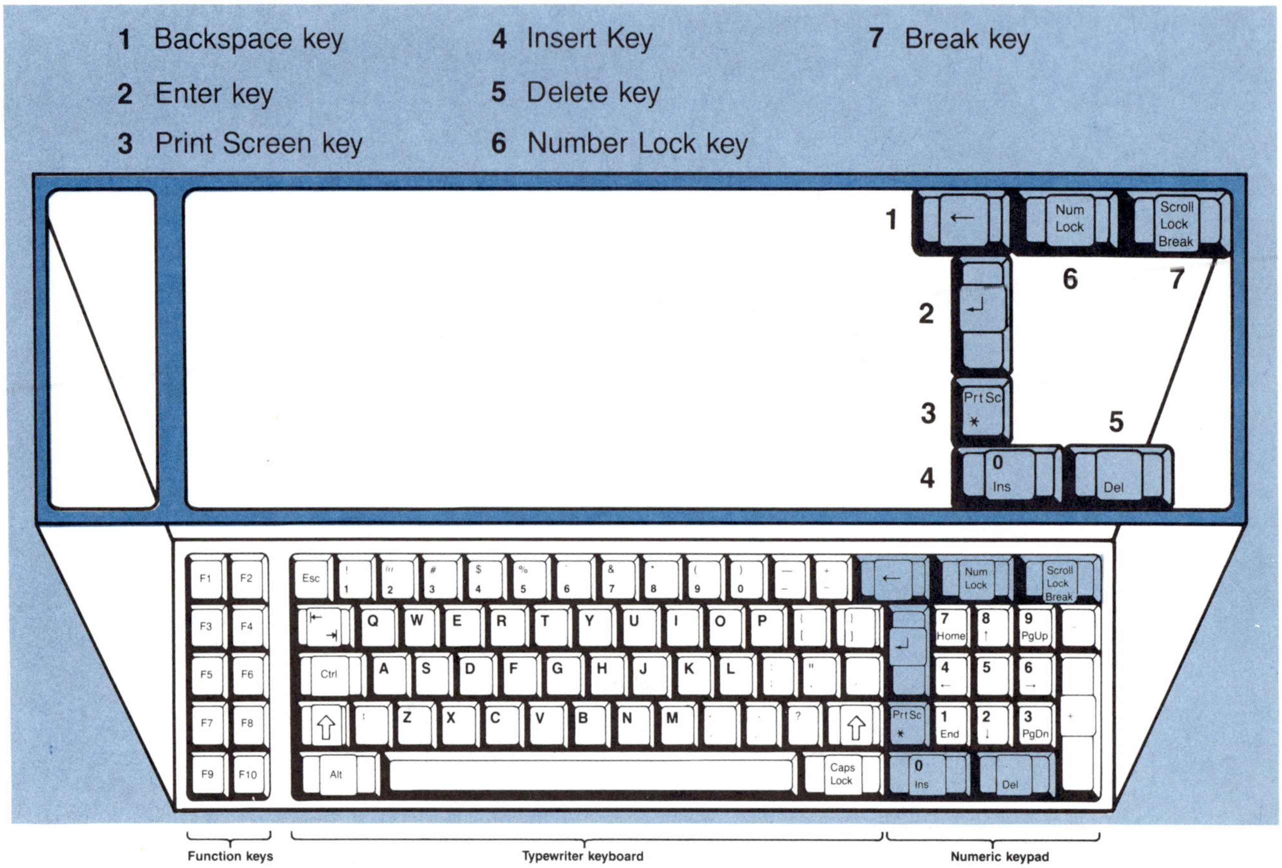

Overwriting Characters

1. Type [^Home **LIST**↵].

Now your program should be listed at the top of the screen with the cursor located at the line under BASICA's "Ok" prompt.

2. Move the cursor to line 140 with the cursor-up key, and then under the *a* in the INPUT prompt with the cursor-right key.

```
140 INPUT "Enter a number ",A
                 |
                Here
```

3. Type [the first].

```
140 INPUT "Enter the first",A
```

Characters typed normally will overwrite existing characters when full-screen editing is being done.

Inserting Characters

1. Tap the key marked "Ins."

This single key toggles on an insert mode. Notice that the cursor has become larger. This indicates that the insert mode is on. Tapping the Ins key again, or typing any noncharacter key (such as a cursor control key or the Enter key) will turn the insert mode off.

2. With the insert mode on, continue by typing [number].

```
140 INPUT "Enter the first number ",A
```

3. Next tap the Enter key, and then type [^Home] [**LIST**←┘].

It is important to note that the computer only recognizes changes in a program line *if* the Enter key is pressed while the cursor is on that line (the cursor may be anywhere on the line). Otherwise the computer ignores any changes made. In this example, the second listing of the program would not have been updated for the changes made to line 140.

Deleting Characters

1. Move the cursor to line 100, and then to under the *T* in *This*.
2. Next tap the key marked "Del." Continue to tap this key until the program line appears as shown here.

```
100 PRINT "s a simple example"
```

The Del key is used to delete characters while full-screen editing is being done.

3. Type [Calculator Program←┘].

```
100 PRINT "Calculator Program"
```

Other Full-Screen Editing Keystroke Commands

Several other keys and key combinations may be used while full-screen editing in BASICA. All of the following will work when you are originally entering a program line, or when you are editing a program line displayed on the monitor screen.

Cursor Movement

- Home key Jumps the cursor to the top left corner of the screen.
- End key Jumps the cursor to the last character of the line on which it is located.
- ^→ Jumps the cursor one word to the right.
- ^← Jumps the cursor one word to the left.

Deleting

- ^End Erases all characters to the right of the cursor.
- Esc key Erases all characters of the line on which the cursor is located.

Controlling Screen Scroll

Screen scroll occurs when more output is going to the screen than its 24 lines can hold. With screen scroll the top lines disappear and the lines below move up as the output is generated.

When you have a long program being listed or have several lines of output from a program's execution, you often will want to temporarily halt the listing or program execution in order to view specific parts of the output. You may do this with the ^Num Lock key combination.

Typing ^Num Lock pauses BASICA operations until ^Num Lock is typed again or any other character key on the keyboard is pressed.

Interrupting BASICA Operations

The important control key combination, ^Break keys, will stop the execution of all BASICA operations including **RUN, LIST, AUTO** (the command to generate line numbers automatically), and more.

The Break key is located on the top row and far right side of the keyboard and is labeled on the top with "Scroll Lock." The front of the key is labeled "Break."

When ^Break is typed, any current operation will be interrupted and the "Ok" prompt will return.

EXERCISE 4: Modifying progone.BAS

You now will modify progone.BAS so that the program will perform any one of four computations, selected by the user, on two numbers input by the user. The purpose of this step in the tutorial is to allow you to use and build a working familiarity with many of the operations and commands discussed so far. In the exercise you will revise, run, and debug the new progone. Knowledge of the program statements used in this modified version of progone is not essential to the intent of this step.

The changes you will make to the program demonstrate that BASICA program lines may have several program statements on them if the statements are separated by colons, and they provide some information about command syntax and program design by example.

1. Use the commands and editing features of BASICA to modify progone.BAS into the following form:

```
1 REM ****************************************
2 REM Assignment # nn
3 REM Program Name -
4 REM
5 REM Prepared for: Course name/number/section
6 REM By          : your name
7 REM Date        : mm/dd/yy
8 REM ****************************************
9 REM
100 REM ----------  Menu Module -----------
110 REM
120    CLS
130    PRINT "Calculator Program"
140    PRINT "=================="
150    PRINT "1) Multiplication "
160    PRINT "2) Division       "
170    PRINT "3) Addition       "
180    PRINT "4) Subtraction    "
190    PRINT
200    INPUT "Enter the number of your choice ",C
210    REM
220    REM ------ Data Entry Module --------
230    PRINT
240    INPUT "Enter the first number ",A
```

```
250     INPUT "Enter the next  number ",B
260     PRINT
270     REM --- Process Selection Module ----
280     REM
290     ON C GOSUB 500,600,700,800
300     REM
310     REM ------- Output Module -----------
320     PRINT
330     PRINT A;C$;B;" equals ";ANSWER
340     REM
350     REM ----- Bottom of Loop Module -----
360     REM
370     PRINT:PRINT:INPUT "Continue (Y/N) ";MORE$
380 IF MORE$ = "Y" OR MORE$ = "y" THEN GOTO 120 ELSE CLS:END
390 REM
400 REM ----- Processing Subroutines -------
410 REM
500 ANSWER = A*B:C$=" times "      :RETURN
600 ANSWER = A/B:C$=" divided by ":RETURN
700 ANSWER = A+B:C$=" plus "       :RETURN
800 ANSWER = A-B:C$=" minus "      :RETURN
999 END
```

2. Run the program and test it to see if all parts of it are working. Use full-screen editing to correct any mistakes that you may have made.

EXERCISE 5: Programming Techniques

The remainder of the tutorial is designed to introduce you to a variety of programming techniques and to some of the peculiarities of the IBM PC and its programming language BASICA.

Using the SAVE Command

1. Type [**SAVE**"progone↵].

The first technique discussed here is brief, but important. Save your programs periodically. It is a quick operation that ultimately will save you time and frustration.

Direct Mode

Direct mode refers to the fact that most of BASICA's statements may be entered without line numbers and the computer will act on them directly.

1. To demonstrate direct mode, type the following:

```
[^Home]
[INPUT "Enter a number ",Z↵ ]
 Enter a number [1234↵ ]
 Ok
[PRINT Z↵ ]
  1234
 Ok
[FOR I = 1 to 10: PRINT I;:NEXT I↵ ]
  1  2  3  4  5  6  7  8  9  10
 Ok
```

Using direct mode is helpful in situations when you are not sure of the syntax or would like to test the effect of a program line before you add or insert it into a program. If you are satisfied with the command's execution in direct mode, you may move the cursor to its display (still on the screen), turn on the insert mode, insert the appropriate line number at the appropriate place, and tap the Enter key to enter it as a line of your program.

2. Type [**RUN**↵].

```
Calculator Program
==================
1) Multiplication
2) Division
3) Addition
4) Subtraction

Enter the number of your choice [2↵ ]

Enter the first number [10↵ ]
Enter the next  number [0↵ ]          (meant to type 10)

Division by zero


10 divided by 0 equals 1.701412E+38

Continue (Y/N) ? [N↵ ]

(screen clears)
Ok
[PRINT A↵ ]
 10
Ok
[PRINT B↵ ]
 0
Ok
[PRINT A/B↵ ]
Division by zero

1.701412E+38
```

The preceding use of direct mode is helpful when unexpected results are occurring during your program's execution. You can stop the program by typing ^Break or wait until it is done executing, then print the values of the variables you suspect may be part of the problem. The values printed will be the last values held by those variables.

Tracing Program Execution

Another useful debugging technique involves the use of the **TRON** and **TROFF** commands of BASICA. These two commands turn on and off program tracing.

1. Type [**TRON**↵**RUN**↵].

```
[1][2][3][4][5][6][7][8][9][100][110][120] (screen clears)
[130]Calculator Program
[140]=================
[150]1) Multiplication
[160]2) Division
[170]3) Addition
[180]4) Subtraction
[190]
[200]Enter the number of your choice [3↵ ]
[210][220][230]
[240]Enter the first number [10↵ ]
[250]Enter the next  number [10↵ ]
[260]
[270][280][290][700][300][310][320]
[330] 10  plus  10  equals  20
[340][350][360][370]

Continue (Y/N) ? [n↵ ]
[380] (screen clears)
OK
```

When program tracing is on, the line numbers of the program lines being executed are displayed on the monitor as the computer executes them. This feature allows you to track the execution of your program while it is running to determine the actual vs. desired order of program line execution.

2. Now type [**TROFF**↵] to turn off program tracing.

Function Keys

Ten gray keys are located on the far-left side of the keyboard. They are Function keys, often referred to as programmable or soft keys.

BASICA automatically programs each of these keys to contain a string of characters used to print entire BASICA commands on the monitor screen. The most frequently used Function keys and their strings are:

F1 (**LIST**)
F2 (**RUN**)
F3 (**LOAD**")
F4 (**SAVE**")

At the bottom of the monitor screen you will see a list of all Function keys and the strings they are holding.

When you press a Function key the string that it holds is placed on the monitor screen for you to enter. In some cases, an Enter keystroke is part of the string so that it is entered automatically. The strings with Enter keystrokes are displayed at the bottom of the screen with an arrow as the last character.

Function Key Commands

Several BASICA commands are associated with the Function keys, one of which allows you to reprogram the string a Function key is holding. To give you experience with Function key commands, complete the following steps.

1. Type the following.

[^Home]	
[KEY OFF↵]	turns off the list at the bottom of the screen.
[KEY ON↵]	turns the list back on.
[KEY LIST↵]	lists the F keys like a program is listed.
[KEY 9, "Portland"↵]	changes the string in F9 from [KEY] to [Portland]. Notice the list at the bottom of the screen reflects this change.

A Function key may hold up to 15 characters and the ability to assign your own characters to these keys can be very useful when you must enter repetitive data.

It may be useful to know that to add an Enter keystroke to a string, type +CHR$(13) after the string. For example typing:

```
[KEY 1,"LIST"+CHR$(13)↵ ]
```

will program the Function key F1 to hold [**LIST**↵]. To include a quote character in a Function key string use +CHR(34). For instance:

```
[KEY 9, "KILL"+CHR$(34)↵ ]
```

will program the F9 key to hold [**KILL"**].

The Alt Key

The key located on the bottom left side of the keyboard and labeled "Alt" is used like the Ctrl key because it is pressed and held while another key is tapped. (The convention of [Alt-key] will mean press and hold the Alt key and then tap the next key shown.)

The Alt key also will produce entire BASICA commands and statements when used with the alphabetic keys on the keyboard. For instance,

[Alt-P] . . . displays **PRINT**
[Alt-I] . . . displays **INPUT**
[Alt-G] . . . displays **GOTO**
[Alt-D] . . . displays **DELETE**

Generally speaking, use of the Alt key is minimal for beginning BASICA programmers. Another use—one that is both fun and appropriate for ending the tutorial—is related to using the Alt key for fancy output in your BASIC programs.

Each key on the keyboard has an ASCII code (a number) assigned to it. If you press and hold the Alt key while typing a character's code on the numeric keypad (the number keys on the right side of the keyboard), that character will appear on the screen. To demonstrate do the following.

1. Type [Alt-65]. Capital A appears on the screen.

Approximately 128 characters are not shown on the keyboard. They are called special characters or, as a group, the extended character set. Their ASCII character codes begin at the number 127 and go to 254.

2. Type the following to view all of these special characters.

```
[^Home]
[FOR I = 127 TO 254: PRINT CHR$(I);: NEXT I↵ ]
```

You may print the special characters directly on the screen by using the Alt key and the numeric keypad keys.

3. Type this program line 325:

Begin in column 11

```
325       FOR I = 1 TO 12: PRINT "[Alt-177][Alt-176]";:NEXT I:PRINT "[Alt-177]"
```

Use the Alt-key convention here rather than literally typing what is shown

4. Now [**LIST** 310–350↵].
5. Move the cursor to line 325 and change its line number to be 335, and then type ↵ (Enter) to enter the change.
6. Now type [^Home] and **LIST** 310–350↵] again.

The last two steps illustrate a handy way to duplicate a line in a BASICA program.

7. Finally, [**RUN**↵] the program to see how its answer output is affected by the two new program lines.

Unfortunately, output on the screen generated by the extended ASCII character set will not print out on most printers because these characters are not accepted as part of the American Standard Code for Information Interchange.

Returning to DOS

The final steps of the tutorial follow.

1. **SAVE** progone.
2. **LLIST** the program.
3. Produce a hard-copy sample **RUN** of the program.
4. Type [**SYSTEM**↵].

SYSTEM is the BASICA command that erases any BASIC program that may be in RAM, and erases BASICA from RAM. You have returned to the DOS level of operation as you can tell by the A> on the screen.

BASICA Quick Reference Command Summary

ABS(x)	Returns absolute value of x
AUTO	Automatic line numbers
BEEP	Beeps the speaker
CHR$(n)	Returns ASCII character
CINT(x)	Returns x as rounded integer
CIRCLE	Draws an ellipse
CLOSE	Closes files
CLS	Clears Screen
COLOR	Alters screen output
CONT	Continues program
CV(I) (S) (D)	Converts strings to numbers
DATA	Holds data elements
DEF FN	Defines a function
DEFtype	Declares variable types
DIM	Dimensions arrays
DRAW	Draws an object
EDIT	Displays a program line
END	Terminates a program
EOF	Signals End OF File
ERASE	Eliminates arrays
FIELD	Defines file buffer
FILES	Lists diskette files
FIX(x)	Truncates x to an integer
FOR NEXT	Establishes a loop
GET	Gets a random file record
GOSUB	Passes control to subroutine
GOTO	Passes control to a line
IF	Sets a condition
INPUT	Takes data from keyboard
INPUT$	Takes data from files
INPUT$(x)	Takes x characters
INT(x)	Returns largest integer
KEY	Controls F key display
KILL	Deletes a diskette file
LEFT$(n)	Returns leftmost characters
LET	Assigns values to variables
LINE	Draws a line or box
LIST	Lists a program on screen
LLIST	Lists a program on printer
LOAD	Loads a BASICA program
LOCATE	Controls cursor position
LPRINT	Outputs to the printer
(R) (L)SET	Moves data into file buffer
MERGE	Merges ASCII file into program
**MID$**(x$,n)	Returns characters from string
MK(I) (S) (D)$	Makes strings from numbers
NAME	Renames a diskette file
NEW	Erases current program file
ON	Passes control by condition
OPEN	Opens a file
PAINT	Fills in an area on the screen
PLAY	Plays music specified by strings
PRINT	Outputs to the screen
PRINT USING	Formats output
PSET	Draws a point on the screen
PRESET	Blanks a point on the screen
PUT	Sends a record to a random file
RANDOMIZE	Reseeds random number generator
READ	Reads DATA elements
REM	Allows for remarks in program
RENUM	Renumbers a program
RESTORE	Allows DATA elements to be reREAD
RESUME	Returns control from error trap
RETURN	Returns control from subroutine
**RIGHT$**(x$,n)	Returns rightmost n characters
RND	Returns a random number
RUN	Begins program execution
SAVE	Saves a program file
SCREEN	Sets screen mode
SOUND	Generates sound through speaker
SPC(n)	Outputs n spaces
SQR(x)	Returns square root of x
STOP	Interrupts program execution
SWAP	Exchanges variable's values
SYSTEM	Exits BASICA
TAB(n)	Moves cursor to column n
TRON	Turns trace on
TROFF	Turns trace off
VAL	Returns numbers from strings
WHILE WEND	Establishes a loop
WIDTH	Sets screen character widths
WRITE#	Outputs data to a file

BASICA File Commands

Diskette File Commands

FILES	Lists a directory of the default disk drive files on the monitor screen. (DOS (A>) equivalent is the **DIR** command).
Example Variations	
FILES"*.BAS	Lists all .BAS files on default drive.
FILES"B:	Lists all files on B: drive.
FILES"B:*.TXT	Lists all .TXT files on B: drive.
KILL"filename.ext	Erases the specified file from the diskette. (DOS (A>) equivalent is the **ERASE** command).
Example Variations	
KILL"B:progone.BAS	Erases progone.BAS from the B: drive.
KILL"*.BAS	Erases all .BAS files on default drive.
KILL"B:*.TXT	Erases all .TXT files on B: drive.
LOAD"filename	Copies the specified BASIC program (.BAS) file from the diskette into the computer's RAM memory.
Example Variation	
LOAD"B:progone.BAS	Loads progone.BAS from the B: drive.
MERGE"filename	Merges a program (.BAS) file, saved in ASCII, from the diskette into the program in RAM. Duplicate line numbers are replaced by lines in the file being merged.
NAME"filename.ext" **AS**"filename.ext"	Renames a diskette file. (DOS (A>) equivalent is the **RENAME** command)
RUN"filename	Loads and begins execution of the specified program (.BAS) file.
SAVE"filename	Copies the program in RAM onto the diskette under the specified filename. If a program with that filename already exists, it is replaced by the program being saved.
SAVE"filename",**A**	Saves the specified file in ASCII.

Current File Commands

CONT	Continues program execution at the line following a break-point caused by a STOP or END statement, a ^Break, or an error.
LIST **LIST** line#-line# **LIST** -line# **LIST** line#-	Lists the lines of the program in RAM on the monitor screen. From one line to another (line#-line#), up to a line (-line#), from a line on (line#-).
LLIST	Lists the lines of the program in RAM on the printer.
NEW	Erases the current program from RAM memory.
RUN	Begins execution of the program in RAM.

BASICA Control Keys

KEY COMBINATIONS

^Alt-Del Reboots the DOS.

^Break Interrupts any BASICA operation.

^Home Clears the monitor screen.

^Num Lock Pauses BASICA operations.

^PrtSc Toggles ON/OFF an echo of screen output to the printer (versions of DOS 2.0 or higher).

Shift-PrtSc Prints the screen on the printer.

Alt-Key Used with alphabetic keys to print BASIC statements.

A	**AUTO**	J	(no word)		
B	**BSAVE**	K	**KEY**	S	**SCREEN**
C	**COLOR**	L	**LOCATE**	T	**THEN**
D	**DELETE**	M	**MOTOR**	U	**USING**
E	**ELSE**	N	**NEXT**	V	**VAL**
F	**FOR**	O	**OPEN**	W	**WIDTH**
G	**GOTO**	P	**PRINT**	X	**XOR**
H	**HEX$**	Q	(no word)	Y	(no word)
I	**INPUT**	R	**RUN**	Z	(no word)

OTHER CONTROL KEYS

Enter Key ↵ Enters the current line into memory for the computer to act upon.

Escape Key Erases a line from the monitor screen at current cursor position.

Num Lock Key Toggles ON/OFF ten-key numeric to cursor control keys.

Function Keys 1–10 User programmable keys that may hold up to 15 characters.

F1	**LIST**	F6	**LPT1:"**↵
F2	**RUN**↵	F7	**TRON**↵
F3	**LOAD"**	F8	**TROFF**↵
F4	**SAVE"**	F9	**KEY**
F5	**CONT**↵	F10	**SCREEN** 0,0,0

To change any of these keys, type KEY #, "The string."

Type [+CHR$(13)] after the last quote to add a ↵.

Type [+CHR$(34)] after the last quote to add a quote (").

BASICA Editing Commands

AUTO	Generates line numbers, starting at 10 and increased by 10, each time the Enter key is pressed. ^Break stops automatic generation of line numbers. An asterisk (*) following a number generated by **AUTO** indicates that a program line with that number already exists. **AUTO** 100 — Starts at line 100, increased by 10. **AUTO** 50,20 — Starts at line 50, increased by 20. **AUTO** ,50 — Starts at line 0, increased by 50.
DELETE line#1-line#2	Deletes all lines from line#1 to line#2, inclusive. Both line#1 and line#2 must exist in the current program. **DELETE** 30-100 — Deletes lines 30 through 100. **DELETE** -60 — Deletes all lines up to and including 60.
EDIT line#	Displays specified program line for editing. Most useful for editing programs from hard-copy listings where several dispersed lines need correcting. **EDIT** 120 — Displays line 120 for editing.
RENUM	Renumbers the current program file. Starts line numbering with 10 and renumbers by increments of 10. All referenced line numbers are changed accordingly.

RENUM ,,20	Starts with 10, increments by 20.
RENUM 100,,20	Starts with 100, increments by 20.
RENUM 100,50,20	Renumbers the program from line 50 on, starts with 100, increments of 20.

Inherent Commands

Inserting a Line

Give the new program line a line number that falls between the two line numbers of the program lines on either side of where the line is to be inserted.

Deleting a Line

Type the line number of the line to be deleted, and then press the Enter Key.

Replacing a Line

Type the new line with the same line number of the line to be replaced.

Moving a Program Line

Use the full-screen editor to change the line number of the line. This will leave two identical lines located at two different places in the new program. Type the first line number (Enter) to delete the original line.

BASICA Editing Keys

Any program line or command displayed on the monitor screen may be edited with BASICA's full-screen editing. The procedure is as follows.

1. Move the cursor to the position in the program or command line to be edited.
2. Make the corrections desired.
3. Press the Enter key to enter that line or command into memory.

EDITING KEYS

Enter Key Enters the line at the current cursor position (the current line) into memory.

Cursor Control Keys Moves the cursor in the direction of the cursor arrow.

Backspace Key Backspaces and erases the character to the left on the current line.

Insert Key Toggles ON Insert Mode. Any non-character key will turn OFF Insert Mode.

Delete Key Deletes the character at current cursor position.

Home Key Moves cursor to top left corner of monitor screen.

End Key Moves cursor to the end of the current line.

KEY COMBINATIONS

Ctrl-Break Exits line being edited without entering that line into memory.

Ctrl-End Erases to the end of the line from the current cursor position.

Ctrl ← or Ctrl → Moves the cursor one word to the left or the right.

BASICA Commands, Functions, and Statements

The following briefly describes many of the commands, functions, and statements available with BASICA.

ABS(x)

Absolute value function. Returns the absolute value of x. The following assigns the value 24 to N.

LET N = ABS(12 * (− 2))

AUTO

Generates line numbers, starting at 10 and increased by 10, each time the Enter key is pressed. ^Break stops Automatic generation of line numbers.

An asterisk (*) following a number generated by **AUTO** indicates that a program line with that number already exists.

AUTO 100	Starts at line 100, increased by 10.
AUTO 50,20	Starts at line 50, increased by 20.
AUTO ,50	Starts at line 0, increased by 50.

BEEP

Sounds the speaker (800 Hz for 1/4 second). **PRINT CHR$**(7) has the same effect.

CHR$(x)

Character string function. Returns the character equivalent of the ASCII code number x. The following prints a capital A on the monitor screen.

PRINT CHR$(65)

CINT(x)

Convert to integer function. Returns the rounded integer value of x. The following assigns the value 6 to the variable B.

LET B = **CINT**(17/3)

CIRCLE

(Graphics mode) Draws an ellipse on the screen.

CIRCLE(120,80),45

The above draws a circle with its center at the screen coordinates 120, 80, and with a radius of 45. Other options allow part of the circle to be drawn and/or the aspect to be changed.

CLEAR

Sets all variables to zero or null.

CLOSE

Concludes input/output to all devices or files. Includes option to close a particular file by specifying the file number under which it was opened. For example,

CLOSE #1,#2

closes files opened as #1 and #2.

CLS

Clears the monitor screen and returns the cursor to the Home position.

COLOR

(Black & White monitor) Sets the foreground, background, and border colors. For example,

0 = Black
7 = White
15 = Bright white

COLOR 0, 7, 15

	sets black foreground (text) on white background with a bright white border. Options include adding 16 to any number for blinking colors.
CONT	Continues program execution at the line following a break point.
CSRLIN	Cursor line function. Returns the current row number of the cursor location.
CVI(x$), **CVS**(x$), and **CVD**(x$)	(Random Files) Convert string function. Converts the string x$ to a numeric-type value as an integer **CVI**(x$), single (**CVS**(x$), or double **CVD**(x$) precision numeric-type variable.
DATA	Used with the **READ** statement, the **DATA** statement holds constants to be read during execution of the program. **READ** ACT,CTY$,AGE,UNIT$ **DATA** 653, "Port., OR",54,IBM PC **DATA** statements are nonexecutable and may be placed anywhere in a program. The items in the **DATA** statement(s) are read from first to last, and are assigned in order to the variables found in the **READ** statement(s).
DEF FN	For user-defined functions. The general form is: **DEF FN**variable-name(argument) = expression
DEF	Declares variable types as integer, single-precision, double-precision, or string—INT, SNG, DBL, or STR, respectively. The following globally defines all variables starting with the letter A and the letters H through M as integer variables. **DEFINT** A,H-M
DELETE line#1-line#2	Deletes all lines from line#1 to line#2, inclusive. Both line#1 and line#2 must exist in the current program. **DELETE** 30-100 Deletes lines 30 through 100. **DELETE** -60 Deletes all lines up to and including 60.
DIM	Specifies the maximum values for subscript variables. Necessary for lists longer than 10 and arrays greater than 10 in any dimension. The following sets the array A$(x,y) to hold a maximum of 20 by 10 strings. **DIM** A$(20,10) Lists and arrays may only be dimensioned once.
DRAW string	(Graphics mode) Draws the object described by the defining string. U Move up E Move diagonally up and right. D Move down F Move diagonally down and right. L Move left G Move diagonally down and left. R Move right H Move diagonally up and left. The string is composed of direction letters followed by distance numbers. The following draws a small triangle in the middle of the monitor screen. **DRAW** "F20 L40 E20" or A$ = "F20 L40 E20" **DRAW** A$

EDIT

Displays the specified program line for editing. Most useful for editing programs from hard-copy listings where several dispersed lines need to be corrected. The following displays line 120 for editing.

EDIT 120

END

Terminates program execution and closes all files. **END** statements may be placed anywhere in the program to stop execution.

EOF(x)

(Files) End Of File function. Returns 1 (true) when an attempt is made to read past the end of the file opened as number x. Most useful when used as a condition to avoid "Input past end" errors.

IF **EOF**(2) THEN . . .

or

WHILE NOT **EOF**(1)

FIELD

(Random Files) Defines field space for variables in a random file buffer.

FIELD #1, 15 AS P$, 10 AS Q$

The above allocates, for the random file opened as #1, the first 15 characters (bytes) to the variable P$, and the next 10 characters to the variable Q$.

FILES

Lists a directory of the diskette files on the monitor screen.

FIX(x)

Truncates x to an integer without returning the next lowest number if x is negative.

FOR and **NEXT**

These two statements cause a series of instructions to be executed a given number of times. The general form is:

```
FOR variable = x TO y
  :
  any program statements
  :
NEXT variable
```

"Variable" is the loop counter; x is the beginning number; y is the ending number.

STEP option allows the loop counter variable to be increased by a value other than one (1). The following will print "Hello" 10 times on the monitor screen:

```
FOR J = 1 TO 10
     PRINT " Hello "
NEXT J
```

and this will print "Hello" twice on the monitor screen.

```
X = 10
FOR Q = 1 TO X STEP 5
     PRINT " Hello "
NEXT Q
```

GET

(Random Files) Reads a record from a random file. The following reads the fifth record in the random file opened as #2.

GET #2,5

GOSUB and RETURN

Transfers control to a subroutine by branching to a specified line. The **RETURN** statement at the end of the subroutine returns control to the statement following the **GOSUB.** The following branches to line 1500 to perform that subroutine.

GOSUB 1500

GOTO

Causes an unconditional branch to the specified line. The following branches program execution to line 500.

GOTO 500

IF THEN and ELSE

Sets a condition and if the condition is true the statement(s) following the **THEN** are executed. As an option, with **ELSE** (if the condition is not true) the statements following **ELSE** are executed. Otherwise control is passed to the next program line.

IF A$="Y" **THEN PRINT** "Done" **ELSE PRINT** " More ": **INPUT** A2$: **GOTO** 500

If A$ equals Y then "Done" will be printed on the monitor. Otherwise, "More ?" will be printed on the monitor and the program will wait for an input. After the input is entered, control will be passed to line 500.

INKEY$

Scans the keyboard for input from the user. The following essentially "freezes" the keyboard, allowing the user to type only a Y or an N.

```
10 PRINT" Continue ? (Y/N)
20 A$=INKEY$
30 IF A$< > "Y" OR A$ < >"N" THEN 20
```

INPUT

Allows for user input from the keyboard. **INPUT** is followed by a prompt string (optional), and then an appropriate variable for the input. The following prints "Enter a number" on the monitor screen and then waits for a number to be entered from the keyboard.

INPUT "Enter a number"; A

INPUT #

(Files) Reads data from sequential files and assigns them to program variables. The following assigns two values, a numeric and a string, to two variables, DEPT and EMP$, from the sequential file opened as #1.

INPUT #1,DEPT,EMP$

INPUT$(x)

Input function. Reads x number of characters from the keyboard. With **INPUT$** it is not necessary to press Enter when answering an input prompt. The program waits until x number of characters are typed, and then continues program execution. The following assigns Q$ the single key character that is typed.

PRINT " Continue ? (Y/N)";
Q$ = **INPUT$**(1)

INSTR(x$,y$)

Instring function. Searches for the first occurrence of a substring (y$) within a string (x$) and returns the starting character position of the substring.

INT(x)

Integer function. Returns the largest integer value that is less than or equal to x. The following prints 5 and −4 on the monitor screen.

PRINT INT(5.675)
PRINT INT(−3.333)

KEY	Sets display of the Function keys (screen-row 25). For example, **KEY ON** or **KEY OFF** turns on or off the Function key display; **KEY LIST** lists the full contents of each Function key on the monitor screen; and **KEY** n, "string" changes the Function key n to contain the specified string.
KILL"	Erases the specified file from the diskette.
**LEFT$**(x$,n)	Left substring function. Returns the left-most n characters of the string x$. For example, A$ = "This is an example" **PRINT LEFT$**(A$,9) prints "This is a" on the monitor screen.
LEN(x$)	String Length function. Returns the number of characters in the string x$. For example, A$ = "This is an example" **PRINT LEN**(A$) prints 18 on the monitor.
LET	Assigns the value of an expression to a variable. **LET** is optional in BASICA. For example, **LET** A = 5 is the same as A = 5.
LINE	(Graphics mode) Draws a line or a box on the monitor screen. For example, **LINE** (200,50)–(300,100) draws a diagonal line from the coordinate 200, 50 to the coordinate 300, 100; and **LINE** (200,50)–(300,100),,B draws a box with its top left corner at 200, 50 and its bottom right corner at 300, 100. BF, instead of B, fills in the box with the foreground color.
LINE INPUT #n	(Files) Reads an entire line from a sequential file opened as file number n into a string variable.
LIST	Lists the lines of the current program on the monitor screen. **LIST** -line# up to a line **LIST** line#- from a line on
LLIST	Lists the lines of the current program on the printer.
LOAD"	Copies the specified file from the diskette into the computer's RAM memory.

LOCATE	Positions the cursor on the monitor screen by row, column. For example, **LOCATE** 12,40 positions the cursor in the middle of the screen. **LOCATE** will not work on printer output.
LPRINT	Directs output to the printer. **LPRINT** may be used with all of the options of the **PRINT** statement.
LSET and **RSET**	(Random Files) Prepares strings to be **PUT** into a random file. **LSET** or **RSET** statements must follow the **FIELD** statement for the variable(s) being (**L** or **R**) **SET**. **LSET** left justifies the string in its field; **RSET** right justifies the string. For example, **LSET** A$ = EMP$ left justifies the string EMP$ in the field defined as A$.
MERGE"	Merges a diskette file, saved in ASCII, from the diskette into the current program. Duplicate line numbers are replaced by lines in the file being merged.
**MID$**(x$,n,m)	Midstring function. Returns a portion of the string x$, m characters long, beginning at the nth character. For example, A$ = "This is an example" Z$ = **MID$**(A$,5,5) **PRINT** Z$ prints "is a" on the monitor.
MKI$**(x), **MKS$(x), and **MKD$**(x)	(Random Files) Make string function. Converts integer, double- or single-precision numeric-type variables into string-type variables.
NAME"	Renames a diskette file. For example, **NAME** "PROG1.BAS" **AS** "PROG2.BAS" renames PROG1 to PROG2.
NEW	Erases the current program from RAM memory.
ON ERROR GOTO	Enables (turns on) error trapping. When an error is detected, control is passed to the beginning of the error trapping subroutine specified by the line number following **GOTO.** For example, **ON ERROR GOTO** 500 will pass control to line 500 if an error occurs during program execution. **RESUME** at the end of the subroutine transfers control back to the line that generated the error.
ON GOSUB and **ON GOTO**	Branches to one of several lines or subroutines, based on the value of n, where the general form is **ON** n **GOSUB** line#1,line#2, ... n is an integer that points to the line# to which control will be passed. If n = 1, then control will be passed to the first line# listed. If n = 5 then control will be passed to the fifth line# listed.

OPEN

(Files) Allows input/output to a file or device. The general form is:

OPEN "filename" **FOR** mode **AS** # fnum

Mode is necessary for sequential files and may be any of the following:

INPUT
OUTPUT
APPEND

If "**FOR** mode" is omitted, the file will be opened for random file input/output. For example,

OPEN "DATA" **FOR INPUT AS** #2

opens the sequential file named "DATA" as the #2 file for input of values from the file to the program; and

OPEN "DATA" **FOR OUTPUT AS** #3

opens the same file as the #3 file for output of values from the program to the file. **OPEN FOR OUTPUT** erases the contents of the file being opened. Further,

OPEN "DATA" **FOR APPEND AS** #3

opens DATA for output without erasing the file. Any values output are added to the end of (appended to) the file.

Once a file has been opened, it must be closed before being opened again.

PAINT

(Graphics mode) (Black & White monitor) Fills in an area on the monitor screen with a selected color. The general form is:

PAINT (x,y),color,boundary-color

x,y sets the coordinate point at which painting will begin. Color is the color that will be used to fill in the area. Boundary-color describes the color that outlines where painting is to stop.

The default foreground color is 3 in medium resolution, 1 in high resolution. Zero (0) is the background color in both resolutions. For example,

SCREEN 1
DRAW "L50 D50 R50 U50"
PAINT (130,120),3,3

sets medium resolution, draws a box on the screen, begins painting inside the box, and quits when it reaches the outline of the box.

PLAY

Plays music as specified by a string.

POS(x)

Position function. Returns the current column position of the cursor. May be used with the **CRSLN** statement to determine the exact location of the cursor.

PRINT

Displays program output on the monitor screen. **PRINT** is followed by a list of variables, constants, and/or expressions. If the list is omitted, a blank line is displayed. The items in the list are separated by: 1) A semicolon (;) which leaves no spaces between items output; 2) A space which acts in the same manner as a semicolon; or 3) a comma (,) which prints the next item in the next Print Zone (every 14 columns).

A comma or semicolon, after the last item in a **PRINT** statement, disables the automatic carriage return.

PRINT USING

Displays output on the monitor screen in a specified format. A string constant or variable, containing special formatting characters, is used to set the fields and formats for printing strings and numbers.

String fields are specified with backslashes (\). Two plus the number of spaces between the backslashes is the allowable length of a string printed in that format.

```
A$ = "This is an example"
Z$ = "     \               \     "
PRINT USING Z$; A$
This is an ex
```

If the number of spaces between the backslashes is greater than the length of the string being printed, the string is left justified and padded with spaces on the right.

Numeric fields are specified by the number sign (#). One sign is used to represent each digit position that will be displayed. A decimal point may be inserted at any position in the field. Numbers are rounded to fit in the field described, and if the number is too large to fit in its field, a percent sign (%) is output to the left of that number.

```
C  = 123.466
L$ ="                  ###.##"
PRINT USING L$;C
                  123.47
```

The dollar sign ($) may be used to the left of the numeric format to print a dollar sign to the left of the number being printed. A double dollar sign to the left causes the dollar sign to be printed to the immediate left of the number. A comma to the immediate left of the decimal in the numeric format, causes a comma to be printed every third digit.

PRINT #

(Files) Writes program output to a file. **PRINT #** outputs to a file in the same manner as **PRINT** outputs to the screen, and **PRINT #** has all the same options as **PRINT** (TAB, SPC, USING, etc.). Semicolons usually are used to separate the items being output. For example,

PRINT #1, A$;",";B,C,D

outputs to the sequential file opened as #1, the values of the variables A$, B, C, and D. Notice that a comma in quotes follows a string to separate it from other items in this **PRINT #** statement.

PSET

(Graphics) Draws a point at the specified coordinates on the monitor screen. For example,

PSET (100,200)

draws a point at the screen coordinates 100, 200. **PSET** also may be used to define the starting point for a **DRAW** string.

PUT

(Random Files) Writes a record to a random file. For example,

PUT #2,5

writes the fifth record to the random file opened as #2.

RANDOMIZE number	Reseeds the random number generator. **RANDOMIZE** keeps the **RND** function from returning the same set of random numbers each time the program is executed. The seed is the number that follows **RANDOMIZE.** Each time the seed is changed the program will generate a new set of random numbers.
READ	Reads values from **DATA** statements and assigns them to the variables listed after **READ.** For example, **READ** ACT,CTY$,AGE,UNIT$ **DATA** 653,"Port., OR",54,IBM PC assigns the values in the **DATA** statement, in order of their appearance, to the variables in the **READ** statements, in order of their appearance: ACT = 653, CTY$ = Port., OR, etc. Once a **DATA** item has been read, it is not read again during the execution of the program. Instead, a marker is set at the next **DATA** item for the next executed **READ** statement to read.
REM	Used to put explanatory notes (remarks) in a program. **REM** statements are not executed. Whatever is typed after **REM** is ignored during program execution.
RENUM	Renumbers the current program file. Starts line numbering with 10 and renumbers by increments of 10. All referenced line numbers are changed accordingly. **RENUM** ,,20 — Starts with 10, increments by 20. **RENUM** 100,,20 — Starts with 100, increments by 20. **RENUM** 100,50,20 — Renumbers the program from line 50 on, starts with 100, increments of 20.
RESTORE	Allows **DATA** statements to be reread. **RESTORE** sets the **READ** marker back to the beginning of the first item in the first **DATA** statement. Optionally, the marker can be set back to the first item in a particular **DATA** statement by typing the line number for the statement after **RESTORE.** For example, **RESTORE** 500 sets the marker back to the first **DATA** item in line 500.
RESUME	Continues program execution after an error trapping subroutine has been completed. **RESUME** 0 — Turns off error trapping. **RESUME** NEXT — Returns control to the next line.
RETURN	Returns control, from a subroutine, to the statement following the **GOSUB** that initiated the branch to that subroutine.
**RIGHT$**(x$,n)	Right substring function. Returns the right-most n characters of the string, x$. For example, A$ = "This is an example" **PRINT RIGHT$**(A$,4) prints "mple" on the monitor.

RND	Random number function. Returns a seven-digit random number between 0 and 1, such as .6291626.
RUN	Begins execution of the BASICA program in RAM. **RUN**"filename — Loads and begins execution of the specified file. **RUN** line# — Begins program execution at the specified line number.
SAVE"	Copies the current program onto the diskette under the specified filename. If a program with that filename already exists, it is replaced by the program being saved. For example, **SAVE**"filename",A saves the specified file in ASCII format.
SCREEN	Sets the screen for text, medium resolution, or high resolution graphics. **SCREEN** 0 — Text (standard screen) 40 or 80 columns. **SCREEN** 1 — Medium resolution (320 × 200) points. **SCREEN** 2 — High resolution (640 × 200) points. **SCREEN** 1 or 2 is required for any of the statements marked (Graphics mode).
SCREEN(x,y)	Screen function. Returns the ASCII code for the character found at the screen coordinates (row = x, column = y).
SOUND	Generates sound through the speaker. **SOUND** is followed by two numbers—one for the frequency and one for the duration. For example, **SOUND** 523,3 generates a sound (roughly, middle C) for the equivalent of three clock ticks (about 1/6th of a second).
SPC(n)	Space function. Prints n number of spaces in a **PRINT** statement. For example, **PRINT SPC**(15);"Test" prints "Test" starting in the sixteenth column position on the monitor screen row.
SQR(x)	Square root function. Returns the square root of x. For example, **PRINT SQR**(16) prints 4 on the monitor.
STOP	Terminates program execution. The program will stop with a break-point message indicating the line where the **STOP** occurred. The **CONT** command will continue program execution at the line following the **STOP.**
STR$(x)	String function. Returns the string value of the numeric expression x. **STR$**(x) is the complement of **VAL**(x$).
SWAP	Exchanges the values of two variables. For example, **SWAP** A$,B$ assigns A$ the value in B$ and B$ the value in A$.
SYSTEM	Exits BASICA and returns to the DOS level of operation.
TAB(n)	Tab function. Prints spaces to the nth position in a **PRINT** statement. For example,

PRINT "This is"; TAB(30);"a test"

prints "This is," starting at the first position, then prints "a test," starting at the thirtieth position on the screen row.

TRON and **TROFF**	These two commands are used to set program execution tracing on and off.
VAL(x$)	Returns a numeric value from a string. For example, A$= "123 Example" **PRINT** VAL(A$) prints the number 123 on the monitor screen. The number to be returned must precede any characters in the string.
WHILE and **WEND**	These two statements execute a series of instructions as long as the condition of the while statement remains true. **WHILE** X => 1 | any statements | **WEND** As long as X is equal to, or greater than 1, the **WEND** statement will pass control to the statement immediately following the **WHILE** statement (causing a loop). X must change in value while the loop is being executed in order to reach a value less than 1, and so stop execution of this loop.
WIDTH	Sets the character size for the monitor screen. **WIDTH** 80 (default width) Sets character size to 80 per screen row. **WIDTH** 40 Sets character size to 40 per screen row.
WRITE	Similar to **PRINT**, **WRITE** outputs to the screen the list of constants, variables and expressions that follow it. **WRITE,** however, outputs a comma between each item in the list and will print the quotes around a string constant or a string assigned to a variable. **WRITE** does not recognize the Print Zones that **PRINT** uses. A$ = "an example" B = 50 **WRITE** "This is"; A$,B "This is," "an example,"50
WRITE#	Writes output to sequential files and is preferred to **PRINT** # since commas as delimiters are automatically included.

Assignment

```
LIST
10 LET A$="Example #"
20 A=1
30   PRINT A$;A
40 READ B$,B
50 DATA Example #,2
60   PRINT B$;B
70 INPUT"Type in the value for C$ :",C$
80 INPUT"                       number ";C
90   PRINT C$;C
Ok
RUN
Example # 1
Example # 2
Type in the value for C$   :Example #
                  number ? 3
Example # 3
--------------------------------------------------------------------------------

LIST
10 A$="Direct assignment"
20 LET A=5
30 B=10
40 C=A+B
50 PRINT A$;A;"+";B;"=";C
Ok
RUN
Direct assignment 5 + 10 = 15
--------------------------------------------------------------------------------

LIST
10    READ A$,B,C$,D
20    PRINT A$,B,C$,D
30 GOTO 10
40 DATA one,2,three,4,five,6,seven,8,nine,10,eleven,12
RUN
one            2              three          4
five           6              seven          8
nine           10             eleven         12
Out of DATA in 10
--------------------------------------------------------------------------------

LIST
10 INPUT"Type in a string value :",A$
20 INPUT"Enter exactly three numbers :",A,B,C
30 PRINT A$;A;B;C
Ok
RUN
Type in a string value :This is an example
Enter exactly three numbers :4,5,6
This is an example 4  5  6
```

Condition

```
LIST
10 A=7:B=15
20 IF A < 10 THEN PRINT "A is less than 10":GOTO 30
25 PRINT "A is greater than 10"
30 IF A > B THEN PRINT "A is greater than B" ELSE PRINT "A is less than B"
Ok
RUN
A is less than 10
A is less than B
---------------------------------------------------------------------------

LIST
10 A=15:B=7
20 IF A < 10 THEN PRINT "A is less than 10":GOTO 30
25 PRINT "A is greater than 10"
30 IF A > B THEN PRINT "A is greater than B" ELSE PRINT "A is less than B"
RUN
A is greater than 10
A is greater than B
---------------------------------------------------------------------------

LIST
10 A=5: B=4: C=3: D=2: E=1
20 IF C > D AND C < A THEN PRINT "C lies between D and A":GOTO 30
25 PRINT"Condition NOT TRUE"
30 IF B > E OR  B = 2 THEN B= 2 * A: PRINT B;: B=2 : PRINT B:GOTO 40
35 PRINT"Condition NOT TRUE"
40 IF A > B AND C > D OR E = 5 THEN PRINT"********************":GOTO 50
45 PRINT"Condition NOT TRUE"
50 END
RUN
C lies between D and A
 10  2
********************
---------------------------------------------------------------------------

LIST
10 A=5: B=4: C=3: D=2: E=1
20 IF C < D AND C > A THEN PRINT "C lies between D and A":GOTO 30
25 PRINT"Condition NOT TRUE"
30 IF B > E OR  B = 2 THEN B= 2 * E: PRINT B;: B=2: PRINT B:GOTO 40
35 PRINT"Condition NOT TRUE"
40 IF A < B AND C < D OR E = 5 THEN PRINT"********************":GOTO 50
45 PRINT"Condition NOT TRUE"
50 END
RUN
Condition NOT TRUE
 2  2
Condition NOT TRUE
```

Iteration

```
LIST
10 FOR X = 1 TO 5
20    PRINT X;
30 NEXT X
40 PRINT"****"
RUN
 1  2  3  4  5 ****
------------------------------------------------------------------------------------

LIST
10 FOR T = 1 TO 3
20     FOR X = 1 TO 5
30       PRINT X;
40     NEXT X
50     PRINT"****";
60 NEXT T
RUN
 1  2  3  4  5 **** 1  2  3  4  5 **** 1  2  3.  4  5 ****
------------------------------------------------------------------------------------

LIST
10 FOR X = 1 TO 3
20     FOR Y = 1 TO 5
30       READ INFO$(X,Y)
40     NEXT Y
50 NEXT X
60 FOR X = 1 TO 3: PRINT INFO$(X,1) "....... "INFO$(X,3): NEXT X
70 DATA Allen,Greene,244-3396,Mktg.,#7763
80 DATA Carol,Lundey,236-1718,Acct.,#6658
90 DATA Terry,Bright,775-0668,Mgmt.,#7204
RUN
Allen....... 244-3396
Carol....... 236-1718
Terry....... 775-0668
------------------------------------------------------------------------------------

LIST
10 HGHT = 10
20 WHILE HGHT > 1
30     BOUNCE = BOUNCE + 1
40     HGHT = HGHT * .75
50     PRINT "Bounce";BOUNCE;" - ";HGHT;TAB(25);"feet"
60 WEND
RUN
Bounce 1  -  7.5          feet
Bounce 2  -  5.625        feet
Bounce 3  -  4.21875      feet
Bounce 4  -  3.164063     feet
Bounce 5  -  2.373047     feet
Bounce 6  -  1.779785     feet
Bounce 7  -  1.334839     feet
Bounce 8  -  1.001129     feet
Bounce 9  -  .7508469     feet
```

Output

```
10 A$="This":B$="Example": A=1: B=2
20 PRINT"    5    10    15    20    25    30    35    40    45    50    55    60 ..."
30 PRINT"----!----!----!----!----!----!----!----!----!----!----!----!---- "
40 PRINT A$;"is an";B$;A;B
50 PRINT A$,"is an",B$,A,B
60 PRINT A$;TAB(10);"is an";TAB(25);B$;A;B
70 PRINT A$;SPC(10);"is an";SPC(25);B$;A;B
RUN
    5    10    15    20    25    30    35    40    45    50    55    60 ...
----!----!----!----!----!----!----!----!----!----!----!----!----
Thisis anExample 1  2
This          is an         Example        1             2
This     is an          Example 1  2
This          is an                         Example 1  2
------------------------------------------------------------------------------

LIST
10 A$="This is one way to center a string"
20 DIS =(80-LEN(A$))/2
30 PRINT TAB(DIS);A$
RUN
                      This is one way to center a string
------------------------------------------------------------------------------

LIST
10 INPUT " (;) includes a question mark";A
20 INPUT " (,) omits the question mark",A
RUN
 (;) includes a question mark? 1
 (,) omits the question mark 2
------------------------------------------------------------------------------

LIST
10 PRINT RND;SPC(10);
20 PRINT CINT(RND*10);
30 PRINT CINT(RND*100);
40 PRINT CINT(RND*1000);SPC(10);
50 PRINT CINT(RND*10)/10;
60 PRINT CINT(RND*100)/100;
70 PRINT CINT(RND*1000)/1000;
Ok
RUN
 .9076439          6  19  631           .9  .74  .843
------------------------------------------------------------------------------

LIST                    *
10 FOR J = 1 TO 6        *
20   LOCATE J,20+J        *
30   PRINT "*"             *
40 NEXT J                   *
RUN                          *
```

PRINT USING Statement

```
LIST
10 A=5:B=50:C=500:D=5000
20 PRINT USING "       ###    ";A;B;C;D
30 PRINT USING "   ####.##    ";A;B;C;D
40 PRINT USING " ####,.##     ";A;B;C;D
50 PRINT USING "$####,.##     ";A;B;C;D
60 PRINT USING "$$###,.##     ";A;B;C;D
RUN
       5         50         500        %5000
     5.00       50.00      500.00     5000.00
     5.00       50.00      500.00    5,000.00
$    5.00  $    50.00  $   500.00   $5,000.00
    $5.00      $50.00     $500.00   $5,000.00
------------------------------------------------------------------------------

LIST
10 Z$="TEST"
20 PRTSTRG$= "\   \#   \    \-"
30 FOR X = 1 TO 5
40   PRINT USING PRTSTRG$;Z$;X;"hello";
50 NEXT X
Ok
RUN
TEST1 hello - TEST2 hello - TEST3 hello - TEST4 hello - TEST5 hello -
------------------------------------------------------------------------------

LIST
10 A = 234 :B$="OUTPUT EXAMPLE": C = 567
20 X$="    Form ###   Computer report  \                  \ No. ###.##"
30 PRINT USING X$;A,B$,C
Ok
RUN
     Form 234   Computer report  OUTPUT EXAMPLE      No. 567.00
```

*NOTE: Special formatting symbols (# . , $ \) are covered in these examples. Other formatting symbols (! * _ ^ + −) have special meaning when included in the* ***PRINT USING*** string. A semicolon (;) is the only ***PRINT*** separator allowed with ***PRINT USING.***

Array Operations

The following examples are based on the string array A$(I,J), which is filled with data read from data statements. The data represent a database of employees working for a small retail store. In the following example, the array A$(I,J) is filled with the data:

A$(I,1)	Employee's last name
A$(I,2)	Employee's first name
A$(I,3)	Sex
A$(I,4)	Yearly salary
A$(I,5)	Department of employment
A$(I,6)	Amount owing on the company's personal account

Filling Array A$(I,J) with Data

```
100 DIM A$(15,6)
110 REM -----------------------------------------------------
120 FOR I = 1 TO 15
130   FOR J = 1 TO 6
140    READ A$(I,J)           ' Read loop for array A$(I,J)
150   NEXT J
160 NEXT I
170 REM -----------------------------------------------------
180 REM              Database for array A$(I,J)
190 REM
200 REM    Last        First                     Personal
210 REM    Name        Name     Sex Salary  Dept  Account
220 REM -----------------------------------------------------
230 DATA   Hunter    , Philip , M , 12000 , 3   ,  90.00
240 DATA   Parsons   , Sharon , F , 10500 , 2   ,  50.75
250 DATA   Boronat   , Penny  , F , 16200 , 4   ,  20.50
260 DATA   Carlson   , Scott  , M , 21400 , 1   , 310.00
270 DATA   Jeli      , Krista , F ,  9500 , 3   ,   0.00
280 DATA   Carson    , Cindy  , F , 22500 , 2   ,  75.00
290 DATA   Anderson  , Jeffery, M , 10000 , 2   , 200.00
300 DATA   Harrison  , Glenys , F ,  9800 , 4   , 130.60
310 DATA   Elting    , Charles, M , 17300 , 1   ,  10.00
320 DATA   Cathcart  , Anita  , F , 19000 , 4   ,  95.50
330 DATA   Nickerson , Cheryl , F ,  8700 , 3   , 105.10
340 DATA   Fuller    , Alice  , F , 19000 , 2   ,  45.00
350 DATA   Parks     , Larry  , M , 12600 , 4   , 180.00
360 DATA   Reeves    , Ronald , M , 18700 , 1   ,  92.50
370 DATA   Zimmerson , Dale   , M , 16300 , 1   , 330.00
380 REM -----------------------------------------------------
390 REM Continue program here
```

*NOTE: The data in these **DATA** statements have been entered in columns to improve readability. When data are read from **DATA** statements they automatically are stripped of all leading and trailing spaces if quotes are not used to delimit them as part of the data.*

Once the data have been read into the array, any one or all of the following example reports may be produced. The reports demonstrate how an array may be checked for particular occurrences of data and produce outputs based on those occurrences.

Search on Single 'J' String—A$(I,3)

```
390 REM Report # 1 All male employees
395 REM -------------------------------------------------------
400 PRINT" First        Last       Salary     Account"
410 R$ = " \          \ \        \ \     \    \     \"
415 REM -------------------------------------------------------
420 FOR I = 1 TO 15
430   IF A$(I,3)="M" THEN PRINT USING R$; A$(I,2);A$(I,1);A$(I,4);A$(I,6)
440 NEXT I

RUN
 First        Last       Salary     Account
 Philip       Hunter     12000      90.00
 Scott        Carlson    21400      310.00
 Jeffery      Anderson   10000      200.00
 Charles      Elting     17300      10.00
 Larry        Parks      12600      180.00
 Ronald       Reeves     18700      92.50
 Dale         Zimmerson  16300      330.00
OK
```

Search on Single 'J' String Converted to Numeric—VAL(A$(I,4))

```
390 REM Report # 2 All employees making more than $15,000
400 REM per year salary.
410 REM -------------------------------------------------------
420 PRINT" Last         First       Salary  "
430 R$ = " \          \ \        \  $##,###.## "
440 REM -------------------------------------------------------
450 FOR I = 1 TO 15
460   IF VAL(A$(I,4))>15000 THEN PRINT USING R$; A$(I,1);A$(I,2);VAL(A$(I,4))!
470 NEXT I

RUN
 Last         First       Salary
 Boronat      Penny       $16,200.00
 Carlson      Scott       $21,400.00
 Carson       Cindy       $22,500.00
 Elting       Charles     $17,300.00
 Cathcart     Anita       $19,000.00
 Fuller       Alice       $19,000.00
 Reeves       Ronald      $18,700.00
 Zimmerson    Dale        $16,300.00
OK
```

Search on Multiple 'J' Strings—Logical Operator AND

```
390 REM Report # 3  All Male employees making more than
400 REM $15,000 per year salary.
410 REM -------------------------------------------------------
420 PRINT " Last           First          Salary    "
430 R$ =   " \           \  \         \    $##,###.##"
440 REM -------------------------------------------------------
450 FOR I = 1 TO 15
460    IF A$(I,3)="M" AND VAL(A$(I,4))>15000 THEN PRINT USING R$;A$(I,1);
       A$(I,2);VAL(A$(I,4))
470 NEXT I

RUN
 Last          First        Salary
 Carlson       Scott        $21,400.00
 Elting        Charles      $17,300.00
 Reeves        Ronald       $18,700.00
 Zimmerson     Dale         $16,300.00
Ok
```

Search on Multiple 'J' Strings—Logical Operators AND-OR

```
390 REM Report # 4  All Male employees making more than
400 REM $15,000 per year salary or female employees maki ng
405 REM making more than $20,000 per year salary.
410 REM -------------------------------------------------------
420 PRINT " Last           First          Salary    "
430 R$ =   " \           \  \         \    $##,###.##"
440 REM -------------------------------------------------------
450 FOR I = 1 TO 15
460    IF A$(I,3)="M" AND VAL(A$(I,4))>15000 OR A $(I,3)="F"
       AND VAL(A$(I,4))>20000  THEN PRINT USING R$;A$(I,1);
       A$(I,2);VAL(A$(I,4))
470 NEXT I

RUN
 Last          First        Salary
 Carlson       Scott        $21,400.00
 Carson        Cindy        $22,500.00
 Elting        Charles      $17,300.00
 Reeves        Ronald       $18,700.00
 Zimmerson     Dale         $16,300.00
Ok
```

NOTE: Since AND has precedence over OR it is not necessary to group these conditions with parentheses:

(condition AND condition) OR (condition AND condition)

Search Using Substring Operations

```
390 REM Report #5- Search for data on last name fragment.
400 REM User inputs any part of the last name, beginning
410 REM with the first character. Program will search and
420 REM display information on employees whose last names
430 REM begin with that fragment
440 REM -------------------------------------------------------
450 INPUT "Enter Last Name fragment";N$
460 X=LEN(N$)
470 FOR I = 1 TO 15
480   IF LEFT$(A$(I,1),X)=N$ THEN PRINT A$(I,1);", ";A$(I,2)
490 NEXT I

RUN
Enter Last Name fragment? Carl
Carlson, Scott
Ok
RUN
Enter Last Name fragment? Car
Carlson, Scott
Carson, Cindy
Ok
RUN
Enter Last Name fragment? Ca
Carlson, Scott
Carson, Cindy
Cathcart, Anita
Ok
```

Totals and Averages

```
390 REM Report # 6  Total salaries, personal accounts &
400 REM averages.
410 REM -------------------------------------------------------
420 FOR I = 1 TO 15
430   EMPS=EMPS+1
440   TOTSALS=TOTSALS+VAL(A$(I,4))
450   TOTACCT=TOTACCT+VAL(A$(I,6))
460 NEXT I
470 REM -------------------------------------------------------
480 PRINT "  Total       Total     Average     Total      Average
490 PRINT "Employees    Salaries   Salary     Accounts    Account
500 R$ =  "  ###        $###,###   $##,###    $#,###.##   $###.##
510 PRINT USING R$;EMPS;TOTSALS;TOTSALS/EMPS;TOTACCT;TOTACCT/EMPS

RUN
  Total       Total     Average     Total      Average
Employees    Salaries   Salary     Accounts    Account
   15        $223,500   $14,900    $1,734.95   $115.66
Ok
```

Totals Using Data Cross-Indexing

```
390 REM Report #7 Total employees/personal accounts by
400 REM department
410 REM -----------------------------------------------------
420 FOR I = 1 TO 15
430   DEPT=VAL(A$(I,5))
440   EMPS(DEPT)=EMPS(DEPT)+1
450   ACCT(DEPT)=ACCT(DEPT)+VAL(A$(I,6))
460 NEXT I
470 REM -----------------------------------------------------
480 PRINT "              Total        Total
490 PRINT " Dept#    Employees     Accounts
500 R$ =  "   #          ##         $###.##"
510 REM -----------------------------------------------------
520 FOR DEPT = 1 TO 4
530   PRINT USING R$;DEPT;EMPS(DEPT);ACCT(DEPT)
540 NEXT DEPT

RUN
             Total        Total
 Dept#    Employees     Accounts
  1           4         $742.50
  2           4         $370.75
  3           3         $195.10
  4           4         $426.60
Ok
```

Search for Greatest Amount A$(I,4)

```
390 REM Report # 8  Search for employee with highest
400 REM yearly salary.
410 REM -----------------------------------------------------
420 HOLD = 0
430 FOR I = 1 TO 15
440    IF VAL(A$(I,4))<= HOLD THEN GOTO 490
450    HOLD = VAL(A$(I,4))
460    FOR J = 1 TO 6
470      ANS$(J)=A$(I,J)
480    NEXT J
490 NEXT I
500 REM -----------------------------------------------------
510 PRINT " Last        First     Sex     Salary     Dept#    Account
520 R$ =  " \         \  \      \   \\  $##,###.##     \\     $###.##"
530 REM -----------------------------------------------------
540 PRINT USING R$;ANS$(1);ANS$(2);ANS$(3);VAL(ANS$(4));ANS$(5);VAL(ANS$(6))
RUN
 Last        First     Sex     Salary     Dept#    Account
 Carson      Cindy      F    $22,500.00     2      $ 75.00
Ok
```

Sorting Array A$(I,J) on Last Name A$(I,1)—Bubble sort

```
390 REM Report # 9 Database sorted on last name.
400 REM -------------------------------------------------------
410 FOR PASS = 1 TO 14
420   FOR I = 2 TO 15
430      IF A$(I,1)>=A$(I-1,1) THEN GOTO 470
440      FOR J = 1 TO 6
450         SWAP A$(I,J),A$(I-1,J)
460      NEXT J
470   NEXT I
480 NEXT PASS
490 REM -------------------------------------------------------
500 R$ = "\        \ "
510 REM -------------------------------------------------------
520 FOR I = 1 TO 15
530   FOR J = 1 TO 6
540     PRINT USING R$;A$(I,J);
550   NEXT J
560   PRINT
570 NEXT I
RUN
Anderson  Jeffery   M          10000      2          200.00
Boronat   Penny     F          16200      4          20.50
Carlson   Scott     M          21400      1          310.00
Carson    Cindy     F          22500      2          75.00
Cathcart  Anita     F          19000      4          95.50
Elting    Charles   M          17300      1          10.00
Fuller    Alice     F          19000      2          45.00
Harrison  Glenys    F          9800       4          130.60
Hunter    Philip    M          12000      3          90.00
Jeli      Krista    F          9500       3          0.00
Nickerson Cheryl    F          8700       3          105.10
Parks     Larry     M          12600      4          180.00
Parsons   Sharon    F          10500      2          50.75
Reeves    Ronald    M          18700      1          92.50
Zimmerson Dale      M          16300      1          330.00
Ok
```

Utilities

```
Function Keys Program
----------------------
100 REM Reprograms the function keys F5-F10 then erases itself
110 REM from memory. Type [RUN"fKey] before starting to program.
120 REM -------------------------------------------------------
130 KEY  5, "FILES"+CHR$(13)
140 KEY  6, "KILL"+CHR$(34)
150 KEY  7, "RENUM 100"
160 KEY  8, "KEY 8, "+CHR$(34)
170 KEY  9, " REM ----------"
180 KEY 10, "---------------"
190 REM -------------------------------------------------------
200 NEW
------------------------------------------------------------------------------

Sound Effects Program
----------------------
100 REM Each "Play string" routine produces an interesting sound effect
110 REM -------------------------------------------------------
120 PRINT "Play string #1"
130 FOR I=1 TO 10
140    PLAY "l64 mf ml t255 n40n41n42n43 n50n51n52n53"
150 NEXT I
160 REM -------------------------------------------------------
170 PRINT "Play string #2"
180 FOR I=1 TO 10
190    PLAY "l64 mf ml t255 n40n42n44n46n48n50n48n46n44n42n40"
200 NEXT I
210 REM -------------------------------------------------------
220 PRINT "Play string #3"
230 FOR I=1 TO 10
240    PLAY "l64 mf ml t255 n50n60n51n61n52n62n53n63n54n64n55n65n56n66"
250 NEXT I
260 REM -------------------------------------------------------
------------------------------------------------------------------------------

Graphics Scale Routine
----------------------
100 REM Scale factor (S) for screen graphics LINE heights
110 REM assuming plots for array F(J), DIM F(M), on a
120 REM screen with 180 points vertical being used.
130 REM -------------------------------------------------------
140 MIN=F(1)
150 MAX=F(1)
160 FOR J=1 TO M
170    IF F(J)>MAX THEN MAX=F(J)
180    IF F(J)<MIN THEN MIN=F(J)
190 NEXT J
200 S=180/(MAX+MIN)
210 REM -------------------------------------------------------
220 REM  When plotting graph use:
230 REM  LINE-(horizontal position, 200 - INT(S*F(J)))
240 REM  to scale graph vertically.
```

```
Statistic Routines
------------------
100 REM Accumulations for statistics and frequency distribution
110 REM for list A(I), DIM A(N)
120 REM -------------------------------------------------------
130 REM Calculate Range of data for list A(I)
140 REM -------------------------------------------------------
150 MIN=A(1)
160 MAX=A(1)
170 FOR I=1 TO N
180     IF A(I)>MAX THEN MAX=A(I)
190     IF A(I)<MIN THEN MIN=A(I)
200 NEXT I
210 REM -------------------------------------------------------
220 REM Calculate Mean (Average) for list A(I)
230 REM -------------------------------------------------------
240 FOR I = 1 TO N
250   TOT=TOT+A(I)
260 NEXT I
270 MEAN= INT((TOT/N)*100)/100
280 REM -------------------------------------------------------
290 REM Calculate Standard deviation for list A(I)
300 REM -------------------------------------------------------
310 FOR I = 1 TO N
320     ER=ER+(A(I)-MEAN)^2
330 NEXT I
340 STD = INT(SQR((1/(N-1))*ER)*100)/100
350 REM -------------------------------------------------------
360 REM Accumulate frequency of events for list A(I) given a range
370 REM MIN to MAX into the array SUBT(A)
380 REM -------------------------------------------------------
390 FOR A = MIN TO MAX
400   FOR I = 1 TO N
410     IF CINT(A(I))=A THEN SUBT(A)=SUBT(A)+1
420   NEXT I
430 NEXT A
-------------------------------------------------------------------------

Bubble Sorts / Lists - Tables
-----------------------------
100 REM   A bubble sort routine for single subscript arrays (lists)
110 REM -------------------------------------------------------
120 FOR PASS = 1 TO 9
130   FOR I = 2 TO 10
140       IF A$(I) > A$(I-1) THEN 160    ' Bubble Sort
150       SWAP A$(I),A$(I-1)
160   NEXT I
170 NEXT PASS
180 REM -------------------------------------------------------
```

```
100 REM Bubble sort for double subscript sorted on A$(I,2)
110 REM where A$(I=10,J=6)
120 REM -----------------------------------------------------
130 FOR PASS = 1 TO 9
140   FOR I = 2 TO 10
150       IF A$(I,2) > A$(I-1,2) THEN 190    ' Bubble Sort
160       FOR J= 1 TO 6
170          SWAP A$(I,J),A$(I-1,J)
180       NEXT J
190   NEXT I
200 NEXT PASS
-----------------------------------------------------------------------------
```

```
Shell Sorts / Lists & Tables
----------------------------
320 N=10-1              ' N = number of A$(I)'s - 1
330 M=N
340 M=INT(M/2)
350    IF M=0 THEN GOTO 470
360    Z=1
370    K=N-M
380 I=Z
390    L=I+M
400        IF A$(I)<=A$(L) THEN GOTO 440
410        SWAP A$(I),A$(L)
420        I=I-M
430    IF I>=1 THEN GOTO 390
440 Z=Z+1
450 IF Z>K THEN GOTO 340
460 GOTO 380
470 REM - Continue program here -
-----------------------------------------------------------------------------
```

```
300 REM Shell Sort for double subscript sorted on A$(I,2) where A$(I=10,J=6)
310 REM ----------------------------------------
320 N=10-1                       ' N = number of A$(I, )'s - 1
330 M=N
340 M=INT(M/2)
350    IF M=0 THEN GOTO 480
360    Z=1
370    K=N-M
380 I=Z
390    L=I+M
400        IF A$(I,2)<=A$(L,2) THEN GOTO 440
405        FOR J= 1 TO 6
410           SWAP A$(I,J),A$(L,J)
415        NEXT J
420        I=I-M
430    IF I>=1 THEN GOTO 390
440 Z=Z+1
450 IF Z>K THEN GOTO 340
460 GOTO 380
480 REM - Continue Program Here -
```

Overview of Data Files

Data files are diskette files used to store data that BASICA programs may access. The data on the diskette are typically in the form of a *relational database,* that is the data are organized in records composed of fields having related data items.

The general procedure for using data files involves having the BASICA program open a data file, read individual data items from the file into program variables, manipulate or process the data while they are held in variables, and then write the data back out to the diskette data file in its updated form.

The advantage of data files is having the means to maintain (update) the records in a database through program execution.

There are two types of data files—sequential and random. The fundamental difference between them is how the data are stored on the diskette. Sequential files use delimiters (quotes, commas, carriage returns) to separate the individual data items; random files are structured so that each data item is given a specific length in characters so the location of a data item separates it from other data items in a file.

Sequential Data Files

Data Structure

Sequential data files have their string and numeric data items strung together with commas, quotes, and/or carriage returns separating them. A sequential file may be viewed as one long **DATA** statement kept on the diskette under its own filename [7765,“Example”,32,“Sequential file”,8867.55].

Opening a Sequential File

Before a BASICA program can access a sequential file, that file first must be opened with an **OPEN** statement in the BASICA program. A sequential file may be opened in one of three modes: output, input, or append (add to). Each sequential data file must be closed with a **CLOSE** statement before it is reopened in a different mode. The following is a summary of the syntax involved when using an **OPEN** statement to access the data in a sequential data file.

The OPEN Statement

OPEN "filename" FOR OUTPUT AS #filenum

This statement opens the diskette file named “filename” for data to be placed in (written to) it. If the data file already exists, any data in it automatically will be erased to prepare the file to receive a whole new set of data.

OPEN "filename" FOR APPEND AS #filenum

This statement opens the diskette file named “filename” for data to be added (appended) to it. Opening for append opens the file to receive data without erasing the file. Any data written to a file opened for append are added to the data already in the file.

OPEN "filename" FOR INPUT AS #filenum

This statement opens the diskette file named "filename" for its data to be assigned to variables in the BASICA program (read from). Opening the file for input does not erase that file.

- filename A sequential file is first named at the time it is opened for output. The filename is enclosed in quotes, and must be eight or fewer letter/number characters in length (no commas, spaces, etc.).
- filenum Each data file is given a number when it is opened. This number is then used to identify that file for all program statements referring to it. After a file has been closed, its filenum becomes available to identify other data files when they are opened.

NOTE: BASICA allows (by default) three data files to be open at any given time during program execution. For accessing more than three files at a time, type BASICA/F:# (where "#" is the number of files to be open at a time) when loading BASICA from the DOS (system) operating level.

Other Statements and Functions Used with Sequential Files

- **CLOSE** Closes all data files. Option to **CLOSE** #.
- **INPUT #** Inputs the next data item from the data file into a program variable.
- **PRINT #** Outputs data items to a data file.
- **WRITE #** Outputs data items and delimiters to a data file.
- **EOF** Signals End Of File.

Sequential File Example Programs

Creating a Sequential Data File

The following example programs involve data on gallons of warehoused paint. In this example the data file "INVEN" is created by opening it for **OUTPUT.** The record data are then entered from the keyboard in the field order of color code, name, and the gallons on hand for each type of paint (each record). The set of data items entered is written to the data file #1 which is identified in the **OPEN** statement as being the file "INVEN." After each record is entered, the user has the option of entering another.

```
LIST
10 OPEN "INVEN" FOR OUTPUT AS #1
20     INPUT "Color Code    ";TINT
30     INPUT "Brand Name    ";BRND$
40     INPUT "Gallons       ";GALS
50     WRITE #1,TINT,BRND$,GALS
60     INPUT "More (Y/N) ";ANS$
70 IF ANS$="y" OR ANS$="Y" THEN 20
80 CLOSE #1
Ok
RUN
Color Code    ? 7765
Brand Name    ? Flamingo Pink
Gallons       ? 87
More (Y/N) ? y
```

```
Color Code    ? 4776
Brand Name    ? Shetland Brown
Gallons       ? 45
More (Y/N) ? Y
Color Code    ?
```

(and so on)

As this program is executed the variables TINT, BRND$, and GALS temporarily hold whatever values the user inputs on the keyboard. After those values are input they are written to the data file INVEN (line 50) and the user is prompted "More (Y/N)?". If the user answers anything other than Y or y to this prompt, line 80 (**CLOSE** #1) will be executed. When the **CLOSE** #1 statement is executed the physical writing of the data items to the file will be completed. At this point the data in INVEN are stored on the diskette in the form:

```
7765,"Flamingo Pink",87,4776,"Shetland Brown",45 ............
```

Appending to a Sequential Data File

If you wanted to add data to the existing file "INVEN," you simply would change the **OPEN** statement in the last example. An **OPEN FOR APPEND** (rather than **OPEN FOR OUTPUT**) used in line 10, will cause the program to append any data entered from the keyboard to the existing data file "INVEN."

```
10 OPEN "INVEN" FOR APPEND AS #1
```

OPEN FOR APPEND will not erase the data in "INVEN" although **OPEN FOR OUTPUT** will.

Reading a Sequential Data File

In the next example, the data file INVEN is opened for input and a report is produced showing what types and how much of each paint currently is warehoused. Note that EOF(#) is a BASICA function whose value is 0 (false) until an attempt is made to INPUT (read) past the end of a file. Its value then becomes −1 (true).

```
LIST
10 PRINT "   Color Code         Brand Name            Gallons on Hand"
20 PRINT" "
30 OPEN "INVEN" FOR INPUT AS #1
40    IF EOF(1) THEN 80
50    INPUT #1,TINT,BRND$,GALS
60    PRINT TAB(5);TINT;TAB(22);BRND$;TAB(52);GALS
70 GOTO 40
80 CLOSE #1
OK
RUN
   Color Code          Brand Name             Gallons on Hand

     7765              Flamingo Pink              87
     4776              Shetland Brown             45
     9953              Russian Red                32
     5545              Coppertone Tan             55
OK
```

Updating a Sequential File

The next example demonstrates how a sequential file can be read into a program, altered, or updated, and then written back to the diskette in its new form.

This particular example program allows INVEN to be updated for the number of gallons on hand of each type of paint. A temporary data file TEMPFILE is used to hold the updated data; then TEMPFILE is renamed as INVEN after the new information has been written to it.

```
LIST
10  PRINT TAB(15);"GALLONS IN STOCK":PRINT
20  OPEN "INVEN" FOR INPUT AS #1
30  OPEN "TEMPFILE" FOR OUTPUT AS #2
40      IF EOF(1) THEN 90
50      INPUT #1,TINT,BRND$,GALS
60      PRINT BRND$;TAB(20):INPUT NEWGALS
70      WRITE #2,TINT,BRND$,NEWGALS
80  GOTO 40
90  CLOSE #1,#2
100 KILL"INVEN"
110 NAME "TEMPFILE" AS "INVEN"
Ok
RUN
                  GALLONS IN STOCK

Flamingo Pink       ? 55
Shetland Brown      ? 35
Russian Red         ? 28
Coppertone Tan      ? 26
Ok
```

Searching a Sequential File

The last example is an "Ordering Report" program which assumes that when stock level is below 30 gallons for any given paint, enough should be ordered to bring back up the stock level to 70 gallons.

```
LIST
10 PRINT "    Color Code          Brand Name                 Gallons to Order"
20 PRINT" "
30 OPEN "INVEN" FOR INPUT AS #1
40 IF EOF(1) THEN 100
50    INPUT #1,TINT,BRND$,GALS
60 IF GALS >= 30 THEN 40
70    ORDER = 70 - GALS
80    PRINT TAB(5);TINT;TAB(22);BRND$;TAB(52);ORDER
90 GOTO 40
100 CLOSE #1
Ok
RUN
    Color Code          Brand Name                 Gallons to Order

      9953            Russian Red                     42
      5545            Coppertone Tan                  44
Ok
```

Random Access Files

Data Structure

Random files are data files with their record data items set up in identical packages. Each record has a unique record number, and all data items in the record have a specified amount of record space reserved for them (called data fields).

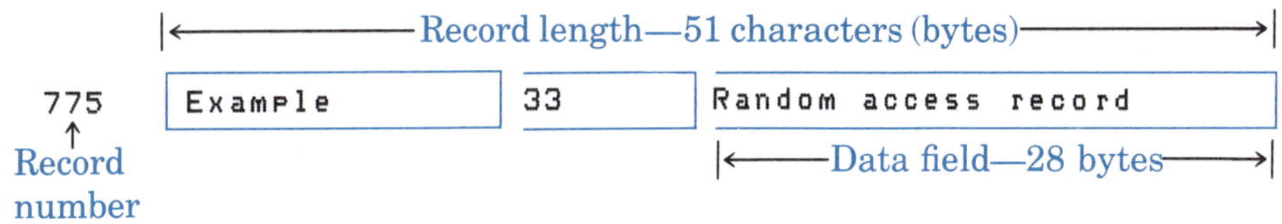

Opening a Random Data File

Before a BASIC program can access a random file, the file must be opened with an **OPEN** statement. Once opened, the random file may have data placed in it (written to), or it may have its data assigned to variables in the BASICA program (read from), with BASICA's **PUT** and **GET** statements.

The OPEN Statement

```
OPEN "filename" AS #filenum LEN = reclen
```

- filename — A random file is first named when it is created. The filename is enclosed in quotes, and must be eight or fewer letter/number characters in length (no commas, spaces, etc.).
- filenum — Each data file is given a number when it is opened. The number is then used to identify the file for all program statements referring to it. After a file has been closed, its filenum becomes available to identify other data files when they are opened.
- reclen — The length of the random file record is the sum of the lengths of all data fields in it.

The Random File Buffer

Data are moved in and out of a random access file through a holding space called a "random file buffer." This space is used to temporarily hold the record being written to a random file or read from a random file.

Defining the Random File Buffer

The size of the random file buffer is defined in the BASICA program by the **FIELD** statement. With this statement, each field in the buffer is given a specific length and a name.

```
FIELD #1, 15 AS A$, 8 AS B$, 28 AS C$
```

In the example above, the **FIELD** statement creates (for the random file opened as #1) a random file buffer that sets aside 15 characters for the field named A$, 8 characters for the field named B$, and 28 characters for the field named C$. The total record length becomes 51 characters (51 = 15 + 8 + 28) as defined by this statement.

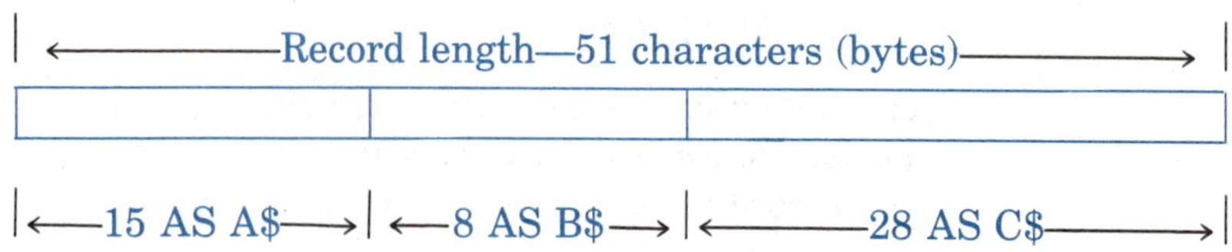

Moving Data into the Random File Buffer

Before data can be written to a random file, it must be placed in the random file buffer. Each data item is assigned to its appropriate field with the **LSET** (left justified) or **RSET** (right justified) statements. If the data item is smaller than its field, the rest of the field is packed with spaces.

Only string values may be placed in a random file buffer, so all numeric values must be converted to strings before placing them in their fields by using the MKI$, MKS$, or MKD$ (Make String) functions.

Writing Data to a Random Access File

After all data items for the record have been moved into the random file buffer, the **PUT** statement is used to write that record to the random file. The following is an example of BASIC code used to write a random file record to the diskette.

Example of Statements Used

This example starts with four program variables, the first of which (RECNO) is the integer used later as the record number.

```
RECNO = 775
TYPE$ = "Example"
AMT = 33
INFO$ = "Random access record"
```

Next the file named "RNDFILE" is opened as the #1 file and its record lengths are set at 51 characters each.

```
OPEN "RNDFILE" AS #1 LEN = 51
```

The **FIELD** statement is then used to create the random file buffer and set aside space for the three fields named A$, B$, and C$.

```
FIELD #1, 15 AS A$, 8 AS B$, 28 AS C$
```

LSETs are used to move the program variables into the random file buffer. MKS$ is used to convert AMT before moving it into its field.

```
LSET A$ = TYPE$
LSET B$ = MKS$(AMT)
LSET C$ = INFO$
```

Finally, **PUT** is used to write this record to the random file opened as #1 (RNDFILE). Notice that RECNO is used to place the record at this time.

```
PUT #1, RECNO
```

NOTE: Since BASICA and DOS block data (512 bytes at a time) before writing to a file, ***PUT*** *will not always result in an immediate writing of data to the diskette.*

In the previous example, a record with the record number 775, 51 characters long, and having three fields, would be written to the random access file, "RNDFILE."

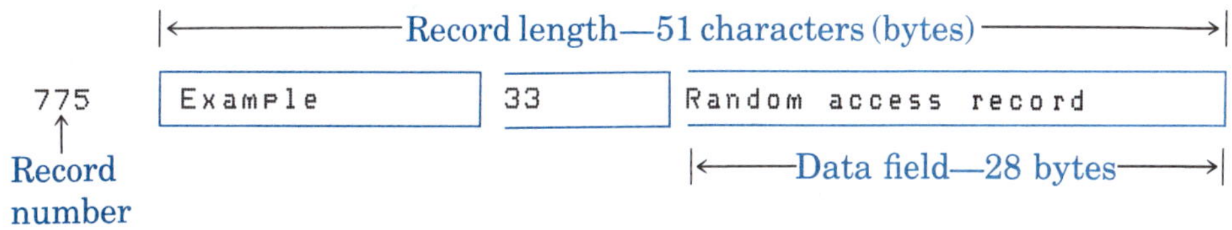

If "RNDFILE" was being created in this example, it automatically would be made large enough to hold 775 records, each 51 characters long. The file "RNDFILE" would then be 38,505 bytes in size. The rest of the space would be there to hold the first 774 records. If the next record **PUT** to the file had the record number 800, the file would be enlarged to hold a total of 800 records, even though it only had two records (#775 and #800) in it.

Reading Data from a Random Access File

Once a record has been written to a random file, the **GET** statement may be used to copy it (identified by its record number) from the diskette, back into a program's random file buffer. After the **GET** statement has been executed, all numeric values previously converted to strings may be converted back to numbers with the **CVI, CVS,** or **CVD** (Convert) functions.

Example of Statements Used

If "RNDFILE" already is open and its fields declared, the following two lines are not necessary.

```
OPEN "RNDFILE" AS #1 LEN = 51
FIELD #1, 15 AS A$, 8 AS B$, 28 AS C$
```

The variable "RECNO" holds the record number.

```
RECNO = 755
```

The **GET** statement will copy the 775th record from "RNDFILE" into the random file buffer field variables A$, B$, and C$.

```
GET #1,RECNO
```

Next the program variables are assigned the values held in the field variables. **CVS** is used to convert the string in B$ to its numeric value before assigning it to AMT.

```
TYPE$ = A$
AMT = CVS(B$)
INFO$ = C$
```

When the string values in the field variables are assigned to the program string variables, they include the spaces that were packed with them before they were written to the random file. In other words, if you were to

PRINT TYPE$;AMT; INFO$;"end"

at this point, the result would be

```
Example          33 Random access record          end
```

Statements and Functions Used with Random Access Files

Statement	Function
OPEN	Opens a data file for program access.
CLOSE	Closes all data files. Option to close #(n).
FIELD	Creates a random file buffer.
LSET	Moves data items into **RSET** the random file buffer in preparation for a **PUT** statement.
PUT	Moves a data record from the random file buffer into the random file.
GET	Moves a data record from the random file to the random file buffer.
MKD$** **MKI$ **MKS$**	Convert numeric data items into string form in preparation for moving them into a random file buffer.
CVD **CVI** **CVS**	Convert random file buffer numeric items, previously converted to strings with MK$ (Make String functions), back into numeric-type variables.

Example Programs—Random Access Files

Creating a Random Access Data File

These example programs involve data on gallons of warehoused paint. In the first example, the data file "INVEN" is created and its records are written to it as they are input from the keyboard. The data items entered in each record include color code, name, and the gallons on hand for each type of paint. The color code is used as the record number. After each set of values is entered, the user has the option of entering another set of values.

```
LIST
10 OPEN "INVEN" AS #1 LEN = 24
20 FIELD #1, 20 AS A$, 4 AS B$
30     INPUT "Color Code    ";TINT
40     INPUT "Brand Name    ";BRND$
50     INPUT "Gallons       ";GALS
60     LSET A$ = BRND$
70     LSET B$ = MKI$(GALS)
80     PUT #1,TINT
90     INPUT "More (Y/N) ";ANS$
100 IF ANS$="y" OR ANS$="Y" THEN 30
110 CLOSE #1
RUN
Color Code    ? 001
Brand Name    ? Very White
Gallons       ? 122
More (Y/N) ? y
Color Code    ? 002
Brand Name    ? Bone White
Gallons       ? 65
More (Y/N) ? y
Color Code    ?
(and so on)
```

Reading a Random Access Data File

In the next example, the random access file "INVEN" is opened and its records are read into the program's variables. A report is produced showing what type, and how much, of each paint is currently warehoused.

```
LIST
10 OPEN "INVEN" AS #1 LEN = 24
20 FIELD #1, 20 AS A$, 4 AS B$
30 PRINT "   Color Code         Brand Name                Gallons on hand
40 PRINT "   ----------         ----------                ---------------
50 FOR TINT = 1 TO 4
60    GET #1,TINT
70    BRND$ = A$ : GALS = CVI(B$)
80    PRINT TAB(8);TINT;TAB(22);BRND$;TAB(52);GALS
90 NEXT TINT
100 CLOSE #1
RUN
   Color Code         Brand Name                Gallons on hand
   ----------         ----------                ---------------
         1            Very White                      122
         2            Bone White                      65
         3            Off White                       88
         4            Bright Light White              23
```

Updating a Random Access Data File

This example demonstrates how a random access data file can be read into a program, altered, or updated, and then written back to the diskette in its corrected form. This particular example program allows "INVEN" to be updated for the number of gallons on hand of each type of paint.

```
LIST
10 PRINT TAB(15);"GALLONS IN STOCK":PRINT
20 OPEN "INVEN" AS #1 LEN = 24
30 FIELD #1, 20 AS A$, 4 AS B$
40 FOR TINT = 1 TO 4
50    GET #1,TINT
60    PRINT A$;TAB(22):INPUT NEWGALS
70    LSET B$ = MKI$(NEWGALS)
80    PUT #1,TINT
90 NEXT TINT
100 CLOSE #1
RUN
              GALLONS IN STOCK

Very White          ? 55
Bone White          ? 35
Off White           ? 28
Bright Light White  ? 26
```

In the previous example, the entire data file was updated by using the FOR NEXT loop counter "TINT" to **GET** and **PUT** each record (1 through 4). It is often the case that a random file is updated by identifying a record, and then updating only that record. For instance, suppose that "INVEN" was updated each evening by entering the number of gallons sold of the types of paint that were sold that day.

```
LIST
10 PRINT "INVENTORY UPDATE                    Gallons sold":PRINT
20 OPEN "INVEN" AS #1 LEN = 24
30 FIELD #1, 20 AS A$, 4 AS B$
40      INPUT "Color Code  ";TINT
50      GET #1,TINT
60      PRINT A$;TAB(35):INPUT GALSOLD
70      GALS = CVI(B$)
80      NEWGALS = GALS - GALSOLD
90      LSET B$ = MKI$(NEWGALS)
100     PUT #1,TINT
110     INPUT "                    More (Y/N) ";ANS$
120 IF ANS$="y" OR ANS$="Y" THEN 40
130 CLOSE #1
RUN
INVENTORY UPDATE                    Gallons sold

Color Code  ? 002
Bone White                            ? 6
               More (Y/N) ? y
Color Code  ? 003
Off White                             ? 4
               More (Y/N) ? n
```

COMMON ERROR MESSAGES AND THEIR CAUSES

Error Messages

Syntax Error

- Generally caused by a misspelled statement or incorrect placement of characters. Check spelling, unmatched parentheses, and/or incorrect use of delimiters (, ; : " '.).
- Line wrap-around. **LIST** only the line with the error. If two or more lines appear, there is a line wrap-around. It probably occurred during program editing.
- If error occurs in a **DATA** statement, check the appropriate **READ** statement for correct variable type. Check if the program is trying to **READ** a string into a numeric variable.
- A reserved word may have been used as a variable name. See "Reserved Words" (p. B–62).

Subscript Out of Range

- An array element may be greater than the array can hold. Check to see if the array has been dimensioned large enough.
- Try using a **PRINT** statement to check the value of the element at the time the program generates the error. It may be more than expected.
- A space in a **TAB** function will generate this error.

Type Mismatch

- A string value occurred where a numeric value was expected. Check variables for correct names and review logic of passing values to them.

Redo from Start

- This error does not stop the execution of the program. It is generated by an **INPUT** statement expecting a particular type or number of values to be entered from the keyboard. Ctrl-Break to stop program execution and examine that line for the logic of passing values to the **INPUT** variables.

Out of Data

- There are fewer **DATA** elements than executed **READ** variable(s). Put a **PRINT** variable(s) directly after the **READ** variable(s) to determine when "out of data" occurs.

Illegal Function Call

- Probably a bad argument value in a statement or function. Usually the argument has something to do with output to the screen. Check parameters to see if they are reasonable.

RETURN without GOSUB

- Usually caused by directly entering a subroutine: entering it from the program lines above it, rather than through a **GOSUB.** Use a **GOTO** to pass control around that subroutine.

FOR without NEXT or NEXT without FOR

- Often occurs in the use of nested loops. Each **FOR** statement requires a **NEXT** statement and vice versa.
- The counter variable in **FOR** must have the same name as the variable in its matching **NEXT** statement.

Bad File Number

- The statement generating the error may refer to a file that is not currently **OPEN.**
- If the error occurs in an **OPEN** statement, the maximum number of files allowed may be currently open, or the filename may be invalid.

File Not Found

- Check spelling and proper file identification. Does the file extension need to be included in that statement?

Input Past End

- Input from a sequential file has been attempted when no data are left to input, or when no data are there. Use the **EOF** function to avoid this error.

Too Many Files

- The filename being used is probably invalid. Use eight or fewer letters or numbers only, and use no spaces, commas, periods, etc. Make sure the name starts with a letter.

Disk Media Error

- Usually indicates a diskette has gone bad.

Reserved Words (BASICA Version 2.0 +)

ABS	DELETE	INT	OPEN	SOUND
AND	DIM	INTER$ *	OPTION	SPACE$
ASC	DRAW	IOCTL *	OR	SCP(
ATN	EDIT	IOCTL$ *	OUT	SQR
AUTO	ELSE	KEY	PAINT	STEP
BEEP	END	KILL	PEEK	STICK
BLOAD	ENVIRON *	LEFT$	PEN	STOP
BSAVE	ENVIRON$ *	LEN	PLAY	STR$
CALL	EOF	LET	PMAP *	STRIG
CDBL	EQV	LINE	POINT	STRING$ *
CHAIN	ERASE	LIST	POKE	SWAP
CHDIR *	ERDEV *	LLIST	POS	SYSTEM
CHR$	ERDEV$ *	LOAD	PRESET	TAB
CINT	ERL	LOC	PRINT	TAN
CIRCLE	ERR	LOCATE	PRINT#	THEN
CLEAR	ERROR	LOF	PSET	TIME$
CLOSE	EXP	LOG	PUT	TO
CLS	FIELD	LPOS	RANDOMIZE	TROFF
COLOR	FILES	LPRINT	READ	TRON
COM	FIX	LSET	REM	USING
COMMON	FNxxx	MERGE	RENUM	USR
CONT	FOR	MID$	RESET	VAL
COS	FRE	MKDIR *	RESTORE	VARPTR
CSNG	GET	MKD$	RESUME	VARPTR$
CSRLIN	GOSUB	MKI$	RETURN	WAIT
CVD	GOTO	MKS$	RIGHT$	WEND
CVI	HEX$	MOD	RMDIR *	WHILE
CVS	IF	MOTOR	RND	WIDTH
DATA	IMP	NAME	RSET	WINDOW *
DATE$	INKEY$	NEW	RUN	WRITE
DEF	INP	NEXT	SAVE	WRITE#
DEFDBL	INPUT	NOT	SCREEN	XOR
DEFINT	INPUT#	OCT$	SGN	
DEFSNG	INPUT$	OFF	SHELL *	
DEFSTR	INSTR	ON	SIN	

STUDY QUESTIONS

1. Which of the following statements are not used to assign values to a variable?
   - a. **LET**
   - b. **PRINT**
   - c. **INPUT**
   - d. **READ/DATA**
2. To delete a program line from your program you must:
   - a. retype the whole line
   - b. list only the line to be deleted
   - c. type the line number then Enter
   - d. use the removal command

What will be output if the following programs are RUN?

3.
```
10 A = 10
20 READ B
30 C = A * B
40 PRINT C
50 DATA 5
60 END
```
- a. 50
- b. 15
- c. 5
- d. 10

4.
```
10 A$ = "Computers"
15 B$ = "    and    "
20 A$ = "Business"
30 PRINT A$;B$;A$
99 END
```
- a. Computers and Business
- b. ComputersandBusiness
- c. Computers and Computers
- d. Business and Business

5.
```
10 W = 6
20 PRINT "W",W,W,"W"
99 END
```
- a. W 6 6 W
- b. 6 0 0 6
- c. 0 6 6 0
- d. W 0 0 W

6.
```
10 A = B + C
20 READ B,C
30 PRINT A
40 DATA 60,40,20
99 END
```
- a. 0
- b. nothing
- c. an error message
- d. 100 will be printed

7.
```
10 A = 32/2^3-(16/2)*4
20 PRINT A
99 END
```
- a. nothing
- b. division by zero error message
- c. 2
- d. −28

8.
```
 5 READ A
10 G2 = INT((A/3)*100)/100
20 PRINT G2
30 DATA 10
99 END
```
- a. 333
- b. error message
- c. 33.3
- d. 3.33

9.
```
10 A = 5
20 READ A
30 PRINT (A+5)^2
40 DATA 2
99 END
```
- a. 49
- b. 100
- c. 25
- d. none of the above

10.
```
10 A = SQR(32/(3+5)+12)
20 PRINT A
30 END
```
a. 256
b. 4
c. 16
d. 64

11.
```
10 READ A$,B,C
20 PRINT A$
30 RESTORE
40 READ A$,B,C
50 PRINT A$,B,C
60 DATA "JACK",10,20,90
70 DATA "SUE",40,50
99 END
```
a. JACK
SUE 40 50
b. JACK
JACK 90 40
c. JACK
JACK 40 50
d. none of the above

Which of the following is the correct BASIC statement?

12. a. `10 PRINT TAB;"X"`
b. `10 PRINT TAB;15;"X"`
c. `10 PRINT (TAB 15);"X"`
d. `10 PRINT TAB(15);"X"`

13. a. `50 IF A NOT = 500 THEN 1000`
b. `50 IF A$ <> 500 THEN 1000`
c. `50 IF A$ <> "500" THEN 1000`
d. b and c are correct

14. a. `10 FOR I = 1 TO 10 STEP 5`
b. `10 FOR I = 10 TO 1 STEP -2`
c. `10 FOR I = N1 TO N2`
d. all of the above are correct

What will be output if the following programs are RUN?

15.
```
10 A = 20
20 PRINT A;
30 GOTO 50
40 PRINT "TESTING";
50 END
```
a. 20 TESTING
b. 20
c. A TESTING
d. none of the above

16.
```
10 A = 15
20 B = 10
30 IF A < B THEN 50
40 PRINT "XXX";
50 PRINT "YYY";
60 PRINT "ZZZ";
70 END
```
a. XXX
b. YYYZZZ
c. ZZZ
d. XXXYYYZZZ

17.
```
10 READ A
20 IF A < 5 THEN 50
30 PRINT A;
40 GOTO 60
50 PRINT "TESTING";
60 DATA 3,6
70 END
```
a. TESTING 6
b. TESTING
c. 3 TESTING
d. 3 6 TESTING

18.
```
10 FOR I = 1 TO 2
20   X = I + X
30   PRINT X; I;
40 NEXT I
```
a. 0 0 2 1
b. 1 1 3 2
c. 0 1 2 1
d. 0 1 1 2

19.
```
10 READ A
20   IF A = 3 THEN 70
25   IF A = 2 THEN 50
30 PRINT "XXX"
40 GOTO 100
50 PRINT "YYY"
60 GOTO 100
70 PRINT "ZZZ"
80 DATA 1
100 END
```

a. XXX
b. YYY
c. ZZZ
d. XXX
YYY
ZZZ

20.
```
10 READ A
20 ON A GOTO 30,50,70
30 PRINT "XXX"
40 GOTO 100
50 PRINT "YYY"
60 GOTO 100
70 PRINT "ZZZ"
80 DATA 3
100 END
```

a. XXX
b. YYY
c. ZZZ
d. XXX
YYY
ZZZ

21.
```
10 FOR X = 1 TO 10
20   PRINT X;
30 NEXT X
```

a. 1 2 3 4 5 6 7 8 9 10
b. 0 1 2 3 4 5 6 7 8 9 10
c. 1 2 3 4 5 6 7 8 9 10 11
d. X X X X X X X X X X

22.
```
10 FOR T = 1 TO 5
20   PRINT T;
30   IF T < 3 THEN 50
40   PRINT "XXX";
50 NEXT T
```

a. 1 2 3XXX 4XXX 5XXX
b. 1 2 3 4XXX 5XXX
c. 1XXX 2XXX 3 4 5
d. 1XXX 2XXX 3XXX 4 5

23.
```
10 FOR H = 1 TO 6
20   READ Z
30   IF Z < 25 THEN 50
40   PRINT Z;
50 NEXT H
60 DATA 10,45,18,90,73,25
```

a. 45 90 73
b. 10 18
c. 45 90 73 25
d. 10 18 25

24.
```
10 FOR I = 1 TO 6
20   READ A$(I)
30 NEXT I
40 PRINT A$(4)
50 DATA CORN FLAKES,RICE KRISPIES,HONEY O'S
60 DATA FRUIT LOOPS,CRUNCH BERRY,CHERRIOS
```

a. KRISPIES
b. FRUIT LOOPS
c. Out of data will occur
d. Subscript error will occur

25.
```
10 FOR A = 1 TO 3
20    FOR B = 1 TO 2
30       PRINT A * B;
40    NEXT B
50 NEXT A
```
a. 1 2 2 4 3 6
b. 1 1 2 2 3 3
c. 1 2 3 4 5 6
d. none of the above

26.
```
10 FOR Z = 1 TO 3 STEP 2
20    PRINT "HELLO    ";
30 NEXT Z
```
a. HELLO HELLO HELLO
b. HELLO
c. HELLO HELLO
d. none of the above

27.
```
10 READ A
20    IF A < 0 THEN 40
30 IF A = 0 THEN 10
40    A = A + 1
50    IF A >= 5 THEN 70
60 GOTO 10
70 PRINT A
80 DATA -5,-6,7,-11,0
```
a. nothing will be printed
b. −4
c. 0
d. 8

28.
```
10 READ N
20 FOR I = 1 TO N
30    READ J
40    IF J < 0 THEN 60
50    PRINT J;
60 NEXT I
70 DATA 5,1,0,-1,-2,5,6,-11
```
a. 5 1 0 5 6
b. 1 0 5
c. 5 1 0
d. 1 0 5 6

29. How many data items are required to fill the arrays in this program?
```
10 FOR I = 1 TO 10 STEP 2
20    READ B$(I),C$(I)
30    FOR J = 1 TO 5
40       READ X(I,J)
50    NEXT J
60 NEXT I
```
a. 70
b. 35
c. 15
d. 10

What will be the output of the following programs?

30.
```
10 DIM X(5,3)
20 FOR T = 1 TO 5
30    FOR U = 1 TO 3
40       READ X(T,U)
50    NEXT U
60 NEXT T
70 PRINT X(3,2)
80 DATA 1,2,3,4,5,6,7,8,9,1,2,3,4,5,6,7,8,9
```
a. 8
b. 5
c. 2
d. nothing will be printed

31.
```
10 FOR I = 1 TO 4
20    READ A$(I),A(I)
30 NEXT I
40 FOR N = 1 TO 4
50    IF A(N) < 5 THEN 70
60    PRINT A$(N);A(N);
70 NEXT N
80  DATA KATHY,4
90  DATA LUCY,6
100 DATA TOM,8
110 DATA MAGGY,2
```
a. KATHY 4 LUCY 6 TOM 8 MAGGY 2
b. LUCY 6 TOM 8
c. KATHY 4 MAGGY 2
d. nothing will be printed

32.

```
10 FOR I = 1 TO 5
20   I = I * 2
30   PRINT I;
40   I = I - 1
50   PRINT I;
60 NEXT I
70 PRINT I
```

a. 2 1 4 3 8 7 8
b. 2 1 4 3 8 7 7
c. 1 1 2 2 3 3 4 4 5 5
d. nothing will be printed

33.

```
10  FOR I = 1 TO 5
20    READ A$(I)
30  NEXT I
40  N = 2
50  PRINT A$(N * (N - 1))
60  DATA SHEILA,HENERY,JOSHUA,CARLIA,LORENZ
```

a. nothing will be printed
b. a syntax error will occur
c. JOSHUA
d. HENERY

34.

```
10 FOR K = 1 TO 5
20   READ D(K)
30   T = T + D(K)
40   C = C + 1
50 NEXT K
60 PRINT T/C;
70 DATA 10,20,30,40,50
```

a. 10 15 20 25 30
b. 30
c. 1
d. 6

35.

```
10 FOR K = 1 TO 5
20   READ D(K)
30   C(K)=D(K) * 2
40 NEXT K
50 FOR K = 1 TO 5
60   PRINT C(K);
70 NEXT K
80 DATA 10,20,30,40,50
```

a. a syntax error will occur
b. nothing will be printed
c. 0 0 0 0 100
d. 20 40 60 80 100

BASICA KEY TERMS GLOSSARY

Advanced BASIC A version of BASIC found on the DOS diskette that has all of the operations and commands of Disk BASIC plus advanced graphics and music commands.

ASCII (American Standard Code for Information Interchange) A standard Data Format that facilitates the interchange of data among various types of software and hardware.

BASIC (An Acronym) Beginner's All-purpose Symbolic Instruction Code, a programming language developed to teach beginning students the constructs of programming theory.

Cassette BASIC A version of BASIC that requires a cassette player and interface cord to save programs.

Data Files Diskette files used to store data that BASIC programs may access.

Disk BASIC A version of BASIC found on a DOS diskette—usually purchased with the computer. This version of BASIC has the operations for accessing and storing data on diskettes.

Firmware A program that is permanently held in ROM.

Random Files Files stored on a diskette that are structured so that each data item is given a specific length in characters so the location of a data item separates it from other data items in a file.

Relational Database Data organized in a database in records with fields holding related data.

Screen Scroll The vertical movement of lines of type on a monitor. As one screen of data is complete, the data at the top of the screen disappears from view to make room at the bottom of the screen for new lines of text.

Sequential Data Files Files stored on a diskette that use delimiters (quotes, commas, carriage returns) to separate the individual data items.

MODULE OUTLINE

DATA TRANSFER BETWEEN APPLICATIONS

Data Transfer between Applications

The Possibilities of Data Transfer

Suppose you have a report to submit that includes a VP-Planner spreadsheet and you want the printed spreadsheet to appear in the body of a text file produced by WordPerfect. Or, maybe you have selected output produced by dBase III, or even a BASICA program, and want that information included in a WordPerfect text file.

Perhaps you want to use the editing capabilities of WordPerfect to create a database for dBase III, or you want to use a spreadsheet to create the database for dBase III. What if you want to use WordPerfect or dBase III to create documentation or data for a VP-Planner spreadsheet?

All of this and more is possible, because you can transfer data between applications softwares. The examples here use the applications covered in this manual, but the fundamentals and basic procedures discussed will be similar for other applications softwares.

ASCII Data Format

The primary key to transferring data from one type of software to another lies in each software's ability to create and accept data stored in the American Standard Code for Information Interchange or ASCII (pronounced "as-key"). This data format standard was established specifically for the types of tasks mentioned earlier—tasks that involve the interchange of information or data.

For computer users (as opposed to computer programmers or professional data processors) it is less important to know exactly what ASCII data formatting is than to know how it can be used and how to identify ASCII files.*

Identifying ASCII Files

The procedure for identifying an ASCII file is straightforward. At the DOS level of operation (A>) you use the **TYPE** command to list the contents of the file on the monitor screen. If every character of data that appears on the screen is a standard keyboard character, the file is stored in ASCII. If not, it is not stored in ASCII.

Software-Produced ASCII Files

Knowing whether or not you are creating an ASCII file is not as simple as identifying one after it has been created. Different softwares' manuals, commands, etc., refer to ASCII files with different terminology. For instance, WordPerfect refers to the ASCII files that it creates as being *DOS Text File Format* files, and dBase III refers to them as *SDF (System Data Format)* files.

The following is a list of the ASCII files created by the software covered in this manual. It indicates each software's ability to accept files for processing.

*For this section's intended purpose ASCII files are defined as files including only those characters numbered 13 and 32 to 126, inclusive.

VP-Planner ASCII Files

VP-Planner produces only its .PRN Print files in ASCII data format. These files are created by printing a spreadsheet or portion of a spreadsheet to a file with the /**P**rint **F**ile command.

VP-Planner readily accepts any ASCII file into its spreadsheets through its /**F**ile **I**mport command.

WordPerfect ASCII Files

WordPerfect will save its document files in ASCII if the proper procedures are followed. The Text In/Out, DOS Text File Format, Save **(Ctrl-F5, 1)** command may be used to save the current document in ASCII format. Another way to save document files and have columns, centered text, footnotes, endnotes, headers, footers, etc. preserved is to use the Print, Select Printers command to define printer #1 as using the default definition of #6, DOS Text Printer. If the DOS Text Printer method is used, an ASCII file named DOS.TXT will be created on the diskette.

Any ASCII data format file can be retrieved into WordPerfect for word processing. The ASCII file will, however, be immediately rewritten to the current format settings (margins, lines spacing etc.).

dBase III ASCII Files

dBase maintains several of its file types in ASCII format. The dBase .PRG command files are stored in ASCII data format.

Its .DBF database files are not kept in ASCII, but a copy of a database in ASCII format can be easily made by using the **COPY TO** <filename> [**SDF**] command. When a copy of a database is made this way it is given a .TXT extension. In addition, any nonediting screen output generated by a dBase operation can be written to an ASCII file by using the **SET ALTERNATE TO** <filename> and **SET ALTERNATE ON** commands. The files created in this manner also are given a .TXT extension.

To read ASCII files into a database the **APPEND FROM** <filename.TXT> [**SDF**] command is used. In addition, any file dBase normally maintains in ASCII can be produced by another software and still be used by dBase.

In general, the commands of dBase III are very effective for moving data between dBase and other software.

BASICA ASCII Files

BASICA programs may be saved in ASCII by using the **,A** option of the **SAVE** command. All BASICA sequential data files are written onto the diskette in ASCII. To direct a program's output to a sequential file the **PRINT** # or **WRITE** # statements may be used. BASICA random access data files are not written in ASCII data format.

Any ASCII file may be opened with **BASICA** program as a sequential data file and be read into RAM memory with the **LINE INPUT** # statement.

DOS ASCII Files

DOS does not actually produce ASCII files itself; but, with versions of 2.0+, you can use DOS to redirect another software's output to an ASCII file as long as the software uses the DOS function calls for its output, and does not generate non-ASCII characters as output.

This feature of DOS can be most useful for canned programs written in a programming language. To cause this redirection (more accurately an echo) of output, you use one or two greater than (>) signs followed by the ASCII file's filename when you load the software. A single > erases any previous ASCII file with the same filename, and two >s append output to any previous file with the same filename. For example, typing

```
A>BASICA LINPRO>>testout
```

loads BASICA and the BASICA program LINPRO.BAS into RAM memory, and begins running the program. If the file "testout" does not yet exist, it is created.

As the program LINPRO.BAS runs, all output that occurs on the screen is echoed to (printed to) the diskette file "testout." If the file "testout" previously existed, the data printed to it are appended (added at the bottom). Typing the **SYSTEM** command after the program is through executing completes the printing of data to the ASCII file and closes it.

Data Structure

Understanding the basics of data structure is the secondary key to transferring data between softwares. For software able to process both strings and numbers, data structure means incoming data is kept in units of data items. The items are separated from each other (delimited) in a way that differentiates the string-type data from the numeric-type data.

The rest of this section presents procedures for specific types of data transfer between softwares, and describes instances where the process may prove useful. The section provides the details about how the data must be structured in each case. As you progress through the material, many principles of data structure will become apparent, enabling you to perform data transfer operations not covered in this section.

Writing Programs with WordPerfect

Two types of user-written programs, BASICA programs and dBase III programs (called command files), have been covered in this manual. Both can be written using WordPerfect rather than the editing modes of the applications designed to execute them (BASICA's full-screen editing and dBase's **MODIFY COMMAND** mode).

Benefits

BASICA's full-screen editing is so powerful that there are only marginal benefits to writing BASIC programs in WordPerfect. The Replace command of WordPerfect can be useful for changing variable names throughout a program, and occasionally it is useful to have the Block/Copy command to perform operations such as writing several similar DATA statements.

With dBase the ability to block text and then copy, delete, move, read, or write the block is very useful. These are operations more easily accomplished using WordPerfect than using dBase's MODIFY COMMAND editing mode.

Procedure

After loading WordPerfect, set the left margin to 0 and the right margin to 254 by inserting a [Margin Set:] code into the document with the Format Line, Margins command. The margin code should occur at the top of the document. Next enter the program. End each line of code with a [HRt] by typing [cr].

To save the program, use the Text In/Out, DOS Text File Format, Save command **(Ctrl-F5, 1)**

Comments

The name you give the file must have the appropriate filename extension for the program to run later. A BASIC program must be named filename.BAS, and a dBase III command file must be named filename.PRG. You can either give the file its appropriate name when you save it or you can use the **RENAME** command of DOS (or the List Files, Rename command **(F5, 3)** of WordPerfect) to change it later.

dBase III automatically saves its command files in ASCII and expects them to be in ASCII when it opens them. BASICA does not. Therefore, if you load a BASICA program written with WordPerfect into BASICA (perhaps to run it to see if it works), you alter the program with BASICA's full-screen editor and expect to edit that program later with WordPerfect. You must be sure the program is resaved with the **,A** option of BASICA's **SAVE** command. The correct syntax is:

SAVE "filename"**,A**

Each line of a dBase III or BASIC program written in WordPerfect must end with an ↵. If a BASIC program written in WordPerfect has anything other than a number (the line number) at the beginning of each line, BASICA will give the message "Direct statement in file" when you try to load it.

Spreadsheets into WordPerfect

In the VP-Planner tutorial, commands were used to save a spreadsheet's data and to print a spreadsheet to a diskette file. You then returned to DOS and used the **TYPE** command to view the file. With VP-Planner, the Print files were perfectly readable. The VP-Planner spreadsheet data file (.WKS) however, was not readable using the DOS **TYPE** command.

In the following, the file shown on the left is an example of what a .WKS file would look like if it were saved in ASCII format. The spreadsheet data file is the file used by VP-Planner to reconstruct a saved spreadsheet in RAM each time the file is loaded with the **/FR** (/**F**ile **R**etrieve) command. The file contains the actual data entered from the keyboard or copied into other cells of the spreadsheet by the user.

Spreadsheet Data File
filename.WKS

```
>D7:+B7-C7
>C7:.675*B7
>B7:1400
>A7:"April
>D6:+B6-C6
>C6:.675*B6
>B6:1410
>A6:"March
>D5:+B5-C5
>C5:.675*B5
>B5:1330
>A5:"February
>D4:+B4-C4
>C4:.675*B4
>B4:1250
>A4:"January
>D3:/--
>C3:/--
>B3:/--
>A3:/--
>D2:/FR"Net
>C2:/FR"C.O.G.S
>B2:/FR"Sales
>A2:"Month
/W1
/GOC
/GRA
/GF$
/GC9
/X>A1:>A4:
```

Spreadsheet Print File
filename.PRN

```
Month          Sales   C.O.G.S       Net
----------------------------------------
January      1250.00    843.75    406.25
February     1330.00    897.75    432.25
March        1410.00    951.75    458.25
April        1400.00    945.00    455.00
```

On the right is shown a file created from the same spreadsheet by using the commands to print a spreadsheet to a file. With VP-Planner, these files are given a .PRN file extension. This file contains the processed data, or output, generated by the software. It appears the same in this file as it appears on the monitor screen or on paper when the spreadsheet is printed.

An important difference between the two is that a Print file cannot be loaded back into a spreadsheet by VP-Planner with the **/FR** (/**F**ile **R**etrieve) command. It is output that, instead of being printed on a piece of paper, was printed on the diskette under its own filename in ASCII data format. If you use a word processor to open the Print file for editing, and then change one of its key values, the rest of the spreadsheet will not recalculate.

With WordPerfect, files can be merged by simply retrieving one file into another. When a file is retrieved, it will be inserted into any existing text at the location of the editing cursor. Any ASCII file can be inserted into a WordPerfect document in this manner.

Benefits

Using a spreadsheet to produce computed values from formulas, printing the results to a Print file, and then reading them into a WordPerfect document file has many practical applications. Corporate reports, term papers, billings, invoices, budgets, appraisals, and estimates are just some of the instances in which such a procedure can be useful.

Procedure

Print the desired area of the spreadsheet onto the diskette with **/PF** (you may want to set the automatic margins top, bottom, and left to zero). Load WordPerfect and retrieve the document file into which you want to place the spreadsheet output. Move the editing cursor to the location where the spreadsheet data are to appear and retrieve the .PRN file. Or, you may simply retrieve the .PRN file and edit around it with WordPerfect. In either case, you will need to specify the whole filename, including its extension, to retrieve the .PRN file for word processing.

Comments

It is important to note that when you create a .PRN file using the /**P**rint **F**ile command of VP-Planner you must exit the Print commands by using **Q**uit. Using the Esc key to back out of the Print commands will result in an empty .PRN file on the diskette.

dBase III Data into WordPerfect

dBase III creates several different types of files, and each has its own type of filename extension. The .PRG (command files) and .TXT (text files) created by dBase are ASCII files. As such, they may be retrieved by WordPerfect for editing, and then saved onto the diskette in "DOS Format Text File" for use again by dBase. The procedure is the same as in writing a dBase program in WordPerfect.

dBase has commands designed specifically for creating ASCII text files (to which it gives a .TXT extension) that are copies of screen output created from a dBase operation, or of a .DBF database file.

The dBase commands used to create ASCII files of screen output are:

SET ALTERNATE TO ⟨filename⟩
SET ALTERNATE ON
SET ALTERNATE OFF

First the .TXT file is created with the **SET ALTERNATE TO** filename. After the file is created, the command **SET ALTERNATE ON** will begin writing (echoing) all output appearing on the monitor screen (with the exception of output generated in an editing mode) to the .TXT file.

The command **SET ALTERNATE OFF** stops the writing of data to the .TXT file. The command **SET ALTERNATE TO,** without a filename specified, closes the .TXT file.

To create an ASCII .TXT file copy of a database the command

COPY TO ⟨filename⟩ SDF

may be used. Once the .TXT file has been created, it may be retrieved for editing with WordPerfect.

Benefits

Although dBase has commands capable of very precise formatting of output for both the screen and printer, they are commands generally used in command files for reports produced often.

When a single report requiring a specific format is needed, or before you have the time, expertise, and/or patience to write the necessary command file, letting dBase generate the raw data and then using WordPerfect to manipulate the data into its final form can be the most effective and efficient means of producing the desired product.

Procedure

From dBase type the commands **SET ALTERNATE TO** ⟨filename⟩, and then **SET ALTERNATE ON.** Type the commands to generate the desired data on the monitor screen, and then use the command **SET ALTERNATE OFF** to stop writing to the .TXT file. Then **SET ALTERNATE TO** to close the file. To obtain as ASCII copy of a database, type the command **COPY TO** ⟨filename⟩ SDF. Be sure to type **QUIT** when you are finished with dBase to close any .TXT files that may be left in an open condition.

After loading WordPerfect, retrieve the .TXT file for editing.

Comments

dBase III seems designed to work quite effectively with word processing software and few (if any) problems occur when these procedures are followed.

Reading ASCII Files into a BASICA Program as Data

BASICA programs can be written to read any ASCII file by using the LINE INPUT statement. It can be particularly useful to have a BASIC program that can read data from a VP-Planner .PRN file, but the fundamentals described here apply to reading dBase .TXT files and any other ASCII file as well.

The following BASICA routine will open a VP-Planner .PRN file, and read the data found there into the variables A$(I) until the end of the file is reached or 1,000 lines are read.

```
90 DIM A$(1000)
100 OPEN "filename.PRN" FOR INPUT AS #1
110 I=1
120 WHILE NOT EOF(1)
130   LINE INPUT #1, A$(I)
140   I=I+1
150 WEND
```

It is important to note that **LINE INPUT** reads a text file one line at a time and that a line is defined as the characters up to a ↵ (also known as Enter, Return, CHR$(13), etc.).

When VP-Planner prints a .PRN file to the diskette, it adds a ↵ to the end of each spreadsheet row as it is printed. Therefore, the following example spreadsheet would be read into the A$(I) variables as:

```
      VP-Planner .PRN file                              Values for A$(I)
      --------------------                              ----------------
Month          Sales   C.O.G.S       Net  A$(1)="Month          Sales   C.O.G.S       Net"
------------------------------------------  A$(2)="------------------------------------------"
January      1250.00    843.75    406.25  A$(3)="January      1250.00    843.75    406.25"
February     1330.00    897.75    432.25  A$(4)="February     1330.00    897.75    432.25"
March        1410.00    951.75    458.25  A$(5)="March        1410.00    951.75    458.25"
April        1400.00    945.00    455.00  A$(6)="April        1400.00    945.00    455.00"
```

Once the data are read into the A$(I) variables (or as they are being read) the substring functions LEFT$(A$(I),n), RIGHT$(A$(I), and MID$(A$(I),n,m) may be used to separate the columns of .PRN file data and assign those values to other BASIC program variables. For instance,

```
LET MONTH$(3) = LEFT$(A$(3),9))
```

would assign "January" to the variable MONTH$(3). The VAL(x$) function may be used to convert the strings to numeric values if needed. For instance,

```
LET SALES(3) = VAL(MID$(A$(3),9,10))
```

would assign the number 1,250 to the variable SALES(3).

Benefits

Although VP-Planner is used in this example, any ASCII file with ↵s separating rows of data items that are organized in columns of specific widths may be accessed and processed the same way by a BASICA program. dBase III database files copied with SDF and WordPerfect DOS Format Text Files with data organized in columnar report format are examples of similar files.

The applications software's ability to process data may seem impressive but simply does not compare to the processing power of a programming language such as BASICA. Operations of extended sorting, compiling frequency distributions, substring data searching, custom screen graphics, matrix operations, and extensive file operations are just some of the processing that can be done with BASICA programs that use applications software files as the source files for their data.

Procedure

Create the source file, making sure that each line of data ends with a ↵ and that the data items in each line occur in similar specific locations. Use the BASICA program to open the file as a sequential data file, then **LINE INPUT** from that file.

Comments

If the software used to create the source file does not produce a file with the necessary data structure, open the file with WordPerfect and edit it before attempting to read it into BASICA program variables.

Spreadsheets into a dBase III Database

It is possible to use the spreadsheet applications to create records for a dBase III database. The dBase command used to read ASCII files into its databases is:

APPEND FROM filename.ext SDF

When dBase appends records this way it looks to the file being appended from for the number of characters equal to the length of the fields defined in that database's record **STRUCTURE.** So, if the database's record structure has three fields, each nine characters long, it will append the first nine characters found in the text file into the first field of the first record, the second nine characters found into the second field of the first record, and so on. The text file must have spaces included where the data for a field will not fill the field.

With the spreadsheet applications this is not a problem. Their Print files are text files set up ideally for appending into a database. Each cell in the spreadsheet is read in as a field of data, and the cells are read from the printed spreadsheet, left to right, top to bottom. Using a previous example:

```
                .PRN file
                -----------
Month         Sales   C.O.G.S       Net
------------------------------------------
January     1250.00    843.75    406.25
February    1330.00    897.75    432.25
March       1410.00    951.75    458.25
April       1400.00    945.00    455.00
```

an appropriate database structure would be created as:

	Field Name	Type	Width	Dec
1	MONTH	Character	9	
2	SALES	Numeric	9	2
3	COGS	Numeric	9	2
4	NET	Numeric	9	2

The only problem is that the first two rows of labels found in the .PRN file are not what you would want (or could) enter into the first and second records of the database. Therefore, you either would 1) not print them to the file, or 2) open this Print file with WordPerfect and delete the first two rows. Then save the file in WordPerfect's DOS Format Text File.

From dBase, after having created the database's structure, typing the command **APPEND FROM** ⟨filename.PRN⟩ SDF would result in a small database with records containing the following data.

```
Record No.      1                  Record No.      2

MONTH       :January               MONTH       :February
SALES       :   1250.00            SALES       :   1330.00
COGS        :    843.75            COGS        :    897.75
NET         :    406.25            NET         :    432.25


Record No.      3                  Record No.      4

MONTH       :March                 MONTH       :April
SALES       :   1410.00            SALES       :   1400.00
COGS        :    951.75            COGS        :    945.00
NET         :    458.25            NET         :    455.00
```

Benefits

Many of the benefits mentioned in the previous section apply to the reading of spreadsheet Print files into dBase as records of a database. Operations such as multilevel sorting, substring searches for reporting, and more, are operations that dBase is designed to do.

Also, the use of spreadsheet formulas and "Copy" (or "Replicate") commands often make creating record-type data a quick and easy process, and the ability to edit a database as you create it is often desired. Therefore, many users prefer to use a spreadsheet to create the records for a dBase III database.

Procedure

Create the .PRN file from VP-Planner using the /**P**rint **F**ile command. Load dBase III and then use the **CREATE** command of dBase III to define the intended database's structure. With VP-Planner the spreadsheet cells may vary in width and the record structure must accurately reflect the varied widths. Next use the dBase command **APPEND FROM** filename.PRN SDF to append the data into the database.

Comments

Again, it is important to note that when you create a .PRN file using the /**P**rint **F**ile command of VP-Planner, you must exit the Print commands by using **Q**uit. Using the Esc key to back out of the Print commands will result in an empty .PRN file on the diskette.

If you are using dBase III Plus and VP-Planner there is a method of transferring data directly into dBase using the **APPEND FROM** command, without the intermediate step of creating a VP-Planner .PRN file. The arrangement of data in the spreadsheet must be the same, each row representing a record of data, and you must create the record structure for the intended database prior to using the **APPEND** command.

The command [**APPEND FROM** filename.WKS **TYPE** WKS↵] may then be used to directly append data from a VP-Planner spreadsheet data file into a dBase III Plus database.

NOTE: See ***APPEND,*** *dBase III Operation and Command Summary Supplement, for information on other file types that can be directly appended to a dBase III Plus database.*

WordPerfect Files into a VP-Planner Spreadsheet

To accept other softwares' data VP-Planner's /**F**ile **I**mport command is used. With this command choosing the option to import a file as "Text" or "Numbers" is the first step in the command operation.

If "Text" is specified, the file being imported into the current spreadsheet will be entered into one column of cells, beginning at the current pointer location and continuing down, with each line of the imported file entered as a Label into a cell of the column.

In the case of a WordPerfect Format Text File, data being imported will exist as labels in the spreadsheet. For instance, if the last paragraph were to be imported into a spreadsheet with the spreadsheet pointer on cell A1 at the time, the paragraph would be entered one line at a time into the cells A1 through A4.

```
      A
1  If "Text" is specified, the file being imported into the current spreadsheet
2  will be entered into one column of cells, beginning at the current pointer
3  location and continuing down, with each line of the imported file entered as a
4  Label into a cell of the column.
```

Each label would extend to the right of the A column as long as the spreadsheet cells to the right remained blank. If spreadsheet data existed in cells A1 through A4 before the Import command operation, they would be replaced by the imported data.

Benefits

Large spreadsheets often require large areas of documentation explaining the assumptions of the model(s) used, and/or summarizing the information generated by the spreadsheet model(s). When such documentation is required it may be more convenient for a person knowledgeable about WordPerfect to use that software to produce the necessary text rather than to use the relatively weak word processing capabilities of VP-Planner.

Procedure

Use WordPerfect to create the text file and then save the document with **Ctrl-F5, 1** (Text In/Out, DOS Text File Format Save) command. Either save the document by specifying a .PRN filename extension or rename the file later to have this extension.

After you have created the text file, load VP-Planner and the appropriate spreadsheet into RAM memory and move the pointer to the top left cell of the area into which you want the text to be imported. Then use the /**F**ile **I**mport command and select "Text" from its menu and specify the appropriate file to import.

Comments

Word processed text files with non-ASCII characters in them may cause unpredictable results when they are imported into a spreadsheet. To protect your existing spreadsheet, you may want to take a more conservative approach. First, import the text file into a blank spreadsheet and examine it for peculiar characters. If no such characters are found, continue by importing the file into the intended spreadsheet. If peculiar characters are found, try using the **F2** Edit mode to delete them, reprint the area to a .PRN file, and repeat the test.

dBase III Database Records into a VP-Planner Spreadsheet

The final data transfer operation to discuss is moving dBase III database records into a VP-Planner spreadsheet. In this example VP-Planner's /**F**ile **I**mport command will be used with the option to import numbers rather than text (see WordPerfect Files into a VP-Planner Spreadsheet).

When the "Numbers" option of the /**F**ile **I**mport command is used, VP-Planner will import an ASCII file with both strings and numbers in it, and will put the data items in the file into separate spreadsheet cells, if the data in that file are structured correctly. With VP-Planner, the strings in the file must be delimited with quotes and the data items must be separated by commas.

Using the database created in the dBase III section, the **COPY TO** ⟨filename⟩ SDF command results in an ASCII file:

```
Pratt John          225-1234M82/06/22 1949.00 1200.00
Smoler Ellen        225-3212F83/09/15 1650.00  300.00
Jones David         292-3832M82/06/15 1550.00  275.75
Sill Sally          224-4321F81/02/15 1507.50  150.00
Knat Michael        221-1235M80/09/15 1800.00  125.00
Smith Paul          244-1010M84/11/15 1700.00  350.00
Martins Mary        222-2123F85/11/01 1600.00  200.50
Nichols Sandy       229-1111F86/02/15 1450.00  175.00
Johnson Frank       223-7928M86/03/20 1500.00    0.00
```

An additional parameter of the dBase **COPY** command is **DELIMITED.** It will copy the records to an ASCII file with delimiters inserted between the fields of data. When this command is used

```
COPY TO testfile DELIMITED
```

the records in the database are copied to the ASCII file "testfile. TXT" in a form:

```
"Pratt John","225-1234","M","82/06/22", 1949.00, 1200.00
"Smoler Ellen","225-3212","F","83/09/15", 1650.00,  300.00
"Jones David","292-3832","M","82/06/15", 1550.00,  275.75
"Sill Sally","224-4321","F","81/02/15", 1507.50,  150.00
"Knat Michael","221-1235","M","80/09/15", 1800.00,  125.00
"Smith Paul","244-1010","M","84/11/15", 1700.00,  350.00
"Martins Mary","222-2123","F","85/11/01", 1600.00,  200.50
"Nichols Sandy","229-1111","F","86/02/15", 1450.00,  175.00
"Johnson Frank","223-7928","M","86/03/20", 1500.00,    0.00
```

This form is suitable for importing into a VP-Planner spreadsheet as "Numbers."

Before importing this file it must be renamed to have a .PRN extension instead of the .TXT extension. When VP-Planner's /**F**ile **I**mport command is executed with the pointer on cell A1, "Numbers" selected as the method by which to import, and "testfile" specified as the file to import, the result will be:

	A	B	C	D	E	F
1	Pratt Joh	225-1234 M		82/06/22	1949	1200
2	Smoler El	225-3212 F		83/09/15	1650	300
3	Jones Dav	292-3832 M		82/06/15	1550	275.75
4	Sill Sal	224-4321 F		81/02/15	1507.5	150
5	Knat Mich	221-1235 M		80/09/15	1800	125
6	Smith Pau	244-1010 M		84/11/15	1700	350
7	Martins M	222-2123 F		85/11/01	1600	200.5
8	Nichols S	229-1111 F		86/02/15	1450	175
9	Johnson F	223-7928 M		86/03/20	1500	0

Each field of each record will be entered into an individual spreadsheet cell in the same data type (string or numeric) as it was held in its database field.

Notice that the spreadsheet column widths may need to be changed for the display of data imported in this manner and that the decimal places displayed for a dBase field of data do not import with that field's numeric data.

Benefits

The greatest strength of any spreadsheet application is its ability to generate formula-based information for decision making. Parametric statistical analysis of an organization's internal data is an example of such information. Database management systems such as dBase III have the strengths of data maintenance, query, and record organization which are useful for reporting purposes, and provide information relevant to a different type of decision making. When the need for formula-based information from record-type data is desired or required, this transfer of data operation may be very useful, and in fact may provide the only way to obtain the needed information.

Procedure

Use the **COPY TO** <filename> **DELIMITED** command to create a .TXT ASCII file of the database with the fields of data properly delimited. Rename the file to have a .PRN filename extension, load VP-Planner and the appropriate spreadsheet (if any) into memory, and then move the spreadsheet pointer to the top left cell of the area into which you want the records imported. To use the /**F**ile **I**mport command, select "Numbers" and specify the appropriate file to import.

Comments

By now you should see that as long as the data are arranged with an appropriate structure, the source of the ASCII file imported as "Numbers" is not important. WordPerfect or BASICA could be used to create the ASCII file.

With BASICA, the quotes and commas automatically will be inserted into a sequential file by using the **WRITE #** statement. With WordPerfect they have to be inserted manually.

Summary

Data transfer between software applications is an important topic, but often is ignored by texts and manuals. This section provides basic information about data transfer and gives some examples to demonstrate its potential application. Now you will need to experiment with it in order to gain a fuller understanding of it.

APPENDIX: ASCII Character Codes

The following table lists all the ASCII codes (in decimal) and their associated characters. These characters can be displayed using PRINT CHR$ (*n*), where *n* is the ASCII code. The column headed "Control Character" lists the standard interpretations of ASCII codes 0 to 31 (usually used for control functions or communications).

Each of these characters can be entered from the keyboard by pressing and holding the Alt key, then pressing the digits for the ASCII code on the numeric keypad. Note, however, that some of the codes have special meaning to the BASIC Program Editor. It uses its own interpretation for the codes and may not display the special character listed here.

ASCII Value	Character	Control Character	ASCII Value	Character	ASCII Value	Character	ASCII Value	Character
000	(null)	NUL	032	(space)	064	@	096	`
001	☺	SOH	033	!	065	A	097	a
002	☻	STX	034	"	066	B	098	b
003	♥	ETX	035	#	067	C	099	c
004	♦	EOT	036	$	068	D	100	d
005	♣	ENQ	037	%	069	E	101	e
006	♠	ACK	038	&	070	F	102	f
007	(beep)	BEL	039	'	071	G	103	g
008	◘	BS	040	(	072	H	104	h
009	(tab)	HT	041	)	073	I	105	i
010	(line feed)	LF	042	*	074	J	106	j
011	(home)	VT	043	+	075	K	107	k
012	(form feed)	FF	044	,	076	L	108	l
013	(carriage return)	CR	045	-	077	M	109	m
014	♫	SO	046	.	078	N	110	n
015	☼	SI	047	/	079	O	111	o
016	►	DLE	048	0	080	P	112	p
017	◄	DC1	049	1	081	Q	113	q
018	↕	DC2	050	2	082	R	114	r
019	‼	DC3	051	3	083	S	115	s
020	¶	DC4	052	4	084	T	116	t
021	§	NAK	053	5	085	U	117	u
022	▬	SYN	054	6	086	V	118	v
023	↨	ETB	055	7	087	W	119	w
024	↑	CAN	056	8	088	X	120	x
025	↓	EM	057	9	089	Y	121	y
026	→	SUB	058	:	090	Z	122	z
027	←	ESC	059	;	091	[	123	{
028	(cursor right)	FS	060	<	092	\	124	¦
029	(cursor left)	GS	061	=	093	]	125	}
030	(cursor up)	RS	062	>	094	^	126	~
031	(cursor down)	US	063	?	095	_	127	⌂

ASCII Value	Character	ASCII Value	Character	ASCII Value	Character	ASCII Value	Character
128	Ç	160	á	192	└	224	α
129	ü	161	í	193	┴	225	β
130	é	162	ó	194	┬	226	Γ
131	â	163	ú	195	├	227	π
132	ä	164	ñ	196	─	228	Σ
133	à	165	Ñ	197	┼	229	σ
134	å	166	ª	198	╞	230	μ
135	ç	167	º	199	╟	231	τ
136	ê	168	¿	200	╚	232	Φ
137	ë	169	⌐	201	╔	233	Θ
138	è	170	¬	202	╩	234	Ω
139	ï	171	½	203	╦	235	δ
140	î	172	¼	204	╠	236	∞
141	ì	173	¡	205	═	237	∅
142	Ä	174	«	206	╬	238	∈
143	Å	175	»	207	╧	239	∩
144	É	176		208	╨	240	≡
145	æ	177	▒	209	╤	241	±
146	Æ	178	▓	210	╥	242	≥
147	ô	179	│	211	╙	243	≤
148	ö	180	┤	212	╘	244	⌠
149	ò	181	╡	213	╒	245	⌡
150	û	182	╢	214	╓	246	÷
151	ù	183	╖	215	╫	247	≈
152	ÿ	184	╕	216	╪	248	°
153	Ö	185	╣	217	┘	249	•
154	Ü	186	║	218	┌	250	·
155	¢	187	╗	219	█	251	√
156	£	188	╝	220	▄	252	^{n}
157	¥	189	╜	221	▌	253	^{2}
158	Pt	190	╛	222	▐	254	■
159	ƒ	191	┐	223	▀	255	(blank 'FF')

Index

Fundamentals of Using Microcomputers

Learning VP-Planner

Learning WordPerfect

Learning dBase III

Learning BASICA

Data Transfer Between Applications

NOTES

NOTES

NOTES

NOTES

WordPerfect
CORPORATION

School Software Direct Order Form

Qualifying teachers, as well as college, university, and other post-secondary students, can now purchase WordPerfect Corporation (WPCORP) software directly from WPCORP at a reduced price. To qualify, a participant must be teaching or currently enrolled as a full-time student, and must agree in writing not to resell or transfer any package purchased under this program.

If you satisfy these qualifying conditions and would like to purchase software directly from WPCORP under the School Software Program, complete the following six steps and sign at the bottom of the form.

Step 1. From the list below, select the appropriate software for your computer (please note that each student is limited to *one* package of WordPerfect) and mark an "x" in the corresponding box(es).

Product	Disk Size	Computer	Price*
☐ WordPerfect 4.2	5¼"	(IBM PC/XT/AT/Compatibles)	$125.00
☐ WordPerfect 4.2	3½"	(IBM PC/XT/AT/compatibles)	125.00
☐ WordPerfect 1.1	5¼"	(Apple IIe/IIc)	59.00
☐ WordPerfect 1.1	3½"	(Apple IIe/IIc)	59.00
☐ WordPerfect 1.1	3½"	(Apple IIGS)	59.00
☐ PlanPerfect 3.0	5¼"	(IBM PC/XT/AT/Compatibles)	99.00
☐ PlanPerfect 3.0	3½"	(IBM PC/XT/AT/Compatibles)	99.00
☐ WordPerfect Library	5¼"	(IBM PC/XT/AT/Compatibles)	59.00
☐ WordPerfect Library	3½"	(IBM PC/XT/AT/Compatibles)	59.00
☐ WordPerfect Executive	5¼"	(IBM PC/XT/AT/Compatibles)	79.00
☐ WordPerfect Executive	3½"	(IBM PC/XT/AT/Compatibles)	79.00

Step 2. Make a photo-copy of your current Student ID or Faculty card *and* a photo-copy of some well known form of identification displaying your social security number, such as your Driver License or Social Security Card. (WPCORP will hold this information strictly confidential and use it only to guard against duplicate purchases.) Your school ID must show current enrollment. If it does not show a date, you must send verification of current enrollment. If you have serious reservations about providing a social security number, call Educational Development at (801) 227-7131 to establish clearance to purchase any of the above software products at these special prices.

Step 3. Enter your social security number: ___ ___ ___ – ___ ___ – ___ ___ ___ ___ .

Step 4. Enclose payment for the total cost of the package(s) ordered with personal check, money order, Visa, or MasterCard.

Account # ______________________________

Expiration Date ______________________________ ☐ VISA ☐ MasterCard

(Make check or money order payable to WordPerfect Corporation.)

Step 5. List your shipping address and the address of your local computer store (dealer) in the space provided:

Ship To ______________________ Your Dealer ______________________

______________________ ______________________

______________________ ______________________

Phone ______________________ Phone ______________________

Step 6. Enclose this signed and completed form, the photo-copies of your identification cards, and your signed check or money order (or Visa or MasterCard account number and expiration date) in an envelope and mail to School Software Program, WordPerfect Corporation, 288 West Center Street, Orem, UT 84057.

The information provided herein is correct and accurate, and I will abide by the restricting conditions outlined by WPCORP in this document. I understand that at its sole discretion, WPCORP may refuse any order for any reason.

Signature ______________________________ Date ______________________

*Utah residents add 6.25% sales tax.

Shell	Super/Subscript	Thesaurus	Cancel
Spell	◆Search	Replace	◆Search
Screen	Switch	Reveal Codes	Help
Move	◆Indent◆	Block	◆Indent
Ctrl	*Shift*	*Alt*	
Text In/Out	Date	Mark Text	List Files
Tab Align	Center	Flush Right	Bold
Footnote	Print	Math/Columns	Exit
Print Format	Line Format	Page Format	Underline
Ctrl	*Shift*	*Alt*	
Merge/Sort	Merge E	Merge Codes	Merge R
Macro Def	Retrieve	Macro	Save

WordPerfect for the IBM PC, PC/XT, AT

Go To	Home
Hard Page	Enter
◆Margin Release	Tab
Soft Hyphen	-
Screen Up/Down	−/+ (num)
Word Left/Right	←/→
Delete Word	Backspace
Delete to End of Ln/Pg	End/PgDn

 TMENWP01 4.2

(Merrill Pub. Co.)

Ctrl Shift Alt TMENWP01/4.2

Shell Super/Subscript Thesaurus Cancel	Spell ◆Search Replace ◆Search
Screen Switch Reveal Codes Help	Move ◆Indent◆ Block ◆Indent
Text In/Out Date Mark Text List Files	Tab Align Center Flush Rt Bold
Footnote Print Math/Columns Exit	FORMAT: Print Line Page Underline
Merge/Sort Merge E Merge Codes Merge R	Macro Def Retrieve Macro Save

WordPerfect for the IBM PC, PC/XT, AT

Go To	Home	Screen Up/Down	−/+ (num)
Hard Page	Enter	Word Left/Right	←/→
◆Margin Release	Tab	Delete Word	Backspace
Soft Hyphen	-	Delete to End of Ln/Pg	End/PgDn

(Merrill Pub. Co.)